THE
XI JINPING
ERA

THE XI JINPING ERA

His Comprehensive Strategy Toward
The China Dream

JAMES C. HSIUNG
Chief Editor

LIU HONG
CHEN YING
ZHOU XINGWANG
TAN HUOSHEN
Contributors

BEIJING MEDIATIME BOOKS CO., LTD.
CN Times Books, Inc.
501 Fifth Avenue, Suite 1708
New York, NY 10017
www.cntimesbooks.com

ORDERING INFORMATION: Quantity sales. Special discounts are available on quantity purchases by corporations, associations, and others. For details, contact the publisher at the address above. Orders by U.S. trade bookstores and wholesalers. Please contact Ingram Publisher Services: Tel: (866) 400-5351; Fax: (800) 838-1149; or customer.service@ingrampublisherservices.com.

ISBN 978-162774-119-4

Printed in the United States of America

CONTENTS

INTRODUCTION A New Era Unveiled by Xi Jinping 1

CHAPTER 1 Who Is Xi Jinping? 37

CHAPTER 2 The Blueprint for the Realization of the China Dream 119

CHAPTER 3 Internal Reform in the Communist Party of China 155

CHAPTER 4 The Major Reforms Deciding China's Fate 201

CHAPTER 5 The Innovation Revolution: Leading China's New Economy 251

CHAPTER 6 The Belt and Road Initiatives 291

CHAPTER 7 A Great Power Requires a Great Military 317

CHAPTER 8 Xi Jinping's New International Thinking 375

CHAPTER 9 Building a New Model of China–United States Relations 413

AFTERWORD The Peaceful Chinese Century Arrives 439

Acknowledgments 445

Index 447

INTRODUCTION
A New Era Unveiled by Xi Jinping

The *Book of Changes*, as annotated by the Chinese sage Confucius, recommends marking the passage of time by observing astronomy, and governing the world by observing human culture. Those who would observe the trends of the time and understand the evolution of historical eras should set about observing the natural laws on earth. The rise of China and the revitalization of the Chinese nation have been among the most significant historical events since humankind embarked upon the twenty-first century. The best way to understand these exciting developing trends in China, from its ancient civilization through the new millennium, is to focus on its current leader, Xi Jinping, who has promoted reform on an unprecedented scale since his election in 2012. The answer to how Xi Jinping will lead China into a new phase of development and forge mutually beneficial relations with the nations of the world lies in his grand reform plan. Like Mao Zedong and Deng Xiaoping before him, Xi Jinping is changing China with his distinctive governing style.

I. A NEW LONG MARCH FOR CHINA

In 1944, the writer and journalist Harrison Salisbury, who was later to become deputy editor-in-chief of *The New York Times*, met fellow American journalist Edgar Snow in the Soviet Union and was told the story of the Long

March of the Chinese communists for the first time. The story of the year-long march, which started in 1934 and covered 12,500 kilometers (circa 7,500 miles), fascinated and inspired him so much, he felt he had no choice but to write about it. In 1972, as President of the Writers Guild of America, he visited China with a delegation of authors from the United States. He asked if he could retrace the route of the Long March but was rejected. However, in March 1984, he returned to China with his wife, and in spite of his illness, he walked (and drove part of the way on) the route of the Long March. In 1985, he published the globally popular book *The Long March: The Untold Story*, which re-triggered interest in China's Long March all over the world.

The Long March is not only a grand historical epic but also a motivational totem of Chinese communism. Whenever China faces difficulties and hardships, China's Communist leaders never hesitate to inspire their people by citing the poems that Mao Zedong wrote throughout the course of the Long March.

On November 29, 2012, when Xi Jinping attended his first public state affair after being elected the general secretary of the Communist Party of China, he once again alluded to "Loushan Pass," a famed poem Mao Zedong wrote while undertaking the Long March, as an attempt to capture the hard and arduous course of revitalization for the Chinese people.

Xi Jinping described how the National Museum of China's exhibition "The Road to Rejuvenation" reviewed the past and presented the future for the Chinese people, offering profound education and enlightenment. The Chinese people's history could be described by Mao's verses, proclaiming that the weight of the hardships and the depths of the sacrifice endured by the Chinese people as they entered modern times was exceptional in the course of world history. "However, the Chinese people never surrendered, they rose to fight over and over again, and finally, the Chinese people became the masters of their own lives, achieving great progress to forge their own country. This demonstrates the great national spirit—with patriotism at its core."

During his visit to The Road to Rejuvenation, Xi Jinping also elaborated for the first time on the "China Dream" he and the Chinese people shared: "to bring about a great rejuvenation of the Chinese nation is the greatest dream of China in modern times. The dream combines the long-cherished wishes of the Chinese people across generations, embodies the overall interests of the Chinese nation and its people, and embodies the future every Chinese person can look forward to."

To bring about the China Dream, the dream of restoring the Chinese nation to greatness, is the culmination of the most breathtaking long march, a march involving everyone in the nation, spanning almost two centuries.

When viewed from the vastness of outer space, Earth is just a small, blue, isolated planet. As the planet progresses around the sun, the beams of the sun seem to hit most prominently on some certain part of the globe; but rest assured, the land receiving this beautiful sunrise is indeed China. The land is high in the west and low in the east, and in this vast land two great rivers flow—the Yellow River and the Yangtze River. With its origins from the loess highland,[1] across the plains of the Yellow and Yangtze River basins, lies the birthplace of one of the earliest human civilizations, the Chinese civilization, which has successfully continued through the last 5,000 years. The Chinese nation, like a great river with numerous tributaries running into it, strives toward unity. Since 221 BC when the First Emperor of Qin unified China, the territory and basic political system have been held in a relatively steady state. This is a country with the largest population on the planet where many fulfilling lives are led. However, opportunity and crisis turn into each other all the time. And inevitably, China fell into a declining valley from the late nineteenth century to the first half of the twentieth century.

No other nation in the world has deeper or more immediate feelings about the rise and fall of history. China was on top of the world for over a millennium (713–1820), sporting a gross domestic product (GDP) that was the world's largest; enjoying peace and comfort; and excelling in art, literature, and science.[2] But the nation was to suffer bitter, purgatorial years— years of hardships, foreign encroachments on its territories, and extreme miseries, from 1840 to 1906, when up to 700 distinct and unequal treaties with foreign powers were signed under coercion, and the national capital was overrun several times during the late Qing Dynasty. In particular, under the villainous "Greater East Asia Co-Prosperity Sphere Plan" concocted by the Japanese, the Chinese people were faced with a cataclysm of subjugation and near extinction. Some 35 million people were injured and killed in wars. The first line of the lyrics to the national anthem of the People's Republic of China, "March of the Volunteers," first composed as a military march during

---

1.　　　*Chief Editor's Note:* On the Chinese civilization originating in the loess highland in today's northwestern China, see Kwang-chih Chang, *The Archaeology of China*, 3rd ed. (Yale University Press, 197); Ping-ti Ho, "The Loess and the Origin of Chinese Agriculture," *American Historic Review* (1969), LVII, no. 1.S

2.　　　According to the aggregate data collected by Angus Maddison, *The World Economy: 1–2030 AD* (Oxford University Press, 2007), p. 379, China's GDP led the world during 1–1820 AD. Also see Joseph Needham, *Science and Civilization in China*, 7 vols. (Cambridge University Press, 1954–2007).

the war with the Japanese, is "Arise! You who refuse to be bound slaves, let's stand up and fight for liberty and true democracy, all the world is facing the change of tyranny, everyone who wants freedom is now crying."

How to save the disaster-ridden Chinese nation and realize national independence, democracy and happy livelihoods for the Chinese people became the most urgent political appeal for China in the twentieth century.

The process of reversing the tragic fate of the Chinese nation and bringing about its rejuvenation has been full of hardship, sacrifice, and heroism—like the great Long March itself—and yet all difficulties in the way have been overcome and the sound of victory has soared skyward.

Looking back on the history of the nation's struggles over 100 years from the nineteenth into the twentieth century, China will have experienced Mao Zedong's era of revolution and Deng Xiaoping's period of reform and opening up. The leaders of the Chinese Communist Party, represented by Mao Zedong, freed the nation and established the new China. Since then, China's fate has been in the hands of its people.

The leaders of the Chinese Communist Party, represented by Deng Xiaoping, led China on a road of transparency and reform. The socialist road with Chinese characteristics crafted by Deng Xiaoping has guided China's return to the center of the world arena, boosting its economic aggregate to the second highest in the world, and leading the nation onto an expressway of rapid development.

At present, the duty of national revitalization is in the hands of the leaders of a new generation, represented by Xi Jinping, at a time when the dream of a great rejuvenation of the Chinese nation has never been so close. How will Xi Jinping shape the new era? What portrait will history paint as he leads the new long march? He has drawn the attention of the world.

II. THE MAO ZEDONG ERA

In a conversation he had in his later years with Hua Guofeng, Wang Hongwen, Zhan Chunqiao, Jiang Qing, Yao Wenyuan, and Wang Hairong, Mao Zedong summarized his life by saying: "A man seldom lives to be 70 years old. I am now in my eighties. Now I always think about what will happen after my death since I am an old man. There is a Chinese saying: 'One's character (and historical place) is accurately judged after his death'. At least I can receive proper judgment now, even though the fact is I am still alive! I have done two things in all my life—first, I fought with Chiang Kai-shek for decades and drove him to stay in those islands in the sea, and second, I fought with the invading Japanese and sent them back to where they came from. There was seldom anyone holding forth against this matter other than those few, who never stopped talking to me with the simple purpose of reclaiming those islands. You are all well aware of that other matter: launching the Great Cultural Revolution. It received quite a few people's objection. Though both matters have not been fully achieved, I have to hand my legacy to the next generation. But how? We must do it in turmoil if not in peace, or there may be conditions that are even more dangerous, blood may be shed. What should you do then? Maybe only heaven knows."

In fact, Mao Zedong's achievements extended well beyond these two matters and the political legacy he left is of immeasurably greater value; few leaders and philosophers can be mentioned in the same breath as Mao. No one can deny the importance of the foundations Mao Zedong has laid for China, and of his ideological accomplishments.

"Political Power Grows Out of the Barrel of a Gun"

It took George Washington, the founding father of the United States of America, fourteen years to fight for the nation's birth, from the first shot fired at the Battle of Lexington in the American War of Independence in 1775, until 1789, when Washington was elected the first president of the United States. America was at war for its independence for about eight of those fourteen years.

In comparison, it took much longer, and with greater hardships, for Mao Zedong to craft the People's Republic of China. For Mao Zedong, it took 28 years from the founding of the Communist Party of China in 1921 until the establishment of the People's Republic of China in 1949, during which China underwent 22 years of brutal warfare. In contrast to how little Washington sacrificed during the American War for Independence, Mao Zedong and his people gave away incomparably more for the cause of founding a new China. Tens of millions of people devoted their lives to wars with the Japanese and to political disputes with the Kuomintang (KMT). Six members of Mao Zedong's own family paid for the revolution with their lives

Mao Zedong battled many adversaries: Japan, the US, the Soviet Union, India, the armed forces led by the US from nineteen participating countries involving the UK, France, Canada, India, and Turkey, as well as the eight-million-strong KMT force led by Chiang Kai-shek—all well beyond the challenges any Western military leaders such as Napoleon, Washington, Hannibal, or Kutuzov might have faced. There has only been one leader in the world who has confronted the US, the Soviet Union, Japan, India, and a slew of other powerful countries without being defeated: Mao Zedong.

George Washington had a military background and was awarded the rank of colonel. Mao Zedong, in contrast, came from a peasant background but loved reading and writing, served less than one year in an irregular force unit, and preferred to be called a teacher. He seldom wore a military uniform and rarely held a gun, but always led the people with his own thoughts. His articles and writings are full of his political thoughts and political strategies, also known as *Maoism* ("Thought of Mao Zedong" in Chinese).

The saying, "Political power grows out of the barrel of a gun," a slogan known to everyone, originated with Mao Zedong. It describes the birth of the new China: the reborn China, founded by war and by fire, by the blood of its people. It is why the brightest red was chosen to adorn the national flag and national emblem of the People's Republic of China.

Mao Zedong is praised as the "father of guerrilla warfare," but he can also claim profound achievements in modern warfare, especially modern strategic deterrence. As early as the 1950s, he was already convinced that nuclear weapons were formidable forces with catastrophic effects far beyond those of conventional weapons. He put forth the idea of developing sophisticated weapons, in an era still reliant on conventional weapons, based on the ever-changing strategic configuration of the world as China was faced with nuclear weapons threat from the US and the Soviet Union. He knew that developing atomic energy and building China's own strategic nuclear force was necessary to break their nuclear monopoly held at the time and overcome nuclear blackmail or extortion for the purpose of national defense; atomic bombs served not only as an important means of military deterrence and counter-deterrence but also became a reflection of a country's military and all-around power. Without nuclear weapons, China would have been unable to contend with hostile forces from other countries. Its military deterrence and counter-deterrence would have been largely compromised.

On January 15, 1955, in an enlarged session of the Secretariat of the Central Committee of the Communist Party of China (CPC), convened by Mao Zedong, China decided to develop its own atomic energy. In April 1956, in a talk to the enlarged session of the Secretariat of the Central Committee of the CPC, Mao Zedong pointed out: "Now China has no atomic bomb. But do not forget that we also had no cannons or aircraft in the past, yet we still defeated the Japanese Imperialists and Chiang Kai-shek—with mallets and rifles. Today is much better than yesterday and tomorrow will be better yet. We will have more cannons and aircraft, and atomic bombs, which we must have if we wish not to be bullied by other countries in the modern world."

To an enlarged session of the Military Commission in July, 1958, Mao Zedong stated: "I hope to establish a navy and make the air force stronger.

I hear that other countries will not recognize your legitimacy, if you do not have an atomic bomb. An object of such small size is essential. Well, we will make some atomic bombs, as well as some hydrogen bombs and intercontinental missiles. I believe ten years' efforts can do the trick. We must work this out and focus on this goal, not once a year, twice a year, or four times a year—but seven or eight times a year."

Chinese missile tests and nuclear test bases were established that year, following instructions by the CPC Central Committee and Mao Zedong. In February 1960, the Soviet Union had reneged on the agreement concerning technical aid to be provided to China for establishing its nuclear industry. China's Central Military Commission (CMC) convened an enlarged session, asserting that the first priority of Chinese strategic posture was to strengthen the national defense industry vigorously, and focus on scientific research and capital construction toward the goal of developing sophisticated technologies. It was proposed that the breakthrough in terms of sophisticated technologies should be achieved within three years. The construction policy for the Chinese defense industry was prioritized as follows: Establish a complete and independent defense industry for China; focus on the atomic bomb and guided missiles; and develop electronic technologies. The research and development of sophisticated weapons was troubled for a time, due to the extremely poor Chinese economy of the 1960s. Some politicians called for its suspension. But Mao Zedong was adamant. "We should remain focused on scientific research, and the development and testing of sophisticated weapons without hesitation or suspension," he declared. During this period, the issues surrounding atomic weapons were also discussed in talks between Mao Zedong and American journalist Edgar Snow, the author who produced the most important western reporting on the communist movement in China.

In October 1964, with the joint efforts and contributions of many excellent Chinese scientists, the first Chinese atomic bomb was a success, followed by the test explosion of a hydrogen bomb in June, 1967. In the meantime, the development of short, mid-, and long-range missiles also progressed, culminating in the successful test launch of a Chinese-designed and manufactured mid- and short-range missile system in June 1964. Two years later, the Second Artillery Corps, China's ground-to-ground strategic missile artillery, was established. Finally, essential to maintaining its independence, China had a strategic nuclear force.

It is a tribute to Mao Zedong's leadership that China acquired such sophisticated weapons, became one of the few countries that had nuclear technology in its own hands, and had mastered the technologies of satellites and guided missiles by relying on its own efforts within such a short time. Mao Zedong's strategic focus on self-defense raised China's position in the international community, providing an effective deterrent against attack by hostile forces, and defending the nation's territorial inviolability and sovereignty.

Khrushchev Can Be Anywhere

Is it harder to carve, or to maintain what has been carved already? This is a question of some philosophical and speculative value to politicians and statesmen. It is also an inevitable challenge to political leaders involved in the founding of a nation.

It is stated in "The Outline of Zhenguan's Reign," that one of the founding leaders of Tang, Emperor Taizong (Li Shimin), along with his ministers, held a special debate on the question: Is it harder to carve, or to maintain what has been carved already? Emperor Taizong of Tang asked for advice from his ministers, and many answered without hesitation: "It is certainly easier to maintain what has been carved, for founding a country requires bloodshed, warfare, and cruel combat, where one always faces the ordeals of life or death."

But the point of view of Wei Zheng, the censorial minister, was quite different: It was not to claim that founding a country was easy, but we cannot deny that such ordeals of life and death are transitory. One tends not to make mistakes when one maintains a defensive posture. Maintaining what has been carved is quite the opposite, because it is an inherently long and tedious task. What is more, no time is spared from the risks of falling into corruption or degeneration. It is common for a ruler or leader to lose willpower when he is surrounded by singing and dancing in celebrations of peace; consequently, he may not be able to maintain a regime that has been lost to dejection and political corruption. Emperor Taizong of Tang respected Wei Zheng's different analysis.

Mao Zedong, who spent a lifetime reading historical works, must have known of this debate well enough. An enormous and unified regime relies on the establishment of an apparatus of state, but the challenges before China were myriad. Internationally, it was known to all that the alliance between Mao Zedong and Stalin, with their nations' uncoordinated strengths, would not form a solid bond; Mao Zedong's opponent Chiang Kai-shek retreated to Taiwan and cultivated a political and military alliance with the United States, which would allow the possibility of a counterattack to the mainland. After failure in the Far Eastern battlefields of North Korea, the US had forged a crescent-shaped chain of alliances with South Korea (Republic of Korea), Japan, China Taiwan, the Philippines, and Vietnam, designed to curb China's influence. What added insult to injury was that the new leader of the Soviet Union, Nikita Khrushchev, launched a series of vengeful counterattacks on his predecessor immediately after the death of Stalin. This began a rift in the Sino-Soviet alliance The Soviet Union became an enormous threat lying to the north of the new China. To make matters worse for China, the Soviet Union and India, a member of the British Commonwealth, became close allies, and India became the main challenger to China's southwest.

In the heart of Mao Zedong, who seemed to be hemmed in on all sides, there was no fear of such encirclement of China, evocative of the verse "cold quick currents are rolling in the high sky." What most worried Mao Zedong was the slack willpower of politicians, as described by Wei Zheng. In other words, politicians were corrupted in all respects by their decadent lifestyles, becoming "people like Khrushchev," who would change the flag of red political power and lose absolute leadership of the proletariat. To prevent the threat that "Khrushchev can be anywhere," and to uncover potential "people like Khrushchev" who hid among his colleagues, and to keep China forever red, Mao Zedong resolutely decided to launch the Great Cultural Revolution.

The Great Cultural Revolution (1966–1975) proved to be a tragedy. In 1981, five years after Mao's demise, the CPC Central Committee adopted the *Resolutions on Certain Historical Issues of the Party since the Establishment of the PRC,* which criticized the Cultural Revolution: "It has been found that 'the Great Cultural Revolution' is not and never will be treated as a revolution of social progress in all senses. It did not 'confuse our enemies' in the slightest, but pushed ourselves into disorder; hence, it never has nor will turn 'great disorder across all of China' into 'great order across all of China'. A clear distinction has been drawn, proffering to history that 'the Great Cultural Revolution' was in its nature a civil disorder launched due to the wrong decisions of leaders, utilized by counter-revolutionary cliques, and the cause of great disasters and tragedies to the Party, China, and Chinese people of all ethnic groups."[3]

Can the principle of class struggle aid in the construction of the socialist cause? The question was debated in the *Resolutions on Historical Issues* as well as discussed many times, and in the broadest terms, by Deng

---

3.   *Resolutions on Certain Historical Issues of the Party since the Establishment of the PRC* (hereinafter referred to as the "Resolutions on Historical Issues") was approved by the Sixth Plenary Session of the 11th Central Committee of Communist Party of China on June 27, 1981.

Xiaoping. Deng Xiaoping pointed out: "One should not say that we did not accomplish anything in those twenty years [from 1957–1978]; in fact, we have done a lot and made many significant achievements, such as atomic bombs, hydrogen bombs, and guided missiles. But it is a disorder from the perspective of the overall situation, and actually represents slowing development and stagnation from the perspective of the entire economy." In a talk with President Gustáv Husák of Czechoslovakia, Deng Xiaoping said, "The technology gap between China and Japan was not tremendously large in the 1950s, prior to the period of twenty years when we closed off China and we failed to place the competition in international markets on our agenda, while Japan turned into a major economic power." In talks with several leaders of the Central Government in August 1991, Deng Xiaoping said, "People talk about 'the Asian-Pacific Century' all the time. Where does China stand? You all know that we used to fall short of the best, but were better than the worst. Now China has trouble being better than the worst. Some countries in Southeast Asia show great potential and may leave us behind." These quotations from Deng Xiaoping may not focus on history, but it is clear that he deplored China's 20 lost years of valuable development time.

Mao Zedong's Tragedy Is also a Legacy of History

"When conditions change, a leader may be unfit for leading the country through periods of change if he himself refuses to change." Lee Kuan Yew, Singapore's senior minister who passed away not long ago, sighed deeply as he spoke of Mao Zedong in his later years.

No one ever doubted Mao Zedong's determination to forge a strong and prosperous path for China. But reality made a cruel joke of this historical figure, in that what he left was a poorly developed China. History has proven that Mao Zedong could never adapt to the new age. He held onto a planned economy in the Soviet mode, perceiving the political and economic system established by Stalin as the benchmark of socialism. He had a fear of the market and a severe distrust of the intellectual.

The *Resolutions on Historical Issues* provides historical context: "Mao Zedong's main arguments for launching the Cultural Revolution included the following points: many representatives of capitalists and counter-revolutionary revisionists have infiltrated all walks of life within the Party, the government, the military, and cultural circles, and the leadership of a great many organizations was neither in the hands of Marxists, nor the people. A capitalist command was formed in the Central Government by people in power within the Party that had embarked upon the capitalist road, and that command had a revisionist political line and organizational line, with proxies at provincial, municipal, and autonomous regional levels, and in various departments of the Central Government. The methods of the past could not solve the problem. Only the Great Cultural Revolution could incite the broad masses of people to blow the whistle on the aforesaid dark side in an open and thorough manner; from the bottom up we can regain the power that has been usurped by 'capitalists'. It is a great political revolution for one class to overturn another class, and will be repeated over and over again in the future"

At that time, Mao Zedong sincerely hoped to confront the long-standing abuses of bureaucracy, and maintained a vision of the ideal socialist world. The *Resolutions on Historical Issues* continues: "Mao Zedong's main arguments for launching 'the Great Cultural Revolution' neither comply with teachings of Marxism-Leninism, nor conform to China's reality."

Coupled with Lin Biao, Jiang Qing, and others who took advantage of it, Mao Zedong's pursuit of his ideals and sincerest wishes was pushed to the extreme, and, consequently, spawned an unprecedented catastrophe. For Mao Zedong, these unanticipated consequences, so contrary to his hopes, felled him irreversibly from glory. His tragic aura was cast.

The cult of personality and the idea that "Maoism tops Marxism" were the critical reasons that Mao Zedong could extend this man-made catastrophe for the ten years that it lasted.

Interestingly, the CPC and Mao Zedong had long ago known of the possibility of this personality cult taking hold long ago, and even took certain preventive measures. In Yan'an, Mao Zedong used to exhort the Party to learn from the failure of Li Zicheng; in the Second Plenary Session of the Seventh CPC Central Committee held on the previous day of the founding of the PRC, he proposed that the Party Central Committee approve a resolution to forbid offering birthday congratulations to leaders of the Party, and to forbid using names of Party leaders as geographical names, street names, and the names of new enterprises—a wise and far-sighted decision.

In the 8th National Congress of the CPC (1982), Deng Xiaoping once again objected to a cult of personality; in his report on amendments to the Party constitution, he wrote: "[the] personality cult is a kind of social phenomenon that has existed throughout history, and this phenomenon may be reflected, inevitably, in certain forms in the Party's life and social life." It had become a Party consensus to prevent the occurrence of such a phenomenon.

However, in 1970, when China was undergoing the Cultural Revolution, in a talk with American journalist Edgar Snow, Mao Zedong said,

"Nevertheless, there should be a personality cult to a certain extent. I used to say that the personality cult did not matter, but now a bit of it seems necessary; a cult of personality has been necessary over the past few years."

Maoism was the source of the Party's wisdom. Though its concepts had philosophical value, they were degraded, turned into empty dogma as the years went on. The personality cult was inescapable during the Cultural Revolution, embodied in common maxims of the time: "Maoism tops Marxism;" "one sentence [of Mao's] is worth ten thousand [of ours];" "ask for instructions in the morning and report in the evening;" and customs such as the mandatory display of the badge with Mao Zedong's portrait on one's lapel. The "Quotation Contest" that remains fresh in many people's memories was a particularly pointed cultural relic of this period.

Rebellious factions from various organizations during the Cultural Revolution arose, gained power and acted as if the law did not apply to them. Some of the rebel factions' illegal and criminal acts referred to the *Selected Works of Mao Zedong* and his "Supreme Instructions" as their "bible."

On the other hand, such a personality cult was responsible for an unprecedentedly large popular movement to study Maoist concepts. The people were intent on understanding the thoughts of their leader. The devotion and the sacrifices of the Chinese people were truly imponderable. The tragedy of an individual will lead to the tragedy of an era. During the Cultural Revolution, when the personality cult hits its peak, none of the following incidents were not consequences of Mao Zedong's arbitrary acts as he lorded over the collective Party Central Committee: the "revisionist" labeling of Liu Shaoqi; the "Headquarters of Capitalists" imposed on Deng Xiaoping; the criticism of the "February Countercurrent;" the condemnation of Lin Bao; and the criticisms of Confucius (actually aimed at Premier Zhou), among others. The tragedy of Mao Zedong spread a tragic pall across the entirety of China and its people, trampling the Party Constitution and the Constitution of the PRC, ruining the normal lives of countless people. The Political Bureau and the State Council existed in name only. Lives were endangered, from Party and state leaders, down to the vast numbers of Party rank and file, and the masses.

The Chinese national economy was on the verge of collapse in Mao Zedong's later years. Statistical data shows that the Chinese gross national product (GNP) accounted for 4.7 percent in the world in 1955 and decreased to 2.5 percent in 1980; the GNP was comparable with Japan in 1960, but was equivalent to a quarter of Japan's in 1980 and even decreased to one fifth in 1985; American GNP was USD 460 billion more than China in 1960, but USD 368 trillion more in 1985. These are only facts about economic strength, let alone scientific and technological strengths—a gap with Japan and the West that was much larger and continued to widen—a sad and cruel consequence caused by 20 years' sinking into leftist thought and practices. According to the statistics, about RMB 120 billion was lost during the "Great Leap Forward" and another RMB 500 billion was lost during the decade of the Cultural Revolution. The total investment in capital construction in China was RMB 650 billion and fixed investment was about RMB 400–500 billion during the 30 years from the establishment of PRC to the Third Plenary Session of the 11th Central Committee of the CPC (1978). Thus it can be seen that the loss of RMB 620 million during these two crises amounted to nearly 124 percent of the total investment of capital construction in the first 30 years of the PRC after its establishment. It is even harder to sort out the intangible and imponderable losses such as missed opportunities to cultivate talent, the population explosion, and other considerable impacts of Mao's rule.

Only those who have profoundly learned from the teachings of history can make it right. One should not only feel the ruthlessness of history manifested in the Mao era tragedy, but heed the warning signs that history exhibits: Without democratic mechanisms to supervise and counterbalance power, the terrible consequences of the personality cult and individual arbitrariness affecting the direction and the overall wellbeing of a nation. It is impossible for China to disregard history, impossible to rush into the objective of building a strong and prosperous China on idle dreams alone. No subsequent statesmen of China have been untouched by the lessons of modern history.

III. THE DENG XIAOPING ERA

Many times in his life, Deng Xiaoping said to foreign friends: "I am a solider and my real specialty fighting in battle."

In 1926, Deng Xiaoping renounced the pen and joined the army to serve as a drillmaster. In the period of the Red Army, he led and launched the Bose Uprising and founded the Seventh Red Army and the Eighth Red Army; during the anti-Japanese War, he served as the Commissar at Division 129 of the Eighth Route Army and his flag was raised over the Taihang Mountain areas; in the period of the Liberation War, he served as the first secretary of the Frontline Committee and led millions of bold and brave soldiers toward the liberation of more than half of China; in the period of socialist construction, he served as the vice chairman of the National Defense Commission and exerted his utmost efforts toward military building; during the Cultural Revolution, he was entrusted with the role of vice chairman of the Central Military Commission, and concurrently that of chief of staff, at a critical and difficult moment as he boldly and resolutely directed the reorganization of the army. Deng Xiaoping took the post of the chairman of the Central Military Commission and became the supreme military commander of China in 1981 when he was 77 years old.

However, Deng Xiaoping is exalted in Chinese history primarily for his leadership role in the reform and opening up of China, even more than for his distinguished military exploits.

There is an old Chinese saying: "A noble-hearted man retains his high aspirations, even in old age." Although he was already in his seventies when he returned to politics for the third time, he was still full of pride in his heart and exerted all his energy in navigating the great ship of China through the proper channels. With his unceasing efforts, the focus of the Party and the state turned toward economic development after the Third Plenary Session of the 11th Central Committee of the CPC (1978).

In the opening up of modernized construction via thousands of new projects, he also reflected on one enormous issue: What should the road to modernization be like for a China that had undergone a decade of disorder during the Cultural Revolution? To Deng Xiaoping, the priority in modernizing China was to amass accurate knowledge of the concrete national conditions of China, in order to choose a path to modernization that conformed to China's national conditions. He stated, "When we carried out democratic revolution in the past, the plan to use the rural areas to encircle the cities developed by Mao Zedong was an example that conformed to China's national conditions; for construction in the present, we must also embark on a Chinese-style road to modernization that conforms to China's national conditions." Deng Xiaoping's reforms started from the idea of "moving steadily by feeling the way over the stones." And, fortunately, the road China chose turned out to be the right one.

"The Soviet Union Had No Deng Xiaoping"

Mikhail Gorbachev was the first and last president of the Soviet Union and, concurrently, the last General Secretary of the Central Committee of the Communist Party of the Soviet Union (CPSU). After he assumed his position as the paramount leader of the Soviet Union in March, 1985, he promoted several reform-minded ideas, including an "accelerating strategy" as well as "democratization," "transparency," and "new thinking," among others, incurring political unrest in the Soviet Union and Eastern Europe.

Finally, on December 8, 1991, during his term, the Soviet Union declared its disintegration. As of now, it remains controversial to appraise Gorbachev, and many Russians claim he was the "sinner of a nation," a characterization by which he surely feels aggrieved. But the West's fondness for Gorbachev was expressed in his earning the Nobel Peace Prize in 1990.

After attending the funeral of former US President Ronald Reagan in 2004, Gorbachev summarized the main cause for the collapse of the Soviet Union in one sentence: "The Soviet Union had no Deng Xiaoping." Among those summaries put forth by several international political figures, Gorbachev's comment was the most interesting one; his implication seemed to be: It is a pity that I am not Deng Xiaoping, and this is the reason for the failure of the Soviet Union's reform.[4]

There is no need to inflate any one individual's role in the course of history, but it is simultaneously impossible to ignore the fact that some key figures have critically influenced the trajectory of history—some will promote the inherent transformations of history, some will put them off. Even if not all responsibility can be placed upon Gorbachev, his direct influence should not be neglected. When he came to power, no republic of the Soviet Union claimed independence; however, the Soviet Union moved towards disintegration after it had been under his rule for less than seven years. There are lessons to be learned from the failures of his reforms. On May 15, 1989, at a press conference in Beijing, when many journalists constantly asked Gorbachev about the Soviet Union's reforms, he replied, "The Soviet Union's priority was to address economic issues. But we found out that issues of openness were more profound and lasting than we imagined when we addressed them, that economic issues could never be addressed without political reform, therefore, we put our hands out to political reform."

It is disastrous to lose the support of the people for reforms that are ahead of the people's needs. Moreover, there is the real possibility that reform can become a game, a scramble for power and wealth among politicians. Those cases are common in the history of reform across the world. The Soviet Union and Gorbachev just allowed the same old mistake: They lost the foundation of the people's support. The Soviet Union was therefore turned into a hollowed-out colossus—strong on the outside but weak within, and it eventually collapsed with a loud crash.

In contrast, China implemented the path of reform in the manner of "moving steadily by feeling the way over the stones" under the leadership of Deng Xiaoping. This path was designed to carry out reforms focused on the peoples' needs; for example, first by addressing the issue of feeding the population by fixing farm output quotas for each household in rural areas and allowing each household to earn provisions; second, by addressing the issue of workers' efficiency by promoting enterprise-level transformation and allowing workers and employees in state-owned enterprises to share the profits earned by enterprises with good economic outlooks.

Originally, "moving steadily by feeling the way over the stones" was a well-known saying among the people of China. Its meaning, that if one must cross an unknown river, without the aid of bridges, or boats, one must test the water, advancing slowly, feeling their way through the current and the riverbed, is the same as that imparted by the two-part aphorism "across a river steadily, by having felt the way over stones—safe and secure." The intent of examining this folk saying in the context of historical study is to reinforce the necessity of gauging conditions, learning rules and laws, estimating risks, and progressing steadily in the absence of sufficient practical experience.

Who exactly proposed the utilization of "moving steadily by feeling the way over the stones" as a practical philosophy? Referring to the available information and data, it was Chen Yun, an important member of the first and second generations of China's central collective leadership, who stressed the method. On April 7, 1950, he employed the phrase for the first time. In a statement in the 27th meeting of government affairs of the Government Administration Council, he said, "Neither price hikes nor declines will do any good for productivity. We need to 'move steadily by feeling the way over the stones.'" This is the earliest context in which such statement was applied to work methods in the CPC literature.

After the reform and opening up, as an important member of the second generation of CPC central collective leadership, Chen Yun spoke of "moving steadily by feeling the way over the stones" as a methodology of reform a number of times. For example, he delivered an important address known as the "Economic Situation and Lessons Learned" in a central working meeting, in which he explored the principles and methods that reform should adopt by summarizing the lessons of history. He asserted that "China needs reform, but we should step forward steadily, because our reform's ramifications are too complex to rush. There is no doubt that reform depends on certain theoretical studies, economic data and projections. What's more important is to set about through pilot projects, in which case, we can sum up experiences at any time—that is, to 'move steadily by feeling the way over the stones'. At the beginning, the steps we take should be small and slow." In the closing session on December 25th of the same year, Deng Xiaoping made it clear that he was in full agreement with Chen Yun's address; he said: "Chen Yun's address correctly summed up the lessons learned on a series of issues regarding the economic work of China over the previous 31 years and henceforth shall serve as the long-term guideline for us."[5]

Deng Xiaoping, the chief designer of China's reforms and opening up, could not agree more with the working philosophy of "moving steadily by feeling the way over stones." To Deng Xiaoping, building socialism with Chinese characteristics was a cause no ancients of the past had attempted. It would be impossible to find answers in the tenets of Marxism-Leninism. There existed no practical experiences anywhere for China to emulate. The only choice was to "move steadily by feeling the way over stones."

At the start of the nation's reform and opening up, Deng Xiaoping reminded the senior cadres of China: "What we are aspiring toward is a new cause. Marx has never taught us anything about it, no ancestor has ever done it, and no other socialist country has ever done this. There is no existing precedent. All we can do is learn by doing and explore while in practice." He also pointed out, "What we are doing is an experiment. It is new to all of us and this is way we need to move forward by feeling the way." He added, "One should be brave and bold for the sake of reform and opening up, and daring, instead of like a woman with bound feet. As long as you are certain, be bold in trying and be bold in going. 'Be bold in trying and be bold in going' applies to rural reforms as well as urban reforms." It can be seen from this that Deng Xiaoping's idea was to guide reform on a reliable and orderly track. And, because of this, "moving steadily by feeling the way over the stones" has been recognized as one of the most important methodologies of reform proposed by Deng Xiaoping, as well as an important token of what we have learned from the great success of China's reform in the era of Deng Xiaoping.

Daring to Embark on a Different Path

No other nation in the world respects its ancestors quite like the Chinese people. Even the American historian Ross Terrill, who spent a lifetime studying Mao Zedong, said at the end of his book *Mao: A Biography* that Mao Zedong was struggling to break though the outmoded conventions and undesirable customs set by ancestors, but that it seemed fated that ancestors' souls still came to him and to the Chinese people in his later years.

What do ancestors mean to the Chinese? A common precept of the Chinese states that whatever ancestors have said should be acted upon, and whatever ancestors have decided should be followed faithfully. After Mao Zedong's death, this concept is just what his successor Hua Guofeng

5.   Han Zhenfeng: *Who Proposed "Moving Steadily by Feeling the Way over Stones" as a Method for the Reform?*

took as Mao Zedong's political legacy. But Deng Xiaoping was different. He employed a down-to-earth attitude toward ancestors, that is, to inherit the correct parts and discard the wrong parts by analyzing the words of ancestors. In contrast to the ancestors people understand generally, Chinese communists of the time also recognized some "foreign ancestors" for their political legacies, including Marx, Engels, Lenin, and Stalin, among others. The "foreign ancestors" had occupied the summits of ideology, their works worthy of study and analysis.

"We cannot discard our ancestors!" This was the first attitude Deng Xiaoping held towards his forebears. Deng Xiaoping said, "That we would focus on economic construction in the midst of reform and opening up does not mean we throw away Marx, Lenin, or Mao Zedong. We cannot discard our ancestors!" The ancestors here mainly referred to the doctrines and thoughts created by Marx, Engels, Lenin, Mao Zedong, and other revolutionary teachers. Deng Xiaoping believed that they offered a theoretical basis to guide the thoughts of the ruling party, and where the roots of the Party's progressiveness grew. The fundamental concepts would be lost without these ancestors, which would lead to confusion, without any doubt.

In a talk with the American journalist Mike Wallace, Deng Xiaoping was always honest about his true state of mind. He said, "I am a Marxist—Marxism is also known as communism—in the past, we fostered revolution, struggled to seize the political power of China, and finally founded the People's Republic of China because we believed in it and we held the dream in our heart." He added: "We also combined the fundamental principles of Marxism and China's reality to construct our country after the victory of revolution." Later, he said that Marxism would not collapse, "not due to the thickness of its books but because the truth of Marxism is able to withstand battering," and "Marxism is unadorned. It tells a simple truth."

"We cannot lay down the flag of Maoism"—a steadfast, fundamental understanding that Deng Xiaoping adhered to from the beginning to the end. In the process of drafting the *Resolutions on Historical Issues*, Deng Xiaoping declared: "One of the most important items is to determine the historical standing of Mao Zedong, and adhere to and develop Maoism; we shall hold the flag of Maoism not only today but from now on." He also said, "*The Resolutions* shall focus on, and recognize, adherence to and development of Maoism as the fundamental issue," and, "A huge mistake will be made in history if we refuse to record or adhere to Maoism." He repeated that China would never totally repudiate Mao Zedong as Khrushchev had done to Stalin: "We must always hold the flag of Maoism while appraising Mao

Zedong's contributions and faults, especially the mistakes he made in his later years, from the facts."

Deng Xiaoping was firmly sticking to his principles and analyzing problems scientifically, and his sense of propriety was of great guiding significance, allowing the CPC to hold a steady political direction in the process of setting things right for China's reform, and opening up. Today, people still praise the foresight and discernment of Deng Xiaoping, who refused to abandon the correct theories passed on by his ancestors.

However, Deng Xiaoping did understand that the ancestors did not provide any plans for China's reform. In another words, there was no answer in books left by political ancestors to the question "What course will China take?" Deng Xiaoping encouraged his colleagues to be brave enough to say what ancestors had not said, and to free their minds.

In 1983, during a visit of the Chairman of the Communist Party of Australia, Edward Fowler Hill, and his wife, Deng Xiaoping said, "Without freeing our minds, our cause will never be improved, nor will it advance, if one only knows how to quote what Marx, Lenin, and Chairman Mao said or wrote."

In 1984, the Third Plenary Session of the 12th Central Committee worked out the *Decision on Reform of the Economic Structure*, which was highly praised by Deng Xiaoping. He said, "My impression is that they have worked out a draft about political economy that combines the basic principles of Marxism and China's practicing socialism. This is my comment;" and, "The document of the reform of economic structure is very good; it explains what socialism is, and where something is new, not derived from ancestors."

In 1987, in a discussion with Japanese visitors about the Party's 13th Central Committee, Deng Xiaoping said, "What we are enacting is a new cause. Marx has never taught anything about it, no ancestors have ever done it, and none of the other socialist countries have ever done it. So there is no existing experience before us. All that we can do is learn by doing and explore in practice." Because of this, on the one hand, Deng Xiaoping paid respect to his ancestors and abided by their teachings; on the other hand, he also called for breaking new roads and embarking on a new path that no ancestor had ever traversed. Deng Xiaoping explored many new things. To summarize, there are three aspects that together made him such an impressive world figure.

First, Deng Xiaoping was the first person in the world to put forth the idea that a market economy could be developed in a socialist country, which was a unique experiment. The courageous breakthrough, followed by successful implementation, allowed the activation, enrichment, and rapid development of China's economic and social advances. His decisiveness in this regard earned China time and gained strategic initiative, evincing his greatest theoretical innovation and contribution to the cause of socialism.

Second, some people were led by a preconception that more public ownership was better for China, and that it would demonstrate the superiority of socialism. Under the allure of collective ownership, and the shibboleth of "each according to labor," the people's commune system was hatched in the past. But, this fanaticism attempted to hasten the realization of what Marx had prescribed for an advanced stage of socialism in the primary stage. Deng Xiaoping drove China back to reality, and calling a spade a spade, he reminded the Chinese people that China was still in the primary stage of socialism and would remain so for a long time. The Chinese people, he importuned, were to proceed from this fact in order to solve all problems, as well as to formulate all policies and guidelines. This understanding provided a solid theoretical basis for the series of important reforms launched under his auspices.

Third, if other people tended to follow rigidly the dictates of socialism in their attempt to achieve and preserve a socialist system, Deng Xiaoping believed that a socialist society needed constant adjustment and reform. Reform, to him, could be interpreted as a revolution from the perspective of freeing and developing productive forces. No one had made such a high evaluation of the role and significance of reform. He also said that a socialist country must open up to the current international environment, whereby the former blockade of socialist China by the international community was broken, turning China from its previously closed or semi-closed state into a country that could accurately acquire various information from other countries and acclimatize itself to economic globalization. A new situation of opening up that had never existed in the history of China or in the history of socialism was taking shape.

The Chief Architect: Sustaining a Century

Professor Ezra Vogel, the former director of the Fairbank Center at Harvard University, conducted long-term studies of Japan and China and wrote the bestseller *Japan as Number 1: Lessons for America* in 1979. In 2013, he published *Deng Xiaoping and the Transformation of China*, a book that took him a decade to complete. Prior to the 110th anniversary of Deng Xiaoping's birthday in 2014, in an exclusive interview in the Chinese newspaper *Global Times*, he said that, after the arrest of the "Gang of Four," whoever became the leader of China would embark on the road of reform, but no one could have made China's reform and opening up as successful as Deng Xiaoping.

Deng Xiaoping is usually praised as the chief architect of China's reform and opening up, but Professor Vogel refers to him as "General Manager," a name that is more popular in the United States. Professor Vogel wrote that Deng Xiaoping had accomplished a mission that all other leaders of China failed to achieve in the previous 150 years—Deng Xiaoping and his colleagues had found a way to enrich people and to strengthen China. In the process of accomplishing his objective, Deng Xiaoping also led China's fundamental transition, both in terms of its relations with the world community and China's own systems of governance, and its society. Indeed, the structural transformation under the leadership of Deng Xiaoping can be called the most fundamental remaking of China since the founding of the Han Dynasty over 2,000 years earlier.

"Deng Xiaoping is not an architect who holds a great blueprint in his hands and dominates changes. In fact, there is no clear, complete, and readily-prepared design for the era of transformation," wrote Professor Vogel, who preferred to call Deng Xiaoping "the General Manager in charge of comprehensive leadership in the process of transformation."

"Chinese or foreigners, it is hard for whoever grows up after the retirement of Deng Xiaoping to imagine how serious were the issues Deng Xiaoping confronted as he embarked on the journey: a country that shuts the door against any completely different and new thoughts; the long-lasting schism between sufferers and persecutors during the Cultural Revolution; military leaders' resistance against disarmament and reduction in military expenditure; people's hostile attitudes towards imperialism and foreign capitalists; socially conservative structures of urban and rural areas; urban residents' refusal to accept 200 million peasant workers; and the disputes arisen due to some becoming rich and others remaining poor," wrote Professor Vogel. He added, "Deng Xiaoping showed greater courage and boldness than leaders in other great powers such as India, Russia, and Brazil in the process of promoting the globalization of China. Although successors advanced the process after Deng Xiaoping, we must remember the fact that the fundamental breakthroughs had been accomplished upon Deng Xiaoping's retirement."

On January 18, 1992, the 88-year-old Deng Xiaoping boarded the special train to South China from Beijing. The tour lasted nearly two months and talks occurred off and on, the contents of which were recorded in *Selected Works of Deng Xiaoping: Volume III*. The article titled "Excerpts from Talks Given in Wuchang, Shenzhen, Zhuhai, and Shanghai (Jan. 18–Feb. 21, 1992)" was called the "Southern Talks" for short, and it was arranged at the end of the official works of Deng Xiaoping, among as the top-ranking works.

In fact, Deng Xiaoping's political successors regard the "Southern Talks" as his true political legacy, in which the most important concept put forth was "the reform and opening up shall sustain a century."

Deng Xiaoping's Southern Talks embodied distinct characteristics with an awareness of China's socialist road being long lasting and full of difficulties, but remaining confident in the ultimate victory ahead; besides, it stressed that it was common for a socialist country to encounter setbacks and frustrations and it was a fundamental law of humanity's development from a low to an advanced level that socialism would inevitably take the place of capitalism after twists and turns. Deng Xiaoping asserted, "Our program of socialism is only decades old and China is still in the preliminary state. To solidify and develop a socialist system, we still need to go through a long historical stage with persistent and arduous efforts of several generations, more than ten generations, or even dozens of generations. In no way will we treat it lightly."

It has been more than 20 years since the Southern Talks. There have been extensive and profound changes in the international situation as well as in modern China, but political successors to Deng Xiaoping adhere to the "basic line" unswervingly. Over more than 20 years, the third generation of central collective leadership of the CPC, represented by Jiang Zeming and the CPC Central Committee with General Secretary Hu Jintao, raise high the flag of socialism with Chinese characteristics and keep pace with the times and constantly enrich and innovate when confronting the new reforms in practice. They have further explored and answered a series of important issues and questions: what kind of Party China should build; how to build that Party; what kind of development the country should accomplish; how to develop; how to balance law-based governance and virtue-based governance. And on the basis of explorations and commentaries regarding the question of how socialism is best defined, how to address other practical problems encountered since the second generation of central collective leadership, represented by Deng Xiaoping, and put into place the essential socio-economic principles, the "Three Represents" and "Scientific Outlook on Development," which further enrich and advance Deng Xiaoping's blueprint of China's road of reform and opening up, a road that has ultimately brought China to the center of the world arena.

IV. A NEW ERA UNVEILED BY XI JINPING

In August 2004, Xi Jinping gave an exclusive interview to Yan'an TV, when he was the Secretary of the Zhejiang Provincial Committee of the CPC. At the end of the interview, the journalist said that he would like to welcome Xi Jinping to consider Yan'an a second home on behalf of his fellow countrymen. Xi Jinping promised warmly, "Absolutely, I will."

Eleven years later, at the Spring Festival of 2015, Xi Jinping, by now General Secretary of the CPC Central Committee, along with his family, returned to his second hometown Yan'an to visit fellow city folk and pay them a New Year's well-wishing call. When news of the visit was broadcast on the Internet, it prompted applause from all over China, and people praised such "a brave man with tender feelings" who was "sincerely for the people."

As well as maintaining an image of being approachable and humane, as a politician, Xi Jinping's democratic, open-minded, and tolerant spirit is praised by the Chinese people. In October 2013, an animated video called "How a Political Leader Was Tempered" was released on the Internet in China. The brief video depicted Xi Jinping as a cartoon—the first time in history that a leader of China had appeared to the public as a cartoon character. "Netizens" and online public opinion welcomed Xi Jinping, affectionately calling him "Uncle Xi." It can be seen from his relaxed and natural interactions with the people that Xi Jinping's attitude is open and liberal. Xi Jinping reveals: "To sum up my governing philosophy: Serve the people and assume the responsibilities I must shoulder." He points out that the essential qualities a good leader must possess include *daringness to be responsible* and *daringness to play*. He sets an example in promoting reform, always holding his responsibilities in the forefront of his mind and carrying the people in his heart, becoming a beacon of inspiration in his dutifulness. Xi Jinping's leadership embodies the notions of *daring to be responsible* and *daring to play*.

How Will Xi Jinping "Play the Second Half" of China's Reform?

Xi Jinping is a big fan of soccer. His Beijing 101 Middle School was known for its embrace of the sport, and Xi Jinping fell in love with it in his youth. At that time, Xi Jinping used to play with some student players of the "second red generation" on the Huiwen football team. During Xi Jinping's term as secretary of Zhengding County Committee of the CPC, Hebei Province, he usually went back to Beijing on weekends and asked his good friend Nie Weiping, the national champion in Wei Qi, to look for tickets for football matches. When Xi Jinping and Nie Weiping watched a match between the Chinese team and Watford FC, then UK First Division runners-up, in Shanghai in the summer of 1983, both left angrily at the end after seeing Watford score five goals against the bewildered Chinese defenders. Speaking of the game, Nie Weiping said that although Xi Jinping "was very saddened by watching it, he did not stop paying close attention to Chinese football."

In 1998, in an article entitled "Advocate for the 'Economic Chorus,'" Xi Jinping wrote about his revelation, realized from soccer games, that the "economic chorus" was about harmony and coordination: "for instance, I am afraid that in a football game an individual's technical skill [is overemphasized], and the important tactic on the field is the coordination of consciousness; the economic work of any place should constitute an organic whole in all aspects." Because Xi Jinping loves soccer, people have employed the game as a metaphor to describe China's reforms under his leadership. A typical analogy is the phrase "how to play the second half of China's reform".

China's reform has been on track for over 30 years. The point when Deng Xiaoping became the supreme leader of China's reform in 1979, to Xi Jinping's succession to it in 2012, can be referred to as the "first half" of China's reform. This first half of China's reform has seen remarkable achievements that have attracted the world's attention, and it is universally acknowledged as "the rise of China" or "the miracle of China."

But not everything that Xi Jinping is faced with can be called optimistic.

The Chinese scholar Professor Sun Liping, a professor of sociology from Tsinghua University, comments, "It is known to all that we call the previous time of more than 30 years the 'period of reform and opening up'. Let us look back at it, we might have simplified something at the beginning of that period and missed something important. What do I mean? At that time, reform, in the minds of the people, was nothing more than a process from a starting point to an end point where that starting point denoted the old system and the end point the new system. What will the consequence of the process be? Based on the logic at that time, we could think out only two consequences—success or failure, that is, the reform would be a success if we reached the end point, or otherwise a failure if we did not. However, there is actually a third possibility, which people did not expect at first: The process may stall halfway. It not only holds still, but will also settle the state into a relatively stable system."[6]

Once the reforms stop, "people may prefer not to continue;" in other words, players quit in the second half. Without a doubt, this is just a metaphor, and the deeper problems of China's reform are even more severe.

---

6.   Sun Liping. "Thirty Years: A Restart of Reform," *Reader*, July 2015.

Xi Jinping examined this, believing that China's reform has entered a critical phase. What has to be tackled will be the tough issues. In this case, we need to have the courage to 'go deep into the mountains, knowing well that there are tigers there' to steadily push reform forward."[7]

In November, 2013, entrusted by the Political Bureau of the Central Committee, Xi Jinping elaborated on the circumstances and difficulties in promoting reform at the Third Plenary Session of the 18th CPC Central Committee:

> Since the 18th CPC Central Committee, the committee has been hammered by the lessons learned through history that reform and opening up is a critical move to determine the fate of contemporary China and also a critical move to accomplish the 'Two Centenary Goals' and bring about a great rejuvenation of the Chinese nation. It will never hit an end point in development, and we must continue to free our minds, and move forward the reform and opening up; we may find ourselves in a blind alley if we stop or go back.
>
> At present, extensive and profound changes are occurring in both domestic and overseas environments, we have already encountered numerous conspicuous contradictions and challenges in the development of China, and there will be many difficulties and problems on our way forward. For example, there will be imbalance, lack of coordination, unsustainable issues in development that remain conspicuous. The current innovative capabilities of the scientific and technological sectors are not strong enough; the industrial structure is unreasonable, and development remains unbalanced; the rural and urban development gap and income distribution gap remain issues, causing more social conflict; there are many problems in terms of the vital interests of the masses, including education, employment, social insurance, medical treatment, housing, ecological environment, food and drug safety, safety in products, public security, and law enforcement and judicature; some people are still living in poverty while problems of bureaucracy, hedonism, and extravagance arise; and corruption tends to occur and concentrate in some sectors and the potential for anti-corruption remains grim. The key to tackling these problems is to deepen the reforms.[8]

---

7.   Speech at the College of Europe in Brugge, *People's Daily*, April 2, 2014.

8.   Xi Jinping. "Introduction to 'Decision of the Central Committee of the Communist Party of China on Some Major Issues Concerning Comprehensively Deepening the Reform,'" *People's Daily*, November 16, 2015.

Xi Jinping has a well-thought-out plan in his mind to play the "second half" of China's reform. In 2014, in a speech to a seminar for provincial and ministry-level cadres to learn and implement the spirit of the Third Plenary Session of the 18th CPC Central Committee, Xi Jinping stated: "From the perspective of forming a more developed and fixed system, we have finished the first half of the socialist program, the main historical task of which includes establishing a basic system of socialism and reform on this foundation; and now we have laid a solid foundation. As to the second half, our main historical task will be to improve and develop the socialist system with Chinese characteristics and provide a more complete, stable, and effective institutional system for the development of the Party-state's causes and the lasting political stability of China."

From a Collective Presidency to a Hero Hunting Tigers

During the period from 2002 to 2013, the Political Bureau of the Central Committee of the Communist Party of China served as the decision-making body with supreme power over the CPC. It was composed of nine members, representing the eight leading groups including the Party, the National People's Congress, the government, the People's Political Consultative Conference, the military, the discipline inspection and supervision, and politics and the law, respectively, in addition to the general secretary. The nine members of the Standing Committee of the Political Bureau had their own divisions of work and were entrusted with different tasks and with coordinating with each other, which constitutes the balance of power with Chinese characteristics. This system was described as a "collective presidency" by Professor Hu Angang, a professor from the School of Public Policy and Management at Tsinghua University.

Professor Hu Angang believes that China's collective presidency concept particularly emphasizes the word "collective," meaning "collective members" instead of "an individual;" it means "multiple institutions" instead of "one institution;" it means "collective intelligence" instead of "individual intelligence;" and it means "collective decision-making" instead of "individual decision-making." It is reflected in five mechanisms during actual operation: collective succession, collective coordination and distribution of responsibilities, collective learning, collective investigation and survey, and collective decision-making.

It is known to people who are familiar with the course of Chinese politics that collective leadership is an institutional arrangement to correct the possibility of an individual reigning over the central government, as in the time of Mao Zedong. Its purpose is to prevent supreme leaders from acting arbitrarily or making decisions out of their own willfulness. As soon as the collective leadership has been turned into a collective presidency, a new pattern emerges in which numerous authorities may counterbalance each other, and which reflects a folk saying that "nine dragons manage the water." The United States implements a separation of the three branches of power in its political system, which can sometimes result in a political environment of extreme disorder; it is not hard to imagine how inefficient the arrangement can become. Therefore, in the case of a collective presidency, because each member has the power to "reject," the possibility of reaching consensus despite unresolved disputes is lower.

In 2010, there were remarks echoing that "few government orders reach outside of Zhongnanhai," indicating that the power mechanism, by focusing excessively on counterbalance, had shown inefficiency, incompetency, and severe internal friction. Any corruption or deterioration of individual members occurring at this supreme level of the power system would create immeasurable damage to political operations. As of now, this could be speculated upon, but no one will ever know the details after the fact, given that high-level political information is classified.

It is obvious that the evolution from collective presidency to the paradigm of "nine dragons managing the water" goes against the original intention to design an efficient collective leadership, hence appropriate reforms and adjustments must be made to the power mechanism to end the dilemma of standstill reform, inconsistent decisions, and poor executive abilities. This challenge has become the responsibility of Xi Jinping.

Richard Nixon, former president of the United States, once pointed out that one will never truly know the magnificence of the highest peak unless they have experienced the bottom of the deepest valley. So one can never understand where a leader's drive comes from if they are not in the leader's shoes.

Outsiders will never understand how much pressure a politician is under when he is faced with the delegation and adjustment of the power dynamic, most especially the risks inherent in trying to eliminate corruption at the uppermost levels of government. There is a Chinese saying: "Punishments do not extend to high officials," meaning that criminal punishments do not extend to officials above the provincial and ministerial level; in ancient China, the toughest punishments to senior officials might be demotion, degradation, criticism, and denouncement, so as to maintain the facade of infallible hierarchies.

Measures intended to reorganize the power structure, rectify poor administration, and crack down on corruption, in accordance with the law, are figuratively called "hunting tigers" by the Chinese people. Confronting a tiger, one risks being eaten alive by the predator. Anti-corruption measures are highly risky: The hunter will suffer if he fails in pursuit of his prey. The hunter must be certain. In earlier times, nine times out of ten, a blind eye was turned to such predators.

At the end of 2012, many Chinese people could be forgiven for harboring doubts when Xi Jinping, who had just ascended to the top of the political arena, declared to the public, "If you want to work with iron, you must be tough yourself," if one is determined to "fight all corruption" and "crack down on any corrupt acts." Previous leaders of China had made similar declarations, but what the public had ultimately witnessed were all words but few deeds.

However, soon afterward, Xi Jinping launched a series of "tiger-hunting" moves that proved his sincerity to the Chinese people. It took only one year, 2014, for him to hunt down four enormous targets: Zhou Yongkang, Xu Caihou, Ling Jihua, and Su Rong.

Zhou Yongkang was a former member of the Standing Committee of the Political Bureau, the former secretary of the Political and Judiciary Commission under the CPC Central Committee, a former senior official at the national level, and a former member of the collective presidency, who enjoyed being received as a head of state when he visited foreign countries. He was called "the Political and Judicial King" by foreign media. Xu Caihou was the former vice chairman of the Central Military Commission, a former member of the Standing Committee of the Political Bureau, and a senior official at the deputy national level, who had been in charge of cadres and human resources in the military for more than a decade. His position in the military was higher than the US Secretary of Defense and the Chairman of the Joint Chiefs of Staff. He was a decisive figure in the Chinese military. Ling Jihua served as the secretary of the Secretariat of the CPC Central Committee and the director of the General Office of the CPC Central Committee, as well as the vice chairman of the Chinese Peoples' Political Consultative Conference and the head of the United Front Work Department of the CPC Central Committee when he was convicted of official corruption. Ling Jihua was the director of the General Office of the CPC Central Committee, a position which was more important and more sensitive than the director of the White House in the US. The role is referred to as "the Manager of the Imperial Palace" by the people of China and is a position near the core of China's power. Su Rong had been the provincial secretary in many provinces, and was serving as the vice chairman of the Chinese People's Political Consultative Conference when he was arrested, and was still a senior officer at the deputy national level.

Furthermore, since the 18th CPC Central Committee, there have been more than 100 corrupt officials above the provincial and ministerial level under investigation and receiving punishments, including many senior officials in high positions.

Young Internet-savvy Chinese people created an online cartoon depicting Xi Jinping riding a tiger, shaking his fist in fury, ready to strike, in emulation of famous hunters of tigers. The Chinese people had recognized Xi Jinping's courage in cracking down on corruption. The assumption of leaders being long on talk and short on action was replaced by an image of one steadfastly devoted to the course of justice. In his case, the image was the reality. He feared nothing, spared no effort for the sake of CPC discipline.

Since the founding of the new China in 1949, until 2012 the officials at the highest level who had been punished for corruption in accordance with the law stayed at the level of vice prime minister, vice chairman, or member of the Political Bureau. No member of the Standing Committee of the Political Bureau or any official at the national level had been held accountable to the law because of corruption. An old Chinese saying went, "anti-corruption has an upper limit," so did accountability for corruption vanish at the level of a member of the Standing Committee of the Political Bureau.

But the exception under Xi Jinping was the first departure in the governing history of the CPC. Now, whoever, at whatever level, regardless of however much power they held, would be held accountable once they break the law or the standards of CPC discipline. The line has been drawn by Xi Jinping.

Lord Acton of the United Kingdom once stated: "Power tends to corrupt, and absolute power corrupts absolutely," which has proven itself to be an inexorable law. How does one tame power? How can we check power before it corrupts? The political history of humankind is the history of humans learning how to handle power properly. In this regard, Xi Jinping's political advances hold special significance. It is beyond the scope of imagination to consider a nation of 1.36 billion people without one powerful helmsman. The primary pursuit must be the establishment of a highly efficient and stable execution of power. In the meantime, it is a great challenge as well to prevent the moral dissipation and corruption of a great power, and uphold the standards of honesty and uprightness.

Wang Qishan, a member of the Standing Committee of the Political Bureau and the secretary of the CPC Commission for Discipline Inspection, told a relevant story once: He met his old American friend, Henry Kissinger, in Beijing after he was assigned to the position of secretary of the CPC

Commission for Discipline Inspection in March 2013. When Wang introduced his position and duties, Kissinger commented, "that is a great job." Later Wang Qishan laughed and said to him, "'a great job', in Kissinger's words, actually meant 'an impossible task', and I know he did not compliment me, but rather he was teasing me. He meant it was impossible for me to do and to control."

It is understandable to describe the elimination of corruption and upholding of integrity within a governing party of 86 million members as an impossible task. Long ago, the saying "eliminating corruption causes the Party to vanish; not eliminating corruption causes China to vanish" appeared in the Chinese media. This so-called "impossible task" is on the agenda of Xi Jinping.

Faced with such a situation, Xi Jinping replies: "The Communist Party of China refuses to believe in heresy." Tough moves should be taken, in accordance with Xi's words. In less than three years, from 2012 to the beginning of 2015, Xi Jinping has proven that his courage, wisdom, and political skills are ready to accomplish the "impossible" task, by means of many bold moves. Without a doubt, it will be a great contribution toward political civility across the world if the "new normal" welcomed by the people, embodied by clear and bright politics, honest and incorruptible officials, and effective governance, is realized in the country with the largest population, the longest history of merit-conscious autocracy, and the deepest long-standing bureaucracy.

Targeting 2049

"Xi Jinping is playing a prodigious game of chess." This has been the relatively consistent comment from international pundits over the two years after he came into power.

The famous scholar of China, Zheng Yongnian, the director of the East Asian Institute, National University of Singapore, contributed quite an accurate analysis. In a speech in October, 2014, he pointed out: "The CPC must take into account long-term goals if they wish to hold power for a long time. It is very important. One only aspires to become president, and plans for matters during the presidency, without thinking of anything after it in most other countries with a multi-party system in the world. From this perspective, people need to know that Xi Jinping does not only think about his own terms. China's constitution requires that the president's term is limited to ten years, so he does not only take into account matters within his two terms; in my opinion, he also has taken into account the 30 years after his terms. This is different from Jiang Zemin and Hu Jintao."

What is the central concept? After 1949, there were 30 years of Mao Zedong, 30 years of Deng Xiaoping; now Xi Jinping is thinking about the 30 years after them, which are very important in the fate of China. The CPC, under the leadership of Mao Zedong, took power in 1949, after which he intended to carry out social and institutional reconstruction. It is a pity that he was an idealist. He proceeded with many revolutionary measures after 1949, which caused many societal problems, including the Cultural Revolution.

Deng Xiaoping learned the lessons of Mao Zedong and turned, in his 30 years, toward modernizing national development. From this perspective, the respective ten years of Jiang Zemin's and Hu Jintao's leadership can be included in the era of Deng Xiaoping. Now China has entered into the post–Deng Xiaoping era officially, with Hu Jintao symbolizing the shifting of the era from Deng Xiaoping into a post–Deng Xiaoping era. Xi Jinping's focus is the next 30 years. The central concept here is that Mao Zedong marks the first generation of the new China, Deng Xiaoping marks the second generation, and Xi Jinping marks the third.

Zheng Yongnian also believes that it is very important for Xi Jinping to end the separation of power inherent in the so-called "collective presidency" and carry out reform by concentrating the central government: "First, politically, it is most important that Xi Jinping ended the previous separation of power and developed it towards concentration of power after he came into office. This is very important. Since Deng Xiaoping's reform in 1979, there was further separation of power in each reform. This was especially so in the 1980s, and after Deng Xiaoping's Southern Talks. Zhu Rongji started to concentrate power economically but there was also further separation of power at the time of Hu Jintao and Wen Jiabao. The separation at that time was not an initiative by the Central Government but a consequence of failure to concentrate. Why does China need to concentrate power now? Xi Jinping said that the easy part of the reform has been accomplished while the difficult part has not. That is, after eating the meat, the bone awaits. China needs to concentrate power. This is the first reason."[9]

Professor Hu Angang, of Tsinghua University, believes that there is a collective presidency in China and an individual presidency in the United States, and the former is better than the latter. But in fact, it is the opposite, because in the end there might be no president or leader to assume responsibility in a collective presidency. The most important link, however, in each political system is who shall assume political responsibility. When there are nine members of the Standing Committee, how will they

---

9.   Zheng Yongnian. *Xi Jinping's Political Roadmap*, Ifeng, October 16, 2014.

counterbalance each other? There is separation of the three powers in the West, but separation of nine powers in China. How is it that the case of Zhou Yongkang erupted in China? It is because of issues in the top-level design, which is the division of individual responsibilities for the nine members of the Standing Committee—that one individual is responsible for one division. This, in Zheng Yongnian's words, is a system of 'feudalism'. It is obvious from the event of Zhou Yongkang that such division does not work. In fact, the leadership at that time was not a true leadership because they might reject each other and no one would be convinced by each other. The people were also confused, and complained that they did not know who was responsible. Such a system made it impossible to accomplish tasks in most cases, but gave rise to the event of Zhou Yongkang. It is now that China needs concentration of power and Xi Jinping's judgment is accurate regarding it."

Zheng Yongnian's opinion quite conforms to the Chinese people's impressions. The open question is how Xi Jinping will lay out the future after the end of the Standing Committee, the "nine dragons managing the water."

On June 16, 2014, the *Financial Times Chinese* published an article entitled "Xi Jinping's Reform and His Mission" written by Robert B. Zoellick, the 11th president of the World Bank (2007–2012), who had served as US trade representative (2001–2005), and the US deputy secretary of state (2005–2006). His observations are thorough and insightful: "About a year since his taking office, Xi Jinping's direction as president of China is increasingly clear. His priority is the preservation of Party control. At present, the central government calls for cadres to watch a movie about the collapse of the Soviet Union, in which Mikhail Gorbachev is not considered a hero.

"Xi Jinping's self-criticism and anti-corruption measures are intended to purify the CPC and enhance power. The speed at which he has consolidated power exceeds expectations. He plays the leading role in the Political Bureau of the CPC Central Committee, he the chairman of the Central Military Commission, the chairman of the new National Security Committee, and the leader of economic reform, as well as several high-level leading groups in the Party.

"Under the premise of regarding the preservation of the CPC as a priority, his reform shall be deemed as a means to realize his goal. Economic reform will not open along with political opening. On the contrary, considering the risk of reform, his belief is to place politics under his control.

"The reform focuses on economic governance and modernization. For the West, these terms seem to be ambiguous. But Xi Jinping's goal is to be one of the greatest leaders of China, enjoying equal popularity and significance with Mao Zedong and Deng Xiaoping. The president's historical mission is to restore China's status as a great country and build a modern economic structure."

If Mr. Zoellick lays particular stress on Xi Jinping's blueprint for economic reform, other observers have noticed that Xi Jinping's overall plans for reform appear ready to come to fruition. Opinions published in the Hong Kong newspaper *Ta Kung Pao*, are the most representative. In June, 2014, several days after Mr. Zoellick published his article, *Ta Kung Pao* analyzed Xi Jinping's new directions in leadership: "Xi Jinping, as the supreme leader of China and the leader of CPC Finance and Economy Group, as well as the chairman of the National Security Committee, the leader of the CPC Network and Information Group, holds the highest state power granted by the constitution. More importantly, he is in charge of politics, national security, foreign affairs, social management, and other important sectors, which is convenient for him to plan the overall course both internationally and domestically, greatly promoting the operating efficiency of power within the complex patterns of influence, in order to perform more efficient high-level plans to deepen reforms. Now, Xi Jinping's image as the 'top designer' of China's new rounds of reform has become clear, and his authority has gradually emerged."

In November 2014, during his visit to Fujian Province, Xi Jinping put forth the "Three-Pronged Comprehensive Strategy," which intends to enact comprehensive measures to "coordinate and finish building a moderately prosperous society, deepen reform, and advance law-based governance."

In his visit to Jiangsu Province, he expanded the Three-Pronged Comprehensive Strategy to a "Four-Pronged Comprehensive Strategy," which aims to implement thorough measures to "comprehensively build a prosperous society; comprehensively deepen reforms; comprehensively govern the nation in accordance with the law; and comprehensively, strictly, govern the Party." Xi Jinping's Four-Pronged Comprehensive Strategy has since been finalized. The *Wall Street Journal* reported that, about two years after he took office, Xi Jinping had presented his political philosophy. The Four-Pronged Comprehensive Strategy was publicized extensively for the first time, indicating that it had been generally accepted at the highest levels of the Party.

The Four-Pronged Comprehensive Strategy is akin to gaining momentum in the game of *Wei-chi* (Weiqi, better known in English by its Japanese name *Go* after it was adopted from China). More than 2,000 years ago, the Chinese father of strategists Sun Wu pointed out, in a vivid passage in *Sun Tzu: Use of Energy*: "For it is the nature of a log or stone to remain motionless on level ground, and to move when on a slope; if [an object is] four-cornered, to come to a standstill, but if [it is] rounded, to go rolling down. Thus the energy developed by good fighting men is as the momentum of a round stone rolled down a mountain thousands of feet in height." Gaining momentum is, in effect, also a means of conserving energy. Master players always devote their complete concentration to the overall roles of their pieces and the effect of timing and position in order to achieve the best outcomes with limited resources.

In conclusion, there are three fundamental challenges facing Xi Jinping.

Economically, how to get out of the trap of a middle-income country and drive China toward its ambition to reach the levels of high-income countries and restore its status as an economically rich country.

Politically, how to realize the modernization of China's governance system and implement lasting political stability, and how to turn China into a democratic and law-based model of fairness and justice.

Culturally, how to regain the creative spirit of the Chinese people and allow them to become the representatives of noble character and morality, to demonstrate that the Chinese spirit can chase away the darkness like a lighthouse, and to ease the voyage of human progress.

To quote the poetry of Mao Zedong (in loose translation):

Oh this land, so rich in beauty,
Has made countless heroes bow in homage.
But alas! Qin Shi Huang and Han Wu Di,
Had it all except in literary grace;
And Tang Tai Zong and Song Tai Zu,
Left but little poetic trace.
And Genghis Khan,
Proud Son of Heaven for a day,
Knew only shooting eagles, bows and arrows ready.
All are past and gone;
Brilliant heroes are those,
For great heroes, look who are here and now!

In February 1936, Mao Zedong and Peng Dehuai, with the Red Army on the Long March they commanded, reached Yuanjiagou Village, in Qingjian County, northern Shaanxi, where they were preparing to cross the river and march eastward toward the Japanese front lines. In order to observe the geographic conditions, Mao Zedong climbed a snow-covered plateau thousands of meters high, where the beautiful rivers and mountains of his motherland, locked in ice for thousands of kilometers, unfolded before his eyes. He couldn't help being filled with a myriad of feelings in his heart, which prompted him to take up his pen and write his famous poem "Qinyuan Spring—Snow." In it, the 43-year-old revolutionary re-assessed heroes and outstanding figures of the Chinese nation in history and relegated them to memories of the past, while announcing that the mission to save the fate of the Chinese nation and to rejuvenate China befell on today's intrepid patriots.

In the early winter of 1969, or, 33 years after Mao composed his poem, 16-year-old Xi Jinping came to Yanchuan County, adjacent to Qingjian County, northern Shaanxi, and started the seven years' orientation for middle school graduates in the countryside. Later Xi Jinping recalled that the seven-year experience in the countryside was the most important period of growth in his life. He became a member of the CPC and started his political career on a stretch of the larger loess highland that had seen the earliest birth of Chinese civilization some 5,000 years ago. Xi Jinping said, "The experience in the countryside allowed me to be connected with the people at the grassroots level…it developed my down-to-earth and self-improving character. Standing on the land among the masses of people, I learned to feel solid and full of energy, for the hard life at the grassroots can hone people's willpower. Then, against whatever difficulties one encounters in the future, as long as the memory remains that people will always manage under hard and difficult conditions, we will know the courage to rise to a challenge, refuse to believe in heresy, maintain the presence of mind in facing difficulties, and move ever forward by overcoming them."

Great heroes of the past must stand in the great arena of history so as to be outstanding. This is an important time for human civilization: from the present, and onwards, until the middle of the twenty-second century in the new millennium. The destiny of humankind depends on the common will of the people of all countries, and political leaders' abilities to guide the courses of their countries. An unprecedented show of reform beckons for China, and at its center stands Xi Jinping. In his era, a China worthy of the attentions of the world will be unveiled.

CHAPTER
1

Who Is Xi Jinping?

It is beyond a doubt that the Chinese people know more about Xi Jinping, the current leader of the Communist Party of China (CPC) and the head of state of the People's Republic of China, than any previous leader. Though it may seem that there is more information available about Mao Zedong, the first chairman of the People's Republic of China, who passed away 40 years ago, than there is about Xi Jinping, most of the vivid descriptions about Mao—many of which are unofficial accounts and fictional narratives—gradually appeared in the years after his death in 1976, during which order was restored out of the chaos and the erstwhile "political clowns" were removed from power. Unlike Mao, however, the present 62-year-old commander-in-chief of China seems to have lifted the veil of secrecy around the nation's top leaders as he shared his actions, words, and thoughts with every Chinese person more than any previous leader, if partly owing to the better facility of modern communication.

For example, in the third week after he assumed the supremacy of China, his visit to Guangdong was first reported by a Weibo microblog user named "Learning from Xi Fan Club," rather than by the usual long press release by the official media.

His visits in China can often be seen in the fond Weibo entries of a grassroots "netizen." Photographs attached to these entries are not of the refined, glossy style of press releases, and have not been elaborately retouched and composed by official presidential photographers, but pictures taken with cell phones—shot at eye level, sometimes containing unwanted passers-by, blurry smiles, and sometimes showing only a stately figure behind the window curtain of a passing automobile. People curious about the leadership of their nation can easily learn where he is visiting, or whether there is a crack on the floor tile of the hotel room where he stayed, or that *Dadao* noodles, dry-fried cauliflower, winter melon, and rib soup are on his lunch menu.

He went to a chain dumpling shop in downtown Beijing to have lunch, and 30 minutes after he left, a photograph of him queuing up holding a dinner plate in his hand was posted on Weibo, and cell-phone videos followed in its wake—the lucky diners stood behind him to take photos with him, while he calmly had his lunch. Three hours later, almost everybody knew that the "presidential combo" consisted of dumplings stuffed with pork and onions, green vegetables, and stewed pig livers and intestines, priced RMB 21 in total, and there was still time for them to copy the menu and arrange for themselves a similar dinner in emulation. Following this example, news from official channels of communication also quickly adopted a more open style.

News came on November 15, 2012, that Xi Jinping was elected at the 18th Party Congress as the general secretary to lead the new Standing Committee of the CPC Central Committee Political Bureau. Five weeks later, on December 23, the Xinhua News Agency released feature stories about Xi Jinping and Li Keqiang, the new premier, reporting on China's top Party leaders' first month in office. The feature story on Xi Jinping, around 15,000 characters in Chinese, detailed his personal life, and, surprisingly, mentioned his falling in love with his wife at first sight. It included details of their married life, and the name of their daughter.

The feature stories of other standing committee members were also released later on. They though were certainly more succinct, they maintained the new format—giving the names and occupations of their wives and their families. This had never appeared before—in the previous twice-a-decade leadership transitions of the CPC Central Committee Political Bureau, as the domestic media were only allowed to release the personal résumés of the Standing Committee members, but no more.

In fact, since the 16th National Congress of China, on every occasion of China's leadership transition, it had become common practice for the Xinhua News Agency to release brief résumés of the seven to nine leaders on whom the future direction of China depended, along with more personal details, to the foreign media. By the time of the 18th National Congress of China, the common practice had been upgraded to a new level, or rather, the common practice had been broken.

All of this came about by "accident"—all of the earlier articles for the foreign media were prepared by the Department of Domestic News for Overseas Services, Xinhua News Agency, before the CPC National Congress was held, and then translated into English. These articles were rarely seen by the Chinese public, due to the media and network "firewall." This changed at the time of the 18th National Congress.

The feature stories, written at such length, with so many details, were totally unprecedented in terms of length, style, and content. In accordance with established procedure, composing such material would not have been the standard procedure of the Xinhua News Agency. Though the material in the articles derived mostly from past media reports, some of the details had been made public for the very first time, including family photos. All of these details were from authoritative information sources as well. The manuscript was still composed by the Department of Domestic News to Overseas Services, Xinhua News Agency, rather than the Central News and Interview Department, which was more experienced in covering the core of the CPC, and its first release by the Department of Domestic News for Overseas Services was clearly intended to cause a reaction.

According to another version of the story, the Department of Domestic News for Overseas Services of the Xinhua News Agency (corresponding with all the overseas Chinese-language media) used to be completely separate from the Domestic Department. However, the *Hong Kong Commercial Daily*, which could receive wire services from the Department for Overseas Services, had been acquired by the *Shenzhen Special Zone Daily*, which decided to publish this new ground-breaking feature, in spite of great risks associated with receiving it, bringing an overwhelming surprise to the domestic press.

In the meeting of the Political Bureau of the Central Committee held on December 4, the 20th day of his presidency, Xi Jinping proposed the Eight Provisions on how to improve the CPC's general working methods and relations with the public, one of which made specific mention of the need to refine the news coverage of leaders in terms of available space, number of characters, and length of time. Three days later, Xi Jinping came to Shenzhen on the first stop of his domestic tour after he assumed office. Thus, it is inevitable that the public would assume that this so-called "accident" was, indeed, intentional.

In any case, the news breakthrough that had occurred and caused such a stir in the public eye and the press had two major benefits:

First, for Xi Jinping and the new generation of leaders who were born after the founding of the People's Republic of China in 1949, and started their careers in officialdom after the reform and opening up of the 1980s, their political careers were unfolded in a relatively transparent political environment—in fact, the long article released by the Xinhua News Agency revealed many details of his political career and life, much of which had been sourced from the papers he wrote himself and published with his own signature. It also included several direct and honest interviews of Xi Jinping and his wife, an opera singer. The general mood was: The past has already been made, and the future has nothing to hide.

Second, Xi Jinping and his colleagues were facing a world in which there is no distinct separation nor decisive barriers between the foreign and domestic environment and between the external and the internal workings of the system—this is a social reality that is manifested not only by the mass-communication revolution. It will undoubtedly bring forth unprecedented challenges to the ruling elite.

Through the ups and downs of his personal life, to his coming of age in a peaceful time (generally speaking); from his engagement in politics after the start of the period of reform and opening up to the gradual increase in transparency in Chinese politics, there are no blind spots in Xi Jinping's résumé. Besides, we have the large number of papers he published, four volumes in total, to trace his progress from Fujian and Zhejiang to Beijing between 1992 and 2014.

In early April, 2015, the Party School of the CPC Central Committee launched a mobile app that collects Xi Jinping's speeches. Once installed, whenever you go near a place where Xi Jinping has given a speech, your cell phone will automatically remind you of the speech the highest-ranking leader of China gave there. New speeches are continuously added to the app. This ultramodern tool will inspire envy in the people who used to carry the pocket edition of the *Selected Works of Mao Zedong* half a century ago.

I. I FIRMLY BELIEVE THAT MY FATHER IS A HERO
The Teenage Chairman in Wartime

As the son of an elder statesman of the CPC, Xi Jinping is unwilling to describe his family background in much detail. The truth is that his family background caused him to suffer quite a lot as a teenager.

Xi Jinping's father, Xi Zhongxun, was born into a land-owning family in rural Fuping, Shaanxi. According to a memoir published by Xi Jinping's mother in *People's Daily* on the 100th anniversary of the senior Xi's birthday, Xi's ancestors moved from Xingan, Jiangxi (present Xingan County) to Dengxian, Henan (present Dengzhou city) in the year of 1369 (the second year of the reign of Emperor Hongwu in the Ming dynasty) in order to flee the famine-stricken area, and then in 1882 (the eighth year of the reign of Emperor Guangxu in Qing Dynasty), once again escaping famine, Xi Zhongxun's grandparents led the whole family to Fupingdan village in Shaanxi. Xi Jinping has called each of these three places his "homeland" on several occasions.

Xi Zhongxun started his revolutionary career at the age of 13, and took part in student demonstrations at the age of 15, for which he was imprisoned. In prison, he joined the Chinese Communist Party. Later on, he joined others in founding the Shaanxi-Gansu (Shaangan) Border Region Soviet Area, and became the chairman of the Soviet-area government at the age of 21. He was dubbed the "teenage chairman."

At the time, the Shaanxi-Gansu (Shaangan) Border Region Soviet government regarded punishing corrupt officials and setting up an honest and clean political atmosphere as a matter of paramount importance. The senior Xi took the lead in implementing a supply rationing system, rationing the everyday necessities, from food and clothes to pens, ink, and paper, per the minimum requirements.

A law adopted at the time declared that any party or military cadre that embezzled over 10 yuan would be executed by firing squad. Consequently, no corruption cases were recorded in the Soviet area.[1]

In mid-1935, when Xi and his comrades merged the Shaanxi-Gansu Border and Northern Shaanxi Soviet Areas to form the Revolutionary Base Area of the Northwest, Mao Zedong had just led the exhausted Red Army out of the muddy grasslands in the northwest of Sichuan—the hardest period of the Long March. Two months later, in a small town on the south of Gansu province, trying hard to find a foothold for the Red Army, Mao discovered one of the few remaining base areas of the CPC—the Northwest Revolution Camp—based on the reports of several out-of-date newspapers, and ended the 25,000-*li* (7,500-mile) Long March.[2]

---

1.   *Biography of Xi Zhongxun*, Central Party Literature Press, August 2013.
2.   In October 1934, the main force of the Red Army led by the CPC was forced to break away from the central revolutionary base in Ruijin (Jiangxi) to begin the Long March, to avoid being encircled. They had fought over 380 battles, crossed eleven provinces, climbed eighteen mountains and crossed 24 rivers, not to mention the desolate and unin-habited grassland and rolling snow mountains, traveled 25,000 *li* (circa 7,500 miles), before

During the Sino-Japanese War, Xi Zhongxun was responsible for guarding the "South Gate" and "North Gate" of the CPC's base of power with Yan'an as the core, and from 1946 right up to 1952, after the founding of the new China, he managed the affairs in the northwest of China. Most of the CPC leaders who worked alongside Xi Zhongxun in the northwest at the time lost their lives in tragic circumstances. For example, the most outstanding military leader in the 1930s, Liu Zhidan, died in a battle after the Red Army arrived; another charismatic leader, Gao Gang, once the vice president of the People's Republic of China, was charged with the crime of "splitting the party and usurping the highest leadership of the Party and the country" in 1954, and ultimately took his own life.

Xi Zhongxun, with less seniority and at a younger age, seemed to have a more successful career as an official. In 1952, he was ordered to Beijing, and at the age of 40, became the secretary of the State Council, the vice premier and the secretary of the State Council at 45, and worked under then Premier Zhou Enlai for over a decade. There, he was in charge of the regular work of the State Council. Due to this job, he was dubbed the "chief of staff" of the State Council.

But due to his history in the northwestern area, his career was always accompanied by dangers. Eventually, they would overtake him.

Imprisoned for so Many Years, the Elder Xi Could Not Recognize his Grown Sons

In 1962, Xi Zhongxun was accused of supporting the novel *Liu Zhidan* and planning to rehabilitate his former comrade Gao Gang. This accusation, of subverting the Party with a novel, become an archetypically absurd case in the history of the CPC.

Xi Zhongxun wrote a letter to Mao Zedong, requesting to return to the countryside to work as a farmer. Soon afterwards, this state leader was assigned to a factory in Luoyang to work as its deputy manager. In the Cultural Revolution that began in 1966, he was subject to humiliation by Red Guards.

When Xi Zhongxun fell out of grace, Xi Jinping was only 9 years old. His father's first wife left three children, one of whom, a girl, died in the Cultural Revolution. Xi Jinping's own mother, Qi Xin, had four children, two boys and two girls. The two girls are older than Xi Jinping, and the other boy is younger than he.[3]

---

finally reaching northern Shaanxi, in October 1935 Some stragglers did not arrive until October 1936.

3.   Xi Zhongxun and his first wife had three children, elder son Xi Zhengning, elder

According to Qi Xin's written memoirs, the two boys were born after they moved to Beijing. She was busy with studying and her work unit, at the Party School of the Central Committee of the CPC, which was located in the northwest suburb of Beijing. Xi Zhongxun, though working as a top official, had to take care of the children in person, bathing them and washing their clothes. He seemed to take these domestic chores as a pleasure: "He was always so happy when he playfully tussled with the boys."[4]

The senior Xi, who was born into poverty and endured many hardships, was very strict with his children. He never carried his family in the government car assigned to him. The children attended boarding school and went home by bus on the weekends. The Xi family lived simple lives: "My two sons often wore their sisters' old clothes and shoes with flower patterns. I remember that, once, when Xi Jinping wouldn't wear his sister's old shoes of his sister for fear that his fellow students would make fun of him, Xi Zhongxun coaxed him, saying, 'a dyeing will make them better.'"[5]

The young boy's experience of "making do" can be seen in his later political life. On the 10th anniversary of the founding of the new China, a plan was put forth to build ten new buildings, one of which would be the office building of the State Council. When Zhou Enlai asked Xi Zhongxun's opinion, Xi Jinping said that Zhongnanhai had been the government office since the Republican Period (1911–1949), and with a simple tidying, Zhongnanhai could serve well as the office building. Besides, building a new office building for the State Council would require tearing down a vast number of residential dwellings. Zhou agreed with him. To this day, the State Council is still situated in Zhongnanhai.

Such a family trait left a deep mark on Xi Jinping. In the early 1980s, when Xi Jinping moved from Beijing to Zhengding County in Hebei as the deputy Party chief of Zhengding County, he took with him an old army quilt and a mattress with various colored patches. Out of curiosity, the local cadres counted the number of patches, and it was said that there were over a hundred. Only later did they learn that the quilt was made by splicing together the fabric of old clothes.[6]

That year, his father had become a member of the Secretariat of the CPC Central Committee, the supreme core institution of the CPC.

Later, Xi wrote in a letter to his father to wish him happy birthday, "Your

daughter Xi Heping (died in the Cultural Revolution), younger daughter Xi Qianping; after he married Qi Xin, they had two daughters: Qi Qiaoqiao, Xi An'an, and two sons: Xi Jinping and Xi Yuanping.

4.   "Recollections about Xi Zhongxun," *People's Daily*, October 18, 2013.
5.   Ibid.
6.   "Loyal and Dedicated Xi Jinping," *Global Characters*, Issue 6, 2015.

frugality is effective. Your strict domestic discipline is well known. We developed the habit of being diligent and thrifty since our childhood under your instruction. This exemplary old Bolshevik and CPC member's family trait shall be passed down from generation to generation."[7]

An unforeseen disaster took a heavy toll on Xi Jinping: Xi Zhongxun was sent into exile, Qi Xin was put under review for several years, their assets were frozen, and their salaries docked. The three older children were sent to work in the construction corps or to the countryside before they came of age—when Xi Jinping left Beijing for Shaanxi as a "sent-down youth," he was not yet 16 years old, and his younger brother, Yuanping, ineligible to attend high school, went to a factory as an apprentice to a lathe operator.

In the winter of 1972, the family finally got to see Xi Zhongxun, who was still in custody at the time. Due to years of separation, the senior Xi could not recognize his grown daughters and sons. The first words he said after seeing his youngest son was, "Are you Jinping or Yuanping?" The whole family shed tears of emotion at the family reunion.

When Xi Jinping talked about this reunion, he said, "He cried when he saw us, so I hurried and passed him a cigarette, and lit one for myself. He asked me, 'How have you learned to smoke?' I said, 'I am too depressed. All these years, we have had too many hardships.' He was silent for a moment, and said, 'You have my permission.'"

Later, Xi Zhongxun gave his own pipe to Xi Jinping, saying that he knew that Xi Jinping did not have enough money to buy cigarettes and he could use the pipe to smoke tobacco. Xi Jinping has said, "I keep the pipe to this day, because it is the gift he gave me during such hard times."[8]

Xi Zhongxun was known for his tenacity and integrity. When he was sent into exile in Henan, he was detained in a small house. Every day he walked in circles, for 10,000 steps, counting from one up to 10,000, and then backwards, counting from 10,000 to one. He often said he was doing physical exercises and honing his willpower in preparation for resuming his work for the country and the people: "I am fully confident in the CPC. I believe that the CPC central authority will come to the right conclusion about me."[9]

Becoming the Most Trusted Person of Hu Yaobang
As he turned 65, with the end of the Cultural Revolution and China getting back on track, Xi Zhongxun was able to continue with his political career,

7.   "One Hundred Years of Xi Zhongxun," *Global Characters*, Issue 27, 2013.
8.   *Biography of Xi Zhongxun*, Central Party Literature Press, August 2013.
9.   "In 1979, Deng Xiaoping Encourages Xi Zhongxun to Fight a Way Out," *Global Characters*, Issue 15, 2011.

a career that had been disrupted by sixteen years of exile. The next decade would prove to be the pinnacle of his life—as a founder of the reform and opening-up policy, and a persistent advocate, his reputation was deeply ingrained in the hearts of the Chinese people.

In April, 1978, Xi Zhongxun was sent to Guangdong, a province adjacent to Hong Kong and Macao, to preside over the work there. At that time, due to the failing economy and the difficulty in maintaining a livelihood in mainland China, there was an unrelenting tide of emigrants to Hong Kong. By ducking under barbed wire, swimming, or climbing mountains, people risked their lives to reach the economically developed Hong Kong. At the peak of the "Great Escape," about 20,000 to 30,000 people attempted to find their way to Hong Kong every month.

At the border, Xi Zhongxun saw with his own eyes the prosperity and bustling commerce of Hong Kong on the far side of the Xiangjiang River, and the desolation and dismay of mainland China on his side. Knowing that escapees would send money back after finding work in Hong Kong and in one or two years their family would have the money to build a new house, he ruminated on the situation. At the time, the escape was considered a point of dispute between people from the mainland and from Hong Kong; escapees were referred to as "illegal border-crossers." Xi criticized the opinions of relevant cadres, saying that these people were emigrants, rather than escapees—that they should not be treated as enemies. Instead, China should let them go: "Rather than arresting people, we should build a strong mainland China."[10]

He advised the central government to delegate powers to lower levels and give full play to the advantages of Guangzhou—being adjacent to Hong Kong and Macao—to lead the economic development. He even said "If Guangdong becomes a 'free country' [of course, he did not mean it literally], maybe its economy will soar in several years, but under the present system, its economy would not go up so easily."[11]

He put forward the measure of zoning plots of land in Shenzhen, Zhuhai, and the Shantou, the hometown of many overseas Chinese, following the example of the foreign processing area, which would be managed separately, and attracting foreign investment to organize production, per international market demands. Such zones were initially named the "Trade Cooperation Zones."

Deng Xiaoping came up with the name "Special Zones," which used to be the name for Shanan-Gangsu-Ningxia Border Region, from which Xi

---

10.   "Xi Zhongxun Biography," *Global Characters*, Issue No. 27, 2013.
11.   Ibid.

Zhongxun started his career and the CPC rallied its forces.

Deng Xiaoping granted him full authority, telling him, "The central government has no money, but we can provide the supporting policies, so you can go find the way for yourself."

This is how China embraced its reform and opening up.

Today, it is generally recognized that Xi's contributions to the founding of the Shenzhen Special Economic Zone were of great significance in China having become currently the second-largest economic power of the world.

In November, 1980, Xi Zhongxun was called back to Beijing to take office as a member of the Secretariat of the CPC Central Committee, the assistant to the renowned reformer. During this period, the reform in China pushed ahead despite so many difficulties, and conflicts of interests began to surface. The turmoil in social ideologies and debates among high-level politicians reached unprecedented levels of intensity, and some thought it might trigger a breakup of the core leadership of the CPC.

According to the memory of Hu Qili, then a member of the Political Bureau of the CPC Central Committee and member of the Secretariat of the CPC, Hu Qili, Xi Zhongxun was a firm supporter and active advocate of reform and opening up; and for this reason, Hu Yaobang trusted him and asked him to oversee many issues of great importance.[12]

After he exited the central political stage in 1988, Xi Zhongxun left Beijing in the 1990s. Though he had worked only two years in Guangdong before, he chose Guangdong, the forefront of reform and opening up, as the place where he would spend his retirement. In October 1999, on the 50th anniversary of the founding of the People's Republic of China, he returned to Beijing, a city he hadn't seen for nine years. He came to the top of Tian'anmen Tower to watch the anniversary ceremony—half a century before, at the age of 35, he had stood in the same place and witnessed the birth of a new China.

When he passed away in 2002, he was buried in Fuping County, Shaanxi, his hometown.

Calm, Self-Restraining Like His Father, and Never Complaining

Xi Zhongxun was not at the core of the political veterans of the CPC—nor was he from Hunan and Hubei, so he was not directly tied to Mao Zedong. He did he take part in the Long March; nor was he a star in the inner-party campaign. He is best known for his integrity, honesty, practicality, tenacity, modesty, the courage to take risks, and his steadfast opposition to extremist left-wing inclination inside the CPC at all historical stages.

12.   "Xi Zhongxun Biography," *Global Characters*, Issue 27, 2013.

He once stated in self-appraisal, "All through my life I've never prosecuted other people and never committed left-wing extremist errors," which were well-known facts in the CPC.

Inside the CPC, which has undergone several brutal inner-party struggles, few of the power holders could make such a self-appraisal.

He once said, "The CPC stresses the 'Party Spirit,' as far as I can see, but being realistic is the best spirit of the party."[13]

His wife Qi Xin's summary of his life was: "He was a hero throughout his rough life."

In his last days, he told his children many times: "I did not leave much fortune to you, [but I did leave] a good reputation."[14]

In the 1980s, many "second-generation reds" took advantage of their parents' social status and influence to do business, some of which verged on illegality, and produced very bad social after-effects. Worrying about this phenomenon, Xi Zhongxun thought that only a morally upright family trait could guide the building of the CPC's working methods. At one time, on hearing his wife Qi Xin say to their children, "The small household matters should not interfere with your work," Xi Zhongxun said sternly, "Bigger household matters should not interfere with your work, either." When Xi Jinping was serving as the governor of Fujian Province, his mother wrote letters to warn him of the "loneliness at the top," telling him to be strict with himself.[15]

In the autumn of 2001, Xi Zhongxun turned 88 years old, the traditional Chinese *Mishou* (because the Chinese character "米" when disassembled forms the number "八十八" or "88"). Xi Jinping, being the Governor of Fujian Province at the time, was absent from the family gathering on Xi Zhongxun's birthday due to busy official duties. Instead, he wrote a letter to wish his father happy birthday. The appraisal of his father in the letter could be deemed his own expectations for himself.

He wrote that his father was honest and authentic, never prosecuted other people, and always struck to the truth; his father was very low-key and treated all his successes and achievements as the water flowing naturally under the bridge, a style telling of his indomitable spirit.

Xi Jinping mentioned his father's persistent pursuit of faith in particular. "Whether in the white terror era, or in the extremist left-wing times; whether when you are framed by other people or in adversity, there is always a bright

13. "Recollections about Xi Zhongxun," *People's Daily*, October 18, 2013.
14. Ibid.
15. "Xi Zhongxun Biography," *Global Characters*, Issue 27, 2013. *Chief Editor's Note:* This Chinese saying, used in this context, cautions on the vulnerability of a top leader, who is exposed to so many temptations.

light in your heart that will forever point to the correct direction."[16]

As Elizabeth C. Economy, the director for Asian Studies at the Council on Foreign Relations, put it in an article published in 2014 on the website of *The National Interest*, an American bimonthly magazine, President Xi "has no kind words for officials who 'worship Buddha'; seek 'god's advice for solving their problems'; 'perform their duties in a muddle-headed manner'; 'yearn for Western social systems and values'; 'lose their confidence in the future of socialism'; or 'adopt an equivocal attitude towards political provocations against the leadership of the CPC.... He may have a revelation later in life, but for now there is no room at the Inn."

According to another commentary, Xi Jinping "inherits his father's character of being realistic, thrifty, and honest, which are directly embodied in each detail of his political strategy. For example, he abandons the state leaders' customary practice of going to the grassroots units during the spring festival—as one does not have to show his enthusiasm for work on the most important festival in China, and the local leaders may enjoy a relaxing family reunion; he simplifies the security arrangement for top government officials going out even on business, abandoning police escorts and traffic closures, giving up the official sedans. Instead, he proposed that all officials take one common minibus. His father once strictly prohibited the practice of having local police vehicles leading the way when he traveled to the grassroots units for studies.

"Xi Jinping is calm, self-restraining like his father, and never complains. When his father was wrongfully sidelined, and his family wrenched apart, he himself narrowly escaped the fate of being sent to juvenile prison; but instead was sent to the rural, barren, loess plateau to be a farmer at school age. Living in the shadow of his father's disgrace, he had trouble trying to join the Youth League and the CPC, and his studies never went well. He said, 'Even in the days when people called us names,' he said, 'I firmly believed that my father was a hero, a father we should be proud of.'"[17]

II. UNCLE XI, THE SON OF THE LOESSLAND
"If I Weren't Sent to Yan'an, Heaven Knows if I Would Still Be Alive Now"

In Chinese folk discourse, state leaders are rarely addressed as a relative by the common people. Mao Zedong was sometimes called "Grandpa Mao" after he passed away. However, starting from Internet comments and grassroots Weibo entries, the nickname "Uncle Xi" (*Xi Dada*, 习大大) appeared less

16.   "Xi Zhongxun Biography," *Global Characters*, Issue 27, 2013.
17.   Ibid.

than a week after the 18th National Congress. What is extraordinary is that this unconventional nickname is often adopted by the official media.

The name "Dada" comes from Shaanxi province, the birthplace of the ancient Chinese, where it is often used to address a father's brothers. Central Shannxi was Xi Jinping's hometown and he spent his youth on the loess plateau in the north of Shaanxi province. The plateau, with the largest loessland area in the world, is situated in the heart of China. The thick loess layer is up to 150 to 180 meters deep in the Northern Shaanxi region. Due to the arid climate, sparse vegetation, and fragile ecology, teamed with the fragmented ground surface, through erosion, the loess plateau releases billions of tons of dust into the Yellow River.

Xi Jinping remained there from the age of 15 to 22. The loess plateau, with the highly fractured mounds and steep and precipitous ridges, witnessed his growth into manhood.

On February 13, 2015, five days from the Chinese lunar New Year, Xi Jinping came back to Liangjiahe Village of Yanchuan county, Shaanxi, with his wife Peng Liyuan. He introduced his wife to the local people in the local dialect: "This is my *Poyi* [wife]."

"Jinping is back"—the local people used this phrase to address him. He purchased the necessities for the spring festival, including wheat flour for dumplings, rice, cooking oil, and the spring festival couplets and traditional new-year paintings for the whole village with his own money, and had a northern Shaanxi farmers' dinner with his Party mentor, the then village Party chief.

The headline of Xinhua News Agency's news release was "The Son of Loessland is Back Home"—22 years ago, when Xi was working in Fujian province, he went back to Liangjiahe once too. An article he wrote to describe his youth was titled, "I am the Son of the Loessland."

This is Beijing at eight past four,
a sea of fingers is waving.
This is Beijing at eight past four,
a magnificent siren is sounding.
The lofty buildings at the Beijing station
suffer a sudden, drastic shutter.
I watch outside the window in surprise,
wondering what has happened.

What is described in these lines is the sight of Beijing's educated youth being sent down to the countryside at the turn of 1968 to 1969. The fifteen-year-old Xi Jinping was on one of the train carriages making its way to northern Shaanxi.

In the Cultural Revolution, the "Up to the Mountains and Down to the Countryside Movement" called by Mao Zedong forced nearly 17 million young people, who should have been receiving educations at school, to be transported to the rural countryside. One tenth of the total population of China was transferred, affecting almost every urban household.

One purpose of the large-scale Up to the Mountains and Down to the Countryside movement in 1968 and 1969 was to end the out-of-control Red Guard movement and, at the same time, ease the unemployment pressure in the cities. However, thanks to this movement, the "educated youth," who learned nothing in high school, would miss their educational opportunities forever, and live a hard life upon returning to the city, and they would be the very first to be affected in the labor retrenchment of the 1990s. What a waste of youth, what a waste of life.

This huge group of people often comprise the protagonists in the "Scar literature" of the 1980s. A rather large part of them were full of disillusions about life and maintain a certain culturally and politically rebellious tendency.

Deng Xiaoping summarized the Up to the Mountains and Down to the Countryside movement in this way: "The country spent RMB 30 billion to buy three dissatisfactions: the dissatisfaction of the sent-down youth, their parents, and the farmers."

However, leaving Beijing, his birthplace, in the midwinter in January 1969, for 15-year-old Xi Jinping, was like an "escape to victory," he wrote in a memoir article.[18] For at the time, after his house was searched and their family property confiscated, he lived with his mother in the Party School of the CPC Central Committee. "As I was stubborn and refused to be bullied, I offended the revolutionary rebels and was written off as the 'black sheep' of the family. They said I deserved 100 deaths by firing squad! So I thought, what is the difference between one death and 100 deaths? What is there to fear?"

He was forced to read the *Quotations of Chairman Mao Zedong* day and night. He was sent to the gate of the police station and turned back, and almost sent to a juvenile prison at one time. However, as the beds in the juvenile prison were all occupied, he had to wait one month to be admitted. It was at this time, December, 1968, that Mao Zedong called on the "educated youth" to go to the countryside. Xi immediately signed up. He chose Northern Shaanxi, the revolutionary base area where his father once

18.   "I am the Son of the Loessland," *National New Book Information*, Issue 12, 2002.

worked. "In their eyes, going to Yan'an was basically equal to being sent into exile, so they agreed," he recalled.

In an interview with "I am a Yan'an Native," a program of Yan'an TV, in 2004, Xi Jinping said that at the Beijing train station, the "educated youth" on the special train to Yan'an were all crying, except him. "I was laughing, for if I had stayed in Beijing, heaven knows if I would still be alive now."

He Lost his Nerve at the Age of Fifteen
After traveling one day and one night, transferring trucks and walking about ten miles of mountain roads on foot, Xi finally reached Liangjiahe village, and settled in a cave dwelling. He carried with him a full case of books, and among the fifteen sent-down youths, he had the heaviest luggage.

The 26,800 young people sent from Beijing to Yan'an at the same time as Xi Jinping were assigned to 2,667 production teams in twelve counties. To manage these young people, later on, Beijing sent 1,200 cadres. Four or five years later, over 98 percent of the educated youth from Beijing had left through recruitment of workers and cadres, military recruitment, or being admitted to universities.[19]

In the commemoration of the 40th anniversary of the Up to Mountains and Down to the Countryside movement in 2009, the *Yan'an Daily* newspaper published the memoir of a local cadre, which mentioned some of the outstanding "sent-down youths" from Beijing. The first of them was a person who moved to the US and became a successful businessman, and the second was Xi Jinping. The article recalled that the local villagers gave special care and love to Xi Jinping. They recommended him to be the "barefoot doctor," work point recorder, and agricultural technician. Later, he was elected him to attend the second Youth Socialist Construction Activist Assembly of Yan'an, at which he received recognition and awards.[20]

But in fact, the teenage Xi Jinping was at a loss when he came to the countryside at that time.

Liangjiahe (Liangjia River) village has no river, only a ditch that flows with muddy water in the wet season. The cave dwellings are carved out of the steep slopes on both sides of the ditch, which had been home for over 200 villagers for generations.

According to Xi Jinping's memory, in this strange environment, with all the disbeliefs around him, he felt very lonely at first.[21]

---

19. "Commemoration of the 40th Anniversary of the 'Up to Mountains and Down to the Countryside' Movement, *Yan'an Daily*, January 5, 2009.
20. Ibid.
21. "I am the Son of the Loessland."

His father Xi Zhongxun used to tell him about the meaning of unity: "Do not do unto others what you would not have them do unto you;" and "to help others is to help yourself." For Xi Jinping, when he first came to Yan'an, he experienced setbacks and learned harsh lessons, both because he had no long-term plan and found it difficult to blend with other people. "The other young people went to work every day, but not I. I did my work at will, for which I left a bad impression on the local farmers."[22]

In an interview with Yan'an TV in 2004, he recalled that the most talked-about of his traits in those days was that he fed bread to dogs—while cleaning a sack, he found half a bread loaf that had gone bad, which he tossed to the dogs. "When the local farmers saw this, they asked me what it was that I fed to the dog, to which I replied that it was a bread. They had never seen bread, let alone tasted it. This story was passed around, and in several days, the whole Yanchuan county knew about this."

He also said that the intensity of the labor there left him in a state of shocked disbelief. Climbing the hill was no less difficult than climbing the Ghost Fear peak of Xiangshan in Beijing. Merely climbing the hill would leave him out of breath, let alone working.

Except for dinnertime, there was only one break, and even that was only enough for him to puff on a pipe of tobacco. "That is how we learned to smoke. We were only trying to get a little rest."

Three months later, he lost his nerve and escaped to Beijing, but soon he was sent to the Taihangshang revolutionary base area.[23] Based on the lessons they had drawn from their revolutionary careers, his aunt and uncle cautioned him to find the opportunity to build good relationships with the broad masses—the local villagers. "Who else can you count on now?"[24]

At that time, the cities were frequently checked for the young people who came back from the countryside. Xi Jinping once wrote in a reminiscence that he was imprisoned with other ousted people at the police station for four to five months, during which they had to do hard labor. "The sewer pipes in Haidian[25] district were laid by us," he said.[26] The relatives of Xi Zhongxun in Fuping county, Shaanxi, recalled that around the winter of 1969, because there were not enough maize grits to eat in Northern Shaanxi, Xi Jinping returned to Fuping with an empty belly, dressed in scanty clothing. After getting a set of cotton-padded clothing, he returned to Yan'an quickly.[27]

---

22.   "I am the Son of the Loessland."
23.   Including the anti-Japanese bases in Shanxi, Hebei, Henan.
24.   "I am the Son of the Loessland."
25.   A district in Beijing.
26.   "I am the Son of the Loessland,."
27.   Ifeng.com.cn, November 15, 2015.

Adapting to the Land that Built His Forefathers

It was not possible to stay in Beijing, and back in Liangjiahe, he was almost on the verge of despair—the fellow young people who came with him were mostly children of military cadres. Half a year later, most of them had left to join the army. Later on, for a period of nearly a year, Xi was the only sent-down youth who stayed on. It was then that the 16-year-old Xi Jinping learned to truly blend into the land that raised and so influenced his parents, working side by side with the local farmers, consciously accepting the hardships in life, and tasting the fulfillment and happiness of overcoming them.

Many times, he would recall the five tribulations of country life he had learned to endure. First, there were the fleas. In the summer, all of Liangjiahe was infested. He had bites everywhere, and due to a skin allergy, the blisters turned to ulcers. But after two years, he got used to the fleas. No matter how the fleas bit him, he could still have a good night's sleep.

Second, the food. All he could get were rough grains—steamed cornbread, milled rice, and wheat flour. For a time, he did not get any meat for several months, so after getting a tiny bit of pork, he ate a piece raw before the meat was fully cooked. He often missed the meals he'd had while in the northern Shaanxi countryside.

Third, the daily toil. He learned to twist wool, make clothes, and quilt. The life of that time laid a solid foundation for his future ability to take care of himself.

Fourth, the labor. At first, the work points given to Xi were not even as high as the work points for women, but after two years, he could get ten work points a day as a strong laborer, and he became a very skilled farmer. He could herd sheep on steep mountain ridges, cut grass among the cave dwellings on rainy or windy days, and look after the cattle at night; when carrying the manure to the field in spring, he could carry 40–75 kilograms of pig or cow manure to the mountain several miles away. At the time of the wheat harvest, he could shoulder 100 kilograms of wheat, walking long distances along mountain roads without stopping for a rest.

Fifth, his own thoughts. He recognized and eventually emulated the farmers' realist, practical, and hardworking spirits. Earlier, he had disapproved of them, for they often had lice. But soon enough he was sharing their *Kang* beds (炕, a platform made of bricks or other earthworks that carry heat from a furnace) and their quilts.

Xi Jinping says the lessons he learned in Northern Shaanxi would benefit him for the rest of his life—he learned what it was to be truly practical, to seek the truth through examining the facts, and of the everyday experiences that made up the people of China.

For example, when he first came to the countryside, he saw things in a very simple way. Knowing that a fellow villager had been labeled a "rich farmer," he would look down on him. Only later did he realize that the villager had been labeled as such only because he had raised several dozen sheep. Xi had not known that, due to destitute agricultural conditions, most of the families were living on chaff and wild herbs for half the year. The women and children went begging for food, leaving the grains for the strongest laborers to consume, so they could engage in spring plowing. At first, Xi had looked down on beggars as "bad elements" or "loafers." His first-hand experience of the hardships of life in the countryside forced him to reconsider.

One year after he came to Liangjiahe, as he grew increasingly close with his fellow farmers, Xi Jinping's cave dwelling became the center of the village. Every night, the farmers, old or young, would come to hear this 16-year-old tell old, new, foreign, and Chinese stories. Gradually, even the village Party chief would consult him on some matters.

However, he could still not forget the gloomy fact that his father was still in prison, and there were no clear conclusions regarding the future.

To join the Chinese Youth League, he wrote eight application letters. To join the CPC, he wrote ten application letters.

"I wasn't feeling miserable or inferior. The only thought I had at that time was that the more good people join the party or the league, the less bad people there will be in the Party. I should certainly be a member, unless there is direct restriction that I should not be recruited," Xi recalled.[28]

In 1973, when all the sent-down youths were preparing for college entrance examinations, once again, Xi's family background became an impassable barrier. In that year, all the sent-down young people from Beijing, except Xi Jinping, left Liangjiahe. He "made the decision not to leave, and to do something for the village through merit."[29]

Biogas Expert

At the age of 20, Xi Jinping was elected the secretary of the Jiangjiahe commune (or administrative village) party branch, a "cell" that constituted the primary level unit of the CPC's system of organization. He worked with his fellow villagers to dig wells, and to build dams and highways. In his heart, Northern Shaanxi had become his second hometown.

When reinforcing the river bank in a bid to prevent soil erosion, he stood in the icy water in the early spring, wearing an old blue cotton-padded jacket,

28.   "I am the Son of the Loessland."
29.   Ifeng.com.cn, November 15, 2015.

a used blasting fuse tied around his waist, and his trouser legs rolled up. To this day, the land formed by the dams built by farmers under Xi Jinping's leadership is still producing plump-eared corn.

In January, 1974, the *People's Daily* newspaper published a report promoting biogas utilization in Sichuan. After reading the report in the dim light of a little oil lamp, he immediately thought of introducing biogas to the loess plateau, which lacked coal and firewood.

He walked over 25 kilometers of mountain roads to the seat of Yanchuan county to tell the county Party committee that he wanted to go to Sichuan to learn how to generate biogas. It so happened that the county Party committee was considering the promotion of biogas utilization. Three months later, six people from Yanchuan went to Sichuan to study this technology, one of whom was Xi Jinping.

Soon, Liangjiahe became a biogas pilot-study location. Xi guided the villagers to dig sands, carry cement, and burn limestone; when the biogas tank leaked water and gas, requiring immediate clearing of the liquid manure, they lifted the liquid manure out of the tank with buckets that very night. They worked full days and nights in the hot summer.

Facing the cameras of Yan'an TV, he recalled that at one time the biogas could not be let out of the tank because the gas pipe was blocked, "when the pipe was pried open, the manure sprayed all over my face," he said.

The biogas tank in Liangjiahe was the first in northern Shaanxi, and also the first in the whole of Shaanxi Province. The village, under the management of Xi, provided enough biogas for over 70 percent of the area's population; it became the number one village in the province. "I walked every corner of the village at that time, working with both the village Party chief and the biogas experts," he said.

There is a monument at the gate of Jiangjiahe village with the inscription stating that Xi led the way in building 60 biogas tanks, which, with some updated technology, are still in operation today.

Gu Xi, a Northern Shaanxi journalist, was probably the first person to mention Xi Jinping in a news report. On September 20, 1975, he wrote a long article entitled "The Story of Fire" in the *Yan'an Correspondence*, describing the full process of how Xi introduced biogas into Shaanxi.

Later, he recounted in his blog that when he went to Liangjiahe to get an interview with Xi Jinping, his Jeep slipped on the steep road leading to the village that year; Xi and several young men pushed it into the yard where the sent-down youths had lived.

Crying Twice in his Life

When the "Story of Fire" was published, Xi Jinping was preparing to say goodbye to Liangjiahe. That year Yanchuan County had two admission quotas for Tsinghua University. Although previously, because of his father, he had been rejected by this renowned science and engineering institution of higher learning in northern China, he still applied to Tsinghua University for enrollment. "To be admitted will bring me happiness, and if I'm not admitted, I shall accept my fate," he said.[30]

The county leaders spoke on his behalf and backed him strongly, and, coincidentally, the two principals who had rejected him earlier were absent. So with the consent of the then first-deputy Party chief of Tsinghua University, Liu Bing, Xi was finally able to go to college.

As remembered by the villagers of Liangjiahe, Xi Jinping was not only hardworking and resourceful, he also loved reading and learning. He was often seen reading "books as thick as bricks" in the dim light of an oil lamp, some of them books of Marxist-Leninist philosophy, some mathematics, chemistry, or physics books.

A journalist of the Xinhua News Agency went to Liangjiahe with Xi in February, 2015. In front of the cave dwelling he had lived in through those years, Xi said, "I loved reading books those days and often read them in the light of an oil lamp till midnight. Sometimes, when I got up the next morning, the phlegm I coughed out was black."[31]

When the chairman of the Writers' Association of Yanchang County, Zhang Siming, visited Xi in 2002, while he was still serving as the Governor of Fujian province, Xi recalled a time when he was on the way from Beijing to Yanchuan. Because Yanchuan was still a long distance away, he stayed a night at the place of Wang Qishan, a close friend of Xi's, who was also a sent-down youth from Beijing, and they slept under the same bed cover. A book on economics that Xi took with him was left at Wang's place.[32]

Later Wang Qishan went to the Northwestern University to study history, and he has become one of Xi Jinping's most important colleagues in the Political Bureau of the CPC Central Committee. Experienced at dealing with financial matters, serving concurrently as the secretary of the Central Commission for Discipline Inspection of the CPC, after the CPC's 18th National Congress, Wang was behind one of the largest anti-corruption campaigns in the history of the CPC.

Xi's reading pals were not limited to people at the same level of society,

30.   "I am the Son of the Loessland."
31.   "Loess Land's Son Is Back," *Xinhua News Agency*, February 14, 2015.
32.   "Wang Qishan and His Friends," *South People Weekly*, Issue 27, 2013.

such as Wang Qishan. Some of them were young native friends of his. Wu Hui, a villager a year younger than Xi, read many Chinese and foreign literary classics like *The Water Margin* (Shui Hu Zhuan), *And Quiet Flows the Don*, and *How the Steel Was Tempered*. Wu Hui applied to the university together with Xi, and became a teacher after he was rejected by the university.[33]

Xi also cut the hair of the young villagers around the same age, taught them how to swim the breaststroke, and gave his shoes to friends in the countryside living in poverty.

On this land, Xi Jinping, a man of strong character who had seldom cried before, would twice shed his tears.

The first time was when his half-sister passed away: "I was digging bomb shelters at the time and I wailed after receiving the letter about her death," he recalled.[34]

The second time was on the morning of October 7, 1975, the day he said goodbye to Liangjiahe. That morning, when he opened the door, he saw the yard filled with his fellow villagers. They had waited there quietly without waking him. Xi shed tears before them, saying, "You are so good to me that I don't want to leave, I want to stay my whole life in this village."

A young villager who had become very close to him retorted, "No, you should go. With you at the Tsinghua University, we will get the chance to visit Beijing—who else could we depend on to prepare meals for us in Beijing? You have to go, even if it is merely to help us realize our dream of visiting Beijing."[35]

That day, nobody went to work on the mountain. They lined up to see Xi off, and walked with him for about five kilometers. Thirteen close young friends walked the 30 kilometers with him to the seat of Yanchuan County. Together they slept on the floor of their room in a state-run hotel.

On the second day, they took a photo together to honor the days they were together—this was the first time these young farmers, except Xi, had their photos taken—spending five yuan for the service. Xi wanted to pay the money, but they wouldn't let him. Instead, they scraped up enough cash by each contributing what they could.[36]

This black-and-white photo came to be known by many Chinese people after the 18th National Congress. Fourteen people, in two rows, the front row in a sitting position and the second row standing, all maintaining quite

33.   Ifeng.com.cn, November 15, 2012.

34.   *I am a Yan'an Native*, Yan'an TV, August 2004.

35.   *Peng Liyuan Talking about Her Happy Family Life*, Zhanjiang Evening News, October 5, 2007.

36.   "Xi Jinping Vice President's Days in Yan'an as a Sent-down Youth," *China Business Newspaper*, December 19, 2008.

serious expressions. The 22-year-old Xi, in the middle of the front row, had a slightly longer brush cut and a thin face, and all the buttons from his neck to the bottom of his coat were fastened. Some of his friends were wearing a *Duijin* jacket (对襟, a kind of Chinese-style jacket with buttons down the front), and some had towels wrapped around their heads.

Later, Xinhua News Agency presented a special report on the basis of this photograph to introduce each of these friends of Xi's. Almost all of them had spent their lives as farmers on the loess land.

Among the youths sent down from Beijing to Yan'an, according to the 1993 statistics, there were eight cadres at the provincial or ministerial level, over 200 at the bureau level, and over 3,000 cadres at the division level.[37]

A Rebirth Through Down-to-Earth Work

Xi Jinping once said in earnest that the two groups of people who had given him the greatest help in his life were the old revolutionary generation and the folks in Shaanxi Village where he lived.

In the nearly seven years he lived in Shaanxi, he could have never done without the protection and help of those around him at critical times.

For example, Shen Yang, then Party chief of Yanchuan County, recommended him to join the CPC, and to be admitted to Tsinghua University. In Yang's eyes, Xi was a "child of northern Shaanxi" and the "offspring of Nanliang," and under a lot of pressure. Shen was a Red Army soldier at the Nanliang Shaanxi-Gansu Border Region Soviet Revolutionary Base area founded by Xi Jinping's father Xi Zhongxun and Liu Zhidan. He had fought in battles under their leadership.

Another example: The director of the commune's Sent-Down Youth Office, sympathetic toward Xi, braved the risks of removing the "dirt" from his file. Xi once stated, bluntly, that he has a "loessland complex."

In the political history of China, northern Shaanxi is a very special place. At the end of the Ming Dynasty (1368–1644), Li Zicheng, the leader of the peasant uprising, rose in rebellion here and proclaimed himself the emperor but lost power before long. Northern Shaanxi is also the place where the fate of the Chinese Communist Party took a turn. Here the CPC broke through an encirclement, restructured their military forces, won the hearts of the people before it finally seized power. The famous debate about "the law of the periodic rise and fall of powers" between Mao Zedong and Huang Yanpei also occurred here—"We've found a new path, and it is called democracy. We can break free of these historical cycles of rise and fall."

---

37.   "Xi Jinping: My Experience in the 'Up to the Mountains, Down to the Country-side' Movement," Fujian Ph.D. *Demeanour*, 2003.

Xi Jinping repeatedly said, "Yan'an is the source and the turning point of my life." The notion that people should have dreams and beliefs, true feelings for the masses, that people should seek truth from facts, and work hard—these life philosophies had been deeply stirred into his blood in those years in Yan'an. When he was still in Liangjiahe, Beijing awarded this model educated youth a motorized tricycle with a trailer, which was very rare in Liangjiahe at the time; but Xi managed to change the tricycle into a hand tractor, winnower, water pump, and yet other farm implements, and lent it out to the village folk for farming.[38]

After he left, he helped the village get access to electric power, build a bridge, and renovate a primary school. When he was party chief of Fuzhou City, in southeast China, he returned to his village on a visit, going door to door to visit people. He gave senior villagers pocket money, and schoolchildren new schoolbags, school supplies, and alarm clocks to remind them to go to school.

In 2009, Xi Jinping, who had become a member of the Standing Committee of the Political Bureau of the CPC and the Vice President, returned to Yan'an during a visit to Xi'an. He wrote the names of nine of his close friends and asked his personal assistant to invite them for a reunion.

Even in the 40 years after he left northern Shaanxi, his connection with this land has never been severed. "Standing on the land, and putting yourself among the masses will make you feel fulfilled and powerful. The hardships at the grassroots can hone a person's will in such a manner that whatever difficulties you run into, the thought that you can achieve something despite such hardships will stiffen your courage to challenge anything, to refuse to be misled by fallacies, devise responses when confronted with disorder, and to overcome all difficulties," he wrote in a reminiscing article.[39]

When he came to the loessland at 15, he was confused, at a loss; when he left the loessland, he had become a new person with firm life goals.

III. DON THE ARMY'S UNIFORM, FOLLOW THE POLITICAL MENTOR

Tsinghua University at the Center of Controversy:
The College Life he Would Rather Not Mention

When he went to Tsinghua University, a premier school that had been at the center of the storm during the Cultural Revolution, another political

---

38.　"The Masses, the Source of Our Strength—on the General Secretary of the CPC," Xinhua News Agency, December 27, 2012.
39.　"I am the Son of the Loessland."

movement was quickly brewing—a movement opposed to Deng Xiaoping. This was to be the last movement, marking the end of the Cultural Revolution.

In August and October of 1975, the first deputy secretary of the party branch in Tsinghua—the man who had approved the admission of Xi Jinping—and three other colleagues wrote letters to Mao Zedong to complain about the left-wing extremism of two principals at Tsinghua University: Chi Qun and Xie Jingyi. They were criticized by Mao, as he suspected that the complaint was an attack on the Cultural Revolution and himself, and considered that Deng Xiaoping, who had transferred the letter, had a hand in such a complaint. At the start of the next year, Mao came back and Deng Xiaoping, who had been presiding over the routine work of the CPC Central Committee for only a year, was once again pulled out.

In no time, once again, Tsinghua University became a site of the political typhoon of the Cultural Revolution. Debates about educational revolution disrupted teaching curricula as tens of thousands of boldly worded posters covered the campus. Hundreds of critical gatherings, mudslinging sessions, contentious meetings, colloquia, and oath-taking rallies became the mainstay of daily work.

From November, 1975, to September of the next year, about 30,000 people from all walks of life came to visit and to learn from Tsinghua University, and the diplomatic envoys and journalists of ten countries came to read the posters, with their enormous, forceful statements.

With such chaos buzzing around, Xi Jinping, as a "worker-farmer-soldier-turned-student," started his college life together with over 3,200 other students. He majored in the study of basic organic synthesis, a branch of chemistry. Based on the realities of the time, such a course of study must have been the result of an assignment rather than his own choice.

The so-called "worker-farmer-soldier-turned-students" label referred in particular to the group of students who went to college between 1970 and 1976. In 1970, four years into the Cultural Revolution, college enrollment was frozen, and enrollment format by unified examination and selection of the best students was abolished. In its place was the new regulation that the students should be recruited from workers, farmers, and soldiers, through a combination of methods such as recommendations of the masses, approval by cadres, and review by colleges, which, of course, could not guarantee the scholastic quality of the students.

The number of worker-farmer-soldier-turned students enrolled in Tsinghua University ranked the first among colleges all over China. Over 70 percent of them had only completed their junior high school education (some even less). The most educated ones had completed specialized secondary education and learned about calculus. The least educated ones might have difficulties adding, subtracting, multiplying, and dividing, and some of them firmly believed that the sun revolved around the earth.

During the "educational revolution," the following ironic story wasn't rare at Tsinghua University: Professors, lecturing as if the students had the appropriate prior knowledge their subjects required, were booed and hissed off the stage because the farmer-worker-soldier-turned students could not understand what they were talking about. Based on the available data, it seems that Xi may not have met what he expected from college-level studies.

In May, 1975, Tsinghua's weekly schedule for the extracurricular activities of students was as follows: In addition to political studies every Tuesday afternoon, there were four hours of politics, as well as the Party and Youth League activities, "educational revolution" discussion groups, and group activities for reading the works of Marxism and Leninism. In this way, in the 21 units of time in one week (four hours each unit), at least four units of time would be used to study non-academic courses.

From the end of 1975 to 1976, Xi's freshman year, as the study hours were mostly taken up by the overwhelming "Criticism of Deng Xiaoping" movement, the minimum study of his major courses was hardly met.

The farmer-worker-soldier-turned-students were told that they were in college to "go to college, manage college, and transform the college with the 'Thought of Mao Zedong.'" In Tsinghua University, the right to manage the college was in the hands of the "farmers' and soldiers' 'Thought of Mao Zedong' propaganda team.'" This was the same as the other colleges in China back then: Intellectuals, such as professors and students, were considered targets of the Cultural Revolution.

In early 1970s, the departments, teaching and research sections, laboratories, and classes at Tsinghua University were divided into battalions, companies, platoons, and squads, the orders of the military establishment—the more famous the college was, the more it was referred to as an enemy territory occupied by intellectuals.

Meanwhile, Tsinghua University also implemented a policy of so-called "open-door" schooling, emphasizing that the college of technology should set up factories in place of teaching, and the students should walk out of the classrooms and labs and directly participate in production as laborers. The results of this approach was that the teaching of basic theories was severely weakened, and the standards in laboratories declined to the levels of the 1950s; some of them were even using instruments and equipment from the 1930s. The proportion of scientific and technical personnel on the faculty dropped from 30 percent to 10 percent.[40]

This was the college environment faced by Xi Jinping—chaotic, with damaged, creaky desks. In fact, due to the recommendation-based enrollment methods, uneven prior academic knowledge levels among enrollees, informal length of schooling, and easy teaching syllabi, the society had a low opinion of the overall quality of the worker-farmer-soldier-turned students. After the Cultural Revolution, related state agencies stipulated that worker-farmer-soldier-turned students should all be granted junior college degrees.

He Dongchang, the deputy Party chief of Tsinghua University during the Cultural Revolution period, said that "the quality of the worker-farmer-soldier-turned students is kind of like a puffy loaf of bread. It may seem bulging, but with a light pinch, it will thin out. If it goes on like this, our national culture might be destroyed."

In the colloquia convened in August, 1977, by Deng Xiaoping with over 30 scientists and educators, a professor from Tsinghua University pointed out that the worker-farmer-soldier-turned students at Tsinghua University had only elementary school educations, and had to supplement their high school educations at college, leaping to college-level standards within only three short years. Deng Xiaoping intervened, saying that, were that the case, the university should be called "Tsinghua High School" or "Tsinghua Elementary School."[41]

In fact, only after the college entrance examination was restored at the end of 1977 did the restructuring and standardization of Chinese universities gradually begin.

Perhaps, because of this, Xi Jinping's college years were rarely mentioned. In this perspective, he was different from his predecessor, Hu Jintao, who completed his college education at Tsinghua University before the Cultural Revolution, and his colleague Li Keqiang, who passed the college entrance examination in 1978 and was admitted to Beijing University. Large portions of the available biographies on Hu and Li concern their college days.

In June, 2012, Xi Jinping, the state vice-president at the time, visited Tsinghua University. In his speech, he said that he felt a sense of warmth coming back to Tsinghua and meeting his teachers, without mentioning any further details, though he often evinced deep impressions of unspoken details, as if they were right at his fingertips.

However, in any case, the passing away of Mao Zedong and Zhou Enlai,

40.   "Comment on Tsinghua University's Educational Revolution," Tang Shaojie, http://bbs.voc.com.cn/

41.   "Deng Xiaoping and the Restoration of College Entrance Examination System," *CPC News.*

the "April 5th Movement" of 1976 that occurred in Tian'anmen Square to protest the Cultural Revolution, and the crushing of the "Gang of Four" in October 1976, which abruptly transformed the supreme authority in China, all took place during Xi's freshman year. In the second half of 1978, the CPC pushed forward a series of significant political initiatives to put an end to the chaotic and corrupt China that had prioritized politic power struggles over the tasks of implementing the correct track of economic development, and the reform and opening up. Xi, facing graduation in Beijing, must have been struck with the changes. Moreover, his father was restored from exile, into the ranks of the top officials.

At the end of 2001, Xi Jinping returned to Tsinghua University to submit his doctoral thesis "Studies on Rural Market-Oriented Construction of the Chinese Countryside" for the PhD program he was enrolled in. This time, he majored in Marxism and ideological and political education. "I did a series of studies, including studies on rural market-oriented construction and poverty reduction in China, and joint development of the mountainous and sea areas in Fujian, modern agricultural theories and practice, the leading basic realization of modernization in the agricultural sector in the developed area of Fujian, the development and improvement of the socialist market economy and Marxist economy, and the rural market-oriented construction and China's entry into the WTO on the basis of practice. I wrote the study results in books and papers." He described the content of his advanced education in this way.[42]

Memorizing Several Hundred Telephone Numbers at the Side of the Defense Minister

In April, 1979, Xi became the personal assistant of Geng Biao, the secretary general of Central Military Commission, after graduating from college.

Geng Biao, a Hunan native, dubbed the "young fellow countryman" by Mao Zedong, shed his uniform and started his over-twenty-year diplomatic career after the founding of the new China, and became the first "General Ambassador" to western countries. On October 6, 1976, on the very night that the CPC Central Committee crushed the "Gang of Four," he was ordered to supervise the propaganda efforts, support the debate on the criterion of truth, and called on the veteran cadres like Deng Xiaoping and Chen Yun to resume their work. Later, he served as the vice premier of the State Council, state councilor, defense minister, and vice chairman of the National People's Congress.

42.　"Xi Jinping: My Experience in the 'Up to the Mountains, Down to the Country-side' Movement," *Fujian Ph.D. Demeanour*, 2003.

In late 1930s, Geng Biao was stationed in Qingyang, Gansu, when Xi Zhongxun was the county Party chief of Huanxian county in Qingyang at the time. The two had established a profound friendship while together at this time. Geng Yan, the youngest daughter of Geng Biao, said, "Both of them were upright and got along well in those years."[43]

This connection between the "elder generation and the sons" was so profound that when Geng Biao passed away in 2000, Xi Jinping and Geng Biao's son Geng Zhiyuan took up Geng's ashes and placed them in the cinerary casket together; two years later when Xi Zhongxun passed away, Geng Zhiyuan accompanied Xi's family through the course of the funeral. "This is what the son, and only the eldest son should do," Geng Yan said.[44]

His father's old comrade-in-arms became the 26-year-old Xi's mentor in political life.

"My father felt that Jinping was a down-to-earth young man who studied diligently. My father had three personal assistants at the time, among whom Xi Jinping was the youngest," Geng Yan said.[45]

In the spring of 1979, when Xi Jinping received an appointment from the General Office of the State Council, Geng Biao was serving as the vice premier of the State Council, in charge of foreign relations, the civilian airlines, tourism, and military industries. But before Xi reported to duty, Geng Biao was transferred to another post, the secretary general of the Standing Committee of the CPC's Central Military Commission, to assist the chairman and vice chairman of the Central Military Commission in handling the routine work of the Central Military Commission. Two years later, he served as the defense minister.

Xi Jinping became a serviceman, donning the green uniform with the red collar tabs and red cap badge (at that time, the Chinese army had not yet restored the rank system). He was ranked as a deputy company-level cadre, according to his education background, his salary was 52 yuan each month. He had no house of his own, and as his work was very busy, most of the time he could not make it home, and stayed in the dormitory provided by his work unit.[46]

Kong Xiangxiu, a personal assistant to Geng Biao, said that when Xi Jinping reported for duty in March that year, Geng Biao was still in the

---

43.   "Geng Biao: Staying Behind in the Anti-Japanese Base, Geng Ying and Geng Yan Telling Stories of Their Father," *China Economic Weekly*, Issue 29, 2010.
44.   Mentor, Blog Weekly, Issue 146, 2013.
45.   "Geng Biao: Staying Behind in the Anti-Japanese Base, Geng Ying and Geng Yan Telling Stories of Their Father," *China Economic Weekly*, Issue 29, 2010.
46.   Mentor, Blog Weekly, Issue 146, 2013.

headquarters, directing the Sino-Vietnamese War.[47] In the three years at the side of Geng Biao, Xi Jinping widened his field of vision, learning a great deal in the process.

The media has used the term "old-time knight's squire" to describe Xi's first job as a confidential clerk.

It's said that there were many things that Geng Biao did not allow Xi to write down. For example, Geng required him to learn several hundred telephone numbers by heart.

Geng Biao attended many meetings of the CPC Central Committee and handled numerous activities. As his personal assistant, a lot of documents from the central government went through Xi's hand, which opened his eyes to the operations of the top political hub.

Geng Yan said, "When [Xi Jinping] was transferred from Shanghai to Beijing, he went to visit each of the senior politicians he encountered as a confidential clerk. In his own words, they were familiar to him. If he had been in the provinces all the time, coming to the central authority, he would have been an outsider: a rural farmer entering the city for the first time. Luckily, this was not so with him, because he was familiar with these men from his career. This is an advantage for him."[48]

Xi used to accompany Geng Biao on his visits to foreign countries and the provinces in China, which greatly widened his horizons.

In their spare time, Geng Biao and Xi Jinping had a common hobby: playing the game of *Weiqi* (better known in the West by its Japanese name, *Go*). The advance and retreat of black and white oblate stones among the 361 points on the grid chessboard can be used to simulate the strategies and tactics of the military formation and to expound the traditional Chinese "way" (道, *Dao*). Geng Biao encouraged the staff around him to play Go, as a means of training their intellects to see the big picture. The Chinese master player Nie Weiping, a good friend of Xi Jinping, said that Xi learned the rules of the game early on. When Xi asked for advice on how to improve his skills, Nie refused. Later Nie explained that he was worried that after improving his skills, Xi, as smart and young as he was, might easily beat Geng Biao and upset the old man.[49]

In that era, Nie Weiping beat Japanese players on behalf of China and became a national hero worshiped by the whole nation. He often acquired tickets to soccer games, tickets that were in great demand, in order to satisfy Xi's craving for watching soccer in the stands of Beijing Workers' Stadium.

---

47.   Mentor, Blog Weekly, Issue 146, 2013.
48.   Ibid.
49.   Nie Weiping. "Why I Didn't Teach Xi to Play Go," *Sports Weekly*, January 8, 2014.

Xi also liked to listen to popular songs, long before he met his wife, a talented songstress. According to the memory of Yang Xilian, then a driver for Geng Biao, Geng Biao's car was a Mercedes-Benz 250, later replaced with a Mercedes-Benz 280, which included a built-in cassette player. Xi could not drive. When they were waiting for Geng, or went out, they often listened to the songs of Deng Lijun (Theresa Teng). "The cassette 'Stories of a Little Town' was almost worn out."[50]

An important responsibility of Geng Biao in the Central Military Commission was presiding over the development of the Program of the Central Military Committee for Downsizing and Restructuring, in accordance with Deng Xiaoping's thoughts on streamlining the military and reforming the system.

At a time when China was sparing no efforts to reinvigorate its decaying economy, the streamlining of the overstaffed military system was imperative. Although the shocking lay-off of a million redundant army personnel was not formally initiated until 1985, three waves of downsizing and restructuring were carried out between 1980 and 1982, including two in 1982. One key element of the program was to downsize the military institutions, concentrating the staff noncombatants and the supporting troops.

In the spring of 1982, Xi Jinping waved goodbye to his political mentor Geng Biao and left the army to become the deputy Party chief of Zhengding County in Hebei.

"At the time, there were four members of staff at the side of Geng. Within about two months, Geng's wife was promoted to deputy commander, and the two other personal assistants were senior to Xi. So either Geng's wife or Xi had to go," Kong Xiangxiu said. "Xi understood Geng's concerns, so he resigned from the job."[51]

Kong said that in the farewell dinner for Xi, they ordered some pork head meat and a fine bottle of spirits. They proposed several toasts to bid him farewell.[52]

Taking the Initiative to Enter Politics: A Road of Great Risks and Low Autonomy

Among the collection of personal photographs of Xi released in the past years, among the most notable is a photo of him in military uniform, shot when he was working at the side of Geng Biao: bright eyes, steady eye contact, and strikingly distinct lines of the face. There is a noteworthy Korean drama

50.　　Mentor, Blog Weekly, Issue 146, 2013.
51.　　Ibid.
52.　　Ibid.

series, "My Love from Another Star," a phenomenally popular TV show. The hero that earned the affections of thousands of Chinese girls appears quite similar to the young Xi Jinping in this photo—his wife Peng Liyuan says that she and their daughter totally agree on this resemblance. It can be seen from the old photos that even though it had been a rather long time after he was transferred to a civilian job, being a thrifty man, he still wore his old military uniform, just without the collar insignia.

It was around the time he left Beijing that he ended his short-lived first marriage. His first wife, the daughter of an ambassador, wished to study overseas—a deviation from Xi's intended life path.

Many people say that, like his mentor Geng Biao, Xi is pragmatic and efficient, and likes to think. Geng Biao's eldest daughter Geng Ying said that in the three years that he followed Geng Biao, Xi was very hardworking and had the momentum required for progress. Perhaps this is why he could seize the chance to create the indelibly precious experiences of his life. She also said that Xi's excellence was due largely to his family's influence and his honorable personal qualities, which laid a solid foundation for him.[53]

Geng Ying's assessment of his "younger brother" (i.e., Xi Jinping), is that he is upright, intolerant of crooked or evil thoughts, strong in character, has a firm will behind a gentle appearance, and hates injustice like poison. He will inevitably finish the things he starts. Perfect or not, everything within his control has a start and an end.[54] Facing the media, her comments on Xi Jinping's actions in his first two years since taking power are that, first, he is a man of action; second, he is a man of strategy and tactics. "He has a clear mind. He is very clear about what he wants, as well as what his people, his country, and his party want."

The "Questions presented by Geng Biao," in 1991, produced a great impact. When Geng Biao returned to Qingyang, he saw that some of the villagers were forbidden by the local cadres to file complaints, so he sent his daughter to receive the complaint letters quietly. He harshly interrogated the local cadres: "In the years we were stationed here, when a boy soldier was to be shot to death according to military discipline because he harassed the daughter of the landlord, the folks kneeled down to plead for him." He asked of them: "If you make a mistake today, do you think the folks will plead for you?"

In Xi's first days as the state president, he began by emphasizing that "the mass line" was the magic weapon of the CPC for solving the deterioration of

---

53.　　"Daughter of Geng Biao: Xi Jinping is Righteous and Hates Injustice like Poison," www.12ccom.net, March 24, 2015.

54.　　Ibid.

the relations between the Party and the masses. Leaving Beijing in the spring of 1982 was Xi Jinping's own choice. Later he said that entering the realm of politics was a road of great risks and low autonomy.[55] However, looking back, this milestone decision was to be the choice that could best manifest his autonomy.

Geng Biao's advice to him was that, if he wanted to go to the grassroots level, he could go to the field army units, instead of the regional government. The princelings of the same family background did not understand his choice. "Finally back from the red land, black land, loessland, and the green grass fields, some of them are of the opinion that they've experienced their fair share of suffering. They think that, from now on, they will not suffer; and some others think that they should be compensated and seek the pleasures of the moment without concerns for the future," Xi Jinping said.[56]

Later in a review, Xi said, in history, the people that passed the palace exams, if awarded local posts, would go thousands of miles to a different locality. "Some of us are not even as good as the literati and officialdoms in traditional times. What is even more pitiful is that the radius of our sphere of activities is not more than fifty kilometers. We would not leave Beijing, would not go to other provinces for fear of losing a registered residence in Beijing."[57]

In addition to Xi Jinping, another princeling who left Beijing in those days was Liu Yuan, the son of Liu Shaoqi, the previous PRC chairman, who went to work in Henan as the deputy secretary of a commune after he graduated from Beijing Normal University.

Thirty years later, Liu Yuan was promoted to the rank of admiral, the political commissar of the People's Liberation Army (PLA) General Logistics Department, and played an important part in assisting Xi in the fight on corruption in the military. But back then their choices seemed rather unusual. In a get-together before they left Beijing, many people professed puzzlement. Xi Jinping said, "In the Cultural Revolution, we were forced to go to the mountainous areas and the countryside. Despite this, we learned and felt a lot of things. Now that everything has returned to normal and those 'leftist' notions that imprisoned us have been lifted, we have more reasons to work, to fight, and to achieve something big."[58]

Xi Jinping's new job was as the deputy secretary of Zhengding County, a post at the deputy division level. It is from this time on that he truly started

55. "Xi Jinping: How I Entered the Political Circle," *Chinese People, Sons and Daughters of China*, Issue 7, 2000.

56. Ibid.

57. Ibid.

58. Ibid.

his long climb toward his current position as supreme leader of the CPC and the state.

Later, in summarizing his experiences in his career as a government official, he said that one should aspire to do big things, rather than to reach a lofty position. Don't take personal development and promotion for granted, because this is no hard and fast law of officialdom. Your pursuit will be realized when you combine opportunity with factors of success, though this can be quite difficult. If you actively pursue promotion, but do not get it, your life will be full of disappointment and pain.

He believes that as long as you hold on, you will accomplish something. "Now that you decide to take this road, no matter how many difficulties and obstacles you run into, you'll have to push forward like a soldier into enemy territory. My political career is also full of ups and downs, hardships, tests, and challenges, all these inescapable things," he said.[59]

In the spring of 1982, for the 28-year-old Xi Jinping, the challenges were just beginning.

IV. TOWARD THE PINNACLE OF POWER IN CHINA
There Are Rarely People Who Worked as County Party Chiefs Among Top Officials of the CPC; He Is an Exception

On January 12, 2015, the general secretary of the Chinese Community Party held discussions with the 206 participants from the county-level Party chiefs in the Party School of the Central Committee, when they met at the People's Great Hall in Beijing. According to the grand training plan, over 2,800 county-level Party chiefs from all over China will be trained in three years. The plan has attracted much attention for its size and range.

Xi Jinping warned the county-level Party chiefs that there were four things to keep in mind: The Party, the people, their responsibilities and warning signs. In addition, they should exercise self-discipline and never be distracted by offers of money, power, or sex.

In the Chinese political structure, the county-level Party chiefs hold a special place. Though they may be at a rather subordinate level (generally at the division level, eight or nine levels away from the top of the power structure), they are granted many rights.

In *Political Tittle-Tattle*, published by Xi in 1990, he wrote: "If China is a net, more than 3,000 counties in China [after multiple subsequent adjustments, there are now more than 2,800 counties in China] are the

---

59.   Ibid.

knots in the net. If the knots get loosened, there will be political unrest; if the knots are tied securely, there will be political stability." He even directly asserted that "the work of the county-level government concerns the fate of the country."

Xi's understanding of the role of the county-level Party chiefs is closely tied to his own experiences. His own political career started when he served as the deputy Party chief of Zhengding County—an ancient town with a history of over 2,000 years in Hebei Province, 240 kilometers to the south of Beijing, only 15 kilometers from Shijiazhuang City, the capital of Hebei Province—in the spring of 1982.

Starting from here, it took Xi Jinping 30 years to finally become the supreme leader of China, in which 25 years were spent outside of Beijing.

In the *Political Tittle-Tattle*, Xi Jinping cited an old saying: "Prime ministers originate from counties." In the ancient bureaucratic system of China, most civil officials had to gradually accumulate governing experience and political seniority from the lower levels. In the contemporary political circles of China concerned about career completeness, one would be surprised to find that though there are few top officials that enter the core leadership by climbing the ranks, the ones with the county-level governing experience are extremely rare.

For example, in the fifth-generation core leadership of the CPC, only Xi Jinping has the experience of working as the county-level Party chief after 1949; and among the successive general secretaries of the CPC since 1949, no more than five have worked as a county-level Party chief (two others are Hua Guofeng and Zhao Ziyang); among the members of the Standing Committee of the Political Bureau of the CPC Central Committee in the most recent three terms, only Xi has the grassroots-level local official experience.

The main reason lies in the fact that in the 30 years since the opening up and reform of China, most of the top officials were trained as engineers, and they officially came into the Party and government departments starting at deputy positions at the municipal level at least, after climbing to certain higher-level positions within factories, research institutes, or the industrial sectors. The majority of leaders with Youth League backgrounds are promoted to positions at the ministerial level and then sent to work at the provincial level.

In fact, in the Chinese political context, the official's first job as the "head" of a locality is very critical, as it is a highly challenging test of a politician in all aspects, including his ability to grasp the big picture, understand the actual situation in China, and remain mindful of the proper application of political resources, as well as the overall quality of his governing.

The predecessors of Xi, Hu Jintao and Jiang Zemin, as well as his colleague Li Keqiang (the premier), all started from governing a province or a municipality directly under the central government, while Xi started from managing a small northern county with a population of 42,000.

An article published in *The New York Times* in 2012 looked back at Xi Jinping's days as the deputy Party chief of Zhengding County, stating that this experience laid a solid foundation for his gradual promotion. Compared with other legacy politicians, or "princelings," with well-developed relationships, Xi seems to have higher credibility when he is speaking on behalf of the grassroots.[60]

This Young Man from Beijing Is Not Here to Get Gilded

When he first came to Zhengding, Xi, still not yet 29 years of age, became the deputy Party chief, the third-most responsible person in charge of the rural economy, spiritual civilization construction, redressing of unjust, wronged, and misjudged cases, and the culture, education, healthcare, sports, and family planning aspects. In fact, originally he requested actively to work as the Party chief of a commune in the county. After prudent consideration, the then provincial officials decided to appoint him the deputy Party chief of Zhengding County.[61]

Xi recalled that his superior, the prefectural-level Party Chief Xie Feng, had a talk with him, saying, "The reason why you did so many things in the countryside in those years is because you were trying to find a way out of an impasse; you have to keep going, as that is your only way out. That is perhaps why you succeeded. But now the situations are different. The other people may wonder why you choose to go down to and remain at the grassroots level."[62] There had indeed been all sorts of speculation about the young man from Beijing: Some thought that he was the son of a high-ranking official, just there for the sake of appearance—maybe in less than half a year, he would pack up and leave this place, unable to endure the hardship.[63]

Wearing his faded military uniform, his large stature made him look like a mess sergeant, or perhaps a rural peasant in the big city.

No dormitory was specially arranged for him, so he lived in the office, a bungalow. Two wooden benches and a plank made up his bed, on which he laid a cotton-padded mattress made by splicing old fabrics and an old

60.   "Xi Jinping's Days in Zhengding as the Deputy Party Chief," *The New York Times*, 2012 (undated).

61.   "Xi Jinping in Zhengding," *Shijiazhuang Daily*, May 18, 2007.

62.   "Xi Jinping: How I Entered the Political Circle," *Chinese People, Sons and Daughters of China*, Issue 7, 2000.

63.   "Xi Jinping in Zhengding," *Hebei Daily*, January 4, 2014.

military quilt. There was also a desk with three drawers, two brick-red chairs, a thermos, and a light bulb. As there was no bookshelf, the books were stacked on the desk or lined up on the window sill. The most appealing things in the room were two *faux* glazed ceramics of the Tang Dynasty— a camel and a horse, both souvenirs from friends in Beijing.[64]

He waited in line to eat at the "commons" for dinner with other people, and squatted beside the table built with concrete slabs, chatting while eating. If he missed dinner because of trips to the countryside, he would cook vermicelli on an oil stove in his office.

"Zhengding is an ancient town near the capital city with radiant thoroughfares, a place that gathers talents from a long time ago," Xi wrote in the foreword to the *Chronicle of Events in Zhengding County 1949–1983*.

But when Xi assumed office there, Zhengding was a poor county, with an annual income per capita of RMB 148, or about 40 cents per day.

Xi liked to ride a bicycle everywhere to get a clear picture of his surroundings. He saw that the small county seat was full of ruined walls, broken bricks and tiles, mixed manure and firewood, and randomly dumped household garbage. The bumpy streets were flowing with sewage.[65]

This young man from Beijing did not sit in his office. Instead, he visited the villages and the peasant households, and humbly consulted the local people. He told them, sincerely, that whether they were county-level cadres or general cadres, young or old: "I am here to learn from you. I hope I can receive your help and advice."[66] Riding bicycles to the countryside, when passing the beach or a muddy road, he would carry the bicycle on his shoulder. He often said that there were three benefits about riding bicycles: exercising the body, being near the masses, and saving gasoline.

He was reluctant to mention that he was the son of Xi Zhongxun. In the countryside, he ate cornbread and pickles at villagers' houses, his favorites, and he would leave money and food coupons with them.

A town cadre recalls that Xi kept a low profile. He had gone through a lot—he was familiar with the folks, and good at bringing people together. "Back then, according to the central government's policy, the people had to pay education funds themselves. As they knew very little about this, mixed feelings were apparent among the people. Instead of blindly carrying out central directives, he went to all the towns under his county's jurisdiction to do ideological work in a prudent and amicable manner." Thus the educational

---

64.   "Friends—Records on the Communication between Xi Jinping and Jia Dashan," Xinhua News Agency, April 20, 2014.

65.   "Xi Jinping in Zhengding," *Hebei Daily*, January 4, 2014.

66.   Ibid.

fund in Zhengding was smoothly collected.[67]

In the early 1970s, Zhengding enjoyed quite a reputation as a major grain-producing county in northern China. However, because of an undue emphasis on grain production, the tillage for cotton, oil crops, and melons and fruits was greatly reduced. With 52,000 *mu* of tillage, the county was required to turn in 38 million kilograms of grain. Not enough grain was left, and many of the villagers had to buy grain from other places.

Though he was a newcomer, he planned to start his work by solving this sensitive problem, though it was a taboo for many, so that the local folks would not suffer from hunger. He and the other deputy Party chief took the task upon themselves actively. They submitted reports to the provincial government and to Beijing, putting forward the request to lower the required quota of grain purchased by the state. The then Party chief worried that this matter would affect his political career, but Xi Jinping said, "Reflecting on a problem is a fine tradition of the CPC, so you don't have to worry."

In the early summer of 1982, the State Council sent an investigation team to look closely at Zhengding in cooperation with the provincial and municipal Party committees, and later decided to reduce the quotas of grain purchased by the state by 14 million kilograms, which greatly eased the local farmers' scarcity. Wang Youhui, then deputy county mayor of Zhengding, wrote in an article: "This issue concerns the interests of 420,000 people in Zhengding County, and it shows Xi's bold and vigorous work. He does not simply follow the orders of superiors, instead, he handles the matter according to the actual situations."[68]

Some regions of south China were already promoting the "household responsibility system" in agriculture production—a remarkably original and forceful first step in the reform that changed the fate of China—but Hebei hadn't started. The county government officials wanted to act only after receiving documentation from the central government, "for fear of being too conspicuous." Xi suggested that Zhengding should take the lead in carrying out the experiment.

At his urgings, Zhengding launched the trial of the household responsibility system of agriculture production. In that very year, the agriculture production value of the pilot villages doubled, increasing the income per capita to RMB 400, for which Zhengding attracted a lot of visitors from both inside and outside of Hebei Province.

---

67.   "Zhengding: the Starting Point of a Political Career," *Economic Observer*, July 11, 2013.

68.   "My Contact with Xi Jinping," *Culture and History Vision*, Issue 11, 2011.

The Youngest County Party Chief Respected his Elders

In the second half of 1983, 30-year-old Xi Jinping became the Party chief of Zhengding County, the first time he headed the administration of a locality; he was also the youngest Party chief ever in the history of Zhengding County.

The Chinese political circles back then were pressing ahead with the building of a "revolutionary, younger, well-educated, professionalized" cadre force, so as to accelerate the upgrading of the official personnel. Xi's personal conditions met these requirements perfectly. Another example from that same year was a colleague of Xi Jinping in Zhengding County, the Deputy County Mayor Wang Youhui, non-CPC, aged 49, and a college graduate. He was abruptly promoted to the position of the deputy director of Hebei People's Congress, advancing four ranks. At the time, some of the old cadres of the same rank were 90 years old.

But even by these new standards, Xi was still one of strongest performers, who continued to grow rapidly. In the mid-1990s, the average age of the officials elected in the list of the top 100 excellent county Party chiefs was 50 years old; among the sixteen who were promoted to the provincial- or ministerial-level positions, the average age at which they were originally promoted to county-level Party chief was 38, the youngest being 32.[69]

At the beginning of 2015, according to the statistics of the *Shandong Business News*, the average age of the county-level Party chiefs in Shandong province is 50.

Immediately after he became county mayor, Xi promoted reform in Zhengding County, reducing the average age of the members of the Standing Committee to 41, with 45 percent of them having received at least a junior college education. For the general rules of the political circle, it is inevitable that reformers have to face criticism. Though Xi pressed ahead and carried out many progressive measures, he received wide recognition in the conservative city. One of his secret weapons was his respect for veteran cadres.

He had said on several occasions that the veteran cadres are a great treasure: "None of our present life would be possible without their past struggles and contributions. So there is nothing to be diminished about the veteran cadres."

He often went out riding his bicycle and assigned the only 212 Beijing Jeep of the Standing Committee to the old cadres, and later bought a sedan for them. There was no common recreational space for old cadres, so he emptied the meeting room shared by the Standing Committee and the county government and converted it into a recreation room for old cadres. He also

---

69.   *Decision*, Issue 2–3, 2015.

kept an eye on their medical expenses. He always sent for the representatives of old cadres to consult them before making major decisions, and visited them at home on holidays.

His practice of showing respect for the elders and the sages was described by the *People's Daily*, *Hebei Daily*, and other official media. He himself wrote an article entitled "The Young and Middle-Aged Cadres Must Respect their Elders," in which he analyzed how to deal with the cooperation and gap-bridging between the older- and younger-generation cadres within the historical context of institutional reform as a large number of veteran cadres retired to secondary and tertiary positions.

"Realizing the transition from the older to the young inside our cadre force represents neither the transfer of power between individuals or opposing groups, nor a power struggle, but an operation for the same objective and the same cause. Therefore, the handover from the older to the young must be a process of cooperation and a kind of graduation. The respect for the elder is the condition for cooperation, and frictionless transition. Cooperation is the necessary basis for the transition," he wrote. This editorial was published in the *People's Daily* on December 7, 1984. It is very rare that an article by a county-level Party chief is published in one of the most important media outlets of the CPC.

The old cadres in Zhengding gave this view of Xi Jinping: He is amicable, honest, prudent, articulate, confident, and humble. He was young but he acted older than his years.

In Chinese political circles, the two human factors that play a most decisive role are two groups: the veteran cadres, and the people. The former represents the core political force, many of whom, though retired, still have far-reaching influence in high-level decision-making processes and personnel scheduling; the latter represents the legitimacy of public opinion. Though they do not vote directly, sometimes their voices still are the key weights on the balance.

Xi fulfilled the well-known requirements for a local official's work methods: The county-level Party chief must visit all of the villages under the jurisdiction of the county; the prefecture-level Party chief must visit all the towns under the jurisdiction of the prefecture; and the provincial-level Party chief must visit all counties and cities under the jurisdiction of the province.

At the same time, Xi and other successful officials detest the bad bureaucratic habit of discussing something without reaching a decision, reaching a decision without carrying it out, speaking lofty-sounding but empty words, and indulging in insubstantial talk. Instead, he vigorously advocates for speaking succinctly, holding short meetings, and by all means avoiding vacuous and worn-out clichés, thereby concentrating all available energies toward achieving big and practical things. He has consistently stuck to these principles in his work from Zhengding to Beijing in the past 30 years.

Hua Luogeng and Yu Guangyuan: The Think Tank of the Small County

As a county-level Party chief, Xi's primary goal was economic reform. Borrowing the famous economist Yu Guangyuan's "semi-suburban economy"[70] concept, he quickly turned the traditional agriculture production in Zhengding county into a commercial success that "earns money from the city people" by producing and processing whatever was needed in the city.

In order to develop edible fungi cultivation in Zhengding, he wrote a letter to a fertilizer producer in Jiangsu to ask for help, and sent people to pick up an important raw material, tailings, from this producer.

In 1983, with its diversified economy, the income of Zhengding County was increased to RMB 43 million, with a per capita income of RMB 100, and the peasant's income per capita increased from RMB 100 to over RMB 200.

Xi also urged the cadres at all levels to open their minds and widen their horizons. He took the cadres to the pioneering areas of reform and opening up in south China to look for inspiration and to visit and study Zhejiang, Jiangsu, and Tianjin, where the township enterprises had started earlier.

On June 16, 1984, no more than one year after he took office, the *People's Daily* reported the new changes to the economy in Zhengding at length. This was the first time that Xi Jinping's name had appeared in the official organ of the CPC, and according to Zhao Derun, the Xinhua News Agency journalist who wrote the report, a lot of the most vivid and interesting ideas were from Xi, but considering that one name could not appear too many times in one article, his name only appeared twice.[71]

Zhao Derun also said that he was favorably impressed by Xi when he met him for the first time in mid-April 1984. "He was very easy-going, talked unhurriedly and he seemed to me a very honest man." And unlike many county-level Party chiefs, he was "an honest man with ideas."[72]

They talked in Xi's office which by now contained a plain desk piled with books; Xi smoked fifteen-cents-per-packet Lotus cigarettes, a brand usually smoked by the local peasants.

70.   Defined as an intermediate economy, with both the characteristics of the suburban economy (such as reliance on cities, advanced commodity production, close urban–rural relations, and the close connection between agriculture and industry) on the one hand, and the characteristics of a rural economy on the other.
71.   "Interviewing Xi Jinping in Zhengding," www.people.com.cn, February 1, 2015.
72.   Ibid.

What left the deepest impression on Zhao Derun was that Xi was good at seeing the big picture and connecting the development of Zhengding with the whole country. He first talked about liberating the mind, then stressed that there should be a long-term guiding plan, instead of just taking one step at a time; he also talked about making scientific decisions to solve some cadres' blindness, and change the randomness and fickleness of the past decisions. He even talked about passing legislation to form a ten- or fifteen-year perspective long-term plan.

This broad-minded young official had a lot of ideas that seemed ahead-of-time, not only in rural areas but in the whole country at that time. For example, he placed recruitment advertisements to the whole nation, and issued nine regulations on recruiting talents, posting them all over Zhengding County and on the front page of the *Hebei Daily*, which aroused a great response inside the province and all around the country. Many intellectuals and engineering technicians requested to work in Zhengding.

He also proposed to organize an economic think tank to offer intellectual support. He sent over 100 invitation letters to famous masters like the mathematician Hua Luogeng and the economist Yu Guangyuan, inviting them to be a counselor to the small county seat. "He is from Beijing, so using his relations, he invited first-class talents to the county. This was an unusual practice," Zhao Derun said.[73]

Xi is bold in employing people. This can be seen when he appointed a peasant who cultivated a superior cotton species as a government cadre; when visiting Wuxi, he found a person who was an expert on management and operations, so he privately persuaded him to work as the manager of a nozzle and oil pump factory that had lost over RMB 500,000 and was on the verge of bankruptcy. On the second day that expert worked in the factory the stocked products were sold out, and in less than one year, the output of the factory doubled.

The medical cosmetics developed by Wu Baoxin, an engineer in Shijiazhuang, sold well all over the country, but he was not appreciated at his original enterprise. Hearing that Zhengding County attached great importance to talent, he sent word that he would like to work in Zhengding. Xi immediately decided to take him on. One day after work, he took the county mayor and deputy mayor to the community in which Wu lived. As he had no exact address, he looked for him from door to door. When this failed, he cried Wu's name at the top of his lungs. Later Wu Baoxin brought the medical cosmetics project developed by himself to Zhengding, and earned over RMB 300,000 in one year.

---

73.   Ibid.

Xi also values education. During his office term as the Party chief of Zhengding County, in addition to dedicating himself to improving the dilapidated school buildings, he also laid a foundation for Zhengding to become a center for the game of ping-pong. There was an extracurricular ping-pong school in Liucun Village that cultivated a number of excellent players. Xi believed that the ping-pong school should be moved to the county seat and be able to choose its trainees from children all over China. Nowadays, this school has become the training base for the national ping-pong team. It is a point of pride for China, with the talented team members training there before almost every big match. It has now also become a major tourism attraction for Zhengding.

Constructing "Oriental Hollywood"

Another initiative of Xi Jinping's that has produced a lasting effect on Zhengding is in the cultural field.

On the night he came to Zhengding, he visited the writer Jia Dashan, an employee of the county's cultural museum, who was less than 40 years old. His novel *Pilgrimage* had won a national award and his work was studied in high school textbooks. "I read several of his novels. The humorous language, philosophical analysis, real and beautiful depictions and ingenious and unique plots totally amazed me," Xi wrote in a memoir.[74]

As Jia was talking with other people, Xi sat down and waited quietly. Knowing that this young man was the new county Party chief, Xi turned his head and said absentmindedly, "Here comes the wet-behind-the-ears young man who is going to take care of us." The words left so deep an impression in Xi's memory that he recalled them when he returned back to Zhengding 20 years later.[75] This impolite joke did not prevent them from becoming close friends. They often talked deep into the night about literature, social issues, intellectuals, and dreams. Sometimes they talked so late that the gate of the county's standing committee's yard had been locked; Xi would hunker down to let Jia stand on his shoulder and climb over it. This close friend became an important assistant to Xi in Zhengding.

Zhengding has a long history. Xi Jinping read the county annals and historical materials carefully, in detail, and wandered about the streets to explore the ancient sites. He realized that with concentrated ancient buildings and well-developed transport routes, Zhengding should restore the ancient ruins and develop cultural tourism.

Jia Dashan was an old Zhengding hand who knew quite a lot about the

74.   "Recollections of Dashan," *Contemporary People*, Issue 7, 1998.
75.   "Xi Jinping Back in Zhengding," *Prose Parterre*, Issue 7, 2009.

existing ancient buildings and cultural relics in Zhengding. Recommended by Xi Jinping, the non-Party persona Jia Dashan was promoted from the deputy curator of the cultural museum, subordinate to the Cultural Affairs Bureau, directly to the head of the Cultural Affairs Bureau.

Zhengding's Longxing Temple is a world-renowned large temple built in the Song Dynasty (960–1279) and a cultural relic considered a national treasure. But due to its age, it was seriously damaged. For its complete restoration, a fund of RMB 30 million would be needed. Such a huge investment was second only to that invested in the restoration of Potala Palace in Lasa, Tibet, in the whole country's cultural relics system back then.

Xi repeatedly invited authoritative experts from all over China to inspect and evaluate it. Jia, running between the capital, Beijing, the provincial capital, and the county seat, was so exhausted that he had gastrointestinal ulcers and had to curl up in the backseat of their Jeep because of his pain. Eventually they got support from their superiors, and the money required for the restoration was appropriated.

To carry out this huge project, they also needed to acquire land of 60 *mu* and relocate 60 households. Despite all the difficulties, the Longxing Temple restoration project was eventually successfully completed.[76]

In 1983, China Central Television (CCTV) was shooting the epic TV series "Dream of the Red Chamber," and decided to invest RMB 800,000 to find a local government to work jointly on the building of the temporary exterior set of the "Rongguo Mansion." Xi wished to introduce the Rongguo Mansion to Zhengding, and build it into a permanent building and form a tourism-based link with Longxing Temple. Despite some reluctance from county-level officials, Xi managed to get the go ahead to build the mansion with loaned money.

During the building, due to inside problems concerning the Dream of the Red Chamber crew, additional investment was needed to finish the construction, which put a major question mark over the project. Xi immediately wrote a letter to a friend in Beijing, asking him to intervene. Finally, CCTV agreed to provide a one-off investment of RMB 380,000. In addition, Xi also drummed up financial support from Shijiazhuang City.

In August, 1986, more than one year after Xi left Zhengding, the Rongguo Mansion scenic area, which cost RMB 3,500,000, and had a total floor area of 37,000 square meters was completed. The cast and crew of Dream of the Red Chamber spent more than two months filming there. Since then, more than 170 movies and television productions have been filmed there.

---

76.   "Friends—Records on the Communication between Xi Jinping and Jia Dashan," Xinhua News Agency, April 20, 2014.

Rongguo Mansion was once dubbed the "Oriental Hollywood." In the 1990s, the annual number of tourists visiting Rongguo Mansion reached a record of 1,380,000, creating the "Zhengding model of tourism."

Xi also attaches great importance to Zhengding's image and publicity. In October, 1984, he invited the directors of *Guang Ming Daily*'s bureaus in 27 provinces, municipalities, and autonomous regions to visit Zhengding and hired them as special information advisors.[77]

The media summarized Xi's administration in Zhengding as a time of economic reform, and of receiving the superior's inspection. In the *Chronicle of Events in Zhengding County 1949–1983* reviewed by Xi, seventeen events concerned economic reform—among which, fifteen events occurred between 1982 and 1983; and among the 23 inspections by superiors, ten inspections occurred between 1982 and 1983.[78]

Despite the emphasis on affirmation and support from high levels, every time the inspectors visited, Xi offered them the traditional dishes of Zhengding, such as buckwheat bread, pork head meat, wonton, bread baked in a tank furnace, buckwheat noodles, and if they wanted to have a drink, he would serve the Zuibaxian and Changshanxiang, the local spirits of Zhengding.

How the Political Strongman Avoided Becoming a "Political Bully"

In the mid-1980s, a novel entitled *New Star* was very popular in China, telling the story of a young county Party chief. It is said that Xi, working at Zhengding, was one of the prototypes. "Now looking back, if we can say we indeed achieved something, it would be the liberation of mind. That we can achieve this end is not only because we have the ability but also because we have the consciousness and wishes to be consistent with the central authority, as well as the sincerity to learn and to try," Xi Jinping proclaimed.[79]

Talking about his personal experience of those years, he said, "I was young in those years, and trying my best to do a good job, I burned the midnight oil, and often stayed up all night. For this reason, almost every month I had a serious illness." Eventually he knew that he could not go on like this. He attained the proper mindset: "Despite the passions in my heart, I had to learn to take my time." He added, "You have so many tasks on hand, each of them like a thread, but at one time only one thread can be pulled through the eye of a needle."

---

77.   "Zhengding: The Starting Point of a Political Career," *Economic Observer*, July 11, 2013.

78.   Ibid.

79.   "Xi Jinping Back in Zhengding," *Prose Parterre*, Issue 7, 2009.

Xi said that the experience hit him right between the eyes. Since then he faithfully goes to bed every night before midnight and restart his work the next day.[80]

His easy grace and prudence gradually became a distinct characteristic. His close friend Jia Dashan said that Xi was an "aggressive reformer, always with a smile on his face," adding "he is not a progressive, nor a hard-edged reformer that wears a rigid suit, but a reformer that persuades people to accept historical reforms while taking ease and having a drink."

The historical reforms are still happening, and the baton of overseeing the reforms in China has been passed to Xi, who has gone through all manner of tests and trials.

At the beginning of 2015, when Xi Jinping faced the county-level Party chiefs that came to participate in the training, he encouraged them to engage in the reform in China, despite the fact that it is beset with numerous contradictions and turbulent undercurrents, and warned them not to be distracted by temptations and risks—after over 30 years of development, as the important governance unit of the second-largest economy of the world, the importance of the county level will become increasingly prominent and the problems unprecedentedly severe.

In the current Party and government hierarchical structure of China, the central authority focuses on the top-level design of the country's development, while the provincial and prefectural (municipal) authorities mainly deal with the common services in larger regions, and only the county-level institutions have three non-substitutable functions: Accepting and implementing the policies of superiors; directly commanding the local governance; and evaluating the governing performance and earning the public's trust.

How much power does a county-level Party chief hold? Some say that the power a county-level Party chief holds is almost no different from that of the central authority, except in the realms of diplomacy, the military, and national defense. As there is the provincial and municipal government between the central authority and the county level, situated at the edge of political geography and with almost zero oversight, the county-level Party chief has a distinct concentration of power, and strong dominance over local political situations. At the same time, with the growth of economic strength in the county territory, funds and major projects that can be controlled by county-level finance are also increasing day by day. Therefore, it is entirely possible that the county-level Party chief may carry out the roles more

---

80.   "Xi Dada's Talk on Time Management: The Young People should Refrain from Staying Late into the Night," Weibo entry, www.people.com.cn, January 12, 2015.

properly undertaken by the government head, company executives, or judges, and thereby become an arbitrary "political strongman."

Xi Jinping wrote an article arguing that the hardest position is that of the county-level official, because they must possess all kinds of knowledge, and great abilities, or else they will fall down on the job.[81]

When doing a field survey during his tenure as the provincial Party chief of Zhejiang, he said that the county-level Party chiefs and county mayors were more important and had more leeway than the deputy prefectural mayor, though their rank was lower than that of the city mayors. Promoting the county Party chiefs and county mayors, who aspire to the deputy prefectural mayor position, was in fact transferring them to an unimportant position. He proposed that the county-level Party chief and county mayors should be raised to the deputy departmental level.[82] In fact, the county-level Party chiefs in some counties were already enjoying this higher rank.

The more important the position is, the higher the risks there will be. In a seminar for county-level Party chiefs, Xi warned: "You will be the targets of all kinds of temptations, calculations, flattery, and adulations—prey in the hunting."[83]

In fact, over the years, the county-level Party chiefs have been ranked as the most affected by corruption. For example, in Shanxi Province, with its high incidence of corruption cases, among all the cadres investigated in 2014, at least fourteen were county-level Party chiefs. Shanxi Provincial Party Chief Wang Rulin even conducted grassroots research, centered on the question, "how to elect good cadres to the office of county-level Party chief, how to prevent the promotion of cadres with faults, and which precautions should be taken when selecting the county-level Party chief."

Political commentator Zheng Yongnian, director of the East Asian Institute, National University of Singapore, pointed out that political reform in China should start at the county-level government. He said that the root cause of corruption and the spread of organized crime is the marginalization of the county-level government in China's overall political and economic system. He believed that after the opening up and reform, the change from the management of cadres two ranks below to one rank below, makes it very hard for the county-level Party chief to see the top leaders in the central government. On the other hand, over a long time, the country's important policies rarely tilt toward the county-level government.

81.   "Political Tittle-Tattle," *Get Rid of Poverty*, Fujian People's Press, 1990.

82.   Ifeng.com.cn, November 15, 2012.

83.   "Sincere Exchange, Solemn Entrust—Sketch of the Discussion between General Secretary Xi Jinping and the Participants of the Seminar for the County-Level Party Chief," Xinhua News Agency, January 12, 2015.

The solutions prescribed by Zheng Yongnian were as follows: Establish a direct connection between the central authority and the county-level government; the main leaders of the CPC should put more efforts into the training and immediate supervision of county-level Party chiefs and mayors; the central fiscal transfer payment shall tilt towards the county-level government, and the central taxation shall devolve power to the county-level government.

He believes that once the reform of county-level government delivers results, it will provide a solid foundation and strong motivation for the overall systemic reform of China.

It is because the county-level Party chiefs shoulder important responsibilities, and can therefore become highly prone to corruption, that the first seminar for the county-level Party chiefs after the 18th National Congress attracted so much attention, and the discussions between Xi and the participants were all the more convincing thanks to his personal experience.

One of Xi Jinping's "idols" in his political career was a county-level Party chief in the 1960s—Jiao Yulu, the Party chief of Lankao County in Henan—who worked desperately to treat the issue of salinized soil and fight hunger until he died of illness while still in office. Xi published a poem in the *Fuzhou Evening News* in 1990 to mourn Jiao Yulu: "The road of life is long and tough, and you exit the world penniless. Where you served as the official, there you benefited the populace, which were the very wishes of your life." Apparently this poem reflects his own political ideals.

In the past, the realization of such a political ideal relied on hard work, but nowadays, such a dream counts more on reform strategy and firm resolution.

V. THE MATURATION OF THE STATESMAN
The City in which he Would Take Office:
Like a Beautiful Maiden in Rags

The day he took office as the deputy mayor of Xiamen in Fujian Province happened to be Xi Jinping's 32nd birthday.

Back then, Xiamen, established as one of four special economic zones of China along with Shenzhen, Zhuhai and Shantou, was considered a benchmark for the reform and opening up. In February, 1984, one year before Xi assumed his post as the deputy mayor, Deng Xiaoping inspected Xiamen, and agreed to expand the Xiamen Special Economic Zone from the original 2.5 square kilometers to the entire Xiamen island, and to enforce the free port policy in Xiamen.

When he came from the heart of northern China to Xiamen on the coast of the Taiwan Strait, traveling over 1,900 kilometers, Xi itched to do something: "Back then I was eager to come to Xiamen to try out the reform and opening up."[84]

At that time, Fujian, along with Guangdong, was referred to as a pioneering site of reform. The first Secretary of the Provincial Party Committee Xiang Nan pushed for reform and later was listed as one of the "eight reform advocates"—the eight men who made great contributions to the reform and opening up in China, of which Xi's father Xi Zhongxun was one. One well-known expression of Xiang Nan was: "Making mistakes shall be allowed in reform. What shall not be allowed is the avoidance of reform."

It can be imagined what an enormous appeal the turbulent and passionate reform and opening up was to Xi Jinping. And it was a rare opportunity for Xi, who had served as the chief of a locality for only two years, to be promoted to work in the special economic zone.

Xi Jinping said that back then the whole Fujian Province did not seem to be as developed as he had imagined. The road trip from Fuzhou to Xiamen took eight hours, due to the poor traffic conditions and narrow roads. Xiamen, though dubbed China's "marine garden," appeared very old. "The beautiful Xiamen island was like a young maiden in an old garment."[85]

Following this promotion, Xi spent seventeen-and-a-half years in Fujian, rising through the ranks from deputy mayor of Xiamen, Party secretary of Ningde, a prefecture-level city, and deputy Party chief, and then ultimately becoming the governor of Fujian. His Fujian career consisted of five positions in total, through which Xi gradually developed a mature style of governing. His experience of working in this locality in this period was of the greatest importance for him: "The wonderful days of youth in my life were spent in Fujian," he recalls.[86]

When Xi Jinping was working as the deputy mayor of Xiamen, he was in charge of agricultural and rural issues. He put forward that to do a good job resolving the agricultural issues, he first had to go up to the mountains and down to the islands.

With the expansion of the Xiamen Special Economic Zone, Xiamen needed to have a development strategy. Led by Xi, in one and a half years, over 100 experts and professors studied 21 subjects and finally worked out

84.   "Zhejiang Provincial Party Chief: Wishing for the New Round of Development in the Special Economic Zone to be Smooth and Rapid," *Xiamen Daily*, December 12, 2006.
85.   Ibid.
86.   Ibid.

a blueprint for the development of Xiamen over the next fifteen years. This was the first economic and social development strategy and plan compiled by the economic zones in China.

There are not many records of Xi's concrete actions over the three years he worked in Xiamen. He said, "Working in the special economic zone was the first time I took up the city-level posts, the first time I directly participated in the reform and opening up in the richer coastal areas, and the first time that I personally experienced urban construction and management." He added, "These three years were a process of comprehensive studies. It was a very hard, assiduous study process, because, first, I had never worked in such a position; secondly, no one had experience dealing with works in the special economic zone. It can be said that the work in the special economic zone filled the dual deficiencies, and Xiamen offered many experiences to my life."[87]

In this period, Xi got married to the singer Peng Liyuan in Xiamen. They prepared a wedding feast with one round table in a hotel to return the kindness of colleagues and friends. "After the dinner, the four of us went to his house to have a talk, only to find that they had merely four cups including the two cups used for tooth brushing. So they washed two bowls to serve tea. Peng bought some candies on the street for us," Xi's colleague in Xiamen recalled.[88]

Keeping the Fire Alive

In 1988, Xi was transferred to Ningde to work as the prefectural Party chief. This was the second time he had served as the chief leader of a locality. Ningde, at the time, with its backward economy and traffic inaccessibility, was known as the "rift of the gold beach." Six of the nine counties in Ningde were poverty-stricken counties, and for this reason, Ningde was identified as one of the eighteen contiguous impoverished areas. Because its economic level was at the absolute bottom of the list in Fujian, every time they came to the provincial capital to attend a meeting, the cadres from Ningde always sat in the last row.

The then deputy Party secretary and director of the Organization Department of Fujian Province, Jia Qinglin, had a talk with Xi. He said that Ningde had a weak foundation, slow development, no strength, and therefore dared not to speak out. "The provincial committee wants you to be in charge of Ningde and change Ningde's outlook." Xi was also required to adopt

---

87.   Ibid.
88.   "Always Have Mutual Affinity with People," *Fujian Daily*, October 30, 2014.

extraordinary measures to change the backward economic situations.[89] The Party secretary and governor of Fujian at that time also gave him support and encouragement.

But these "extraordinary" expectations coincided with the currency inflation and the overheated economy at the end of 1980s. The central authorities started upon the necessary improvements and rectifications, which suddenly changed the circumstances. Xi Jinping knew that "the people wanted to see changes, they wished that I could lead an effort to change the situation there. They did not see that, all on my own, I could not perform wonders for them."

He meant that the people often began introductions of him by saying that he was the son of Xi Zhongxun, and that there was hope for Ningde now, because as Party secretary, Xi would get projects for Ningde. Xi himself believed otherwise. Later, he told his friend, "This kind of introduction scares me. I've never stretched out my hand to ask for projects from Beijing. The locality has to design its own projects."[90]

He did not intend to follow the practice of "lighting [the proverbial] three big fires after assuming a new post." Instead, he was going to "light a small fire to warm up the water, keep the fire burning, and now and again pour some more cold water in."

Eager to help the people of Ningde get out of their difficulties, the Ningde cadres wanted to get three things done: Develop ports, build railways, and change Ningde Prefecture to Ningde City. But Xi was of the opinion that since it had a weak economic foundation, it should not bite off more than it could chew. Instead, it must act on the principle of seeking truth from facts and lay a solid foundation.[91]

In the three months after he assumed office, Xi Jinping visited each of the nine counties and then most of the towns. Xiadang Town, the remotest mountainous area of Shouning County, was not founded until 1988. There were no highways, no running water, no electric light, no fiscal revenue, and no government offices. In the hot summer, Xi walked over ten kilometers with the local officials for an inspection of the town. With a straw hat on his head, and a towel on his shoulders, Xi walked with the officials over two hours on the mountain roads under the scorching sun. The steep and dangerous roads were full of bushes, so dense they could only be cleared with an ax.

89.   "Xi Jinping: How I Entered the Political Circle," *Chinese People, Sons and Daughters of China*, Issue No. 7, 2000.

90.   *Celebrity's Offspring Tracing, Vol. 1*, Chinese Ancient Books Publishing House, 2009.

91.   "Xi Jinping: Walking Ahead by the Red Ship," *Mother Earth*, December 1, 2006.

One day, they traveled by car for five hours, walked four and a half hours, and had a two-hour meeting. Only after they got back to the county seat did many cadres find that the soles of their tired feet were covered in bloody blisters. Xi often described this travel to Xiadang town as "extremely arduous and unforgettable." Later in his tenure in Fujian, he went to the town twice more.

Xi was not particular when he was visiting the countryside. Unlike some officials who took with them their own thermos and cup, he drank the tea offered by the villagers, and if he took meals in the village, he would pay for the meal in full.

One year, a flood devastated the country road. He walked nearly 13 kilometers to direct the relief activities. In a mudslide section, when someone offered to carry him, he said with a smile: "I am so young. How could I ask you to carry me?"

After the inspection, Xi Jinping decided to guide his governance of Ningde with the saying that "steadily dripping water can hollow out a stone"—rather than being anxious to make his mark, this 33-year-old prefecture-level cadre showed an unusual rationality and persistence.

In October 1988, in an interview with the *Economic Daily*, Xi again put forward the idea that "steadily dripping water can hollow out a stone." Later, he repeatedly expounded on this, saying that in a backward locality like Ningde, only long-time strenuous efforts could bring economic development. It was necessary to overcome naive thoughts, impatience, and short-term solutions and strive to develop a mindset of creating long-term momentum and sustainability in his tenure.

The natural landscape he beheld when he was sent down to Shaanxi, an illustration of "water hollowing stone," left an indelible impression on him: "One drop of water, small and weak, will surely break into pieces when it splashes on a stone. Its value and results, not visible at the moment of the splash, are manifested by the successive splashing of numerous water drops, until it bores a hole in the stone below," he wrote in an article[92] Xi believed that there were no shortcuts for the economically lagging regions. The Great Wall was not built overnight. The changes are a progressive process from quantitative change to qualitative change, like the splashing water hollowing out the stone.

"If the mention of reform and opening up brings in mind help from all directions, we will have yet more impractical, unworkable illusions, and less spirit to do hard work; if the mention of economic development

---

92.   "Revelations from Dripping Water Wearing Stone," *Get Rid of Poverty*, Fujian People's Press, March 1990.

brings to mind the construction of tall buildings and the running of huge manufacturing plants, if we only pursue the dramatic effect and forget the essential infrastructure, in the end, all our efforts will be spent in vain," he wrote.[93]

When Xi Jinping left Ningde, 94 percent of the poverty-stricken families had essentially solved their food problems. On December 12, 1990, the *People's Daily* reported his performance in an article entitled "Ningde Rises Above the Subsistence Level."

Whom to Offend: The Thousands of Cadres, or the Millions of the Masses?

Stressing progressive improvement does not indicate a lack of decisiveness. Xi Jinping whipped up an anti-corruption storm in Ningde.

At the end of the 1980s, seizing land to build personal homes became a common practice for the local cadres of Ningde. In the narrow downtown, rows upon rows of illegal properties were built on the hillside, and were quite offending to the eye. The public greatly objected to this "roadside corruption," but the removal of these illegal properties would have involved thousands of cadres, who had complex connections.

At that time, there were 7,392 cadres with illegal personal houses, 242 of them above the deputy county level, 1,399 above the bureau level, each accounting for 49 percent and 46 percent of the total number of cadres. This set of figures was in great contrast to the poverty of the area.[94] Xi Jinping resolved to solve this problem. He criticized his colleagues' fears at a prefecture-level work conference: "This is a problem concerning whom to offend, the thousands of cadres, or the millions of the masses?"

At the end of 1990, the whole prefecture punished 3,782 cadres for occupying land and building houses against the rules; 99 were above the division level, 476 were above the bureau level, and financial penalties were imposed on 3,446 cadres in total, collecting penalties totaling RMB 1,980,300.

This bold action was reported in the *People's Daily* in May, 1990, and the CPC central authority's official organ also wrote an editorial entitled "Perseverance Creates a Force Without Equal" to passionately praise the prefectural standing committee under the leadership of Xi Jinping.

Apart from removing the illegal properties, Xi also focused on the

---

93.   "Revelations from Dripping Water Wearing Stone," from the book *Get Rid of Poverty*, Fujian People's Press, March 1990.
94.   "Do One Good Thing, Win the Hearts of Thousands of People," *People's Daily*, May 21, 1990

major corruption cases involving Lin Zengtuan of Fubing County and Zheng Xixuan, the vice chairman of the Association of Overseas Chinese of Ningde Prefecture. He stressed in particular that corruption would be strictly separated from necessary explorations of the means to reform, and the cadres who dared to carry out reforms and related explorations would be protected.

At the end of the 1980s, a craze for going into business emerged in the coastal area. Xi warned the subordinate officials: "If you think that being a cadre is not worth your while, you can resign and go into business or start a company, but never try to be both an official and a businessman, and use your official power to seek gain for private interests. The connection of officials and businessmen will inevitably lead to corrupt bureaucratism."[95]

In Ningde, Xi also pioneered the complaint-reception system. Applying to an audience of higher officials to file complaints is a very special "political relief" system in Chinese society, by which the common people pass over relevant grassroots executive branches to make complaints directly to the higher or central administrations. Though the ratio of problems solved through this system is rather low, it is still considered an important safety net of Chinese society. A system that operates outside the judicial system and administrative levels generates great controversy. The number of such applications from the people in each province to the central authority is also a performance metric, used to assess the local government's performance. The higher the number is, the lower the assessment of a local government's efficiency. Xi Jinping turned the system around. In December, 1988, he launched the first reception event in Xiapu County. In fact, when he was still in Zhengding Hebei, he often set a table on the street to hear questions, complaints, and advice from the masses.

In Xiapu, the first person Xi received was Shu Huiying, an employee of the county's bus company. The local government had built a house on the bank of the river beside her house, causing river channel sedimentation and floods. The flood washed away her grain, and parts of her property. She required that the county government dredge the river and compensate her economic loss.

On the first reception day, he had face-to-face exchanges with 102 applicants, received 86 cases, and solved twelve cases on site. He ordered the local government to handle the rest of the cases in one month.

In the summing-up meeting of that day, Xi Jinping said that the officials should be responsible not only to the superiors but also to the masses:

95.   "Xi Jinping's Seventeen Years in Fujian: Iron in Official Control, and Constant Dripping Water Wearing out Stones," www.ifeng.com.cn, November 15, 2012.

"The officials at all levels must get off their perches and rid themselves of bureaucratic airs."[96]

"The emphasis of the petition work should be placed on the grassroots unit, receiving the complaints at the lower governments, send your services to the people, from the prefecture, to county, to town, and then to the villages, and solve the problems at their source, instead of pushing the conflicts to the higher government." This is how Xi Jinping described the complaint-reception structure.

In his eyes, the reception of complaints at grassroots level would not only solve the problems of the people but also strengthen the connection between the Party and the people—maintaining close ties with the masses has always been considered a magic weapon by the CPC to gain power and win the hearts of the masses. It is just that some officials could not carry it out strictly.

When he assumed the office of municipal Party secretary of Fuzhou, Xi continued this practice. On May 14, 1990, merely half a month after he took over, he held a "reception week" in Gulou District, and solved a land dispute for one citizen that had lasted over half a year.

In Fuzhou, Xi Jinping proposed the "do-it-right-away" practice, another attempt to change the government's work style and improve government efficiency. This slogan still hangs in the building of Fuzhou Administrative Service Center's building in the yard of Fuzhou municipal Party committee, situated at the entrance of the Fuzhou Mawei Tunnel of National Road 104 in Fujian Province.

The biggest Xi's moves when he was heading the Fuzhou government was prompting the rapid development of the Mawei Economic Development Zone. Dissatisfied with the working efficiency of the previous government, he stipulated that "the matter concerning Mawei shall be treated as a special issue, to be handled immediately."

Later, this thought was disseminated throughout the Party and government departments of Fuzhou, requiring all the public servants to accelerate the work rhythm and increase the handling efficiency.

In an interview with the media, he explained that the "do-it-right-away" practice required not only work efficiency but also the fastest and most prudent reaction from people in the environment of fierce market competition. Only if everyone can maintain sensitivity can the cause be kept young.

His colleague said that although Xi was only 37 years old when he

96.   "Always Have Mutual Affinity with People—Records of Xi Jinping's Practice of the Mass Line in Fujian," *Fujian Daily*, October 30, 2014.

assumed the office of the Fuzhou Party chief, he had the courage to think and act, was never aggressive, and was always reliable.

The One who Unites the People Is Not a Coward

When he assumed the office of the governor of Fujian in 2000, Xi Jinping proposed and personally participated in the organization of the Fujian Government Advisory Group to collect all kinds of experts as a think tank for Fujian—an extension of his practice in Zhengding, Hebei. The experts personally selected by Xi were not necessarily famous ones, but "Young Turks" who were active in the front lines, daring to think and act.

This advisory group offers comments to Fujian provincial government every year. Xi also invited them to attend important meetings, such as the annual economic analysis meeting. It is said that Xi Jinping is good at listening to other people's advice, and rarely makes a summary conclusion or criticizes other people in the standing committee meetings. Instead, he puts forward the problems for discussion. Furthermore, he rarely says harsh words.

Being good at handling interpersonal relations and uniting other people is another characteristic of Xi Jinping. This leader's style and capability grew increasingly mature in his seventeen years in Fujian and received broad recognition. In his eyes, unity is the prerequisite for a person wishing to be in an invincible position in politics. He lists the historic figures like Liu Bang, Liu Xiu, and Liu Bei to prove his idea. "These figures may seem cowardly to us, but they all have a big ability—that is to unite a group of capable men."

He knows the importance of integrating a team and the drawbacks of blindly highlighting an individual. In a cadre meeting in Ningde, he compared the cadre team with a soccer team to expound on the importance of teamwork: The most important factor of success is the organic cooperation of overall strengths, and an individual's skills rank second. Blindly highlighting an individual's skills without integrating them with the whole team will lower the whole team's prowess and affect the whole team's fighting capacity.

In Fujian, Xi Jinping rose through the ranks from deputy bureau-level to the governor of a province that covers an area of 124,000 square kilometers and has a population of over 30 million—three times the total population of Switzerland. This was an important stage in which he gradually shaped his state-governing skills and tested and adjusted his thoughts in practice.

Fujian has a complicated topography with mountains and seas, and it contains special economic zones, important ports, a poverty-stricken countryside, and mountainous hinterlands. It also directly faces Taiwan, an issue that tethers the country's core interests. It went through a conversion process from the "Taiwan-Strait front line" to the "west coast of the Taiwan Strait." In the mid-1990s in particular, cross-strait tension was nearly on the verge of breaking into war. These numerous factors inevitably deepened Xi's understanding of the issues in the big picture and his thinking on major national interests.

Facing an even more complicated administration, Xi Jinping put forward and put into practice many new concepts, such as the "ecological province," limited and efficient government, a digital Fujian, the maritime economy, forestry rights reform, and food security. These measures were all developed under careful consideration, and after he left Fujian, they were expanded to Zhejiang. Some of his initiatives were promoted all over China.

When he walked out of Zhengding, he was a young cadre full of dreams; when he left Fujian in 2002, he had become a mature and prudent statesman.

A Firm Believer in Limited-Government Theory

In October, 2002, Xi Jinping was transferred to work in Zhejiang as its governor, and a month later was promoted to the provincial Party chief. This was the first time that he became a commander of a border province and headed the administration of a province.

Zhejiang is to the northeast of Fujian. Though the two provinces are neighbors, there is a big gap between them in economic strength—by GDP rank, Zhejiang is usually in fourth place, and Fujian is often in eleventh or twelfth place. Zhejiang is the province with the smallest area in China, but the activity of its economy—its private economy in particular—is virtually unrivaled. Its residents' per capita disposable income ranks the highest in China for the past decade, for which it is known as the "richest province in China."

According to an insider, Xi Jinping's transfer from Fujian to Zhejiang was totally beyond his expectations. Before the transfer, he was prepared to be transferred to Shannxi or some other province in western China. After he arrived at Zhejiang he said, "I did not expect that one month later I would be appointed the Party chief. At the time, I made the decision to do a good job. Because if I failed, it would affect not only me but the population of 46 million in Zhejiang."[97]

In 2006, in the "China Economic Forum" program on CCTV, Xi Jinping said, "The higher the mountain, the more difficult it is to climb; the faster the car, the harder it is to drive" to describe the challenges he faced when he took over the strong economic province.

There are people who assert that Xi was a "firm believer in limited

97.   "Xi Jinping: Walking Ahead by the Red Ship," *Mother Earth*, December 1, 2006.

government theory," which happens to fit with his status as leader of a province with a large private sector.[98]

Intensive inspection is the basic working method of Xi Jinping. In his own words: "One should first be a student," and "not like the blind man touching an elephant." In the two months after he assumed office, inspections took up half of his time, getting up at 6:00 or 7:00 a.m. every morning and going to sleep at 1:00 or 2:00 a.m. every night. Nine months later, he had visited 69 of the 90 counties and cities in the province. Once, when he was visiting one of Zhejiang's sister provinces in Sichuan, due to the high altitude, many cadres stopped half way, but Xi not only went through the whole visit, he stepped out of his car from time to time to speak with the local residents.

Xi often says that when going to the grassroots level, officials do not have to aspire to perfection, but must give opportune help, go to the places where there are problems, great difficulties, and hard circumstances, just to get things done.

The complaint-reception practice he created continued in Zhejiang. In August 2006, he led a complaint-reception delegation made up of the Zhejiang Province's Party and government cadres to receive complaints in Quzhou. That morning, he met 167 people, and solved 76 problems on the spot.

In Zhejiang, and later in Shanghai, a slogan of Xi Jinping was made familiar to all the cadres: "The cadres that go to the grassroots to receive complaints shall go to the regions with numerous conflicts; only in this way, the CPC can earn the people's trust."

Two years after he assumed office in Zhejiang, the challenges he faced were no longer "the high mountain and fast car," but the "pain of growth"— Zhejiang, with the high marketization of its economy, was faced with the shackles of resources, power, money, land and water; due to its high dependence on exports, with the exacerbation of trade conflicts, where zippers, leather shoes, and textiles suffered sanctions overseas. In general, the region was under high ecological and environmental pressure.

When he was working in Hebei and Fujian, for a rather long time the core issue he needed to address was subsistence; now, in economically leading areas of Zhejiang and Shanghai, the challenges he faced were economic growth models and strategic adjustments of the economic structure. The latter adjustments represent a breathtaking leap the whole of China must face now, or several years in the future. It matters, as it concerns whether China can overcome the middle-income trap and realize the China Dream.

The solutions to Zhejiang's problems were as follows: to strengthen

98.   "Xi Jinping and the Model Transformation in Zhejing," *Decision*, October 14, 2005.

economic and technical exchange and cooperation with Shanghai and Zhejiang; to actively urge the private sector to enter the advanced high-tech manufacturing industry, infrastructure-constructing industry, and new service industry, with high added value; to sort out and revise the policies and regulations that limited private-sector development; to treat private enterprises on par with the state-owned enterprises; and to expand powers to strong counties and towns. It was also imperative that he break the restriction of administrative systems on the economic sectors with promising, high-growth momentum.

He even decided not to assess Lishui City, which has an outstanding ecological environmental advantage by GDP, because "the environment is the productivity, and a good ecological environment is akin to GDP; it will push the localities to walk on a road of sustainable ecological development."

He Emerged at a Time of CPC Leadership Changes

On March 24, 2007, the front page of *Zhejiang Daily*'s "New Sayings from Zhejiang" column published a short essay entitled "Pursuit of the Ultimate Realm of 'Restraining in Privacy,'" the last of the columns Xi Jinping wrote for four years under the name "Zhexin".

On that day, the central authority decided to appoint Xi the municipal Party chief of Shanghai.

In the autumn of 2006, the Shanghai pension scandal erupted, and Shanghai Party Chief Chen Liangyu and several other high officials were removed from office. Chen became the most senior party member to be dismissed at the time. Would Shanghai, the benchmark of the Chinese economy and political situation, fall into the turbulence caused by this storm? Xi Jinping focused primarily on the transformation of economic growth models and the promotion of a modern service industry. He set the goal of building Shanghai into "four centers"—an international economic center, international financial center, international maritime center, and international trade center.

He summarized his mission in Shanghai in this way: "I strive to stabilize the general situation, unite differing thoughts, balance emotions, and arouse the cadres' enthusiasm." In just seven months and four days, when he was called to Beijing, the city of Shanghai had recovered its stability and confidence.

Before he assumed office in Shanghai, Xi's image overseas was of a reform-minded and pro-business statesman. In China, when the ordinary people talked about this local satrap, they would still mention his father, the veteran CPC member, and were not necessarily impressed with him, based on legacy alone. His transfer to Shanghai, however, made him the focus of attention, especially at the sensitive time when the core leadership of the CPC was undergoing a power shift. In the 17th National Congress of the CPC in mid-October 2007, Xi entered the nine-person core leadership of the CPC Central Committee. Li Keqiang also joined at the same time— he would become Xi's governing partner five years later.

In the five years since then, Xi Jinping served as the principal of the Party School of the CPC Central Committee, was ordered to lead the preparation of the 2008 Beijing Summer Olympic Games and 2008 Paralympic Games, draft the CPC's report on the 18th National Congress, and revise the CPC charter. Now, he has risen to the peak of power and became the general secretary of the world's largest political party, and the helmsman of the second largest economy in the world.

Looking back to the beginning of 2007, when the media asked Xi to grade his own performance in the past five years, he said, "How could I grade myself? If I give myself a high grade, you will say I am conceited, if a low grade, you will say I feel inferior." He explained that his performance should be graded by the people; an official should work for the people, and the people should have their opinions about the official's performance.

Now, the 1.36 billion Chinese people are watching his every move, evaluating him in their minds.

VI. "FIRST LADY" PENG LIYUAN, A 35-YEAR MILITARY VETERAN
There Is a Love Called "Uncle Xi and Mama Peng"

At the Beijing APEC meeting of late November, 2014, what attracted as much notice as Xi Jinping's description of Beijing's blue skies as "APEC blue" was an interesting interaction between the Chinese supreme leader and his wife. In the group photo session of the banquet, decked out in a silken high-collared Chinese tunics, Xi, First Lady Peng Liyuan, and other APEC leaders stood in two rows. When they waved to the cameras, according to the custom, Xi Jinping only smiled. The First Lady Peng Liyuan turned to him to give him a nudge, and Xi immediately held up his right hand to wave.

This funny and warm gesture was soon made into an animated image file, called a "GIF," by the *People's Daily* WeChat account, which collected several photographs of the couple's affectionate moments taken on their foreign visits, naming it "There Is a Love Called 'Uncle Xi and Mama Peng,'" and remarking: "This is the indigenous love of our great China."

Around the same time, several musicians from Henan wrote a song called "Uncle Xi Loves Mama Xi," and produced a video that contained 33 photos and two cartoon pictures. The pop ballad's lyrics included verses such as: "This sort of love is legendary, the realm with lovers is the strongest. Men should study Xi Dada, and women should study Peng Mama, love like they do, people in love can win everything." In the six days that the video was online, it received 45 million hits, and became a hit song for street dancing. In fact, since Xi Jinping's first foreign visit after he became the supreme leader of China, each time he attends a major foreign affairs event, one of the focuses of public opinion is inevitably the First Lady Peng Liyuan.

Apart from her elegant and fashionable personal style, people are fascinated to discover those natural and sweet details between the couple—the intertwined arms and the umbrella Xi Jinping holds for Peng when they walk down the steps of an airplane; at a Costa Rican ranch, Xi picked a white coffee blossom and held it before Peng's nose; when the two of them were sharing a dessert, Peng lightly picked up the crumbs that fell on Xi's trousers; when they went aboard the icebreaking research vessel *Snow Dragon*, Xi stepped into a cabin door, turned and reached a hand to his wife, whispering lightly to her, "Come." In the Australian governor-general's house, when Peng reached out a hand to lightly caress a tiny kangaroo, Xi reminded her, smiling all the while, that the animal might not like being touched on the head.

Seeing these images, many commentators always try to analyze the so-called "First Lady effect," her "soft strength," and similar notions. But for the Chinese public, the strategy or tactics are not so important. They prefer to learn any information they can about the "First family"—after all, the Chinese political figures are always mythic. Apart from their several-hundred-word personal résumés, the public seldom has the opportunity or access to learn more details about them, including their families. When they appear at magnificent venues, they are like symbolic isolated beings. In order to show their affection for the people, they shake hands with the elders and hug the children, but their concerning glances or natural smiles to their family are hidden from us. In short, they are not quite accessible as "people."

However, Xi Jinping and Peng Liyuan are very different from previous leaders and their wives. One of the main reasons is that the First Lady Peng Liyuan was a household name before her husband received such widespread attention. Her ambitions for a career, struggles, and family life are not unfamiliar to the Chinese people.

In the spring of 2007, when Xi Jinping was transferred to be Shanghai Party chief, or at most no later than the holding of the 17th National Congress of the CPC in October 2007, Peng Liyuan was the singer and artist who best represented China's bearing in the world of the arts. She sang the finales at evening parties, and had no tabloid scandals. She was not trendy or popular due to fashion; after 2007, she left the stage and only occasionally appeared in public service campaigns. However, after the 18th National Congress, she suddenly turned into a fashion icon, thanks to her colorful, stylish, and gentle image that integrated western and oriental fashions—and refreshed the reputations of Chinese leaders abroad and at home. To match her outfits, Xi Jinping even wore some tender pink, orange, purple and light-green neckties in addition to the more typical red or blue ties. These livelier colors were rarely seen on previous Chinese politicians.

She Is Not a Star, but a Role Model

In fact, even if her husband was not Xi Jinping, Peng's life was already bright and motivational enough.

She was born in a small county in Shandong in 1962 and went through a lot of hardship and setbacks. In her 30 years' career, 13 years were spent on studies from technical secondary school to graduate school. She was the first in China to obtain a master's degree in traditional ethnic music; she became a representative and also one of the cofounders of the contemporary traditional ethnic music scene. She has won many honors and all the songs she sang are the grave and grand type that promote the national spirit or positive feelings about the native land; the figures she has played in operas are all classics. In the past 30 years, she has regularly appeared on the annual CCTV New Year's Gala, the program with the highest audience rating in the world. She is also an active-duty military woman, serving as the president of the People's Liberation Army Arts College.

During their courtship, Xi said to Peng, "Though we've suffered a great deal, we kept an intrinsic simplicity and goodness." Though they are nine years apart in age, they have a lot in common in their life experiences.

In the 1960s and 1970s—during the Cultural Revolution—Peng's father, originally working as the curator of the county's cultural center, was sent down to the farms to be reformed through labor, and her mother, the leading light of the county's touring opera company, was categorized as one of the "monsters and demons," and hounded off the stage, all because her uncle was in Taiwan—an "overseas relation." At the age of nine, Peng and her mother were driven back to the countryside.

The girl who used to travel with her mother on a bullock-cart was blessed with a beautiful voice. As hardworking and assiduous as she was, she was admitted into a technical secondary school at the age of 16, and participated in the national ethnic and folk music performance in Beijing at the age of

18, creating a sensation among the Chinese people. In the same year, she was enrolled into the art troupe of the PLA. "As a platoon cadre wearing a cadre's uniform with four pockets, I was very majestic," she said in an interview with the CCTV's "Culture Interview" program in 2007.

She told the interviewer that she was more than happy when she became a soldier. It was more like a "political relief," as if a heavy burden had been lifted.

In the Chinese show-business world, Peng seems to be the only person with no negative news attached to her. She is never tainted with rumors of quarrels or rifts, and even on the Internet, which is notorious for spreading malicious gossip, she has never received any bad comments. She is simple and unadorned, candid, warmhearted, and frank, and loves lending aid to an injured party. She once cried because the name of a set designer was omitted on her performance posters. She keeps a low profile but never hides her career ambitions.

In 1996, in an interview with a People's Liberation Army (PLA) magazine she recalled that she wrote on the title page of her diary, "Career ambition is supreme, it is the foundation to climb the heights of the arts" when she was attending the technical secondary school. She added, "As a vocalist, voice, musicality, intelligence, persona, and physique are all very important. With the good natural traits my parents gave me, and my own hard work and opportunities, there is no doubt that I can stand out from the rest."[99]

In the 1980s and 1990s, the Chinese pop music scene was very hot and it became common practice for some PLA performers to earn extra money without prior approval from the unit they belonged to (meaning the actors of art troupes in the system moonlighted in informal commercial performances organized privately in the 1980s), and "star-making" crazes occurred repeatedly. Many performers belonging to PLA art troupes became involved in this craze, and some of the famous ones approached the officials and businessmen and were drawn into corruption cases.

Peng kept herself away from the whole craze. With three years in technical secondary school, four years in junior college, four years in undergraduate college, and three years to pursue a master's degree, she spent thirteen years of her life above elementary school, furthering herself educationally.

She wrote in her diary, "My dream is not to sing songs for several years. Maybe I am hitching a wagon to a star, but I really think that Chinese national ethnic music lacks a systematic aesthetic theory. Some of our pioneers sang beautiful songs, for dozens of years, without knowing really why they did so.

---

99.   "Peng Liyuan: A Life Story Conveys Positive Energy, True Ability Creates Fame and Wealth," *China Pictorial*, August 8, 2013.

If this goes on, how can our national ethnic music develop? Now with the industry and agriculture taking off, the art should also spread its wings and soar high. We should take the national music to the international art forum, an obligatory task of our young generation."[100]

In the early 1990s, the famous lyricist Qiao Yu wrote a short article to support Peng's artistic choices. He commented that in vocal music circles, most performers focused on their skills, few on their artistry, and a lot of excellent performers were prone to fall into "self-made traps." He believed that to pursue perfection in the arts, only relying on skill won't get you there. To be a true master, the performers must have surpassingly high and rounded talent, and a broad-minded cultural horizon.

It's apparent that Peng did not fall into this "self-made trap." She made painstaking efforts to study opera. In September 2005, the semi-stage opera *Legend of Mulan* starring Peng was performed at Lincoln Center in New York. This was the first Chinese opera to be presented in the US since the founding of the new China. The famous critic and Grammy Award judge Joshua Cheek said, "Peng is the germ of the Chinese people" after seeing the performance.

In 2004, as a prominent figure of the Chinese national ethnic music, Peng changed her style in a new album, combining national folk music with international popular musical elements. She said in an interview with the CCTV that she first thought of trying this combination a decade ago, because she hoped that the Chinese folk songs could be loved by young people all around the world.

In 1991, CCTV held an evening party to celebrate the 70th anniversary of the founding of the CPC. As Peng sang "People from Our Villages," she suddenly fell to her knees on the stage, an act which moved the whole audience; some of the cadres watching the show sobbed.

Peng says she loves the lyrics of the song: "the high tree never forgets the root." She said, "A person, no matter what achievements you have made, or what a prominent figure you've become, a leader, a statesman, or a star, no matter how high a position you are in, you would always want to find your roots, and never forget the place you lived as a child—the place you had little food, the place where you enjoyed a cup of tea."

She thinks that it is because the lyrics of the song fit the feelings of the common people that she is loved by the audience.[101] In 2001, a CCTV director interviewed Peng on a television program. She saw that quite a few young people were fans of her. A 19-year-old girl said that she loves Peng as

---

100. "New Missions of Peng Liyuan," *Global Characters*, Issue 17, 2011.
101. Ifeng TV, *Weekend Star Show*, 1999.

she loves her mother. "This is the first time that we felt that someone could love a singer as she loves her mother. We used to think that the idols might become a 'dream lover' for members of the audience. It was not until today that I learned this love can be used to celebrate performers as a family," the director said.[102]

Yuan Dewang, a CCTV director, said many years ago, "It is hard for one person's art to satisfy all the people, from the state leader to the housewife, and be accepted by people of different educational backgrounds, different ages, and different ethnic groups. But I think this is what Peng has done."[103]

In the mid-1990s, Peng bought two pianos, and sent one to her alma mater, Shandong Yuncheng No. 1 High School, and the other to her first music teacher. At the end of 1990s, she took out the money she had saved in the past decade to build an elementary school for her hometown village, and later raised money to construct new educational facilities for her alma mater.

Some media have said, "It is an impossible mission to find someone more appropriate to represent the image of Chinese women than Peng Liyuan: She has a face like a full moon, shining eyes, and white teeth, and she is upright and straightforward, frank and friendly. She meets both the refined aesthetic standards and the popular conception of beauty, her charisma crosses both the royal and imperial court and all corners of the country."[104]

After Love at First Sight, a Phone Call Every Day

At the end of 1986, the 24-year-old Peng Liyuan met Xi Jinping, then the deputy mayor of Xiamen, for the first time. Back then, she was already well known all around the world as an actress in the General Political Department of the PLA, the most prestigious arts company of all, and a student in the vocal music school of the China Conservatory. She had also sung three songs on the CCTV's New Year Gala that year—one of the most popular TV programs, watched by millions of Chinese people, and she had just won a championship in the CCTV Youth Singer Television Grand Prix—the only talent show in the 1980s and 1990s in China.

The 33-year-old Xi Jinping was relatively unknown at the time, and a divorcee. Peng described their first meeting:

On that day, she deliberately wore her sloppy green army uniform to test if Xi only valued appearances. To her surprise, Xi was plainly dressed too, and Peng was attracted to him after he spoke his first words. He did not ask,

---

102.   "First Lady Peng Liyuan," *Southern People Weekly*, Issue 10, 2013.
103.   Ibid.
104.   "50 Most Beautiful People in China," *Southern People Weekly*, March 2014.

"what is the most popular song nowadays?" or "how much are you paid for each performance?" but instead, "how many singing techniques are there in vocal music?"

"My heart sped when I heard this—isn't this the ideal husband in my mind? He is humble and full of ideas. Later, Xi told me, 'In less than 40 minutes I've decided that you are to be my wife.'"

Xi Jinping recalled their love at first sight.

However, Peng's parents were not keen to marry off their daughter to the son of a top official. Xi told Peng that his father was the son of a peasant, and the spouses of his sisters and brothers were the children of common people.

On September 1, 1987, Peng Liyuan and Xi Jinping had a simple wedding. Before the dinner that served as their wedding banquet, Xi's colleagues did not even know that his wife was the renowned singer Peng Liyuan.

On the last day of 2013, when Xi gave his New Year's Speech to people all around China, people saw from the TV screen that there were six photos on his bookshelf in the background, one of which was the photo of the couple taken in Dongshan Island in Fujian in 1987. In the photo, Xi is in a blue shirt, and Peng in a red dress and a pair of red shoes—the standard Chinese bridal dressing.

As an active-duty military service member, Peng had busy performance schedules and her workplace was in Beijing; and as Xi Jinping was transferred to increasingly important posts, the two of them lived largely separate lives. But Xi would not like Peng to leave the stage. "That would be too selfish," he said.

In 1988, while attending the 5th National Conference of the China Federation of Literary and Art Circles, the famous performing artist Tian Hua lived in the same room with Peng. Tian recalled that Peng made a long-distance phone call to her husband, and hearing that Xi was suffering from a fever, Peng said, "I am really sorry. I will go visit you as soon as I am free." Xi replied, "Don't worry, I don't blame you."[105]

There was no heating in southern China in the winter, so Peng made a cotton-padded quilt for her husband, because "the quilts sold on the street are too small, and Jinping is tall. I am afraid that his feet would be bare at night." She asked her mother to fluff three kilograms of new cotton, bought the quilt covers, and made the quilt by herself.

Back then, she was on a national tour, so she carried the quilt to the northeast of China and then to Fujian, finally delivering the new quilt to her husband working in Ningde, Fujian.

Xi Jinping is very strict with himself and his family. Wherever he worked,

---

105.   "First Lady Peng Liyuan," *Southern People Weekly*, Issue 10, 2013.

he warned his relatives and friends not to engage in any commercial activities at his work place or seek personal gains in his name. Even on occasions he was allowed to take his wife with him, he would not let Peng go, because, he said: "If I always take you with me, other people will talk behind our backs, and it would be a bad influence." He also required Peng not to do commercial performances, saying, "As I am a Party member and cadre, you'd better not perform outside."

During their physical separation, he would make at least one phone call to his wife each day, no matter how busy he was.

For 30 consecutive years, Peng performed in CCTV's New Year Gala on New Year's Eve. As long as he was back in Beijing, Xi Jinping would sit down to watch the program while making Chinese dumplings and waited for Peng's return, and they would cook the dumplings together, as northern China's custom would have it.[106]

Like many Chinese wives, Peng understands and supports her husband. "I should say that my husband puts in a lot of efforts for me. He does not have a normal family life like other people do. I think this is the biggest sacrifice he makes for me." In 1999, on a program on iFeng TV, Peng said that she can cook Shandong-style noodles, bake pancakes, and cook several dishes. Once they got the chance to be together, she would manage the household and cook delicious dinners for the family.[107]

Peng expressed her hopes that there could be one week she can stay at home, watch TV, wash clothes, or measure a piece of fabric to sew a bed sheet with a sewing machine. She acclaims that her husband is a great man, and a "decent husband and father." In September 2009, when she was attending the first international Qi culture festival in Zibo, Shandong, she said, "I think in all my life, the most important thing is my family."

In her eyes, her husband is an ordinary person, though he is special in many ways. He likes eating the home cooking of Shaanxi and Shandong, and having drinks with friends. He likes swimming, hiking, watching basketball, soccer, and boxing, and sometimes he stays up late to watch the sports programs on TV.

At the end of 2012, the Xinhua News Agency released a collection of Xi Jinping's family photos, one of which was a photo of him giving his daughter a ride on a bike—with the shade of trees in the background. Xi is in a shirt and tie and riding an exquisite lady's bicycle, and on the backseat of the bicycle is his 3-year-old daughter in a dress.

---

106.   "The Masses, the Source of Our Strength—on the General-Secretary of the CPC," Xinhua News Agency, December 27, 2012.

107.   "First Lady Peng Liyuan," *Southern People Weekly*, Issue 10, 2013.

Chinese leaders' families are rarely exposed to the public eye, let alone their children. The release of this photo aroused exclamations all round China.

Xi's daughter, Xi Mingze, was born in 1992, and nicknamed "Muzi"—the names of Xi Zhongxun's grandson and granddaughters all contain the *Ming* (明) character. The meaning of Mingze is "live a simple and clean life and be a person that is useful to the society." She studied in Hangzhou Foreign Language School and in 2009, she was admitted to the Foreign Language School of Zhejiang University. Peng has said, "I wished for a son, while Xi wished for a daughter. I gave birth to a girl, just as he wished. Our daughter was like him a lot. When I am taking care of her, she is very mischievous. But every time she is with her daddy, she turns into an obedient girl."

Xi did not get to witness the birth of his daughter. When his wife went into labor, Fujian was experiencing a strong typhoon. He commanded the relief activities at the front lines and did not come home for three days.

Peng said she felt sorry for her daughter because she did not have the chance to give her much of her time. But when their daughter learned that her mother had hugged an AIDS orphan, she praised her, saying, "Mom, you are so brave." Peng told her, "I will take you with me when I get the chance. You can make friends with them."

In 2008, the 16-year-old Xi Mingze went as a volunteer to the area affected by the Sichuan earthquake as a volunteer. Peng told a CCTV journalist: "In the first few day after the earthquake occurred, my 16-year-old daughter asked for a leave from her teacher, and went to Hanwang Dongqi Elementary School in Mianzhu, Sichuan, from Beijing to be a volunteer." She participated in the rescue of the injured and offered psychological counseling for the masses in the areas affected by the earthquake.

Peng's comment on her daughter's choice was that "in those seven days, she worked very hard as a volunteer and never complained about the hardship." When Xi Mingze returned home, she said, "Despite enduring such a huge disaster, Sichuan's people did not fall. Their care for the volunteers fills me with confidence about the future."

In an interview with Yan'an TV, Xi Jinping said, "Though I usually get no time for my child, and could not find the time to watch her do her homework or help with her lessons, I really care about her growth." Peng has told the media that their daughter reads a great deal. "Studying is the right choice for her. As for a future career choice, that is totally up to her."

Running the Front Lines, Risking Gunfire, Singing in the Trenches

Since Peng joined the performance troupe of the local PLA in the 1980s, she has served in the military for 35 years. She often goes to the frontline sentry posts, remote and harsh areas, and disaster relief sites to give morale-boosting performances. At present she is in charge of the best art school of the PLA. "I am a soldier, and obeying orders is my duty," she often says.

Morale-boosting performances are a tradition of the PLA. For at least nine months each year the various troupes containing over 2,000 personnel undertake performances for the army at different levels. In recent years, due to restrictions imposed on such personnel participating in commercial performances, many PLA performance stars have chosen to leave their posts and become commercial artists.

On a mid-autumn day in 1985, Peng came to the Laoshan front line at the Yunnan border, where the war against Vietnam was raging. People can still find the collection of photos taken of Peng at Laoshan. Wearing no make-up, with thick braided hair and in plain uniform, she stood among the soldiers and signed autographs for them.

In 2008, on Culture Interview, the CCTV program, she described her experience at the Laoshan front lines: "We traveled by Jeep braving the storms of gunshots and artillery shells." Some superior bosses specially warned them that even one mouthful of phlegm spit out or a flicked cigarette butt might trigger a landmine. Peng and her colleagues traveled to the front lines in a roaring storm of shells.

As recalled by another singer who traveled with Peng, at 5:00 a.m., the five of them set off in a Jeep to get to the foxhole where the frontline command post was. To reach the post, they had to first go through the enemy's gunfire blockade zone. Every one of them put on a helmet, and the soldiers traveling with them loaded their guns. The Jeep ran at a very high speed, and in the gunfire blockade zone, it zigzagged its way through. After about 20 kilometers, they finally got to the command post, and could hear the coming and going of cannonballs. They ran along a path and sang in the trenches.

At the performance, their songs were interrupted by gunfire from time to time. Fearing that they may be shot, some of the soldiers shielded them with their bodies.

In the foxhole of the command post, they sang for the soldiers nearest to the enemy lines via phone. "They can hear us sing wherever the telephone line goes," Peng recalled.

After so many years, she isn't shy about telling of the fears she felt at the time: "To tell you the truth, I was very afraid. I was thinking: 'I am still young, I don't even have a boyfriend. If by any chance I am hit by a stray bullet, my life will come to an abrupt end."[108]

Following her morale-boosting appearances for the soldiers, she went to the borderlands of China and Laos, Burma, Vietnam, the Soviet Union, and Korea. Peng said there was one time she traveled 48 hours by train to their home in Fujian, but on the second day she received a phone call telling her that she must go to carry out a task. "I felt very upset. Indeed, you can never imagine how upset I was. But I am a soldier, and obeying orders is the duty of a soldier," she said.

In the spring of 2003, the SARS (Severe Acute Respiratory Syndrome) epidemic broke out in China. In just seven days, a field hospital for infectious disease with 1,000 beds was established at Xiaotangshan in northern Beijing, with health workers temporarily dispatched from military hospitals. This SARS contract hospital treated more than one seventh of SARS patients in the whole country.

At the time, Peng was at their home in Hangzhou—her husband had been transferred to the office of provincial Party chief of Zhejiang. A phone call came telling her that the General Political Department was going to the front lines to convey appreciation to the doctors and nurses in Xiaotangshan. There were only a dozen passengers on the airplane from Hangzhou to Beijing, each wearing a mask; "I am afraid too but I had to go," she said.

In 2008, after the Sichuan earthquake that caused the deaths and injuries of 110,000 people, Peng immediately donated RMB 200,000 to the stricken area, and went to the hard-hit region to give a special performance as an expression of gratitude and appreciation. On the stage, wearing her camouflage uniform, with her hair tied into a ponytail, she sang "The People from My Villages" and "My Soldier Brothers." The lyrics expressed "the true feelings she had after arriving at the earthquake-stricken area." The people listened to her songs in tears, waved enthusiastically to her, and shouted her name.

Once, six soldiers could not go to listen to a performance of hers because they were on duty. Peng decided to hold a special concert for them. She went to their posts and sang the songs as meticulously as she would on stage, outside in the drizzling rain.

In the first half of 2012, Peng took up the post of president of the PLA Arts Academy, the best art school of the PLA. This school has trained numerous writers, singers, and film stars. It is said that after she assumed the office, she strengthened the discipline and management of the institute. In November,

---

108.　"Peng Liyuan: Positive Energy Transferring China Charisma," *China Pictorial*, August 8, 2013.

2014, she accompanied the wife of the president of Mexico to visit the PLA Arts Academy.

Orphans of AIDS Called her "Mama Peng"

In recent decades, an increasing number of Peng's titles have been related to her public service campaigns. In June 2011, at the headquarters of the World Health Organization (WHO) in Geneva, Switzerland, the director-general of the WHO, Dr. Margaret Chan, announced the appointment of Peng as the WHO Goodwill Ambassador for tuberculosis and HIV/AIDS.

The WHO knows that she has a compassionate heart, and at the same time, there is in her a kind of diligent and unyielding spirit.

In fact, Peng had accepted the invitation from the Ministry of Health of China to be the advocate of AIDS prevention obligations as early as the beginning of 2006, and put on the red ribbon of AIDS prevention.

Two months later, she visited Fuyang in Anhui province to visit the more than 200 children under the care of the AIDS Orphan Salvation Association. Most of these children's parents had died of AIDS, and they were born with AIDS. Peng drew pictures, sang songs, and played games with the children. She specially went to their school to see if they received equal education opportunities, like other children. One of the children loved singing very much. So Peng took her back to her hotel to personally give her singing lessons.

The parents of Gao Jun, another AIDS orphan, had died from AIDS. He had been raised in a pig sty by his aunt and uncle. When Peng saw Gao Jun and heard about his misfortune, tears appeared in her eyes. She held him in her arms and fed him dumplings. Since then, Gao Jun has always addressed her as "Mama Peng".[109]

In 2012, to publicize World's AIDS Day, Gao Jun and Peng appeared in an anti-discrimination public-service short film called "Be Together Forever," produced by the Ministry of Health. In the seven-minute long film, Peng was seen teaching the children to play piano, draw pictures, and run with them; at one point, she tied Gao Jun's shoelaces.

The number of children orphaned by AIDS is still increasing. "In the past years, helping them has become the focus of my life," Peng has said. She keeps calling for the psychological care of these children: "Many efforts put in to help with the implementation of relevant policies cause complications, redundancy, and disorder in the forms of healthcare. I think, for these children, the psychological care from families, schools, and society is the most important. What cuts them the deepest is the discriminating and

109.   "New Missions of Peng Liyuan," *Global Characters*, Issue 17, 2011.

indifferent eyes," she said during the national CPPCC.[110]

Peng also put forward detailed measures, such as "the country shall establish the registration, reporting, and routine follow-up of young children of patients with suspected or confirmed viral infections, so as to promptly understand the psychological needs of these kids and offer help." The country must also "provide specific psychological counseling through their adoption by families or communities, family foster care, foster care by small families, and institutional support, to tackle the psychological isolation and inferiority complexes of AIDS-orphaned children."

In 2007, Peng became the "national ambassador for TB prevention." Two years later, she had new titles: "tobacco control ambassador" and China's ambassador for the "For Tomorrow" public welfare campaign, dedicated to preventing juvenile delinquency.

After assuming the title of "national TB control ambassador," she visited many areas with high TB incidences to meet patients, show concern for their diseases, and eagerly express her wish for them to benefit from a scientific method to protect themselves. She described her feelings as "a bit heavy, but comforting and excited."

In 2009, Peng appeared on the government plaza in the Guangcheng District of Dongguan City in Guangdong Province to teach migrant workers about TB preventative measures. She said, "I want to tell them what I know by questioning them, and share knowledge through word of mouth."[111]

Apart from being a famous and renowned singer, Peng also has a very important identity—she is a member of the 8th, 9th, 10th, and 11th Chinese People's Consultative Conference (CPPCC), and has been participating in the most important political processes in the past 20 years. At the time of the habitual Two Sessions (of the NPC and the CPPCC) each year, she would put on her military uniform or the *Tang* suit to reach the venue with other members by bus.

Children Are Forever: The Thrust of her Policy Proposal

Peng suggests that "developing rural educational causes and improving the education level of rural youth are measures at the core of solving agricultural, rural, and development issues."

Peng told a journalist that she started to notice this issue because of a child of her cousin in her hometown in Shandong. Her cousin wanted to use the money Peng gave her to build houses and compensate living expenses.

110.   "First Lady Peng Liyuan's Road to Charity: The AIDS Orphans Call her Mama Peng," *Beijing News*, January 17, 2014.

111.   "New Missions of Peng Liyuan," *Global Characters*, Issue 17, 2011.

However, Peng believed that the money should be spent on the education of the child, in order to raise the economic status of the family fundamentally.

Every time she went home, Peng would pay extra attention to the current educational status of the villages. She noticed that the overall fund input into the compulsory education in rural areas was reduced greatly, the teachers in the rural elementary school and high school were not stable, and the turnover rate of key teachers was very high, which had become a major factor in the rural education dilemma.

Peng stated in the session of CPPCC: "The educational support for rural children shall not be limited to a cutting of tuition and fees, but also the living expenses or even the medical bills of their family. If a problem occurs in any of the links, the child's studies may become troubled."

She hopes that society can extend its hands to help the youth in rural areas to receive better educations. For more than a decade, she has personally supported 50 to 60 college, high school, and elementary school students to finish their education.

A magazine published by the *People's Daily* press praised Peng for appearing in public, and relating to her husband, to the people, and to those children, women and elders who need care.[112]

The publisher of a fashion magazine in China has said, "Peng has a remarkably positive meaning for China and China needs such a female role model. Imagine what the effect will be if she becomes a first lady like Michelle Obama?"[113]

Who would have thought that this songstress in military uniform would truly turn into the first lady? After eagerly watching her performance at foreign visits, the Chinese media proudly believe, "China has a versatile, beautiful, and kind 'First Lady';" "they have Michelle Obama in the US, and we have Peng Liyuan in China."

VII. WHAT KIND OF MAN IS THE LEADER OF CHINA?
What Does it Take to Lead China?

Some scholars say that the social public's overall anticipation of the leader's image can be summarized in three points: Nobility, seniority, and a civilian perspective. As to China, the word *nobility* refers to the ancient Confucian tradition that the leader shall be a philosopher king. He shall have a saint's ethics: self-discipline, sincerity, and prudence. He shall be patient, and at the same time have the righteousness and benevolent wisdom to "run the family,

112.   "New Missions of Peng Liyuan," *Global Characters*, Issue 17, 2011.
113.   "First Lay Peng Liyuan," *Southern People Weekly*, Issue 10, 2013.

moralize the country, and appease the world." The word *seniority* means the leader shall have the ability to both deal with complicated situations and reasonably delegate and deploy political resources. And, the *civilian perspective* attribute means that the leader shall attain a solid understanding of what the people need, and be like a real "person." To sum up, the leader shall be a proper combination of Confucian moral sense, Machiavellian shrewdness, and the quality of Plato's philosopher king.

Some commentators say that since the death of Deng Xiaoping in 1997, Chinese politics changed from "strongman politics" to "ordinary-person politics." The public could indeed see that the supreme leaders were paying increasing attention to revealing their ordinary side.

But at the same time, some commentators say that although the Chinese economy have realized a market transition and "miraculous" high-speed growth, problems such as the widening gap between the rich and the poor, rampant corruption, and the sluggishness of reform, just as described by the political scientists, China has fallen into a "small-scale pattern"—behind many policies and measures, there are the shadows of the interests of an individual, a family, or an influential circle—the single statesmen can only bring small changes to the country.

The words of the Italian Marxist Antonio Gramsci are often mentioned: To be a ruler for a long time, the party must surpass its own interests.

From this angle, empathy for the people is only one of the characteristics expected by the Chinese people from their leaders. What's more important is that he shall not be bound by cowardice or venality, and have the courage to surpass the Party's interests, as well as the bearing to make the toughest decisions, maintain a strong will and continually develop adept political skills.

Political commentator Xiao Gongqin once analyzed the three political abilities possessed by reform advocate Deng Xiaoping. First, he was a veteran politician, and different from most "Young Turks" in history, he had deep political experience within the system, an acute sense of political propriety, and an awareness of the boundaries of his actions. Second, he had high political prestige, and a talent for rallying allies. Third, he had rich organizational abilities to establish the reform mobilization system.[114]

Thirty years after the start of China's reform and opening, what kind of leader can properly deal with the present complicated situation, wherein "to reform means to court death, and to not reform means to wait for death?" What kind of political resources does he have to possess?

---

114. "From Deng Xiaoping to Xi Jinping: Another Starting Point of Reform in China," Xiao Gongqin, *Phoenix Knowledge Salon*, Issue 2, December 2013.

After the 60-point decisions about reform were announced at the Third Plenary Session of the 18th Central Committee of the CPC held in November, 2013, just one year after he assumed the office as the supreme leader of China, Xi Jinping was considered the practitioner of a "new authoritarianism 2.0." Xiao Gongqin believed that by virtue of Xi Jinping's influence and actions, China had entered the "golden age of authoritarianism."

Mao Zedong and Deng Xiaoping, the two most influential statesmen of the 30 years before and after the CPC came to power, are often compared to Xi Jinping by elite scholars and the grassroots people. This has never happened to a predecessor of Xi Jinping's.

You can see this as the public's heartfelt wishes, or the era's urgent calls for the rebuilding of a roadmap of reform based on "cat theory"[115] or the theory of "crossing the river by feeling one's way across the stones"—though such calls may contain contradictory motives.

In the first year of Xi Jinping's administration, he took overall charge immediately, pushed through new concepts, set a new agenda, and attracted high levels of attention both in- and outside of China. Looking back, it becomes clear that Xi Jinping possesses the following characteristics.

First, he rules with an iron hand, and he dares to shoulder the heaviest responsibilities. To get where he is today, he was the young peasant who took the lead to work in the icy mud; he was the diligent young military officer, the prefectural-level Party chief who firmly believed that "sometimes it is necessary to pound the table," and who "insisted on finishing what he started." As general secretary of the CPC, he required "leaving footprints on stone, scratching steel with his fingers" in the rectification of officials' working styles—his firmness, as settled as a massive rock, is being constantly strengthened in the course of his life.

Second, he has the character to adopt the happy medium in order to bridge opposing views. Though he has an iron hand, his disposition is measured, pragmatic, and reasonable, and never abrasively aggressive. An old friend says of him, "He is an aggressive reform advocate with a smile on his face." His colleagues say he has never spoken harsh words.

Zhao Derun, a journalist of the Xinhua News Agency, interviewed Xi Jinping when he started his career in officialdom, and was referred to by Xi as "a friend in Xinhua News Agency." They have kept in contact throughout the years, and when Xi Jinping was serving as the provincial-level Party chief of Zhejiang, the two of them had a long talk.

Zho says that it is no coincidence that Xi Jinping became the leader of

---

115.   "Cat theory" is a reference to Deng Xiaoping's pragmatism, as captured in his pithy remark: "No matter if the cat is black or white, it is a good cat so long as it catches mice."

the Party and the supreme leader of the country, adding, "From his starting point in Zhengding, to the seventeen-year toughened rule in Fujian, his career in officialdom was not entirely a smooth journey. There were difficult times and setbacks. But he is broadminded, good at uniting himself with people whose ideas differ from his own, and especially able to tolerate the people that have made mistakes or hurt him in the past. Ordinary people cannot do this."[116]

This ability to be good at uniting people and finding balance is a statesman's tradition passed down from his father. Some people complain about the "red second-generation."[117] Yet others compare them to the political legacies in Japan or in the US, believing that the "red second-generation" are more familiar with political logic and better at handling the available political resources.

Perhaps it is not right to make such a sweeping generalization. But at least with Xi Jinping, an extraordinary sense of propriety and a balancing ability can be discerned. For example, he promoted forceful reform in Zhengding while taking good care of the veteran cadres, which apparently eliminated many frictions. When he was back in Beijing, and about to enter the core of the central leadership, he visited the homes of the founders of the new China one by one. This is both an expression of his affectionate disposition and an astute political instinct.

In the 18th National Congress of the CPC, he proposed that the direction of reforms shall adopt neither a closed rigid route nor the haphazard way of perfunctory conversion. This means he will resolve any social conflicts in a moderate and rational way, to draw the reform into a deeper level, and thus resolve the issues that China faces.

Third, Xi Jinping underscores how important it is for officials to have strict morals and diligently carry out the tenets of self-discipline. One quotation from the *Analects of Confucius* is always cited deferentially by Xi Jinping: "He who exercises government by means of his virtue may be compared to the north polar star, which keeps its place as all the stars turn toward it."

Eleven years ago, he wrote an article in the magazine *Seeking Truth*, an official organ of the Central Committee of the CPC, counseling that to exercise their rights to bring good benefits to the people, the officials must emphasize both laws and morals, exercise their rights according to both laws

---

116.   "Interviewing Xi Jinping in Zhengding," www.people.com.cn, February 1, 2015.
117.   "Red second generation" is an apt phrase used by the Chinese today for descendants of first-generation communist leaders.

and morals. All in all, their exercise of rights reflects their morality.[118] This can be understood as his interpretation of power.

He has said, looking back across all the generations, with each collapse of an emperor's rule, even the destruction of a dynasty, a ruling regime's stepping down from the political stage was always attributable to its officials' failure to establish, cultivate, and exercise morality, and the ruling regime's wrongful working style, raging corruption, and failure to win the hearts of the people.

To exercise governance by means of virtue, the ruling party must, first of all, win the hearts of the people; and second, must discipline itself and improve its own moral integrity to educate and move the people.[119]

When it comes to how to treat the issue of one's own advancement in officialdom, Xi Jinping says that after he decided to enter politics, his policy was to push ahead like a soldier in the opponent's territory; but as to career advancement, just let it be. If you actively pursue your own promotion but do not get it, he advises, your life will be full of disappointment and pain.[120]

So in Zhejiang, when he talked about a tragic fire that caused the death of 40 people, he requested that the officials involved do things holding the "black gauze cap" in their hands, rather than acting in a conspicuously official capacity, wearing their caps on their heads. One person present at the scene relates that after hearing this, the people fell silent.

Regarding official morality, Xi Jinping especially stresses inner concentration and self-discipline.

In the Two Sessions of the NPC and the CPPCC in 2013, he said in a seminar with the Jiangsu's representatives that training a cadre in China was far more expensive than training a pilot. Therefore, the officials shall hold onto the bottom line and remind themselves that the power in their hands is given to them by the people, and they must focus on self-improvement.[121]

From his riding bicycles to the countryside, paying for his own meals, not taking his wife when attending official events, requiring his family not to do business in places under his jurisdiction, and the issuance of the "Eight Provisions" on rigorous enforcement of economy and improvement of Party working style immediately after the holding of the 18th National Party Congress, his prudent attitude can be seen.

---

118.   "Exercise Rights by Moral and Follow Rules in Communication," *Seeking Truth*, Issue 19, 2004.
119.   "Be a Person and Be an Official," *Zhejiang Daily*, February 7, 2007.
120.   "Xi Jinping: How I Entered the Political Circle," *Chinese People, Sons and Daughters of China*, Issue 7, 2000.
121.   "Xi Jinping: The Officials shall Face the Wall for Self-Reflection and Know the Prohibitions," *Yangzi Evening News*, March 9, 2013.

Fourth, Xi Jinping emphasizes that you must tell the truth and show true temperament.

Xi's diction may make people think of Mao Zedong—with a combination of plain words interspersed with ancient classics. However, the words spoken in his leisurely Beijing dialect make them sound more gracious and calm.

His fundamental truths include: Fairly well-off or not, just take a look at the villagers; if you eat the meals provided by the CPC, do not smash the pot of the CPC; tie the cage tightly, for a farm shed could let in a cat; if you want to do anything, do it clearly; the Party shall not be reduced to a private club; you should not mess up a region or the world, all for your personal ends. Whether addressing domestic affairs or foreign affairs, he always disseminates his ideas with humorous, interesting, and vivid turns of phrase.

Regarding Xi Jinping's diction, the book *The Amicable Xi Jinping*, published in Shanghai, and *Xi Jinping's Dictions*, published in Beijing, cite and analyze his words from both the vernacular and classical perspectives. In fact, telling the truth, he does not reflect a superb language art or technique, but he has a true disposition, based around honesty, straightforwardness, and seeking the truth through available facts.

Local cadres who once worked under Xi Jinping said that his words often hit the nail on the head. Though he never speaks harsh words, he makes his attitude clear.

Watching videos of his TV interviews through different periods, you will find that, unlike those overbearing officials sitting stiffly, he recounts his stories smoothly, and talks about sensitive topics frankly, and never deliberately maintains his official image when coming to the details. Though he is amicable and peaceful in attitude, a strong sense of confidence always impresses the people who hear him speak.

When he went to the US on an inspection trip as the Fuzhou municipal Party chief, a Chinese student helping with translations found that Xi Jinping was very attentive, asked questions where he did not understand, and was never embarrassed by his questions.

When Natsuo Yamaguchi, the head of the Japanese Komeito Party, talked about his four meetings with Xi Jinping, he later remarked that sometimes Xi's face looked very serious, "but that is a natural revelation of his feelings." He felt that Xi is a trustworthy statesman, a politician you can be frank with, who does not get over himself because of the rise of his position, never puts on airs and has always been calm and prudent.[122]

---

122.   "Special Interview with Natsuo Yamaguchi," *Xinhua Daily for Overseas Chinese in Japan*, February 2013.

We can often find some topical elements in his talks. For example, in his 2015 New Year's Eve speech to the nation, he used a popular Internet phrase to praise the hard work of the cadres, saying he offered the "thumbs-up" sign for them. Sometimes, he also mentions popular songs and stars. These elements are sincere, humorous, and relatable to China's young people.

In February, 2012, when he was visiting a local sports association in Ireland, he walked onto the grass field and kicked a soccer ball far away in front of the crowd.

The media consensus is that he "perfectly conveys an amicable image," and "shows the Chinese charisma." A journalist witnessing the scene in Dublin, Ireland, speculated that his kicking the ball was an impromptu act, and such acts on diplomatic occasions can carry risks. But the spontaneous and smooth kick showed his love of soccer, and his extraordinary confidence and ease.

Fifth, Xi Jinping loves to read books and excels in the sharing of information.

Xi Jinping has spoken several times about his personal hobbies in front of foreign media. This keen sports fan learned to swim at the age of four, enjoys hiking and walking and is familiar with soccer, volleyball, basketball, tennis, and the martial arts.

However, due to his intense work schedule, the only hobby he can enjoy with any frequency is reading books. "Reading has become a lifestyle of mine," he says.

Thanks to the historical background of his youth, he has read many books by Russian writers like Krylov, Pushkin, Gogol, Lermontov, Turgenev, Dostoyevsky, Nekrasov, Chernyshevsky, Tolstoy, Chekhov, and Sholokhov, and has a clear memory of the brilliant passages and plots.

He has also read many works of philosophy, such as ancient Greek classics and Herbert Marcuse's studies of post-modernism.

Chinese traditional Confucius classics, history, philosophy, and literature are also among his reading materials. The words he cited all come from the *Analects of Confucius, Shih Chi (Historical Records), The Spring and Autumn Period*, the *Books of Songs*, the *Books of Rites,* and *The Guang Zi.*

In the seventeen years he worked in Fujian, he wrote many investigative reports. Li Junru, the former deputy president of the Party School of the Central Committee of the CPC, thought that Xi Jinping's articles were unadorned, but full of wisdom, with no cliché-like empty words. He added that Mao Zedong once required Party leaders to write reports and editorials personally, in order to form a studying and working style based around considering problems and drawing conclusions from steady practice. But there are not many officials who have ideas and are willing to put pen to paper quite like Xi Jinping in the CPC.

Xi Jinping also highlights an emphasis on media publicity. His work in Zhengding and Ningde was reported in the *People's Daily* and, in 1990, there were two stories about his work in three months, a frequency almost unheard of for such a low-ranking Party member.

When he was working in the provincial government, he often had interviews with TV stations, or made speeches on the economic class of the CCTV. From February, 2003, to March, 2007, he wrote a column in *Zhejiang Daily* over four consecutive years and published 232 short essays to answer questions of concern to the public with a language of equality and equanimity.

Since he assumed office in the central government, dramatic changes have occurred in methods of disseminating information, and the Internet has become the primary platform.

First, there is the Weibo account "Learning from Xi Fan Club," which broadcasts Xi Jinping's schedule of official visits at a faster speed than the official media, and sometimes forecasts the next stops on his visits.

The official media has also broken away from the routine practices. The urgent and compelling information of the high-level leaders is no longer solely published by Xinhua News Agency or the CCTV's news broadcasts. Social media has become the first outlet.

Soon several short animated films produced by Fuxing Road Studio and Chaoyang Studio went viral on the Internet—the cartoon image of the national leader began to appear in a light, lively, and humorous fashion. "How the Chinese Leader is Tempered" described the Chinese officials' promotion and assessment system, "Following Uncle Xi to Boao" illustrated the flexible Xi-style diplomacy; "The Party's Mass Line" series shows the cartoon image of Xi Jinping brandishing a club to fight tigers.

Some media compare this new method of publicity, different from the traditional, somewhat mechanical, adulatory style, with the banner reading *Xiao Ping Nin Hao* ("Hello, Xiaoping") that appeared in the National Day's parade team in 1984—in the days when the cult of personality was being phased out; "Xiao Ping Nin Hao" is an expression with a strong sense of modesty and affection, that highlights the leader's "plebeian" image, making him more easily accessible to the masses.

In fact, the series of animated videos have become the necessary venue for the CPC's association with other parties and for foreign publicity. The appearance of the leader's cartoon image in China, a country with so many political taboos, draws the following conclusions from foreign media—from now on, the CPC government can no longer be deemed as an out-of-date, dogmatic, and rigid government.

Sixth, Xi Jinping gets close to the people, and values personal relations. Many international commentators once thought that Xi Jinping was an unfathomable, mighty, formidable figure. But soon they changed their view and now define him as an amicable and gallant statesman.

Looking back at Xi's career, one characteristic that cannot be ignored is his talent for finding a way to get close to the people at all times. He often changes the route of his inspections, in order to go to people's homes, or to receive complaints so that he can address some urgent livelihood problems demanding his immediate attention. This contact with the people is in no way a fanfare, but a political and personal instinct of his.

In fact, for all the CPC's paeans to the "mass line," quite a few cadres liked to keep the people at a distance, and some of them even feared the people. The experience of Xi in his youth left a deep mark on him: The people can protect him, and can re-create a new him.

In a summary meeting after coming back from a complaint reception day, he told the cadres that while in ancient days, the county magistrate held court trials to right wrongs for the people, nowadays we were busy in meetings and seldom actively held court trials. This was not right.

On New Year's Eve, 2014, Xi Jinping delivered a televised speech to the people of China, and the close-up shots in the four-minute video showed the details of the supreme leader's office for the first time: There were six photographs on the shelves, including a picture of Xi with his parents, wife, and daughter, plainly showing the personal side of him as a son, a husband, and a father.

Xi Jinping can get nostalgic about the old days. When Lv Hou, the peasant friend he met when he was sent down as an educated youth to Shaanxi, was taken ill, he took him to Fujian for better medical treatment, went to visit him almost every night and paid his medical bills. When his friend Jia Dashan in Zhengding had a terminal illness, he specially went to visit him and wrote an article to commemorate him.

He invited the friends he met in the days when he was sent down as an educated youth to Shaanxi to have dinner at home, and his wife Peng Liyuan cooked the meals. Meeting these friends, Peng said, "As a 'daughter-in-law'[123] of Liangjiahe, I should go back to the village to sing songs for my people on the barn's threshing floor." Xi chimed in, "If we have the chance,

---

123.   By Chinese custom, Peng was referring to the fact that being married to someone (Xi) who felt Liangjiahe was like his second hometown, she was like a "daughter-in-law" from the same village.

let's go back together."[124] They kept their word. In the spring of 2015, the two of them went back to the Shaanxi village.

In fact, apart from the foreign affairs assignments, Peng rarely accompanies her husband on his domestic inspections. In November, 2013, when Xi Jinping went on an inspection in Shandong, Peng was there too— as Shandong is her hometown. The old Chinese tradition of a couple going home to visit one's family filled the political activity with extra warmth.

Xi extends greetings to his former teachers every New Year's Day, and when he was in Fuzhou, he provided long-term funding to the children in poverty-stricken families to help them study in school long enough until they could find jobs. In Shanghai, on a field survey, a farmer sent a picture to him, and was a little embarrassed because he had no frame for it. Not long after that he received a collection of frames sent by Xi Jinping. The Chinese overseas student who served as interpreter for Xi on his visit to the US receives New Year cards from Xi each spring festival. He is not the only one. Many people who have met Xi also receive cards from him. "Calm, controlled, and willing to shoulder the responsibilities for the country…he has a competitive spirit and is dissatisfied with China's second-place status… true to himself"—these are just some of the positive comments about him from US media.[125]

Asian politicians seem to have more understanding of the turbulence in contemporary Chinese politics.

Singapore's Senior Minister Lee Kuan Yew, who died recently, visited China in November, 2007. Back then Xi had just entered the Standing Committee of the Political Bureau of the CPC Central Committee. The one-hour meeting between the two of them left a deep impression on Lee Kuan Yew. He said of Xi, "I think he is a man of ideas. He went through many trials and sufferings in his life. I put him in the same class as Nelson Mandela— strong emotional self-control, and he does not let his individual misfortunes and hardships influence his greater judgment."

"It is not only the self-control," Lee added, "The individual's hardship and misfortune—against the backdrop of the country's own hardship and misfortune—will be refined into a profound sense of duty, and of sympathy. This overcomes his rigidity and distance as a politician, and presents an affectionate, righteous, and warm image to the people."[126]

---

124.   "Loyal and Dedicated Xi Jinping," *Global Characters*, Issue 6.

125.   "Several Anecdotes about Xi, the State President of China," *National Interest*, (website), October 15, 2014.

126.   "Loyal and Dedicated Xi Jinping," *Global Characters*, Issue 6.

CHAPTER
2

The Blueprint for the Realization of the China Dream

The China Dream is a dream held by the Chinese people to return to the status of a leading nation of the world. To the Chinese people, to realize the China Dream serves not only as an objective to fight for, but also a compelling duty given by the history of humankind. To realize one of the greatest dreams in history, Xi Jinping has unfolded his own governing plan: the "Four-Pronged Comprehensive Strategy." It is critical for the success of Xi Jinping's reform plan to break through the distractions and obstructions of vested interests, to wash away every conservative barrier inherited from the past, and to summon up all of China's courage and energy to move towards the goals laid out for 2049.

I. THE CHINA DREAM

Around the same time, at the end of 2012, the leaders of China and the United States both spoke of the "dreams" of their nation's hearts. Both nations had undergone transfers of power that year. With the 56th presidential election of the United States decided, President Barack Obama delivered a speech on election night, in which he stated: "We believe in a generous America, in a compassionate America, in a tolerant America open to the dreams of an immigrant's daughter who studies in our schools and pledges to our flag. To the young boy on the south side of Chicago who sees a life beyond the nearest street corner. To the furniture worker's child in North Carolina who wants to become a doctor or a scientist, an engineer or an entrepreneur, a diplomat, or even a president. That's the future we hope for." This is what China endeavors to achieve as well.

Around the same time, the new General Secretary of the CPC Central Committee Xi Jinping visited the exhibition "The Road to Rejuvenation" at the National Museum of China, unveiling his "China Dream" for the first time. To bring about the rejuvenation of the Chinese nation is China's greatest dream of modern times. The dream combines the long-cherished wishes of the Chinese people over many generations, embodies the overall interests of the nation of China and its people, and represents the culmination of all that the Chinese people look forward to.

Obama, an African-American, was elected as the president of the United States—a living embodiment of the American dream. The modern history of China is the story of the Chinese nation's century-long struggle to soar beyond the label of "Sick Man of East Asia," to become a great nation maintaining the balance of the current world—a splendid dream.

Why is the Chinese population, well beyond a billion strong, overcome with emotion about the China Dream? How can they make the dream into reality? How will China cope, when President Obama has said "the United States will lead the world for the next century?" It would appear that dreams are more than just the blueprints of ambitions, but are sometimes destined to become veritable conflicts in the real world.

Understanding the China Dream; Understanding the History of China

One autumn night, November 11, 2014, with a clear moon and heavy winds, was destined to play an essential part in the history of relations between China and the United States. In accordance with diplomatic arrangements, President Xi Jinping and President Obama were to take a walk, focusing on matters of diplomacy, at the Zhongnanhai Compound in Beijing. The original plan called for the leaders to take a walk at Yingtai Bridge at 6:30 p.m., followed by a small meeting at Hanyuan Hall, then dinner at Xiangyi Hall, and a last tea at Yingxun Pavilion. All activities were to be finished by 9:15 p.m.

But in fact, the two heads of state enjoyed their talks so much that each phase of the evening was spontaneously extended, and the 30-minute meeting lasted 90 minutes. Xi Jinping invited Obama to dinner in case Obama was hungry, and Obama showed an interest in talking with Xi

Jinping on additional issues. As a result, the 90-minute dinner lasted nearly two hours; the 30-minute tea lasted nearly one hour. They ended up waving goodbye after 11:00 p.m.

Why were both Heads of State so interested in such talks, despite the wind and the cold? We can interpret it logically.

First, why was Yingtai Bridge chosen as the location for the walk? The Chinese characters *Yingtai* (瀛台) were written by the Qianlong Emperor in the Qing Dynasty of China. The good environment, with China's "APEC-blue" skies, can be described in one word: beautiful. Surrounded by waters and embellished with pavilions, terraces, and open halls, it seems as if the legendary fairyland of Yingzhou truly exists at the Yingtai Bridge.

During the walk, Xi Jinping described to President Obama the history of Yingtai, which has witnessed the vicissitudes of China over the centuries. Xi Jinping explained that Yingtai Bridge was built in the Ming Dynasty and later emperors of the Qing Dynasty stayed here to preside over court, to avoid the summer heat, and to entertain guests. Here, Emperor Kangxi formulated the national strategies to crack down on civil strife and reclaim Taiwan; after that, China had faced decline. The Guangxu Emperor was hosted here by Empress Dowager Cixi after the failure of his "Hundred Days of Reform" in 1898.

Obama understood immediately. The same cycles can be discerned in the history of the United States: It is an invariable law that reform will encounter obstruction. Within this context, it can be understood why the historic Yingtai Bridge was chosen for the talk between the two heads of China and the United States: Xi Jinping wanted to give President Obama an *in situ* history lesson.

What Xi Jinping said later reinforced the crucial point: Knowing the modern history of China is essential to understanding the Chinese people's ideals today and the trajectory of their desired development.

To the inanimate world, history makes no inherent sense; it is merely a scale that records time. But to a nation and a people, history and time denote destiny and unforgettable memories. From the European Renaissance in the fourteenth century, the English Civil War in 1640, to the Industrial Revolution in the West in the eighteenth century, the United States ratifying its Constitution in 1787, and the French Revolution in 1789—the civilization of Europe and America rose impressively, and the West became the leading force of globalization.

Meanwhile China had been in decline since the fourteenth century, when the progress of history seemed to abandon the eastern nation, casting a tragic shadow as it found itself a passive, beaten bystander. In the First Opium War in 1840, the Qing Dynasty was defeated and conceded Hong Kong; in the Sino-Japanese War in 1885, the Qing Dynasty was thoroughly defeated and conceded Taiwan; the Eight-Power Allied Forces invaded Beijing in 1900 and signed the *Peace Protocol of 1901* with the Qing Government in 1901, sinking China further into the depths of failure. Japanese invaders occupied the three northeast provinces of China in 1931; Japan stepped up its invasion of China in 1937, and occupied Beijing and Nanjing in succession and then carried out the brutal and shocking Nanjing Massacre—a mirror of the old China, full of humiliation and bitterness, indignation, and salvation. How could the Chinese nation break away from this condition, of always lagging behind and being vulnerable to attacks? How could the Chinese people stand straight again and win back their survival and dignity? Chinese descendants were suffering, hesitating over ways to go forward, seeking answers, and contending.

No one has deeper feelings about the vicissitudes of the Chinese nation's position than overseas Chinese immigrants. Once a Kuomintang (KMT) veteran told a story of his exile in South Africa after the KMT retreated to Taiwan in 1949. In the middle period of the twentieth century, South Africa still enforced the stubborn racial separation policies of Apartheid. On the bus in Cape Town, the whites always sat in the first compartment while people of color such as Africans and Asians sat in other compartments in the back. Each time he boarded, the veteran got on the bus at the first compartment, bought a ticket, and then walked to the back. This changed all of a sudden on a day in 1964. He got on the bus and bought a ticket as usual, but the conductor held onto him when he was about to walk to the back, saying, "From now on, you can sit in the first compartment." The veteran was confused: "I am one of the colored, one of the 'second class', and I should sit in the back," he said. The white conductor told him, "You probably don't know, but your motherland, China, has successfully detonated an atomic bomb. No nation that can develop atomic bombs can be regarded as second class. Therefore, from now on, please sit with us."

Chinese people still cannot help shedding tears when reading such a story, even after more than 50 years. Only a nation that has suffered such global humiliation and undergone such hardships as China can be aware of the true taste of oppression.

China successfully detonated its first atomic bomb on October 15, 1964; henceforth, China put its hand to the development of the hydrogen bomb immediately. Compared with atomic bombs, it is much more complex to develop and manufacture hydrogen bombs. In the first instance, Chinese experts at the atomic laboratories were given several lectures by military scientists and engineers from the Soviet Union on how to make atomic bombs while Chinese scientists started from the very beginning in making hydrogen bombs. The Chinese scientist Deng Jiaxian, involved in hydrogen bomb design, forced himself to complete the theoretical design for the hydrogen bomb with a manual calculator and an abacus.

China successfully exploded its first hydrogen bomb on June 17, 1967. From an atomic bomb to a hydrogen bomb, it took the Soviet Union four years, the UK four years and seven months, France eight years and six months, while China, only two years and eight months.

When the Soviet experts left China in 1959, they were very dismissive, saying, "Without our help, the Chinese will make nothing but potato bombs."

Not one foreign country ever believed how far China's development of nuclear weapons could go. But the Chinese people were never convinced by fate and tried to win credit at the critical moment. Western scientists were confused all along about how Chinese people could successfully make both an atomic bomb and a hydrogen bomb in such a short period of time. Professor Chen-Ning Franklin Yang, who worked in the United States, recalled that "it was universally believed in the scientific community of the United States that it would be impossible for Chinese scientists to develop atomic and hydrogen bombs without the participation of foreign scientists."

When asked, in August, 1971, whether any foreigner had participated in China's development of atomic and hydrogen bombs, Deng Jiaxian wrote that, apart from minor assistance from the Soviet Union prior to the end of 1959, China's atomic weapon engineering had not engaged any foreign advisors or consultants. The thought of China achieving such a feat is still a source of great pride.

Wars Between China and Japan

More than 120 years ago, in the year 1892, the First Sino-Japanese War took place. It ended in utter failure for China.

The trajectory of China's descent from prosperity to the bottom can be reflected in the comparison of strengths between China and Japan in East Asia. There was tension between the two countries as early as the third century. During China's Tang Dynasty, Japan prepared to invade Korea and then coveted China not long after its initial rise. In 663 AD, the Tang navy destroyed Japanese naval forces at Baekgang, Korea, convincing Japan that China's strength was much stronger than it had previously known; in the next millennium, Japan remained non-aggressive. But in 1592, after Toyotomi Hideyoshi took over the political affairs of state in Japan, dreams of aggression against China were rekindled; history would call this war the

"Japanese Maritime Invasion of 1592." The Ming Government of China sent forces to assist the Korean regime and the Allied Forces defeated the Japanese army again, forcing Japan to remain quiet for another 300 years. In Sino–Japanese conflicts from the 1870s to the 1880s, China's strength was greater than Japan's, but this changed sorrowfully in the decade after the Kapshin Coup in Korea. During this period, Japan kept an eye on China. Yamagata Aritomo, an important official in the military of Japan, pointed out "the stronger China's military force is, the less complacent we should be." Consequently, after 1890, Japan invested 60 percent of its state revenue into navy and army development. In 1893, the Mikado decided to allocate JPY 300,000 from his palace coffers and extract one tenth of officials' remunerations to supplement shipbuilding costs. The whole nation from top to bottom seemed to unite to fight for the goal of surpassing China and prepared to "bet on the fate of Japan."

In 1890, China's Beiyang Navy had seven warships over 2,000 tons, with a total tonnage of more than 27,000, while there were only five warships above 2,000 tons, with a total tonnage of around 17,000 in the Japanese Navy. In 1872, Japan launched its ten-year military expansion plan, and by 1885 had established an army composed of 63,000 soldiers and 230,000 reservists, including six field divisions and one guard division by the eve of the First Sino-Japanese War. Meanwhile, the Japanese Navy now contained 32 warships and 24 torpedo boats with a total displacement of 72,000 tons, much stronger than the Beiyang Navy. Japan also sent Le Shan Tang, Xuan Yang She, and other spies to sneak into China to gather intelligence in all aspects. After the outbreak of the First Sino-Japanese War, the Qing Government was defeated on both the Korean and Chinese battlefields due to the corruption and incompetency of its military leaders. As soon as Japan occupied the Liaodong Peninsula, the Qing Government started to appeal for peace through diplomatic channels. After Weihai Port fell into Japan's hands, the Qing Government sought more urgently to establish peace. Li Hongzhang was assigned as the fully authorized representative to negotiate peace in Japan. On April 17, 1895, the Qing Government and Japan signed the *Treaty of Shimonoseki*, which was full of humiliating terms that included the surrender of China's sovereign rights, in which the Qing Government conceded Liaodong Peninsula, Taiwan, and the Penghu Islands, compensating 200 million Chinese taels for Japan's military expenditure, allowing Japan to set up factories in China, and opening up Shashi, Chongqing, Suzhou, Hangzhou, and other commercial ports. After the intervention of Russia and other countries, Japan gave back Liaodong Peninsula but asked for another 30 million Chinese taels as "ransom." The *Treaty of Shimonoseki* was imposed on the Chinese people. The money Japan looted from China, amounting to tens of millions of taels, laid a material foundation for it to wage further aggressions against China. Japanese's military might continued to expand, allowing it to become the dominant force in East Asia, and culminated in the attack on Pearl Harbor on December 7, 1941, thus provoking war between Japan and the United States in World War II.

In an important meeting on December 27, 2013, Xi Jinping expressed his thoughts: "Once a country's military lags behind, it will have a fatal impact on that country's national security. I read historical documents on modern China often. It pains me to see such miserable scenes of lagging behind, and being vulnerable to attacks." To know what the China Dream means to the Chinese people, one must understand the history of China; only by fully understanding the history of China can one apprehend the pain of poverty and stagnation that comes upon a defeated nation.

How Do China's Goals Resonate with China's People?

To the old version of me,
Sitting before your window,
Looking back in the past;
What choices I make
What life I live
Whether to live in such a country that,
Even far from the coast, a mountain, or a river
Blossoms of flowers everywhere
Without thousands of masks,
People still laugh without concern.

Live the life closest to life;
Safe food and secure homes
No fears, no worry of illness,
Loneliness for no one.

Rainbows and dragonflies in the eyes of children
Learning freedom from teachers, the cars slow down for them.
Snug sleep on quiet nights, to wake in joyful days;
Home stays where it is, it never moves.
Strange friends are
Full of good faith
Sharing, not showing off,

Caring not for backgrounds
Caring not for status;
Encountering the sunshine, as if for the first time.
Never hurrying through fair nor foul
Not eager to boast, magnanimity in heart
Diverse hobbies with firm beliefs.
Without thousands of masks,
People sing to the heart

Live the life closest to life;
Safe food and secure homes
No fears, no worry of illness,
Loneliness for no one.

Born with dreams, live with wishes
Just as everyone will die;
Everyone's dream will come true.

These are the lyrics of a song called "To the Old Version of Me" created by a post-1980s independent musician for NetEase's reports on the Two Sessions—the annual meeting of the National People's Congress (NPC) and the Chinese People's Political Consultative Conference (CPPCC)—of China in March, 2013. After the song was published on the Internet, numerous Chinese Internet users showed an appreciation for it. The songwriter, even in the March smog, remained optimistic and yearned for a happy life on behalf of those who are sunk in difficulties. Such a spirit of holding fast to dreams seemed to strike a chord in the heart of Chinese youth. In addition to receiving praise, the song also moved people to discuss the China Dream.

Undoubtedly, the China Dream is a dream of China, of the nation, of politicians. More importantly, to work in concert with the people, it should be a dream of the people—closely linked to everyone. Xi Jinping gave an appropriate summation of it in the 2013 Two Sessions. In a speech to the National People's Congress on March 17, Xi Jinping elaborated on the connections between the China Dream and the Chinese people: In the long run, the China dream is a dream of the people; its realization closely depends on the people, it will bring stable benefits to the people. To the common people, it is the fundamental will to have safe food, clean water, clean air, secure homes, and comfortable families. To realize these ideals can mobilize people to work harder than grand, but abstract, national goals.

Journalist and author Thomas Friedman has written in his articles of

China's many challenges, "from widening income gaps to massive rural-urban migration to choking pollution and environmental destruction. The only way to square all that is with a new Chinese Dream that marries people's expectations of prosperity with a more sustainable China."

CPC leaders have gone through a winding three-step process with to articulate the China Dream. As early as the founding of China, Mao Zedong once boldly predicted that China would soon clean up the filthy mires left by the reactionary government, heal the wounds of wars, and build a brand new people's republic worthy of the name. However, despite the beautiful dream, we needed to see the reality, namely poverty and emptiness; Mao Zedong spoke of China's available resources in a bitterly ironic tone: "What can we make now? We can make chairs and tables, teapots and teacups; we can grow food and grind flour, and make paper, but we cannot make a car, an aircraft, a tank, or even a tractor." With such a low production capacity, Mao Zedong still set industrialization as the main objective to tackle. In 1956, he proposed a goal of industrial modernization. Then, people could hardly recognize China only four or five decades after the revolution of 1911, namely the Xinhai Revolution. In another four or five decades, to the year 2001, at the turn of twentieth century, China had transformed beyond recognition. China has become a socialist industrial power.

Based on such an understanding, the CPC Central Committee put forward the mission to build China into a great and industrialized country with an advanced level of modern civilization in the 1950s, which was later called the goal of the "Four Modernizations"—in agriculture, industry, national defense, and science and technology.

However, it did not go well on the way to that dream. To realize the goal as soon as possible, Mao Zedong launched the "Great Leap Forward." But the Great Leap Forward did not lead China forward; on the contrary, a great regression occurred, accompanied by a sharp decline of living standards. Mao Zedong and other leaders also instituted the political tenets of communism, in which there was no private property, all men were equal, and distribution was carried out according to labor. The "old culture" was to be abandoned entirely in order to achieve the goals of communism, so they launched the Cultural Revolution that subjected China and its people to a decade of catastrophe. The Cultural Revolution, lasting a decade, not only forced China's economy to the verge of collapse, but also further widened the gap with developed capitalist nations. Meanwhile, the United States' economy grew rapidly without hindrance for 106 months from January, 1961, to October, 1969, so that Americans called the 1960s their "decade of prosperity." Japan developed more rapidly and its GDP grew 7.2-fold from 1955 to 1970; the economic conditions in China and Japan had little difference at the beginning of 1950s, but by the end of the 1960s, Japan had left China far behind.

Mao Zedong's exploration on the road to develop China in his later years indicates that it is valuable to have dreams, but the point is to find a realistic path to make them come true.

In 1979, Deng Xiaoping took over the position as China's navigator and started a new round of unprecedented explorations. Deng Xiaoping's reforms emphasized improving people's livelihoods.

Whenever Wan Li, who used to serve as the chairman of the Standing Committee of the National People's Congress, recalled an experience he had when he was the secretary of the Anhui Party Committee, he could never help shedding tears. In the late winter of 1977, Wan Li visited the countryside of Huaibei, Anhui, which had suffered the most severe famine conditions. When he walked into a peasant household, he saw an old man and two girls, covered in worn cotton tunics, crawling beside their stove. Wan Li greeted the old man, but the old man did not respond. Wan Li thought the old man might be deaf, so he raised his voice, but the old man remained silent. Other cadres ran over, and said into the old man's ear, "This is our provincial secretary coming to visit you." Then the old man stood up slowly, but Wan Li was too surprised to speak because the old man did not have pants; he was naked beneath the worn cotton. Wan Li was embarrassed, so he turned to the two girls, but the two girls also did not respond. Another cadre said, "Secretary Wan, they do not have pants, neither." Wan Li then saw the point that the naked father and two daughters spent the cold winter by the residual heat from the stove. He could not prevent his tears, and decided that no matter how the left wing attacked him, he would support the reform of fixing agricultural output for every rural household. The rural areas of Anhui Province became the pilot area of China's reform with the purpose of allowing the people to have adequate food and clothing, instead of arguing "what is the socialist path and what is the capitalist path" with nothing in their stomachs.

His first time meeting with Chinese and foreign journalists after being elected as the general secretary at the 18th CPC National Congress, Xi Jinping declared that his most important political views included responding to the people's hearts, and overseeing the improvement of their livelihoods: "the Chinese people love life, look forward to better education, more stable jobs, more satisfying incomes, more reliable social programs, medical and health services of a higher quality, more comfortable living conditions, more beautiful environments, and they hope their children can grow better, work better, and live better. Meeting the people's expectation for a better life is our goal." The China Dream can never be fulfilled in all its potential without being grounded in reality, connecting to the vital interests of every individual. The China Dream is closely associated with better living standards for the people of China.

II. THE FOUR-PRONGED COMPREHENSIVE STRATEGY
The Grand Strategy of China

On September 16, 1993, in a talk with his brother Deng Ken in his later years, Deng Xiaoping said, "How to help the 1.2 billion–person population become rich and how to distribute wealth after they become rich are big problems. Distribution is very important. We aim to prevent polarization, but actually, polarization is inevitable. These problems should be settled by a multitude of means, methods, and strategies. If a minority of people has so much wealth, while the majority has none, one day it will all go wrong. Unfair distribution of income will cause polarization, which will bring about problems at some future time. These problems must be solved. We used to say 'develop first', but we now see there might be more problems after development than during it."[1]

It can be seen from Deng Xiaoping's reflections on the road for China's development that he had sharp intuitions regarding the problems of post-development China—"there might be more problems after development than during it;" "[the income gap] will bring about problems at some future time"—these were Deng Xiaoping's profound reflections for China after the reform and opening up, indicating that he had seen past the limitations of reforms based solely on development.

Deng Xiaoping passed away in 1997. But the problems he confronted in his later years did not go away with him but were left to successors who must face those problems, seek answers, and devise effective plans.

Development comes with challenges, but fortunately, challenges that arise in a nation's development can be solved by development itself. The leaders of China since Deng Xiaoping have been required to understand the logical evolution of China's road toward advancement in a dynamic manner and to solve new problems faced by China, as appropriate, with flexible ways of thinking. Essential to this is discerning problems present before development from problems brought about by development.

Lack of development is a major problem; and development always

1.   Ju Lingrong, Wang Zuoling. *A Chronicle of Deng Xiaoping's Life: 1975–1997*, p. 1364, Beijing: Central Party Literature Press, July 2004.

comes with new problems. How does China solve new problems provoked by development? Now, the insights of Deng Xiaoping are in the hands of Xi Jinping.

The "Last Window" for China's Reform

In the 1980s, when Chinese people started to see the world, many neighbors such as Japan, Korea, Malaysia, the Philippines, Thailand, Singapore, Indonesia, and Taiwan Province, were well ahead of mainland China in terms of development. Professor Zhang Weiwei, who used to serve the Chinese Ministry of Foreign Affairs as a translator, retains his memories of first going abroad, as if they were fresh: "Near the beginning of the 1980s, I followed leaders of China to Thailand for the first time. I was shocked to see that there were expressways, supermarkets, and shopping malls bustling with activity. At that time, I felt Thailand was at least 30 years ahead of China."

But in the last 30 years, it seems that Japan has been stuck in stagnation while Thailand, the Philippines, Malaysia, Indonesia, and others have not made great progress, except for Korea and Singapore, who have carried on boldly and entered the ranks of high-income developed countries. Professor Zhang Weiwei asserts that "Thailand is at least 20 years behind Shanghai, and the Philippines is nearly 30 years behind Shanghai."

The Chinese people's perceptions are partially supported by the analysis by the World Bank, and the World Bank's grouping criteria over recent years, which have been based on the "map method"—similar to market rates of exchange, in which an economic entity with gross national income (GNI) per capita of less than USD 975 ranks in the low-income group, an economic entity with GNI per capita between USD 975 and USD 3,855 ranks in the below-average-income group, between USD 3,859 and USD 11,905 ranks in the above-average-income group, and more than USD 11,906 ranks in the high-income group. Observed according to the above dynamic criteria, a country may fall into the trap of average income if it fails to graduate and ascends to the rank of a high-income country after sufficiently long-term growth as an average-income country.

In fact, according to the above criteria, putting aside those wealthy countries dependent entirely on oil exports, it seems obvious that besides those developed countries in Europe and America, only Japan, Korea, Singapore, Taiwan, Hong Kong, and Macao of China have stepped into the ranks of high income nations so far. Meanwhile those countries in Latin America that once ranked on an equal basis with European nations and those in Asia that have ascended to average income levels have not become a member of the high-income tier countries yet; even when certain Latin

American countries surpassed the average–high threshold for a period, they eventually fell back.

There is another conjecture about the trap of average income: No country with a population of more than 100 million has ever broken out of the trap by itself during the 30 years from the 1980s to now. Japan was the only exception because it has been a "developed" country that could run at the pace of the great powers in Europe and America before World War II. In other words, the vast developing countries have been drifting, suspended in sluggish development.

Now the open question is: Will China take the lead to break through?

When China's economic aggregate leapt to the second place in the world and its GDP per capita became USD 4,382 in 2010, it just barely ranked in the above-average income level as defined by the World Bank. But warnings from experts and scholars came soon afterwards: Owing to numerous potential dangers and unsustainable factors during economic growth, the odds were 70 percent that China would follow the rule of deceleration.

Besides, the realistic threat incurred by China's aging population is close at hand: Aging is considered one of the important causes of a slowdown in economic growth. The aging of the population means reductions in the growth rate of the working-age population and its absolute size, with no more increases, and a subsequent decrease in the proportion of the working-age population to the total population. Accordingly, the demographic dividend, adequate labor supply, and high reserves for economic growth will begin to fade. In 1990, the aging level in Japan reached as high as 11.9 percent, meaning that the population of citizens over 65 years old accounted for 11.9 percent of the total population, followed by a rapid increase of the dependency ratio of the population—the ratio of dependents to working-age citizens. At about the same time as these changes in the population structure, Japan's economic growth also changed sharply from deceleration to stagnation. China's 8.9 percent population over 65 years old in 2010 was quite close to the aging level slowing down the economic growth of Japan in the 1990s. Like Japan, China will undergo an increase in its dependency ratio during the Twelfth Five-Year Plan. Losing the comparative advantage in labor-intensive industries and being out of reach of the comparative advantage in technology and capital-intensive industries, China is facing the challenge of an "absent comparative advantage".

In the report of the 18th CPC National Congress, the risks and challenges China faces are summarized. Unbalanced, uncoordinated, and unsustainable development remain big problems. The capacity for scientific and technological innovations are weak. The industrial structure is unbalanced.

Agricultural infrastructure remains weak. Resource and environmental constraints have become more serious. Many systemic barriers stand in the way of promoting development in a scientific way. The tasks of deepening the reform and opening up, and changing the growth model, remain arduous. The development gap between urban and rural areas and between regions is still large, and so are income disparities. Social problems have increased markedly. There are many problems affecting people's immediate interests in education, employment, social security, healthcare, housing, the environment, food and drug safety, workplace safety, public security, law enforcement, and the administration of justice, among other issues. Some people still lead hard lives. There is a lack of ethics and integrity in some sections of society. Some officials are not competent enough to pursue development in a scientific way. Some community-level Party organizations are weak and lax. A small number of Party members and officials waver in the Party's ideals and convictions and are not fully aware of its purpose. Hierarchies and bureaucracies, as well as extravagance and waste, are serious obstacles. Some sectors are prone to corruption and other misconduct, and the fight against corruption remains a serious challenge for China. The nation must take these problems very seriously and work harder to solve them.

As urgent as these difficulties are, the danger of losing this window for reform is more urgent. After the 18th CPC National Congress, CPC senior leaders recommended two books to Party cadres: *A Memorial of 20 Years for the Collapse of USSR and its Party* by the Chinese scholar Huang Weiding, and *The Old Regime and the Revolution* by the French scholar Alexis de Tocqueville. In the first book, the author comprehensively reflects on the causes of the Soviet Union's sudden collapse following Gorbachev's reforms. How does such a powerful party, which had led the Soviet Union for more than 70 years, vanish overnight? This subject frightens CPC senior leaders. The second book is a comprehensive analysis of the French Revolution, when the French royal family had implemented several reform measures and French society foresaw many opportunities; in contrast, the French people launched a revolution that resulted in Louis XVI and his Queen, Marie Antoinette, being beheaded, with the country engulfed in a horrific bloodbath. In the book, de Tocqueville asks, why did measures meant to accommodate the people aggravate them instead? Such a historical quandary causes the leaders and the people of China to consider the ramifications of the current reforms.

Samuel Phillips Huntington, one of the most influential American political thinkers, reveals in his famous work *Political Order in Changing*

Societies that political instability has its roots in modernization, which breeds stability, while the process of reaching modernity incites disturbances.

After investigating many countries, Huntington pointed out that both economically developed and backward countries were relatively stable in politics, while political disturbances always occurred in countries that had just developed their economy to an extent. The primary cause is that development of an economy, the consequent differentiation of groups, conflicts of interests, transformation of value systems, and increased expectations of public participation are well beyond what the political system can withstand, and thus can lead to social disorder.

China is in the critical period, leaping from average income to high income, a life-or-death period in which the Party enters the decisive battle against corruption, a period thorny with contradictions. All signs indicate that the leaders of China, headed by Xi Jinping, do not have much time.

Xi Jinping came out with his own political decisions in the latest phase of China's reform. In the introduction to the *Decision of the Central Committee of the Communist Party of China on Some Major Issues Concerning Comprehensively Deepening the Reform*, he pointed to all members of the Central Committee. Upon completion of the 18th CPC National Congress, the Central Committee set out to determine the topics for discussion at the Third Plenary Session of the 18th CPC Central Committee. The Party's 18th National Congress set the goal of finalizing the construction of a moderately prosperous society in all respects, and emphasized that the Party must, with greater political courage and wisdom, lose no time in deepening reform in key sectors and resolutely discard all concepts and institutions that hinder efforts to pursue development in a scientific way. It also pointed out that the Party should set up a well-developed, scientific, standardized, and effective framework of systems and ensure that essential administrative bodies in all sectors are fully functioning. To achieve the strategic goals and carry out the plans set forth at the 18th National Party Congress, China must waste no time in promoting true reform.

Comprehensively strengthening reforms through anti-corruption mandates, and a genuine search for both temporary and permanent solutions, are important missions. China can implement temporary solutions, but only to buy time for permanent remedies. Taking the structure of law as a foundation, maintaining strategic focus, and averting a dangerous situation through the modernization of China's system of governance are clear and necessary steps put forward by Xi Jinping.

With repeated polishing and refinement, these ideas for reform constitute Xi Jinping's "Four-Pronged Comprehensive Strategy." Up to now, Xi Jinping has submitted his first plans for reform to the international and domestic communities.

The Four-Pronged Comprehensive Strategy will eliminate the income trap first. The strategy centers around finishing the building of a moderately prosperous society, deepening reform, advancing the law-based governance of China, and strengthening Party self-discipline.

As time progressed, the complete strategy was gradually formed in different high-level meetings. In November 2012, the 18th CPC National Congress put forward the goal to finish building a moderately prosperous society in all respects. A year later, the Third Plenary Session of the 18th CPC Central Committee proposed deepening reforms comprehensively.

Early in October, 2014, the Fourth Plenary Session of the 18th CPC Central Committee made the decision to advance the law-based governance of China. And on October 8, 2014, in the summary meeting of the mass line education and practice activities, Xi Jinping proposed strengthening Party self-discipline.

In November, 2014, during a visit to Fujian Province, Xi Jinping first put forward the "Three-Pronged Comprehensive Strategy," which aimed to take comprehensive measures to "finish building a moderately prosperous society, deepen reform, and advance law-based governance." On a visit to Jiangsu Province in December, 2014, the Three-Pronged Comprehensive Strategy rose to become the Four-Pronged Comprehensive Strategy, which aims, in total, to "finish building a moderately prosperous society, deepen reform, advance the law-based governance of China, and strengthen Party self-discipline." At this point, Xi Jinping's Four-Pronged Comprehensive Strategy had been finalized, constituting the general framework for the new term of central collective leadership of China to rule the state and manage political concerns.

To finish building a moderately prosperous society in all respects is the general goal put forward by the 18th CPC National Congress, while to deepen reform comprehensively and to advance the law-based governance of China will, together, ensure swift progress toward the goals of building a moderately prosperous society; together, the two strategies work in unison to soar, like the wings of the phoenix. In the process, strengthening the Party's self-discipline comprehensively functions as a fundamental guarantee for success in each endeavor and every goal. In the eyes of pundits as well as experts and scholars, Xi Jinping's Four-Pronged Comprehensive Strategy is the strategic plan for him to rule the country.

Professor Xu Yaotong, of the China National School of Administration, has stated: "This is an official declaration, pronouncing that the Four-Pronged

Comprehensive Strategy has become the new blueprint of governance, where the Central Committee with Xi Jinping as the general secretary rules China and manages all political concerns."

Xu Yaotong believes Xi Jinping's stratagem is innovative because of its emphasis on being *comprehensive*: "On one hand, it shows a certain continuity, in that it derives from the same strain of previous directions and paths, and the new generation of central collective leadership refuses to abandon or deny the past; on the other hand, the term "comprehensive" is not an understatement—the stratagem is to be applied broadly, without any blind angles, with a strengthened intensity, depth, and breadth."

Political commentator Liu Ruishao believes that Xi Jinping is advancing the realization of the China Dream by proclaiming it upon taking office, and following up with his Four-Pronged Comprehensive Strategy two years later.

Differing from the interpretations of experts and scholars, the Chinese people pay more attention to the stricter aspects of Xi Jinping's Four-Pronged Comprehensive Strategy, that is, the possibility of mandatory quotas and tough measures. What the Chinese people see is the goal of a moderately prosperous society: that China must double the 2010 GDP and per capita income for both urban and rural residents by the year 2020, which is known as the Chinese version of the "Income Doubling Program" that originated in Japan. In 1960, Hayato Ikeda, then prime minister of Japan, adopted economists' suggestions on village governance and put forward the original Income Doubling Program. To realize the goal, Japan took an economic leap. By 1976, Japan had doubled average incomes after only seven years, bringing about the so-called "Japan Miracle." In 1968, Japan surpassed West Germany and became the second largest economy in the world, a rank it held until China surpassed it in 2010.

The Chinese Income Doubling Program focuses on China's economic aggregate surpassing the US and its per capita income ranking among the high-income countries by 2020, in order to break away from the trap of average income and embark on a sustainable track of development. To be more specific, China wishes to create another 300 million middle-class people during decade from 2010 to 2020, so as to change the pyramidal shape of China's income distribution fundamentally, into an ovoid shape, which is an economic society led by the middle class—healthier, and more stable. Only when the people have mastered theory can it be turned into material strength. The wisdom of Marx is taken as the main point of his theoretical dissemination of policies. To adopt forms of expression beloved by the people is to allow them to comprehend, and to master, vast and elaborate political philosophies.

Shi Zhihong, who used to be the deputy director of the China Central Policy Research Office, the think tank serving senior Chinese officials, also published comments and articles in the news media. He summed up Xi Jinping's general philosophy in verse:

> One, two, three, four, and five;
> To hunt tigers on mountains high above,
> To lead the new normal,
> To create wealth, so that people may live.

After it was reported by the media, the verse spread widely on the Internet. Shi Zhihong interprets it as follows: One, two, three, four, and five stand for "*one* China Dream," "*two* centenaries," "*three* strategies," "the *Four*-Pronged Comprehensive Strategy," and "the *fifth* modernization."

The one "China Dream" was put forth by General Secretary Xi Jinping on his visit to the exhibition The Road to Rejuvenation on November 29, 2012: "To bring about a great rejuvenation of the Chinese nation is the greatest dream of the Chinese nation since modern times."

"Two centenaries" was a goal put forth by Xi Jinping when he was in charge of drafting the report of 18th CPC National Congress from January to November in 2012: "To finish building a moderately prosperous society in all respects by the time the Communist Party of China celebrates its centenary in 2021; and to turn China into a modern socialist country that is prosperous, strong, democratic, culturally advanced, and harmonious by the time the Republic of China celebrates its centenary in 2049."

"Three strategies" was another goal, described by Xi Jinping in the Central Economic Working Conference on December 9, 2014: "The three strategies include 'The Belt and Road Initiatives', the Beijing-Tianjin-Hebei Region, and the Yangtze River Economic Zone."

The Four-Pronged Comprehensive Strategy was eventually summarized by Xi Jinping during his visit to Jiangsu Province in December, 2013: "To enact comprehensive measures to finish building a moderately prosperous society, deepen reform, advance the law-based governance of China, and strengthen Party self-discipline."

A "Fifth modernization" was put forth in a speech delivered by Xi Jinping at the opening ceremony for the special seminar for major provincial and minister leaders on February 17, 2014: "We have mentioned many modernizations, including agricultural modernization, industrial modernization, scientific and technological modernization, and the modernization of national defense. This is the time to assert the urgency of the modernization of China's system of governance and its governance capacity."

"To hunt tigers on mountains high above" refers to Xi Jinping's ongoing tough stance against corruption, a zero-tolerance policy—full enforcement, and uncompromising, limitless principles, without exception.

"To lead the new normal" refers to the concept of the "new normal" in economic development that was first put forth in a speech delivered by Xi Jinping at the Central Economic Working Conference on December 10, 2013. A newly sustainable rate of economic growth at a high-to-moderate speed occurs after China's economy has kept growing for more than 30 years—it is a new status quo, a "new normal," that complies with the laws of economic growth. The concept embodies China's respect for the objective laws of economics.

"So that people may live" refers to the CPC Central Committee's commitment to the people first—continuing to increase investments in people's livelihoods, building up a basic social safety net, ensuring there is a cushion for those who are in need and making proper institutional arrangements; and still inputting more than 70 percent of fiscal revenue in people's livelihood in 2014, though the growth of 2014 fiscal revenue was slowed down under the pressure of expenditures.[2]

Historians outline ten important reforms in China's history of thousands of years, including Guanzhong's Reform, Shangyang's Political Reform, the Political Reform of Wang Anshi, Zhang Juzheng's Reform, and other historic measures; however, there were only three successful reforms, and none of them were free of resistances and regressions. The great reform for the century, launched by Deng Xiaoping and enhanced all around by Xi Jinping, can be regarded as an unprecedented reform—one that cannot be compared in its scope to any earlier reform in the history of China. Consider the plan *On Deepening Reform in An All-Around Way* approved in the Third Plenary Session of the 18th CPC Central Committee as an example; one may say this plan to reform the words of Party policy, and strengthen meaning between the lines, is composed of only 20,000 words, but it involves fifteen fields and 60 specific tasks. Each line contains a multitude of directives; great changes will be made to the institutional dynamics of the field if the tasks are successfully implemented. During the drafting of the plan, Xi Jinping made two requests: First, to incorporate content relevant to reforms only, especially important ones—and specific tasks for development should be excluded in principle; second, during amendments, unless on sufficient grounds, any

---

2.   Shi Zhihong: "The 'Two-Pronged Comprehensive Strategy' Will Last Two Centuries," *Global People*, Issue 7, 2015.

amendments that may weaken the intensity of reform or actions necessary to reform will be rejected. Furthermore, any content relevant to reforms, as long as it captures the greatest common denominator and reaches a certain consensus, must be incorporated. Reform is imperative to Xi Jinping and his colleagues. They are ready to assume their responsibility to history.

A Decisive Battle Against Vested Interests

How difficult is it to reform China? The famous writer of modern China, Lu Xun, once joked: "Blood will be shed even if one tries to move a table in China." Mao Zedong agreed with Lu Xun. In 1912, Mao Zedong wrote a political essay entitled "On Shang Yang's Establishing Credibility by Moving a Wood Pole," examining Shang Yang's Reform when he was studying at Hunan Provincial High School. Mao Zedong, at the time not yet 20 years old, wrote sorrowfully:

> Shang Yang's method is a good one. By looking through the historical records of China over 4,000 years, today we must see that Shang Yang is second to none amongst those great politicians that seek the best for their countries and benefit the people, isn't it so? Shang Yang lived at the time of Duke Xiao of Qin when the Central Plains were undergoing countless wars, like a seething cauldron— the land was troubled and unsettled. It was of the utmost difficulty for rulers to pursue victory against the other warring states and unify China. Shang Yang launched the reform in Qin and promulgated decrees to punish malefactors based on laws for the protection of people's entitlements. It called for developing farming and weaving in order to enhance Qin's strength and the people's capacity to lead an abundant life, to enhance military forces for the national prestige of Qin, and to help put people to work. It was a great policy that was truly unprecedented in the history of China. But the people refused to believe in the reform, to such an extent that Shang Yang had to establish credibility by erecting a wooden pole, asking one of his subjects to move it, while promising to pay if he did so [and fulfilling his promise, despite the subjects' earlier disbelief]. What I learned was how painstaking a ruler can be, how foolish the people can be, and the reasons for the people's ignorance. The source of China's near subjugation in the previous thousands of years, is its rulers' policy of keeping the people in ignorance.

Mao Zedong pointed out profoundly: The people could not understand and believe in reform, however great its measures, due to their undeveloped wisdom. It is nothing but a joke that Shang Yang was forced to motivate the masses to favor reforms that would benefit them by posting a reward.

It can be said that the failures of reforms in the history of China are closely associated with the people's ignorance, ignorance imposed by the ruling class. And Xi Jinping's promotion of reform is forced to confront another strong opponent—the obstruction imposed by vested interests, and by the established government itself.

The media describes 2014 as the first year of deepening all-around reform. Compared with the reform that has taken place in the past 30 years, Xi Jinping's round of reform is, in ways, more arduous, and certainly subject to more exacting standards. Professor Wang Yukai, a professor of the China National School of Administration and the vice president of the China Society of Administrative Reform, explains, "China's development has entered a new stage and the reform has approached the phase of solving the most difficult problems. To fight against vested interests is surely the greatest difficulty of reform; we have not gotten through the danger yet. It is hard to conclude whether we will defeat these vested interests or be swallowed by them. So, to a large extent, the success of the second reform depends on whether we can effectively curb and defeat the entrenched vested interests." He added, "What they call the 'vested interests' is the group that obtains large amounts of influence by means of unfair competitions, and by virtue of public power and policy resources. I delivered an article in 2011, in which I systematically analyzed the patterns in which the vested interests are represented. There are the 'three grays': gray power, gray capital, and gray profiteering."[3]

To Jiang Yukai and other experts on China's national conditions, the obstruction inflicted by the vested interests on reform is a reality, and it could be fatal. He explains: "The vested interests cash out capital in the market through their children, spouses, relatives, and friends, depending on the influence of public power, and become billionaires overnight. This is truly the greatest corruption. There are at least three forms of the vested interests in China: (1) interests represented by corrupt officials; (2) representatives of industrial monopolies; (3) interests representing the real estate and natural resources extraction industries. The three great vested interests hold power, resources, and capital, full-fledged and with enormous potential, and exert considerable social influence on China. In the current environment of China, at least three hostilities have been incited by the vested interests: (1)

---

3.   Jiang Yukai: "Government Reform is the Core of the Reform," *Economic Informa-tion Daily*, September 23, 2014.

official–citizen hostility; (2) capital–labor hostility; (3) rich–poor hostility. China's society is saturated by a hostile attitude against officials and the rich. We can see the shadow of the vested interests behind mass incidents."

China's top leadership never stopped making estimations on the entire reform after the 18th CPC National Congress. There are statements asserting that the deepest reform needs to tackle the toughest issues, that no reform goes smoothly, that reformers must wade across dangerous shoals, and reform will encounter great difficulties, resistances, and risks in the current environment. Xi Jinping repeats in his speeches that we need to have greater courage and determination and must break the barriers raised by vested interests. Xi Jinping has never explicitly used the term "vested interests," but to academic circles and think tanks, he employs the phrase "interest solidification" in reference to the vested interests. Other tough expressions describing the urgency of anti-corruption measures that he has employed are particularly vivid, such as "scraping the poison off the bone;" "to cure with strong drugs;" and "to carry off the black sheep," indicating that the vested interests have become the greatest obstruction to China's reform.

The famous economist Wu Jinglian, who has participated in the process of designing China's economic reform, is called "Market Wu" in academic circles. To him, the greatest concern about the new round of reform by Xi Jinping and China's top leadership lies in the potential resistance of groups of vested interests with closely allied power and capital. In an interview on China Central Television (CCTV), he said, "It takes as many as 20 years to change, to give play to the basic role of the market that was conceived of during the Third Plenary Session of the 14th CPC Central Committee, and to give full play to the decisive role of the market put forward in the Third Plenary Session of the 18th CPC Central Committee. At present, the vested interests formed in the process of high-speed growth over the years have replaced ideological concerns as the greatest obstruction to reform, and they, supported by public power or resources, are testing China's determination to reform."

It can sometimes seem as if every Party authority's irresistible and intrinsic impulse to take advantage of the power of government for revenue, and particularly, to take advantage of power to advance their self-interests. Therefore, the expansion of government power, especially approval power, has become a common fault of China's government departments from top to bottom over the recent years.

"The process of administrative approval is too complex to be completed within a day and a night." In the 2014 Hainan Province Two Sessions, the deputy to the Hainan People's Congress, Xing Yichuan, showed the "Long

March Flow Chart" of administrative approval that he had devised. Five pieces of A3 paper detail the tedious and convoluted process of approving an investment project, from the acquisition of a piece of land, to the completion of all formalities, including more than 30 items of approval and hundreds of official seals; the whole process requires at least 272 approval days.

Xing Yichuan said that the statutory period for the whole approval process is 272 business days, but actually, it always takes longer than 272 working days. For many projects, it can take one to three years. Another developer, in Hainan Province, told the media that it took five years for the government to approve a project, from land acquisition to the commencement of construction.

To standardize government power, and to restrain the power of the Party and government by law, China must allow power holders to operate by themselves, which has to be the greatest challenge every reformer is up against, undoubtedly. The Premier of China State Council Li Keqiang has said many times, quite emotionally, that it is harder "to touch the vested interests than [it is] to touch the soul." But Xi Jinping warns Party officials and government authorities in a forceful tone not to cut down on reform measures: "To deepen reform will inevitably run against someone's 'loot', and encounter various barriers and convoluted networks of influence. It is impossible to satisfy all. To break though the vested interests and stake the reform requires courage, superior judgment, and the ability to assume responsibilities. It will be difficult to implement new measures and advance essential work if we are afraid of making bold moves."[4]

Apart from the responsibilities as the general secretary of the CPC Central Committee, the president of China, and the chairman of the Central Military Commission, with the purpose of promoting the new round of reform on an unparalleled scale, Xi Jinping also holds the posts of the chairman of the China National Security Council and leader of four leading groups responsible for implementing the new initiatives: the Central Committee Deepening Reform Leading Group, the Central Committee Network Security and Informatization Group, the CMC Deepening Reform Group for National Defense and the Military, and the Central Committee Finance and Economy Leading Group. We can be assured that Xi Jinping has devoted painstaking efforts toward the new round of reform; the great determination toward reform, as well as the intensity, the depth, and the breadth of the vested interests that will be uprooted, all are unprecedented.

---

4.   *Excerpts of Xi Jinping's Statements on Deepening Reform*, p. 152, Central Party Literature Press, May 2014.

III. THE TWO CENTENARY GOALS: CHINA'S TURN AS THE PROTAGONIST

At the beginning of 2015, Professor Joseph Stiglitz of Columbia University published an article entitled "The Chinese Century" in *Vanity Fair*. He wrote that, measured by purchasing power parity (PPP), China's GDP surpassed the United States' in 2014 to become the first in the world. From 2015 on, the world is entering "the Chinese century." Will 2015 become the first year of the Chinese century? Believers argue that there are also other trends, in addition to the fact that China's PPP-based GDP has surpassed the US, supporting the argument that the Chinese century has begun, trends such as strong advocacy for the Free Trade Agreement of the Asia Pacific (FTAAP) and BRICs Development Bank, and China's carrying out the vast and ambitious Belt and Road Initiatives, as well as hosting the World Internet Conference, among others. However, those who disagree believe that China's economic growth has his its upper limit recently, and will even claim that the era of China is about to end. The Chinese Academy of Social Sciences has published the *Yellow Book of the World Economy* for 2015, which argues that China may become the country that makes the greatest contribution to global economic growth. Professor Jin Canrong, Renmin University of China, argues that the contemporary China is best viewed through the historical analogy of the United States in 1872, when the PPP-based GDP of the US surpassed the UK for the first time. But the world did not enter the "American century" until the end of World War I; in Jin's view, the first year of the Chinese century still has many years to arrive.

China's goal to become the world's most prosperous nation is unshakable in the hearts of the Chinese people, although most of them are too afraid to accept the title of "world's number one" at the time. Xi Jinping did not say "world's number one" when he put forth the Two Centenary Goals, but it is the utmost goal that China's leaders and the Chinese people share—to make China the most prosperous nation in the world. Now, the mystery is *when*.

Surpassing the United States: Not the Ultimate Goal

"When the history of 2014 is written, it will take note of a large fact that has received little attention: 2014 was the last year in which the United States could claim to be the world's largest economic power. China enters 2015 in the top position, where it will likely remain for a very long time, if not forever. In doing so, it returns to the position it held through most of human history."

In "The Chinese Century," Professor Stiglitz writes that, in many ways— for instance, in terms of exports, household savings, and infrastructure construction—China long ago surpassed the US. China still trails America when it comes to the number of patents awarded, but it is closing that gap. He also called on the US Government to face up to the emergence of a new order of global politics and economics. He lent context by analyzing previous tectonic shifts in global economic power. Great Britain acted as the world's dominant power for a century, and still remained so for a time, even after being surpassed by the United States economically in the 1970s.

Premature claims of the arrival of the Chinese century emerge frequently in the American media. BloombergView published an article entitled "China Steps in as World's New Bank," which stated, ironically, "Thanks to China, Christine Lagarde of the International Monetary Fund, Jim Yong Kim of the World Bank and Takehiko Nakao of the Asian Development Bank may no longer have much meaningful work to do." The article also claimed that Beijing's recent currency assistance to Russia, Venezuela, and Argentina was a sign of putting an end to the Bretton Woods System, which utilizes the US dollar at its core. But what have America and its allies done? Europe is asking for Beijing's help to save the euro market. And Laos and Vietnam understand quite well that China seldom writes checks without conditions, yet China seems a more appealing option than IMF loans, with their myriad of restrictions.

The New York Times published articles asserting that China's leaders had revealed "the great national ambition" of trying to prove that China was not a fearsome warlike country, but one that would love to help small countries. Due to the poor fortunes of modern China, it always trailed international conditions; but China has now participated in the causes of great powers, shifting world order and setting new rules.

Professor Stiglitz's aim is to advise the American government not to attempt to curb China because a new order of global politics and economics is forming as a result of the new economic reality that the US cannot change. His article warns that if the United States reacts to China in the wrong manner, it risks a backlash that could result in a dysfunctional global economy. Nevertheless, his proposal that the Chinese century began in 2015 still provokes lively discussions in international political circles.

Given the rapid development of the economy, an overconfident view believing the Chinese century has come has emerged, and a new global mentality that the "China model" beats the "American model"—the view most popular at the height of the subprime crisis in the US; the other response is to recognize that in some western countries' views, China will overtake the US as the world's number one, due to a conspiracy with the purpose of imposing more international responsibilities on China's shoulders. But most

Chinese people see the title "world's number one" and the concept of the "Chinese century" as excessive—an exaggeration, albeit a flattering one.

On March 15, 2015, soon after issues concerning China becoming the world's largest economic power were publicized, the Premier of China State Council, Li Keqiang, offered an honest response: "This kind of statement frequently comes to my attention when I am abroad, which always makes me feel as if it is a joke. According to statistics from international authorities, China, at the most, is the world's second economic power. More importantly, China is ranked after 80 other places if we consider per capita GDP. Before the spring festival not long ago, I visited two households in a village in west China. One was a mother and a son living in a damaged tile-roofed house. The son was in his forties but was too poor to have a wife. The other one raised a college student with so many efforts and hardships, but his sister was still working in another place in order to put the brother to college. It was a heartache. In fact, there are many families like this out there. The World Bank's criteria will say there are still nearly 200 million people in poverty and China is an authentic developing country."

The current refusal of the Chinese people to admit that their country has become the "world's number one" certainly does not indicate that the Chinese people are willing to stay still as the "world's number two," or accept the position of a second-class country.

Followed by the Two Centenary Goals put forward in the report of the 15th National Congress, it is reiterated in the report of the 18th National Congress to finish building a moderately prosperous society in all respects by the time the Communist Party of China celebrates its centenary in 2021; and to turn China into a modern socialist country that is prosperous, strong, democratic, culturally advanced, and harmonious by the time the Republic of China celebrates its centenary in 2049.

Xi Jinping repeatedly stresses that the Two Centenary Goals is akin to a military order, an unshakable goal we should spare no effort to achieve, since he was elected as the general secretary of the CPC Central Committee at the 18th CPC National Congress in 2012. In a meeting with representatives of Boao Forum for Asia on October 20, 2014, Xi Jinping stressed: "The Chinese people are working in unison to complete the building of a moderately prosperous society in all respects, and to comprehensively deepen reform, advance law-based governance, and enforce strict Party conduct. Our objective is to realize the Two Centenary Goals."

People have different ways of interpreting China's Two Centenary Goals, but however they are analyzed, they still need to place China within a historical context in order to obtain insight of the true meaning of the "dream to strengthen China" that the Chinese people hold in their hearts.

In the report entitled "China and the World" in the eighteenth century, the famous Chinese historian of the Qing Dynasty, Dai Yi, pointed out that in 1900, the world had a population of 900 million, including 300 million Chinese people; China's grain yield also accounted for one third of the world's, putting it first place in world production. In the meantime, the value of China's industrial output remained 33.3 percent of the world's, while the entirety of Europe accounted for 28.1 percent. In the eighteenth century, there were ten metropolises with populations greater than 500,000; six of them were in China—Beijing, Nanjing, Yangzhou, Suzhou, Hangzhou and Guangzhou. The French enlightenment thinker Voltaire pointed out that the Chinese nation "is second to none in respect to ethics, morals, governance, and politics—owing to its identity as the world's oldest nation."

But China fell into failure due to decline in the following two centuries. In those dark days after China was defeated by Japan in the First Sino-Japanese War, Sun Yat-sen, the pioneer of China's revolution still called out the slogan—China was to be "the world's most prosperous nation." In the petition to Qing Viceroy Li Hongzhang in 1894, Sun Yat-sen said that China would "outpace and exceed Europe;" in *How China's Industry Will Develop* in 1919, he wrote that as long as China's industry prospered, "we would not only keep pace with America, we would be four times as productive."

To Mao Zedong, catching up to and surpassing the United States was not China's foremost goal; China's goal was to make great contributions to humankind. However, Mao Zedong did believe that China could only contribute to the cause of humanity by surpassing the US. On October 29, 1955, in a lecture at a forum on the transition of industry and commerce from capitalism to socialism, Mao Zedong said: "Our goal is to catch up to America, and to surpass America. They only have 100 million people, and we have 600 million. We should be able to catch up to America. Even if it takes decades; depending on how hard we work, it could take as little as 50 years, or even 75 years—but 75 years is still just fifteen five-year plans. Only on the day we catch up to America, and surpass America, can we exhale." In 1956, in his "Memorial to Mr. Sun Yat-sen," he wrote: "China is a country with 9,600,000 square kilometers of land and 600 million people. It is only right that we make major contributions to the human race. And for a long time in the past, we've barely contributed anything. That's a fact that makes us ashamed."

Mao Zedong believed in China, as a country with vast territory and the largest population, with a history of civilization one should be proud of: "so if in 50 or 60 years you still cannot catch up to America, what's the matter with you? You deserve to have your membership in the human race revoked!"[5] For the sake of "surpassing the UK and US," China, under the leadership of Mao, Zedong carried out the Great Leap Forward. The consequence was that China suffered a great deal. But the Chinese people still hoped to realize the rise of China and become the world's timekeeper through innovative development. The dream never rests.

Deng Xiaoping spent his life following the goals of a prosperous and strong nation and built a socialist and modernized power. Deng Xiaoping said on May 24, 1977, "The Meiji Restoration is the modern incarnation of a bourgeois national rejuvenation. As the proletariat, we should be able to do even better." In 1985, he highlighted the strategic concept to bring about national revitalization by reform: "We are doing something today that China, in its thousands of years of history, has never accomplished. This reform influences more than just China; it influences the world." On April 7, 1990, in his keystone speech "Revitalizing the Chinese People," Deng Xiaoping said, "We need to use our opportunities and develop China. In the coming century, there is hope for us."

To realize China's development goals, Deng Xiaoping developed the "Three-Step Strategic Plan" for China in the 1980s: The first step, basic sustenance for all, would take ten years; the second step, healthy growth, would take another ten years; and the third step, the grand goal of national revitalization, would be accomplished within the first 50 years of the twenty-first century.

By tracing history people can clarify the logic that China's revitalization plan for this century is not to surpass the US but to meet its own needs, that is, the pursuit of making great contributions to humankind out of the Chinese people's own will.

In 2009, China's *Global Times* invited 85 economists from all around the world to participate in a survey—80 of whom turned in their answers. To the question of how many more years it would take China's economy to catch up to the United States, 23 percent of the experts believed it would happen in ten years; 45 percent believed within 20 years; 17 percent believed within 30 years; and 6 percent and 2 percent believed it would take longer or never happen at all. Now after only five years, China continues to accelerate on the way to catch up to the United States. According to most economists' anticipations, as long as no stagnation or downturn occurs in the future, even with conservative estimation and based on purchasing power, China's economic aggregate will catch up to the US in 2020, and surpass it in 2030.

---

5.   *The China Dream*, pp. 10–11, Liu Mingfu, China Friendship Publishing Co., Ltd., 2010.

The timetable fits Mao Zedong's prediction in 1955, give or take. China's conception of their century is entering the home stretch.

As the helmsman of the great vessel that is China, Xi Jinping knows well his duty is to navigate properly. When Xi Jinping attended the APEC Summit on October 7, 2013, he delivered a speech saying: "China is a great country that allows no disruptive mistakes on fundamental issues; because once such a mistake occurs, there is no turning back, and no remedy. We should explore boldly and be brave enough to blaze new trails; we must also be reliable and prudent, and 'look before we leap.' We must stick to the correct direction of reform and openness, and be certain not to hesitate during the reform."

In the speech, he also stressed: "I hold firm confidence in maintaining the healthy development of China's economy; we must remain vigilant about issues and challenges such as reduction in demand, excess production capacity, local debt, and shadow banking; and pay close attention to impacts that might be caused by external forces. We are taking proper countermeasures to nip [these potential challenges] in the bud."

It is widely believed by commentators that the current term of Chinese leaders is holding a strong hand of cards. As long as they are not rash, avoid disruptive mistakes, refuse to take on evil ways, and don't look back, China's national goal will certainly be realized.

Undoubtedly, as a mature politician who has lived through many tests, Xi Jinping lays an additional ballasting stone to the stability of China's sailing course. Henry Kissinger, who has visited China hundreds of times and has met all of China's previous top leaders, made such a prediction about Xi Jinping. Kissinger understands that Xi shoulders heavy responsibilities, that he is trying to change a country with a population of 1.3 billion, and change the course that China has established over many years. In Kissinger's opinion, at this turning point, where China's population is becoming heavily urbanized, and the world's economy is more and more complex, Xi Jinping will be remembered as a leader bringing great reforms to China, some of which will be of great historic significance.[6]

Are the Chinese Mentally Prepared for Reclaiming the Role of the World's Top Country?

A famous host of CCTV once told of her experience of stepping into the position of a main host from that of a supporting host: As a supporting host at a local TV station in an inland province of China, she answered a call one day from an important news producer of CCTV offering her a new job. "Are

6. *Caixin Weekly*, Issue 11, 2015.

you mentally prepared for becoming famous?" the producer asked.

"I am already famous," she told him. She believed she had been as famous as a main host in the province.

"I mean," the producer stressed, "are you ready to be known by every household in China?"

What does it mean to be known by every household in China?

She figured it out later: People recognize you wherever you go, and people ask for your autograph even when you are shopping in a supermarket. Privacy, or solitude, were no longer possibilities. What bothered her most were the countless calls and emails she would receive every day, asking for help. "You are an A-list celebrity now!"

Standing in the center of the arena, you must face numerous tests and challenges from all angles. This is a feeling all first-time stars and celebrities have in common. China's course of development is similar to the host's experience: In the previous century, China was a "walk-on" figure on the world arena. After the establishment of the Republic of China, it remained unimportant, although it was ever closer to the center of the arena. Over the next 30 years, China was inclined to keep a low profile and focused on economic development, hiding its capabilities and biding its time, with no intention of becoming a major player. But, one day, all of a sudden, China was pushed to the center of the world's arena, surrounded by people proclaiming—"you are the protagonist of the global stage!" It is not hard to imagine the surprise, and the stage fright, in the hearts of the Chinese people.

An American media agency published an analysis report a few years ago showing that the features news story people read most frequently over the previous decade was headlined "China Rises as an Economic Superpower"— even more so than the Iraq War or the 9/11 attack on New York's World Trade Center.

The American Global Language Institute searched newspapers, electronic media, and the Internet with an algorithm to find out people's search trends. The Institute reported that people had a strong interest in the economic engine of Asia. The head of the Institute, Paul Payack, explained that China, by its leaping to a new economic level, has changed the international order, and goes on changing current international orders, and the ramifications of the ongoing transformation might explain why it is such a popular news story over the past ten years. According to Payack, the list was based on statistical analysis of the number of citations on the Internet and in blogs, as well as 50,000 paper media and electronic media websites. The Institute also declared in its report that the rise of China was the most important news story over ten years, leaving the second place far behind by 400 percent; the second place was occupied by stories on the Iraq War.

"The rise of China" became the hottest search-engine terms on the global Internet, indicating that China had certainly become a major player on the world's stage. Like reports on many famous Hollywood stars, the world's attitudes towards the new star, China, were diverse—ranging from positive affirmation to unavoidable negative reports, from embellished stories to malicious gossip. But nevertheless, the previously shy Chinese people, who were used to keeping a low, down-to-earth, profile, suddenly found themselves facing tens of thousands of cameras for the first time.

"Their Own Worst Enemy," published in *The Atlantic*, and written by James Fallows, their senior journalist stationed in China, and "How Can China Understand Other Countries More?" published in Lianhe Zaobao, Singapore, by Lu Yiyi, a special researcher of the Royal Institute of International Affairs and researcher of the China Policy Institute at the University of Nottingham, both reflected similar themes: that the Chinese people barely knew foreign countries; knew little in terms of culture, politics, and systems of foreign governments, had no idea about how different societies operated, and always misjudged foreign trends of policies. The lack of expression shown by their government spokesmen also concerned other countries. To foreigners, the main concern over China was that it would exert more and more influence on the world, but it barely knew anything about the world's views, which could lead to many misconceptions and disputes.

In general, it is a widely held belief that China remains a developing country and its priority lies in domestic affairs; while the world's expectation of China is raised to a level that its people find hard to accept. "G2 collegiality," proposed by the political circle of the United States, is a typical example.

"G2 collegiality" is also known as "Sino-US collegiality," derived from a new word, *Chimerica*, a concept introduced by American economic historian, Niall Ferguson, in *The Sunday Telegraph* on March 4, 2007. He defined "Chimerica" as a community of interests consisting of the greatest consumer, the United States, and the greatest saver, China, and its impacts on the world's economy. Following on from the more famous concept of the "G2" (Group of Two), it clearly shares the same result with "Chimerica." In July 2008, C. Fred Bergsten, the director of the Peterson Institute of International Economics, published "Equal Partnership" in the highly regarded journal *Foreign Affairs*, which proposed a solution for the United States to "cope with the challenge of China's economy," to establish a "G2" model between the US and China, a model of consultation on an equal footing, and leading the global economy. But in regard to "G2 collegiality," Chinese scholars believe instinctively that the "G2" concept is unrealistic and does more harm rather than good.

First, it is noteworthy to doubt whether the US sincerely wants China to play the leading role alongside it. Cooperation within limits has been the terms of the American government's keynote policy towards China; will it give away a part of the leadership? And it also does not fit China's position as a large developing country and its basic diplomatic policy—China never intends to pursue hegemony. Secondly, in addition to China and the US, there are also the other greatest economic entities: Europe, Japan, the three other countries that constitute the "BRICs;" each one with different interests. China's strength is not as the leader, its challenge will be to co-manage and co-govern along with the United States. The Chinese people cannot deny that to strengthen cooperation between China and the US will be beneficial for the world, but doing so in practice is a different matter.

No matter how scholars argue, the balance of power in the international community has not fundamentally changed: The premier position of the United States has not been altered, and China remains a developing country. As a country with important influence in the world, enhancing the dialogue level between China and the US (including leaders' regular or irregular meetings), working together on strategic cooperation, coordinating official positions and policy, will undoubtedly be conducive to world peace and development, and major international security issues should be properly addressed and resolved. Therefore, strengthening China's relationship with the US is a notion beyond reproach, but the most important issue is still for both countries to follow their own paths, and develop toward their own betterment, so they can make greater contributions to the world.

One Xi and Two Roosevelts

In the history of the United States, there were two presidents named Roosevelt: Theodore Roosevelt, known as "Teddy," who served as the 26th president, and Franklin D. Roosevelt, known as "FDR," the 32nd President.

The former adopted reform policies with a tough stance, which made him one of the greatest presidents in the history of America. His fair trade laws included consumer protection provisions, his antitrust laws ensured punishment for monopolistic behaviors within industries, and he focused on the maintenance of American wildlife habitats and American wildernesses. In foreign policy, he expanded the US Navy and constructed the Panama Canal, and some scholars believe that he is the creator of modern America, calling him the founder of American modernization. It was in the hands of

Theodore Roosevelt that America became the world's number one country and overtook Great Britain in total economic output and, in international affairs, took the initiative to exert the influence of America. He also won the Nobel Peace Prize due to his successful mediation of the Russo-Japanese war.

Franklin D. Roosevelt led America out of the mire of the Great Depression, led the country to victory in World War II, and firmly established the "big brother" role of the US in the world today. With his wide vision and firm determination, he ended American isolationist policy, led the US to compete with Europe, debuted a strategic design for his country after World War II, and made a crucial contribution to the creation of the United Nations. Thus, FDR is a well-deserved founder of contemporary America's international position.

The accomplishments of the two Roosevelts enabled the US to realize its economic rise and coordinate international and domestic situations. Domestically, the US pursued reform with keen determination, the shackles of monopoly capitalism and the interference of vested interest groups were broken. A new system, making rule of law play a leading role in the order of the market economy, was established and pushed the US into the orbit of a modern country. In the international political and diplomatic fields, the two Presidents Roosevelt helped build a platform for the country to lead the international new order and succeeded in making the US the principal power. Chinese scholars such as Liu Yongtao have pointed out that in analyzing the experience and enlightenment of America's rise, there are certain similarities with the rapid development of China, through the problems and challenges encountered by the US in the second half of the nineteenth century. Both countries developed at an alarming speed, cities expanded, material wealth accumulated, and lives were enriched. The US took the opportunity of the second industrial revolution, and became the world's economic and technological leader.

In the 30 years after implementing a policy of reform and opening up, against a background of globalization, China has promoted a four-pronged modernization plan with unprecedented speed, and become the world's second-largest economic entity. However, sharp social conflicts and contradictions have seriously restricted the pursuit of the country's goals toward achieving further development of its overall national strength. Therefore, the government, the people, and all elements of society must adapt to social and cultural changes stimulated by industrial and urban development, and adjust legal and administrative management methods to adapt to an era full of change and restructuring.[7]

More plainly, under the leadership of Xi Jinping, China is faced with the problem of future development, which is, in essence, similar to the problems faced by the two Roosevelts. On the problem of economic development, a powerful law-based government should be established to advocate a "Fair Deal" philosophy aimed at protecting the interests of consumers and restricting the monopolies of large enterprises. Theodore Roosevelt described his presidential role as the "citizen's housekeeper," and made himself a true leader in order to fulfill his self-described role. After he took office, he proceeded to resolve existing major national issues at that time, put forward feasible solutions, and gain the support of voters and the congress.

As far as Theodore Roosevelt was concerned, industrial monopolies were a major problem. The authority of federal executive departments had to be established, and antitrust laws were used to deal with monopolistic enterprises, or unjust business practices, involving the American Tobacco Company, DuPont, the New Haven Railway Company, and Mobil Oil. But Theodore Roosevelt also realized that industrial development was inevitable: big enterprises won leadership roles in world industry, and the government needed to maintain trust with industry and business leaders. The US needed large industrial and commercial enterprises, but required a strong government to supervise them.

Similarly, modern-day China must break down the barriers imposed by vested interests, promote fair competition between large and small enterprises, especially between state-owned monopolies and private capital enterprises, and, at the same time, the international competitiveness of China's leading business enterprises must be maintained. China's world-leading position in manufacturing must also be maintained, and in international affairs China needs to adapt to the transition from a supporting role to a leading position, and even eventually to the premier position.

China needs to lead the world to rectify unreasonable old rules, establish new rules, and become the steward of world peace and justice. It must occupy the moral high ground, strongly object to totalitarianism, terrorism, and extremism; this is a responsibility given by history to China, and a sincere aspiration of developing countries for China. The strategy of keeping a low profile is not out of date; it emphasizes that China needs to be pragmatic and humble, and avoid overestimating its own strength and ability. It should also firmly hold the bottom line, that is, putting its own country in order should always be the first priority. At the same time, the domestic development of China is closely reliant on the international environment; if it does not open

7.   *Beijing Daily & Theory Weekly*, September 15, 2014.

up a new situation and construct international policies accommodating of the national development goals of China, it would be impossible for China to achieve its strategic objective of returning to the top of the world. In this aspect, there is a similarity with Franklin D. Roosevelt working hard to persuade the American people to end isolationism, and take the initiative to guide the establishment of a new post-war international order.

Throughout the history of the rise of the world's great powers, it seems that it is often most difficult to be second in the world. France and Germany tried to challenge Britain's imperial hegemony, but ultimately sank like stones. Even the mighty Napoleon had to suffer imposed exile, and eventually death, on Saint Helena Island. Japan and the former Soviet Union poured all their resources into competing for global supremacy against the US, but ultimately failed. Now Xi Jinping is at the stage of transformation from the world's number two toward gradually becoming its leader. It will be fascinating to see if this miracle can be achieved.

In the autumn of 2014, *Xi Jinping: The Governance of China* was published, systematically compiling Xi Jinping's important articles and speeches from the 18th National Congress of the Communist Party of China from November, 2012, to June, 2014. It presented an opportunity for the international community to understand Xi Jinping's core beliefs on domestic and foreign affairs. Former German Chancellor Helmut Schmidt wrote a lengthy review of the book, commenting that *Xi Jinping: The Governance of China* told foreign readers the philosophy the Chinese leader followed, and the strategy on which China's development depended. The world can better understand the development of China, especially China's domestic and foreign policies.

Former German Chancellor Gerhard Schroeder wrote in the preface of the book that since Xi Jinping began serving as the general secretary of the CPC Central Committee and president, the Chinese government has proposed ambitious reform programs, covering various fields. *Xi Jinping: The Governance of China* explains the position of President Xi Jinping and the Chinese leaders, and can guide all readers to understand the dynamics of Chinese politics. The book establishes that the realization of the dreams of the Chinese nation—rejuvenation, openness, a stable and prosperous China—is consistent with the interests of Europe. Jon Taylor, of the University of St. Thomas in Houston, Texas, believes that the book can provide insight into Xi Jinping's thoughts on the China Dream, and under his leadership and the Communist Party of China, how the country will be run for the next few years and how its plans will be realized.

On March 28, 2014, Xi Jinping delivered a speech in Germany, and highlighted the collective consciousness of China, ready to follow the path of peaceful development he has consistently advocated: "History is the best teacher, it faithfully records the footprints of every country, and provides inspiration to the future development of every country." He explained that, in the century from the Opium Wars in the 1840s to the founding of a new China in 1949, war was frequent in Chinese society—internal wars and foreign invasions occurred in cycles, bringing painful suffering to the Chinese people. An aggressive war launched by the Japanese caused a tragedy with casualties numbering around 35 million in total. This tragic history has left an imprint on the Chinese, who have always believed "Never do unto others what you would not have them do unto you."

China needs peace, just as living things need air, like trees need sunshine to grow. Only by following the path of peaceful development, only with countries all over the world working together to maintain world peace, can China achieve its own goals, and make greater contributions to the world.[8]

---

8.   *Xi Jinping: The Governance of China* (Chinese), p. 266.

CHAPTER
3

Internal Reform in the Communist Party of China

On July 11, 2014, Liu Yunshan, a member of the Standing Committee of the Political Bureau, attended an international conference, The Chinese Communist Party in the Eyes of European Scholars, and delivered a speech entitled "Several Aspects by which to Know the Chinese Communist Party." He believed that "to know the Communist Party of China well is the best way to know China. Why? The answer to that question is quite simple, that is, the Communist Party of China (CPC) is China's governing party and the leader of China's revolution, construction, and reform. Under the CPC's leadership, China has achieved its current level of development; and the CPC's leadership acts as the most essential feature of socialism with Chinese characteristics. To understand the CPC is to hold the key to unlock the mystery of where China is coming from, and where it is going."[1]

People should know this; unfortunately, it has been overlooked for a long while in the West.

In 1991, the Soviet Union failed to make a stable transformation to democracy, collapsing in an instant. The fact shocked the Soviet Union's onlookers in western countries. All China watchers of the time believed that China was also sitting on a volcanic vent, and eventually an inability

---

1.   Liu Yunshan. "Several Aspects by which to Know the Chinese Communist Party," *People's Daily Online*, July 10, 2014.

to cope with increased and intensified social contradictions would result in the governing party leading the regime toward falling apart. However, the "theory of China's collapse" that arises every couple of years has brought no bad luck to China, and the CPC has not fallen from power due to the stress of social contradictions as some had expected; instead, China's development momentum has just become stronger and stronger, as has the people's support of the CPC.

Western scholars were urged to reflect upon the fact that the CPC and the Communist Party of the Soviet Union (CPSU) shared nothing in common in regard to their fates—what helped the CPC to withstand the stress, to swim against the stream and do an incredible job when the fate of socialism was in question? In 1997, Professor Bruce J. Dickson of George Washington University provided one possible explanation: He believed that the CPC's effective response to the external stress could be attributed to its adaptability.[2] In 2003, Professor Andrew J. Nathan of Columbia University, who had maintained a negative point of view towards the CPC, changed his tone and thus made a relatively positive judgment, specifically attributing the CPC's survival to the Party's inherent "resilience."[3] Either adaptability or resilience will naturally lead to the capacity for internal Party reform.

The CPC described it in a customary way: "If you want to work with iron, you must be tough yourself." It requires every member of the Party to be tough in morality and ability. The Party organizations must have a firm leadership, be able to respond to various problems of the reality of current society, and shoulder the responsibility as the core leadership of the nation. It is also important to take tough measures when needed to reform and to self-reform the Party.

Xi Jinping stressed that "to work with iron, you must be tough yourself" upon his first appearance at a press conference covered by foreign and Chinese media on November 15, 2012, immediately after he was elected as the general secretary of CPC Central Committee. He said that, under the new situation, the CPC still faced many serious challenges; and there were still many problems demanding prompt solutions in the Party, especially corruption, isolation from the masses, formality, and bureaucratism among some Party members and cadres. By employing the maxim "to work with iron, you must be tough yourself," he requested that the entire Party be prepared for increased discipline, and make great efforts to tackle these problems, so as to give the CPC a strong core of leadership in the cause of

2.   Dickson, Bruce J. *Democratization in China and Taiwan: The Adaptability of Leninist Parties.* New York: Clarendon Press 1997.

3.   Nathan, Andrew J. "Authoritarian Resilience." *Journal of Democracy*, 14(1).

building socialism with Chinese characteristics.[4]

It is clearly in the mind of the CPC that only in the following three ways might the governing position of the CPC be shaken: first, failure to do its job, causing the people to rise in revolt; second, defeat by foreign enemies; and third, problems within the Party. The first two are extremely unlikely, while being ruined internally seems to hold the greatest possibility. Therefore, "the Party should supervise its own conduct and run itself with strict discipline to fully solve the prominent, open problems it has." It is a task demanding prompt solutions from the 18th CPC National Congress. Xi Jinping set the keynote for the subsequent anti-corruption storm by delivering a speech at the press conference.

I. HUNTING TIGERS

It is a useful visual metaphor to imagine those corrupt officials as tigers; generally, it is only corrupt officials above the vice-ministerial level who are called "tigers," while those above the deputy national level are called "big tigers." Few tigers, and even fewer big tigers, were caught during anti-corruption purges in the past; hence, there is a popular saying in Chinese society: "Just swat the flies only, do not hunt the tigers." Since the 18th CPC National Congress witnessed the CPC's determination to hunt tigers and regain people's confidence in the Party, four "big tigers," namely Zhou Yongkang, Xu Caihou, Ling Jihua, and Su Rong, have been dealt with. According to survey results provided by the China Anti-corruption Research Center at the Chinese Academy of Social Sciences (CASS), 93.7 percent of leading cadres, 88 percent of general cadres, and 75.8 percent of urban and rural citizens have shown confidence in initiatives combating corruption.[5]

The Fight Against Corruption will Be Harder in Ten Years if it Is Not Attempted Now
Ten years ago, Kenneth G. Lieberthal summarized the challenges the CPC was facing into the following two aspects: first, lack of an inspiring ideological state that can motivate Party members to be competent as public servants and endure personal sacrifice; second, corruption, which has extensively

---

4.   Party Literature Research Center of the CPC Central Committee. *Collection of Important Literature—Since the Eighteenth CPC National Congress (I)*, Beijing: Central Party Literature Press, 2014, p. 70.

5.   China Anti-corruption Research Center, Chinese Academy of Social Sciences: *2014 Report on Implementation of Combating Corruption and Upholding Integrity*, Social Science Academic Press (China), December 2014, p. 59.

penetrated certain organizations of the Party, and can grow to such an extent that it brings harm to the Party's moral authority and discipline and to economic growth and social stability in practice.[6] Apparently, the CPC shared deeper feelings and used more stringent words than Lieberthal. In the report of the 18th CPC National Congress, phrases such as "fatal damage," "the collapse of the Party and the fall of the state" were adopted to emphasize potential dangers caused by corruption problems, to lay stress on the necessity of diligently combating corruption and upholding integrity, and keeping vigilance in mind against all corrupting influences. Such warnings were proven to be no mere rhetoric intended only to frighten people from those "big tigers" and "small flies." Subsequent anti-corruption actions proved their seriousness.

The inventory of the confiscated possessions of Xu Caihou, the former member of the Political Bureau of the CPC Central Committee and former vice chairman of the Central Military Commission, shocked well-informed investigators—piles of cash, US dollars, euros, and renminbi flooded the basement under the 2,000 square-meter luxury property, loot weighing more than a metric ton. The cash was followed by gold, silver, jewelry and various antiques, as well as calligraphic scrolls and paintings dating back to the Tang, Song, Yuan, and Ming dynasties. Dozens of trucks were used to carry it all away. A leader of the Central Committee said with bitter hatred about the case of Xu Caihou: "Xu's crazy accumulation of wealth by unfair means is unimaginable!"[7]

As unimaginable as the excesses of the big tigers could be, small flies were also a shock to people's eyes. For example, more than RMB 200 million was confiscated from Wei Pengyuan's home, the former deputy director of the Coal Department of the National Energy Administration, constituting a case involving the greatest amount of illicit money discovered by the investigating and prosecuting apparatus since the establishment of the People's Republic of China (PRC).[8] In the home of the "billionaire water official" Ma Chaoqun, the disciplinary inspection department found tens of millions in RMB, 37 kilograms of gold, and 68 certificates of real estate, an unbelievable extent of corruption.[9] And Ma Chaoqun was merely the

---

6.   Lieberthal, Kenneth G. *Governing China: From Revolution to Reform*, translated by Hu Guocheng, et al., Beijing: China Social Sciences Publishing House, 2010, pp. 340–341.

7.   Zhong Jian. "An Inside Story on Confiscation of the Traitor Xu Caihou," *Phoenix Weekly*, Issue 32, 2014.

8.   Zhang Lei. "The Supreme People's Procuratorate: More Than 35 Thousand Were Charged in Previous 9 Months," *China Discipline Inspection and Supervision*, November 1, 2014.

9.   Qi Leijie. "Sledgehammer Fight against Corruption in Hebei Province: 14808 Cas-

general manager of the General Water Supply Company for the Beidaihe District, Qinhuangdao City, at the most a cadre at the section level. Such "arch corrupt official at low levels" are not rare by any means across China, frequent corruptions occurred among cadres at the section and the lowest level whose titles are even inferior to a "Grade 7 Petty Official." Data from *Southern Weekly* show that during the ten years following 2001, among those corruption cases involving an amount of ten millions RMB or more, which have been reported by the media, there were at least seventeen officials at or below the section level, including six cases involving around 100 million RMB. Cases involving these small figures, such as "Land Lady" Luo Yaping, "Roving Bandit of the Official Circle" Mu Xincheng, the "Red Head official merchant" Hao Pengjun, "Gang Sheriff" Guan Jianjun, "Billionaire Subsection Chief" Li Huabo, and the "Social Player" Li Zhiqiang, among others, can stun people, even if they are not high-ranking officials.[10] The aforementioned statistics do not cover all convictions, and are not even close to all the corruption crimes that have taken place.

A larger, sinister, reality is that the big tigers and the small flies have spun a large network of vested interests. It is known from the CNPC Nest Case, CMCC Nest Case, and China Southern Airlines Nest Case, as well as the landslide corruptions in Chongqing, Shanxi, and other places, that appealing advantages and interests have made those officials who hold power form a community of interests with a complicated set of social relations and a complete chain of influences. From 2013 to 2014, when a "mine disaster" occurred in Shanxi political circles, seven out of the thirteen members of the Standing Committee of Shanxi Provincial Party Committee elected in 2011 were either transferred or removed from office, and Yun Chunqing, the provincial secretary, and Tang Tao, the minister of organization, were also transferred. Jin Daoming, Ling Zhengce, and Du Shanxue were in the "three groups" of the Shanxi Provincial Party Committee, Provincial People's Political Consultative Conference, and provincial government, respectively, thus the capture of them was considered the raiding of a "corruption nest." At the municipal level, three secretaries of the Taiyuan Municipal Party Committee and three directors of the Public Security Bureau were taken under investigation; at the county level, two secretaries of the Gaoping Municipal Party Committee and their mayors, and one secretary of the Commission for Discipline Inspection were taken under investigation;

es during 10 Months," *Xinhua Net*, November 12, 2014. http://news.xinhuanet.com/2014-11/12/c_1113217687.htm

10.   Su Yongtong, Ren Mina, and Nie Meng. "Corruption at Section Level Becomes a Hidden Danger, More "Arch Corruption Officials" Involving Tens of Millions under Investigation for Ten Years," *Southern Weekly*, April 1, 2011.

at the village level, during the investigation of a case for an urban village, dozens of cadres of the Party and government were found guilty, including one cadre at the municipal bureau level, and were found to possess dozens of properties in Beijing and Shanghai as well as family properties worth more than 10 million RMB.[11] In the Hunan Hengyang "Bribery Case" revealed at the end of 2013, Xu Shousheng, the secretary of Hunan Provincial Party Committee was understandably shocked as, upon investigation, a total of 56 elected deputies to the Provincial People's Congress were involved in bribery for support votes, involving RMB 110 million given to 518 deputies to Hengyang Municipal People's Congress and 68 staff members at the congress.[12]

On March 22, 2015, in an interview by a journalist from the overseas edition of the *People's Daily*, Professor Zheng Yongnian, the director of the East Asian Institute, National University of Singapore, pointed out that the present represent a window of opportunity hard to come by again for China to combat corruption. If Xi Jinping does not do so, the chances of success will be very small in another ten years, when groups of vested interests will become too powerful. If they are turned into political oligarchs from economic oligarchs, China will be in a situation like Russia in the past, or Ukraine today. China must be sure to seize the opportunity and unearth corruption from the root.[13]

Plainly speaking, in ten years' time China's anti-corruption mission will not be possible if we do not exert great efforts toward it now. Over the past 30 years, China has always industriously struggled against corruption, however, neither such a great effort nor determination was comparable to the renewed efforts after the 18th National Congress. Evidently, the CPC has been well aware of the fact that decades of efforts in previous decades failed to obtain significant results and the Party hit a bottleneck in fighting against corruption, one which will be difficult to overcome without sufficient determination, willpower, and courage.

Xi Jinping revealed his determination in regard to anti-corruption measures with the statement, "If you want to work with iron, you must be tough yourself," upon his first appearance on November 15, 2012. Two days later, in the first collective learning session of the 18th Political Bureau of the CPC Central Committee, he then used the statement, "Matter decays first,

---

11.   Wang Rulin. *Three Features of Shanxi Sliding Corruption, Phoenix Information—High-level Talks at the Two Sessions.*

12.   "Hunan Province Strictly Investigates Sabotaging Election Case in Hengyang," *Xinhua Net*, December 28, 2013.

13.   Zheng Yongnian, National University of Singapore. "Current China Needs an Aggressive Xi Jinping," *People's Daily Online*, March 22, 2015.

vermin comes soon afterwards," to caution officials. He also stressed that, "to allow corruption to grow more prevalent and entrenched will eventually lead to the collapse of the Party and the fall of the state." From Xi Jinping's determined "voice of anti-corruption," people hold hopes and expectations as to how much effort the Central Committee will exert to crack down on corruption.

Zero Tolerance for Corruption

After comparing the governing performances between Hong Kong's Independent Commission Against Corruption (ICAC) and Korea's anti-corruption agency, Korean scholar Choi found that the reason why Hong Kong was more successful in this regard primarily lay in the fact that the leaders have stronger determination and commitment to crack down on corruption.[14] The CPC described the issue in a customary way: "Our tolerance for corruption is zero."[15]

Hong Kong was once a severely corruption-affected area. Only 30 years ago, it turned itself into a city known to everyone as a hub of honesty and high efficiency. The Hong Kong government advocates an attitude of "zero tolerance" for corruption, and as an expression of that attitude, it formed the ICAC, which plays an important role in the struggle against corruption. Tony Kwok, an international anti-corruption expert and the former ICAC deputy commissioner, expressed the consistent anti-corruption philosophy of the ICAC: the ICAC pays no attention to the amounts involved in a case but adopts a standard of "zero tolerance," that under no circumstances can even a single dollar be taken by unethical means, and "corruption does not become entrenched through an official collecting millions on their first day, but developed step by step, over time."[16]

In January, 2014, in the Third Plenary Session of the 18th Central Commission for Discipline Inspection, Xi Jinping stressed that China should

---

14.   Choi Jin-Wook. 2009. "Institutional Structures an Effectiveness of Anti-corruption Agencies: A Comparative Analysis of South Korea and Hong Kong." *Asian Journal of Political Science*, 7(2): 195–214.

15.   "Zero tolerance" derives from the Broken Windows Theory introduced by James Q. Wilson and George L. Kelling; their hypothesis: Consider a building with a few broken windows. If the windows are not repaired, the tendency is for vandals to break a few more windows. Eventually, they may even break into the building, and if it's unoccupied, perhaps become squatters or light fires inside. It is a psychological theory that reveals the relations between minor violations and crimes, indicating we must punish minor criminal acts severely. James Q. Wilson and George L. Kelling. 1982. "Broken Windows." *Atlantic Monthly*, 249(3): 29–38. Xi Jinping has quoted the Broken Theory more than once.

16.   Li Xiangyu, Ren Haoming. "Hong Kong's Antiseptic Ideas of 'Zero-Tolerance' and Their Clue," *Academic Search for Truth and Reality*, Issue 5, 2008.

"hold a determination equal to that of curing illness with strong drugs, governing disorders with strict laws and regulations, have the courage to scrape the poison off the bone, to firmly carry out the reconstruction of proper Party conduct, and of an honest and clean government, and maintain the struggle against corruption."[17] He went on to say that "a small leak will sink a great ship. We must nip evil in the bud to advance anti-corruption measures, and accept only 'zero tolerance' and 'zero corruption'; we must remove the source of corruption, practice 'zero tolerance' and capture and punish anyone guilty of corruption. Only by these means can we 'scrape the corruption off the Party.'"

The CPC does what it says. The stronger and stronger storm of anti-corruption efforts following the 18th National Congress has lived up to, and surpassed, not only the expectations of officials at all levels, but also of the whole international community; it had not occurred to anyone that the CPC's determination and intensity could be so strong. The "storm of incorruptible government" that is changing China has shocked the world, with unprecedented raids on more officials, at higher levels, in a wider range of sectors, and with stronger accountability efforts than ever.

Li Chuncheng, the former deputy secretary of the Sichuan Provincial Party Committee, was arrested as soon as the curtain of the 18th National Congress was lowered. If doing so did not raise too many eyebrows, the subsequent series of anti-corruption dramas indeed captured the attention of the nation. According to the data provided by the working report of the Third Plenary Session of the 18th Central Commission for Discipline Inspection, there were a total of more than 24,000 violations taken under investigation by the Discipline, Inspection, and Supervision Department in 2013, during which more than 30,000 individuals were dealt with, including 7,600 who were given Party disciplinary punishment and policy disciplinary punishment.[18] In 2013, the Discipline, Inspection and Supervision Department investigated 37,551 cases involving 51,306 individuals of crimes taking advantage of their positions including bribery, corruption, malpractice, and infringement, containing 2,581 major cases involving an amount of more than RMB 1 million.[19]

---

17.   Propaganda Department of the CPC Central Committee. *A Reader of Xi Jinping's Important Addresses*, Beijing: People's Publishing House, 2014.

18.   Party Literature Research Center of the CPC Central Committee. *Collection of Important Literature—Since the Eighteenth CPC National Congress (I)*, Beijing: Central Party Literature Press, 2014, p. 727.

19.   China Anti-corruption Research Center, Chinese Academy of Social Sciences. *2014 Report on Implementation of Combating Corruption and Upholding Integrity*, Social Science Academic Press (China), December, 2014, p. 16.

In the subsequent year of 2014, the CPC's anti-corruption efforts reached a peak in history; the year of 2014 is also called China's "first year of anti-corruption." According to the *Blue Book of Rule of Law: An Annual Report of China's Rule of Law* published by the Institute of Law, CASS, on March 18, 2015, the number of anti-corruption cases under investigation rose in 2014 compared with the same term in 2013. An average of 500 persons were taken under investigation including two officials at the bureau level, more than 80 local officials above the provincial level, and more than 30 senior military officers. In the first three quarters of 2014, China's investigating and prosecuting apparatus registered 27,235 cases of corruption and bribery, involving 35,633 persons, which was higher than the same term in 2013, by 9.9 percent and 5.6 percent, respectively.[20]

Although most people were shocked when a batch of officials from Sichuan Province were detained, today people have started to understand that the CPC's tough stance against corruption has become the new norm; and they know that anti-corruption measures will result in punishment and will continue to do so under the CPC's genuine and tangible policies and measures.

People have recognized and put their trust in the CPC's steadfast determination to tackle corruption and the great achievements it has made so far; the CPC's zero tolerance for corruption is now widely accepted, and has become a common understanding within Chinese society. The anti-corruption storm during the previous two years is an implication that the CPC is replicating Hong Kong's successful experiences in a promising way. "Zero tolerance" not only stands for the political will against corruption that the highest levels of the Party hold; more importantly, the entire society of China can now see that our tolerance for corruption is zero. Anti-corruption initiatives will not be reduced to a one-man show, played out by our leaders only. In the past, if there were ten instances of corruption, only one person was brave enough to inform the authorities; now, if there is one instance of corruption, ten people are willing to condemn and disclose it. Furthermore, more than 70 percent of the common citizens of Hong Kong use their real names in reporting unethical acts.[21] Only when the entire society's tolerance for corruption is zero, and all of the people participate in the struggle against corruption, and make corruption an evil hated by everyone, will there be no room left for corruption to hide.

Nowadays, when the entire society is motivated to support the CPC's anti-

20.   Li Lin, Tian He, et al: *Blue Book of Rule of Law: Annual Report of China's Rule of Law*, Beijing, Social Science Academic Press, 2015.

21.   Li Hui. *A Research on the Anticorruption System in Contemporary China*, Shanghai, Shanghai People's Publishing House, 2013, p. 236.

corruption measures, petition letters and reports have become important sources for leads toward building new anti-corruption cases. According to the data provided in the report of the Third Plenary Session of the 18th Central Commission for Discipline Inspection, in 2013, all discipline inspection and supervision departments of China received as many as 1,950,000 petition letters and reports, and 18,000 persons applied by letter.[22] In the first half of 2014, there were as many as 1,320,000, an increase of 65 percent compared with the same term in 2013.[23] The Central Inspection Team will not enter suspected organizations unless it has received a whistle-blower's report and obtained associated leads and evidence. The people's petition letters and reports make it possible for the CPC to shoot the arrow at the target and fight against corruption accurately. In Zhejiang Province for example, 29.8 percent of the 21,613 petition letters and reports received by the discipline inspection and supervision departments across the province in the first half of 2014 contributed to case investigations.[24]

The Internet plays a powerful role in corruption. China is an Internet powerhouse. According to the McKinsey Global Institute, affiliated with McKinsey & Company, the population of cyber-citizens in China reached as many as 632 million in 2014, and the Internet plays an important role as the participatory channel that people are willing to use. The research center of *China Youth News* conducted an online survey showing that in answer to the question, "What channel would you prefer to use to report corruption?" 71.5 percent chose "will participate by myself", and 78.3 percent believed that Internet reports plays a great role in prevention and enforcement of corruption.[25]

At midnight on April 19, 2013, simultaneously, eight Central Committee media online sections and four large-scale commercial websites, including Sina, Sohu, NetEase, and Tencent, launched an "Internet Report and Supervision Area" on their home pages with a uniform design.

In September, 2013, the Central Commission for Discipline Inspection and Ministry of Supervision launched its website, with fields for reporting corruption available at a conspicuous location on the home page, which

---

22.   *Party Literature Research Center of the CPC Central Committee. Collection of Important Literature—Since the Eighteenth CPC National Congress (I)*, Beijing: Central Party Literature Press, 2014, p. 729.

23.   China Anti-corruption Research Center, Chinese Academy of Social Sciences. *2014 Report on Implementation of Combating Corruption and Upholding Integrity*, Social Science Academic Press (China), December 2014, p. 23.

24.   Ibid.

25.   Education Classroom, Central Discipline Inspection Commission. *10 Hot Spots about Anticorruption*, China Fangzheng Publishing House, 2011, p. 91.

made "click to the Central Commission for Discipline Inspection" come true. On average, it receives more than 800 reports every day.

Internet-based anti-corruption measures quickly curtail corrupt officials. One dramatic example: Upon the closing of the 18th CPC National Congress, on November 20th of the same year, Lei Zhengfu's scandal video was posted on the Internet; on November 23rd, only 60 hours later, he was dismissed from his position and taken under investigation.[26]

Set No Limits when Hunting Tigers

The mission of the CPC's anti-corruption initiative is to "set no limits for tiger hunting, and leave no dead space for flies." "Set no limits" means that anyone who is found guilty of violating Party discipline and the laws of the state will be punished severely, without any tolerance, no matter how much power they have acquired or how high their position is. The theory of "set no limits" derives from a speech delivered by Xi Jinping in the Second Meeting of the Fourth Plenary Session of the CPC Central Committee on October 23, 2014, where he stated that China must "further advance to combat corruption, continue to hold a tough stance; we should retain the attitude of zero tolerance, the determination of curing an illness with strong drugs, the courage of scraping the poison off bones, the force of severe punishment; investigate upon the discovery of any possible corruption, investigate all such discoveries, without setting a limit, crack down on anyone found guilty of corruption and exterminate evil once and for all."[27]

The speech was not disclosed to the public at the time. Now, when the public looks back at it, Xi Jinping must have had a plan in mind, because soon afterward several tigers, including Su Rong, the former chairman of the Chinese People's Political Consultative Conference, Xu Caihou, the former vice chairman of the Central Military Commission, and Zhou Yongkang, a former member of the Standing Committee of the Political Bureau of the CPC Committee and former secretary of the Political and Judiciary Commission, were detained one after another.

By arresting Zhou Yongkang a signal was sent to all: Set no limits when tiger hunting. The tigers getting caught are from higher and higher levels. Scrutinizing the situations of senior officials at the provincial and ministerial levels that have been caught since the 18th National Congress, it becomes clear that the capture of Zhou Yongkang pushed the anti-corruption drama to a climax, given the fact that no official at the national level and in the ranks

---

26. "An Inventory of 2012 Internet Anti-corruption," *Hexun Net*, February 4, 2013.
27. Excerpts of Xi Jinping's Statement on the Construction of the Party Conduct and of an Honest and Clean Government.

of the Political Bureau has been caught before; besides, Zhou Yongkang's investigation breaks the fantasy that "punishments do not extend to officials," and reiterates that no amount of gold can prevent one from being taken under investigation, even if they are a member of the Standing Committee.

By capturing Xu Caihou a signal was sent to all of China—there is no safe space for corruption! The CPC's struggle against corruption jumps from one area to another now that the anti-corruption storm has blown into the military, which was always regarded as a restricted zone. As of March, 2015, more than 30 military officers above the level of general have been detained.

On July 22, 2014, the Ministry of Public Security launched a half-year action called "Fox Hunting 2014" to arrest suspects of economic crimes who had fled overseas, reinforcing the truth that there is no place for corruption to hide in the world. The CPC is determined to arrest corrupt officials even if they have fled to the ends of the earth. This fact also alarms those officials who may have intended to flee. Overseas shall no longer be a haven for corrupt officials. By December 31, a total of 680 economic criminals had been arrested, a 4.5-fold increase from the number of arrests made in 2013. Among those criminals, 290 were arrested, 390 turned themselves in; 208 cases involved an amount of more than RMB 10 million; and 117 suspects had fled overseas and stayed for more than ten years.[28] In April 2015, the upgraded version of "Fox Hunting," known as "Sky Net," was activated, where the CPC's net of anti-corruption, pursuit of evasion and recovery of ill-gotten gains has been consolidated and become tighter and firmer. China's overseas arrest actions received strong support from foreign law enforcement, many countries including the United States agreed to cooperate with China and simplify the process of extradition for Chinese people who fled abroad.[29]

The world recognizes that "tiger hunting" has obtained favorable results in the recent rounds of the CPC's anti-corruption actions. Compared with tigers, there are more flies that are closer to the people. In fact, ordinary people have no immediate feelings of those tigers' extravagant and dissipating lives; on the contrary, buzzing flies near at hand conform to the people's impressions of corruption. Even though they are small, these flies reach out for any chance to profit; their ranks are low but they get hold of considerable power, especially in water, electricity, gas and other essential areas of people's livelihoods, where there is much space for corruption to breed. It is almost the norm for them to take advantage of their duty by seizing people's food, taking over people's properties, or obstructing people's

28.   "The Ministry of Public Security. 680 Economic Criminals that Fled to Overseas were Arrested during 'Fox Hunting,'" *China Police Network*, January 8, 2015.
29.   "'Sky Net' Eliminates Corrupt Official's Dreams of Freedom," Xinhua News Agency, April 3, 2015.

ambitions if not bribed. If we fail to crack down on these corrupt officials at low levels, China's people may not experience or enjoy the true benefits of anti-corruption actions. Therefore, anti-corruption is intended not only to "hunt tigers," but to exert great efforts to "swat flies." Only by fighting against corruption and focusing on people's vital interests can their expectations be satisfied. At the beginning of 2013, the Supreme People's Procuratorate implemented a special two-year program to investigate and prevent criminal activities by officials that are near the people and cause harm to the people. By November, 2014, 14,512 cases involving 20,403 persons had been taken under investigation.[30]

Anti-Corruption: From a Movement to an Institution

In May, 2014, in an article written by Professor Minxin Pei, of Claremont McKenna College, it was asserted that Xi Jinping's anti-corruption measures had entered a critical stage. His determination to crack down on corruption in the Party and the state received strong support from the public, but he was facing a tougher challenge—how to maintain it. The movement launched from the top to bottom would cost more and more with smaller and smaller effects.[31]

The focus of concern now is whether these anti-corruption measures will have a long-lasting effect. People have shown concern as to whether this current round of anti-corruption is another movement like many others in previous years. There is a popular folk saying in Chinese that describes the movement of anti-corruption as merely a "short-lived campaign." That it is like a wind flying by—even if it triggers some ripples on the surface of the water, the water itself is hardly impacted—wind blows and corrupt acts are restrained; after the wind passes, corruption makes a comeback, or is even further intensified. Xi Jinping is well aware that, to avoid short-lived anti-corruption results, there must be reforms to support and reinforce current anti-corruption initiatives. In addition to combating corruption in the Party, or of a central leader's individual willpower, there must be laws and institutional norms as well as more far-ranging democratic supervision.

"A good institution may prevent bad people from wrongdoing, or even guild them toward good acts; while under a bad institution, good people may be forced into wrongdoings" Corruption is rooted in poor supervision over power, so the best way to prevent corruption is to control power that

---

30.   Zhang Cancan. "Tighten the 'Fence' of Supervision to Curb 'Arch Corrupt Officials at Low Levels'," *Procuratorial Daily*, March 16, 2015.

31.   Pei Minxin. "Xi Jinping's Anti-corruption Enters a Critical Stage," *Reference News*, April 15, 2014.

should be exercised within institutions, where the power must follow the standards and chains of command of the institution. For example, in the first half of 2014, the CPC unveiled a series of fresh policies:

- **January 2014**: revised version of the *Work Regulations on Selection and Appointment of Party and Government Leading Cadres*, defining the move to clear "exposed officials" for the first time and advance the process of anti-corruption greatly;
- **January 2014**: the *Notification on Further Accomplishing Individual Work Reports of Leading Cadres*, urging and supervising Party members and cadres to report information strictly and according to the facts;
- **January 2014**: *Methods for Spot Check and Verification of Individual Matters of Concern of Leading Cadres (Trial Implementation)*, sorting out leads on corruption by spot checks;
- **February 2014**: the *Notification on Publishing and Disclosure of Cases of Cadres of Discipline Inspection and Supervision Violating the Central Committee's Eight Rules*, strengthening the self-supervision of the system of discipline inspection and supervision;
- **April 2014**: *Notification on Clearing Non-Licensing Approval Matters in Departments of the State Council*, preventing corruption at the source;
- **April 2014**: *Implementation Opinions on Pilot Projects for Reform of Institutional Mechanisms of Corruption Investigations*, exploring experiences for further reform;
- **June 2014**: the *Embodiment for Institutional Reform of Party Discipline Inspection*, deploying 29 reform measures.

The CPC is striving to "establish and strengthen a multi-level supervision system, improve various open administrative systems, and make sure that leading bodies and individuals of the Party and the state exercise their rights according to statutory jurisdiction and procedure."[32] Most importantly of all in establishing an anti-corruption institution of "zero tolerance" and trapping undisciplined power is that the trap should be transparent, allowing the people to know, to perceive, and to supervise. Over the past decade, the CPC has been focused on exploring a way that allows power to operate openly; it formulated the *Regulation of Government Information Disclosure*, and carried out pilot projects in many sectors. For example, participatory

---

32.   Xi Jinping. The Speech at the 60th Anniversary Celebration of the National People's Congress, *People's Daily*, September 6, 2014.

budgeting, that is, disclosing the approval of prospective budgets to the public; in the past, local governments' drafts of budget and final settlements were classified documents known only to finance departments and the people's congress, and the public barely knew anything; past procedure made it difficult to establish an external supervisory mechanism. The situation has been changed by adopting participatory budgeting in Shanghai, Zhejiang Province, and other places, where citizens are now invited to participate in the process of allocation of budgets and funds. In doing so, it allows distribution of funds more systematically and democratically, strengthens people's trust in the government, and effectively establishes a social supervisory institution for budgeting. In March 2014, the *Notification on Deepening and Advancing Open Local Budgeting,* issued by the Ministry of Finance, required local government departments to further refine their methods of open budgeting.

"If you want to work with iron, you must be tough yourself" is a particularly popular notion in the system of the CPC Commission for Discipline Inspection. The construction of anti-corruption organizations is a critical factor in institutional anti-corruption measures while the Commission for Discipline Inspection is responsible for the CPC's anti-corruption actions; so the commission must be tough, so that in no way shall corruption rise within it, and the commission must be competent as well. Indeed, after the 18th CPC National Congress, the commission did start with itself, constantly strengthening by internal restructuring. On May 27, 2013, the commission issued the *Notification on Clearing and Returning Membership Cards in Nationwide Discipline Inspection and Supervision System,* which asked the staff of the discipline inspection and supervision system to clear and return all membership cards that were accepted in different names, prior to June 30, 2013. At the time, all of the 810,000 full-time and part-time cadres submitted a "zero-holding" report on time, without delay.[33] As small a matter as a membership card, the action still represented the commission's determination for self-purity.

At the Third Plenary Session of the 18th Central Commission for Discipline Inspection (CCDI), Xi Jinping pointed out: the Commissions for Discipline Inspection at all levels must properly handle the problem of "shadows under lights," and comply with Party discipline and the laws of the state. If your job is to investigate others, then who shall investigate you? Wang Qishan, the secretary of the Commission for Discipline Inspection, showed an unshaken attitude on the matter; in 2014, as many as 1,575 Discipline

---

33. "The Nationwide Clearing and Returning of Membership Cards in Discipline Inspection System Completes. 810 Thousands Cadres Submitted 'Zero Holding' Reports," *People's Daily Online,* June 28, 2013.

Inspection and Supervision cadres were punished by the Commission for Discipline Inspection at all levels for violation of the law. There was no lack of "VIPs," such as Shen Weichen, a member of the Central Commission for Discipline Inspection, Wei Jian, the director of the Fourth Inspection Office for Discipline Inspection, CCDI, Cao Lixin, a deputy-director-level investigator and ombudsman of the CCDI. Moreover, since the 18th National Congress, CCDI has briefed four open notifications by name for general information of nineteen typical cases of discipline inspection and supervision initiatives of cadres who have violated Party ethics and law.[34]

In addition to maintaining its own purity, the commission never stops innovating in regards to the working dynamics for anti-corruption; the inspection team and international anti-corruption efforts provide good examples of this. In 2014, thirteen central inspection teams were assigned to 20 provinces (autonomous regions and cities) and the Xinjiang Construction Regiment for two rounds of routine inspection, during which they discovered a great number of valuable leads. Severe cases of disciplinary violations were found during the inspection, including those by Su Rong, Shen Peiping, and Wan Qingliang. During the second round, at least 3,351 officials were punished, including 66 above the bureau level. At the same time, the central inspection team also carried out a special inspection at six units, also in two rounds, for the Ministry of Science and Technology, the China Oil & Foodstuffs Corporation (COFCO), Fudan University, the Chinese Academy of Science, General Administration of Sport, and the First Automobile Group (FAW).[35]

After the pilot "Fox Hunting 2014" initiative by the Ministry of Public Security (MPS), MPS's "Fox Hunting 2015" was incorporated into the upgraded "Sky Net Actions." New members participate in the latter's leading departments, including the Central Organization Department, the Supreme People's Procuratorate, the People's Bank of China, and numerous other departments. They adopt comprehensive methods, combining police affairs, inspection affairs, diplomacy, and finance, to inspect deeply, leaving no stone unturned, and by no means will they allow corrupt officials to hide away, avoiding conviction."[36]

In 1959, the first Prime Minister of Singapore, Lee Kuan Yew, said that

34.   Li Zhiyong: "To Supervise Others, You Must be 'Tougher' on Yourself First," *China Discipline Inspection and Supervision*, February 5, 2015.
35.   China Anti-corruption Research Center, Chinese Academy of Social Sciences. *2014 Report on Implementation of Combating Corruption and Upholding Integrity*, Social Science Academic Press (China), December, 2014, pp. 19–20.
36.   "Sky Net" Action is Launched for International Pursuit of Evasion of Recovery of Ill-Gotten Gains, CCDI & Ministry of Supervision, Mar. 26, 2015.

the newly independent Singapore was "badly sick, greedy, corrupt, and full of decadency" immediately after it was rid of colonial rule. Today, it has retained its top position in global lists of least-corrupt countries for many years.

When the Independent Commission Against Corruption (ICAC) was established in 1974, corruption had been a way of life in the Hong Kong police force, as routine as slumber is at night, and waking is in the morning. But now, Hong Kong's people can say with pride: "Hong Kong's superiority is earned by us and by the ICAC."

Today, Xi Jinping is placing unprecedented emphasis on building an incorruptible government in China. China should feel assured that the CPC will give clean consciences back to the people.

II. SETTING UP RULES

This round of tiger hunting handled corruption that had accumulated over years, but setting up rules is essential for handling the possibility of future corruption creeping up again in increments. The former removes the necrotic tissue, scraping the poison off bones; the latter promotes tissue regeneration, upholding the body's energy and vitality. Both aspects are equally important and China should be tough on both fronts.

A Circle or Square Cannot Be Drawn Without a Gauge

There is a proverb in China—"a circle or a square cannot be drawn without a gauge." Without rules, an entity as large as a country, or as small as an individual, will be in a state of disunity. The fact holds graves importance for a governing party with a great historical mission on its shoulders. One of the important reasons that the CPC succeeded in developing and growing stronger from a small party composed of little over 50 members to a party that defeated the Kuomintang (KMT), with a much stronger foundation, and thereby establishing the PRC, is that it is well-organized and highly disciplined. The CPC's opponent, Chiang Kai-shek, knew this quite well. After escaping to Taiwan, he expressed his complaint that the KMT was defeated due to undisciplined organization and demoralization.

Indeed, the CPC and its opponent, the KMT, are both apprentices of the CPSU; the difference is that the CPC performed better in its studies. The CPC learned the quintessence of the Leninist party, and established an organization in extremely tight formation. Its political program was clear and strong, its central, local and primary-level organizations were complete, its internal information channels were unobstructed, its actions were coordinated in lockstep, in no circumstances would it allow Party members to act outside of established guidelines and policies, and it cracked down on such violators. Compared with its mentor, the CPSU, we can say that the CPC excels its master. All in all, the CPC won its victory after 28 years of bloody battles, through thousands of escapes from death, and those innumerable trials and hardships were beyond the CPSU's imagination. The Bolsheviks took over the regime with almost no fight during the October Revolution. The CPC survived in a brutal environment, doggedly depending on a discipline as tough as iron and thereby developed and grew stronger and stronger.

The CPC had said that a "discipline as tough as iron" must be upheld at the Second CPC National Congress; later the "Three Rules of Discipline and Eight Points for Attention" became the key to the success of CPC's revolution; the Rectification Movement in Yan'an united the Party as if it was formed into one person with an iron discipline. Mao Zedong once offered a visual metaphor: "The Monkey King Sun Wukong's hoop is made of gold; Lenin says the communist party's discipline is a discipline of iron. I say, it is fiercer and tougher than King Sun's golden hoop."[37] Later, when Mao Zedong summed up the lessons learned from the New-Democratic Revolution, the work of party building containing this iron discipline was praised as a "magic weapon."[38]

Compared with parties in the United States, the CPC's main features are quite prominent. In the United States, both the Republican Party and the Democratic Party exist for elections only; they are very active during the general elections but go into a dormant state afterwards; the political parties are poorly disciplined, even compared with European political parties. In the United States Congress, no matter how hard a party tries, its members may not stay in line with the party establishment's preference in policies.

Xi Jinping visited Xibaipo Village in June, 2013. In the house that the Political Bureau of the CPC Central Committee used as a conference room in the past, he said: "this is where rules are made. The establishment and enforcement of our rules and institutions have promoted the construction of the working style and discipline of the Party," and "today, as a great governing party with more than 86 million members, facing profound and lasting changes of worldly affairs, national conditions, and party conditions, the political discipline and political rule of the Party must remain stricter

37.   *Collected Works of Mao Zedong, Volume 2,* Beijing: People's Publishing House, 1993, p. 416

38.   *Selected Works of Mao Zedong, Volume 2,* Beijing: People's Publishing House, 1991, p. 606

and more impartial than ever."[39]

In saying so, he was picturing how the CPC had acted with extreme caution, as if treading on thin ice, 64 years ago when they went to Beijing for "examination." In March 1949, the Second Plenary Session of the Seventh CPC Central Committee was held in Xibaipo. In order to prevent the possibility of apathy and slackness in the Party after the victory of revolution, the CPC introduced the "Six Rules:" (1) do not celebrate birthdays for leaders of the Party; (2) do not give gifts; (3) seldom propose toasts; (4) do not applaud unnecessarily; (5) do not name a place, street, or enterprise after names of Party leaders; and (6) do not place Chinese comrades on a par with Marx, Engels, Lenin, or Stalin. The Six Rules seem as simple and unadorned as the "Three Disciplines and Eight Points for Attention" 20 years ago, but they work quite well.

Like Mao Zedong at the time, Xi Jinping is also facing a new "examination" upon taking office; furthermore, his pressure is not at all second to the expectations faced by Mao Zedong. Mao Zedong set up the Six Rules at Xibaipo to cope with the "examination in Beijing" 64 years ago; and today, Xi Jinping set up the "Eight Rules" in Beijing only 20 days after he was elected as the general secretary. In the past, with the help of the Six Rules, the CPC surmounted the possibility of being conceited, self-satisfied, and indulgent in a life of pleasure and conformity; they held off the attack from the "sugarcoated bullets" of complacency, and did not lose a battle before new challenges. Today, Xi Jinping hopes that the Eight Rules will also bring an altogether new aspect to the working style of the Party and the atmosphere in governing bodies, so that the CPC may be able to shoulder the great trust of the people among the complexity of intersecting social conflicts, and ever-changing domestic and international conditions.

The Eight Rules have been developed in the name of goodness. They are well operable, just like their predecessor, the Six Rules.

The Eight Rules

Old Zhong, a retired worker in Hebei Province, was a Party member for many years. Immediately after he watched the Central Committee introduce the Eight Rules on TV, he told everybody whom he met that "the CPC goes through the motions. Do not expect many lasting effects." But he was a man of intention, and he paid close attention to analyzing those cases under investigation by the central government and local authorities that came to light after the Eight Rules, and he also recorded in his diaries the changes in

---

39.　　Li Qinggang. "Xibaipo, Where 'Rules Were Made'." *Beijing Daily*, September 30, 2013.

the working style of other Party members he observed and the general mood of society. One year later, he was well aware of the changes in the working style of the Party and the atmosphere in government bodies, as well as how determined the CPC was to put the Eight Rules into practice. Now, he tells everybody he meets that "the Eight Rules comply with the wishes of the people, understand the wills of the people, and most importantly, they are 'the real thing'!"[40]

Like Old Zhong, most Chinese people did not expect that the CPC was serious, because so many such rules had been issued in the previous 20 years that people had become accustomed to them, and thus became inured to the usual. The CPC introduced new rules concerning specific corrupt behaviors almost every year. As early as 1993, which was also the year following Deng Xiaoping's Southern Talks, the CPC had already begun to confront the issue of outbound tourism, and to confront indiscriminate fundraising activities, even though the former had only newly emerged and was not as prevalent as today. After the 15th National Congress, the CPC focused on clearing up the matter of communications equipment and sedans purchased at public expense, as well as engagement in trade among Party and government organizations; after the 17th National Congress, the CPC directed its focus toward construction projects of halls and guest-houses such as office buildings for Party and government organizations and cleared problems present in officials' rights to sell off state-owned land.[41]

However, with so many rules issued, the results were not as good as expected—not only did they fail in restraining tourism misappropriations, private use of government vehicles, and the construction of halls and guest-houses, the situation became further intensified. At this time, Xi Jinping did not let the Chinese people down. Like Old Zhong, many people's attitudes were doubtful, waiting and watching, and then were satisfied and inspired by the changes brought about by the Eight Rules. At the end of 2013, Xinhua Net reported that, in the "2013 Top Discipline Inspection Words Approved by Cyber Citizens," the Eight Rules ranked highest—cyber citizens, considered the most informed demographic group of the Chinese population, had approved of the Eight Rules.[42]

Reuters correspondent Ben Blanchard wrote on his MSN website to introduce the achievements of the Central Commission for Discipline

40.   "Survey Shows: 75.8% of Urban and Rural Citizens Look at the Bright Side of Anti-corruption," *People's Daily Online*, February 23, 2015.

41.   Li Hui. *A Research on the Anticorruption System in Contemporary China*, Shanghai: Shanghai People's Publishing House, 2013, p. 191.

42.   "2013 Top 10 Internet Trends for Discipline Inspection," *Xinhua Net*, December 31, 2013.

Inspection: "China has punished almost 20,000 officials by administrative sanction or disciplinary action within the Party in the last year for breaching rules to cut down on bureaucracy, as well as pomp and ceremony. More than 5,000 officials were found to have breached rules connected to the use of official cars, while 903 were guilty of organizing overly elaborate celebratory events. Others were singled out for being 'mediocre' or 'indolent.'" The article triggered a wave of discussion among American Internet users. Some commented that, "this is a good beginning for a responsible government;" "they have punished corrupt officials, it seems they are not simply 'acting.'" And another commenter reflected on the United States: "All that the US government does is accuse China, they really should learn something from China."[43]

Following the Eight Rules, the CPC issued injunctions one after another, covering education and training, government credit cards, office occupancy, artistic performances, and cadre appointments—this was truly an unprecedented refinement of enforcement measures. We can see the cage tightening and tightening by looking into the regulations introduced by the CPC in 2013:

- **March 30**: *Regulations on Further Strengthening Trainees Management in Education and Training for Cadres*;
- **May 27**: *Notification on Clearing and Returning Membership Cards in the Nationwide Discipline Inspection and Supervision System*;
- **June 23**: *Notification on Stopping Construction of New Halls and Guest-houses and Clearing and Returning Office Occupancies for Party and Government Organizations*;
- **August 13**: *Notification to Stop Organizing Overly Elaborate Celebratory Events and Promoting Economized Events*;
- **September 3**: *Notification on Implementation of the Spirit of Eight Rules Issued by the Central Committee to Firmly Prevent Giving Gifts by Using Public Funds and other Harmful Practices During the Mid-Autumn Festival and the National Day*;
- **September 13**: *Administrative Measures on Conference Expense for the Central and State Organs*;
- **October 19**: *Opinions on Further Normalizing Problems of Party and Government Leaders Concurrently (fully) Holding Posts in Enterprises*;
- **October 31**: *Notification on Prohibition in Purchasing, Printing,*

---

43. Americans Talk Over China's Fight Against the Four Undesirable Work Styles is "Awesome", *People's Daily Online*, December 31, 2013.

Making, or Sending New-Year's Cards and the Like with Public funds;
- **November 21**: *Notification on Prohibition of Purchasing and Presenting New-Year's Gifts and Festival Presents such as Fireworks and Firecrackers with Public Funds during the Spring Festival;*
- **November 25**: *Regulations of Rigorous Enforcement of Economy and Combating Waste for Party and Government Organizations;*
- **December 2**: *Notification on Strict Normalization of Publishing Work of Party Newspapers and Publications and Prohibition of Breaching Rules;*
- **December 8**: *Administrative Regulations on Domestic Official Reception for Party and Government Organizations;*
- **December 19**: *Opinions on Party Members and Cadres Setting an Example to Promote Reform of Funeral Interment;*
- **December 12**: *Administrative Measures on Funds for Unscheduled Trips Abroad on Business;*
- **December 23**: *Notification on Strict Rectification of "Noxious Style in Clubs" During Party's Activities of Mass Line Education and Practice;*
- **December 29**: *Administrative Measures on Funds for the Central and State Organs.*

The issuance of these rules and regulations became more and more frequent, and more importantly, no rules and regulations in the past were so specific, detailed, and rigid. Expressions such as "generally" and "in principle" that were commonly used in previous laws and regulations within the Party were rarely used, replaced by firm wordings such as "prohibited," "completely," and "must." In addition, vague wordings disappeared, replaced by specific figures. For example, the *Administrative Regulations on Domestic Official Reception for Party and Government Organizations* specifically provided: "The host organization can arrange one working meal with strict control of the number of companions only if the job demands. If the number of people to be received is less than ten, the number of companions shall be no more than three; if more than ten, the number of companions must not be more than one third of the people to be received."

It was reported in the *People's Daily* that, as of December, 2014, a total of 77,606 cases were taken under investigation for breaching the Eight Rules, in which 102,168 people were dealt with, including 31,338 people that received Party disciplinary actions and/or policy-based disciplinary punishments.[44]

---

44.   Sheng Ruowei, Zhao Bing. "The Stricter Control Exercised over Discipline, the Solider Impartial Rules Become," *People's Daily*, January 27, 2015.

Start with the Central Political Bureau

This is easier said than done. Xi Jinping showed his determination in implementing the Eight Rules by saying, "rules are rules. The absence of a 'trial implementation' is to make clear our steadfast determination. The rules must be followed," and "the most important thing is to focus on implementation. One must stand by one's words and must not stop one's action until success is achieved."[45] After the Eight Rules were issued, Xi Jinping stressed repeatedly that China should start with the Central Political Bureau.

Xi Jinping visited Guangdong Province on December 7, 2012, which was his first local visit after he was elected as the general secretary, and after issuing the Eight Rules. During the visit, roads were not blocked, buses, taxis, and private cars were allowed to travel with his fleet side by side. A cyber citizen, "@陆亚明" (Lu Yaping) posted to a microblog on Weibo, saying of his encounter with Xi Jinping's fleet: "The police cars had on lights but no sirens. The minibus's window was not covered by curtains, the speed was about 60 kilometers per hour. Traffic conditions were as usual on Shennan Street. Most probably the working style of the president has changed for sure— there was no big deal, they didn't even block the road! I salute you! We don't mind you visiting us, General Secretary Xi."[46]

Xinhua Net posted a photograph in which Xi Jinping was holding his own umbrella during a visit, at 12:38 on July 21, 2013. Cyber citizens were moved. On the morning of that day, Xi Jinping visited Xingang, Wuhan, with no entourage present, no welcome banners hung. At 11:50, as the rain started coming down, Xi Jinping rolled up his trouser legs, held an umbrella, and continued his visit in spite of the rain; his shirt was soaked. A cyber citizen, "圆规画方" (Yuan Gui Hua Fang), commented: "Rolled-up trouser legs and holding an umbrella, awesome! I hope leaders and cadres at all levels can be as realistic and pragmatic as General Secretary Xi Jinping is."[47]

On December 28, 2013, a microblog on Weibo mentioned the time-restaurant, Qingfeng Dumpling Shop, well known to the whole nation. At 1:20 p.m. of that day, a cyber citizen, "四海微传播" (Si Hai Wei Chuan Bo), posted a comment: "Folks, I cannot believe my eyes! Uncle Xi had dumplings at Qingfeng! Here's the picture." One minute later, the cyber citizen posted another comment: "Uncle Xi waited in the line for his dumplings. He paid

45.   Xi Jinping. A Speech on "Improving Work Styles and Maintaining Close Ties with the Masses" at the Meeting of the Political Bureau, December 4, 2012.

46.   "What Does General Secretary Xi Jinping's Visit in Guangdong Reveal?" *Xinhua Net*, December 15, 2012.

47.   "General Secretary Xi's Visit in Xingang, Wuhan in Spite of Rain Touched Internet Users," *People's Daily Online*, June 21, 2013.

for them, carried the tray and took them by himself. Qingfeng can introduce a Xi Jinping Package in the future." He Yuanli, manager of Qingfeng, recalled that, during the three or four minutes that Xi Jinping was waiting in line, people came over to shake hands and take pictures with him; when he sat down for his meal, he also talked with the people around him at the same time.[48] "Uncle Xi" is a nickname of Xi Jinping used by his fans. "The general secretary sets an example for us. If he fulfills the Eight Rules, other leaders ought to do so, too." This is the true feeling of officials at all levels.

The ancients said: "If the ruler himself is morally upright, all will go well, even though he does not give orders. But if he himself is not morally upright, even though he gives orders, they will not be obeyed." Under the leadership of the new term of collective leaders, the CPC's officials at all levels have improved their working styles markedly.

People are delighted to see that:

- Meetings are shortened and more efficient; meeting agendas have changed and become more simple and unadorned; there are fewer and shorter documents, and they are more honest; formats of documents have been changed to be more easily understood and accessible; and Party members and cadres are freed from the mountains of paperwork and their many redundant meetings.
- Fewer people use government vehicles for private errands, and "extravagance on wheels" is controlled.
- Officials no longer feast on public funds, and the "bite of corruption" has been effectively curbed.
- Some clubs located in scenic sports and tourist attractions have been shut down, and entertainment, power-for-money deals, and power-for-sex deals have been stopped. Those upscale clubs that used to open for big money and under-the-table dealings have turned themselves into "happy teahouses" for the public.
- Local officials no longer run to Beijing to offer bribes during holidays and festivals; luxury liquor and cigarettes have been reduced in both quantity and price, returning to rational amounts; and thereby holidays and festivals have recovered their original simplicity.

From these vivid changes, people again can feel how determined high-level CPC officials are in implementing the Eight Rules, and witness the

---

48.   Zhao Li, Li Dandan. "The President Arrived at Qingfeng Dumpling Restaurant without Advance Notice," *Beijing News*, December 29, 2013.

practical style of the CPC—node by node, helping them to make the best Party, even in the details.

Node by Node

The high-level officials' examples are clearly not enough to implement rules effectively. Since the 18th CPC National Congress, the most important part of setting up rules and establishing discipline is the way in which the CPC has concentrated its efforts on details, moved its focus node by node, and proceeded steadily and with confidence.

On September 19, 2013, it was the first Mid-Autumn Day after the Eight Rules were issued. Half a month earlier, the Central Commission for Discipline Inspection (CCDI) issued the *Notification on Implementation of the Spirit of Eight Rules Issued by the Central Committee to Firmly Hold on Giving Gifts by Using Public Funds and other Harmful Practice During the Mid-Autumn Festival and the National Day*, which made this a different Mid-Autumn Day than previous ones. High-priced moon cakes, gift cards purchased with public funds, and Yangcheng Lake crabs that used to be everywhere in the past became less prevalent than ever. Sedans full of various gifts and offerings were reduced in number, improving Beijing's traffic conditions. In Pudong, Shanghai, where once people needed to pull all the strings they could to buy a box of moon cakes at RMB 1,988 or 2,988 each at a five-star hotel, at that Mid-Autumn festival almost no one bought them. On the contrary, inexpensive moon cakes in bulk were warmly welcomed.

Even so, some organizations still breached the rules to grant favors and festival gifts. According to a brief by Jiangsu Provincial Commission for Discipline Inspection, the City Inspection Detachment of Qiandengcheng, Kunshan City, purchased 58 moon cake coupons worth RMB 199 each with public funds and distributed them to city inspectors, and purchased shopping cards totaling RMB 10,000 and distributed them to some inspectors and cooperative organizations; Zhu Xiaobing, the head of the detachment received a punishment as a warning within the Party, and was asked to pay compensation of RMB 10,000 for the gift cards, and the costs of the moon cake coupons were borne by the inspectors who were given them.[49] At this Mid-Autumn festival, Zhu Xiaobin was not the only one who was punished. Fu Shigan, president of Hunan Provincial Health School, Gong Zukang, head of Naning Central Blood Bank, He Ningyu, secretary of the General Party Branch of the Blood Bank, Zhang Xianliang, dean of the Chinese Academy of Fishery Sciences, Ministry of Agriculture, Jiang Guojin, general manager

---

49.   "Jiangsu Provincial Commission for Discipline Inspection Notified 8 Cases for Breaching the Eight Rules," *People's Daily Online*, January 23, 2014.

of COFCO Meat Investment Co., Ltd., Li Changqing, deputy director general of the Urban Construction Bureau of the Shahekou District, Dalian City, and others, were punished for moon cake–related scandals.[50]

At the time of the New Year and Spring Festivals, the CCDI had issued the *Notification on Prohibition in Purchasing, Printing, Making, or Sending New-Year Cards and the Like with Public funds* and the *Notification on Prohibition of Purchasing and Presenting New-year Gifts and Festival Presents such as Fireworks with Public Funds during the Spring Festival* in succession respectively on October 31 and November 21, 2013. Due to lessons learned from the Mid-Autumn festival, the New Year's and the Spring Festival in 2014 went on in peace and quiet, and served as corruption-free and exemplary holidays.

One might wonder: Does a box of moon cakes or a gift card matter so much? Wang Qishan, CCDI secretary, displayed a very decisive attitude in response to the question. He said, "we should steel our wills to rectify the 'Four Undesirable Work Styles'. Practice makes perfect, establishing a long-lasting effect. In doing so, we can change normality by persistence; and maintain it by long-lasting institutional restructuring."[51] As it turns out, the CPC must haggle over every penny and move its focus, node by node. "An order is made for every festival," nipping problems in the bud and focusing on details, as well as curbing some cadres' poor conduct.

Emphasizing implementation requires not only will, but also means. Details often determine success or failure. A good example is the resolution of the trend sometimes known as "extravagance on wheels."

In January 2013, Luan Songwei, a sixth-grader at Erligou Central Elementary School, Haidian District, Beijing, tabled a proposal that China should place red license plates on government vehicles for unified management and surveillance by the masses, in order to curtail the private use of government vehicles.[52] His suggestion was soon turned into reality in some places. On May 16, 2013, Jiyuan City, Henan Province, took the lead to require that government vehicles must be identifiable as such, displaying vehicle number, organization, vehicle license-plate number, and a supervisory hotline number.[53] Linfen City, Shanxi Province, Qujing City,

---

50.   "CCDI Recovered 'Weekly Notification' for the Eight Rules, and 4 Officials were Punished For Moon Cakes in the First Week," *People's Daily Online*, August 12, 2014.

51.   "CCID named 885 People for Severe Breach Rules to Grant Welfare During the Two Sessions," Tencent Website, February 22, 2015.

52.   "A Pupil's Suggestion of Using Red Plates on Government Vehicles for Supervision Received Wide Praises," *Xinhua Daily Telegraph*, February 21, 2013.

53.   "All Government Vehicles in Jiyuan, Henan were Labeled with Pink 'Government Vehicle'," *People's Daily Online*, May 18, 2013.

Yunnan Province, Wenzhou City, Zhejiang Province, and Shaya County, Xinjiang, one after another, also issued similar measures in next to no time. Private use of government vehicles was greatly reduced in these regions. For example, in the first quarter after government vehicles were labelled in Shanya County, Xinjiang, fuel consumption decreased by 30 percent compared with the same term in previous years.[54]

In some places, government vehicles were equipped with GPS to supervise them by means of an "eye in the sky." Since September, 2013, 420 government vehicles in Si County, Anhui Province, were equipped with GPS; from then on, every movement would be recorded by an electronic surveillance system. Private use of government cars in Si County was curtailed.[55]

Technology serves as a means only, but it provides no help in confronting the apathy in one's mind. Many people become afraid to touch those high-voltage lines of power and influence, despite repeated orders issued by the CCID. However, it is difficult to eliminate some other bad habits, such as "not making big mistakes, but making small ones constantly," habits that were formed over a long time. For example, to some people, asking others to sign in for them at work, asking others to attend meetings for them, being late and leaving early at meetings are small mistakes. The Municipal Mobilization Meeting for Urban Construction, City Management and Environment Protection was held in Nanjing on January 25, 2014, and the deputy director of the Lishui Urban Management Bureau appointed other people to attend the meeting for him, without permission or adhering to the procedure of asking for leave, due to private affairs in his home. The appointed proxy was ten minutes late for the meeting, and he was caught in the act by Liao Ruilin, the major. The next day, the Lishui District Committee decided to remove the deputy director from office and punished him by circulating a notice of criticism.[56]

This round of the CPC's establishing rules makes Party members and cadres dare not consider unethical practices, an important shift in outlook in such a short period. This round of implementation concentrates efforts on details, considers them from all angles, and takes one practical step followed by another one. A cadre in Hubei Province spoke of what was on many people's minds when he said, "now less of my time is used for social

54.   "1/3 Year-on-Year Decrease of Fuel Consumption of Government Vehicles in Sha-ya County," Xinjiang, Yaxin Net, March 28, 2013.
55.   "420 Government Vehicles of Si County Were Equipped with GPS," Ifeng, October 12, 2013.
56.   Zhang Haiying. "'Removal From Office Due to Tardiness' Triggers Hot Online Discussions," *Workers Daily*, January 29, 2014.

engagements, more of my time can be spent with my family; there are no longer so many courtesies and reciprocities, allowing me to make true friends. I feel at ease with my family and my friends."

Officials Travel with Light Luggage and Few Attendants

Officials' now travel with light luggage and few attendants, and the change in atmosphere in government bodies has triggered a rapid chain reaction in society. A typical example is the "emptied-dishes initiative"

"Have you emptied your dish today?" At the beginning of January, 2013, attention was drawn to a public benefit with the theme of "emptied dishes." It was not a commonwealth organization, but a group of nearly 30 young adults in Beijing who formed ties of friendship in a training session, who decided to call for an "emptied dishes initiative." The action started with several microblogs on Weibo, and it was forwarded about 50 million times in just over a week.

In addition to Weibo, they also distributed 60,000 flyers in Beijing and posted more than 5,000 posters in restaurants on commercial streets and in back lanes. "Over 1 billion people in the world are hungry! An average of 10 million die of hunger every year, one child dies of hunger every six seconds! If we reduce wasted food every day by 5 percent, we can save more than 4 million famine refugees!" read the flyer. One should no longer have the heart to waste food senselessly after seeing the shocking figures.[57]

Xinhua News Agency captured the dynamic accurately and brought it to the eyes of high-level officials by the *Proof of Domestic Dynamics*. On January 17, Xi Jinping gave instructions in reaction to the *Proof,* requiring greater publicity and guidance, striving to make conservation of food and other resources a common practice in society.[58]

The high-level officials and the people echoed each other, and activities centered around themes of food conservation were spontaneously started in the community. Reasonable à la carte orders and packaging leftovers became a vast majority of consumers' response to the emptied-dishes initiative. In the past, when people were dining out, they often felt embarrassed if they did not order many dishes; in most cases, many of the dishes were not finished. Due to the perceived necessity of saving face, people were embarrassed to package leftovers. According to the World Food Program (WFP) of the United Nations (UN), the food discarded each year by China's catering

57.   Cao Ping, Fang Min. "The 'Emptied Dishes Initiatives' was Forwarded 50 Million Times," *People's Daily*, January 25, 2013
58.   Party Literature Research Center of the CPC Central Committee. *Collection of Important Literature—Since the Eighteenth CPC National Congress (I)*, Beijing: Central Party Literature Press, 2014, p. 119.

industry simply for reasons of saving face could feed 200 million people.[59] Now, the people and Xi Jinping share the same view: "understanding that there are over 100 million people subjected to rural poverty, tens of millions of people mired in urban minimum living-standards, and numerous other needy people, the very existence of waste makes me feel very sad."[60] Driven by the emptied-dishes initiative, it has become the fashion to order less food and package leftovers to take home when people dine out.

In February, 2013, the Department of Student Affairs, the Youth Communist League, and the General Affairs Management Office of Yantai University called on the teachers and students to actively participate in the emptied-dishes initiative. Wu Minghua, a 62-year-old member of the cleaning staff in the dining hall of Yantai University, along six other colleagues, responded to the call by eating the students' leftovers, such as dumplings and rice. Speaking of food waste, Wu Minghua was quite frustrated: "We are a conservation-oriented community while the students are a consumer-oriented one." The cleaning staff acted as a mirror in which the students saw their own shortcomings. As a result, many students participated in the emptied-dishes initiative. Yin Shanlong, another member of the cleaning staff, said with deep feeling, "there would be several receptacles of leftovers in the past, and now there are just two, filled only with some soup and water." Zhang Jinlong, director of the Food Service Center at Yantai University, told the media that now with the emptied-dishes initiative, amounts of swill were reduced by two thirds every day, and more than 98 percent of dishes were emptied.[61]

In the second half of 2014, China Agricultural University conducted a survey on various communal canteens, restaurants, families, and managers and consumers of farmers' produce, and the results indicated that the emptied-dishes initiative had achieved good results; according to preliminary estimations, food waste was reduced by half in the communal canteens, restaurants, and other consumer sectors, compared to the same period in 2013.[62]

59.   "China's Severe Waste in Catering Industry Each Year Can Feed 2 Million People," *Chinese Radio Network*, Oct. 17, 2012.

60.   Party Literature Research Center of the CPC Central Committee. *Collection of Important Literature—Since the Eighteenth CPC National Congress (I)*, Beijing: Central Party Literature Press, 2014, p. 119.

61.   A "Record of Saving Action in Yantai University: the Action of Emptied Dishes Enjoys Popular Support," *Jiaodong Online*, June 20, 2014.

62.   Jiao Jian. "'The Emptied Dishes Initiative' Obtains Good Results—An Interview of Committee Member Wu Weihua, Vice Chairman of Jiusan Society and Academician of Chinese Academy of Sciences," *Guangming Daily*, Mar. 16, 2015.

III. WHERE DOES THE CPC'S LEADERSHIP DERIVE FROM?

On March 23, 2015, news was announced of 91-year-old former Prime Minister of Singapore Lee Kuan Yew's death. The great statesman of this small country had utilized concepts of good governance, saying that "the western democratic system can realize effective accountability, however, it cannot guarantee a good government or leaders." Lee's observation contains a grain of truth. Because of their design, the western democratic system and political system are not intended for the selection of an outstanding leadership team. Western parties and the CPC are different. The CPC is an organization that stands for the interests of a part of the community, and no party is better than other parties; if we were to simply presume which party was better, then there might be no need for elections. The basic assumption of elections is that men are equal and no man is better than others and the candidate who most accurately reflects the aspirations of the people will win the election, and thereby take power. Dong Biwu presented a subtle criticism of this logic: "Some comrades think that the mass line means there is no need for the Party to lead. This is wrong. In the absence of the Party's leadership, the people's interests cannot be achieved." He added: "The long-term interests of the people are often invisible to the masses themselves; hence, there must be the Party's leadership, so that the masses will not go astray."[63]

As a Marxist political party, the CPC presupposes that it is better than other parties. Because the CPC bears a noble historical mission, it can claim an insight into laws of social and historical development, and most adequately represent the interests of the people, representing the interests of the entire community, instead of just a subsection. In the CPC's own words, they represent "the fundamental interests of the overwhelming majority of the people." The Marxist party's vanguard logic and traditional Chinese Confucian scholar's political logic align to a certain extent: Both philosophies emphasize that there should be an outstanding leadership team to shoulder the responsibility of leading the people and to build a more perfect order, which is why Marxism ultimately wins in modern China's ideological competition. The outstanding leadership team shall not only be able to discern the laws of historical development and natural laws, but

63.   Dong Biwu. *Our Financial Mission and the Mass Line: Selected Works of Dong Biwu*, Beijing: People's Publishing House, 1985, p. 174. This is different from the democratic system's hypothesis of the rational man, which believes that everyone is rational and self-interested, and they know best their own interests, no one else knows better than himself where his own interest lies. Therefore, all a party need to do is to accurately reflect their aspirations.

also be able to respond to the people's aspirations. The former is a necessary requirement of the vanguard logic, while the latter is a requisite component of democracy. The CPC believes that the two can be unified. In terms of specific strategies of action, the CPC's own words are that it is necessary to maintain an advanced nature, and to adhere to the mass line so as not to become divorced from the wishes and the needs of the masses. Therefore, the CPC ensures that members stay advanced in both morality and competency through constant self-improvement; at the same time, also through a variety of institutional arrangements to ensure its leadership of China, the CPC ensures positive interactions with the community through the mass line, so that the state and society will revolve around this core—the political party. This is the source of the CPC's leadership, which, on the one hand, produces an outstanding leadership through precise selection and appointment, and allows that leadership to develop scientific and rational public policies; on the other hand, it implements these policies effectively through appropriate institutional arrangements.

Why Is Party Discipline Stricter than National Law?

On November 26, 2014, the Central Discipline Inspection Commission was briefed on the results of the investigation of four corrupt officials in Shanxi. The brief's wording included "adultery with others" to describe two female officials. As soon as the news came out, it led to a heated discussion among the public. "Adultery" refers to a married person who consensually has sexual relations with an individual other than his or her spouse. It is not a crime, but it is a violation of ethics. In China's criminal law and related statutes, there is no provision made for prosecuting adultery. However, in the CPC's disciplinary provisions there is a punishment for adultery. Article 150 of the *Chinese Communist Party Disciplinary Regulations* states: "Adultery with others, if resulting in adverse effects, shall be handled with a warning or a serious warning; if the circumstances are relatively serious, offenders shall be removed from Party posts or placed on probation; if the circumstances are gravely serious, offenders shall be expelled from the Party."

Why is Party discipline stricter than national law? This is essential to the nature of the CPC. As a political party with the nature of vanguard, Party members are a part of the vanguard—they are people with special abilities, and they should play an exemplary role, unite ordinary people around themselves by political mobilization, and thereby lead them to join in the struggle for the cause of human liberation.

Party members should adhere to a more stringent standard for self-requirements, in terms of morality and competency. Party members must conduct themselves better than average citizens do, in order to deserve the title of a Party member, which is the logic that party discipline is stricter than national law. National law is a requirement for citizens, and it is a fundamental requirement for citizens; while Party discipline is a requirement for Party members, and it is set to a higher standard for the sake of the Party's advancement.

So, Who Is a Qualified Party Member?

On March 18, 2014, Xi Jinping went to Lankao County, Henan Province. This was not the first time he had been there. At the end of March, 2009, Xi Jinping took a special trip to pay respects at the tomb of Jiao Yulu at Lankao. In Xi Jinping's mind, Jiao Yulu is a monumental leader, and the model of a qualified party member. As early as 1990, Xi Jinping composed a poem to express his admiration for Jiao Yulu: "Who among the masses does not like a good official? Great efforts were made, as if tears were made to rain of the Jiao Tong. Never forget the dunes, either live or die, the people lie at his heart. Snow in the evening and frost in the morning, the will and spirit of a hero never changes. He brought benefits to the people he governs, satisfies their wills for a lifetime."

This is the realm Xi Jinping aspires to. In the past, when Xi Jinping chose to leave the capital, his heart was always filled with this ideal; and when Xi Jinping came to Lankao, his heart was also filled with a hope to learn from Jiao Yulu and encourage more Party members and cadres to be a good cadre like Jiao Yulu.

Jiao worked in Lankao for only 470 days, but in the hearts of the people, he became an eternal legend. His spirit has been able to cross over a half-century and remains timeless, which is because he had at the heart of his public service he upheld the intention to keep all the people in mind, not just himself. He embodied the spirit of struggle and plain living, an integrity driven by the maxim "a revolutionist needs to be a hero in the face of difficulties," and a staunch moral character.

Three months later, at the National Organization Working Meeting, Xi Jinping elaborated the standards of a good cadre: "The major aspects of a cadre are competence and integrity;" "good cadres should have steadfast ideals and beliefs, serve the people, be diligent and pragmatic, have the courage to go outside of their comfort zones, and be clean and honest." Of these five aspects, Xi Jinping laid stress on ideals and beliefs and "daring to play"—maintaining the courage to step outside one's comfort zones.[64] He

---

64.   Party Literature Research Center of the CPC Central Committee. *Collection of Important Literature—Since the Eighteenth CPC National Congress (I)*, Beijing: Central Party

believes that the foremost requirement for a good cadre is holding solid ideals. He has a vivid metaphor: "Belief is the communist spirit's 'marrow';" "if ideals and beliefs are lacking, or if the ideals and beliefs are infirm, the person will be deficient in spirit," which "could lead to political deterioration, greed, moral depravity, and a corrupt life." The status quo is that some Party members are afraid of being responsible and refuse responsibility.[65] Xi Jinping stressed that adherence to principles and having the courage to step outside of the status quo are the basic qualities of a good cadre; "an official should be ashamed of himself for a lifetime if he avoids responsibility" and one's courage to blaze trails is equal to how grand their cause is.

Maintaining the progressive nature of Party members as individuals is the premise of the advanced nature of the Party. To maintain the Party's progressive nature, there is one job that is extremely important: selecting a good successor carefully. At the beginning of the reform and opening up, Deng Xiaoping stressed: "carefully selecting a good successor is a strategic problem, and it is a big challenge related to the long-term interests of the Party and the country."[66] Thirty years later, Xi Jinping has repeatedly stressed that the training and selection of young cadres is related to passing the Party's cause to generations to come and is a matter of the long-term stability of China.[67] The CPC attaches great importance to this work, and the Central Organization Department, responsible for selecting and appointing cadres of the Chinese Communist Party, has thus become the most powerful department in the national government. On January 14, 2014, the *Regulations on Selection and Appointment of Party and Government Leading Cadres* that had been in practice for more than a decade were revised by the CPC to further improve the methodology for selecting and appointing cadres and their procedures for supervision and management.

Who Can Be a Member of the Standing Committee of the Political Bureau?

In the old revolutionary base in Liangjiahe Village, Yanchuan County, Yan'an City, on the wall of the living room of the old secretary Liang Yuming hung

Literature Press, 2014, pp. 337–340.

65. Propaganda Department of the CPC Central Committee. *A Reader of Xi Jinping's Important Addresses*, Beijing: People's Publishing House, 2014, p. 159.

66. Deng Xiaoping. *Senior Cadres Should Take the Lead to Carry Forward the Party's Fine Tradition: Selected Works of Deng Xiaoping (Volume II)*, Beijing: People's Publishing House, 1983, p. 222.

67. Party Literature Research Center of the CPC Central Committee. *Collection of Important Literature—Since the Eighteenth CPC National Congress (I)*, Beijing: Central Party Literature Press, 2014, p. 347.

five framed photographs, one of which was a yellowed seven-inch black-and-white photograph. It depicts fourteen young men dressed in tunics. Xi Jinping, then secretary of the Party branch of the Liangjiahe Unit (now Liangjianhe Village) at the time, sits in the center of the photo. He was 22 years old, and to his right is seated Liang Yuming, nine years older than him.

In January, 1969, Xi Jinping, and more than 20,000 graduates of junior and high schools together were sent to Yan'an to live and work in rural production teams, and be trained by poor peasants. That year, he was 15 years old. Here he saw the most basic and most authentic social reality of China. At that time China was very poor, especially the old revolutionary regions. These children from cities lived in earth kilns, slept on adobe platforms, and ate corn dumplings; the rural life was very hard. Xi Jinping had to shovel manure, transport coal, help to erect dams, and cultivate the land—the poorest life he has ever experienced. But he regards the experience as a valuable asset in life. During the Two Sessions in 2008 when he served as a member of the Standing Committee of the Political Bureau of the CPC Central Committee and the secretary of the CPC Central Committee, Xi Jinping participated in the consideration of the Shaanxi delegation, and he said, "This period of time was a turning point in my life. It can be said that Shaanxi is the root, and Yan'an is the soul. I still remember a lot of things, and a lot of thoughts are associated with that period of time. Like He Jingzhi's poem, "Back in Yan'an," which describes "returning to Yan'an in many of my dreams."[68]

Xi Jinping stayed in Yan'an until October 1975, for nearly seven years, and this was his first experience at the grassroots level. Seven years later in 1982, Xi Jinping voluntarily withdrew from his superior position in Beijing, withdrew from serving as secretary of the Central Military Commission, and went back to the grassroots level from Beijing, this time as the deputy secretary of the Zhengding County Party Committee, Hebei Province. Many years later, Xi Jinping often talks to people about the experience of research in the countryside when he served as the secretary of Zhengding: "I often ride a bike to the countryside when I am in Zhengding, from the north shore of the Hutuo River to the commune to the south of the river—I had to shoulder my bike and walk along the shoreline of the Hutuo River. Although it was difficult, the situation was soberly evaluated, and the distance between the grassroots cadres and the people was narrowed, and sentiments improved."[69]

---

68.   "Empowerment at the Primary Level: Xi Jinping's Youthful Days," *The China Press*, November 16, 2012.

69.   "'Governance of County' by Xi Jinping: Build 'Front Line Headquarter' and the Secretary of County Party Committee Should Have 'Four Haves,'" *People's Daily Online*,

From 1982 to his return to Beijing again in 2007, Xi Jinping worked at the grassroots level for 25 years. It is from this small county, Zhengding, that Xi Jinping rose to the pinnacle of power step by step. We can simply browse the résumés of other CPC Political Bureau Standing Committee members to find out if the "grassroots experience" is a shared experience among them, and whether any members have experienced work at the grassroots level for longer than Xi (Table 3.1).

It is not only the Political Bureau Standing Committee members but almost all CPC leaders at all levels that have some grassroots work experience. When the CPC selects and appoints cadres, whether or not they have grassroots frontline work experience is an important condition, especially work experience in tough environments. Therefore, the CPC has a special system arranged, and requires cadres to work at the grassroots, and hopes that through grassroots experience they will deepen and reinforce their roots. The embryonic form of this system was implemented when the border region government assigned intellectuals, cadres, and students to go to the countryside on a massive scale, and to reform rural society during the Yan'an period. It was formally established in 1991, when the CPC issued the *Decisions on Pushing Forward Training and Educating Young Cadres*, and aimed to cultivate promising young cadres by purposefully selecting them to serve at the grassroots level. The decision also stipulates that when Party and state organs at the city level or higher promote leading cadres to department level or higher, they must have more than three years work experience at the grassroots level.

In the opinion of the CPC, only those who have grassroots work experience can understand people and empathize with their suffering. In this regard, Xi Jinping has deep experience: "after participating in grassroots work, experiencing something difficult and urgent, large-scale and complex ideas in an ordinary post can be felt more deeply in the national conditions, social conditions, and the conditions of the people, and that is often said by people 'at ground level.'"[70] Only through grassroots experience can one's will get the most effective exercise. Since the late 1990s, one cadre in Mission Central, after finishing his master's degree at Peking University, was assigned to work in the famous poverty-stricken county of Luliang in the mountainous area of Shanxi Province. He was not provided housing, and he lived in a ruined temple for two years with no running water, no telephone, and no electricity. Later, when he meets with difficulties in his work, he

April 8, 2015.

70.   *Party Literature Research Center of the CPC Central Committee. Collection of Important Literature—Since the Eighteenth CPC National Congress (I)*, Beijing: Central Party Literature Press, 2014, p. 349.

TABLE 3.1 Experience and Time of Working in Local Authorities for the Members of the 18th Standing Committee of the Political Bureau

Name	Local principal position	Duration of local principal position	Duration of local position
Xi Jinping	Deputy Secretary of Fujian Provincial Party Committee, Secretary of Zhejiang Provincial Party Committee, and Secretary of Shanghai Municipal Party Committee	12 years	25 years
Li Keqiang	Deputy Secretary, Secretary of Henan Provincial Party Committee, and Secretary of Liaoning Provincial Party Committee	9 years	12 years
Zhang Dejiang	Secretary of Liaoning Provincial Party Committee, Secretary of Zhejiang Provincial Party Committee, Secretary of Guangdong Provincial Party Committee, and Secretary of Chongqing Municipal Party Committee	18 years	28 years
Yu Zhengsheng	Secretary of Hubei Provincial Party Committee, and Secretary of Shanghai Municipal Party Committee	12 years	38 years
Liu Yunshan	Deputy Secretary of Nei Monggol Autonomous Regions Party Committee	2 years	25 years
Wang Qishan	Vice Governor of Guangdong Province, Secretary of Hainan Provincial Party Committee, Deputy Secretary of Beijing Municipal Party Committee and Major of Beijing	7 years	17 years
Zhang Gaoli	Vice Governor of Guangdong Province, Deputy Secretary of Guangdong Provincial Party Committee, Secretary of Shandong Provincial Party Committee, and Secretary of Tianjin Municipal Party Committee and Major of Beijing	24 years	43 years

remembers this affirmation: "Nothing can be harder than [Luliang]."

Grassroots experience has another very important role—it can rapidly enhance the ability of young cadres to deal with practical problems. In contemporary China, which is in a rapid transformation period, old and new contradictions interweave, knowledge from books alone is not enough, and more practical experience is needed to build up wisdom and local knowledge. "The harsher the conditions, the greater the difficulty and the more conflicts there are, the more people can exercise their practical tenacity," and "for those young cadres who see accurately, have true potential, and are promising, this process is not a feel-good exercise, but should be a requirement for many different Party positions, over a long time, and with no presupposed promotion forthcoming, to let young cadres gain practical experience."[71]

Through this effective system, arrangements for grassroots experience within the CPC enables the ability to select cadres not only with the relevant work experience, but who also have the wisdom to deal with complex issues. This is an important source for the CPC's leadership.

The Engine of Innovation

In 2006, when Bruce Dickson assessed the future development trends of the CPC, he thought the CPC was not in danger of imminent collapse due to internal decay or external pressure. Although the CPC is facing many serious problems, it proves repeatedly that it has enough flexibility and adaptability.[72] The question is begged: Where does this adaptability come from? Danish scholar Kjeld Erik Brodsgaard and National University of Singapore East Asian Study Institute Professor Zheng Yongnian believe that the CPC's adaptability derives from its organizational adjustments and its willingness to learn. The scholars' work also dedicates a chapter to discussing the CPC's Party school, emphasizing that the CPC's Party school is a unique and indispensable mechanism.[73] Since the 1990s, the CPC has taken on Party education as an essential tactic. Although learning is a time-honored tradition in the CPC, top-down training in the Party and learning mechanisms were established very early on, namely at all levels of the Party

71.   Party Literature Research Center of the CPC Central Committee. *Collection of Important Literature—Since the Eighteenth CPC National Congress (I)*, Beijing: Central Party Literature Press, 2014, pp. 342, 348.

72.   Dickson, Bruce J. "The Future of the Chinese Communist Party." In Jae Ho Chung, ed., *Charting China's Future: Political, Social, and International Dimensions*. Lanham, MD: Rowman and Littlefield, 2006.

73.   *The Chinese Communist Party in Reform*, Kjeld Erik Brodsgaard and Zheng Yongnian, eds. Abingdon, UK: Routledge, 2006.

school and administration institute. With the reform and opening up as a symbol, the meaning and content of the CPC's educational directives has changed quite a bit. During the era of Mao Zedong, "learning" was primarily focused on political enlightenment and a member's political progress. Then, in the era of Deng Xiaoping, requirements of professional knowledge and abilities were added to the educational directives. After 1978, the central leaders of the CPC began to repeatedly stress the importance of learning about the world, and the importance of learning modern science, technology, and new management theories.[74]

The most famous educational institution of the CPC is not the central Party school, it is the Political Bureau of the CPC Central Committee collective learning system. This institution was formally established on December 26, 2002, on the day the Political Bureau of the 16th CPC Central Committee held their first collective learning session. This was an important institutional innovation. Supreme leaders carrying out collective learning was not a part of the CPC's traditional learning system. The 16th and 17th Political Bureau carried out learning sessions 44 and 33 times respectively, and the educational standards are high.

On November 17, 2012, members of the Political Bureau of the CPC Central Committee who had just been elected two days previously carried out a collective learning session for the first time since the 18th National Congress. Until the end of March, 2015, the Political Bureau of the 18th CPC Central Committee has conducted 21 collective learning sessions, with an average frequency of 1.3 months. The educational content is extensive, involving politics, economics, society, culture, ecology, party building, the rule of law, the military, national defense, and historical contexts. From these subjects, collective learning embraces important issues of governance, and is closely intertwined with the needs of the people. Collective learning not only helps the CPC unify thinking and build consensus, but also promotes the introduction of policy. Political Bureau collective learning has become a form of governing process.[75] In a sense, the Political Bureau of the CPC Central Committee's collective learning activities have become an important window for us to observe socio-political trends in China, and an emphasis on learning is often the prelude to a major policy decision.

74.   CPC Central Literature Research Center. *Selected Important Documents since Third Plenary Session of the Eleventh Central Committee (I)*, Beijing: People's Publishing House, 1982, pp. 282–283.

75.   Wang Lixin. "Nation Learning Ability Construction: A Case Study on CPC Central Committee Political Bureau Collective Learning System," which was cited in Chen Mingming. *Comparison of Modern Country Construction in the View*, Shanghai: Shanghai People's Publishing House, 2013, pp. 67–85.

Participants in the Political Bureau of the CPC Central Committee's collective learning sessions not only include members of the Political Bureau, but also include responsible persons from the National People's Congress and the Chinese People's Political Consultative Conference—learning topics are related to their respective government departments. Through learning, the CPC not only maintains powerful governing capacity, but also leads officials to achieve huge successes, showing a strong adaptability.

National University of Singapore researcher Bo Zhiyue who specializes in the study of the political elite, believes that the "China model" actually represents a mode of learning.[76] In addition to the Political Bureau's collective learning, nationwide Party and government organization leading groups have also established a central group study system to strengthen the daily learning of principal leaders. The theory learning center group is like a "party committee version" of the Political Bureau collective study sessions, and is a key platform for the CPC to lead cadres to study politics.

The leading group should carry out regular collective learning sessions and general Party members and cadres should partake in rotating training sessions at Party schools and within the administrative college system. As professor of political science and international affairs David Shambaugh has said, "the Party school system is a vital organization; nationwide, 2,700 Party schools are not only responsible for the training of more than 40 million Party members and cadres at certain levels, but they also play a role in think tanks, conceptualizing reform ideas, and policy formulation." Training at all levels of the Party school and administrative college generally includes four aspects: (1) Marxism-Leninism and new policy documents; (2) the Party's organization and management dynamics and methods; (3) administration, management, and leadership theory; (4) basic knowledge such as economics, accounting, statistics, history, international politics, and philosophy, to expand horizons.[77]

After the 16th National Congress, in order to adapt to a new era of strategic needs for large-scale training of cadres and a great improvement in cadre quality, the CPC established three cadre colleges: Pudong Cadre College, Jinggangshan Cadre College, and Yan'an Cadre College. The themes and classes are different in each college, with rotating training tasks completed by the Party school system, and special subject classes provided. For example, the most important class at Pudong Cadre College is the special training

76.　　Bo Zhiyue. "Political Bureau Collective Learning System and Chinese Mode," *Nanfengchuang*, Issue 3, 2010.

77.　　Shen Dawei. *The Communist Party of China: Contraction and Adjustment*, (translated by Lv Zengkui, Wang Xinying), Beijing: China Compilation & Translation Press, 2011, pp. 205–206.

course for bureau-level members, and three major themes are covered: (1) urbanization and urban modernization; (2) international financial systems and modern financial management; and (3) learning from the reform and development experience in the Yangtze River Delta and promoting scientific developments of the rural west.

Due to faculty restrictions in the Party schools, they cannot always meet the demand of Party members and cadres at all levels for modern knowledge. Since 2000, the CPC has strengthened its cooperation with universities, taking advantage of the complete range of university knowledge, through special training that lets Party members and cadres at all levels keep up-to-date in the subjects of political science, economics, public management, and social management.

In order to encompass all aspects of Party members' and cadres' views, the CPC Organization Department has also established training cooperation initiatives with many foreign universities, regularly sending them overseas to receive special training. Now, many local cadres have overseas learning experience.

It can be said that after decades of effort, the CPC has established an expansive educational system, and has the ability to train all cadres from the central to the local government, from Party committee to industry. Through regular and systematic learning, the CPC is able to continuously improve its ruling ability. It is no wonder that, in February 2015, Xi Jinping stressed in his preface to a textbook written specifically for cadre learning and training, that "Chinese communists rely on learning to get ahead today, and are bound to rely on learning into the future," and "all Party members, especially leading cadres of all levels, should have no lack of ability, for the spirit of time waits for no man. Be diligent in learning, be sensitive in thinking. Through learning, educate others in turn; through learning, cultivate moral character; and through learning, enhance natural talents."[78] Learning has become the constant engine of renewal for the CPC.

The Secret of a Country Lead by a Communist Party

The CPC can effectively realize the leadership of the state, in addition to continuing to strengthen its ruling ability and ruling level, it also needs an institutional mechanism to connect the Party and the country, to effectively hone the will of the Party into national policy, and to guarantee that various departments can effectively implement these policies. Among the many mechanisms of distilling policy, three are quite unique, and very important.

78.   Xi Jinping. "Leading Cadres at All Levels Should Constantly Enhance Skills," *Chinese Youth Daily*, February 28, 2015.

The first is the "leading-group" mechanism. In December, 2013, only a month after convening the third plenary session of the 18th CPC Central Committee, the CPC set up a new mechanism, the Comprehensively Deepening Reform Leading Group, with Xi Jinping as the group leader. For those who do not know Chinese politics, it may be difficult to understand why the group leader of the leading group is the general secretary, and the specifications of the group are so high that four of the seven Political Bureau's standing committees serve on it.

The Central Work Leading Group does not have any influence on the Party constitution but is widespread in the Party's and the country's political procedures, and plays a role in decision, deliberation, and coordination. This organization is essential to China's political operations. The number of leading groups is high; there are both permanent and temporary groups, and they are complementary to the government's conventional administrative methods, and have trans-departmental coordination powers. The higher the status of a group leader, the stronger the team's capacity for coordination and execution. For example, in 2006, the country set up a Deepening Medical and Health System Reform Ministerial Coordination Working Group. Because many departments are involved, the healthcare reform package's inception was protracted. On December 20, 2008, the State Council enhanced the group's specifications by approving the Medical and Health System Reform Coordination Group to the Medical and Health System Reform Leading Group, with State Council Vice Premier Li Keqiang personally taking command. With this news, the media used phrases such as "new medical reform entering the fast lane" to describe the new progress in healthcare reform.[79]

Because of this, the Comprehensively Deepening Reform Leading Group established after the Third Plenary Session of the 18th CPC Central Committee has very high specifications, and it can be said to be China's most powerful leading group. The Comprehensively Deepening Reform Leading Group is responsible for overall conceptualization, coordination, supervision, and implementation. As the nerve center of the mission to comprehensively deepen reform, eleven meetings have been held since its establishment, and it has successively examined at least 50 documents, including "Comments on Further Promoting Household Registration System Reform;" the "Supreme People's Court Setting up Circuit Court Pilot Scheme;" "Comments on Strengthening Socialist Deliberative Democracy;" and "Guidance on City Public Hospital Comprehensive Reform Pilot." It has also passed many high-impact plans, and confronted many sources

---

79.   "New Medical Reform into the Fast Lane, *Xinhua Net*, August 14, 2009.

of resistance to reform, sources that had been causing problems for many years. Judicial reform is the issue gaining the most attention in this round of deepening reforms. Seven meetings out of eleven involved the substance of these reforms, and up to twelve relevant plans and mandates were passed successfully.[80]

From the operation of the Comprehensively Deepening Reform Leading Group, it can be seen that important decisions of the CPC occur by drawing up plans in special groups, then handing them to the Standing Committee and Political Bureau to deliberate, for future implementation by the relevant departments. The Central Work Leading Group is one of the most important mechanisms for the CPC to realize the state's and society's overall leadership, and acts as a bridge between the Party and top state leaders and departments. Every leading group in their related functional areas guides an aspect of the Party, government, or military institutions. The so-called "centralized management" in Chinese political life is usually achieved through the Party's leading-group system.[81]

The second mechanism is the Party group system. On January 16, 2015, a meeting of the Political Bureau Standing Committee of the CPC Central Committee was held, and was devoted to listening to a Party group report of the Standing Committee of the National People's Congress, State Council, Chinese People's Political Consultative Conference, Supreme People's Court, and Supreme People's Procuratorate. Xi Jinping, at the meeting, stressed that a very important method by which the Party's Central Committee will lead the Standing Committee of the National People's Congress, the State Council, the Chinese People's Political Consultative Conference, the Supreme People's Court, and the Supreme People's Procuratorate, is to set up Party groups in these institutions. Party groups are organizations set up by the Party Central Committee and local Party committee at all levels in non-Party organization's leading agencies, and they are important in realizing the Party's lead in non-Party organizations.[82]

The Party, through various committees, operates at all levels in non-Party organizations. As agencies, the Party committees are different, the Party members are elected, but the members of the non-Party organizations

80.   "The Eleventh Deepening Reform Group Meeting Chewed over Many 'Tough Is-sues'—Highlighting 'Four Issues of Importance,'" *Xinhua Net*, April 2, 2015.
81.   Zhou Wang. *China Group Mechanism Research*, Tianjin People's Publishing House, 2010, p. 13; Ken Lieberthal. *Governance in China: From Revolution to Reform*, translated by Guo Chenghu, et al. Beijing: China Social Sciences Press, 2010 edition, p. 219.
82.   "Xi Jinping Presided over Political Bureau of The Central Committee Standing Committee Meeting And Delivered An Important Speech," Chinese People's Political Con-sultative Conference Net, January 16, 2015.

are not necessarily elected. However, the non-Party organizations accept the leadership of the Party committees at the corresponding levels. It is through the Party committees that the Party can effectively realize all kinds of non-Party organization's leadership. In the National People's Congress, for example, when the People's Congress is not in session, the National People's Congress Standing Committee within the Party implements the Party's will, and Party members in general are led by the chairman and vice chairman of the Party (and the standing committees of local People's Congresses by the director and deputy director of the Party members) and secretary. In practical terms, the People's Congress Party is, to a considerable extent, the core of leadership of the NPC Standing Committee. Party control is actually shared between the Party committees and the Standing Committee via a joint channel of communications. The Party committees implement the decisions of the Party into practical actions to the Standing Committee of the National People's Congress. Then, the Standing Committee of the National People's Congress passes on relevant referrals and reports to the Party committee at the same level. Party committees at the corresponding levels belonging to the People's Congress and the Party have two different systems from the perspective of inner Party relations.

The third mechanism is the CPC leader's service in national institutions. For example, Xi Jinping is the Party's general secretary and Central Military Commission chairman, but at the same time he is president and chairman of the State Military Commission, and on other standing committees of the Political Bureau he serves as vice president, premier of the State Council, vice premier, and chairman of the National People's Congress.

Through these three mechanisms, the CPC can more easily overcome mutual vetoes and disadvantages of inefficiency, which may occur under a decentralized system. American political scientist, political economist, and author Francis Fukuyama has said, "the United States' two-party system sends American politics into polarization periodically, and the separation of powers makes a certain part of the political system relatively easy to obstruct in other parts, so as to form 'vetocracy', and the whole system is subject to veto power."[83] In divided government, if political parties are not able to effectively coordinate the relationship between the legislative institutions and administrative departments, then political impasse is reached, and even federal governments sometimes have to bring their workings to a halt. In the nineteen years from 1977 to 1996, the US federal government closed seventeen times, an average of almost once a year, and the most instance

---

83.   Conversation of Li Shimo and Fukuyama: Sino-US System Comparison, *Observer Net*, March 30, 2015.

occurred in October, 2013. At that time, the French newspaper *Le Monde* published a review with the title "Jefferson, wake up! They've become idiots!" In contrast, the CPC's party policy can not only make decisions based on long-term goals, and not be swayed by interest groups in the decision-making and implementation process, but also through the Party it can effectively coordinate legislation and administration and relations between different administrative departments, to make policy formulation and implementation more seamless.

Pragmatism, Honesty, and Moral Stature

On May 9, 2013, the CPC issued the *Notes on Carrying out the Party's Mass-Line Educational Practice in the Party*, which requires members to maintain the Party's mission for advancement and purity, and to carry out educational directives with the themes of pragmatism, honesty, and moral stature. As a mobilized "party of the masses," it is not surprising that the CPC has launched this directive, because the CPC has committed to the idea as a way of governance.[84]

One maxim often spoken by Xi Jinping is "one point deployment, and nine points implementation." To implement the intensive introduction of reform measures, in addition to achieving effective leadership of the country, it is necessary to encourage effective social mobilization, and strengthen society to identify the CPC's route to progression, principles, and policies. The Third Plenary Session of the 18th CPC Central Committee proposed 60 reform tasks, which may be one of the most ambitious reform programs in the history of humankind. It will require speedy and tough reforms. Such an arduous task is not possible without the public's support.

Mao Zedong, in summing up the successful experiences of the Chinese revolution, emphasized that the "mass line," the culmination of the correct ideas the masses gain in everyday life, is the Party's ruling foundation, and is essential to guarantee that the "three magic weapons" will play their respective roles. In 1979, just after the Cultural Revolution, China was devastated, reform was beset by difficulties, and Deng Xiaoping brought the concept of the mass line to the fore once again: "as long as we maintain close ties with the masses, work deeply and speak reason to people clearly, we can earn people's sympathy and understanding, and bigger difficulties can also be overcome."[85]

84.   Lieberthal, Ken. *Governance in China: From Revolution to Reform*, (translated by Hu Guocheng, et al.) Beijing: China Social Sciences Press, 2010, p. 73.
85.   Deng Xiaoping. *Senior Cadres Should Take the Lead in Developing Party's Fine Tradition: Selected Works of Deng Xiaoping (Volume II)*. Beijing: People's Publishing House, 1983, p. 229.

Today, reform has entered deep waters, and Xi Jinping once again has brought up the mass line as his "magic" instrument; he uses a vernacular to elaborate general requirements of mass-line educational practices: "educational practices should focus on self-purification, self-improvement, and self-cultivation." He implores Part members to "look in the mirror, dress well, take a shower, maintain good health."[86]

Mass-line educational practice is the Party's means of self-purification, and this is the premise of the Party's social mobilization. Only with self-perfection can the Party through unite the masses around itself. As Deng Xiaoping said, in China, with the introduction of any major policies, facing major adjustments of interests, "without the high prestige of the Party and the government, it is impossible."[87] Educational practice and the Party's self-purification are means of repairing the foundations of trust between the Party and the masses, maintaining the credibility of the Party line, its principles, and policies, and strengthening the masses' identification with the Party leaders.

In the CPC's ideological discourse, "mass line" has connotations across three aspects: First, its political meaning, that is, the basic political course of the Party and its fundamental organizational line. Second is its methodological meaning, namely "from concentrating on the masses to insisting upon the masses to forming a correct opinion of leadership as the basic leadership method."[88] The third meaning is one of style, that is, when maintaining close ties with the masses, the Party is at its finest.

The mass line as an organizational directive, which, in addition to requiring Party members and cadres at all levels to maintain close ties with the masses, also needs to maintain specific organizational mechanisms.

These organizational mechanisms have both direct and indirect aims. For the former, the CPC has been trying to strengthen its organizational system, striving to achieve full integration into society. In recent years, the CPC Organization Department has vigorously carried out measures that are embodiments of this effort. An example of the latter is the people's organizations . They are the link bridging the CPC and the masses, and an important starting point for the CPC to carry out social mobilizations. Westerners seldom comprehend the people's organizations in the Chinese

---

86.　"The Party's Mass Line Educational Practice Work Conference is Held, Xi Jinping Delivered an Important Speech," Xinhua Net, June 18, 2013.

87.　Deng Xiaoping. *Senior Cadres Should Take the Lead in Developing Party's Fine Tradition: Selected Works of Deng Xiaoping (Volume II)*. Beijing: People's Publishing House, 1983, p. 217.

88.　*Selected Works of Mao Zedong Volume III*, Beijing: People's Publishing House, 1991, p. 900.

political system, and often confuse them with general social organizations. In fact, the difference between the two is quite large. Social organizations are managed by the State Council, and people's organizations are led by the CPC's Secretariat of the Central Committee. In accordance with the CPC's principles, one belongs to government, and one belongs to the Party. People's organizations are peripheral to the Party, so it is easy to understand why they are a link between the CPC and the masses. The CPC attaches great importance to the role of people's organizations. Released on February 3, 2015, *Notes on Strengthening and Improving the Party's Alliance Work* emphasizes "unifying the broad masses more closely around the Party."[89]

People's organizations include the Labor Union, the Communist Youth League, and the Women's Federation which were founded after the establishment of the PRC. A huge organizational system was instituted from the top down. At the grassroots level, these people's organizations and the Party's grassroots organizations are intertwined, and weave an expansive network, to provide effective organizational means for the CPC to carry out its social mobilization goals. In recent years, people's organizations, including the Labor Union, the Communist Youth League, and the Women's Federation, have been actively seeking to transform themselves, trying to assume the function of social hubs for their members while supporting relevant social organizations. For example, in Guangdong Province, the Guangdong Communist Youth League has 30 "cultivation and incubation" sites, and has established more than 366 new social organizations.[90] These social organizations have become an extension of the people's organizations, and make it easier to lay the foundations for social mobilization.

89.   "The CPC Central Committee Issued 'Opinions on Strengthening and Improving Party's Alliance Work'," Xinhua Net, February 3, 2015.
90.   Shi Yong. "Social Organization Reconstruction under Transformation of Communist Youth League," Nanfengchuang, Issue 10, 2014.

CHAPTER
4

The Major Reforms Deciding China's Fate

Early in 2013, Zhang Weiying, a professor at Beijing University, wrote an arresting turn of phrase in the Foreword to a new version of the book *Reform*: "The thirty-five-year reform and opening up went through many ups and downs. In the past decade, perhaps the most extraordinary ten years, totally different or even opposite evaluations can be drawn from different perspectives. My basic evaluation is this: By the economic growth index, it has been the best ten years; by the incidence of social contradictions, it has been the worst ten years; and by the outcome of the reform, it has been ten lost years." And he believed that "the ten coming years will be a 'window period' of reform in China."[1] Many people agree with Zhang Weiying's views.

The Third Plenary Session of the 18th Central Committee of the Communist Party of China (CPC), held in November 2012, put forth the major decision of "comprehensively deepening reform." Xi Jinping's statement in the decision shows that the CPC is clearly aware that "many people inside and outside the Party, both at home and abroad, are concerned with the reform and opening up of China, and the entire Party and all walks of society have high expectations. To face the future, to solve the difficulties brought about by development, resolve the risks and challenges from

1.　Zhang Weiying (chief editor). Foreword to: *Reform*, Shanghai: Shanghai People's Publishing House, 2013, pp. 1, 7.

all sides, and give a better play to advantages of "Socialism with Chinese Characteristics," as well as to promote sustainable and healthy economic and social development, China has no options other than to deepen the reform and opening up."[2]

The CPC's determination to launch the reform, as well as the scale of the reform, is rare in human history. It involves over 60 different tasks and 336 concrete reform measures, including the economy, politics, culture, society, ecological preservation, national defense and the military, and the Party itself. Several days later, State Councillor Liu Yandong visited the US. When she introduced the enormous reform package to the American people, they were stunned. On December 12, 2013, a leading group for the comprehensive deepening of reform was created, which came up with an intensive series of concrete reform measures, and in November 2014, all 60 reform projects were essentially started.[3] The sketches outlined by the Third Plenary Session of the 18th Central Committee of the CPC have become a series of distinct roadmaps and projections for reform.

Many people couldn't help asking questions like: What kind of glory and dream will China continue to pursue, after it has been marching on the reform road for over 30 years? What are the prospects of this vigorous reform? What kind of influence will it produce on China and on the world? Is it still too early to evaluate its influence? Many people see the hope of China's future in Xi Jinping, and many people worry about the reform's prospects. Among these people, the shifts in Professor David Shambaugh's opinions offers food for thought. In 2008, he had a fairly optimistic view about the prospect of CPC reform, stating that "so far, the Chinese are doing rather well," and "in order to solve the problems it faces, the CPC is carrying out fairly (though not completely) effective adjustment and reform."[4] But in the face of the bold and resolute reforms instituted by the CPC, he wrote an article in the *Wall Street Journal* on March 6, 2015, stating that this reform will take China to the verge of collapse.[5] But no matter how we judge the prospects of the reforms, pessimistic or optimistic, there is one thing China can be sure of—this is a reform that will decide China's fate.

---

2.   *Selection of Important Literature Since the Eighteenth National People's Congress (Vol. I)*, Beijing: Central Literary Contributions Publishing Bureau, 2014, p. 508.

3.   Li Gang. "Sixty Reform Tasks Basically Started," *Qilu Evening News*, November 3, 2014.

4.   Shambaugh, David. *Communist Party of China: Atrophy and Adaption*, (translated by Lv Zengkui, and Wang Xinying), Beijing: Central Compilation & Translation Press, 2011, p. 11.

5.   Shambaugh, David. "The Coming Chinese Crackup," *The Wall Street Journal*, March 6, 2015.

I. POWER IS NOT TO BE USED ARBITRARILY
Defining the Borderline Between Government and Market

Among the reform tasks put forward by the Third Plenary Session of the 18th Central Committee of the CPC, the most important will be the economic reforms, the core problem of which is to resolve the relationship between the government and the market.

Since Deng Xiaoping delivered the Southern Tour speeches in 1992, the CPC has established the setting up of a market economy as the goal of economic reform. In the two decades following that, the relation between the market and the government became a topic that the CPC tried its best to resolve. From the 14th Central Committee to the 18th Central Committee, the basic direction of the efforts has been "to give play to the basic role of the market in resource allocation to a larger extent and in a large scope."

The Third Plenary Session of the 18th Central Committee of the CPC made an important theoretical breakthrough by putting forward that the market shall play a decisive role in resource allocation, simultaneously stressing that the government shall play a stronger role.

It is a great leap from the "basic role" to a "decisive role," though only a single word is different. The notion that the government must play the stronger role springs from the simple idea that the government and the market weaken each other and stresses that they must actually complement each other. The establishment of a complementary relationship between the government and the market will greatly facilitate further digging into the economic growth potential and improvement of growth quality. The primary reason that it is increasingly difficult to tap potential is that market distortion seriously suppresses the release of potential, and government overreach and bloated state-owned enterprises (SOEs) are the two main causes of market distortion. To enable the market to play the decisive role, efforts must be put into government reform and SOE reform.[6]

An Effective Government, an Effective Market

"It was another day in the spring of 1992. An old man composed a poem on the South Sea coast of China." This is a lyric from a popular song in China, and the old man in the song is Deng Xiaoping. The poem written by Deng Xiaoping by the South Sea coast in 1992 not only started the market economic process but also started the course in which the market forces the government to act, embracing a new launchpad for the market economy and

---

6.   Zhang Wenkui. *Liberating SOEs*, Beijing: Citic Press, 2014, p. 233.

government reform in China.

Before 1992, though the newly emerging market mechanism had massively stepped onto the stage of the Chinese economy, its position and function were not high priorities, and the CPC was not quite certain about it. The Chinese economy switched from a structure that relies primarily on a planned economy with market adjustments to a structure of combined planned management and market forces, a top-down structure in which the government regulates the market and the market leads the business enterprises, and then back into the structure that combined a planned economy and market forces in 1989.

The economic overheating, economic disorder, and price distortion problems that appeared around 1991 caused the CPC to doubt and waver about market reforms. It was at this crossroads that Deng Xiaoping's Southern Tour speeches launched the reform of China onto a new track, and the market economy was set free from the debate on socialism versus capitalism and became the direction of all efforts put into economic reform in China, and thus started the process in which the market forces enabled the government to make reforms.

Some people say that present-day China is a bit like China in 1992.

In 1992, the reform in China was at a stalemate, and people were at a loss about the future direction of reform.

In 2013, China was at a hard time in the reform, with the consensus about reform broken down, and the question about where China will go in the future, once again, surfaced.

In 1992, Deng Xiaoping took a tough stand: China will face a dead end without reform.

In 2013, like Deng Xiaoping, Xi Jinping took a tough stand as well: pausing and withdrawing are not a way out. Reforming and opening up only has a present tense, not a past tense.

In 1992, Deng Xiaoping decided that the market economy shall play a basic role in resource allocation.

In 2013, Xi Jinping decided that the market economy shall play a decisive role in resource allocation.

But after all, China in 2013 differs widely from China in 1992. The biggest difference lies in the fact that the current Chinese economy has found a "new normal."

The so-called "new normal" economy, in Li Keqiang's word, is in "triple simultaneous transitions," which are, respectively, a slowdown of economic growth—which is decided by the objective law of economic development; difficult structural adjustments to be made—which is an initiative conceived to accelerate the transformation of economic development modes; and the absorption of the effects of previous economic stimulus policies—an inevitable stage in which to resolve the deep-seated conflicts that have accumulated in the past years.

Under this new normal, China is facing more new problems and new challenges in handling the relations between the government's "visible hand" and the market's "invisible hand," realizing a soft landing for the national economy, from the soaring momentum of high-speed growth, to normal steady growth, while maintaining sustainable development.

"The best government is that which governs least," Adam Smith said long ago.

"A better government means a bigger government and stronger control of enterprises," Prime Minister of India Jawaharlal Nehru believes.

"The best government is that which governs right," China's experience in the past 30 years has taught economists and policy makers.

To allow the market to play a decisive role in resource allocation does not mean that the smaller the government is or the less it governs, the better, but that we have to better define the borderline between the government and the market. A smaller government might be a weak government that could not support an effective market; a strong government might be a government that destroys the operational mechanisms of the market; only an "effective government" and "effective market" should be the goal of our pursuit.

The "ways" are the criterion to check if the government is efficient, or the government's governance is right or wrong. "Simple is the way," Li Keqiang used one ancient Chinese saying to interpret the way of government. "A public spirit will rule all under the sky when the great Way prevails."[7] The government must stick to the tenet of serving the people. It cannot be both a player and a referee at the same time, and therefore lose its sacred duty as the guardian of public interests in the contentions of profits and the people.

"Hold up the principle of sincerity, and perform one's duties with simplicity, without disrupting the people."[8] An effective government must be a limited government, a self-restraining government. A limitless government will inevitably suppress the activities of enterprises and individuals. The government's visible hand, if omnipresent, will seriously damage the market, the "invisible hand."

But neither is it right to "hold up the principle of simplicity and discharge one's duties with simplicity."[9] A brusque government with no laws

---

7.   *Book of Rites: Evolution of Rites.*
8.   Yong Ye. *Book of Analects.*
9.   Yong Ye. *Book of Analects.*

and no achievements is a neglectful government, an inefficient government. An effective government must be a law-based government that works out the regulations for the market, carries out administration and judicial justice according to laws, effectively maintains the market order, constantly improves administrative efficiency and service quality, and promotes the healthy development of the economy.

Under the pressure of the aforementioned triple simultaneous transitions, the government must put its abilities to good use to lead the steady economic transition of China.

The lesson China drew from its successful development in the past three decades is to reduce organizational and institutional costs through reform and opening up and thus liberate the creativity of Chinese people as well as their social productivity.[10] Nowadays, under the pressure of the new normal economy, China's status in the global competition, and the future lives of the Chinese people, depends on whether it can accelerate the reform of government itself, define the borderline between the government and the market, constantly reducing the market's organization costs and institutional costs.

Streamlining administration and delegating power to the lower levels, no matter how painful it is, must be carried out.

At the National Party Congress (NPC) and the Chinese People's Political Consultative Conference (CPPCC) in 2015, Premier Li Keqiang stressed that "it goes without saying that power shall not be used arbitrarily" in the government's work report; it was spoken in all seriousness, and yet retained a sense of humor. This phrase grabbed the audience's attention and soon became another Internet catchphrase.

"Power shall not be used arbitrarily" pinpoints the working focus of the government. What is government? It is the executive organ of state authority—the symbol, carrier, and actualizer of the national public executive power. So how should the government exercise its executive power? As described by the premier, the government shall not use its power arbitrarily. Instead, it shall handle its power with reverence, and discharge its duties with simplicity, aspire toward streamlined administration with a reverence for the people. It shall hold the people in awe and veneration and care about the people, and not disturb the people through its actions.

But for a long time, the holders of power have been too arbitrary. They forgot that the power in their hands is entrusted by the people, and could only be owned and executed with the people's authorization. They turn state

---

10.   Zhang Weiying (chief editor). Foreword to: *Reform*, Shanghai: Shanghai People's Publishing House, 2013, pp. 188–191.

power into a privilege and a personal power, and use it to seek personal gains instead of using it to serve the people. The power that should be delegated to the lower levels is not delegated, and the affairs they should attend to are not attended to.

The Arbitrariness of the Power Holders

At the 2013 session of the Guangzhou People's Political Consultative Conference (GPPCC), Cao Zhiwei, a GPPCC member and the CEO of Guangzhou NewCity Investment Holding Group, drafted a "Long March Flow Chart" to depict the administrative approval process of construction engineering projects based on his own enterprise's tough experiences in obtaining an approval. This chart grabbed the attention of all soon after it appeared in the national NPC and CPPCC: "At present, the whole approval process of an investment project in Guangzhou involves 20 commissions, offices and bureaus, 53 departments, sections, centers, and stations, 100 approvals, and 108 official seals, as well as 36 administrative fees. The total number of business days required by the whole approval process is 2020. Even the shortest and optimal process will take 799 days."[11] In the words of Zhou Dewen, the vice director of the China Association of Small and Medium Enterprises, "with such a complex process, when the process is finished, the original project may be outdated."

Feng Lun, president of the Vantone Group, wonders why the government is always so concerned with the market: "I was going to make an investment in New York. My company was registered in Huairou, the governments at all levels, from the county government, to Beijing municipal government and the State Reform and Development Commission, asked if we can make money. What is there for the government to fear when the shareholders do not worry about losing money?" In fact, the government is not worrying about whether an enterprise can make money but whether it can make money for itself. According to the analysis of the economist Wu Jinglian, in the 1980s, about 40 official seals were required in the enterprise registration process, while at the turn of the century, the number of seals required had been increased to about 100. This is what is called "rent-seeking activities" in economics. With each seal comes a rent-seeking opportunity, which involves both rights and interests.

The administrative reforms after the 18th National People's Congress convey a determined effort to cut off the chains of powers and special interests. Streamlining the administration and delegating more power to the lower

---

11.   Lian Qingqing. "The Political Dream of a Millionaire," *Guangzhou Daily*, September 4, 2013.

levels are, in essence, to remove the bonuses of those power holders. This is nothing short of asking a tiger for its skin, so we can imagine how difficult it can be. This is why Li Keqiang said that this requires great determination, and that no matter how painful it will be, the reform must be carried out. In fact, since the 18th National People's Congress, the streamlining of administration and the delegation of authority to lower levels have become one of the chief subjects of the State Council's work. Li Keqiang promised that after he assumed office he will take this as his paramount task.

The most important task of streamlining the administration and reforming the delegation of authority to lower levels is the restructuring of the administrative approval system. In 2013, the State Council canceled and sent 416 administrative approval items to the lower-level governments, and revised the *Catalog of Investment Project Subject to Government Verification*, along with canceling and reduction of 348 administrative service fees.[12] The cancellation of an increasing number of administrative approval items with high value is becoming a highlight of the reform.

On January 8, 2014, shortly after the New Year, the executive meeting of the State Council decided to promote further deepening of the administrative approval system reform, continue to take on streamlining as the paramount task, and turn the streamlining into a continuous reform activity. This task will be aimed at the administrative reform system itself, requiring that the approval items shall gradually stride toward the "negative-list" management mode, and see that all the items not covered in the negative list shall be decided by subjects at their own discretion. The "negative-list" management mode suggests that the streamlining has shifted—from the quantitative requirements of pure cancellation and decentralization of administrative approval items, toward improving the quality of the administrative approval system itself. Through the year 2014, Premier Li Keqiang held many executive meetings of the State Council, most of which were intended to tackle administrative streamlining and decentralization measures.[13] In 2014, 317 administrative approval items were canceled or delegated to lower levels, and in addition to the 416 items canceled or delegated to lower levels in 2013, the total number has amounted to 733, accomplishing the target of this government—reducing the over 1,700 administrative approval items of the State Council departments by more than one third—ahead of schedule.

In the NPC and CPPCC sessions of 2015, Li Keqiang reasserted calls for "expanding administrative streamlining and delegating more powers

---

12.   *2014 Government Work Report*, www.people.com.cn, March 5, 2014.
13.   Zhang Guo: *2014: 40 Standing Committee Meetings of the State Council, 21 Times Stressing Streamlining Administration*, January 9, 2015

to lower-level governments and to society in general, while improving regulations. The National Reform and Development Commission said it will comprehensively review the non-administrative license approval items and cancel and delegate a batch of administrative approval items, and thereby greatly reduce the pre-approval process and regulate the management of administrative approvals.

The streamlining reform warms the market and loosens the ties around business enterprises. The 27.6-percent increase in the number of new companies registered and the growth of the private investment ratio to 63 percent are clear proof of the effects of such reform.

Even so, in the NPC and CPPCC sessions of 2014 and 2015, the administrative approval system still provoked furious responses from many NPC delegates and CPPCC members.

In the NPC and CPPCC session of 2014, Cheng Long, a CPPCC member and a famous actor, cried foul in a panel discussion: "I have been going through the formalities for a plot of land in China for eight years. The government departments push around responsibilities. I am going to give up this land," he said, "I just want to know what formalities I should go through."[14] In the NPC and CPPCC sessions of 2015, Zong Qinghou, a NPC member and the CEO of Hangzhou Wahaha Group Co., Ltd. complained that "one bottle of water has to be reviewed for half a year. This year, a Shenzhen subsidiary of mine was applying for approval for a packaged drink. After half a year, and only after using my professional connections did I get the approval. This approval system is seriously influencing private innovation."[15]

Why is the approval system like this?

Li Keqiang's words speak the truth. The administrative streamlining in some departments is like "releasing a hand brake but still keeping one's foot on the brake pedal." Some of the administrative approval items are canceled on paper, and appear again in the name of filing and confirmation, or their operations are picked up by secondary government entities or mediators. For example, in January 2014, the State Council canceled the "Class-A environmental protection (pollution regulation) facility operator qualification accreditation," which used to be managed by the environmental protection departments, and afterwards the General Office of the Ministry of Environmental Protection notified the environmental departments at the provincial, prefectural, and municipal levels to abolish the Class-B

---

14.   Lin Qiling. "Cheng Long: Seven Long Years in Going Through Formalities for a Plot of Land, to No Avail," *Beijing News*, March 12, 2014.

15.   Chen Yuanyuan. "Applying Approval for A Bottle of Water Takes Half a Year, Testing the Quality of Administration Streamlining," *Jinan Daily*, March 9, 2015.

qualification accreditation and temporary qualification approvals. But a month later, the China Association of Environmental Protection Industry issued a notice, specifying that it was in charge of the relevant assessment work. From the obstruction of administrative streamlining by this secondary government entity, we can see the consequences of the arbitrary use of administrative power.[16]

All the localities and departments are actively exploring ways of solving these problems.

On May 1, 2013, the Pilot Program for Optimized Approval Process of Construction Engineering Projects in Guangzhou came into formal implementation. It resolves the administrative approval difficulties in policy, and according to Cao Zhiwei's statistics, the administrative approval process has been shortened from 799 to 37 days. Guangdong Guanghong Holdings Co., Ltd. is one of the first beneficiaries of this policy. According to Huang Xiangqing, the vice president of the company, project approval used to take a long time. Often they could not get the approval documented in half a year, or sometimes, they had to set up a team to deal with approval and certification matters. They didn't expect to get the document until August, but in fact, they obtained the document in no more than ten business days and saved a great amount of time and costs.[17]

On January 1, 2015, the Government Affairs and Service Hall of the National Development and Reform Commission was put into operation officially, which uniformly receives and responds to applications for thirteen categories of administrative license items. "Changes are taking place in NDRC, the big holder of approval powers. It has thrown aside its superior feelings, which makes me a little bit unaccustomed"—this is the feeling of a local official who goes to the Government Affairs Hall to handle his business.[18]

Since the 18th National People's Congress, China is determined to seize the breakthrough in the administrative approval reforms to better match the operation of powers and markets, further release the economy's and society's vitality, and create a healthier market competition environment. This is the key to the government and market problems. As Li Keqiang said, there are still a lot of problems in the promotion of administrative streamlining—for example, keeping silent about major charges while admitting the

16.   Shen Qi. "Administration Streamlining: Not Allowing Arbitrary Use of Power," *Shanghai Law Newspaper*, March 18, 2015.

17.   Liu Huaiyu. "Guangzhou Planned Construction Project Approval from 134d to 11d, 90% Process Compressed," *Southern Daily*, June 7, 2013.

18.   Yang Shisheng. "Streamlining Administration: the Last Mile," *China Times*, January 12, 2015.

minor ones, middle-management obstructionism, obstacles in the final stages of approval, and a lack of connection and coordination between the departments. But there is no turning back. The streamlining of administration and the delegation of powers to lower levels will be a continuously carried-out reform measure. "In the next round, we will continue to promote the reform and strive to fight the battle steadfastly," said Li Keqiang.

Both subtractions and additions shall be made.

In August, 2013, the Public Security Bureau of the Shenzhen Municipality uncovered sales of pork from dead or sick pigs. The criminal offender Zhou claimed that he had been producing fine-grained rib meat made of pork from dead or sickened pigs since March, 2012, selling over 150 tons of pork in total to the Shenzhen market. A veterinary medicine, harmful to human beings, was measured in his pork at twelves times the standard amount.[19]

This is not the first report of such a case, but it attracted the public's attention in a stunning way. According to the current food-safety management system, animal quarantine, business, quality inspection, industry and commerce, healthcare, food and drug supervision, and city management departments are all technically in charge of supervisory oversight of the pigs, from husbandry, slaughtering, processing, circulation and sales, to consumption. There is a food safety office in charge of guidance and supervision as well. With so many government departments involved, the supervision network they built should have been airtight, or as long as one of the departments could perform its duties with due diligence and ensure that its area of oversight has no problems, the criminal will not get away with their criminal acts so easily, and the case would have been uncovered long ago, rather than in one-and-a-half years. But this extraordinary case, in which "eight departments could not manage one pig" indeed happened right under the nose of all eight departments.

If the Long March Flow Chart of administrative approval reflects the arbitrary use of power by the administrative departments, then this case reflects the inaction of the administrative departments, because of overlapping functions.

Xi Jinping said, "the market should play a decisive role in resource allocation, but not all the roles."[20] The goal of this reform is not a smaller government and bigger market but an effective market and an effective government. Building a powerful national institution is more important than merely introducing free-market elements. When the government

19.   Yanghui. "150t Pock from Sick Pigs Flowing in to Shenzhen from Maoming, Containing 12x Standard Veterinary Drug," *Yangcheng Evening News*, August 30, 2013.

20.   *Selection of Important Literature Since the Eighteenth National People's Congress (Vol. I)*, Beijing: Central Literary Contributions Publishing Bureau, 2014, p. 500.

has the ability to effectively provide political stability and public products (including infrastructure), it can, in return, secure a good environment for the development of market and political domestic systems.[21] To better distinguish the borderline between the government and the market, the government does not only have to perform a subtraction—not meddling with what is not its business—but also perform an addition—being responsible for its own business.

Reflecting on the addition to the government's responsibilities since the 18th NPC, there are indeed some remarkable trends to review.

Adopting New Legislation to Safeguard the Market Economy

Since the 18th NPC, the legislation programs that promote economic development and improve the market-economy mechanism are currently playing a dominant role. The 12th NPC passed amendments to tourism laws, special equipment safety laws, trademark laws, consumer interest protection laws, budgetary laws, production safety laws, and environmental protection laws, and considered the drafting of an assets-assessment law, waterways law, an amendment to the trademark law and an amendment to the securities law.[22] On April 21, 2015, the Standing Committee of the State Council passed the *Administrative Measures for the Franchising of Infrastructure and Public Utilities*, further opening up franchising in five areas of infrastructure development and public utilities, breaking the long-time monopoly of the SOEs, and inspiring private investment through institutional innovations.[23]

Fighting Monopolies and Maintaining Fair Market Competition

In February 2015, the US-based Qualcomm Incorporated was fined RMB 6.08 billion for monopolistic practices, and was ordered to make rectifications. This is the largest anti-monopoly penalty in the history of China; two months later, the Mercedes-Benz company and its distributors were fined RMB 357 million for maintaining a monopoly, which is the largest anti-monopoly penalty in China's automobile industry. These two largest penalties reflect the constant improvement in the Chinese government's capability and dedication in anti-monopoly investigations and enforcement.

21.   Zhang Jun (chief editor). *Market, Government Governance and Chinese Economic Transition*, Shanghai: Shanghai People's Publishing House, 2014, p. 14.

22.   Zhao Chao, Chen Weiwei. "Galloping on the Fair and Just Track: Scanning of Promotion of Sustainable and Healthy Development of Economy since the 18th NPC," www.xinhuanet.cn, October 15, 2014.

23.   Wan Jing. "Franchising Aimed at Increasing Benefits, Not Price Inflation," *Legal Daily*, April 24, 2015.

These measures are playing an increasingly important role in China's economic reform and transition.[24]

Innovation Instills New Economic Vitality

On September 29, 2013, the new Shanghai Pilot Free Trade Zone was officially put into operation. In the year and a half after its founding, it achieved great institutional innovations—as in the basic establishment of foreign investment management systems with a "negative list" as the core operational formula; the effective implementation of trade supervision systems that focus on providing convenience for traders; the orderly promotion of the financial systems that target the accountability and opening up of the financial service industries; the initial formation of interim- and ex-post supervision systems that take the governmental transformation as their core concerns. On April 21, 2015, the China (Guangdong) Pilot Free-Trade Zone and China (Tianjin) Pilot Free-Trade Zone and China (Fujian) Pilot Free-Trade Zone were officially established at the same time, and the building of China's free-trade zones officially entered the "2.0" phase. The experience of the Shanghai Free Trade Zone will be studied and the relevant lessons applied in an orderly manner in the new free-trade zones to create a new blueprint for reform and opening up and innovative development.[25]

Strategic Planning Creates Favorable Conditions for the Economic Transition

In September and October, 2013, Xi Jinping put forth "The Belt and Road Initiatives," opening the possibility for a new round of opening up. This strategy boosts the opening up of the middle and western areas and the border areas, driving the open economy in the eastern coastal areas to take the lead in transformation and upgrading, and thus to form a new pattern for opening up, a pattern characterized by overall planning between sea and land, complementary cooperation between the East and the West, as well as the new intention of facing the rest of the world. Also in October, 2013, Xi Jinping launched an initiative to prepare for the establishment of the Asian Infrastructure Investment Bank (AIIB), which was not only welcomed by Asian countries but also received lively responses from western and other industrial countries (with the exceptions of Japan and the United States). By April 15, 2015, the Asian Infrastructure Investment Bank had accumulated

24.   Yang Yichen. "Anti-monopoly: New Dynamics behind the Largest-amount Fine," www.xinhuanet.cn, April 23, 2015.

25.   Jin Shuyang, Chen Yong. "Three Free Trade Zone in Guangzhou, Fujian and Tianjin Put into Operation, Urging 2.0 Era," *Securities Times*, April 22, 2015.

57 prospective founding members, 37 of them in Asia and 20 of them outside Asia. The AIIB strategy lifts China to a new level in the world's economic structure, and provides a new buttress for China's industrial upgrades and the internationalization of the financial service industry. At the same time, China is also creating an upgraded version of the China-ASEAN free trade zone. It has signed free trade agreements with Switzerland, Iceland, and South Korea; and a free trade agreement between China and Australia is expected before the end of 2015. These great achievements are expected to create favorable conditions for China's economic transition.

II. STATE-OWNED ENTERPRISE REFORM

Reform, in China, adopts a progressive strategy that addresses the easy issues and avoids the difficult ones. Despite a clear target, platform, and policies, the reform of core departments could not budge.

State-owned enterprises are one type of such core departments. "Promoting the state-owned enterprises to a perfect modern corporate system," a mission put forward in the Third Plenary Session of the 18th Central Committee, was put forward in the Third Plenary Session of the 14th Central Committee 20 years ago; "actively developing a mixed-ownership economy" was a program devised ten years ago in the Third Plenary Session of the 16th Central Committee. The aims of earlier state-owned enterprise (SOE) reforms were to: "relax control over market entry in the monopoly industry, introduce a competition mechanism; carry out the separation of the functions of the government from those of enterprises, state assets management authorities, and public institutions; deepening the administrative approval system reform, and shifting the government's function to serving main market players and creating an excellent development environment." These goals were long ago completed, before at the Third Plenary Session of the 16th Central Committee of CPC.[26] It is a pity that after ten years, such significant measures still haven't been carried out, and the reform of SOEs is still progressing with great difficulties.

The Third Plenary Session of the 18th Central Committee used phrases such as "treading the dangerous shoals" and "biting the hard bones" to describe the reform of core departments like the SOEs. The reason why the reform of SOEs is beset with such difficulties is that the two biggest sources of resistance to reform—reform-perplexing ideologies and vested interests—are most prominent in the SOEs' reform. The state-owned assets

26.   "Decisions of the CPC Central on Several Questions Concerning Improving Market Economic System," *Xinhua News Agency*, October 22, 2003.

worth trillions in yuan is to some extent the largest share of the interests. As Li Keqiang said, "touching their interests seems more difficult than touching their souls." But no matter how deep the water is, we have to wade into it.

The history of the past three decades shows that the difficulties in SOE reform is not to identify the problems or put forward a target and a program, but the ability to carry out such a program. The warning by Xi Jinping that "the deployment is ten percent, implementation is ninety percent," is especially important for SOE reform.

As the leader of SOE reform, the State-Owned Assets Supervision and Administration Commission (SASAC) of the State Council set up a central leading group for to study the major problems in the SOEs, and in July, 2014, launched the "four reforms" pilot project in the central SOEs: (a) launch the pilot program to restructure the State Development and Investment Corporation (SDIC) and COFCO Limited into state-owned capital investment companies; (b) launch the pilot program to develop a mixed-ownership model in China National Pharmaceutical Group Corporation and China National Building Materials Group Corporation; (c) launch the pilot program to allow the board of directors to exercise top management personnel recruitment, performance evaluation and salary management rights in Xinxing Cathay International Group, CECEP, China National Pharmaceutical Group Corporation, and the China National Building Materials Group Corporation; and (d) dispatch discipline inspection groups to two or three central SOEs whose main leaders are managed by the SASAC.[27] These four reform pilot programs basically display to the people the action points in this round of SOE reform.

Driving the Reform of State-Owned Enterprises

On December 19, 2013, Huang Shuhe, the deputy director of the SASAC of the State Council, appeared at the Press Release of the State Council Information Office and introduced the road map to SOE reform. In his eyes, the highlight in this round of state-owned assets and enterprises reform will be to drive the reform of SOEs with the reform of state-owned assets, and the government, as the sponsor, will manage the state-owned assets instead of the SOEs.

From "management of state-owned enterprises" to "managing state-owned assets," may ultimately be only one word's difference in nomenclature, yet great changes will occur to the content, subject matter, and the way the management acts.

---

27.   SASAC of State Council Holds News Release about Four Reform Pilot Project, website of SASAC of State Council, July 15, 2014.

In the past, the SOEs were managed by the SASAC departments at different levels as if they were managing a company; they managed the personnel, procurement, and assets. From now on, as required by "state-owned asset managements," under the framework of the company law, the representative institution of the state-owned assets shall manage the assets as a shareholder.

From "managing state-owned enterprises" to "managing state-owned assets," the orientation and functions of the SASAC are also going to change. In the past, the SASAC has had a strong voice in the appointment of top management, the making of major investment decisions, and the identification and assessment of operation indexes in SOEs. But according to its new orientation, the SASAC will exercise its duties as the contributor, and implore its stock rights as a true shareholder, and carry out the contributor's responsibilities revolving around "assets management," without meddling in the detailed operations activities nor the corporate property rights and operating autonomy of the SOEs.

On December 22 and 23, 2014, in a meeting of the executives of the central SOEs and local SASAC organizations, the executive of the SASAC of the State Council said that the reform of the SASAC's supervision work shall not be merely superficial tinkering, but shall represent the results of deep, substantial, investigations, or a thorough remolding of some aspects. The SASAC of the State Council will have to take the lead to enact self-reform or self-revolution.[28]

"Managing state assets," though seemingly simple, is in fact much harder. The Third Plenary Session of the CPC's 18th Central Committee put forward a call for: "reforming the authorized operation mechanism for state-owned capital, establishing a number of state-owned capital operating companies, and supporting qualified SOEs to reorganize themselves into state-owned capital investment companies."[29] This means that the two-tier management structure of a "SASAC-enterprise" will be broken to form the three-tier structure of a "SASAC-state-owned capital operating company, and an investment company-enterprise." Part of the responsibilities will be assigned to the investment and operating companies as in the areas of enterprise restructuring, mergers and acquisitions, and securities offerings. And the SASAC will be responsible for establishment of systems, formulation of rules, and the supervision and assessment of the state-owned capital operating

---

28.   Wang Yajie. "SASAC Deciding the Focal Point of Work in 2015, SOEs Classification and Supervision Put on Agenda," *National Business News*, December 23, 2014

29.   *Selection of Important Literature since the Eighteenth National People's Congress (Vol. I)*, Beijing: Central Literary Contributions Publishing Bureau, 2014, p. 515.

company or investment company.

If the current SOEs are compared to "players" and the SASAC is compared to a "referee" or "coach," after the launching of a new round of state-owned capital and enterprise reform, the "referee" function of the SASAC shall be further clarified, and the state-owned capital operation and investment companies shall become relatively independent "coaches." Marketized tools will be introduced to inspire the competitive vigor of SOEs—the main market players.[30]

Shanghai, as the local center of state-owned assets and SOEs in China, has an inventory second only to the centrally controlled assets and enterprises in scale. In this round of SOE reform, Shanghai acts as the vanguard. In 2014, Shanghai conducted the "mixed-ownership reform" of the financial industry and initially formed two state-owned capital liquidation platforms for physical and financial state-owned assets. In it, the Shanghai International Group, the market outlier that looks neither like an administrative institution nor like an enterprise, became the first target of the reform. Shanghai International Group was stripped of its enterprise operator's role, and is now merely serving as the contributor. This reform built the Shanghai International Group into a professional state-owned capital investment and operation platform. In the first eleven months of 2014, Shanghai released state-owned assets of about RMB 80 billion in total.[31]

Classification: The Basis of SOE Reform

On December 22, 2014, the SASAC of the State Council said that the focus of the state-owned assets and enterprises in 2015 includes defining the functions of different SOEs, and developing mixed-ownership enterprises in a reliable, standardized, and orderly manner. This shows that there is hope that the classification of SOEs, which has been a controversy for a long time, will be further clarified in 2015.[32]

SOE classification is the basis of SOE reform, for only by clarifying how the SOEs shall be classified can the reform be launched to supervise enterprises of different classifications with different manners. It was because the SOEs were not classified properly in the past that people had so many low opinions of them. The SOEs that engage in pro bono services, such as the

30.   He Xinrong. "From Managing Enterprise to Managing Assets: Three Questions Concerning Deepening State-owned Assets Reform," http://www.banyuetan.org, March 19, 2014.

31.   Lu Ning. "2014: Shanghai 'Mixed-ownership Reform' Stories," *SOE*, Issue 2, 2015, pp. 28–35.

32.   Wang Yajie. "SASAC Deciding the Focal Point of Work in 2015, SOEs Classification and Supervision Put on Agenda," *National Business News*, December 23, 2014.

bus operations, and the postal service, should be the reasonable recipient of state subsidies, while the SOEs that engage in competitive businesses should not be entitled to receive these subsidies. So far, there has been no consensus on the classification as such of SOEs in both official and academic circles.

Time waits for no one. In practice, some localities have already started to try their own classification. Since Shanghai fired the first shot in the reform of state-owned assets and enterprises on December 17, 2013, by September 19, 2014, some seventeen provinces and municipalities including Shanghai, Guangzhou, Beijing, and Jiangsu have issued their opinions on local state-owned assets and enterprises reform. The wild fire of reform is spreading across China.

In the state-owned assets and enterprise reform program of Tianjin and Shanghai's Pudong region, the SOEs are divided into *competitive, public service*, and *functional* classes. The competitive enterprises orient themselves towards the market, take the maximization of economic benefits (i.e., profits) as their main goal, and at the same time take into account potential social benefits, and strive to become the most dynamic and influential enterprises in the business at home and abroad; the public service enterprises provide public products or services to ensure the normal operation and stability of cities and the realization of the social benefits of such stability; the functional enterprises take the completion of a strategic task, or significant specific tasks, as their goal, and at the same time take into account the potential social benefits of their actions. The SOEs of different classifications are not only different in orientation, but also in the form of ownership.

Shanghai SASAC has finished the detailed classification of the SOEs under its jurisdiction. Among over 40 SOEs, most are classified as competitive SOEs, such as SAIC Motors, Shanghai Electric, Bright Food (Group) Co., Ltd.; the functional SOEs include the Shanghai Guosheng Group, Shanghai Real Estate Group Co., Ltd., Shanghai Shendi (Group) Co., Ltd.; and the public service enterprises are Shanghai Shenergy Group Co., Ltd., Shanghai Shentong Metro Co., Ltd., Shanghai Jiushi Corporation, and the Shanghai Municipal Investment (Group) Corporation.[33]

Relatively speaking, the classification of local SOEs is easier than the classification of central SOEs, because most of the central SOEs touch on many different business sectors, with different operational requirements and relationships. For example, for the China National Petroleum Corporation (CNPC), gasoline and gas extraction are its main functions, but its pipeline

---

33.   Wang Daojun, Ji Simin. "Detailed Annotation about Shanghai SOE Classified Supervision: Most of Over 40 SOEs Identified as Competitive Enterprises," *Oriental Morning Post*, July 4, 2014.

business and terminal gas stations are its main competitive businesses. Therefore, a better approach would be to divide the enterprise by business sector, rather than the entire enterprise. There is still a long way to go before reaching a scientific method of classifying the central SOEs.

Mixed Ownership

February 19, 2014 is a day that should be remembered in the progress of SOE reform. On this day, the Chinese Petroleum & Chemical Corporation (Sinopec Limited) made a blockbuster announcement: It proposed to restructure its oil product sales business sector on the basis of an audit and assessment of current assets and liabilities, and at the same time, encourage the investment of social and private capital, in order to realize the mixed-ownership operational model.

On the same day, a work conference on Guangdong state-owned assets and enterprise reform development was held, announcing the official launch of the new round of state-owned assets reform. On that day, the Gree Electric Appliance Co., Ltd. and Gree Real Estate of the Gree Group were among the first to announce their reform program. The reform of the Gree Group includes two important aspects. First, separating Gree Real Estate, Port Corporation, and Zhuhai Gree Aviation Investment Co., Ltd., and Gree Group's liability to Gree Real Estate for free, and instill such assets to the newly incorporated Zhuhai Holdings Investment Group Limited. Second, the Gree Group separation will introduce strategic investment by transferring no more than 49 percent of the company's shares through public listing.

The reform of central SOEs in Beijing and local SOEs in Zhuhai marks the beginning of mixed-ownership reform.[34]

It's no doubt that the mixed-ownership reform is a major factor of SOE reform. Driving the SOE reform with state-owned assets reform is intended to pave the way for the eventual completion of SOE reform; the mixed-ownership reform directly focuses on the fundamental ownership issues of SOEs. Without SOE ownership reform, the SOE market reform will be just an insubstantial reflection, like the moon in the water or a flower in a mirror. "Just like you cannot wake up a person who is pretending to be asleep, you can never wake up an enterprise that lies in the warm bed of state ownership."[35]

Since the Third Plenary Session of the 18th Central Committee, the localities and some central SOEs have put forward all kinds of mixed-

34.   Zhao Chunling. "Guangdong: Mixed Ownership Reform Tide," *SOEs*, Issue 2 2015, pp. 36–40.

35.   Zhang Wenkui. Foreword to: *Liberating SOE*, Beijing: Citic Press, 2014, p. xxii.

ownership reform programs. Among the seventeen provinces that have issued their opinions on mixed-ownership reform, seven of them have identified their time-lines and reform goals in detail,[36] and are exploring stock-based incentives and employee stock ownership, attracting private capital to participate in the projects controlled by state-owned assets and SOEs by means of equity investment, and opening some partners and subsidiaries of the industries to private capital. These means have become the main operating mechanisms of the locality's exploration of SOE reform.

In the exploration of stock-based incentives and employee stock ownership, Shanghai is one step ahead. Shanghai International Port Group (SIPG) became the first SOE to implement the employee stock ownership system. The "SIPG reform program" that came out at the end of 2014 can be described as a "mixed-ownership reform test" with the largest amount of stock subscribed by employees in the state-owned assets and enterprise reform in China. It is also the calmest case. A conspicuous feature of the SIPG reform program is that it refuses to assign the largest shares to the top management. According to the effective and legally binding 2014 Employee Stock Ownership Plan, SIPG issued less than 420 million shares of private stock to its employees, raising funds of no more than RMB 1.8 billion, 1 percent of which is held by members of the top management of SIPG like its president, and the rest (99 percent) is subscribed to by over 16,000 employees. Over 70 percent of SIPG's employees benefit from this program, perhaps the largest proportion in similar reform cases in history.[37] In fact, as far as Shanghai is concerned, there are dozens of municipal competitive SOEs waiting to try the employee stock ownership plan. At the very beginning of 2015, the SASAC's central leading group for comprehensively deepening the reform considered the *Guidance for Implementation of Employee Stock Ownership Pilot Program in Mixed-Ownership Enterprise.* Typically, employee stock ownership will become a key part of the SOE reform.

In attracting private capital to invest in SOEs, the private capital owners have much to consider. On July 15, 2014, Liu Shengjun, the executive VP at CEIBS Lujiazui International Financial Research Center, stated at a symposium on the current economic situation, as chaired by Premier Li Keqiang, that presently the private capital owners are mainly concerned with three aspects of the mixed ownership mechanism: "First, what will the government contribute to the mixed ownership? Second, what proportion

36.   Liu Dong. Over Half Provinces Issuing State-owned Assets Reform Opinions: High Overlapping Content, Low Quality, 21th Century Economic Report, September 20, 2014.

37.   Lu Ning. "2014: Shanghai 'Mixed-Ownership Reform' Stories," *SOE*, Issue 2, 2015, pp. 28–35.

will the private capital account for? Third, will the mixed ownership be unduly interfered with (by any quarter)?"[38] Liu's concerns were not groundless. In June, 2014, the mixed-ownership reform in Eastern China Nonferrous Metals Investment Holdings Co., Ltd. ended up in failure and was restored to state ownership. One of the important causes of the failure was the conflict between administrative logic and market logic after the reform. In the half year after the reform, the president and vice president resigned and the shareholders engaged in six lawsuits. The disputes between shareholders caused by personnel turnovers exposed, on the one hand, the danger of too large an amount of state-owned shares, and on the other hand, the conflict between governmental will and shareholder's value as well as the conflict between the market players' consciousness and the state-owned sector's consciousness.[39]

The Eastern China Nonferrous Metals Investment Holdings Co., Ltd. is by no means the only case of failure. For private enterprises, it is not easy to love mixed ownership models. If the three issues feared by Liu Shengjun cannot be handled properly, mixed-ownership reform may follow the old disastrous road. In one sense, mixed ownership still has a long way to go.

Breaking the "Iron Bowl"

On November 12, 2013, Wang Jianzhong, the CEO of Xiangtan Hengdun Group Co., Ltd., leaped to his death from Xiangtan's government office building. Wang's company was facing operation difficulties and tight finances. For several months, he had been seeking help from the government, wishing to change the nature of a plot of land his company was using from industrial to commercial, and thus pull the company out of the mess it was in. But things did not go as planned, and in desperation, he exited the market by ending his life.[40]

Coincidentally, beside Xiangtang Hengdun Group Co., Ltd., Hunan's well-known SOE Valin Group had been experiencing heavy losses for several years, but the president of Valin did not end his life in desperation as Wang did, because the government is generously using tax payers' money to help the SOE. The government not only provided land and mineral deposits but also coordinated banks in making loans, and offered benefits like tax

38.   Liu Shengjun. "China SOE Reform Avoiding Pains," *FT Chinese* (website), January 27, 2015.

39.   Peng Jieyun. "Mixed Ownership Practice in Awkward Situation: East China Non-ferrous Ownership Reform Dilemma Investigation," *First Financial Daily*, March 20, 2014.

40.   Zhu Liumiao. "Hunan Private Business Owner Jumped to Death from Government Building," *Beijing News*, November 14, 2013.

breaks and cash bonuses to the SOE. In 2010, Valin lost RMB 2.644 billion, and was included in the list of trading losses on both the Shanghai and the Shenzhen stock exchanges. In 2011, Valin got RMB 1.165 billion in government subsidies, and realized a net profit of RMB 7 million in the same year. But in 2012, after the government subsidies were cut off, Valin went into the red once again with a net loss of RMB 3.25 billion.[41] Under such difficult conditions, the top management of the SOE would go on to commit embezzlement. After the 18th Central Committee, the first SOE manager in the iron industry that fell into disgrace was Zheng Boping, the vice president of Valin Group.[42]

But why? In a word, the root cause of such a situation is: bureaucracy. "Living, he towered above all men; dead, he was a hero of ghosts." This proverb, relevant to all aspects of society, depicts the mentality of some SOE leaders.

The saying strikes at the heart of the problems with the SOE governance structure. For a long time, the country has cared for SOEs, paid for all their losses, and offered enviable jobs with excellent benefits. The top management of SOEs, especially those of central SOEs, enjoy both the glory of being an official and a good largess. They move between official circles and the business community. As long as they do not make big mistakes, generally, they could comfortably do this work until retirement. In such a comfortable environment, it is almost impossible for them to be as adventurous and innovative as real entrepreneurs.

Even after mixed ownership reform, it will still be very hard to realize joint governance by all the shareholders. Especially in the state-controlled mixed ownership enterprises, the top management will still be government cadres, and there is great difficulty in implementing market-oriented recruitment systems and salary systems and in turning the top management personnel into true entrepreneurs and professional managers. Their behaviors have to cater to political requirements first and foremost, which will be a great obstacle to such enterprises' commercial operation.[43]

To turn the SOEs into real market players, the government must conduct administrative reforms and cut off the easy sustenance, or "milk supply," recruit the "first hand" of SOEs—especially central SOEs—from the market, rather than let the Central Organization Department appoint its own people, solve the SOEs' top management hiring problem through the

41.   Yi Bing. "Iron Steel Industry Bailout: Valin Steel's Subsidies is Four Times its Net Project," 21st Century Economic Report, August 20, 2014.

42.   Guo Weiwei. "Valin Steel Group's Vice President Zheng Boping Arrested," Oriental Morning Post, April 22, 2014.

43.   Zhang Wenkui. Liberating SOEs, Beijing: Citic Press, 2014, p. 45.

professional management mechanism, and create a batch of SOE officials who are interested in industries do not intend to be officials.

On January 1, 2015, the *Reform Plan for Payment Packages of Executives of Central SOEs* was formally implemented. The reform involves the executives of 72 central SOEs, including 53 central SOEs whose executives are appointed by departments like the CNPO, SINOPEC, and China Mobile, and nineteen other enterprises in the finance and railway industries. It is worth noting that the plan requires that the payment package reform shall match the selection of the central SOE executives. This means that the payment for such executives will be determined according to the SOE's classification and nature as well as the status and selection and appointment methods of SOE senior management. If they are appointed by the organization, and can claim an administrative identity, their salaries will not be market-oriented. Instead, their salaries will be comparable to the pay of public functionaries of the same rank. If they are selected through professional management recruitment, their salaries will be market-oriented. This system breaks the "iron bowl" tenure of SOE executives, and stipulates corresponding incentives, balancing restraints and market incentives.[44]

Anti-Corruption: Helping State-Owned Enterprises Reform

With the intensive advancing of the SOE reform, SOE anti-corruption measures are also being launched at an accelerating pace. In the new economy, the parallel implementations of high-pressure anti-corruption measures and market-based reforms may be viewed as simultaneously overcoming bad institutional habits, the "scraping of poison off the bones," and spurring innovation.

In 2013, seventeen SOE executives fell into disgrace. In 2014, the number of SOE executives that fell into disgrace increased to 70. In the first quarter of 2015, 38 SOE executives were investigated, or over half of the number of executives that fell into disgrace over the course of 2014.[45] Since the central leading groups for inspection work were stationed in 26 central SOEs in March, in one month, eighteen central SOE executives had fallen. Some media call this the "one-day-one-down" pace of anti-corruption actions since the first SOE executive's removal was announced after the NPC and CPPCC's sessions.[46]

44.   "SOE Reform: Hand-in-hand Promotion of Anti-corruption and Reform," *Business Weekly*, Issue 4–5, 2015, pp. 14–17.
45.   Li Wenji, Zhang Ying. "38 SOE Top Management Personnel Fall into Disgrace in This Year," *Legal Evening News*, April 8, 2015.
46.   Pan Yuan. "SOE Anti-Corruption Could not Only Rely on Leading Group for Inspection Work," *China Youth Daily*, April 19, 2015.

Under the new economic normal, the SOEs have entered the ascending phase, and are in urgent need of reform, with a keen determination to release their vitality. However, there is an unavoidable problem, that is, the SOEs' corruption is still not effectively curtailed. Against such a background, the promotion of reform faces difficulties and SOE development was stifled. Since the 18th Central Committee of the CPC, the five rounds of inspection by the central leading groups reflect the central government's emphasis on SOE anti-corruption initiatives, and conveys to the public a strong signal of strengthening anti-corruption efforts, driving the SOE reform to go into true depth through the greater anti-corruption campaign. Hence, the SOE anti-corruption measures are not merely extensions of the broader anti-corruption initiative, but a campaign aimed at deepening the SOE reform, driving it through the "deep-water zone," involving an all-around commitment.[47] "Identify the problems, drive the reform, find out the causes from the institution and management, promote systematic perfection, detail the power list and responsibility list to provide references for comprehensively deepening the reform." Putting forth fundamental means by which to cure problems after they are identified is the new concept developed in the new round of inspection and the future direction of SOE anti-corruption efforts. In the days when great changes are taking place in the ownership system and assets management method and mixed ownership is being gradually promoted, the boundary between state-owned capital and private capital will become increasingly indistinct, and in a great number of fields, they will each have something of the other and mutually integrate. This will impose higher requirements for SOE supervision and the prevention of state-owned asset losses.

To solve SOEs' serious ethical problems, it is essential to solve the insider control issue and SOE executives' oversight issues that have existed for a long time. Under market economy conditions, the solution is to shorten the owner's principal-agency chain, and truly establish a modern enterprise system, implementing a corporate governance structure. The frequent occurrence of corruption cases in the CNPC was rooted in the institutional weakness of the operation and management: the excessively concentrated power of SOE executives and a lack of effective oversight and restraints. One result of such problems is that once the insiders reach an agreement, evidence of their complicity may be hard to discover.[48] In this sense, the SOE anti-corruption initiative must dig out those audacious offenders and punish

47.   "SOE Reform: Hand-in-Hand Promotion of Anti-Corruption and Reform," *Business Weekly*, Issue 4–5, 2015, pp. 14–17.
48.   Pan Yuan. "SOE Anti-Corruption Could not Only Rely on Leading Group for Inspection Work," *China Youth Daily*, April 19, 2015.

them severely, in accordance with Party disciplinary standards and national laws. The even harder task is to perfect a series of oversight systems within the SOEs, and promote the dismantling of impenetrable bureaucracies in SOE management and senior management.[49]

On January 13, 2015, Xi Jinping stressed in the Fifth Plenary Session of the 18th Central Committee's central discipline commission that "we have to focus on improving the SOE oversight system, strengthening the Party's leadership of SOEs and the supervision of SOE leadership, doing a good job in the inspection of SOEs, and intensifying audit and supervision efforts. The state-owned assets resources are hard-won, and they represent the collective wealth of the people." China must improve the oversight system of state-owned assets resources, intensifying the supervision of departments and posts that retain concentrations of power and influence.

III. DELIBERATIVE DEMOCRACY: A BREAKTHROUGH FOR POLITICAL REFORM

On July 4, 1945, Independence Day for the US, as the American people were celebrating, Mao Zedong invited Huang Yanpei to be a guest at his home. They had a long talk in the afternoon about the rise and falls of countries and peoples. When Mao Zedong asked Huang Yanpei how he felt about Yan'an, Huang said frankly, "Having lived for more than 60 years, disregarding what I have heard, from what I have seen, the situation can be described as 'quick to rise, and quick to fall,'—there is not one person, one family, one group, one place, nor even a country, that can escape being dominated by this cycle." He asked Mao Zedong if the CPC could break out of historical cycles. Mao replied, "We have found a new path; we can break free of the cycle. The path is called democracy. As long as the people have oversight of the government, the government will not slacken in its efforts. When everyone takes responsibility there will be no danger that a policy will terminate when the leader dies." Hearing this, Huang said, "You are right. Only if the major policies are decided by the public, the individual's desire for achievement will not disappear. Only if the matters of a locality are announced to the people of this locality, the place will be full of talents that each will do his best to achieve. Democracy may break the cycle."[50]

49.　"Xi Jinping's Important Speech on the Fifth Plenary Session of Discipline Inspection Commission of the Eighteenth Central Committee of CPC," *Xinhua News Agency*, Jan. 14, 2015.

50.　Huang Yanpei. "Return from Yan'an," published in: *A Selection of Literature for Research on the Yan'an Democracy Model*, Yanhan Democracy Model Research Group, ed. Northwest University Press, 2004, pp. 220–221.

But what should the new path of democracy be like? Neither of them dwelt on the details. Huang Yanpei put forth an abstract concept, and Mao Zedong's response stuck to his principles.

After 70 years, Xi Jinping has answered this question. On September 12, 2014, in the meeting held to commemorate the 65th anniversary of the establishment of the CPPCC, Xi Jinping depicted the democratic vistas with Chinese characteristics: "China's socialist democracy has two forms. One is electoral democracy, which ensures that the people exercise their rights through elections and ballots, and the other is deliberative democracy, which ensures that the people conduct consultations before major policy decisions are made. In China, these two forms of democracy are not interchangeable or opposing but mutually complementary. Together, they constitute the characteristics and advantages of the Chinese socialist democratic politics."[51]

"China's Deliberative Democratic System: Superior to the Democratic Systems in Many Western Countries"

In 2002, Xi Jinping headed the administration in Zhejiang. In this year, Wenling, a city of Zhejing, a prefecture-level city under the jurisdiction of Taizhou, began to upgrade their indigenous democratic consultations into an example of Chinese grassroots deliberative democracy.

The democratic consultation, originally a form of ideological and political work, was born in 1999. At the time, under the unified deployment by the Provincial Party Committee, the Taizhou and Wenling municipal propaganda departments selected Songmen Town as the pilot area for the "modern agricultural and rural education forum." Borrowing the form of a press conference witnessed on television, Songmen Town held the forum in the format of a "two-way dialogue with the masses," finding that this forum produced wonderful results, and the people complained that they hadn't had such a chance to speak for 20 years.[52] This is the original format of the "democratic consultation."

The experience of Songmen Town and its success was soon spread to all the towns of the prefecture, and the dialogue-based consultation was quickly developed into a decision-making consultation. At the beginning of 2002, the number of people participating in the democratic consultations in Wenling had reached up to 300,000 people, amounting to one fourth of the total population, over 15,000 entreaties were put forth, near 10,000 replies

51.   Xi Jinping. The Speech on the 65th Anniversary Celebrating the CPPCC Establishment, *People's Daily*, September 21, 2014.
52.   Chen Yimin. "Wenling Democratic Heart-to-heart Discussions: Seeking Growth Space for Democratic Politics." *Decision*, Issue 1, 2005.

were made on the spot, and about one third of the problems brought to light were solved or appropriate programs to address them were carried out.[53]

So far, the democratized consultation is still a way to realize grassroots democracy, and is not connected to deliberative democracy. In 2004, the inference of a foreign scholar changed the situation.

In August of 2004, an academic conference centered on the theme of deliberative democracy was held in Hangzhou. At this conference, Wenling's officials responsible for democratic consultation work met Professor James Fishkin of the Department of Political Science at Stanford University, and learned about the deliberative polling methods he advocated.

Fishkin is the first advocate and practitioner of deliberative democracy theory. Early in 1988, he created the deliberative polling method to connect the advantages of public opinion polling and the deliberative democracy model. According to Fishkin, the results of public opinion polls are about what the public think, and the results of deliberative polling are about what the people would think.[54] In deliberative polling, representatives are selected by random sampling, and through exchanges and consultation among the representatives, consistent decisions are made in the formulation of public policies.

The officials responsible for promoting the democratic consultation felt at the time that this program would be of great help to the promotion of democratic consultation. Jiang Zhaohua, at that time the Party chief of the town of Zeguo, invited Professor Fishkin to Zeguo to arrange the democratic consultation on use of construction funds in a deliberative democratic way. Fishkin readily agreed, and went to Wenling two times with Professor He Baogang of Australia's Deakin University. Together, they privately presided over the questionnaire design. The deliberative democratized method was officially introduced into the practice of democracy at the grassroots level in China, and democratic consultation became the preferred form of deliberative democracy.

In these democratic consultations, twelve experts were invited to join a working force with the town's Party committees and government and to use the scientific random sampling method to select 275 representatives from the town's population of 120,000. Ten days before the consultation, the selected representatives received the explanatory materials on 30 projects and the expert panel's neutral and impartial project introduction.

53.　　Chen Peng. *Countryside Deliberative Democracy Practice Under the Interaction of Country and Society*, Shanghai: Shanghai Century Publishing Group, 2012, p. 83.

54.　　Fishkin, James. *Democracy and Deliberation: New Directions for Democratic Reform*. New Haven, CT: Yale University Press, 1991, pp. 1–4.

On the day of the meeting, 259 representatives attended the meeting and filled out a questionnaire concerning the degree of importance of the 30 projects. In the morning, the 259 representatives were divided into sixteen panels by random sampling to enter the panel discussions, which were presided over by a trained chairperson. After the panel discussion ended, the representatives participated in the discussion portion of the conference, with the problems of biggest concern and the most concentrated opinions. In the afternoon, the representatives were once again divided into small panels, and then participated in the second conference discussion session with new problems and opinions. All the government officials were present in the two conference discussion sessions. After the democratic consultation ended, the same questionnaires were once again sent to the representative for the second tests.

After the meeting, the town Party committee and government called an office meeting to discuss the advice provided by representatives at the consultation and the primary results of the second questionnaire survey. The twelve top projects in the survey were proposed as the 2005 basic urban construction projects. On April 30, 2005, in the fifth meeting of Zeguo Town's 14th People's Congress, by discussion and vote, the representatives passed twelve projects selected by the representatives through consultation and discussion.[55]

The whole democratic consultation process is very standardized, and the representatives participating in the heart-to-heart discussions behaved very well. Professor Fishkin, who participated in the organization of the whole course of discussions said, "this is better than democracy in the US." Taking the example of Zeguo, he encouraged American citizens to institute more deliberative democracy practices. He also said the deliberative democracy practice in China can directly influence policies, and therefore, it is much more effective than the citizens' assembly in Canada.[56]

When the grassroots deliberative democracy flourished everywhere in Wenling, top-level political consultations were also shining with a new vitality

55.   He Baogang. *Deliberative Democracy: Theory, Method and Practice*, Beijing: China Social Sciences Press, 2008, pp. 168–169.

56.   Ibid., p. 268. In 2004, a deliberative democratic experiment was held in the third largest province of Canada, British Columbia, which selected 160 citizens through a random selection method to compose a citizens assembly to assess and redesign the election system of British Columbia. After a long year's operation, the citizens thought that the selection system should be changed to the single transferable voting system. In May 17, 2005, British Columbia held a referendum about the citizen assembly's advice, but the vote results overruled the advice. For more details see: Mark E. Warren and Hilary Pearse, *Designing Deliberative Democracy: The British Columbia Citizens' Assembly*, Cambridge University Press, 2008.

under the guidance of deliberative democracy theory, and Guangdong, well-known as the frontier of reform and opening up, once again took the lead in adopting this system.

Guangdong chose Guangzhou city as the pilot area. After a year's fumbling, in September 2009, Guangzhou took the lead to introduce the *Guangzhou's Political Consultation Procedure (tentative)*. In May, 2010, on the basis of the pilot program in Guangzhou, the *Guangdong Province"s Political Consultation Procedure (tentative)* was issued; in August 2011, on the basis of a summarization of lessons learned from the pilot program, a standard procedure was officially issued. The procedure explicitly specifies the principles of political consultation, and provides detailed stipulations about the main content, basic form, and procedures of political consultations. This standard marks the first time that political consultation became a rigid constraint on the local Party committee and government's work, and stipulates that when making major decisions, the consultations are not only required, but also must be conducted according to the procedures specified.

Led by Guangdong, Jiangxi, Nanjing, and Xiamen also issued similar regulations in succession. By the end of 2013, 26 provinces, cities, and autonomous regions had developed a political consultation procedure. For the first time, the political consultation changed from a "soft approach" to "hard constraints," and from an attitude that consultations "may be consulted" to one requiring that they "must be consulted."

In November, 2012, the 18th Central Committee proposed to "perfect the socialist deliberative democracy." Deliberative democracy was written into the highest-level document of the CPC for the first time; the Third Plenary Session of the 18th Central Committee a year later further proposed to "promote the extensive, multilevel and institutionalized development of deliberative democracy." Deliberative democracy officially rose from a local or partial practice to a national strategy, and expanded from the political fields to the economic and social fields, rising from a work approach to an extensive system.

Deliberative Democracy Fulfills Potential

In 2000, John Gastil of the University of Washington wrote a book entitled *By Popular Demand: Revitalizing Representative Democracy Through Deliberative Elections*. In the book, he writes that representative democracy is beset with a crisis, and that in order to revitalize representative democracy, during the election, randomly selected panels of citizens should be convened to deliberate on ballot measures and candidates. Voters would learn about the judgments of these citizen panels from voting guides and possibly information printed on official ballots.[57]

Professor Fishkin had similar assumptions and specially designed a deliberative system. Though the idea was good, the realities were not.[58] In 1992, Fishkin planned to hold an "improved primary election" in the way of deliberative polling during the American presidential primary election. But his plan failed because of budget issues.

Just like the people of the US who wish to activate their representative democracy with deliberative democracy, the CPC wishes to use its own systemic potentials with deliberative democracy and, indeed, realize the dream to a certain degree.

This attempt started as early as 2005. Back then the final stage of the "Zeguo experiment" was to submit the resolution formed by the randomly sampled representatives to the town's people's congress for voting. This is indeed a connection between the deliberative consultation and the existing system, and its results amazed Fishkin—the consultation directly influenced the decisions reached. Later, in the Zeguo Township's democratic heart-to-heart discussions on public budgeting held in 2008 and 2009, with two more institutional arrangements, the consultations activated the core mechanism of the original political structure—the people's congress system. The first institutional arrangement was to invite the township's people's representatives to sit in on the discussion process; and the second institutional arrangement was to submit the resolution formed by the randomly sampled representatives to the town's people's congress (PC) delegates for voting. At the same time, the randomly selected representatives were invited to sit in on the discussion by the township's PC delegates. The design of the two links had two effects: First, sitting in on each other's discussions greatly intensified the PC delegates' self-awareness. The PC delegates that came to hear the discussion were very serious, and they felt great pressure, likely thinking "in a few days, the villager representatives will sit in on our discussion, how would their delegates feel if our discussions are not as excellent as theirs?" Second, the dormant functions of the grassroots PC were activated. According to the institutional design, the PC has the right to deliberate on the government budget and supervise budgetary enforcement. But, for a long time, this function had been in a dormant state, though, informally, the PC does sometimes review the government budget. With the launch of the deliberative democracy experiment, under pressure from the villagers' review of the township's financial budget, the township's PC started to truly

57.   Gastil, John. *By Popular Demand: Revitalizing Representative Democracy Through Deliberative Elections*, University of California Press, 2000.

58.   Ackerman, Bruce, and Fishkin, James S. Deliberation Day, *Journal of Political Philosophy*, 10(2), 2002, 129–152.

perform their obligations. At the same time, the villager representatives' deliberative democracy test provided the template for the township's PC review, and taught them how to truly conduct the review.[59]

But the collaboration of randomly selected representatives and the township's NPC creates a problem: What if the decision of the randomly selected representatives is not consistent with that of the township's PC delegates? The experiment in Xinhe Town, Wenling City, provided the solution.

At the end of July 2005, the Xinhe experiment that connects the democratic heart-to-heart discussions with the public budget reform was officially started. Without directly copying Zeguo Town's experiences in the past months, Xinhe made some adjustments of its own. It directly implanted the deliberative democratic techniques into the PC system, activating the power given to the PC by the constitution.

First, the scope of discussions is not limited to just some of the projects' budgets, but reviewed the whole government budget, implementing the PC's budget review rights that has been dormant for many years.

Second, the participants are not randomly selected representatives, but the township's PC delegates and voluntary participants. This does not only activate the PC but also ensures the orderly operation of deliberative democracy in the existing framework. At the same time, in order to overcome the problem that the PC delegates do not know much about budgetary issues, Xinhe Township specially invited financial experts from Zhongshan University—Ma Jun and Niu Meili, as well as Zhou Yanmei, from the Shanghai Municipal PC Standing Committee's training commission—to train such delegates, ensuring the effectiveness of the PC delegates' participation.

Third, a budget amendment system is set up. On the basis of panel discussions, five or more PC delegates may jointly submit a budget amendment. This helps to overcome the bounded rationality of the government-compiled budget, and impose powerful binds on the government budget. In response, Ma Jun said, "this is absolutely the first time that the amendment has been set up, and the first time that the PC delegates have performed the budget amendment right."

Fourth, set up the PC finance task force which is responsible for supervising the government financial budget enforcement. This is a very important institutional innovation, as it eases up tensions caused by

---

59.　　Tan Huosheng. "Deliberative Democracy in China," published in: *A Sociology of Knowledge Perspective, Economic and Political Studies*, Jing Yuejin, Zhang Xiaojin, and Yu Xunda, eds. Beijing: China Social Sciences Press, 2012, pp. 83–100.

information asymmetry, shortens the principal-agency chain and effectively encourages the public to exercise their rights to participate, to know, and to supervise.[60]

What is even more exciting is that from 2008, the institutional innovations of Zeguo Town and Xinhe Town began to spread to other places, and the municipal PC standing committee became a new driving force, which spread such innovation laterally, to Ruoheng, Daxi, Binhai, and other towns, and vertically adds such innovation to the agenda of the municipal PC.

Corresponding to the deliberative democracy's activation effects of the grassroots PC, the deliberate democracy's activation effects on the political consultation system, is also remarkable. Among them, the restoration of a biweekly consultation seminar is the most notable.

In October, 2013, after 48 years, the biweekly symposium of the CPPCC was restored, and is generally held once every two weeks, about 20 times in year. This biweekly symposium refines the consultation procedures, applies new means to make the selection of consultation participants more systematic, the prepared consultation materials more sufficient, and the consultation process more efficient in the organization. It is worth noting that the biweekly symposium is not only of high profile—it is chaired by Yu Zhengsheng, the chairman of the CPPCC, with the participation of the leaders of relevant central ministries and commissions—but each symposium invites different CPPCC members, striving to ensure that each CPPCC member will attend the symposium once in his tenure. Influenced by the CPPCC's demonstration, many local committees are holding similar symposia, and some are maintaining the same frequency (Tianjin, for example), and some at the frequency of once every two months (Qinghai Province, Jinan City of Shandong, and Zhuzhou City of Hunan).

In September, 2013, Stephen Elstub of the University of West Scotland in the UK pointed out in the annual meeting of the American Political Science Society that studies of deliberative democracy are paying increasing attention to the building of deliberative systems and stressing the interactions and connections between different institutional arrangements of political consultation.[61]

Two months later, the Third Plenary Session of the 18th Central Committee decided to "build a consultative democracy featuring appropriate procedures and complete segments." On February 9, 2015, the CPC issued

60.   Chen Peng. *Countryside Deliberative Democracy Practice Under the Interaction of Country and Society*, Shanghai: Shanghai Century Publishing Group, 2012, pp. 175–181.
61.   Elstub, Stephen and McLaverty, Peter. Ten Issues for a Deliberative System, Annual Meeting Paper: American Political Science Association, 29 August–1 September 2013: Chicago.

the *Opinions on Strengthening the Socialist Deliberative Democracy Building*, which clearly delineated their ideals: "continue to strengthen consultation with other parties, the government, and the political consultation conference, and actively launch the consultation with the PC, people's organizations, and the grassroots, gradually explore the consultation with social organizations. Give play to the advantages of different consultation channels and design good connections and coordination arrangements."[62]

A Roadmap of the Democratization of China

Many western scholars doubt that the deliberative democracy in China should really be called "deliberative democracy." And even if the answer is yes, can it be an organic part of the democratization of China, or become the force that drives the democratization in China?

Regarding this problem, let us first take a look at the western scholars' reflections on the democratization problem.

The most important lesson brought by the first wave of democratization that started from mid-1970s to the theories about democratization is this: Democracy does not always equal good governance. The operation of elected governments and its governance performance are often not as wonderful as people may have wished, and many emerging democratized countries have pretty bad records in human rights and liberties despite the establishment of a competitive election system. Larry Diamond, a political sociologist and leading contemporary scholar in the field of democracy studies, lamented that "the present problem is not the collective withering away of democratic states, but that many countries' democracies are gradually hollowing out, leaving only the shell of multi-party election."[63] This tendency of excessive emphasis on competitive election and negligence toward other dimensions of democracy is called the "electoralism fallacy" by some scholars. In other words, democratization has to focus on not only whether impartial elections will be held at fixed periods, but also elements beyond elections, the problem of governance in particular.

In 2009, Canadian scholar Mark E. Warren put forward the concept of "governance-driven democratization," which is relative to election-driven democratization. He took China as the example to explain that even without the multi-party competition, governance-driven democratization is possible, and the CPC actively encourages the development of deliberative democracy. The reason why the CPC chooses to walk the path of governance-

62.   "Opinions On Strengthening Socialist Deliberative Democracy Building," *People's Daily*, February 9, 2015.

63.   Liu Junning (editor). *Democracy and Democratization*, Beijing: Commercial Press, 1999, pp. 408–409.

driven democratization is because of the diversification and growth of social competencies released by social and economic development, rather than the pressure from election-driven democratization.[64]

Though Warren's article was not aimed specifically at China, it is very astute of him to grasp the western countries' two core concerns about the democratization of China: First, should the democratization of China be election-driven or governance-driven? Should it focus on the establishment of competitive elections first and then set about building participatory democracy or the deliberative democracy that aims at improving the democracy quality? Or should it reverse the order? Second, under the leadership of the CPC, is it possible to realize democratization without multi-party competition?

For the first problem, paralleling the election and governance is itself a breakthrough, as it abandons the simple thinking that democracy equates to elections only, and is aware that democratization has two dimensions: election and governance. Elections concern the sources of power, while governance concerns the operations of power.

Those who equate democracy to elections only often stress that an election system must be established to realize democracy. Even if they admit that democracy is also about governance beyond elections, they will resort to the experience of Western European countries to prove the view that "election is foremost, consultation is secondary" and that the government could only establish the democratic election and then improve the democratic governance quality through deliberative democracy. But the experience of the third wave of democratization shows that equating democracy to elections is misleading; generalizing the Western European countries' experiences and believing that democratization means first elective democracy, and then deliberative democracy, is also misleading. Early in the 15th Central Committee, the CPC has defined the connotations of democracy as "democratic election, democratic decision, democratic management, and democratic supervision," fusing election and governance into one. Xi Jinping emphasizes constantly that "deliberative consultation has been integrated into the whole process of Chinese socialist democracy." Election and consultation, these two forms of democracy, are not interchangeable nor opposite, but mutually complementary. In the eyes of the CPC, it makes no sense to plan China's democratization process in accordance with the Western European countries' experience. China will take a road to democratization different from that of the Western European

---

64.   Warren, Mark E. 2009. Governance-Driven Democratization, *Critical Policy Studies*, 3(1), 3–13.

countries.

The CPC has never denied the importance of democratic election, nor the importance of competitive elections. In fact, in the past two decades, the CPC made many institutional innovations to the grassroots democratic election, and was constantly attempting to introduce competitive mechanisms in the inner-party democracy. If we look again at the case of Wenling of Zhejiang, you may get the wrong idea that the CPC is trying to substitute deliberative democracy for electoral democracy; but if we look beyond that and see the big picture in China, you will find that in many localities, the grassroots elections are adopting many institutional innovations, such as the "audition" in Lishu County of Jilin Province, and combined elections in Anqing and Suzhou Counties of Anhui Province.[65] At the same time, in the past 30 years, the NPC delegate selection system has also undergone numerous reforms, constantly expanding the scope of direct election and better manifesting the principle of equality. The inner-party democratic election is also making progress. In Shanxi Linyi, Zhejiang Hangzhou, Sichuan Ya'an, and many other places, they are testing "split-ticket voting" or "public recommendation and direct election," and other competitive election mechanisms. In the discreet and incremental reform process, a road to democratization with Chinese characteristics is growing increasingly clear.

The CPC does not defy the notion of competitive election. What it really defies is the competitive election marked by a rotation of ruling parties, which is in fact a denial of the CPC's leadership. To many western scholars, without the establishment of a multi-party system and the rotation of ruling parties through election, there will no real democracy, and even the further development of deliberative democracy will be meaningless. This involves the second problem: Is it possible to realize democratization under the CPC's leadership, that is, without multi-party competition?

Since the start of the twenty-first century, some western scholars have started to take the development of democratic politics under the CPC's leadership seriously, advocating for placement of the Party in the center of any analysis. In 2004, Brantly Womack, Cumming Memorial Professor of Foreign Affairs at the University of Virginia, explored the possibility of party-state democracy. He believes that the CPC is striving to increase its efficiency and tolerance, and quickly responding to the demands of the people, and thus building a party-state democracy under the condition of not changing its leadership.[66] Womack believes that this is a feasible democratization

65.   Liu Jianfeng. "Anhui Combined Election Test," *Reform in China*, Issue 2, 2012.
66.   Womack, Brantly. "Party-state Democracy and Three Representatives: Insight into the Theory," in Lv Zengkui (chief editor) *Ruling Transformation: Overseas Scholars' Studies on the Building of CPC*, Beijing: Central Compilation & Translation Press, 2011, pp. 96–118.

method that can minimize the pains of transformation. David Shambaugh also does not believe that a western democracy will appear in China. He believes that what is more likely to happen is that the CPC will further develop broad consultation channels with non-CPC organizations and grant more powers to the NPC.[67] Professor He Baogang points out that, in China, consultation without the multi-party competition seems to be better than the multi-party competition without consultation. It can be imagined that, in the coming decade, the CPC will still stand atop institutional governance, while the deliberative democracy system will spread through the local level, and push China's politics in a democratic direction.[68]

An increasing number of people have given up observing democratization in China in the context of the Western European experience, and are starting to recognize it based on the political practices of the past three decades of reform and opening up (especially the institutional innovations at the local governance level). More people have started to recognize that democratization in China is possible under the condition of sticking to the CPC's leadership. There are two important characteristics about democratization under a one-party regime: First, the democratization of China is an endogenous evolutionary process. Its basic framework and basic elements of democratization is endogenous, "proceeding from within," rather than exogenous, "from external influences." The Party's leadership, electoral democracy, and deliberative democracy are all an extension or expansion of the CPC's political tradition. In this sense, the deliberative democracy in China is indeed different from the deliberative democracy in western countries, and the CPC's deliberative democracy is first a standardization of a form of democracy: political consultation, and the promotion of the successful experience to other territories. Evolution means that the democratization is empirically minded and progressive, as written by David Shambaugh, the CPC is following the same strategy in the political reform that it used in the successful economic reform: testing new approaches everywhere, and then gradually promoting the successful ones into the whole country, welcoming the successful experiments and giving up the failing experiments.[69] Second, the democracy of power operation and

67.   Shambaugh, David. *China's Communist Party: Atrophy and Adaptation*, (translated by Lv Zengkui and Wang Xinying), Beijing: Central Compilation & Translation Press, 2011, p. 243.

68.   He Baogang. Deliberative Democracy and Deliberative Governance, (meeting document), Nankai University: "Deliberative Democracy Theory and Practice International-al Research Conference", November, 2013.

69.   David Shambaugh, *China's Communist Party: Atrophy and Adaptation*, (translated by Lv Zengkui and Wang Xinying), Beijing: Central Compilation & Translation Press, 2011,

the democracy of power sources would go hand in hand. Different from the democratization processes in Western Europe or other regions, the democratization of China is not meant to solve the democracy of power sources, and then solve the democracy of power operations, but to give full play to the late-mover advantage of promoting democracy of both aspects simultaneously.

IV. THE RULE OF LAW

The Fourth Plenary Session of the CPC's 18th Central Committee, held in November, 2014, attracted the eyes of the world. This was the first time "rule of law" had been identified as the theme of the plenary session of the Central Committee in the 65 years the CPC has ruled China.

Looking back over the 65 years, from rule by man to rule by law, from management to governance, the CPC's governance's conception has taken a tortuous and difficult path.

In Mao Zedong's era, the governance of the whole country had the deep stigma of Mao himself. In the Deng Xiaoping era, the CPC drew bitter lessons from the Cultural Revolution, and from rule by man, to rule by law, and then to rule of law. The concise guideline "there must be laws for people to follow, these laws must be observed, the enforcement must be strict, and law breakers must be dealt with" gradually took shape. In the Xi Jinping era, the modernization of the state governance system and governance capacity has become the guiding ideology for comprehensively deepening reforms, and the concept of the rule of law is further deepened, toward good law and good governance.

When he was heading the administration of Zhejiang, Xi Jinping had put forward the concept of "rule by law in Zhejiang" and went to over 40 villages, communities, and units at the grassroots level to conduct a special survey. In 2006, the Zhejiang Provincial Party Committee issued the *Decision of Zhejiang Provincial Committee of the CPC on Building Zhejiang under Rule of Law*. The "overall rule of law" is an upgrade and expansion of the "rule by law in Zhejiang."

In April, 2015, the *Implementation Plan on Carrying out the Decision of the Fourth Plenary Session of the Eighteenth Central Committee of the CPC and Further Deepening Judicial System and Society System Reform* was issued. The plan supports the 84 reforms put forward in the Fourth Plenary Session and explicitly states the work schedule and milestones. According to the time-line of the *Implementation Plan*, these reforms will be made into

p. 250.

concrete policies and measures in the three years from 2015 to 2017.[70]

Good Laws, Good Governance

July 5, 2009, was a special day, as it was the fifteenth anniversary of the promulgation of the Labor Law, and the second anniversary of the promulgation of the Employment Contract Law, a day that the legal world should have been celebrating. But on that day, everything was quiet. Two years before, the Employment Contract Law was issued amid immense celebration, and came into effect on January 1st, 2008. At the time, Vice Chairman of the NPC Sheng Huaren proclaimed it a significant milestone, and the media used all kinds of magnificent words to praise it.

However, this "good law" that is aimed at connecting the international regulations and protecting laborers' rights and interests was controversial from the day it was issued. Many critics bluntly called it an "evil law." The economist Zhang Wuchang posted ten articles in his blog to oppose the Employment Contract Law. Professor Dong Baohua of the East China University of Political Science and Law, one of the drafters of the Employment Contract Law, was also the first legal scholar to criticize the law.[71]

In practice, the ramifications of the Employment Contract Law should have put people's minds at ease.

Despite the significant growth of the labor contract signing rate, the number of labor dispute cases grew dramatically, spiking in coastal areas like Shanghai and Guangzhou. In the first half of 2008, the number of labor dispute cases in Shenzhen and Dongguan increased by 20 percent year on year, so that the officers in Guangdong had to hear one case every 1.8 hours.[72]

The mass disturbances caused by labor disputes became more acute, and incidents of violence became a common occurrence. In Shenzhen, the number of mass disturbances caused by labor disputes increased at the largest rate, with 637 occurrences in 2008, up 119.7 percent from the previous year.[73] On a nationwide scale, there were over 40 homicide cases caused by labor disputes in 2009. Also, in this period, there were the highly publicized suicides of ten employees of Foxconn that jumped from a building, as well as the Guangzhou Nanhai Honda workers organizing a strike.

Liu Ji, honorary president of China Europe International Business School (CEIBS), pointed out in the 2008 annual meeting of economic observers that,

70.   "Coming out With Concrete Measures for Judicial Reform in Three Years: The director of the office central leading group for judicial reform answering questions from journalists," *Southern Metropolis*, April 10, 2015.
71.   He Yong. "Labor Contract Law Besieged," *China Business*, January 25, 2010.
72.   Ibid.
73.   Yang Lin. "Employment Conflict and Misery," *Outlook*, Issue 50, 2009.

according to a survey, the Employment Contract Law increases enterprises' direct costs by 20 or 30 percent, leading to the shut-down of many small- to medium-sized enterprises (SMEs). This confirms Zhang Wuchang's criticism of the law:[74] "Employment Contract Law is an important contract for the comprehensive interference of markets, and will seriously damage the whole market."

Faced with the criticisms from all sides, the NPC had to start its revision program not long after the law was promulgated. On December 28, 2012, the Third Meeting of the 11th NPC Standing Committee passed the *Decision on Amending the Employment Contract Law of the People's Republic of China*. In Dong Baohua's eyes, the Employment Contract Law has become a lesson in legislative history. "It is not only an evil law, but also a stupid law that cannot be afforded by society."

The exact meaning of "rule of law" is not simply governance according to law, but good laws plus good governance, and a precondition of the rule of law is the passing of good laws, not "evil" laws, nor "stupid" laws.

Since the reform and opening up, China has experienced a quick and economical law-making period, initially forming a legal system in just 30 years. According to the statistics, up to September, 2014, it had 242 laws currently in effect, 737 administrative regulations, 8,500 local regulations, and over 800 autonomous and separate ordinances.[75] Almost all the laws required have been made, and some other laws are still in the making. But in this huge legal system, some laws and regulations conflict with the constitution; some others are in discrepancy with each other; some are of low quality and have a considerable gap with the social reality.

The most important cause of such a phenomenon is that the law-making movement in the past 30 years is just a transplantation of laws, with sufficient efforts to be in line with international standards, but not sufficient consideration given to the realities of China, to the extent that the "legal kingdom" built by the lawyers is more like a "castle in the air." These groundless laws cannot escape the fate of "evil laws" or "stupid laws," and such groundless rule of law will only produce bad governance.

Evil laws could do more damage to society than the unfair justice system, as the latter only harms individuals while the former harms all the objects governed by the law. An unfair justice system will incite hatred of the law enforcer, while the evil laws will directly endanger people's belief in

74.　　Liu Ji. "Do Not Blame All the Problems of China on Financial Storm," http://finance.ifeng.com/

75.　　Qiao Xiaoyang. *Historical Achievement of the Socialist Legal System Construction*, posted on *Decision of the CPC Central on Several Major Issues Concerning Comprehensively Promoting Rule of Law*, Beijing: People's Publishing House, 2014.

the rule of law itself. So how to ensure that the legislation is a good law and how to connect other places' laws to the people's secular life are the greatest challenges faced by the building of the rule of law in China, and the key to success in legislative reform.

In October, 2013, the amendment of the Legislation Law officially came into the legislation program of the 12th NPC's Standing Committee. On March 15, 2015, the Plenary Session of the 12th NPC voted to adopt the *Decision on Amending Legislation Law of the People's Republic of China (draft)*.

In the amendment process of the Legislation Law, 46 amendments and the addition of over ten articles represented a total overhaul of the law. On the afternoon the amendment was adopted, Xinhua News Agency released an enthusiastic report, proclaiming it a milestone, leading to good laws and good governance.

The amendment to the Legislation Law strengthens the democratic nature of legislation. Like the constitutions of other countries, China's constitution takes popular sovereignty as the first principle. But this principle shall be embodied by various systems and concrete norms. Due to a lack of knowledge, technique, and experience, the Legislation Law made in 2000 failed to completely meet the requirements of this principle of the constitution, and the government-led legislation was very fierce. The amendment to the Legislation Law reflects a requirement put forward in the Fourth Plenary Session of the 18th Central Committee of the CPC: "complete structures and mechanisms for the people's congresses with legislative power to lead legislative work, enhance the role of the people's congress in the planning, drafting, and amendment stages, and take care to highlight the dominant status of the NPC. At the same time, stress the people's participation in legislation, attract the people's advice through multiple channels, including conducting legislative consultation, completing legislation reasoning and hearing mechanisms, and soliciting ideas on the published draft laws, completing channels and methods for all walks of society to participate in legislation in an orderly manner."

The amendment of the Legislation Law improves the procedures and norms of legislation. On the one hand, it improves the review and voting mechanisms and legislative techniques, strengthens the record review of laws and regulations, prevents the abuse of local legislative power, avoids conflict with laws of higher levels, avoids regional protectionism in the local legislatures, and eliminates fighting in the legal system, as well as enhancing the authority of the constitution.

On the other hand, it stresses the reforms according to the law, regulates the authorization process, and sets out to solve the problems existing in the authorized legislation. Since the reform and opening up, all fourteen authorizations from the NPC and its standing committees failed to address two critical problems: First, what is the basis of, and restrictions on, the authorization? Second, how should the power granted be monitored? Among the most criticized instances are the two times the NPC generously and unreservedly authorized the State Council to draft taxation legislation in 1984 and 1985. This legislation method does not only provide the basis for the State Council's legislative power expansion, it causes a divisional legislation problem—80 percent of the draft laws are prepared by the administrative department, and legislation has become the means for the governmental department to obtain power and allocate favors to vested interests.[76]

The amended Legislation Law specifies that the authorization decision has to state clearly not only the purpose and scope of authorization, but also the authorized matters, and the terms and the principles the authorized organ shall follow in implementing the authorization decision. The term of authorization shall be no longer than five years, and to renew the authorization, relevant opinions shall be submitted to the NPC or its standing committees for decision. This will avoid the problems of a "package decision" or "indefinite authorization," and ultimately restrain the locality's and department's arbitrary use of power. For example, the government does not have the final say in the automobile license plate purchase restriction and house purchase restriction. Instead, it must go through legislation by the regional people's congresses, avoiding the exercise of power in the name of laws.

The amendment to the Legislation Law is expected to open the door to good laws, making laws to be followed by the people no longer "castles in the air," but granted a solid basis. The three main points of the aforementioned guideline "these laws must be observed, the enforcement must be strict, and law breakers must be dealt with," shall be strengthened. In real life, the rule of man that can manifest itself in the implementation of the rule of law can be found everywhere, and the rule of law has been reduced to powerful departments' tools to rule the people. How to embody the requirements of rule of laws in law enforcement and the judicature is the second difficulty faced by the comprehensive rule of law.

Justice and Fairness in Every Legal Case
On March 12, 2015, the Third Meeting of the 12th NPC, Chief Justice and

---

76.   Cai Dingjian, Wang Chenguang (chief editor). *Twenty years of Reform and Development of NPC System*, Beijing: China Procuratorial Press, 2001, p. 422.

President of the Supreme People's Court, Zhou Qiang, and the Procurator-in-Chief and the Procurator General of the Supreme People's Procuratorate, Cao Jianming, mentioned the Huugjilt Case in the work report and blamed themselves for the mishandled case.

On April 9, 1996, a rape and murder case occurred in a wool mill in Hubhot, Inner Mongolia Autonomous Area. At the time, an 18-year-old wool mill worker called Huugjilt was identified as the murderer, and 61 days after the case was disclosed, the people's court sentenced him to death and executed him immediately.

In 2005, Zhao Zhihong, the serial rapist and killer dubbed "homicidal devil" was caught. The first case he confessed to was the April 9 toilet stall rape-murder, attracting wide concern from the media and public.

In March 2006, the Committee of Political and Legislative Affairs of the Inner Mongolia Autonomous Region set up a case review team to reopen the case.

On November 20, 2014, the Huugjilt Case entered into retrial procedure. On December 15, 2014, the Inner Mongolia Higher People's Court made a retrial judgment to the Huugjilt intentional homicide and hooliganism criminal case, revoking the criminal ruling of the second instance about the Huugjilt case made by the Inner Mongolia Higher People's Court in 1996, and the criminal ruling of the first instance made by the Hubhot Intermediate People's Court, acquitting him and delivering the retrial ruling to his parents.

On December 19, 2014, Inner Mongolia's public security, procuratorate, and courts started the Huugjilt Case liability investigation proceeding. On December 30, the Inner Mongolia Higher People's Court determined to offer state compensation of RMB 2,059,621.40 to his parents, Li Sanren and Shang Aiyun.

The Inner Mongolia court redressed the Huugjilt case, and returned delayed justice to the related party and respect to the relevant laws. Though the whole process was eventful and the results were inseparable from the outsiders' unremitting efforts, it was the court system that finished the normal legal procedures within the legal framework, and compared with the "rehabilitation" in the "rule-by man" era, rule of law is now apparently much better. In this sense, the Huugjilt case is a milestone in the promotion of the rule of law.[77] But in fact, the exoneration of Huugjilt was by no means unique. As of December 15, 2014, the day Huugjilt was exonerated, 23 major mishandled cases have been corrected since the 18th NPC, most of

---

77.   "Foreign Media Comments on Correction of Huggjilt Case: Rule of Law is the Final Winner," www.ifeng.com.cn, November 17, 2014.

which were corrected by the judicial authority following the principle of the presumption of innocence, only a few of them corrected because the real criminals had been captured.[78]

It is impossible to restore the deceased, but true justice is worth waiting for. Xi Jinping stresses that the people should be able to expect justice and fairness in every legal case. All in all, the effect of the judicial system reform should be judged by the people. Xi Jinping's words point directly to the core of the judicial system reform. Philosopher and essayist Francis Bacon once wrote that "one foul sentence doth more hurt than many foul examples. For these do but corrupt the stream, the other corrupted the fountain."[79] Xi Jinping uses the analogy "$100 - 1 = 0$" to describe the importance of judicial fairness. The negative influence of one mishandled case is sufficient to destroy the good image accumulated through 99 fair judgments. Moreover, for the individuals involved, one mishandled case means the total destruction of their lives.[80]

In the new round of judicial system reform, the Huugjilt case happened to be an opportunity to make the modern judicial concepts—innocence until proven guilty, equilibrium of prosecution and defense, and centering on trial—to be the consensus to push forward the rule of law in China; to turn the judiciary into the developer of institutional improvement, promote the reform of relevant institutions through actual cases, and hold up the ideal of judicial fairness with institutional components.[81]

Judicial system reform is among the biggest concerns of Xi Jinping. As of April, 2015, the Central Leading Group for Comprehensively Deepening Reform, in which Xi Jinping served as the leader, has held eleven meetings, seven of which involved judicial reform, and passed up to twelve relevant programs and opinions.[82] Starting from July, 2014, Shanghai, Guangdong,

78.   Li Yunfang, Ma Shipeng. "23 Major Mishandled Cases Corrected Since the 18th NPC," www.thepaper.cn, December 16, 2014.

79.   Bacon, Francis. *The Essays*, (translated by Shui Tiantong), Beijing: Commercial Press, 1983, p. 193.

80.   Wang Lin. "Driving Consensus on Rule of Law by Controversy of Disputed Case," *People's Daily*, December 15, 2014.

81.   In the retrial process of the Huggjilt case, the relevant systems are being gradually improved. In July 2013, the Commission of Politics and Law issued the first guiding opinions on practically preventing mishandled cases, requiring strict punishment of the act of extortion of confession by torture, and resorting to violence to obtain testimony. Later, other political and legal organs respectively formulated detailed opinions as per the guiding opinions, for example, the Supreme People's Court issued the *Opinions on Establishing a Work Mechanism to Prevent Mishandled Criminal Cases*, and the Supreme Procuratorate formulated the *Several Opinions on Practically Performing Procuratorial Function and Prevention and Correction of Mishandled Cases* to prevent recurrence of mishandled cases.

82.   "11 Meetings of the Leading Group for Comprehensively Deepening Reform Bite

Jilin, Hubei, Hunan, and Qinghai have launched pilot judicial system reform programs. On February 26, 2015, the Supreme People's Court issued the *Opinions on Comprehensively Deepening the Reform of the People's Court*, putting forth 65 concrete reform measures in seven aspects.

The core of this round of judicial reform is to ensure that the people's courts can independently and fairly exercise judicial authority according to the law. It requires that "in the process of adjudication, the judicator shall be subject to only legal requirements and the conscience, rather than any influence, interference, or control from either inside or outside the court."[83]

The arch enemy of judicial independence is the administrative organ's interference in judicial activities. To enable the courts to independently exercise judicial authority, first of all, the court shall be independent from the lateral administrative organs at the same level, while in the structure of state power, the courts have to maintain relative independence in personnel and financial budgeting. In China, the local party committee's control of power over personnel and the local government's control of the courts' financial budget enables them to impose their influence on the courts' operations. A case recounted by Zhang Siha, the former deputy director of the Research Office of the Supreme People's Court, is illustrative of the problem: A county court's justice disagreed with the local party committee's opinion, asserting that he would rather die and insist on independent adjudication. But he was transferred to another position before the judgment could be passed. He said half-jokingly that he was not even allowed to die at the post.[84]

In this round of reform, the judicial authority's power of personnel administration and financial independence issues that have been called for over many years will finally break the surface. In June, 2014, the CPC launched the pilot program for reform of unified management of personnel, financial, and material resources of provincial-level courts and procuratorates or lower, removing the interference from administrative organs at the same level. The unified management of people is mainly about establishing a mechanism so that the judges and prosecutors shall be uniformly nominated, managed, appointed and dismissed by the provincial government according to legal procedure. Specifically, a selection commission of judges and prosecutors will be elected at the provincial level to select personnel from a professional perspective, the organization, personnel and discipline inspection department will inspect their political quality and self-discipline, and the

into Multiple 'Hard Bones', Highlighting Four Reforms," www.xinhuanet.com.cn, April 2, 2015.

83.   Chen Ruihua. *Visible Justice*, Beijing: China Legal Publishing House, 2000, p. 129.
84.   Wang Feng. "What Kind of Judges and Courts does China Need?" *21st Century Economic Report*, August 13, 2014.

people's congress will be responsible for their appointment or dismissal following the relevant legal procedures. The unified management of financial and material resources is mainly about establishing a mechanism in which the funds for local courts and procuratorates under the provincial level will be managed by the provincial government's financial departments.[85] It is expected that this reform will remove the assumption that "faith in the law is no better than applying for an audience with a top official," and "three verdicts are not as good as a note from a top official."

The second enemy of judicial independence is the self-administration inside the judicial organs. This requires that the superior and lower courts shall keep vertical independence, and that when the judge or collegial panel is hearing a case, they shall be free from the influence of the relations with their superiors inside the court. The practice in courts nowadays is that of separation of trial and verdict, and of layers of approval inside the trial-work system, which have led to unclear divisions in power and responsibilities in the trial-holding process. The systematic reform in Shanghai "tightly holds the nose of the judicial responsibility system," taking the jurisdiction as the core to establish improved mechanisms for dealing with cases that consist of a presiding judge and collegial panel, and setting up the court officer power-list system. The principles of unified power and responsibilities must be adhered to, in order to establish improved mechanisms for dealing with cases that consist of a presiding judge and collegial panel, and to solve the problem of unclear divisions of power, responsibilities, and accountability.[86] The highlight of the reform in Shenzhen is to remove all the administrative positions of all the prosecutors, so that they can concentrate solely on handling cases to the best of their abilities.[87]

To enable judges to independently and fairly exercise jurisdiction according to law, it is essential to minimize the influence of internal administrative burdens through institutional restructuring. Without the meticulous care of the system, any "golden heart" will dim. The Fourth Plenary Session of the 18th Central Committee of the CPC proposes to "establish and perfect the protection mechanism for judicial personnel carrying out statutory duties. The judges and prosecutors shall not be

---

85.   Xu Xiaotong. "Mixed Feelings about the Unified Management of Personnel, Financial and Material Resources for Courts and Procuratorates Under the Provincial Level," *China Youth Daily*, June 27, 2014.

86.   Peng Mei, Wang Dianxue, Shang Xi. "Shanghai Pioneering in Headcount Mechanism, Break the Lifelong Tenure of Judges and Assess Them Annually," *Southern Metropolis*, March 12, 2015.

87.   Zhang Shuling. "Shenzhen Judicial Reform Removes the Hat of Prosecutors," *Beijing Times*, April 27, 2015.

transferred, dismissed, removed—or demoted for any legal cause or for following extra-legal procedure."[88] Shanghai fully strengthened the safeguard measures, established the judicial personnel management system that fit the appropriate occupational characteristics, highlighting judges and prosecutors' dominance in the process of handling cases and dividing the workers of the courts and procuratorates into three categories: judges/prosecutors, ancillary judicial personnel, and administrative personnel, each accounting for 33 percent, 52 percent and 15 percent of the total payroll.[89] At the same time, it promotes the reform of the judge/prosecutor salary system, temporarily arranging for the salary of judges and prosecutors within the above-mentioned proportion—43 percent above the salary of common public servants, and tilted towards the front-line judges and prosecutors.[90]

Another enemy of judicial independence is local protectionism, one of the main factors that has been influencing judicial fairness for a long time, which is especially outstanding in the trial of trans-jurisdictional and cross-domain civil, business, and administrative cases. Local protectionism has fragmented judicial power in China. For this reason, the Fourth Plenary Session of the 18th Central Committee proposed that "the supreme people's court shall set up circuit courts to hear the major administrative, civil, and business cases that cross administrative regions." On December 2, 2014, the Seventh Plenary Session of the Central Leading Group for Comprehensively Deepening Reform adopted the *Pilot Program for Setting up Trans-Regional People's Courts and Procuratorates* and the *Pilot Program of the Supreme People's Court for Setting up Circuit Court*. On December 28, the No.1 Circuit Court of the Supreme People's Court settled in Shenzhen and was officially put into operation with the judicial circuit of Guangdong, Guangxi, and Hainan. Three days later, the No. 2 Circuit Court of the Supreme People's Court was set up in Shenyang, Liaoning, with the judicial circuit of Liaoning, Jilin, and Heilongjiang. These intensive reform measures ensure that any cases that are tried in the local courts can be referred to the circuit court and the circuit court will make judgment through independent trial. This aids in overcoming local protectionism and reducing unfairness in trials.

---

88.   *Decision of the CPC Central on Several Major Issues Concerning Comprehensively Promoting Rule of Law*, Beijing: People's Publishing House, 2014, p. 21.

89.   Wang Xuanhui. "Judges and Prosecutors: Shall Implement Life-long Tenure System," *Legal Evening News*, October 28, 2014.

90.   Hao Hong, Huang Qingchang. "Income of Judges and Prosecutors: 43% Higher than that of Ordinary Public Servant," *People's Daily*, April 24, 2015.

Gain Hold of the "Critical Minority"

"The law must be believed, or it will be void."[91] The words of American comparative law expert Harold Berman has become a frequently cited saying in present-day China.

"The law must be believed." Not only the common people, but the leaders and cadres at different levels, should believe in it. To encourage the common citizen to believe in the law, the government has to ensure that the people can enjoy fairness and justice in each judicial case; to encourage the leaders and cadres to believe in the law, the idea of rule by law must be absorbed into their blood through self-education, and converting rules into actions through institutional structuring. For the common people, they have to feel that the law is the protector of their rights; to the leaders and cadres with great power, they have to realize that the laws bind their power.

To turn laws into beliefs, the government must gain a hold of the "critical minority," constituted by leading officials, just as Xi Jinping has said. Because they are the power holders, and it is their interference with judicial actions that can lead to the vicious cycle of "believing in power, in man, and in bosses, but not in the law" in a society. In this sense, only if the leading officials can take the law as their belief, can the law become the belief of every citizen. Gaining a hold of the critical minority of leading officials is the key to confronting bureaucratization and influence-peddling in the judiciary.

On March 30, 2015, the General Office of the Central Committee of the CPC and the General Office of the State Council issued the *Regulation on Blacklisting, Naming Publicly, and Punishing the Leading Officials for Illegal Interference on Judicial Activities and Meddling with Case Investigations*; on the same day, the Commission of Politics and Law of the State Council issued the *Regulation on Recording and Punishing Insider Personnel of Judicial Organs for Meddling with Cases*. The issuing of these two regulations shows two sides of the judicial de-administration.

What these regulations are trying to prevent is the administrative organ's interference with judicial activities. This interference has two primary forms: First, asking for favors directly or through other people. Second, by making notes on legal documents. The motives of the officials asking for favors or making notes on documents center around private interests or departmental benefits; some are doing it out of kindness, for example, thinking about local economic development, or hearing complaints and feeling that the judicial organ did not do a good job. But, as judicial activities are different from administrative work, whether to advance private interests, or out of

---

91.   Harold Berman. *Law and Religion*, (translated by Liang Zhiping), Beijing: Joint Publishing House, 1991, p. 42.

kindness, the officials' interference in the judiciary may lead to an imbalance of the scales of justice, and the destruction of judicial credibility. Even the note "handle it according to law" from a leading official, if it appears on a legal document, might impose pressure on the presiding judge of the court or lead to an unfair ruling.[92] The aforementioned regulations build a firewall to prevent interference in judicial activities on the outside by setting up recording, public naming, or punishment systems, and vastly constricting the ability of leading officials to interfere in judicial matters.

The *Regulation of the Commission of Politics and Law* prevents interference from administrative management functions inside the judicial organs. According to the requirements, the insiders of the judicial organs shall not, "as an individual," "breach the regulations to ask about or interfere with cases being dealt with by other personnel nor breach the regulations to pass materials related to the case or ask about information, or in any other manner say a good word for the party to the case" (Article 2). Besides, the insiders of the judicial organs, as well as public servants deployed elsewhere, shall prevent their activities from imposing improper influence on the judiciary when performing their duties (Articles 4 and 5). The former would represent an act of corruption, and the latter, a lapse in job performance. For the prevention of interference by the administrative functionaries inside the judicial organ on judicial activities, the latter situation is more worth noting, as it is more common, and its ill effects more secretive.

Like the courts in the US, the courts in China have two parallel systems, one system is responsible for holding trials, the other is the administrative system established to safeguard and support the trial functions. In theory, the former shall be dominant and the latter auxiliary, but in practice, these two systems are often conflated, their assumed dominant-auxiliary relation inverted. For a long time, judges with no administrative titles inside the courts were accustomed to thinking that they worked under the leadership of the president or vice president of the court or the division, and they were used to reporting to and asking for instructions from such presidents, whether regarding procedural or other matters. This unwritten practice has been taken on as an unquestioned routine in courts at all levels. It creates opportunities for administrative leaders' direct interference in open cases. If the practice is not confronted, even after the courts take control of their own budgets and personnel rights and gain more independence from the administrative organs, administrative influence will not necessarily fade, but

---

92.   Zhou Bin. "Supreme People's Court and Procuratorate: Ensure the Judicial Personnel Dare to Keep Truthful Records of Cadres' Interference in Judicial Activities," *Legal Daily*, March 31, 2015.

may grow stronger.[93] It is based on this consideration that Article 4 of the *Regulation* stipulates that "if the leading cadres or superior judicial organ's workers have to put forth guidance for in-process cases, in their performance of leadership or supervision duties, they should put forth such guidance in writing, and any oral instruction they put forth shall be recorded on file by officers of the court," in order to prevent the administrative functionaries inside the court usurping their power, and imposing improper influence on the judicial process.

Another circumstance in practice is the pernicious combination of external and internal administrative interference. Many external attempts at interference act through the internal administration—that is, the leading officials contact the direct manager of the case-handling officer or the court president to convey his instructions. So if the court president receives such a request for favoritism, the president shall keep records in details, and the officer receives the suggestion from the president, the officer shall keep detailed records.

These records will test the judicial personnel's courage, and their belief in the rule of law, and whether the system safeguards in place are effective. If judicial personnel suffer professional consequences by their keeping truthful records, if promotions are influenced by the records, or personnel are not protected from retaliation, many staff members will not dare to keep records. So to guarantee the actual implementation of these two regulations, the Commission of Politics and Law is working with relevant departments on drafting supporting institutional methods. For example, the Supreme Procuratorate will further safeguard the system against wrongs, and further refine the prosecutorial appeal and complaint system, so that prosecutors and all supporting staff can freely keep records.[94]

---

93.   Su Li. *Court's Trial Function and Administration,* edited by Zairian Chunying and Li Lin, *Rule of Law and Judicial Reform,* Beijing: Social Science Academic Press, 2008, pp. 319–336.

94.   Zhou Bin. "Supreme People's Court and Procuratorate: Ensure the Judicial Personnel Dare to Keep Truthful Records of Cadres' Interference in Judicial Activities," *Legal Daily,* March 31, 2015.

CHAPTER
5

The Innovation Revolution: Leading China's New Economy

The new economy stems from knowledge and imagination, which are key aspects of modern China's transformation. The transformation and upgrading of the economy became the only choice left when the energy-intensive and high-consumption growth mode of the economy came to an end.

Dan A. Kimball, an undersecretary of the United States Navy, once claimed that wherever renowned Chinese rocket scientist Qian Xuesen went, he was worth the military strength of five divisions. Sir Winston Churchill, former prime minister of the United Kingdom, once said: "I would rather lose India than Shakespeare." These comments indicate how outstanding elite figures play such a critical role in the rise of nations.

Following the rapid 30-year march of China's economy, its resources and ecological burden are being pushed to the limits, and thus Xi Jinping is facing his most severe test of his time—to alleviate the economy's pressure on China's resources. Thankfully, China is able to avoid the familiar pitfalls faced by industrialized countries of "treatment following pollution" and break new ground in sustainable development with its eastern wisdom, leading the world's sustainable development. China's success depends on the realization of an innovation-driven economic breakthrough under the leadership of Xi Jinping. "Fate" is too passive a term to portray China's economic future;

strong action is now called for. The "new normal" will exemplify the new ways of economic development.

I. THE "NEW NORMAL" OF CHINA'S ECONOMY

On October 26, 2014, *USA Today* named the world's top 20 most profitable companies on its website, according to the enterprises' net income for the preceding fiscal year, as provided by the US financial data software companies. The Industrial and Commercial Bank of China (ICBC) was the world's most profitable enterprise.

USA Today also announced the world's top ten most profitable enterprises, which were: the ICBC, Apple, OAO Gazprom, China Construction Bank, ExxonMobil, Samsung, the Agricultural Bank of China, the Bank of China, BP, and Microsoft.

Outsiders would have been forgiven for thinking that Chinese people would be delighted and inspired after seeing the report, but they would have been wrong. The Chinese people were not happy. Apple is a world-renowned technological innovator, and a typical private enterprise per China's classifications, while the ICBC is a wholly state-owned and monopolistic financial group company and its president enjoys the treatment of a cadre at the deputy ministerial level. The fact that the ICBC defeated Apple by the advantage of its massive volume seemed to be of no honor, because of the unequal nature of the enterprises.

Soon afterwards, the media put forth the question: All of China's four great stated-owned banks have climbed into the top ten most profitable companies; should we be delighted, or concerned?

For sure, there was obvious delight that China's economic volume was larger, enabling it to retain the position of second place in the world.

But there was major concern that none of China's innovative enterprises had entered the global top 20. Moreover, none of China's private enterprises had entered the top 100; while nine of the United States' innovative enterprises, represented by Apple and Microsoft, were ranked in the top 20 most profitable companies. More admirably, Samsung, a science-and-technology enterprise of China's neighbor, South Korea, had ascended into the world's top ten.

Therefore, to a certain extent, this list meant a race between China and the United States in terms of economic competitiveness, and also completely exposed China's economic drawbacks—large but not strong, and weak in innovation.

Will the future of China's economy be lifted up by state-owned enterprises that simply depend on policy advantages and monopoly positions? The answer to that question is *no*.

However, will China's economy break the curse of weak innovation and step toward a "new normal" of sustainable and sound development? The answer to the question will be given by Xi Jinping and China under his leadership in the coming years.

Zhu Rongji's Warning

On January 27, 2003, Zhu Rongji, the premier of the China State Council, presided over his last plenary session. All the members of the plenary session of the State Council attended. Zhu Rongji delivered his outgoing speech, in which the "veteran," who had worked at the forefront of China's economy, presented his concerns and warnings about China's economy without mincing words:

Given that this term is about to end, I am still a little worried about one issue. I would like to talk about it too, and remind those comrades who will stay behind and continue this work. What I am concerned about most is the overheated economy, which I have been worried about for over a year. I will not talk about it in public and only at the level of the leadership. I am quite worried about the overheated economy. There have been many symptoms of this trend and China's economy will be out of control if we do not pay attention to it. I have been engaged in economic inner circles for over 50 years, and believe me, I am well aware of such 'syndromes' in China—as long as our lives improve, most people will become complacent in their working styles and make uninformed decisions. I mentioned the overheating of real estate, but I find that most comrades still have not realized the severity of the issue, and will instead come up with the answer that 'everything is in excellent condition as a whole' in the first place, and only later admit there is a bit of a problem. This is absolutely not the case! This overheating is not a small problem. Because of the overheating of the real estate market in 1993, Hainan Island is still "a mass of bruises" now. In foreign newspapers, they all say China's bubble economy has formed, the real estate market is overheating, and there are big risks. Comrades engaged in banking must pay attention, because the money is from the banks.

I am also worried about 'urbanization.' At present, 'urbanization' is associated with house building—the government buys out farmers' land at a low price and sells to foreigners and real estate developers, and fails to make proper arrangements for the farmers. This way of working is very dangerous. It completely fails to adhere to the policies and spirit of the Central Committee. We have discussed this, and it frightens us the most.[1]

Zhu Rongji's "outgoing warning" points out a potentially fatal snag for China's economy: Economic boosting that is overly dependent on the government's investment will create a dilemma for macroeconomic regulation and control—for once the government releases its control, the economy will be disordered; if the government tightens control, the economy will come to a dead end. In addition to this, governments at all levels seem to be keen to seek money by selling land and increase income by relying on real estate, which will cause a country-wide overheating of the real estate markets.

It turns out that Zhu Rongji's warning seemed to fall on deaf ears, and his words were neglected by his successors. The ten years following Zhu Rongji's departure became the most severe decade of China's economic overheating and governments at all levels had to invest RMB tens of trillions successively, including the Central Government's one-time investment of RMB 4 trillion to boost the economy, which allowed China's economy to grow at an annual rate of more than 10 percent. "Money is not a problem" became the pet phrase of China's government at all levels. This comment—that money was not a problem—derived from the enormous earnings generated by the real estate industry. Housing prices in the central areas of the megacities such as Beijing, Shanghai, Guangzhou, and Shenzhen rose between five-and ten-fold during the decade and the coffers of many first-tier municipal governments also doubled.

For example, in 2009, when real estate development was at its hottest, according to data from the National Bureau of Statistics of China (NBSC), a total of RMB 3.623 trillion was invested in real estate development throughout the country, an increase of 16.1 percent compared to 2008; RMB 2.562 trillion was invested in commercial housing, an increase of 14.2 percent, accounting for 70.7 percent of real estate development. In the same year, the nationwide real estate developers' floor space under construction was 3.196 billion square meters, an increase of 12.8 percent compared with 2008; newly constructed floor space was 1.154 billion square meters, an increase of 12.5 percent; and floor space completed was 702 million square meters, an increase of 5.5 percent. That included the fact that floor space completed for

1.   *Zhu Rongji on the Record, Vol. IV*, People's Publishing House, 2011, pp. 480–489,

residence was 577 million square meters, an increase of 6.2 percent. Taking a closer look at the figure of 3.196 billion square meters of floor space, if you take the measure of 30 square meters per capita, the housing developed in 2009 alone could accommodate 120 million people, which amounts to one out of every three persons in the United States moving into a new residence.

Overheated development and rapid rises in income are enough to cover up the cracks of deep-seated problems in an economy. This is like a company constantly getting windfalls—its president will seldom think there are risks inside the company. A song called "Walk in the Sun" voiced the attitude that a considerable amount of China's local officials held about the economic situation from 2003–2013: "Walking through the spring and autumn, and walking in the sun. The smiling faces of flowers tell me the sky is so clear. Figures chasing dreams, running to embrace hope. Walking with friends on the road warms the heart."

Humming the lyrics, many people felt optimistic about China's economic prospects. Even some leaders within China's government made the judgment that "China has taken the lead in walking out of the global financial crisis."

An economy based on increasing income depending on strong investment and real estate never goes too far, and the consequence of not heeding Zhu Rongji's warning was eventually felt. On October 21, 2013, Li Keqiang, the premier of the China State Council, was invited to deliver a report on China's economic position at the 16th National Congress of Chinese Trade Unions, in which he revealed the dilemma he encountered in the economic conditions he had inherited. He said, "Since the establishment of a new term of government, we have been faced with complex domestic and international situations. In 2010, our economic growth was in the double digits, reaching 10.4 percent. But in the fourth quarter of last year, affected by intertwined multiple and complex factors both in the international community and China, the economic growth rate was only 7.8 percent. This year, it continued the downward trend, 7.7 percent in the first quarter, and 7.5 percent in the second. Why would I tell you about GDP once I am here? Comrades may say that we cannot lay stress solely on GDP. This is correct. But China is a developing country after all, meaning development remains our basis and key for solving all the problems. More importantly, the way we are concerned about the GDP is, in fact, a concern about employment. In the past, each percentage point in China's GDP growth would provide about one million jobs. After years of adjustment of economic structure, especially with the accelerated development of the service sector, currently each percentage point in GDP growth is able to provide 1.3 million, or even 150 million jobs. I asked the Ministry of Human Resources and Social Security

(MHRSS) and the concerned parties to repeatedly estimate our required growth for success, and they all believed that an economic growth of 7.2 percent is required to ensure 10 million new jobs with the registered urban unemployment rate at around 4 percent. In the final analysis, the reason why we want steady growth is to protect employment."

Li Keqiang admitted that China would want to adopt a way of expanding government investment to boost the economy, but issuing more currency was no longer an option. In the face of the pressure of the economic downturn, what should we do?

He said, "We have two options to maintain steady growth and preserve employment—one option is to expand budget deficits and increase the supply of currency. In doing so, to boost investment by creating deficits and issuing currency may be effective at the time, but that requires appropriate operation room for fiscal and monetary policies. More importantly, it is difficult to sustain by this kind of short-term stimulus because our deficit rate has reached 2.1 percent. What does that mean? The EU set a standard that deficit cannot exceed 3 percent of GDP, but we all know that many member states did not comply with it and exceed the standard. The consequences are known to us all: The European debt crisis emerged and lasted from the past few years to the present. Some countries' economic growth was weak and even declined, the unemployment rate surged, and the previous benefits could not be guaranteed. Regarding currency, the balance of China's broad money supply (M2) had reached more than RMB 100 million by the end of March, already twice over the GDP. In other words, the "pool" has been stuffed with sufficient currency, and issuing more currency may lead to inflation. As we all know, hyperinflation not only interferes with or disrupts the market, it also brings enormous pressure and side effects to people's lives, or even causes public panic."[2]

Statistics show that as of 2012, China's M2 inventory quantity was 1.5 times the size of the US, 4.9 times the size of the UK, 1.7 times the size of Japan, and was RMB 20 trillion more than the currency supply in the eurozone. At the same time, M2-to-GDP ratio had gradually climbed to nearly 190 percent, indicating that, during the reign of Xi Jinping, the government will no longer pay for a massive investment-led economy. It has become an unsustainable policy, and the era of "the government's generosity" will never return again.

---

2.   *Workers' Daily*, November 7, 2013.

Xi Jinping: Maintaining Strategic Focus

As we all know, the most recent 30 years' worth of economic development in China was mainly driven by the "troika," which refers to government investment, driven by foreign trade, and driven by domestic demand. At the time when the driving engine of government investment faced fizzling out due to shortages of fuel, with the spread of the global financial crisis, China's foreign trade also took a nosedive. In 2014, China's total import and export value was RMB 26.43 trillion, an increase of 2.3 percent over 2013; the export value was RMB 14.39 trillion, an increase of 4.9 percent; the import value was RMB 12.04 trillion, a decrease of 0.6 percent; the trade surplus was RMB 2.35 trillion, an expansion of 45.9 percent. China's foreign trade growth was only 4.9 percent in 2014, which was a low rate that was unthinkable in the first decade of the twenty-first century. For example, according to statistical data in 2008 of Chinese Customs, China's foreign trade amounted to USD 2.561 trillion, an increase of 17.8 percent compared with the previous year (similarly hereinafter). Among this, the export value was USD 1.428 trillion, an increase of 17.2 percent; the import value was USD 1.133 trillion, an increase of 18.5 percent; the trade surplus was USD 295.47 billion, an increase of 12.5 percent over the previous year, and a net increase of USD 32.83 billion.

According to the data of the World Bank, in 2007, China's consumer spending accounted for 34 percent of GDP, lower than the mean level of the world's average-income countries, 60 percent, and even lower than the mean level of low-income countries, 41 percent. For a long time, China's domestic demand only accounted for one-third of GDP, its contribution of economic growth was also about one third, and the growth rate was quite slow.

At the core of a shortage in national domestic demand is slow income growth. In 2010, Zhang Jianguo, then the director of the Contract Department, All-China Federation of Trade Unions (ACFTU), told the media that in the Chinese mainland, the ratio of residents' labor compensation to GDP continued to decline after it reached a peak of 56.5 percent in 1983, and it had dropped to 36.7 percent in 2005—falling by nearly 20 percent in 22 years. From 1978 to 2005, in stark contrast to the declining share of labor remuneration, the ratio of return on capital to GDP increased by 20 percent. A related ACFTU survey also showed that 23.4 percent of workers did not have a wage increase during the five years observed, 75.2 percent of workers believed that the distribution of income was unfair in the current society, and 61 percent of them believed that the greatest injustice was that ordinary workers had low incomes.

On the other hand, the income share of GDP continued to decline, widening the income gap. According to NBSC data, the national Gini coefficient was 0.473 in 2013, which was an undervalued level of the domestic residents' income gap that a lot of people considered; even so, in accordance with the international general standard, a Gini coefficient above 0.4 represents the income gap running into the high-risk zone. More extreme statistics were shown in unofficial estimates. Gan Li, dean of the Institute of Economics and Management, Southwest University of Finance, published a report in February, 2014, and stated that the distribution of family assets in China was very uneven: 10 percent of Chinese households possessed 63.9 percent of assets. In other words, 10 percent of the richest households owned more than 60 percent of China's family assets. No matter which way you look at the statistics from all sectors, China's gap between the rich and the poor had grown dangerously wide.

Such a gap will seriously affect social harmony and stability, and it will restrict the elevation of overall consumption if it is too wide, making China's domestic progress stagnant.

Faced with this grim macroeconomic situation, Xi Jinping made a quick basic conclusion: The long-term fundamentals of China's economic and social development are getting better, but China is in a stage of "Three Periods Superimposed," including a shifting period from a high rate of growth to a medium–high rate of growth, a difficult period of structural adjustment, and an absorption period of previous economic stimulus policies. Together, these trends are referred to as the "Three Periods Superimposed," marking Xi Jinping's determination to lead China's economy to a new normal.

Xi Jinping has pointed out: "China's development is still in an important period of strategic opportunities. We should boost confidence, start from the current features of economic development, adapt to the new normal, and maintain a balanced state of mind strategically."

Over the past 30 years, China's economy has maintained long-term double-digit growth. An important symbol of the new normal of the economy is that economic growth gradually declines to a medium–high rate of growth. This is a rate for sustainable economic development. Xi Jinping stressed: "We should fully understand the relationship between sustainable and healthy development and GDP growth."

A non-blind pursuit of the high rate of economic growth helps to optimize the allocation and full utilization of various resources, improve the quality and efficiency of economic development, and effectively make economic development benefit all people. The shift in economic growth is only a modest reduction relative to the high rate of growth in the past, but China's economic growth is still significantly higher than the growth of the mature, developed economies, and even many emerging market economies. However, China's initiative to decelerate its economy still triggered worldwide concerns and questions, and also led to negative rhetoric by some forecasters—after China's initiative to slow down its economy in 2014, the West set off on a new round of criticism of China. Prior to the NBSC announcing the economic growth data of the first quarter of 2014, some overseas investment banks launched a bearish "chorus" over the Chinese economy following Goldman Sachs' prediction that China's economic growth rate would be only 6 percent in the first quarter; but the final data of 7.4 percent that the NBSC released provided a strong counter to international investment banks' forecasts.

Chi Fulin, the president of the China Institute for Reform and Development, said that China's long-established "trinity" mode of economic growth—investment-led, government-led, and emphasizing competitive local governments—played a major role in promoting rapid economic growth; but under conditions of profound change in internal and external environments for development today, this mode of growth would fail to maintain a sustainable development, and had even become an institutional factor that may increase economic conflicts and economic risks.

Li Zuojun, deputy director of the Development Research Center of Resources and Environmental Policy Institute, State Council, said in his previous analysis that: "In the new situation, reducing the GDP growth target is more of an initiative, and thus it will be easy for enthusiasm and motivation to shift modes and adjust." He added that the current emphasis on the efficiency and quality of development was being gradually accepted by the people, which would be "very favorable" for the promotion of economic restructuring, and for building the "upgraded version" of China's economy.

Obviously, Xi Jinping hopes to decelerate China's economy appropriately and to promote the transformation of China's economic structure. But to him and his colleagues, the transformation of China's economic growth is considered a lasting battle, of a scale comparable to the Huaihai Campaign.

Economic stories of the Huaihai Campaign go back to the year 1949. In that autumn, the grain-producing regions of northern China suffered natural disasters and crop failures, and the already tight food situation became more severe. In planning the war of price gouging with capitalists, Chen Yun, the top leader of the CPC Central Finance front, was very worried that speculators in the north might attack the food price—and if food prices rose along with textiles, the north and south would be at war, and China would be threatened by both sides and the situation would be uncontainable. Chen Yun devoted three months and soon calmed down the price in Shanghai. Thus the economy in Shanghai, which was plagued by hyperinflation for twelve years since the beginning of the war in 1937, was finally brought under control by Chen Yun. As spring changed to summer in 1950, the country's prices were basically stabilized. Mao Zedong spoke very highly of Chen Yun's victory in this economic war and believed the victory was as important as the success of the Huaihai Campaign. This is the origin of allusions to the Huaihai Campaign among the economists of the CPC.

How difficult will it be to adjust the economy and transform economic growth in China? Ni Jinjie, the visiting researcher of the China People's Insurance Institute, asserted that although "structural adjustment" has become a common term in policy documents, it still has a long journey ahead before being implemented in practical strategies. Over the past ten years (2000–2010), the structure of GDP growth has been deteriorating, which could explain the high difficulty of implementing structural adjustments to the economy. In 2009, the ratio of investment to GDP reached an alarming 67 percent, while in 2000, this ratio was merely 37 percent, which some economists already considered too high.

Wu Jinglian, a veteran Chinese economist, bluntly stated: "In fact, it is not the government that will adjust the [economy's] structure. For so many years, we have taken protective or suppressive measures according to different conditions, so the Third Plenary Session of the 18th CPC Central Committee made the correct decision that we should think of ways to play the role of the market."

Xi Jinping holds to a firm philosophy of allowing the market to play a decisive role in economic growth by clarifying the relationship between government and the market. In the *Explanation on "Decision of the Central Committee of the Communist Party of China on Some Major Issues Concerning Comprehensively Deepening Reform,"* he pointed out that the mission of deepening reform all around remains focused on economic reform, and handling the relationship between the government and the market remains the core issue of economic reform.

Adjustment of the economic structure is not without consequence. Inevitably, in order to transform the mode of economic development and optimize the role of industry, many enterprises and companies will be affected, and some may even withdraw from the market. The price we must pay is the "growing pains" during the structural adjustment. GDP growth, which many officials considered as the primary performance indicator, will also be given up reluctantly, a decision made by Xi Jinping. The significance of the new normal will gradually emerge in the future.

Chinese Academy of Social Sciences (CASS) Vice President Li Yang and other scholars believe that after this round of global financial crisis, actually, the global economic situation will enter a new period of development. Internationally, the new normal is passively reflected as more of a long-term periodic shift in economic growth since the 1980s. In China, the new normal constitutes strategic planning for better development in the future, not only emphasizing the necessity of China's economic transformation, but navigating the course of, and understanding the dynamic structure of, that transformation.

China's economic growth is the like the running of a marathon; when runners have consumed too much energy by bolting through the first half, they need to make some metabolic adjustments in the middle by slowing down and conserving energy, which helps them run a good second half. China's economy still tends toward the positive side. Some experts have estimated that we will see a stable upward trend in China's economy in 2016. Now, as some critics rush to speak ill of the Chinese economy, they are being injudicious once again.

Sweatshops: The Truth Behind the "World's Factory" Label

Generally, the "world's factory" is the honorific title for the world's strongest industrial countries, especially manufacturing countries.

Prior to the late nineteenth century, Britain was recognized as the world's factory; by the end of the nineteenth century, the United States replaced Britain as the world's leading industrial power and was ranked in the forefront in both production scale and export share in many manufacturing fields including steel, automobiles, chemicals, machinery and heavy equipment, aircraft manufacturing, electrical products, medical technologies, and military hardware; therefore, the United States was called the world's factory. Then, from the 1960s to the 1980s, Japan's industry gradually turned from the export of heavy chemical products to high exports of value-added machinery and electronics products, and thereby Japan became a technology-intensive production and export power including mechanical and electrical equipment, automobiles, household appliances, and semiconductors. Thus Japan could then be considered the world's factory.

The purpose of such a manufacturing economy is to provide a large number of export products for the world market, and not just consume the total amount of its industrial products. If looked at from the perspective of total production, China's many industrial products will have been ranked first in the world, such as coal, steel, cement, plate glass, televisions, home refrigerators, washing machines, air conditioners, microwave ovens, all kinds of textiles and consumer-grade light industrial products. However, due to China's large population and cheap labor, a majority of industrial products per capita were still below the world's average level. China is a big country in terms of industrial products, and also a large consumer of all kinds of industrial products. Now, products are provided for domestic consumption first, followed by export. Beginning of the twenty-first century, China's exports have enabled it to access the global top three, where its export of electromechanical products ranks first in the world, and thus China ascends to the status of the "world's factory."

But behind such an accomplishment, there are many little-known and awkward truths.

For example, it is acknowledged by experts that there are three reasons for the fact that US senators are concerned about the Sino-US trade surplus: First, the demand structures of American and Chinese markets are different because people's consumption choices are closely related to their income levels and the great differences of economic development between the two countries incur different structures of residents' demands; China's production of labor-intensive products are mostly daily necessities, while US production of high-tech products are high-end products. Given that the income level of Chinese residents is relatively low, the Chinese market is incapable of the purchasing power for sufficient and effective demand. Second, the United States' discriminatory export controls against China are a "double-edged sword" that, in addition to bringing harm to US industries, also weakens its export competitiveness in many ways, leading to the decline in exports to China. Third, the direct cause for the trend of greater China-US trade surplus is global industrial transfer. Since the mid-1980s, China's neighboring countries' and territories' upgrades and adjustments in industrial structure have lost their comparative advantage in labor-intensive industries and handed them to China, forming production and trade patterns in which the Chinese import raw materials and spare parts from these countries for processing and assembly, and then export to the US and European nations. The changes of international division brought by the economic structural adjustment of the Asia-Pacific region allowed the United States to reduce the imports of these countries and territories, and increase imports from China, where South Korea and Japan's trade surplus with the United States and other countries showed a downward trend, and the Sino-US trade surplus grew year after year.

On the third reason, Professor Lu Feng, of Peking University, who used to serve as a member of the Third Advisory Committee of China National Information Technology, has a more in-depth analysis: In the history of the world's economic development, it is typical that China lasted nearly 20 years in "double surplus" patterns. From the basic principles of economics in terms of the balance of payments, the trade surplus means that China is a capital-exporting country, namely China's rate of savings is sufficient to support a very high rate of domestic investment without having to supplement by introducing large-scale inflow of foreign direct investments (FDIs). But in fact, China maintains a trade surplus and a large number of foreign investments at the same time, leading to a surplus in the capital account. "Double surplus" allows China to accumulate huge foreign exchange reserves. In fact, China's foreign exchange reserves broke USD 1 trillion in 2006 and then reached USD 3.181 trillion by the end of 2011, accounting for a quarter of total global foreign exchange reserves. However, China's huge foreign exchange reserves lack effective investment outlets, which are mainly used for the purchase of assets such as US Treasury debts and the like. As a matter of fact, China attracted foreign investment at a very high price, but again built up foreign exchange reserves for the purchase of low-yielding assets and overseas debt.

The fundamental reason for the Sino-US "double surplus" is that US companies move the production link to China, where the US multinationals lead the value chain; and the trade deficit does not mean that US companies are uncompetitive, but illustrates that in this kind of control the core technology is a major transfer of benefits for the US companies. According to surveys, US companies' average return of investment in China is 33 percent; while in contrast, China's return on purchases for the US Treasury is estimated to be no more than 1 to 3 percent. Accumulated foreign exchange reserves from attracting foreign investment are used for purchase of low-profit debt assets was summed up by Yu Yongding, the prominent Chinese economist, as "tantamount to poor people borrowing money from the hands of the rich at a high price, and then lending it back at an extremely low price."[3]

Actually, with the accolade of being described as "the world's factory," China is in the role of a working boy, whose basic job is to process for others cheaply. For example, among Apple's global manufacturing facilities, China is the most important one, accounting for 90 percent of production. Apple's profit per iPad is about USD 150, which exclusively accounts for 58.5 percent of the profit; raw materials suppliers account for 21.9 percent of the cost (screens and electronic components) and other major suppliers get 4.7 percent, while Chinese labor ultimately only gets 1.8 percent.

In order to squeeze more value out of staff, facilities for Apple take on more extreme means of production by forcing workers to work overtime in order to increase productivity and reduce remuneration. Among these, Foxconn receives the most criticism.

---

3.   *Sustainable Prosperity in the New Economy*, Shanghai Far East Publishers, 2011.

Since Foxconn's first employee committed suicide on January 23, 2010, up to November 5, 2010, fourteen Foxconn employees have jumped from the building. The events caused global concern. According to media reports, Foxconn workers work eight hours a day for RMB 900 a month; and if they want to earn more money, they have to choose more shifts of simple and repetitive work and give up their leisure time. After a series of accusations and protests by the public, in February, 2012, Apple announced on its official website that, at Apple's request, the Fair Labor Association (FLA) were going to conduct an independent audit for manufacturers of final product assembly for Apple, including Foxconn's factories in Shenzhen and Chengdu, China.

Under pressure from public opinion, "sweatshops," represented by Foxconn, have taken some measures to assist workers, but many domestic facilities in China have not fundamentally changed. Guo Jun, the director of the Department of Legal Affairs, ACFTU, told the media in February, 2015, that in some domestic companies, employees work more than ten hours a day and rarely have a day off. Some small- and medium-sized private enterprises don't offer paid leave. Foxconn and other companies force workers to work overtime for a long time illegally, and cause some workers to suffer from a variety of mental issues, resulting in occurrences of "death from overwork" or suicide from time to time.

"Death from overwork" is a term seldom heard in the United States and Europe, but in the current environment of China, "death from overwork" is far from uncommon. On March 24, 2015, Zhang Bin, a 36-year-old graduate of Tsinghua University, was found dead in the bathroom of his hotel room. Before his death, he worked for a software development company and worked overtime frequently—sometimes working into the early hours until 5 or 6 a.m., and then returning to work without rest. His wife said, "He exhausted himself to death." Tragedies of young workers like Zhang Bin, who died from overwork, continue to unfold in China. According to a report of the Chinese Guang Ming Net's survey of "post-80s white-collar workers," 60 percent of employees said they "work overtime frequently," and 70 percent of respondents said they were in a state of "overwork."

The tragic cost of GDP in human blood angers the Chinese more than "death from overwork" and responsibilities to work overtime. For example, in May 2011, an explosion of combustible dust occurred at Foxconn's Chengdu factory, killing three people and injuring sixteen; in August 2012, an explosion of aluminum dust occurred in Wenzhou City, Zhejiang Province, killing thirteen people and injuring fifteen workers; in April 2014, an explosion of hard acid resin dusts occurred in Shuangma Chemical Co., Ltd., in Jiangsu, and eight people died and nine workers were injured; four months later, another accident with more than 260 casualties occurred in Kunshan, Jiangsu.

Yang Dongliang, the head of the State Administration of Work Safety, said that in 2013 the total number of production accidents in China fell from 800,000 to 300,000, a decrease of 61.5 percent, and the number of deaths fell from 136,700 to 69,000, a drop of nearly 50 percent, which was the "best Chinese production safety record ever achieved."

II. BREAKING THROUGH THE "SOFT SPOT" OF INNOVATION

China's economy has many shining examples of achieving success in the world. It is number one in terms of production for steel, coal, fertilizer, glass and hundreds of other industrial products.

China also has the world's largest foreign exchange reserves, is the world's second largest economy, and is also one of the top two import and export trade powers.

China has the highest number of college graduates in the world, the most engineers, and the most doctoral students.

However, there is one ranking that will always make the Chinese people feel ashamed—that is, the innovative competitiveness of China's economy.

According to the *Global Competitiveness Report* released by the World Economic Forum in 2014, the competitiveness of the Chinese mainland ranked 28th among the world's 49 major countries, at a level of below average. Switzerland, Singapore, the US, Finland, Germany, Japan, Hong Kong China, the Netherlands, the UK, Sweden, and other countries and regions have retained positions among the world's top ten in global competitiveness for at least three consecutive years. Despite the upward trend of mainland China in its global competitiveness ranking, it is still far apart from the US, Japan, Germany, UK, and other established economic powers.

In the world's ranking for scientific and technological strength set forth in the "Green Paper of the World's Comprehensive Scientific and Technological Strength" published by *Nature Publishing Index* and the Massachusetts Institute of Technology (MIT), countries are divided into five grades in terms of scientific and technological strength, and China ranks in grade four. Grade I, *core*, is the United Sates, the one and only in the world. Grade II, *developed*, features UK, Germany, France, and Japan. Grade III, *proficient*, includes Finland, Russia, Italy, Israel, Canada, Australia, Norway, South Korea, the Czech Republic, and other moderately developed countries.

Grade IV, *staying at the gate*, includes China, India, Mexico, South Africa, and other developing countries. Grade V, *backward*: other poor developing countries are in this ranking, such as Zimbabwe and Somalia.

Innovation problems and delays have become a constraining bottleneck for China's economic transformation and upgrading. If this constraint cannot be overcome soon, China's dreams of rejuvenation will remain at the stage of an unrealized dream.

Eight Hundred Million Chinese-Made Shirts for One Boeing Aircraft

No one can deny that Chinese people are very industrious and are some of the world's most diligent workers. But why are the industrious and diligent Chinese not rich?

Chen Zhiwu, professor of finance and economics at the School of Management, Yale University, in his book, *Why Are The Chinese Industrious And Yet Not Rich?* has analyzed the matter: China has the world's largest population, and relatively cheap labor, which is an advantage that can make up for the negative impact of the high costs on China's economy in the early stages of economic growth, but cheap labor certainly cannot make the Chinese people's accession into the ranks of the affluent be realized.

What is China's large workforce concentrated in doing? Undoubtedly, the main job is concentrated in low-level industry—primary processing. A few years ago, the Ministry of Commerce of China made a calculation: if they exported Chinese-made shirts to the United States for US dollars, they would need to swap 800 million shirts in exchange for a Boeing aircraft. This figure also shows the urgent need to transform China from a manufacturer into a brand power.

Li Yushi, the vice president of the Chinese Academy of International Trade and Economic Cooperation, MOFCOM, believes that China needs to sell 800 million shirts in exchange for a Boeing aircraft.[4]

As a manufacturer, China has invested manpower and materials and consumed energy and resources, but it can only earn a small share of the processing fees, which still attracts endless allegations of trade dumping from European and American markets. Lu Renbo, of the Market Economy Research Institute, Development Research Center of the State Council, believes that the only way for Chinese enterprises to surpass the technical barriers of Europe and America is to get rid of low-priced competition, strengthen research and development (R&D) capabilities, develop core technologies, and develop new industrial standards.

It is not the Chinese people's willingness, but rather a helpless move to

4.   *Shenzhen Economic Daily*, December 31, 2005.

choose sectors that "are thankless and come to nothing." According to Adam Smith, Arthur Young, and Yang Xiaokai's theories, without considering income distribution or assuming a reasonable income distribution, a person or country's high income level is because of their high productivity level, and the high level of productivity is because of their high level of specialization, and the high level of specialization is because of their developed market trading system. Conversely speaking, the developed market trading system reduces transaction costs; in turn, low transaction costs improve efficiency in the division of labor, efficiency promotes the increase of labor productivity, and increased labor productivity raises the income level. Therefore, the poverty of industrious Chinese people has its roots in its underdevelopment of trading and poor specialized division of labor. In other words, low levels of technology, low capital per worker, and poor specialized divisions of labor combine to keep China stuck in the low end of the industry chain, and it is difficult to extricate themselves.

A more difficult problem for China's economy is that during the pursuit of industrial upgrades, the higher China climbs, the more difficult it is to breathe, as if climbing Mount Everest. Current technology upgrading in China has entered the zone of 5000 meters above sea level, where altitude sickness emerges, and it seems so difficult to climb every step. Li Yang, CASS Vice President, comments that it is easy for a country to improve production efficiency when it has a large gap with the world's technology forefronts; however, when the gap of its technology with a leading edge is narrower, the introduction of cutting-edge production technology will become more difficult, and the cost of production, particularly the advantage of low labor cost will fade away; in that case, the key to raise the level of economic development depends on the country's innovation efficiency of products, where technological advancements will be more dependent than the "innovation strategy." In contrast, the investment strategy focuses on improvement of production efficiency while the innovation strategy focuses on an increase of innovation efficiency.

China's policy makers did not realize this pursuit of technological advances, in particular to acquire core technologies. However, they have been hoping to exchange markets for technologies during the past 30 years, and the effect has been far from satisfactory.

Among China's enterprises, the typical industry that largely implements the idea of "exchanging markets for technology" is the automobile industry. As early as the beginning of the late 1980s, the Chinese auto industry would have wanted to open the market to foreign car manufacturers in exchange for technology in the manner of a joint venture. Thirty years later, what is the situation of China's auto market? An article entitled "The Automotive Industry Paid a Big Price for an 'Exchange Market for Technology,'" published on Guang Ming Net, made a comprehensive assessment of this trial over 30 years: According to the statistics, as much as 90 percent of market shares of China's auto, electronics, and other high-tech products—as well as key areas of engines, transmissions, and other core parts are controlled by multinationals; and more than 60 percent of shares of the parts market are controlled by them. Originally, "exchanging markets for technology" was an expectation that attracted foreign investment, but most multinationals failed to fulfill their commitments to drive China's scientific and technological innovations, and caused a "crowding out" of the scientific and technological innovations of local Chinese enterprises. The Chinese auto industry paid a heavy price. This makes China's auto industry understand the truth: Only engaging in joint ventures and transnational partnerships, rather than creating their own brand, is ultimately wasteful; the better the product was developed, the stronger the multinational companies' brands became, and the smaller the market space for China's automobile brands.

On January 12, 2015, the China Association of Automobile Manufacturers held a conference in Beijing, in which the operational status of the auto industry in 2014 was summarized: In 2014, a total of 19,700,600 cars were sold in China's passenger car market, a year-on-year increase of 9.89 percent. Since the growth in passenger cars of independent brands is lower than the overall market, as of the end of 2014, the independent brands' share in the passenger car market dropped 2.14 percent on a year-on-year basis, which was only 38.44 percent. According to statistics, the sales of cars of independent brands dropped 17.4 percent on a year-on-year basis.

We opened our door and handed over the market share, so that foreign auto manufacturers made a great fortune in China while domestic auto companies did not earn any technology worth mentioning. These harsh lessons tell the Chinese people: China cannot pay for, nor can it trade for, core technologies. China must lean on innovation.

Xi Jinping deeply feels the urgency of the drive for innovation. On March 4, 2013, Xi Jinping attended the Two Sessions. At the discussion with CPPCC members of China's scientific community, he said: "Implementation of an innovation-driven development strategy is the future-focused key strategy, based on the overall situation, and the fundamental measure to accelerate the transformation of the economic development mode, resolve deep-seated conflicts and problems of economic development, and enhance the power and vitality of economic development. In the increasingly fierce global competition of overall national strengths, we have to face a harsh reality, admit gaps, closely track, catch up forthwith, choose the road of independent innovation, take more active and effective measures, and explore boldly in key scientific and technological areas in the future, accelerating the transformation from factory-driven development to innovation-driven development, and acknowledge scientific and technological innovation's leading and supporting role."[5]

From the Needham Question to Qian Xuesen's Question
Time magazine made an inventory of the best inventions of the year that have contributed to a better, more intelligent, and more interesting world. It also selected the "25 Best Inventions of 2013–2014" including a real levitating skateboard, the Mars Orbiter Mission (Mangalyaan), a high-beta fusion reactor, WiTricity, a versatile 3D printer, the Blackphone, which enables secure communications, and a portable refrigeraton unit.[6]

Although this is only *Time*'s magazine's opinion, this list of "the Best Inventions of the Year" is still striking for two reasons: (1) In previous years, the list had no selections that were invented in China; and (2) it is also noted that in recent years the list featured the US, of course, as the "big winners," but countries on China's periphery, including Japan, South Korea, and India also made the list; so why does China miss out on the "best inventions" list every year?

It is not enough just to mention that the Chinese people have never made the list of the world's contribution of major scientific and technological inventions in the past 20 years; they are hardly found in the world's history of major scientific and technological inventions even from the beginning of the eighteenth century. Are the Chinese, who account for a quarter of the world's population, born without the ability to innovate?

Here we have to ask the world-renowned Needham Question, which was originally put forth by the famous British scholar Joseph Needham (1900–1995), a leading authority on the history of China's science and technology. In his fifteen-volume book *Science and Civilisation in China*, he officially presented this question: "Why did modern science, the mathematization of hypotheses about Nature, with all its implications for advanced technology, and the technology revolution not make their meteoric rise in Chinese civilisation despite its earlier successes?" In 1976, Kenneth Boulding, the American economist, called it the Needham Question. Many people have continued to ask the Needham Question, and thus it has become: "Why has China's modern science gone backwards?" and "Why does China lag

---

5.   Xinhua News Agency, March 4, 2013.
6.   *Reference News* December 1, 2014.

behind in modern times?" and other similar questions. The debate over the Needham Question has been very spirited.

In addition to the four great inventions known to the world, as many as another thousand kinds of advanced inventions were also contributed by the ancient Chinese. In his book *The Genius of China*, American scholar Robert Temple wrote: "If the Nobel Prize was established in ancient China, the prize winners would have been undisputedly all Chinese." Of course, it may be a slight exaggeration. But the research results of Needham and others also proved that the ancient Chinese people had an amazing ability to create: From the sixth century to the early seventeenth century, China contributed to more than 54 percent of the world's major scientific and technological achievements, while it dropped to only 0.4 percent by the nineteenth century. Why science and technology took a big drop in China but saw a great rise in the West and thus widened such a large gap, is the long-puzzled-over question Needham found inconceivable.

Admittedly, since the middle and late periods of the last century, China's innovation capability was struggling to catch up, but the status of major innovations are far disproportionate to the superpower with an enormous population of Chinese professionals, and also disproportionate to China's huge research talent base. Zhou Ji, of the Chinese Academy of Engineering, said, "At present, the number of engineers cultivated in China annually is equivalent to the sum of engineers cultivated in the United States, Canada, Europe, Japan, and India combined." As of 2014, China's total professional and technical personnel reached more than 55.5 million, which was 45.6 percent of China's total number of its talent team, and the ratios of high, middle, and junior professional and technical personnel reached 11:36:53, with 68.6 percent claiming college educations. Especially in the last five years, China's new professional and technical personnel was 8.60 million, including nearly 60,000 post-doctoral researchers, 1.0557 million returned overseas students, and 9.4515 million professional and technical personnel who had acquired vocational qualifications.

This talent team dominates the world in quantity, well ahead of the US and EU, but they cannot make major achievements that match them. Why? Qian Xuesen, the famous contemporary Chinese scientist, did not find the answer to the question on his deathbed, and therefore, it is called Qian Xuesen's question.

In 2005, when Wen Jiabao, the Premier of China State Council at the time, visited Qian Xuewen, Qian said with emotion: "I have trained many students over years, but none of them can be compared with masters that were trained during the Republic of China in terms of academic achievements."

He then asked: "Why are our schools always failing to cultivate outstanding talents?"

A total of 20 scientists have been awarded the Chinese State Supreme Science and Technology Award since its establishment in 2000, and fifteen of them graduated from colleges prior to 1951. Qian Xuesen was born in 1911 in Shanghai, China. In 1934, he graduated from National Chiao Tung University, and was then admitted to the study-abroad program of Tsinghua University in June of the same year. In September 1935, he entered MIT's Department of Aeronautics, and a year later, in September, 1936, he earned a graduate degree in aeronautical engineering at MIT, and was transferred to the Department of Aeronautics, California Institute of Technology, and soon became the most important student of the world famous aeronautical scientist and mathematician Theodore Von Kármán. He won a graduate degree in aeronautical engineering and aerospace, and a doctorate in mathematics. From July, 1938, to August, 1955, he was engaged in the fields of aerodynamics, mechanics and solid rocket and missile research in the United States, and with his supervisor, they conducted research on high-speed aerodynamics problems and established the Kármán-Tsien formula. Over his 20-year stay in America, he had become a world-renowned aerodynamicist. In 1945, he served as an associate professor at the California Institute of Technology. In 1947, he served as a professor at MIT. When the news of the establishment of the People's Republic of China in 1949 reached the United States, Qian Xuesen and his wife Jiang Ying discussed returning to the motherland to serve their own country. It was at this time that United States Senator Joseph McCarthy led a "witch hunt" against communists and a wave of employee loyalty to the US government was set off.

Qian Xuesen's certificate to participate in secret research was suddenly revoked by the US military because he was suspected of being a Communist. He was very angry and asked to return to China on this account. In 1950, when Qian Zhong was about to return, he was stopped by US officials, and put in jail. The Undersecretary of the US Navy, Dan A. Kimble, stated: "Wherever Qian Xuesen goes, he is worth the military strength of five divisions." After that, Qian Xuesen was persecuted by the US government and he also lost freedom. In 1955, after Premier Zhou Enlai's constant efforts in diplomatic negotiations with the US, even negotiating the release of 11 captured US pilots in the Korean War, on August 4, 1955, Qian Xuesen received notification allowing him return to China. On September 17, 1955, Qian Xuesen finally realized this desire to return home.

Undersecretary Kimble believed that Qian Xuesen was worth five US divisions. It turns out, this judgment was an underestimation of the

outstanding talents' contribution to scientific and technological innovation—
Qian Xuesen was awarded the Medal of Atomic and Hydrogen Bombs and
Man-Made Satellites; he was hailed as the "Father of China's Space Program;"
"Father of China's Missile;" "Father of China's Automation and Control;" and
the "King of Rockets." Some people think that Qian Xuesen serving China
shortened at least 20 years development of China's launch of its missiles and
atomic bomb. On October 31, 2009, Qian died in Beijing at the age of 98.

Qian Xuesen has gone, but the "Qian Xuesen Question" he left is still
struggling to be answered by contemporary Chinese people; together with
the Needham Question, leaders of contemporary China are compelled to
work out the problem of China's innovation.

Igniting the Innovation Revolution

Xi Jinping graduated from one of China's top universities, Tsinghua
University. From 1975 to 1979, he specialized in basic organic synthesis at
the Chemical Engineering Department of Tsinghua University; from 1998
to 2002, he studied at an on-the-job graduate program in the humanities
and social sciences at Tsinghua, majored in Marxist theory and ideological
and political education, and he received a doctorate in law. Xi Jinping, who
has extensively engaged in both natural sciences and social sciences, is no
stranger to the predicament of China's innovation.

On June 9, 2014, at the 17th General Assembly of the Chinese Academy
of Sciences and the 12th General Assembly of the Chinese Academy of
Engineering, Xi Jinping delivered a speech and again he profoundly analyzed
the so-called Needham Question. He said, "I've been thinking of the reason
why China's science and technology gradually became obsolete from the
end of Ming and beginning of Qing. Scholars' studies show that Emperor
Kangxi was very interested in western science and technology and invited
western missionaries to lecture on western learning, including astronomy,
mathematics, geography, zoology, anatomy, music, and even philosophy.
Only lecturing books in terms of astronomy numbered as many as 100.
What time was that? How long had he learned? Probably, the early stage was
between 1670 and 1682, in which he spent two consecutive years and five
months of uninterrupted learning of the Western knowledge. It was an early
and a sufficient process of learning. But the problem was, he was interested
in the Western learning and learned a lot, but he failed to use that knowledge
for China's economic and social development; instead, mostly they sat and
prattled about general principles and sat pontificating, and conducted idle
talks in the Forbidden City.

"In 1708, the Qing government organized missionaries to draw a Chinese map, and they spent ten years and completed the Map of China in the Kangxi Reign at an unprecedentedly scientific level, which was the highest level of cartography the world at the time. However, such an important achievement had long been favored as confidential and was stored within the government, where society could not see it—and it did not play any role in economic and social development. On the contrary, western missionaries who participated in cartography brought the data back to the West for publication, allowing their people better geographical knowledge of China than the Chinese people for a long period. What problem does this illustrate? It shows that science and technology must be combined with social development; laying aside and neglecting however much we have learned is merely a hunt for novelty, a refined interest, or even considered as a clever but useless trick, and of course it will be impossible to play any role in reality."

Xi Jinping looked far and wide at the history of modern China's vicissitudes. He said, "History tells us a truth: whether a country is powerful or not does not depend solely on the size of the total economy, whether a nation is strong not on the population size or the area the territory covers. In modern history, one of the root causes of our backwardness and being beaten is the backwardness of our science and technology."

Reports from the World Intellectual Property Organization noted that in 2011, China accepted more than 520,000 patent applications; in the United States the figure was 500,000, and Japan 340,000. China had actually overtaken Japan in 2010; it then surpassed the US and became the world's largest patent applicant in 2011.

This data allows Chinese people to feel proud—in the past 100 years, there were only three countries ranking in the field of patents: the United States, Germany and Japan. As a developing country, China had become the world's largest patent applicant overnight. But does it mean that China's ability to innovate has surpassed the established developed countries?

"In fact, almost none of the world's current core technological innovations comes from China," Professor Xu Zhengzhong, Department of Economic Research, China National School of Administration, pointed out, adding that the GDP contribution of Chinese scientific and technological innovation remains low. Looking at the world, the GDP contribution of scientific and technological innovation in innovative countries is as high as 70 percent, and even up to 80 percent in the US and Germany; while it was only 40 percent in China.

So, it is an integral part of Xi Jinping's governing plans to be determined to start the engine of technological innovation. Xi Jinping noted in this regard: "Over the years, there has been the chronic issue of ineffective and obstructed transformation from scientific and technological achievements into practical productivity; one of the most important cruxes is that there are many barriers of institutional mechanisms in the chain of science and technology, and innovation's convergence with the transformation in all aspects is not tight enough. Like a relay race, no one will take the baton, or one may know nowhere to run even as he or she takes it, once the first runners have finished the race.

"To solve this problem, it is necessary to deepen the reform of our science and technology system, to get rid of the constraints of ideological barriers to technological and institutional innovations, to handle the relationship between government and the market properly, to promote the deep-going integration of science and technology and the economic and social development, to break through the channel of turning strong science and technology into strong industry, a strong economy, and a strong nation, to release innovation vitality by means of reform, and to accelerate the establishment and improvement of China's national innovation system, allowing full play to all sources of innovation.

"If the scientific and technological innovation is assimilated to the new engine of China's development, the reform is the essential ignition system to ignite this new engine. We must take effective measures to improve this ignition system and to mobilize the new innovation-driven new engine at full speed."[7]

In March, 2015, the CPC Central Committee and State Council publicly released the *Opinions on Deepening Reform of Institutional Mechanisms to Accelerate the Implementation of Innovation-Driven Development Strategy* (hereinafter referred to as the "Opinions on Innovation"), marking the launch of an innovation-driven strategy that has formally become China's national strategy. This strategy clearly pointed out: "Innovation is an important force to promote the development of China and the Chinese nation, is also an important force to push forward the development of the entire human society. Faced with significant opportunities, challenges in the new round of global technological, and industrial revolution, with changes in trends and characteristics of economic development under the new normal, with historical mission and requirements to achieve the Two Centenary Goals, we must deepen the reform institutional mechanism and accelerate the implementation of innovation-driven development strategy.

"China's strategy to promote an innovation-driven nature is to promote

---

7.   Refer to Xi Jinping's Speech at the 17th General Assembly of Chinese Academy of Sciences and the 12th General Assembly of Chinese Academy of Engineering, Xinhua News Agency, June 9, 2014.

popular innovation and people's innovation: To accelerate the implementation of an innovation-driven development strategy is to allow the market to play a decisive role in the allocation of resources and to better play the role of government, to get rid of all obstacles restricting innovative ideas and systemic barriers, to stimulate the innovative vitality and creative potential of the whole society, to enhance the efficiency and effectiveness of labor, information, knowledge, technology, management, and capital, to strengthen the connection of science and technology with economy, innovation with industry, innovative achievements with industries, innovation with real productivity, and innovative R&D workers' efforts with their interests and incomes, to enhance scientific and technological progress' contribution to economic development, and to create policy environment and institutional environment for popular entrepreneurship and innovation."[8]

Former Soviet writer Viktor Afanasyev has pointed out that innovation requires the smashing of all "walls" that hinder fresh thinking: To carve out a way for all innovators and creators is an important task of administrative authorities and leaders.

It must be admitted that the promotion of innovation is hard for a risk-averse government with a preference for control to adopt. Innovation has its unique rules; those in charge must have the ability to weigh the stakes between opportunities and risks, costs and benefits, long-term and current situations, future trends and existing models. For example, Li Kai, an academic from the American Academy of Engineering, has operated China's high-tech R&D "863 Program" for 28 years. He said: "In recent years, China's state investment funds reached USD 2 billion per year, but we could not find a successful commercial case with a core intellectual property that was generated by undertaking the 863 Program and occupied the international market in the high-tech innovation, especially in the computer field.

"If speaking from the perspective of culturing people, the 863 Program has cultured a group of talents; however, from the perspective of research and innovation, I think it is a failure," Li Kai said. His evaluation was based on three criteria: First, whether to generate disruptive technologies; second, whether or not to occupy a leading position in a field in the international market; and third, whether a core intellectual property creates high margins. Some people think that Li Kai set too high a standard, but he did not agree: "This is a well-recognized criteria in the world's industrial sector, not mine."[9]

Li Kai's advice: The government should not set unified criteria to restrain

8. Ibid.
9. "Innovation: The Government Should not Play the Investor of Venture Capital—An Exclusive Interview with Li Kai, Scholar of the American Academy of Engineering," *China Youth News*, January 5, 2015.

all universities and research institutes, and should delegate authority to universities and research institutes, believe in their judgments, and let them develop their own appropriate measurements.

The facts show that, to China, innovation is no longer altering or tinkering, but a new revolution in terms of order. Chinese scholar Liu Yang believes that there is nothing more difficult in the world than carving out a new order. Exploration and conquest of the unknown has already been quite a consumption of manpower. Potential adversaries will make it even more difficult. Those vested interests of the old order, which were indifferent to changing the status quo, and those that stagger, because of the fear of failure, will become a hampering force to reform that should not be overlooked. It is human born compliance with nature, which will not be overcome by system, not changed by technology, not awoken by enlightenment, or even conquered by force. Moreover, these opposite sides to innovation tend to connect with each other and form in a line: Given the chance, they will attack reformers with as much venom as religious fanatics.[10]

Innovation has been the only way to break through China's reform by stimulating innovation through reform, optimizing development through innovation, and achieving stability through development; innovation should be integrated into the core strategic arrangements for governing China and dealing with politics in China and allow reform, development, stability, and innovation to become essential elements of China's governance strategy.

III. ECOLOGY FIRST: BUILDING A BEAUTIFUL CHINA

In early 2014, more than 90 percent of China's government work reports involved air pollution and control, and at least fifteen provinces signed a military order for management of smog and preservation of a blue sky. Tough wordings and expressions occurred commonly in some provinces' government work reports, such as "strong," "iron fist," and "the most stringent." However, an NBSC statement showed that after monitoring 161 cities, air quality of more than 90 percent of them was not up to standard.[11]

To most provinces and cities of China, to control air pollution has become an urgent and overwhelming task.

The harsh reality that only 9.9 percent of cities have qualified air quality not only makes some provinces and cities' specific targets appear futile, but also lets down Chinese people's hopes and expectations for a blue sky. One

10.   Liu Yang. *The Innovation War*, Hunan Science and Technology Press, 2012, pp. 134–135,
11.   Xinhua Net, March 16, 2015.

wonders why so many commitments for haze governance vanished like soap bubbles in the air. Was it because the original target was set too high, or was local governance not strong enough?

Under no circumstances will the control of air pollution become a "random project" based on random decisions and guarantees. Ultimately, what is the problem with the unfinished target? Is it because of supervision and law enforcement? Or the launch of new projects? We should identify the reason and clarify it to the public. Otherwise, the Government's annual military order will become a "paper tiger" that can be either fulfilled or not. Consequently, the commitment to pollution control will inevitably be criticized as a lie to fool the public.

Environmental pollution and the ecological dilemma are not only a danger to public health, but will also shake public confidence in the government if protracted, leading to a crisis of public opinion. In particular, if the government's operations are seen as unprofessional and undedicated, they are more likely to cause widespread public resentment, which can easily become a political issue in the long run. On April 1, 2015, at an on-the-spot work meeting attended by hundreds of persons in charge of different monitoring states, Wu Xiaoqing, the Deputy Minister of the Ministry of Environmental Protection, admitted that there were "fraud issues" in terms of monitoring data in some places. He also warned that, the bottom line, reliability and authenticity of monitoring data, were absolutely untouchable, and environmental monitoring staff must treat monitoring data as if their lives depended on them.

Smog is an issue that China's Minister of Environment Protection cannot avoid. In the NPC Press Conference on March 7, 2015, Chen Jining, the new Minister of Environmental Protection, said that his first thing in the morning was to think about the students when he was the President of Tsinghua University in the past; and now, serving in the Ministry of Environment Protection, his first thing in the morning was to check in the sky.

In fact, not just air pollution, water crisis, soil pollution, and resource shortcomings—like the Sword of Damocles—hang over China and threaten its sustainable development. Once China's ecological chain is broken, China's development will reach a dead end. This is not alarmist, but the crisis of the reality.

Smog: The Most Gripping Crisis

In the past, Chinese folk liked to say, "Well-off or not, the key is ourselves." Now they say, "Well-off or not, the key is the sky."

Xu Dongqun, the Deputy Director of Institute of Environmental Health and Related Product Safety, China CDC, introduced an example in 2013: The continuing large-scale pollution of haze covered seventeen provinces, municipalities and autonomous regions of China, affecting a quarter of China's land area and a population of about 600 million.

On December 18, 2012, *An Assessment Study on the Health Hazards and Economic Losses of PM$_{2.5}$* jointly released by Greenpeace and the Peking University School of Public Health also stated that the pollution of PM$_{2.5}$ (particle pollution) was a deadly hazard to public health. With the existing air quality, as many as 857 people died above quota (premature death) due to the pollution at levels of PM$_{2.5}$ in Beijing, Shanghai, Guangzhou and Xi'an in 2012, and the economic losses due to excess mortality reached RMB 6.8 billion.

Many multinationals have long been aware of the potential hazards of Beijing's air. A Mr. Higashiyama, from a Japanese chemical company, told *China Business Weekly* that many Japanese companies have equipped offices with air purifiers for employees from January to February of 2013. If an employee was dispatched from Japan with his family, then the company would equip air purifiers in the employee's home based on the size of the family or family rooms. A considerable amount of Japanese companies including the aforesaid chemical company prepared 3M masks for employees in China.

Smog is common in autumn and winter. Although both fog and smog are considered obstacles to visibility, there is a huge difference between them— fog is a natural phenomenon of weather caused by moisture condensation in the air, which is not necessarily linked to man-made pollution. Smog, on the other hand, is the aggregates composed of dust, smoke, or salt, as well as other aerosol particles emitted into the air due to air pollution. They can be distinguished largely by humidity; generally, it will be foggy if the relative humidity is greater than 90 percent, with smog, or, "haze," if less than 80 percent, and a mixture of fog and haze if between 80 percent and 90 percent. Haze is not purely a natural phenomenon; the emergence of it is considered as a weather problem and an environmental problem.

Smog is a regular meteorological observation in China. According to the statistical analysis of observations over the years, the number of haze days in China in 2013 was significantly more than the same period of previous years; the average number of haze days from January to October daily of 2013 were the greatest compared with the same period since 1961. In January 2013, the average number of haze days in China was 4.4 days, an increase of 1.4 days compared to the same period of previous days; 4.7 days in October, an increase of 2.3 days. A large number of haze days were seen in northeast China, north China, Huanghuai, Jianghuai and other eastern regions. For example, among provincial capital cities, Hefei had up to 30 haze days in January, both Nanjing and Hangzhou had 29 days when they were almost shrouded in haze for the entire month; Beijing had 25 haze days, an increase of 13.6 days compared with the same period in the previous year, and the largest number of the same period since 1954.

Reductions in air quality and visibility due to smog impose severe effects on public health, travel and traffic and daily lives of people. In January, 2013, the number of admittances to hospitals in Beijing, Tianjin, Shijiazhuang, and other places increased significantly. Patients with respiratory infections accounted for more, and they showed significant allergic symptoms, such as runny noses, sneezing, itchy eyes, dry coughs, phlegm, suffocations, and shortness of breath. Haze also inflicts severe effects on aviation and road transportation. Jinan Airport canceled nearly 70 flights due to haze on January 17, 2013, and Beijing Capital International Airport canceled 49 flights due to the same reason on January 29.[12]

The smog is not accidental; its frequent and large-scale emergence is caused by super massive consumption of resources and energy in the process of China's industrialization.

In the period of rapid industrialization, emissions of large quantities of industrial waste, gas and coal dust into the air and the gradual increase in automobile exhaust are the major sources of air pollutants. The near-surface atmosphere's temperature inversion can cause the spread of pollutants so that, if the inversion layer maintains for a long time, the accumulation of contaminants and photochemical reaction occurs, which may result in substances of more toxicity, leading to vicious air pollution, causing heavy casualties.

In December, 1930, in the Maas Valley of Belgium, an industrial region situated in a narrow basin, there was a strong inversion layer over the river valley for a period of two weeks, which meant that industrial discharge and smoke accumulated, and piled thicker and thicker. From the third day, thousands of people in the industrial zone suffered respiratory illness, and 60 died within a week. In 1948, a similar event occurred in Donora, a small town in a valley of Pennsylvania, which had a concentration of sulfuric acid plants, steel mills, and zinc smelling plants. From October 26 to 31,

---

12.   "Cause Analysis and Considerations for Response for Haze." *Rescue CN*, February 24, 2014.

1948, there was a persistent heavy fog and temperature inversion layer in the town, and smoke from the plants was enclosed in the valley, affecting 6,000 people and causing the deaths of 20. In 1952, the shocking "London smog" occurred in the UK. From December 5 to December 8 of that year there was an inversion layer over London, without any wind controlled by the high pressure center for the next few days. A heavy fog enveloped the city, coal dust, soot and other pollutants accumulated without spreading in the absence of wind, and patients with respiratory tract illnesses increased dramatically. In only four days, the death toll reached 4,000 people, and another 8,000 people died in the following two months.[13]

The causes of air pollution in China are similar. *The China Ecological Urban Construction Development Report* (2014) jointly issued by the Social Development Research Center of the Chinese Academy of Social Sciences, Institute of Urban Development in Gansu Province, and Lanzhou City College, shows that China's primary energy consumption was 3.62 billion tons of coal in 2012, consuming 20 percent of the world's energy sources. The consumption per GDP was 2.5 times the world average, 3.3 times the US, 7 times that of Japan, and higher than Brazil, Mexico, and other developing countries. In China's energy consumption structure, coal accounts for 68.5 percent, oil 17.7 percent, hydro 7.1 percent, natural gas 4.7 percent, nuclear 0.8 percent, and others 1.2 percent. In other words, in 2012, China consumed nearly half of the world's coal, while thermal power consumed nearly half of China's coal.

Coal is the "dirtiest" fossil fuel and many pollutants such as CO_2, SO_2, and others, are coal-fired emissions. For a long time, China's coal-dominated energy structure has been its base, and the long-term share of it accounts for 66 percent in China's energy consumption, the status quo of which is difficult to change in quite a long time. Unbridled consumption of coal is a manifestation of China's extensive development; non-renewable resources formed over hundreds of millions of years would have been depleted in just a few decades in such a rapid manner. One should see that this outrageous development path cannot go on forever.

Zheng Jingping, the former NBSC chief engineer, pointed out: "The price to pay for an extensive development mode is very clear—first, a hard constraint of resources will be formed due to consumption of many resources that are already scarce. For example, China's dependence on foreign oil has reached nearly 60 percent and dependence on foreign iron ore has exceeded 50 percent. Second, the increasingly serious environmental pollution has become a hard constraint of economic growth and social stability. Third, it

---

13.   Ibid.

is contrary to the situation of China as a developing country. Developing countries should not have long-term surpluses and accumulated large amounts of foreign exchange. The reason is that it is hard for China to increase value of its substantial foreign exchange reserves due to drastic fluctuations of exchange rate of major international reserve currency, narrow channels for investment with foreign exchange, and lack of investment experience and other factors, which is contrary to the stages of development for developing countries. Fourth, it is difficult to digest the huge excess capacity."[14]

If this rough model of development is not reversed, it will be very difficult to control the presence of smog in a relatively short time.

Qing Dahe, Vice Chairman of China Association for Science and Technology, and former Director of China Meteorological Administration, said: "There is a great difficulty for China in that 70 percent of China's energy reserves is coal, and it is difficult to overcome the fact that coal is the primary energy. If we say that we need 30 years to control haze, people will be disappointed; if we say that we only need three to five years, it is not realistic. So I think the elimination of haze will depend on changes in energy structure, changes in the industrial structure and the results of the joint efforts of all the people. In this case, I do not have the answer to how many years we need, but I think 30 years might be long, and three to five years might be unrealistic; so I say, we need a certain historical period."

Qin Dahe added: "The priority remains in great efforts in science and technology. China must have its independent green industry and technology so as to improve the output for each unit of energy consumption, and thereby reduce haze and emissions of carbon dioxide. Just think, if our consumption, and consumption per GDP are similar to the United States, our GDP must be tripled—undoubtedly, we would soon be the world's number one. So, what should we rely on to change the situation? The correct answer will be science and technology as well as all the people."[15]

China's Growth Limit: The Water Crisis

"If we do not save water, the last drop will be our tears." The public service announcement repeatedly aired on China's major television stations highlights the crisis of water resources in China.

China is a drought-hit country. China's total fresh water resources are about 2.8 trillion cubic meters, accounting for 6 percent of global water resources, ranked fourth in the world and second only to Brazil, Russia,

---

14.   Zheng Jingping: "To Establish and Improve a Law-Based Socialist Market Economic System, *China Economic Times*, August 29, 2013.

15.   *People's Daily Online*, March 29, 2014.

and Canada. However, China's water resource per capita is only 2,300 cubic meters, only a quarter of the world's average level, and China is one of the world's poorest countries in per capita water. However, China is the world's largest water consumer. In 2002 alone, China's consumption of fresh water reached 549.7 billion cubic meters, accounting for about 13 percent of the world's annual consumption, and 1.2 times of the US fresh water supply of 470 billion cubic meters in 1995.

China's water resources per capita are in severe shortage, and distribution of water resources is extremely uneven. Heilongjiang River and Yarlung Zangbo River located in China's border have the most fruitful freshwater resources places, but both rivers are located in inaccessible frontier regions, little of which can be used. In China's most densely populated areas, the Beijing-Tianjin-Hebei region, the degree of water shortage surpasses Israel.

According to the 2010 Beijing Water Resources Bulletin, Beijing's total water consumption was 3.52 billion cubic meters, while the total water resources throughout the year was only 2.31 billion cubic meters, though 6 percent more than in 2009, but 38 percent lower than the annual average of 3.739 billion cubic meters. In Beijing, from 1956 to 2000, the average of total annual water resources was 3.74 billion cubic meters; but since 1999, Beijing has entered a continuous dry season and 59 percent of surface water resources, 37 percent of groundwater resources and 77 percent of water entry resources have diminished, while over the same period, Beijing's urban population has increased rapidly. Both factors jointly led to the reduction of water resources per capita in Beijing, even to an extent of less than 100 cubic meters per capita, less than one twentieth of the national average level, and thus it has become the region with the lowest water resource per capita.

Such water resources per capita is far below the international standard for extreme water shortages, and it is significantly lower than the bottom line of the catastrophic standards that threaten human survival. This state of water resources is poorer than the Middle East, North Africa, and other regions that are described as arid. Even in Israel and the Middle East, which lack water, the water resource per capita is 387 cubic meters, more than three times higher than Beijing.

A more vivid example than the figures is the cut-off of Beijing's mother river, the Yongding River, and the Chaobai River, which is one of five major river systems in Beijing. According to statistics, since 1980, all of the 21 major rivers across the watershed that Beijing relies on have undergone a cut-off.

"The first thing to do every morning is to fill up water tanks and buckets. I am too afraid to pour away water that has been used to wash and I keep it for flushing toilets," explains Ms. Liu, a resident of the area, who deliberately asked her son to buy some buckets to reserve water when there were water cut-offs in many communities—Majuqiao Town, Tongzhou District, and in Beijing, such as Wenxin Jiayuan—during a period in the second half of 2014.

There was less rain in the year and more residents had moved into the new projects in the region. However, the groundwater table was lowered, and there was a serious shortage of water supply.

This scene in Beijing's suburb, Majuqiao, is the epitome of an increasingly severe water shortage in northern cities of China.

"Severe shortage of water, heavily polluted water environment, and severe damaged water ecology, the three interact with each other and superimpose on each other." This was a comment on Beijing-Tianjin-Hebei Region's water safety after an investigation on ecological and environmental protection in the region by a joint research group composed of seven departments such as the Ministry of Environmental Protection.

The *2013 China Environmental Bulletin* showed that there was a light pollution of surface water, and water pollution in the five major river systems including the Yellow River, Huaihe River, Haihe River, Liaohe River, and Songhua River. Among 4,778 groundwater monitoring points all across China, about two thirds have poor or very poor water quality.

Look at the lakes. The *Bulletin* showed that among important lakes under the national monitoring of China, 39.3 percent had polluted levels of water; among the 31 large freshwater lakes, seventeen were moderately polluted or slightly polluted, including Baiyang Lake, Yangcheng Lake, Poyang Lake, Dongting Lake, and Jingbo Lake; and Dianchi Lake was heavily polluted. Moreover, a large number of natural lakes had disappeared or been reduced in large areas. Boyang Lake, "the largest fresh water lake," and Dongting Lake, which is "steaming over the dreamy and cloudy leak," have been significantly reduced in surface area; in Hubei Province, known for its "lake conditions, which are the provincial circumstances," there has been a sharp decline in lake surfaces and wetlands.

The reality is worrying in that among 657 cities of China, more than 300 of them fall into the categories of "serious [water] shortage" or "[water] shortage," according to United Nations-Habitat Evaluation Criteria.

The trend is grim in that China's water pollution has extended to river trunks, spread from the cities to rural areas, infiltrated from surface water into groundwater, and developed from inland to the sea.

"At present, China's total national annual consumption is nearly 620 billion cubic meters, a lack of more than 500 million cubic meters in normal years. With the intensification of economic and social development and global climate change, the imbalance between water supply and demand will become more acute," warns Chen Ming, Deputy Director of the Division of Resource Management, Ministry of Water Resources Water.

The World Bank issued a report warning: "With the widening of the gap between water demand and limited supply, as well as the deterioration of a large area of water quality caused by pollution, it is possible a severe crisis of water shortages will be caused in China."

In no way is the warning alarmist, because it is becoming a real threat.

Lv Zhongmei, Dean of the School of Economics, Hubei University, has 30 years' experience in the study of environmental law. She sharply pointed out: "A wide range of smog occurs, people often encounter it, so it is called the 'heart and lung diseases' of China; and water safety is becoming the 'scourge' of the Chinese nation."

Vice President and Chief Engineer of China Environmental Planning Wang Jinnan said, "In the Haihe River Basin where the water environment situation is extremely serious, the development of high energy consumption, high pollution industries such as steel, coal, chemicals, building materials, electricity, and paper-making is promoted everywhere that they focus on development only regardless of the environment."

Water pollution aggravation is largely caused by human factors, and it is because people's solutions to nature that already scarce and dirty water becomes scarcer and dirtier.

Take Suzhou, Jiangsu province, as an example. As Suzhou folk said, "There was the washing of rice and vegetable in the 1960s, irrigating and watering in the 1970s, water quality deterioration in the 1980s, fish and shrimp extinction in the 1990s." This is about antecedently industrialized areas of China represented by Suzhou, an "antecedent area" of water pollution. If you take the "water quality deterioration" in China's coastal area represented by Suzhou in the 1980s as a reference, water quality in most parts of the country began to deteriorate in the 1990s.

Li Junfeng, director of the National Climate Change Strategy Research Center and International Cooperation Center, said, "China is a country of energy shortages, and water resource shortages. Water security and energy security are important and closely related, but water security is more important and more complex than energy security, and also needs more attention. From the national level, 60 percent of China's oil depends on imports, which still can be maintained; but if 10 percent of freshwater resource is needed to be imported, for a populous country and manufacturing industry country such as China, it would be unimaginable."

Li Junfeng further pointed out that as for China, whether in a "high-coal" or "low-coal" era, energy and water are inseparable. China's future energy distribution should take water as its important factor. According to the current assumption, we hope that the usage amount of coal can be reduced by one percentage point each year, the proportion of other energy increases by one percentage point per year. Coal mining, coal washing, coal power, cooling, de-dusting, and slagging need plenty of water. Some people may think that reducing the use of coal will save a lot of water. But we should note that some alternative energy also needs to consume a lot of water. Take shale gas for example. China predicts that the annual output of natural gas and shale gas will reach 400 billion cubic meters in 2030, and mining would consume at least 15 billion cubic meters of fresh water every year. Coal power generation and gas power stations consume a lot of water in China. Wind and solar energy projects also need water. So water security will determine the future of China's energy structure.[16]

All the signs indicate that carrying the capacity of the water will determine capacity of China's future development. Whether China's development can be extended to a certain extent depends on the affordability of its water resources.

"Never Sacrifice the Environment for Short-Term Economic Growth"

In the process of industrialization, growing first, cleaning up later and transferring high pollution industry abroad is an approach all the developed countries in the world have gone through. History has proved that this is a curved road, and it has a costly dead end.

China is in a period of rapid industrialization: Can the same errors be avoided, and a new trail be blazed with rapid development and improvements to the environment?

The world is nervously concerned about China under the leadership of Xi Jinping.

"Gold, silver mines, green hills, and clear waters are needed, and green hills and clear waters are gold and silver mines. We must never sacrifice the environment for short-term economic growth." This is Xi Jinping's consistent attitude.

On February 26, 2014, after hearing the Beijing and Tianjin synergistic development work report, Xi Jinping pointed out that the water shortage problem had been very serious in North China: "If we do not attach importance to protect ecological space with water conservation such as

16.　　Li Junfeng: "Why Is Water Crisis in China More Important than Energy Security?" *Strategic Network*, October 22, 2014.

forests, lakes, wetlands, and if we continued to over-exploit the groundwater, the efforts of nature's revenge will be greater."

The outstanding problems such as a seriously damaged ecology, frequent ecological disasters, and huge ecological burdens, have become the biggest drawbacks of building a moderately prosperous society. What does China need to do to solve these problems? Xi Jinping has a deep understanding. Xi Jinping conducts a deep analysis in his "Two Mountain Theory."

"Three stages are passed to know the relationship between green hills and clear waters, and both gold and silver mines in practice. The first stage is to use green hills and clear waters to change gold and silver mines, to not consider or rarely consider the carrying capacity of the environment, and obtain resources blindly. In the second stage, both gold and silver mines, and green hills and clear waters, are needed, contradictions between economic development, a lack of resources and environmental deterioration begin to be highlighted at this time, and people realize that environment is fundamental to our survival and development, only by keeping green hills can we have firewood. The third phase is to learn that green hills and clear waters can bring gold and silver mines constantly; green hills and clear waters are gold and silver mines. Evergreen trees we plant are money-making machines, and ecological advantage becomes economic advantage and develops seamless, harmonious and unified relationship; this stage is a higher realm."

This deep understanding of Xi Jinping about the relationship between green hills and clear waters, and gold and silver mines dates back to the long-term practices of forestry and ecological construction.

The ecological changes in Changting, Fujian province, is a microcosm for China and a lesson to all. Changting County is an important habitation of the Hakka people. Historically, its scenery was beautiful, with lush forests, fertile crops, and the people lived and worked in peace. But in modern times, the forest has been severely damaged, and Changting became one of the most seriously soil eroded areas in China at that time. In 1985, the soil erosion area in Changting was 1.462 million *mu*, occupying 31.5 percent of the county area, and many places were uninhabitable, with "dirty water, infertile fields, and poor people."

If green hills and clear waters are gone, who can talk about gold and silver mines? During his work in Fujian province, Xi Jinping went to Changting five times, visited villages, visited farmers, got to understand the actual situation, sought measures, and supported the management in Changting. After ten years of continuous efforts, 1.628 million mu of soil erosion were managed in Changting, 0.988 million *mu* of soil erosion were reduced, forest coverage rate was increased from 59.8 percent in 1986 to 79.4 percent now, and "barren mountain, oasis and ecological home" historic change was realized.

The 18th National Congress held in November, 2012, for the first time took "beautiful China" as a major theme with a grand goal of ecological civilization construction, and made ecological civilization construction as a strategic target.

The report, with Xi Jinping as head of the drafting group, reflects China's new, deeper understanding of the characteristics of Chinese construction and development.

Ecological environment protection has become a global consensus, but the CPC is the first to take on ecological construction as an action platform of a political party, especially a ruling party.

Since the CPC's 18th National Congress, Xi Jinping, regardless of holding important meetings, home and abroad, attending international conferences and activities, often emphasizes ecological civilization construction and ecological safety maintenance. In fact, his related key speeches, discussions and instructions on the subject number more than 60.

On February 25, 2014, haze shrouded Beijing, and residents had to wear masks. That evening, on the TV news program, people were surprised to see that Xi Jinping, accompanied by Secretary of Beijing Municipal Committee Guo Jinlong and Mayor Wang Anshun, visit the alley in South Luogu Lane, Beijing, and meet the "old folks." People noted that Xi Jinping did not wear a mask, and his accompanying staff did not wear masks. After this investigating Beijing operation, Xi Jinping proposed a synergetic development strategy in Beijing, Tianjin, and Hebei Province, and one of the core tasks was through adjusting development to improve air quality. After his tour of the area, Xi Jinping told the person in charge of Beijing: "The primary task of dealing with haze pollution and improving air quality is to control $PM_{2.5}$ smog. Although it is early for the whole China to control $PM_{2.5}$ and beyond our development according to the international standard, we should see this issue has aroused the concern of the cadres, the masses and international society, so we must solve it. The people are calling, I shall respond!"

On February 26, 2014, when listening to the Beijing, Tianjin, and Hebei province synergistic development report, Xi Jinping again stressed the importance of collaborative governance. He called for more effort to be put into expanding environment capacity and ecological space, strengthening ecological environment protection cooperation, on the basis of starting atmospheric pollution prevention and controlling synergistic mechanism, improving cooperation mechanisms in forest protection, water resource protection, and clean energy use.

Xi Jinping repeatedly stresses that China's reform is driven by its problems. So, reform is to start from problem-oriented policies. International public opinion notes that Xi Jinping has set aside a red line for ecological construction in China. On May 24, 2013, Xi Jinping at the CPC Central Committee Political Bureau's sixth collective learning session, pointed out that the concept of an ecological red line should be firmly established. On the ecological environment protection issue, no one should overstep the line, otherwise they should be punished.

Environmental problems that occurred over hundreds of years in developed countries in the past, had been focused to emerge in the past 30 years of China's rapid development, and if this economic development mode is not changed, resources and the environment will be difficult to support the sustainable development of China. Xi Jinping stressed: "We owe too much to the environment, if this work is not precisely managed from now on, we will pay more in the future."

Ecological construction is not intended to give up industrial progress and return to original production and living modes, but on the basis of the environment and resource-carrying capacity, to take natural law as the criterion, to take sustainable development, human and natural harmony as the goal, and to construct a civilized society of production and development, affluent life, and a healthy environment. Such harmony can hardly be found in the wisdom of western civilizations, so we must seek enlightenment from the wisdom of the Oriental civilizations.

Distinguished British historian Arnold J. Toynbee firmly believes that the Western world after the disintegration of the Roman Empire developed industrialization and nationalism in politics. Thus, the consequence of the West conquering the world is that all non-Western countries imitated Western industrialization and technological modes, and so there was more and more demand for political unity in a global sense, because through industry and technology, the fate of mankind was inevitably closely linked. The key to the next step is China. The understanding of Taoism in China on esoteric issues between the universe and humans, and not believing that human society dominates the universe, is a philosophical foundation for moderate and rational concepts of progress, provided by China's Taoists for the human civilization.

Rachel Carson in her landmark 1962 environmental science book *Silent Spring* lashed out at American farmers for extensively using the pesticide DDT and causing an ecological disaster. The harvest of staple crops, and environmental conservation are both necessary, but western scientists have no convincing solution without resorting to unnatural methods.

However, this quandary is easily solved by Chinese peasants well versed in Taoist thought. In Zhejiang, Hunan, Guizhou province, local farmers have widely adopted the "fish in a paddy field" method. By putting fish in their paddy fields, fish-derived products can be obtained, fish eat the pests and weeds in the paddy field, and the fish excrete manure to fertilize the growth of rice, which can increase the rice output by 10 percent, gaining hundreds of pounds of fish. When today's scientists conduct research into low-toxicity pesticides, the Chinese people realize that their ancestors were simply using the "fish in a paddy field" method to sustain generation after generation.

When ecology thrives, then civilization thrives; when ecology declines, then civilization declines. Xi Jinping's foundation of Chinese philosophy and literature includes deep thoughts on the continued development of civilization.

Looking at human civilization, and looking at contemporary China, the Chinese civilization has lasted 5,000 years. Can it be extended another 5,000 years, and realize truly sustainable development?

"The contradictions inherent in the environmental concerns of our country have a historical context. [The environment] did not decline in a day, but it could become worse and worse in our hands. The CPC shall have the mind and the will [to confront the issues]." Xi Jinping's words resonate with truth.

CHAPTER
6
The Belt and Road Initiatives

As a leader trying to push China to the political center of the world, Xi Jinping has presented his grand strategy—"The Belt and Road Initiatives"—before the world. This is not just a financial competition, but a strategy that encompasses economic development and geopolitics. The global economy and even global politics could be rewritten.

I. THE ASIAN INVESTMENT BANK

The "excellence" of a leader is shown not only in the capabilities of his leadership, but also whether through his strategic vision he can see how the world will change in the next two to three years, and push the development of global patterns over the next two or three decades and even longer.

Xi Jinping used to administrate Zhejiang Province and Shanghai City, the most affluent areas of China, and later entered Zhongnanhai in Beijing. All the while, he has been closely following domestic and international development trends, and saw the huge demand in Asian countries and the huge potential of China when the world economy was weak.

Over the past 30 years, the basic experience of development in China was to drive investment and strengthen infrastructure construction, as the

Chinese saying goes, "to be rich, build roads first;" and there is another Chinese saying: "As long as the train sounds, tons of gold are gained." The large-scale construction of highways, high-speed railways, ports, and airports has stimulated the development of building material, cement, steel, and other industries in China, providing employment opportunities for the surplus labor force in rural areas, and laying the foundations for economic growth.

Many Asian countries are not as courageous as China—a lack of strong central government is one reason, but lack of money is the main reason.

According to the calculations of the Asian Development Bank, the investment demand of infrastructure in Asia will reach USD 730 billion each year before 2020, any form of cooperation among the World Bank, the IMF, or the Asian Development Bank cannot meet the need for such large capital requirements. It is very difficult for the private enterprises to spend large sums of money on infrastructure construction due to the large capital demand of infrastructure investment, the long-term implementation cycle, uncertain income and other factors.

The harsh conditions given by the World Bank, the IMF, and the Asian Development Bank, have discouraged many countries. Especially some Asian countries, many of which have painful memories. During the Asian financial crisis in 1997, Malaysia had to ask the IMF for help. But the IMF offered a range of tough conditions for Malaysia to get loans, including opening financial markets, relaxing foreign exchange control, reducing deflation and inflation and cutting spending to the maximum extent, and even political reform. These "dramatic measures" clearly infringed upon Malaysia's national sovereignty. Therefore, hearing of these conditions, Malaysian Prime Minister Mahathir bin Mohamad swore: "it is better to let Michel Camdessus [then IMF president] work as the president in Malaysia."

By contrast, China had a foreign exchange reserve of USD 4 trillion, and China has always had a generous foreign aid policy, without additional harsh conditions involving human rights, although western countries have accused it of actually encouraging violation of human rights and damage to the environment. Most of the aid-receiving countries were pleased because they had finally found a quality creditor who did not want to manipulate them. Now the Asian Investment Bank has emerged as an alternative, but will it be good for Asian countries?

Xi Jinping's Big Initiative

Xi Jinping certainly does not give money for free. His plan to set up the Asian Investment Bank is based on deep considerations toward maximizing the national benefits of China.

First of all, there should be return on investment. So far, for the Asian Investment Bank, the revenue is low, but there is still some. More important is that China has a foreign exchange reserve of USD 4 trillion, but about one-third has been invested in US treasuries, which is undoubtedly risky.

For example, one of the favorite motifs of American political cartoonists is the depiction of a heavyset Chinese creditor (sometimes it is the representative of China, a giant panda) knocking on a door arrogantly, and a sore-headed creditor, Uncle Sam, standing behind the door respectfully. The implication is that though the United States is domineering in the world, it must kowtow to China because China is America's largest creditor!

American political cartoonists are, naturally, ridiculing Washington, but in fact, many countries borrowing money are in dominance! Especially in the United States because the yield rate of US treasuries is relatively low, about 2 to 3 percent per year. In the past few years, the appreciation of the renminbi (RMB) has greatly exceeded this ratio, which means that China's foreign exchange assets are actually depreciating. Moreover, China cannot sell such a large amount of debt, otherwise it will lead to the collapse of the US bond market, and China will incur more harm than good.

In fact, this is truly a "dollar trap." As more and more foreign currency reserves are invested by China, the traps are becoming deeper and deeper. Moreover, it must be noted that although the sovereign credit rating of the United States has remained at a AAA level (but degraded by Standard & Poor's because of the recent congressional struggle), it is the currency of America after all, and if Washington really wants to enact any shameless policies, China can only go down the drain. However, part of the foreign reserves for investment will help reduce the risk.

The economic benefits cannot be ignored. The Asian Investment Bank is an important booster to push the planning of the Belt and Road Initiatives in China, and also helps external transfer of capacity in China, thus contributing to the integration of the multinational economy and the Chinese economy; economic development in other countries will also contribute to the economic development and export of products in China. Of course, this new international financial institution headquartered in Beijing will be a positive impetus toward the internationalization of the RMB.

The geopolitical gains cannot be avoided. There are certainly some countries that will refuse to pay off debts, but most countries will undoubtedly strengthen cooperation with China in order to obtain investment and projects, and China will gain more friendship instead of hostility. It can be seen that Vietnam and the Philippines have actively joined the Asian

Investment Bank, although they have territorial disputes with China.

Finally, it will enhance China's right to speak up and influence the international financial sector. We have to point out that the inefficient reform of the international financial system has provoked outrage in China, and urged China to make a fresh start.

As products of the Bretton Woods System, the World Bank and the IMF have set up their headquarters in downtown Washington DC, only a few hundred meters away from the White House. The United States has held the sole right of veto for over 70 years, and the president of the World Bank must be American, the IMF president can only come from Europe, and the first vice presidential position is still held by an American.

In 2008, financial crisis swept through Wall Street. The western world realized that the world situation had undergone major changes, but the seven major western countries of the G7 group could not solve all the problems. So the Group of Twenty (G20) replaced the G7 as an important platform for world economic consultation, and reforming the irrational international financial order was thus placed on the agenda.

At the end of 2010, the G20 agreed to continue to reform the IMF, by asking developed countries to transfer more than 6 percent of their shares to emerging markets in order to enhance the voting power of countries with emerging markets, at the same time European countries should transfer two executive director seats to developing countries so as to promote the influence of developing countries represented by China in the global financial system.

Once the IMF reform is implemented, China's share in the IMF will rise from 3.8 to 6.39 percent, and become the third-largest shareholding country behind the United States (16.75 percent) and Japan (6.98 percent), and voting rights will also rise from the current 3.65 to 6.07 percent.

Former US Treasury Secretary Lawrence Summers said the reform program could supplement IMF resources and boost confidence in the global economy; and more importantly, it can give China, India, and other countries vote shares more commensurate with their new economic weight.[1]

Although this reform does not match the actual position of China as the world's second largest economy, and China still has valid complaints, the final result made the entire international community shocked and helpless: the Republican-controlled congress refused the reform program approved by the Obama administration, and the IMF reform was blocked on Capitol Hill.

The World Bank and the IMF have been in the control of the western

---

1.   *Financial Times Chinese*, April 8, 2015.

countries, Japan and the United States have the final say to the ADB headquartered in Manila, and the reforms meant to weaken the influence of western countries has also suffered a great deal of resistance. Thus, as the world's second largest economy, China has often been overlooked in international financial decision-making. China will inevitably still be controlled by others without financial decision-making power.

It is very dangerous to break and transform the old world, but ultimately China will create a new world.

By the same token, the BRICS Bank and Fund, Silk Road Fund, and the SCO Bank, which are intended to be formed, are all reiterations of the Asian Investment Bank, and China is playing a pivotal role in the whole process. Xi Jinping began the initiative for the active layout of a new international financial system by changing the previous diplomatic strategy of keeping a low profile, and achieving mastery by striking only after the enemy has struck.

Persuading Southeast Asian Nations
to Join the Asian Investment Bank

According to the *Memorandum to Build the Asian Investment Bank*, the authorized capital of the Asian Investment Bank was USD 100 billion, the target of China's initial subscribed capital was about USD 50 billion, China invested 50 percent and became the biggest shareholder. Each founding member with intention will agree to take the economic rights measured by gross domestic product (GDP) as a basis of share distribution in each country. In 2015, a trial operation of paid-up capital was taken as 10 percent of the initial subscribed goal, which is USD 5 billion, including China's investment of USD 2.5 billion.

Although the capital scale of USD 100 billion for the Asian Investment Bank is less than USD 220 billion and USD 175 billion respectively for the World Bank and the Asian Development Bank, this fund can be enlarged 50 times through financial leverage. This means leveraging loans of USD 500 billion to USD 1 trillion which will greatly contribute to development and construction in Asia.

Xi Jinping saw the demand in Asia and China's strength, he chose to open up a new battlefield rather than confront opponents face to face, and he can claim many allies. He took initiative in Indonesia, not only because Indonesia is the largest economy in the Association of Southeast Asian Nations (ASEAN), but Indonesia has been the largest and first engineering contracting market of China in the world and Southeast Asia for three consecutive years. The Indonesian market has a lot of expectations on

Chinese capital and infrastructure construction.

The Chinese media stated that Susilo Bambang Yudhoyono, the former president of Indonesia, had a "positive response" to this concept, but there were signs that Indonesia was very hesitant about the new financial institution dominated by China at first and were not sure whether they should join the organization.

Xi Jinping has prepared plans to engage any possibility. On October 4, 2013, one day after he met Yudhoyono, Xi Jinping appeared in the prime minister's office located in Malaysia's capital Kuala Lumpur, and he described the same initiative to Malaysian Prime Minister Najib Tun Razak. Malaysia was clearly much more enthusiastic than Indonesia and Najib said Malaysia would give "full support" to China's initiative and take it into account.

Two days later, as Xi Jinping attended the Asia-Pacific Economic Cooperation (APEC) summit in Bali, he held a conversation with Yingluck Shinawatra, the former prime minister of Thailand. Among ASEAN countries, Thailand is different from the communist states such as Vietnam and Laos, has no territorial disputes with China like the Philippines, and maintains a close relationship with China. So Yingluck immediately agreed to the initiative.

In the fall of 2013, China started a prudent and sharp diplomatic offensive. When Xi Jinping went back home after putting forth the initiative of the Asian Investment Bank, the Chinese Prime Minister Li Keqiang began a visit to ASEAN. On October 9, he held talks with leaders from ten ASEAN countries. In the *Joint Statement to Commemorate the 10th Anniversary of the Establishment of China—ASEAN Strategic Partnership*, published after the meeting, ten ASEAN countries agreed that they "appreciated China's initiative to establish the Asian Investment Bank to give priority to ASEAN interconnection projects."

China is not only targeting Southeast Asian countries. On July 4, 2014, in talks with South Korean President Park Geun-hye in Seoul, Xi Jinping told his "sister," who has a close relationship with him, that China would like to strengthen cooperation with South Korea in the building of the Asian Investment Bank. Although Park Geun-hye and Xi Jinping have reached consensus on many issues, as for the Asian Investment Bank, Park Geun-hye only showed that she appreciated China's initiative, and said she "would like to maintain communication with China," but did not mention whether South Korea would join.

Canada and Australia held similar attitudes on this issue. On October 20, 2014, Australian Treasurer Joe Hawkey said Australia was "actively discussing" whether to join the Asian Investment Bank; Canadian Finance

Minister Joe Oliver said Canada could understand and support China's initiative.

The hesitation of Korea, Australia, Canada, and other countries was due to pressure from the US. America was well aware that the establishment of the Asian Investment Bank would be bound to impact on their monopoly in the international financial system, as soon as the initiative was brought up, the United States publicly expressed a dissenting opinion and claimed that it might reduce environmental standards if the Asian Investment Bank grants such a loan.

But the resistance from the United States did not affect the countries which have closely cooperated with China to show their favor in the establishment of the Asian Investment Bank. As of October 24, 2014, a total of 21 countries had signed the *Memorandum to Build the Asian Investment Bank* in Beijing, including ten ASEAN countries, Mongolia, Uzbekistan, Kazakhstan, Sri Lanka, Pakistan, Nepal, Bangladesh, Oman, Kuwait and Qatar.

It is noteworthy that India is the only large economy to have signed this treaty in the Great Hall. In a visit to India, Xi Jinping specially invited Indian Prime Minister Narendra Modi to attend the event in Beijing, but Modi did not appear in Beijing in the end.

Hit Back by the United Kingdom

What took the United States by surprise was the critical blow from the UK. In a National Security Council meeting, some British diplomats warned that to join the Asian Investment Bank might "alienate" the United States, but the British Chancellor of the Exchequer, George Osborne, believed that this concern was unnecessary, and that the business interests brought by joining the Asian Investment Bank would outweigh any possible "diplomatic uproar."[2]

In the end, British Prime Minister David Cameron had the final say and Britain became the first western developed country to apply to join the Asian Investment Bank. It was undoubtedly a crucial moment: the old capitalist financial power of Britain would be partnered to greatly enhance the credibility and financing capability of the Asian Investment Bank, and many countries which were afraid of US pressure would no longer be hesitant.

On March 12, 2015, George Osborne said in a statement: "I'm very pleased that Britain is the first developed country to become a founding member of the Asian Investment Bank. To strengthen cooperation between the United Kingdom and Asia is the pillar of our long-term economic

2.   *Xinhua Feature Articles*, March 31, 2015.

program in the United Kingdom and will help British companies to get business and investment opportunities in the most significant growing market of the world."

China was very happy with Britain's decision. In Beijing, the Chinese Ministry of Finance immediately issued a statement that China welcomed the decision of the United Kingdom, and would seek comment from the current founding members with the intention of joining.[3]

In faraway Washington DC, the White House knew what the possible consequence of this move would be. The United States publicly expressed strong anger with the defection of this close ally. A senior official of the Obama administration said Britain made the decision "almost without consultation with the United States," and the "Group of Seven" even discussed how to deal with the newly established Asian Investment Bank. Another US official accused Britain of "constant accommodating," and stated that "this is not the best way to deal with a rising power."

It has long been thought that the US and the UK are special allies—the US seldom publicly expresses dissatisfaction with the UK with stern words, thus the reaction clearly highlights the impact this move by the UK has had on the US.

The British naturally had their own interpretation. According to the statement of the British Treasury, the British chancellor of the exchequer had previously expressed to the US Treasury Secretary Jacob Lu, that they intended to become a founding member of the Asian Investment Bank. Osborne knew that his decision would not be welcomed in Washington but he believed this move was in line with British interests.

It is clear that the Asian Investment Bank led by Xi Jinping was an irresistible temptation to Britain.

Britain saw the huge infrastructure market in Asia, and it was also clear that the Asian Investment Bank would play an increasingly important role in the world's financial structure in the future. Boycotted by the United States, the influence of the World Bank and the IMF has shrunk, but the UK does not want to lose influence. It wants to become a founding member and participate in the rule-making so that the Asian Investment Bank will be more in line with their own interests.

The US and the UK have natural links as Anglo-Saxon countries, but the world situation is changing in the post-crisis era. China has already become the second-largest economy and according to data from the IMF, China has surpassed the United States to be the world's largest economy if calculated in accordance with the purchasing power parity.

---

3.   *Financial Times*, March 12, 2015.

With the enhancement of China's economic strength, the RMB will inevitably become one of the main international reserve currencies. The British must cooperate with China if they want to make money and retain London's existing international financial status. Britain cannot put all their eggs in one basket. Regarding criticism from the United States, British Prime Minister David Cameron's spokesman said the decision to join the Asian Investment Bank belongs to Britain's national interest: "We sometimes have different ideas than the United States."

The Benefits of the Asian Investment Bank

Great benefits have made the Asian Investment Bank attract developing countries in Asia and developed countries in Europe like a magnet. For China, the Asian Investment Bank is called a clever act of diplomacy because it has succeeded in making more friends and effectively differentiating the opponents. Xi Jinping has included clever designs in some rules of the Asian Investment Bank, which impelled Britain to urgently announce it wanted to join the Asian Investment Bank.

The equity allocation of the Asian Investment Bank will be based on GDP, and the equity of the Asian members accounts for 70 to 75 percent. China certainly accounts for the vast majority; countries outside Asia will allocate the remaining 25 to 30 percent equity with three board seats. After repeated analysis of the role and status of the Asian Investment Bank, the western nations are clear even if they do not join, the Asian Investment Bank will be implemented smoothly. It is better to join and get rights in decision-making rather than lose the right to speak in an international financial institution. Hearing that France, Germany, and Italy would soon announce they wanted to join the Asian Investment Bank, Britain taking finance as an economic pillar had a greater sense of urgency, and took the lead by extending an olive branch to the Asian Investment Bank.

Of course, China certainly has made a commitment to Britain in secret negotiations, and perhaps even conducted some constraints to their original dominant right so that western countries would recognize they will certainly not lose out in cooperation with China.

After Britain, the snowball effect began to show. On March 14, 2014, France, Germany, and Italy announced they would also like to become founding members of the Asian Investment Bank. By March 31, 2014, the deadline to apply to become a founding member, only the United States and Japan of the G7 nations did not join the financial organization, the United States suffered from their own public pressure.

South Korea and Australia have been very hesitant, taking into account the position of the United States. Before March 31, 2015, they and other countries set off a boom to join the Asian Investment Bank.

As of March 31, 2015, a total of 57 nations and regions had submitted applications to join the Asian Investment Bank. There are four seats from the five great permanent members of the Security Council: China, Britain, France, and Russia.

There are also thirteen seats for the G20 countries: China, India, Indonesia, Saudi Arabia, France, Germany, Italy, Britain, Australia, Turkey, South Korea, Brazil, and Russia.

Overall, there are 35 countries from Asia, 18 countries from Europe, two states from Oceania, one country from South America, and one country from Africa, with a total of 57 countries.

The Ma Ying-jeou authority from the Taiwan region also applied to become a founding member. This move was strongly criticized by Taiwan's opposition faction and was thought to lose honor to the Chinese mainland. As Beijing always considered Taiwan a province to be unified, Taiwan's application was eventually turned down by the Chinese mainland, and that attitude was not surprising. But Beijing subsequently expressed goodwill: welcoming Taiwan to join the Asian Investment Bank with a proper identity. Indonesian President Susilo Bambang Yudhoyono immediately became an active supporter of the Asian Investment Bank. When he visited Beijing in November 2014, he tried to persuade Xi Jinping to set up the headquarters of the Asian Investment Bank in Indonesia. Southeast Asia is an important target market of the Asian Investment Bank after all, and Indonesia accounts for 40 percent of the economy in Southeast Asia.

However, when he heard the decision had been made to set up the headquarters in Beijing, Yudhoyono immediately corrected himself and expected to become the first deputy chairman as Indonesia was the founding member after China, and the first chairman of the Asian Investment Bank must be a Chinese official. According to an informed source, the first deputy president was intended to be given to Japan, as Japan is the second largest economy in Asia, and also has a large number of financial management personnel. But Japan did not want to join the Asian Investment Bank, and naturally missed this post.

The United States is the most angry and disappointed of dissenters. They provoked a financial struggle with China, but it ended in defeat. It is also considered to be the biggest failure since the United States returned to Asia. Its threat and pressure failed to secure their own camp, one after another, its allies became shareholders of the Asian Investment Bank instead.

On the one hand, this reveals changes in the global situation. While the

United States is still the only superpower in the world, its leadership has shrunk in today's multipolar world, "a hundred responses to a single call," is gone forever; on the other hand, the success of China's Asian Investment Bank strategy will only bring anxiety to the world-leading America, but America can do nothing at all to stop it.

This is a contest between a rising power and a conservative power, but the poor practices of the United States has changed it into a competition between a constructive power and a declining power.

Former US Treasury Secretary Lawrence Summers said that March 2015 would be written in the annals of history as an historic moment, marking the moment the United States lost the role of guarantor of the global economic system.[4] "Indeed, the United States has experienced many frustrating periods, sometimes it was not really the behavior of multilateralism, such as the Nixon decision to end convertibility of gold with USD in 1971. But with the exception of the Bretton Woods system, no event can be compared with the combination of the following two things: China seeking to build an important new institution; and the United States failing to persuade dozens of traditional allies not to join this institution, starting with the United Kingdom."

The competition of the Asian Investment Bank has also attracted great concern from the international community. However, it has become a hotspot not only because of the importance of the institution itself, but the reflection of the transformation of the international order, as well as the major and subtle changes of the power dynamic.

II. CHINA'S BACKYARD

The Asian Investment Bank displayed only a small part of Xi Jinping's talent in its diplomatic offensive. As a political leader trying to push China to the political center stage of the world, he has a more ambitious strategy: The Belt and Road Initiatives. Many Westerners call it the Chinese version of the Marshall Plan.

The Belt and Road Initiatives is an abbreviation of the "Silk Road Economic Belt" and the "Twenty-First Century Maritime Silk Road," which is a bit difficult to pronounce in Chinese. But the twenty-first century is added in the front of "Maritime Silk Road" without "economic belt" behind. Just like Deng Xiaoping described China's reform and opening up as "wading across the stream by feeling the way," Xi Jinping's Belt and Road Initiatives are also a feeling-out process.

4. *Financial Times*, March 12, 2015.

"Opening to the West"

The Silk Road Economic Belt appeared first. In the morning of September 7, 2013, Xi Jinping visited China's western neighbor Kazakhstan, where he made a speech at Nazarbayev University, named after the President of Kazakhstan, proposing the initiative to build the Silk Road Economic Belt.

He told the students of Kazakhstan that Zhang Qian of China's Han Dynasty visited Central Asia twice with the mission of peace and friendship 2100 years ago, and opened the door to a friendly exchange between China and Central Asian countries, as well as the Silk Road connecting the East and the West, Asia and Europe.

Zhang Qian is a legend in Chinese history. In 164 BC, the ingenious Emperor Wu of the Han Dynasty sent him to the Western regions to contact the Da Rou Zi ethnic group who held a grudge against the Huns to fight againt the powerful Hun Empire in northern China. This journey was quite dangerous; Zhang Qian was detained by the Huns, and arrived in the Western Regions many years later. Although the Da Rou Zi refused an alliance, Zhang Qian was considered to be the first person who blazed the trail that would become the Silk Road.

This path goes through the Guanzhong Plain, Hexi Corridor, and Tarim Basin in China, Transoxiana between Syr Darya River and the Oxus River in Central Asia, then to Iran, and westward to Europe. It was first used to transport ancient Chinese-produced silk, porcelain, and other goods, and later became one of the main routes for trade and communication between East and West. But its name appeared much later, as it was named the Silk Road by German geographer Ferdinand Freiherr von Richthofen in the 1870s.

The Silk Road is a major contribution of Chinese civilization to the world. According to the study of some linguists, the source of the name "China" was likely to be the pronunciation of "silk" in Chinese. China has been translated as porcelain in western languages because most ancient porcelains came from China.

Xi Jinping said in his speech that his hometown Shaanxi was just the starting point of the ancient Silk Road. The places the ancient Silk Road went through from Shaanxi to the West, including Kazakhstan, made important contributions to linking the civilizations in the East and West, and promoting the interaction and cooperation between different nationalities and cultures.

"Standing here to look back through history, I seem to hear the sound of camel bells reverberating around the mountains, and see the solitary smoke floating in the desert every night. All of this makes me feel very warm," Xi Jinping said at Nazarbayev University.

If we say Deng Xiaoping opened the door of the East to the world and realized China's economic takeoff, Xi Jinping started opening up to the West and realized the great ambition to connect China with Central Asia, even Asia with Europe. This is the Silk Road Economic Belt.

During the leadership of Xi Jinping, a number of regional cooperation organizations have been established between Europe and Asia, including the Russia-led Eurasian Economic Community and the Shanghai Cooperation Organization helmed by Russia and China.

But the latter was first set up to solve the problem of border demarcation between China and the former Soviet Union, although it was later turned to economic cooperation, it was still more like a political organization. From the perspective of the development of China and Central Asia, the flourishing of trade cooperation should be promoted by a new form of economic organization.

Xi Jinping thinks it is time for the "Silk Road Economy" to play a big role. From the perspective of trade, the Silk Road Economic Belt involves a total population of 3 billion people with huge market potential; from the perspective of traffic, there is China in the east, and Western Europe in the west, if the transportation channels from the Pacific Ocean to the Baltic Sea can be connected, the whole market in Central Asia, West Asia, and Eastern Europe will be revitalized.

Moreover, this move is also conducive to the internationalization of the RMB. In the speech made at Nazarbayev University, Xi Jinping said China, Russia, and other countries had carried out good cooperation in local currency settlement, achieved gratifying results, and also accumulated a wealth of experience, thus it is necessary to promote this good practice. It can greatly reduce distribution costs, enhance the ability to resist financial risk, and improve the international competitiveness of the regional economies if each country can realize local currency exchange and settlement in the current account and capital accounts.

In other words, the construction of the economic belt will also boost the Chinese RMB toward becoming a world reserve currency.

Some Russian experts believed that the proposal of the Silk Road Economic Belt was directly related to the inefficient and slow work of the Shanghai Cooperation Organization (SCO). As the organization has two core members, Russia and China, China's intentions could not be effectively implemented, and therefore, this economic belt is a new version of the SCO, the "pure Chinese version."[5]

5.　　Sergey Luzyanin. "China: The Rise of the 'Silk Policy'," Voice of Russia Radio (website), March 19, 2014.

The deputy director of the Russian Far East Institute, Sergey Luzyanin, believes that, in regards to the action of Xi Jinping to primarily target the containment strategy against China built up by the United States once the "Silk Road Strategy" was successfully implemented, "it would become an effective weapon to contain the United States and drive it to the distant Atlantic Ocean."

Greater "Development Space"

As a country with a vast territory, northwest China and Tibet can apparently link with the Silk Road Economic Belt and therefore have access to the development of new power; Xi Jinping has planned a new twenty-first century Maritime Silk Road in the southeast and southwest regions of China. Over 2,000 years ago, ships loaded with Chinese silk, porcelain, and other cargo departed from Chinese ports and finally reached the ports of India, Arabia, and Africa through the Strait of Malacca. In 2007, when China salvaged a complete ancient merchant ship wrecked over 1,000 years ago bearing thousands of pieces of precious porcelain, the entire heritage value of the merchant ship was estimated at USD 100 billion.

Xi Jinping worked in Fujian province on the southeastern coast of China for a long time, Quanzhou is attached to Fujian and is considered the starting point of the Marine Silk Road. Many Christians, Muslims, and Manichaeans came to live here at that time, and seven mosques were built here. The *Travels of Marco Polo* describes one of the largest ports in the world, found in Fujian Province, "it's really hard to imagine the amounts of businessmen gathered here and goods were piled up mountain-high." Xi Jinping intended to reproduce the brilliance of the Marine Silk Road, and get closer with Southeast Asia. On October 3, 2013, Xi Jinping delivered a speech to the Indonesian parliament, mentioning that the Southeast Asian region has been an important hub of the Marine Silk Road since ancient times and China would like to strengthen maritime cooperation with ASEAN countries for the common building of the Twenty-First Century Maritime Silk Road.

It is noteworthy that Xi Jinping said China proposed to build the Asian Investment Bank and would like to carry out the construction of infrastructure connecting with developing countries in the region, including ASEAN countries, before this concept was first put forth.

It can be said that the Asian Investment Bank is just a tool of The Belt and Road Initiatives, a tool that will help China advance the project of The Belt and Road Initiatives.

If the common prosperity is an important selling point of The Belt and Road Initiatives, we should say Xi Jinping has clearly focused on the geopolitical landscape, rather than the economy alone. His well-prepared idea is an extremely ambitious strategy which will not only help to quell suspicions of China's rise but is also likely to change global patterns in the future. From an economic point of view, after the breakout of the world financial crisis in 2008, global economic performance has been mediocre. President of the International Monetary Fund (IMF) Christine Lagarde, coined a phrase to describe it: "a new mediocre." The main characteristics of this era can be generally described as "fragile, uneven, and constrained by risks."

The biggest problem of the global economy is the lack of demand; the biggest resistance is surplus of funds. The Belt and Road Initiatives will bring huge demand to Asian infrastructure construction, involving railways, highways, bridges, energy, and hundreds of other projects. The world will be expected to share their experiences and lessons of development with China so as to achieve economic prosperity.

Most importantly, this program will be introduced to more of China's partners and friends. A big country needs support from plenty of countries. However, many countries had conflicts with China during the 60 years when it was governed by the Communist Party in addition to Pakistan, which was called "close friend" by the Chinese. China has had fierce border conflicts with Russia, Vietnam, and India, as well as heated arguments with North Korea, which has depended on China over the years. It is a clear signal that after Xi Jinping became China's top leader, he did not adhere to the convention of visiting North Korea first; he did not visit for a long time.

The Belt and Road Initiatives will be expected to put a lot of Asian countries into China's development track where they can benefit from the economic boom in China; at the same time, they will also open their markets to China and allow the introduction of Chinese standards to their countries.

Take Xi Jinping's favorite term, "interoperability," as an example. "Interoperability" does not only refer to project construction, but includes three aspects: "hardware" construction based on infrastructure and transportation; "software" construction based on the convergence and cohesion of institutions and rules; and the cross-border contact and exchange of personnel between countries, which is a trinity of shared infrastructure, institution and regulation, and the exchange of personnel and expertise.[6]

When Xi Jinping proposed the idea of the Silk Road Economic Belt in the capital of Kazakhstan, Astana, he said bluntly that the global economic

---

6.   Xi Jinping delivered a lecture on the "Common Construction of the Silk Road Economic Belt" at Nazarbayev University on September 7, 2013.

integration was being accelerated, and regional cooperation is in the ascendant. In other words, Xi Jinping has clearly recognized that the future of the world is not competition within a country, but competition within a region. The Silk Road Economic Belt will be able to connect Eurasian economies closely, and provide all countries with greater opportunities to develop.

This is what Xi Jinping has contributed to the world: He is rewriting the international economic order. The world was western-centric in the past and China followed the steps of the West. The Belt and Road Initiatives have encouraged China to open to the West, and will drive the opening in western China, as well as Central Asia, Mongolia, and other inland countries and regions, change the poor and turbulent "economic depression" in these regions, and essentially contribute to getting rid of terrorism and war, which are a bane to these regions.

China is trying to do what Britain could not do, the former Soviet Union did not do, and the United States did not want to do.

Economic integration and financial facilities will inevitably bring about political friendship. These countries will become close allies of China, even those which have poor relations with China will not throw down the challenge. In other words, in the twenty-first century, China will finally restore all the glories it used to have, become the center of Asia with a vast "backyard," and these countries will also benefit from the close relationship with China.

Breaking the Containment of the United States

In ancient East Asia, China formed a "tributary system," with its neighboring countries as a middle kingdom. The ruler of China (the master of both China and the fringe areas) was called the emperor. The emperor performed direct administration of the "kingdom" (China), the regions outside the directly ruled area were called "marginal areas" (or "fringe areas") where local rulers were canonized by the emperor to rule. The rulers of marginal areas recognized the leadership of the emperor, and got seals awarded by the emperor for recognition of their legitimate rights. We can find these seals given by the middle kingdom in museums in Japan, Korea, and Vietnam today.

To show the richness and generosity of the central kingdom, the Emperor always gave a lot of rewards to people to pay tribute in line with the principle of "receiving less, and giving more," the value of the reward was far more than the tribute, so the vassal states were always ready to pay tribute to China, and even felt very unhappy when they were restricted from doing so.

This relationship was broken after Britain launched the opium war against China in 1840, and many nations belonging to China were colonized by the West. China itself was almost carved up.

But some scholars think this tributary system referred to as "Chinese imperialism" by the West is similar to the free trade system, and also highlights the wisdom of eastern civilization. Modern countries obviously will not repeat this system, but the mutual respect, mutual benefits, and win-win concepts should be inherited and developed.

Xi Jinping has a passion for reading and has clearly realized the wisdom of his Chinese ancestors. He attaches great importance to peripheral diplomacy; he thinks the basic principle of China's peripheral diplomacy is persisting in building a neighborly relationship and partnership with its neighbors, fostering an amicable, secure, and prosperous neighborly environment, and highlighting the concept of intimacy, honesty, credit, and tolerance.

It is also used to hedge the strategic threat caused by America to China by returning to Asia. With the rise of China, the original balance of the Asia-Pacific region has been broken. China is increasing its influence and control on the surrounding areas, and extending the growing military strength to the East China Sea and South China Sea islands, a source of anxiety among its neighboring countries.

The United States made a high-profile announcement to return to Asia for the purpose of preventing China's expansion; it incited some surrounding countries to challenge China on territorial disputes by using their power of influence, and caused friction between China and its neighboring countries through the implementation of its "Rebalancing the Asia-Pacific Region" strategy.

Professor Huang Jing, of the Lee Kuan Yew School of Public Policy at the National University of Singapore, thought that to break up the containment of the United States, Xi Jinping should always persists in the principle that China's core interests should not be violated, grasps the trend of the Asia-Pacific economic integration, puts forth the blueprint for realizing The Belt and Road Initiatives, actively seeks the cooperation and development with surrounding regions, and seeks stability on the basis of development.[7]

Based on this strategic layout, China has led the way towards implementing a series of measures, including the establishment of the Asian Investment Bank and the development fund of the Silk Road, promoting economic development of neighboring countries and the building of a community of fate on the basis of cooperation and development. He also

---

7.   *People's Daily Online*, April 22, 2015.

"pays attention to morality and justice, follows principles, seeks fairness and win-win solutions, firmly grasps the high moral ground in international affairs, makes no concessions on questions of principle, and does not hurt others," according to Professor Huang Jing.

III. ALL ROADS LEAD TO BEIJING

On March 28, 2015, Xi Jinping went to China's southern island of Hainan Boao once again after two years, and delivered a keynote speech at the Boao Forum for Asia. The Boao Forum for Asia is one of the international forums dominated by China, which follows the pattern of the Davos World Economic Form, aims to break through the dominance of western public opinion, and delivers China's voice and influence more accurately and objectively.

Xi Jinping preferred to talk naturally in comparison to the formalized speech styles used by some Chinese leaders. There was none of Obama's American humor in his words, but he was more honest than others. Perhaps this is the difference between western speeches and eastern speeches: The former focus more on laughter and applause, and the latter focus more on honesty and thought.

"The Belt and Road Initiatives," and the Countries along the Road

This was a special speech. Just a few days before, Singapore's "Father of the Nation," Lee Kuan Yew, passed away. Lee Kuan Yew had many contacts with Xi Jinping after Xi Jinping was elected as a member of the Standing Committee of the Political Bureau in the 17th CPC national congress in 2007—as the eventual successor to China's top leader, the first dignitary Xi Jinping met was Lee Kuan Yew.

It is said that Lee Kuan Yew guided the West to have an understanding of China. He did not think highly of many Chinese leaders, but particularly admired Xi Jinping. He compared Xi Jinping to Nelson Mandela in his book *One Man's View of the World.*

Lee Kuan Yew has said, "Xi Jinping impressed me with his generosity. He has broad vision, looks at problems thoroughly and insightfully without showing off his abilities and knowledge. Gravity is my first impression of him. I further thought about the sufferings and trials he experienced, how he went to live and work in Shanxi in 1969, and struggled to the top step by step without any complaints. I think he could reach a level as high as Nelson Mandela."[8]

8.   Lee Kuan Yew. *One Man's View of the World.* Singapore: Straits Times Press Pte. Ltd., 2009.

Five years later, Xi Jinping became China's top leader, Lee Kuan Yew gave full affirmation to him, and he thought Xi Jinping would be able to draw attention to the handling of different issues during the current critical period in China. "I believe that he can keep calm in the face of changes, and cope with challenges appropriately. Xi Jinping is influential, I believe he can be a good leader of the communist party of China, and his military background will also help him to establish authority in the army."

After Lee Kuan Yew passed away, Xi Jinping sent a message of condolence to Singapore. In his message, he affirmed Lee Kuan Yew was a respectful elder, "I am full of respect for him. We will never forget the important contribution he made to our bilateral relations."

Lee Kuan Yew's funeral was replete with posthumous honors. The leaders of ASEAN, South Korea's president Park Geun-hye, Japanese Prime Minister Shinzo Abe and Australian Prime Minister Albert went to Singapore for the funeral on March 29. It was expected that Xi Jinping would also attend the funeral. He did not, in possible consideration of political interests. China's top leaders have never attended the funeral of other country's leaders, and Singapore has closer relations with the United States than China. But it was more likely due to the time conflict, because Xi Jinping was set to announce his grand program, The Belt and Road Initiatives, in Hainan Boao. He didn't want to reduce people's attention to its conception due to other activities.

In this well-prepared speech, Xi Jinping told leaders attending this meeting that he proposed The Belt and Road Initiatives to fit the development needs of China, countries along the road, and the native regions in line with the common interests of relevant parties, and conform to the trend of regional and global cooperation.

Xi Jinping clarified doubts and criticisms from outside one by one. He said The Belt and Road Initiatives are in compliance with the principle of joint discussion, joint construction, and sharing, which is open and inclusive, not closed; it is not unique to China, but a chorus sung by countries along the road.

The Belt and Road Initiatives are not going to replace the existing regional cooperation dynamics, but rather promote countries along the road to achieve connections and complementary development strategies on the basis of existing relations.

The Belt and Road Initiatives construction is not an empty slogan, but a real and tangible measure which will bring tangible benefits to each region and country. Through the joint efforts of all relevant parties, the vision and action documents of The Belt and Road Initiatives construction have been set, the preparation of the Asian Investment Bank has made substantial progress, the Silk Road fund has been launched smoothly, and a batch of infrastructure interconnectivity projects have made steady progress. We can see the broad prospects of The Belt and Road Initiatives through these early achievements.

Xi Jinping has stated that there were more than 60 countries along the road, and international organizations expressed their positive attitude toward participating in the realization of The Belt and Road Initiatives. China's Belt and Road Initiatives projects and the Asian Investment Bank are open to all. He called this conception a "grand event," he welcomed the countries along the road and all Asian countries to actively join on behalf of China, and did not exclude countries outside of the historical Silk Road region.

A New Geopolitical Master

To address the outside world's fears surrounding China's rise, Xi Jinping offered a highly emotional new phrase: "a community of fate."

He said Asia has occupied one-third of the world's economy and had become one of the most dynamic and ambitious regions in the world; its status in global strategy is rising. But Asia is also facing all kinds of challenges, and there are still some problems left over by history and the practical contradictions of the region: the tasks of developing the regional and state economies; improving people's livelihoods; and eliminating poverty, all are arduous tasks still complicated by a variety of traditional and non-traditional security threats.

He has said that Asia will be well if the world is well; the world will be well if Asia is well. In the face of changing international and regional conditions, we must grasp the world's trends, keep up with the trends of the times, jointly build regional order, which is more advantageous to Asia and the world, and advance the construction of humankind's "community of fate" by moving forward the Asian "community of fate."

He made a series of strategic concepts for The Belt and Road Initiatives construction. There is a Silk Road fund in addition to the Asian Investment Bank. This is a fund completely dominated by China and was announced by Xi Jinping on November 8, 2014, in Beijing. China invested USD 40 billion, aiming to boost the construction of The Belt and Road Initiatives. In April, 2014, when Xi Jinping visited Pakistan, the fund, the large-scale water conservancy construction company of China, the Three Gorges Group, as well as the Pakistan Private Power and Infrastructure Committee signed a cooperation agreement to develop hydropower projects in Pakistan and address power shortages; this was the first project supported by the Silk Road fund.

China is setting up an international order led by itself with the help of The Belt and Road Initiatives program. Xi Jinping, who likes competition, is taking aim at the most urgent practical demands of regional cooperation, basing his ideas on the comparative advantage of self-development and transformation, focusing on the most essential intersections of Chinese and foreign interests, planning and upgrading economic diplomacy and peripheral diplomacy—a series of Chinese strategies are coming out one after another.

If we say China was just a participant and follower of the international rules previously, it is now turning to the role as a leader and a shaper more and more. In this era of the international stage, Xi Jinping is undoubtedly a new geopolitical master.

Xi Jinping places China's national interests as a number one priority, but never forgets his responsibility to the international community. He clearly knows that China is returning to the world's center stage, and is likely to overtake America as the world's largest economy in his tenure. Power brings responsibility, therefore China must make contributions and the implementation of The Belt and Road Initiatives will help some of the poorer and smaller countries to take advantage of China's development programs.

The United States has many suspicions and plans to slow China's expansion. If China seeks breakthroughs in the military and political fields, it will attract even tighter encirclement from the United States; however, China uses economic weapons like the Chinese Taiji Kung Fu to create a gentler image and improve its regional influence gently, yet powerfully. It is welcomed by other countries, but the United States has no alternative.

Asian patterns are likely to be rewritten. For example, China has invested USD 46 billion in a model project, the "China-Pakistan Economic Corridor" which belongs to The Belt and Road Initiatives program. In this project, Xinjiang Kashgar of China and the Gwadar port of Pakistan would be connected. Chinese engineers are cutting mountains for roads and laying tracks. Pakistan's President, Mamnoon Hussein, said this project was "a milestone of this century; not only China and Pakistan, but the whole area with a population of billions will benefit from it."

This will help stabilize Xinjiang and Tibet in China, and help Pakistan avoid economic collapse, and let China get in and out of the Indian Ocean ports. Although Indian experts thought the establishment of the China-Pakistan Economic Corridor, as an auxiliary project of The Belt and Road Initiatives, would greatly change China's strategic ability in southern and western Asia, and promote the power of the China-Pakistan strategic alliance in the region.[9] But China thought it could contribute more economically to regional development.

Thus Xi Jinping was warmly received by the parties of Pakistan in his state visit in April, 2014. When his plane entered Pakistani airspace, the air force sent eight XiaoLong fighter planes made in China as an escort. The Pakistani president and prime minister were present at the airport to meet him, highlighting the close relationship between China and Pakistan.

In a speech Xi Jinping delivered in Pakistan's parliament, he said China and Pakistan should develop their ties and realize shared development goals. Chinese culture advocates "wishing oneself to be established, seeing that others are established, and wishing oneself to be successful, seeing that others are successful." China adheres to righteous ideas of morality and profit; to aid Pakistan is to aid China.

In Xi Jinping's opinion, the cost of the China-Pakistan Economic Corridor is huge, but it is an important link to achieve common development between China and Pakistan. This sample project of The Belt and Road Initiatives will take corridor construction as the core, focus on the Gwadar port, energy-related projects, infrastructure construction, and industrial cooperation.

"Corridor planning and layout should take account of various areas in Pakistan so that achievements in development will benefit the Pakistani people, and benefit all the peoples of the region." Xi Jinping's sincere speech was warmly received by Pakistani lawmakers, receiving applause no less than 57 times.

In South Asia, China is considering extending the Qinghai-Tibet railway from Lhasa to Nepal's capital Kathmandu at the request of Nepal. Wang Mengshu, Chinese tunnel engineering expert and academic of the Chinese Academy of Engineering, has stated that the railway is intended to cross the Himalayas, and a long tunnel will need to be built. He has said that China has started the necessary preparation work.

After the Nepal earthquake in April 2015, Xi Jinping quickly expressed his condolences, and promised that China would provide all necessary assistance. The Chinese international rescue team quickly flew to Nepal to help with the rescue operation and a large number of Chinese relief supplies were sent to Kathmandu. China's pride and sense of responsibility to countries in need was witnessed by the world.

---

9.   Cole Hariharan, China Research Center, Chennai, India. "Afghanistan-Pakistan Dilemma Faced by China," *Indian Defense Review*, September 8, 2014.

Not a New Marshall Plan

The West regarded The Belt and Road Initiatives as the Chinese version of the Marshall Plan. In July, 1947, in order to help European countries which had been damaged by the war to regain development, the United States launched the European recovery program in western Europe, including finance, technology, equipment and other forms of assistance with a total of USD 13 billion. If the inflation factor is taken into account, the aid would be equivalent to USD 130 billion in 2006. The plan, which was named after US Secretary of State George C. Marshall, substantially helped western European countries to restore their economies, promoted capitalism in Europe, and also put Western Europe under the wings of the United States.

Clearly, The Belt and Road Initiatives in China is not the Marshall Plan. China's investment will be far more than USD 130 billion, and this new economic cooperation body will cover more than 60 percent of the population and a third of the world's economy.

Moreover, China's foreign minister Wang Yi argued that The Belt and Road Initiatives was older than the Marshall plan with over 2,000 years of history, and it is now glowing in a new era of light. At the same time, The Belt and Road Initiatives is younger than the Marshall Plan because it is born in the era of globalization, and it is the product of China's opening up and cooperation.

Wang Yi has also said that The Belt and Road Initiatives is not the product of geopolitical maneuvering and cannot be regarded with outdated Cold War thinking. But there is one aspect in common: the Marshall Plan avoided the collapse of the economy in Europe, and narrowed the psychological distance on both sides of the Atlantic Ocean helping the United States become the world's superpower. If The Belt and Road Initiatives are successful, they are bound to establish closer relations between China and neighboring countries, and rewrite the economic and political landscape in Eurasian countries.

Certainly, there are some challenges. The core of the Silk Road Economic Belt is in Central Asia, which has been rife with wars. Large investments may change the conditions of the region, but may also be swallowed up, to no constructive end. Moreover, this area traditionally belongs to the sphere of influence of Russia, and Russia is in confrontation with the West on the issue of Ukraine, and urgently needs the support of China; therefore, Russia has acquiesced to the plan. But Russia only announced that it wanted to join the Asian Investment Bank at the last minute, implying that Russia was still wary of the financial institution led by China.

Even in Pakistan, China's most loyal ally, the construction of the China-

Pakistan Economic Corridor must overcome the extreme environment of the Karakoram Mountains, as well as the security problem that have always been a major challenge, especially in regions with frequent terrorist activities and local separatist militias. In 2004, three Chinese engineers engaged in the building of Melon Tal port were killed by terrorists. Chinese military power is growing, but it belongs to a defensive troop on the whole and is unlikely to interfere in the internal stability of Pakistan. During a visit to Pakistan, Xi Jinping made a point to meet with Pakistan's military leaders, possibly for this reason.

The challenge may be bigger for the implementation of the Maritime Silk Road. At one time China maintained a close relationship with Sri Lanka, which ended its civil war lasting for 26 years with the help of China; Sri Lankan President Rajapaksa regarded China as an old friend. However, in the general election of January, 2015, Rajapaksa failed to win. The new President Xi Li Senna first made a visit to India, and only then to China, and some projects invested in by China are being reconsidered.

In the past, China liked to bet on a certain foreign leader, but the unstable political situation in these countries brought great uncertainty as a result. After a leader was overthrown, many Chinese projects would be unsustainable and a large number of bad debts were formed. In Libya, after the collapse of the Qaddafi regime, Chinese people were evacuated from the war-torn areas quickly, but a large amount of equipment and projects were abandoned with huge losses. China's Ministry of Commerce spokesman Yao Jianzeng revealed that there were a total of 50 large projects contracted to China at that time in Libya, with all contracts amounting of USD 18.8 billion.

It has been proven that it doesn't work to carry out construction in a closed environment in the era of globalization. As the United States has returned to the Asia-Pacific region, China's strategic space is compressed and must seek a breakthrough. The Belt and Road Initiatives proposed by Xi Jinping may be affected by British strategist Michael Mackinder.

In 1902, Mackinder proposed the concept of the "World Island" to the British Royal Geographical Society. This World Island does not refer to Greenland, nor Australia, but to the entire landmass linked by the continents of Asia, Africa, and Europe. Mackinder thought that the centerpiece of the earth was the World Island made up of these three continents, but that the heartland could not be controlled by a single power due to the backward transportation conditions. But the presence of the railroad in the early twentieth century changed the situation: "when Eurasia was covered by a dense railway network, a strong continental country would dominate this vast land." Mackinder could only conceive of railroads. Actually, the traditional railroad, with slow speeds and different track gauges, had no ability to realize integration such as he envisioned; but the present-day high-speed trains, moving at speeds of 300 kilometers per hour, may change the theory into reality. Of course, the integration process is long, and twists and turns are inevitable; but human beings are destined to come together through the modern technology, especially high-speed rail and the Internet.

The high-speed trains in China will become an important tool of integration. And China's Prime Minister Li Keqiang is also known as the most enthusiastic promoter of China's high-speed rail. In the past, all roads led to Rome. Now, all roads will lead to Beijing!

Xi Jinping delivered a speech at the APEC CEO summit at the Beijing Olympic venue called the "Water Cube" on November 9, 2014.

The Water Cube enclosed the indoor swimming events of the 2008 Olympic Games in Beijing. Xi Jinping certainly had vision in arranging the international conference there, and hosted a banquet for APEC leaders on the second day. According to Xi Jinping, water was symbolically important in Chinese culture. More than 2,000 years ago, Lao Tzu said, "the greatest kindness is to be like water, for water benefits all things and goes against none of them."

Xi Jinping can understand the concerns of the outside world about China becoming a hegemony. He quoted this famous saying to tell other countries that China would never seek hegemony. China has a history of more than 2,000 years, and the Chinese people have always preferred to live in harmony, rather than to seize and plunder indiscriminately.

He told these gathered global elites that the prospect of Asia-Pacific development depends on today's decisions and actions. China has a responsibility to realize the dream of the region's people. He stressed that "a grand time requires a grand plan, and a grand plan requires grand wisdom." The business leaders of the world applauded him, for they could all see clearly that the "grand wisdom" Xi Jinping alluded to might just be his own.

CHAPTER
7

A Great Power Requires a Great Military

Thirty-six years ago, when college graduate Xi Jinping donned an army uniform and became the confidential secretary of the Central Military Commission Secretary General Geng Biao in 1979, the Chinese army was beginning to understand the need for major reforms.

At that time, fierce fighting on the southern border stimulated the need for streamlining and mechanization of the People's Liberation Army (PLA). The most salient example of this need was the fact that the army had no identifiable military rank system, resulting in disorder on the battlefield. Bloody lessons inspired the PLA's ardent pursuit of organized combat effectiveness, and the discussion on army reform was unprecedentedly intense.

The China-Vietnam border war lasted for ten years and was the last battlefield experience of the Chinese army. From the late 1970s to 1980s, this massive fighting force also experienced its first drastic change since 1949.

The establishment of diplomatic ties between China and America at the beginning of 1979, the whirlwind visit of Deng Xiaoping to the United States, the outbreak of border war in the spring of that year, the constantly changing external situation and national strategy—all these factors must have been perplexing for the young Xi Jinping at the time, who found himself at the center of the decision-making process of the armed forces.

Now, 36 years later, as Xi Jinping has became the supreme commander of an army of 2.3 million people, he is still facing a "war with reform"—aiming to put a stop to long-standing abuses in the PLA, and to promote a thorough transformation of the army at the same time, so as to match the security and development needs of the world's second-largest economy.

As media analysts have pointed out, many of the world's leaders served in the army before the age of 30, but it is quite rare for one to serve as supreme commander of the army, and to have personally witnessed the decision-making processes of the high-level national military. "At this age, Barack Obama was studying at university, and Angela Merkel was in a research institute studying physical chemistry—both working toward their degree. Vladimir Putin and David Cameron worked at this age, the former was the cryptographer of Leningrad, and the latter was the director of corporate affairs at a communications company."[1]

When you take this into account, and when you look at photos of the young Xi Jinping in his military uniform, could one still claim he looks like the handsome star of a Korean soap opera?

I. IS THE PEOPLE'S LIBERATION ARMY A "PAPER TIGER?"

On November 15, 2012, when Xi Jinping took over the supreme power of the Central Committee of the Communist Party of China, he also succeeded in becoming the president of the Military Commission of the Central Committee of the Communist Party of China. Since November, 1989, when Deng Xiaoping resigned, the role of commander in chief of the Chinese army was taken on by a former politician in a military uniform once again after 23 years.

As early as two years previously, it was striking when Xi Jinping was appointed as the vice chairman of the Central Military Commission at the fifth plenary session of the 17th Central Committee of the CPC—for in China's political system, once a leading member of the Central Committee of the Communist Party from the civil service system joins the Central Military Commission, this serves as a signal that a most important personnel arrangement in the future is certain.

When Xi Jinping appeared behind Hu Jintao, who was the chairman of the Central Military Commission, in his dark green Chinese tunic suit, which is called "casual uniform," *The Guardian* newspaper described this as

---

1.   "Xi Jinping: New Commander in Chief of the People's Liberation Army," *Phoenix-net Phoenix Military*, May 13, 2014.

a "crucial military position."

It prompted a wave of attention from foreign media for Xi Jinping. Writer Robert Lawrence Kuhn, who interviewed Xi Jinping, said, "He's very enthusiastic without any official airs." *The Times* said Xi Jinping was known as a reliable person, and the former US Treasury Secretary Henry 'Hank' Paulson said that he was the kind of person who knew how to excel.

Many foreign media also noted Xi Jinping's comments when he met and discussed with overseas Chinese on a trip to Mexico in the spring of 2009: "There are some foreigners who had eaten their fill and have nothing better to do, pointing their fingers at our affairs. China neither exports revolution, nor exports hunger and poverty, we don't involve ourselves in their affairs, what else can you really say?"

The blunt and confident demeanor of this Chinese politician let many people, for the first time, feel the strong will under his gentle appearance. And this kind of straightforwardness, confidence, and strength was soon familiar to the government and people after the 18th National Congress of the CPC. At the executive meeting of the Central Military Commission held on November 15, 2012, he put forth a strong, succinct demand, that the army "fight a victorious war."

The handover of top leadership of the Chinese army was completed in the enlarged meeting of the Central Military Commission held the next afternoon. Xi Jinping said his predecessor, President Hu Jintao, had offered not to serve as the supreme leader of the Chinese Communist Party and army, which fully reflected his long-term vision, broad mind, and upright moral character as a Marxist statesman and strategist. President Hu Jintao called him the "qualified chairman of Central Military Commission."

Needless to say, to integrate the supreme power of the Party, the government, and the army will mean, in essence, controlling the large and complex country. Xi must mobilize various resources to effectively promote his own governing ideas, and the post of the Central Military Commission chairman also marks a special significance. Deng Xiaoping, who served as chairman of the Central Military Commission, did not work as the highest leadership of the People's Republic of China at the same time, but he still had unchallenged authority and influence.

There was a delay in the handover of this position for the previous two top leaders before Xi Jinping. Jiang Zeming took the role of chairman of the Central Military Commission and after five months he adopted the Communist Party of China; while Hu Jintao took over the position of Military Commission chairman from Jiang Zeming, and after nearly two years he worked as the general secretary of the CPC Central Committee.

For the CPC, "the party commands the gun" is an ironclad law, and the unified power of *party* and *gun* is the necessary premise toward realizing the "effective concentration" and efficient decision-making envied by the outside world.

After Hu Jintao handed over control, the office located in the Central Military Commission "Bayi Building" by his predecessor Jiang Zeming was immediately removed. According to media reports, Jiang Zeming also had an office in the grand building 6 kilometers west of Zhongnanhai since the year 2000, in addition to his office in Zhongnanhai.[2]

The Chinese people are accustomed to seeing Xi Jinping in service dress or camouflage clothing on television—the practice that rank would not be awarded to the chairman of the Central Military Commission was first adopted by Deng Xiaoping in 1988, who told the legislative institution that the rank of marshal was not set in peacetime, and he would not be a marshal.[3] Now, when the commander in chief of the People's Liberation Army appears, they have no rank, and most wear the Chinese tunic suit in coordination with their army uniform, forgoing shoulder adornments and neckties.

On November 23, 2012, Xi Jinping elevated the rank of Wei Fenghe, the new commander of the Second Artillery Force, to General at the "Bayi Building." Two weeks later, Xi Jinping joined troops in Guangzhou, climbed into an amphibious assault vehicle with front-line troops, and went aboard the Haikou guided missile destroyer, a warship armed with the latest type of radar and robust air defense missile systems known as the "China Aegis."

During his first military inspection after he served as the supreme commander of the Chinese People's Liberation Army, Xi Jinping shared his thoughts on governing the military: Ensure the absolute command of the Communist Party of China over the army; conduct construction and make preparations according to war-time standards; and govern the army strictly in accordance with the law to ensure a high degree of centrality and unification, as well as safety and stability. Within less than one month, Xi Jinping crystallized the China Dream, already integrated with his strategic thinking, into the "Army Dream" for the military.

During a one-week inspection visit to the war zone in Guangzhou, five ships of the East China Sea fleet completed a training maneuver far into the western Pacific, and patrolled the Diaoyu Islands on the voyage home. The navy of the Nanjing military region held the annual largest practice exercise,

---

2.   "The Decryption of the Standing Committee Office of the Political Bureau: Two Red Phones Are Standard Equipment," *Southern Metropolis Weekly*, January 10, 2014.

3.   "Comrade Xiaoping Did Not Act as Marshal," *Legal Daily*, August 20, 2014.

combining with the army, the Airborne Warning and Control System (AWACS), fighter planes, and reconnaissance aircraft.

China Does Not Want Peace Without Dignity

Let us have a look at the dilemma Xi Jinping is facing in terms of defending China. Tension continues to boil in the South China Sea. In April, 2012, Chinese fishing boats had been in conflict with aggressive Philippine warships for months. On December 5, 2013, the new Chinese aircraft carrier *Liao Ning* was closely tracked by the US Navy's Ticonderoga-class guided-missile cruiser *USS Cowpens* as it carried out naval exercises in China's waters, and a confrontation between the Chinese and American warships arose. Between May and June of 2014, Vietnam offended Chinese civilian ships on many occasions, and also sent diving frogmen to interfere with the normal operation of a Chinese oil-drilling platform.

In September 2012, two months before the 18th National Congress of the CPC, the Japanese government decided to purchase the Senkaku Islands, known to the Chinese as the Diaoyu Islands, which caused anti-Japanese demonstrations in many cities in China. A territorial dispute now applies to the waters around the Diaoyu Islands, with sea and air patrols continuing. From April to May of 2013, confrontations occurred between the Chinese and Indian armies in a border zone at a distance of 300 meters, eventually lasting for 20 days. In September, 2014, the Indian army built an observation post in the China-India boundary region with an elevation of 5500 meters, sparking clashes for three weeks, involving nearly 1,000 Chinese and 2,000 Indian soldiers. At the same time, underground nuclear tests in North Korea and fighting at the Sino-Burmese border have added to the insecurity around China.

China became the world's second largest economy in 2010, overtaking Japan, which fell into long-term economic stagnation and suffered natural and man-made disasters such as a tsunami, earthquake, and nuclear accident. In the same period, the United States and Europe were emerging from the devastating subprime crisis and debt crisis.

In 2011, the US put forth a policy to "Return to Asia," and further generalized this notion into an "Asian-Pacific Rebalancing Strategy" in 2012. It is said that the Xi Jinping era started when "the west and the east were in disorderly crisis."[4] And his own judgment is that China is facing the dangers of being invaded, subverted, and divided. He believes that China is unprecedentedly close to the center of the world stage, on the verge of

4.   "Xi Style Maneuver: The Strategic Support of the China Dream," *Phoenixnet Phoenix Military*, May 13, 2014.

achieving the great renewal of the Chinese nation, and can now claim the unprecedented ability and confidence to achieve this goal. But the road ahead will never be easy.

Fears of China becoming a worldwide threat have been voiced for many years. The western world has repeatedly stressed the "Theory of Thucydides' Trap," that inevitably "strong nations must bully the weak, and strong powers must fight each other," and that this is a historical destiny, one that cannot be avoided on the path to becoming a superpower. In January, 2014, when Xi Jinping accepted an interview with *World Post*, a subsidiary of the online tabloid *The Huffington Post*, he delivered a firm retort: The assumption that great powers will inevitably pursue hegemony does not apply to China, and China does not have the genes for such a pursuit.

However, not pursuing hegemony does not mean to halting development of the army. On the contrary, rich countries with a weak military will not ensure the safety of themselves, and may also cause regional crises, let alone neglect the necessary international responsibility they should undertake.

Therefore, Xi Jinping put forth an overall national security theory, including political security, homeland security, military security, economic security, cultural security, social security, digital and information security, ecological security, resource security, and nuclear safety: "Make the country rich and the military efficient, and a powerful army will defend the country." He emphasized that he would attach importance to both China's own security and common security, creating a "community of fate."

Professor Jin Yinan, of the University of National Defense, has written that peace and security are two different concepts: Peace can be gained in the absence of dignity, and security is the effective safeguard of our rights. Today China is pursuing national security, not peace without dignity. The research interests of Jin Yinan are national security strategies, international conflicts, and crisis management; Xi Jinping has recommended his works to senior cadres. "Now the behavior of some Chinese lead the world to think the Chinese people are very utilitarian. This impression will bring disaster to our nation. And some countries will infer that, 'As long as I am strong, China will be weak.'" In view of the Sino-Japanese War, Professor Jin Yinan has stated that "what China needs now is not to argue whether to fight or not to fight, win or lose, but to show the vision that we must defend the interests of the state and our national dignity by any means. This is beyond notions of victory and defeat."[5] In other words, the army must produce deterrence, or why would we build the military forces?

Therefore, while the new ideas of the China-US "new power relations"

---

5.   "The Duties of Chinese Soldiers," *Global People*, February 2014.

and the underlying "intimacy, honesty, beneficence, and tolerance" principles were put forth, on the other hand, Xi Jinping stressed "remembering the bottom line." China must make a well-defined stand on issues of core national interest without any concessions. This includes accelerating the strengthening of necessary facilities in the South China Sea reefs; conducting combat patrols by the Chinese navy and air force around the Diaoyu Islands, setting up an air defense identification area in the East China Sea; training and conducting exercises of ships and planes continuously across the island chains; and simultaneously implementing a "hurricane action" training mission during the China-India border standoff. The official newspaper of the Central Military Commission, the *Liberation Army Daily* published fifteen photo features entitled "Diary of No Man's Land," depicting the combat exercises in this highly sensitive area.

The Army Force Can No Longer Endure

As the commander in chief of the People's Liberation Army, Xi Jinping took strong measures in applying his judgment of the outside world to the security situation in China, as well as taking the teachings of history into account. The year 2014 marked the 120th anniversary of the China-Japan war, also known as the "War of Jiawu." The outbreak of the China-Japan war in 1894 altered the fates of the two nations. Japan became an emerging capitalist power in Asia, but China's attempt at modernization failed, and it was forced to cede Taiwan and other territories; the nation was divided by outside powers like vultures tearing at meat, and reached the edge of extinction.

Introspection on the anniversary of the war, especially the China-Japan naval battle, prompted Chinese experts to analyze the war and its impact. Liu Yazhou, the political commissar of the National Defense University, and an expert in military strategy, believes that the true failure of the China-Japan war was not the defeat of the army, but the failure of the state and the system.

Xi Jinping has also mentioned the lessons of the China-Japan war twice, describing it as the "pain of a broken heart." At an important meeting held at the end of December, 2013, he explained: "If the military falls behind, the impact on the national security will be fatal. I often read historical data from modern China; unbearable pity came to my mind every time I saw the tragically backwards conditions!" Xi Jinping has stated that the China-Japan war has a special meaning for the Chinese nation. Liu Yazhou understands this to mean that the China-Japan war should become a symbol for China to maintain an everlasting "consciousness of suffering" in mind.[6]

---

6.   Liu Yazhou. "Get out of the China-Japan War, Welcome Reform, Create Brilliance,"

The idea of a "consciousness of suffering" stems from a feeling that complacency has been allowed to creep in because of the long-standing habits of peacetime allowed to form in the People's Liberation Army. There has been no war for nearly 30 years, morale has sunk, corruption has increased, preparation for war is relaxed, and this detachedness has become a public nuisance.

Observers have seen luxury cars with military license plates driving through the streets, inappropriate extravagances have crept up among some senior officers, and it is not rare to hear of buying and selling official positions.

Former deputy commander of the Nanjing military region Wang Hong-guang believes that a slackness has gradually formed in the army: "some senior commanders have no memories of off-road jeep command vehicles. In recent years, our army has become equipped with 'warrior' and 'brave warrior' brand command vehicles, but senior and intermediate commanders rarely use them."[7]

Military "exercises" have become mere "acting;" one hears that "training exercises are not for war; training is for spectators." Military swimming became no more than practice in the swimming pool. Soldiers did not live in field tents for camping exercises, but had a barracks, with sidewalks, running water, and electric lighting; air conditioning was even installed in the campgrounds and phones and Internet browsers were installed. Before maneuvers, terrain reconnaissance was made in advance, and plans were pre-prepared, with fixed targets, routes, and directions.

Vice Chairman of the Military Commission Fan Changlong instituted special requirements for true-to-life exercises, not simply for show. China should not passively ensure security at the expense of losing fighting capacity. After Xi Jinping took over the supreme leadership of the Chinese army, he started to govern army forces with an iron hand, almost without any transitional or buffer period, requiring soldiers to "have soul, have skill, have spirit, have morality." He said, "The army should do what the army should do." He especially set an "ironclad rule" for senior cadres to consider themselves forewarned.

People soon discovered that the army gave the first response to the national reform actions with a faster pace and stricter requirements in comparison to other militaries of the region. Anti-corruption measures marched forward in the army, and many cadres who were found to have fallen below ethical

---

People's Liberation Army Daily, May 15, 2015.

7.   Wang Hong-guang. "Soldiers Need More Exercise for Courage and Uprightness in Peace Time," *Global Times*, July 15, 2013.

standards were culled. The scale and magnitude of exercises were increased, even casualties were no longer strictly kept confidential—it was considered to be a strong signal that training had become "closer to true combat."

The official media also constantly reminded the Chinese people: "To some extent, the current reforms and anti-corruption struggles are 'forced' by a high-pressure situation. The temptation of hedonism, and the lowered morales of soldiers are issues. People become addled with complacency by the extended peacetime, and through indulgences, corruption is bred.[8] The public can see the changes brought about by strengthening discipline, which brews a positive atmosphere and creates the proper conditions for self-directed "invisible changes." Military reform has also entered a critical phase in its synchronization with the overall reform process in China.

The new military revolution launched by the United States has been compared to carousel—it is easy to be flung off if you only stay at the edge, so we must enter the center. Especially after the attack on the Chinese embassy in Yugoslavia in 1999, the Chinese people, who had concentrated on economic development, made a decision that the army cannot tolerate such events. Deng Xiaoping said that army building should take care of the overall situation of national reconstruction, and, giving way to large-scale reforms in 1985, that China should "endure for a few years." The end of the twentieth century was the limit of endurance predetermined by this master tactician.

In this round of reform focused on information, intelligence, and innovation, the United States, Russia, Japan, and other developed countries made the first move; India, Brazil, Vietnam, and other developing countries followed suit. The People's Liberation Army faces serious challenges in the mechanization initiatives that have not yet been resolved, while the information and intelligence initiatives should be proceeding at the same time. Although the armed forces are being upgraded, the system set-up and command system of the PLA are still based upon a semi-mechanized war environment. Some policy systems closely related to national defense and military reconstruction grew out of the planned economy era, and national defense and military upgrades have not been well integrated into the overall development of the nation.

Even some foreign media have asked: Is the People's Liberation Army just a paper tiger? In this context, when the Chinese military refers to the China-Japan war, they should not simply examine history, remember suffering, but also make decisions for the future.

---

8.   "The New Designer Xi Jinping: Military Governing," *People's Daily*, November 14, 2014.

As Liu Yazhou said, a backward military may not have inferior equipment, but it will have old ideas: "Money can buy advanced weaponry and equipment, but it can never buy advanced military thoughts and culture. Before the China-Japan war, the Qing government bought the world's most advanced warships and weapons, but the army was ruled by the corrupt Qing dynasty and a generation of backward ideologies and military tactics—backward in comparison with the Japanese army, which had experienced the Meiji Restoration—had emerged."[9]

Although 120 years have passed, the sea battle that completely annihilated China's Northern Fleet, with its first-class equipment, in March, 1895, is still felt like a curse. The Chinese people need to be constantly aware and unceasingly introspective as to how to transcend a conservative national psychology, backwards ideas, and the cultural stagnation formed in the interregnum. How can China finally escape the shadow of the China-Japan war? This is Xi Jinping's mission.

II. WHY SHOULD CHINA BE LOYAL TO CHAIRMAN XI JINPING?
The Army of the Communist Party of China
Is Not a Peasant Uprising Troop

In late October, 2014, Xi Jinping, chairman of the Central Military Commission, addressed more than 400 top generals of the People's Liberation Army at the PLA's political work meeting in Gutian Town, west of Fujian province. In the Chairman Mao Memorial Garden, he climbed over 151 steps and offered a flower basket to Mao Zedong's statue. This town has become an important landmark in the history of the Communist Party of China and the PLA due to the "Gutian Meeting" held in 1929. Several former chairmen of the Military Commission have been here; Xi Jinping worked in Fujian for many years, and had visited to conduct surveys on several occasions.

The PLA has always regarded "ideological and political work" as a lifeline, and has been strictly controlled by the system formed by army Party organizations. The General Political Department is an important management department of the army juxtaposed with the headquarters of the general staff, the General Armament Department, and the General Logistics Department.

An American who fought with Chinese soldiers on the battlefields of

---

9.   Liu Yazhou: "Get Out of the China-Japan War, Welcome Reform, Create Brilliance," *Liberation Army Daily*, May 15, 2015.

North Korea once said that he had never found a perfect communist unit broken by combat. No matter how severely the unit was damaged, they still had the ability to resist, as long as the Party organization was intact.[10] American, Japanese, and Indian troops have no particular political labor system to equate to communism, but their national consciousness, values, and patriotic educations become important buttresses for their fighting capacity. At the same time, the PLA General Political Department is also responsible for cadre management and political supervision of the entire army.

Fifteen army political work meetings have been held in the 88 years since the PLA was established, but Gutian had never been chosen as the conference site, and the last meeting was held in 1999. The meeting was formally proposed by Xi Jinping early in May, 2013, and he personally selected the site. The Gutian meeting was held on December 28 through December 29, 1929, and was the 9th Party Congress of the 4th Army of the Red Army. The main forces were led by Mao Zedong and Zhu De, and a large number of farmers from Jiangxi to Fujian had joined the army, but strong concepts of clan identity, exclusionary attitudes, and a hedonist philosophy made them lax in discipline. For example, a town was taken by bloody fighting, but when the soldiers saw that the paddies were mature, they all went home to harvest rice; the town was undefended and eventually was lost again.

The important value of the Gutian meeting lies in the fact that a traditional peasant army was transformed under the leadership of the Communist Party of China. "In the previous peasant uprisings in Chinese history, the army came into the city and took power, but finally broke down. The Communist Party of China did not become the 'tail' of any peasant uprising, and did not follow their old routines."[11]

The Communist Party of China group was composed of young leaders aged around 30 years old, and there had been disagreement, debate, and even struggle between them before this meeting. Therefore, researchers believe that the results of the Gutian meeting were not only to make clear the ironclad law that "the party commands the gun," and put forth the principle of "building the Party with ideology, building the army with politics," but more crucially, it witnessed the maturity of CPC leaders, and forged a new army by the efforts of this exploratory committee.

---

10. *The United States Army in the Korean War: Policy and Direction—The First Year,* James F. Schnabel National Defense University Press.

11. Jin Yinan. "Where Does the Spirit of the Great Gutian Conference Come From?" *National Defense Reference,* December 3, 2014.

Mao Zedong said, "Advance military power for the Party, instead of individuals, otherwise it will be unable to complete its mission; the minority of people will influence the majority of people." The farmers abandoned the old ideas, and joined together under the flag of the Soviet Union, like iron filings to a magnet.

"During the 85th anniversary of the Gutian meeting, we come here again to trace its origins, thoroughly think where we set out from, and why we did it," said Xi Jinping.[12] The philosophical propositions of where we set out and why we did it have very practical meanings, not just for the PLA-based political work of Party cadres, but also for the 88-year-old army, and the 94-year-old party.

Politics and the Military

The official discourse has employed the name "new Gutian meeting" to apply a historical context for the 2014 meeting hosted by Chairman Xi Jinping. In Xi Jinping's era, he puts emphasis on the notion that "the party commands the gun," which has become quite different since its origins, when the CPC set up its own forces. On one hand, the Party itself is undergoing a modernization process; on the other hand, the army has no advantage in systems, talent, and culture, as compared with the entire society, and can no longer be closed off as a whole. The army must connect with society, so governing the military in accordance with the laws of the nation has become the inevitable option.

According to Zheng Yongnian, a researcher of Chinese studies, the control of politics on the military is not too much, but not enough, in China. "The Party seemed to relax control of the Chinese army in the past ten years; this is the biggest problem."[13] He thought the Communist Party of China should primarily focus on the control of personnel, and less on systems. "When the ruling party lacks institutional control of the army, the army's autonomy will inevitably lead to abnormal behavior of the army. Corruption is just one of many forms of abnormal behavior."[14] There are even more radical views for caution: China must alert the army to get involved in political disputes.

On the other hand, systemic reform toward modernization of the Chinese army has not been put on the agenda. And the current direction is toward army professionalization, connecting the legal system of the army with

---

12.　　"Highlights of Xi Jinping Attending the Army Political Work Conference," *Liberation Army Daily*, November 2, 2014.

13.　　Zheng Yongnian. "Re-evaluation on the 2nd Anniversary of the 18th National Congress," *Phoenix Weekly*, January 30, 2015.

14.　　Ibid.

civilian laws. The army is not a "land outside the law." Only in this way, can the army really become a pillar of China's sustainable development.[15] Three days before the meeting—on October 27, 2014—the Military Procuratorate ended an investigation into suspicions of bribery by the former vice chairman of the Central Military Commission, Xu Caihou, and transferred the case for examination before prosecution. Xu Caihou had been in charge of army political work for many years, and had been involved in a web of complex corruption relying on the power of personnel organizations.

Back in March 2014, as national defense was being prioritized and the army reform leading group of the Central Military Commission was set up, Xi Jinping acted as group leader, to "plan and command in person."[16] The move aimed to "disrupt military oligarchs," and focus on strengthening reform, so that the Party could truly control the army's forces.[17]

Over the years, as long as it comes to the political system and the leadership system, there have always been voices critical of the control of the Communist Party of China over the army, regarding it as the biggest obstacle for China's continuing political development, especially for China's democratization, and called for a nationalized military unaffiliated with any political party.

Zheng Yongnian feels that this would be a grave mistake: "China is a special case among all of the late-developing countries in terms of the military's position in the country. China has two national systems—the Party and army. Most developing countries have only two forces: the military and their religion. The military and religion lack legitimacy. The characteristic of political legitimacy is rule by the educated classes now." He added: "The difference of China is that through the power of the Party, the essence of army nationalization would be control of the army by the intelligentsia; the Party is already the intelligentsia, and we do not need to copy the Western concepts."[18]

At the first executive meeting of the Military Commission presided over by Xi Jinping, he particularly stressed that we must think clearly and take decisive action in adhering to the fundamental principle of the Party's absolute leadership over the military.

15.　　Ibid.

16.　　"Xi Jinping's Plan: Personally Oversee the Reform of National Defense and the Army 'in Unison,'" *Ta Kung Pao*, March 20, 2014.

17.　　Zheng Yongnian: "Re-evaluation on the 2nd Anniversary of the 18th National Congress," *Phoenix Weekly*, January 30, 2015.

18.　　Ibid.

We Are Not Flexing Muscle, but Gaining Support

Shortly after the close of the 18th National Congress, it was noticed that every time Xi Jinping participated in large activities or launched an investigation, he also arranged to inspect the local garrison at the same time. He has inspected infantry units outside Beijing nearly 20 times thus far, including seven divisions of land, sea, air, and armed police forces. Each inspection has lasted a long time and included much pageantry. He has reviewed the troops, boarded vessels, fighting vehicles, and new bombers, personally sat at controls and inspected instruments, watched live firing, signed navigation logs, and even performed guard duty with soldiers at border posts.

He has focused on the day-to-day lives of grassroots infantry units, and has often sat down to eat with soldiers at the same table for a simple canteen meal, shaken hands with the cook-house squad, and apologized for delaying soldiers from their rest. He has shown that he cares that platoon troops have fresh vegetables to eat, whether it's convenient to see a doctor, and even tested whether the temperature of their bathwater was to their personal preferences. He has urged soldiers who delayed marriage for military service to get married as soon as possible. In the winter of 2014, Xi Jinping met with a group of soldiers patrolling a snowy field in Inner Mongolia, and he took off his gloves and shook hands with them in the freezing weather.

The official media always makes for rapid and full reports on Xi Jinping's inspections of military forces. CCTV broadcasts regular reports of his inspections, and the People's Liberation Army newspaper also tracks Chairman Xi Jinping through a real-time blog and carries photos of his army inspections, demonstrating the earnest attentions and familiarity of the supreme commander for the army.

In fact, although it has been 25 years since Xi Jinping took off his military uniform, he has never been far removed from the army and national defense. By convention, when he served as a local chief leader, he would also have a related position in the local military zone or national defense mobilization committee, and always had a good reputation for giving "active support to the army." According to China's political system concerning the coordination of the relationship between the army and a locality, the deputy secretary of the Provincial Party Committee also acts as the first commissar of the provincial reserve's high-artillery division, as the reserve forces are traditionally responsible for air defense, and the high-artillery division becomes the first division of provincial reserves in the operational sequence. Provincial and municipal government leaders often take office in national defense mobilization committees.

However, after Xi Jinping was promoted to the post of provincial governor of Fujian province from his former role as deputy secretary of a party committee, he still worked as the first commissar of a provincial reserve's high-artillery division: a rare occurrence in the army, according to the *National Defense* magazine.

As the first political commissar, the governor of Fujian province Xi Jinping approved the investment of more than RMB 2 million in the construction of a training center for the reserve high-artillery army in Fujian. A photograph of him sitting in the firing position of an anti-aircraft gun in a camouflage uniform was published in *National Defense* magazine. In this photo, Xi Jinping has turned the brim of uniform's cap to one side of his head, in order to get close to the gun sight.

In his term of office as Fuzhou municipal party committee secretary, the former chairman Li Xinanian's wife Lin Jiamei visited Fuzhou in January, 1993. The provincial party committee arranged a luncheon reception in Fuzhou, with a visit to the army in the morning of that day. "Xi Jinping had the experience to give priority to the needs of the army, so he went to the army as planned. When he got to the radio facility[19] he solved its dispute within one unit on site. He left the provincial military region and went to his next engagement without eating dinner."[20]

Xi Jinping often attended reserve service ranking and promotion ceremonies after taking office in Shanghai. Some reports said that his strong principles demanded that such ceremonies be attended, no matter how busy he was. At the same time, he often went to the local army units for inspections and greetings, not only during the Spring Festival and the Army Day. Thus, it was no surprise that the new Military Commission chairman was very familiar with the military hardware, his ability to handle the equipment appealed to the rank and file, and he spoke with the soldiers naturally and intimately. As media have followed Xi Jinping's inspections the army's new equipment, and even certain military bases, rarely seen previously, have entered the public eye.

For example, Xi Jinping went on board the vessel *Jinggangshan* in Sanya, which was the largest warship in the Chinese navy. Before the aircraft carrier *Liao Ning* entered active service, the *Jinggangshan* ranked first, with a displacement of 19,000 tons. It was able to carry enough soldiers, fighting vehicles, helicopters, and hovercrafts to attack and occupy an island.

During Xi Jinping's tour of the *Jinggangshan*, the internal workings of the ship were exposed for the first time. Based on experience acquired since the Gulf War of 1991, large amphibious landing ships or aircraft carriers

---

19.   Former Chinese People's Liberation Army Fujian radio station.
20.   *The Literature of Fujian*, 04, 1994.

have been deployed as naval bases. In previous years, when Chinese leaders visited a naval base, they usually boarded a typical guided missile destroyer. Before Xi Jinping visited the *Jinggangshan*, it had just completed a war readiness patrol and offshore training in the South China Sea and western Pacific, and had been tracked by foreign patrol airplanes, reconnaissance aircraft, and destroyers.

Early in 2015, Xi Jinping climbed into the cockpit of an H-6K long-range strategic bomber. *Jane's Defense Weekly* noted: "This is the first time a wide perspective of the cabin of the latest H-6K bomber has been provided." It is said that the combat radius of the H-6K bomber is about 3,500 kilometers, and coupled with the KD-20 cruise missile's range, it would be sufficient to cover the cluster of US bases to the northeast of Asia and Guam. The long-range bomber is the symbol and embodiment of China's powerful air force.

Revealing equipment and capabilities is not merely China's means to "flex its muscles," as foreign media has speculated. For Xi Jinping, who has a deep understanding of the military, he would prefer to arouse the confidence and pride of all officers and soldiers of the army, and to arouse all citizens to support and admire their military forces.

Who Is the Watchman of the Communist Party?

Commissar of the East Sea Fleet Wang Huayong also participated in the new Gutian meeting. He told the media: "Chairman Xi Jinping made a very poignant statement. He said the comrades present here, we have big responsibilities. In fact, it was directed to all political cadres! Political cadres at various levels are the most reliable men in the Party, which is to say, they should be the night watchmen of the party."[21]

Obviously Xi Jinping did not only direct the remark to the political cadres. He emphasized at the new Gutian meeting that the army should behave like an army, in particular those senior and intermediate cadres. He thought the root of corruption over the army forces was due to "the loose management of cadres." Originally, "the army should behave like an army" was a phrase coined by Deng Xiaoping in his important speech entitled "The Army Needs Rectification," published in 1975. This phrase is regarded as the typical expression of Deng Xiaoping's thoughts on governing the military: The Party commands a gun in the army, the gun does not command the Party; in other words, "the army cannot have its own flag;" the army exists to win wars and contain wars, and combat effectiveness must be steadily improved. This simple and straightforward philosophy has been revisited

---

21.   "The Sound of China," The Central People's Broadcasting Station, November 4, 2014.

and polished by Xi Jinping after 40 years.

Jin Yinan, a professor at the National Defense University, said to the media that the courage and moral character of the military do not depend on the training and innate talents of officers and soldiers, but on the ambition, pursuit, and spiritual states of senior officers. A leader of the military commission said: "Today's gaps in ability primarily refer to the difference between the cadres, the goal to build a strong army cannot be achieved if these problems cannot be solved."[22]

Former supreme leaders only met cadres more senior than division commanders. However, Xi Jinping often meets regiment cadres in his inspections of infantry platoons, so that lower-ranking officers can have an intuitive understanding of the thinking and determination of the Central Military Committee.

Since the close of the 18th National Congress until the end of 2014, Xi Jinping held talks with 90 newly promoted cadres more senior than the corps on five occasions in the Qinzheng Palace of Zhongnanhai and the Bayi Building. Before that, the chairman of the Central Military Commission talked to promoted cadres more senior than the deputies of large military regions. Xinhua News Agency reports that the face-to-face communications allow these generals to have in-depth understanding of the important army-building initiatives of Chairman Xi Jinping, and feel pride in the close attention of the commander in chief.[23] On Army Day in 2013, six PLA senior officers were promoted to the rank of general by Xi Jinping. At the same time, the largest personnel changes at the highest levels of the People's Liberation Army in the past ten years had been implemented, and more than 20 major military generals are in place. This is seen as the signal that the new Military Commission chairman has truly asserted his control. Hong Kong's *South China Morning Post* asserted: "Xi Jinping is becoming an influential PLA commander in chief."

This round of adjustments had been prepared long before the opening of the 18th National Congress, and the newly promoted generals belonged to the older generation, those aged beyond 50 years. Many of them had joined the army when they were young, such as Air Force Commander Ma Xiaotian, the Commander of Lanzhou Military Region Liu Yuejun, and Commander of Jinan Military Region Zhao Zongqi. Many people started at the level of the infantry, eventually led troops, and several had fought in the

---

22.   "The Duties of Chinese Soldiers," *Global People*, February 2014.

23.   "The Lifeline Is Shining in the Great Journey to Build a Strong Army—Documentary of Chairman Xi Jinping, the Central Military Commission Leader," and "Advancing the Army's Political Work under the New Conditions," *Xinhua News Agency; People's Liberation Army Daily*, Nov. 3, 2014.

Sino-Vietnamese war and earned commendations.

For example, Lieutenant General Liu Yuejun fought on the Fakashan battlefield as the company commander and earned a second-class merit; Lieutenant General Zhao Zongqi was a reconnaissance section chief, and he often disguised himself as a Vietnamese soldier and slipped into the enemy camp to gather information; the Chengdu military region commander, Lieutenant General Li Zuocheng, suffered multiple injuries in battle, but he insisted on fighting on the front lines, leading the officers and soldiers of his entire company in combat with the enemy for 26 days and nights.

These senior generals also appeared more open and more characteristic of a new wave of military leaders.

On the evening of April 29, 2015, China's Navy Admiral Wu Shengli and the United States Chief of Naval Operations Admiral Jonathan Greenert talked via a video call. The background behind their talk concerned US wariness of construction in the South China Sea reef initiated by China. Wu directly criticized the close reconnaissance of an American helicopter near China, and ensured that construction in the Nansha Islands area would not threaten navigation nor free over-flight in the South China Sea—it would improve the capabilities of beneficial activities in the area such as meteorological forecasting, marine salvage, and fulfilling the international obligation to maintain the security of international waters. He welcomed international organizations, the United States, and other concerned countries to use these facilities when they are ready in the future, and carry out humanitarian cooperation in disaster relief and rescue. Such straightforward and clear talk on this sensitive issue of the South China Sea was tactful and sincere.

Before the end of February, 2014, the People's Liberation Army completed another reassignment of senior generals, and more than 30 deputy military generals assumed new posts, including six promoted from army commander and political commissar, two from the southern Xinjiang military region and Yunnan military region. The two regions have always been the border positions with a heavier duty to maintain stability in recent years.

The two personnel arrangements covering the important army posts highlighted Xi Jinping's thoughts on military governing and selecting talent: Some of these people have rich grassroots experience, some are army chiefs who led troops on the front lines, some are scientific and technological talents engaged in research and development of cutting-edge weaponry and equipment. Critics have claimed that this move conformed to the idea he had stressed several times: "to insist on promoting military preparations according to the standards of wartime." At the same time, it has become a trend to promote across divisions and services, the intention to upgrade the army and strengthen the integration of multi-service cooperative combat is quite clear.

The Central Military Commission led by Xi Jinping is trying to guide officers to rid themselves of their dependence on professional networks and relationships, base their achievements on moral character and talent, and give preference to appointing officer candidates from the grassroots level, and to the strongest recruits. Starting in April 2013, the Central Military Commission focused on an examination to the leadership above corps commander in the army and armed police force, an examination personally decided upon and arranged by Xi Jinping, for nine months. Official media described this examination as having a "wide range, high standards, and a deep level," and thought it reflected a determination to correct the conduct of the officials hiring and appointing posts. At the same time, disadvantages of cadre appointments were purged from the army, violations of promotion and of the emigration of spouses and children abroad were checked, and all cadre archives were cleaned up.

Xi Jinping also personally approved the planning of deepening the reform of the military cadre system. The assessment of cadres, reserve cadres, qualifications, secretary management, the evasion of duties, and other matters and regulations were gradually finalized. One example is that the requirements to assume the post of the secretary to a senior officer are more stringent. The "airborne" units will face severe tests, and people promoted from the grassroots level will be favored.

According to the official media reports, Xi Jinping, as chairman of the Military Commission, took up many matters personally. He led and authored *The Decision on Several Problems about the Army Political Work under the New Conditions*; personally approved plans to mobilize 40,000 troops for the "Mission Action 2013" inter-district training exercises and put forth clear requirements. He personally approved the Central Military Commission to hold theoretical study seminars for senior cadres, and determined the trainees, and devoted attention to teaching arrangements as well. He personally reviewed the prepared speeches of Central Military Commission members and talked heart-to-heart with them in preparation.

The year 2014 was very critical for Chairman of the Central Military Commission Xi Jinping. On February 20, Xi Jinping's important *Selected Statements on National Defense and Army Building* was published, approved by the Central Military Commission and issued to cadres above regimental commander. Three days later, a senior cadre seminar based on the spirit of Chairman Xi Jinping's speech was opened at the National Defense University; there were three consecutive periods and sixteen days for each of them.

This seminar was thoroughly determined by Xi Jinping, from solutions to participants.

Xi Jinping's idea on the governance and strengthening of the military have been compiled as teaching materials, which were disseminated by thousands of cadres above regimental commander into the grassroots infantry units so that they could take root. In early April, the People's Liberation Army newspaper published the speeches of 35 senior generals at the senior cadre seminar—an unprecedented move. In the speeches, they clearly expressed their support for and loyalty to Chairman Xi Jinping. It is said that this was the first time such a large section of senior generals made a declaration to support the chairman of the Military Commission since Deng Xiaoping returned in the late 1970s.

In December, similar scenes recurred. After the 4th Plenary Session of the 18th Communist Party of China Central Committee, 37 generals above the military area command published articles in *Chinese Military* magazine in a strong array to support the notion of "governing the country and the army in accordance with the law" put forth by Xi Jinping.

The chief of the General Staff stated that he would "resolutely implement the accountability system of the chairman of Central Military Commission" and "ensure the smooth implementation of the governmental decree and military order." The director of the General Political Department said, "The party's absolute leadership over the armed forces is not only the highest political demand, but the insurmountable legal bottom line." The minister of the General Logistics Department said he would "resolutely safeguard the authority of the Central Committee, Central Military Commission, and Chairman Xi Jinping."

A professor from the National Defense University described it as "the year to make rules, the year to follow rules." He thought the accountability system of the chairman of the Central Military Commission had been continuously strengthened, a rare quality execution in the army had been demonstrated, the entire army was transforming the focus toward the improvement of discipline and battle effectiveness.[24] The notion that "the Party commands the gun" has been epitomized in the era of Xi Jinping.

---

24.   Gong Fang Bin. "Xi Jinping Stimulates Frontline Soldiers' Confidence by Governing the Army with an Iron Hand," *People's Daily Online*, March 4, 2015.

III. WEALTH MUST BE SHARED FOR COMBAT EFFECTIVENESS

Soldiers Will Not Work for Corrupt Officials; Corrupt Officials Will Not Die for their Country

On December 5, 2012, Xi Jinping, who had only served as the chairman of the Central Military Commission for a mere twenty days, went to inspect the second artillery installation, about 20 kilometers from Zhongnanhai, located in the center of Beijing, to a destination in the northern suburbs. He specifically told officials not to close off traffic, although they would pass through a number of potential traffic jams. He had said in a meeting of the Central Political Bureau: "It is worth spending a few more minutes to win the people's support!"

As commander in chief of the armed forces of the world's second-largest economy, Xi Jinping placed his emphasis first on frugality. Although some voices outside China have described Chinese troops, with their freshly upgraded equipment, as "*nouveau riche*," Xi is well aware that money is not equivalent to fighting capacity.

Deng Xiaoping used the words "overstaffed, loosely disciplined, arrogant, extravagant, and idle" to sum up the problems that existed in the People's Liberation Army. After more than 30 years, these are still problems that Xi Jinping has to face in military governing, and the severity of some problems have even increased by several magnitudes. In early March, 2015, the military authorities released the news that fourteen senior officers had been investigated for corruption. In the middle of January, the military publicized the corruption cases of sixteen cadres above the rank of army commander, including Xu Caihou, the former deputy chairman of the Central Military Commission, and Guo Zhenggang, the son of the former Deputy Chairman of the Central Military Commission Guo BoXiong. The administrative system and logistics system became the worst-hit areas.

Previously, Vice Minister of the General Logistics Department Gu JunShan, was publicly found guilty of corruption charges involving RMB 20 billion. It was heard in court that he would bribe officials by filling up a Mercedes with gold bars and simply handing over the keys. In the past, such corruption cases involving the military were kept secret by the Chinese government, but the rumors were never completely silenced.

Commissar of the General Logistics Department Liu Yuan, described the corruption of Xu Caihou and Gu Junshan as "embezzling military funds, selling military property, accumulating wealth in a crazy way, selling official appointments." He told the media the self-reform of the army forces in all countries was normally conducted internally and confidentially. But now, in response to public concern, the corruption of some senior army cadres was publicized immediately. Such secrecy would continue in other countries, but now a precedent was set for the Chinese army to become the most transparent in the world.[25]

Liu Yuan is the son of former Chinese President Liu Shaoqi, also one of a handful of the second generation of the Communist Party of China who chose to leave Beijing along with Xi Jinping in the early 1980s. After he took office at the General Logistics Department, he pushed for the investigation of Gu Junshan and other military corruption cases, and told colleagues that he would rather "die than let corruption continue unchecked" in a speech made internally. Liu Yuan said anti-corruption measures were actively driven by the army under great pressure, and also strictly implemented within the system. The cases of Xu Caihou and Gu Junshan were decided, supervised and handled by Xi Jinping in person: "The army will not be saved without the courage, boldness, and sense of responsibility of Chairman Xi Jinping!" he declared.[26]

It has been said that only one thing in the world can overcome the strength of the Chinese military—and that is corruption.

The corruption of the PLA has been carried out for many years. In the early 1950s, Mao Zedong was required to "catch tigers" in the military, and he demanded the axing of the Zhongnanhai art team, and slashed the numbers of the art ensemble and sports teams so as to contain the trend of extravagance. In 1975, Deng Xiaoping called out the army as "a bit extravagant," claiming it was too focused on enjoyment, unable to make a clear distinction between the public and the private, giving feasts, receiving gifts, seizing property from the local people at random, or buying at unfairly low prices, establishing farms and businesses, and spending money without control.

The PLA discipline inspection commission was established in January 1980. Around 174 corruption cases were detected in the entire army in 1982 and 1983, involving smuggling, bribery, embezzlement, illegal enterprises, tax evasion, and other offenses. In the middle and late 1980s, army business increased the corruption level. The finances were concentrated on the development of the country's economy at that time, the military disbursement was not enough, the army experienced more than ten years of enduring these conditions, and from the mid-1980s to the late 1990s, they developed

---

25.   Liu Yuan. "The Army's Anti-Corruption System Is Advancing Step by Step," *People's Daily Online*, March 13, 2015.
26.   Ibid.

and ran factories, established mines, and set up companies to supplement the gap of budget funding. The rapid expansion of the military's commercial interests had grown into a huge network, involving thousands of loosely connected enterprises and companies, hotels, nightclubs, karaoke bars, and golf courses, airlines, pharmaceutical companies, mobile phone networks, cosmetics, stock brokerages, and electronics companies.[27] According to the statistics of a Hong Kong expert, more than 15,000 enterprises had military background, and the sales might have reached as much as RMB 150 billion.[28]

Some military enterprises were also involved in smuggling activities, and caused losses of about USD 12 billion to USD 25 billion to China every year. In some cities, companies run by the police sold illegal satellite receiving antennas.[29] Business benefits were quickly obscured by this negative influence—and this not only caused violations of law, corruption, and logistical chaos, it also eroded the combat effectiveness of the army.

As the saying goes, "the army must eat 'imperial rations.'" Almost the entire Chinese army had withdrawn businesses under strong consolidation by the end of 1998. But the detour of army business still had influence, and new forms of corruption appeared with the rapid development of the economy. For example, in the infrastructure and barracks area of the General Logistics Department, the three senior generals who came under investigation were responsible for the construction of army barracks, including housing, manufacturing facilities, and libraries. They were in charge of the approval of all military lands and construction projects. They also had the rights to allocate tens of billions worth of capital in the process of monetizing military housing. At the same time, the army has a huge stock of land assets, and a lot of military land located in the prime areas of the city were sold. The benefits were enormous. Another feature of the army corruption case was sectarianism. Personal attachments are easier to be had due to a vertical management system, excessive discretion rights of individual leaders, lack of objective oversight, as well as the feelings of shared fates that bond soldiers.

Military corruption means failure in wartime, Xi Jinping said bluntly.

A military expert explains that the strong anti-corruption measures implemented in the army after the appointment of Xi Jinping were designed to boost morale and improve battle effectiveness. "Soldiers won't fight for corrupt officials, corrupt officials will not die for their country, military expenditures will not be used to buy equipment, and there is a lack of

27.   Kuhn, Robert Lawrence. *He Changed China: Biography of Jiang Zemin*, Shanghai Translation Publishing House, 2005.

28.   "Speed up Anti-Corruption in the Army," *VISTA*, Issue 3, 2015.

29.   Kuhn, Robert Lawrence. *He Changed China: Biography of Jiang Zemin*, Shanghai Translation Publishing House, 2005.

urgently needed equipment. How can such an army win victory?"[30]

The People's Liberation Army newspaper disclosed that cases of fraud transferred by the audit department of the army forces in 2014 were more than the entire sum of the past 30 years. Full oversight, zero tolerance— Xi Jinping holds the same attitude of anti-corruption toward the army and local Party officials, even demanding that the army take the lead. He doesn't mind the expression that "anti-corruption will cause havoc in the army," or "anti-corruption will destroy the Party," but places more emphasis on the standardization, normalization, and long-lasting benefits of anti-corruption measures.

In late October, 2013, the army formally established a patrol system, set up a patrol agency, and focused on supervision of the top party committee group and its members, especially the main leadership. The patrol system was originally started up in China's Han Dynasty 2,100 years ago, when the emperor sent a team solely responsible for the central institution, which always grasped the power dynamics of governors. This way of supervision is known to be a powerful supplement to the insufficient supervision within the Chinese Communist Party. After years of trials, this "anti-corruption weapon" was introduced to the army for the first time, the inspection of seven major military regions had been completed by the end of 2014, and a lot of important evidence had been unearthed.

In November 2014, the People's Liberation Army audit office, affiliated with the General Logistics Department, was led by the Central Military Commission, which is primarily in charge of the audit work of the entire army. The locality can emphasize supervisory relationships, and the military can emphasize the unification of military authority and leadership. This determines that anti-corruption measures in the army can't be carried out through power dissolution and power restriction. The change of the PLA audit office is regarded as a way to adapt to the characteristics of the military's surveillance.

In December, 2014, the People's Liberation Army newspaper commented that anti-corruption initiatives amounted to a "life-or-death battle that we can't afford to lose." Answering questions of doubt regarding "will the public feeling be broken up to go on with anti-corruption" and "can [the popularity and persistence of such initiatives] be continued?" the commentary asserted that it was a critical moment: "Corruption and anti-corruption are in deadlock." It stated bluntly: "Who can't be removed? Even the 'big tigers' like Zhou Yongkang and Xu Caihou have been removed."

---

30.   "'Catching Tigers' in the Army," *Global People*, Issue 3, 2015.

Senior Officers Equipped With Private Ranks

On December 24, 2012, the liquor stocks in the Chinese stock exchange fell greatly, and stocks in the renowned wine Guizhou Maotai fell by 5.55 percent. This may have been connected to the fact that, days before, the Central Military Commission had issued ten rules on strengthening the constitution of the army. One of them stated "no banqueting, no drinking, no gourmet meals."

Although there was a lot of satisfaction with this provision, because it meant fewer and shorter meetings, strict control of the use of police cars, no troop formations for meetings, no welcome mats, no special art performances, no souvenirs, and special local products, and no more accommodations in local hotels, this rule led by the Central Military Commission and followed by the entire army to rectify discipline was called "prohibition" by the public.

This is because alcohol has deep connections with the army. In accordance with the Chinese practice of ancient times, before soldiers fight the enemy, they must drink to boost their confidence and drink to celebrate in triumph. But in peacetime, lethal battles are rare, and drinking sometimes becomes a way to match wills, and is even distorted to be a litmus test to measure loyalty and courage. "How can you lead a unit to fight if you cannot even drink?" This sentence is widely recognized in the army. Army units have also been big liquor consumers, some high-grade liquor brands even began as custom products for troops. Thus the market's reaction was swift as soon as the prohibition was issued.

Seventeen days before the issuance of the prohibition, the Political Bureau of the CPC Central Committee issued eight rules for improvement, the ten rules made by the Central Military Commission followed up the previous measures of the central government with a more strict scale, more detailed regulations, and deeper implementation. Investigators looked for evidence in restaurants near army headquarters, even set up surveillance teams to keep an eye on soldiers and military vehicles; alcohol testing instruments were installed at the gates of some military camps, and drinkers were immediately impounded. As a matter of fact, the prohibition is only form of theater; the key motive is to strengthen military discipline, reviving the fine tradition of strict management of the army and military orders is imperative.

Official media summed up the extravagances of the army as "waste on the tip of the tongue," "corruption on wheels," "entertainment at the table," "the unhealthy practices seemed impossible to be stopped in the past," and the "persistent problems" have been accumulated for many years.[31] These

---

31.   "The Lifeline Is Shining in the Great Journey to Build a Strong Army—Documen-

extravagant habits inevitably permeated the military culture, and have had enormous influence on mid- and low level officers and soldiers whose appointments and promotions were susceptible; at the same time, serious misuse of limited military spending harmed the morales of officers and soldiers.

Before the China-Japan war, the advanced armored fleet of the Qing Dynasty navy visited Japan, and the Japanese made an accurate judgment on their fighting capacity from their idle and corrupt manner, and ultimately buried this army like sand at the bottom of the sea.

Xi Jinping harshly criticized the army, demanding of them: Do you feel comfortable getting drunk all day? The new commander in chief set an example by personally taking part in army activities and the Central Military Commission implemented all measures in full, and the long-standing alcoholic culture was soon weakened and has since collapsed. At the reception dinners of many divisions, teacups replaced bar glasses and home cooking replaced restaurant dishes. Official receptions are uniformly held in guest-houses for accommodation without banquets, liquor, fruit, and flowers. The results of medical examinations of an armored division showed that fatty liver disease, high cholesterol, high blood pressure, and other physical symptoms have been visibly reduced.

After the implementation of the ten rules, in the first quarter of 2014, the PLA administrative consumptive expenditure and official reception expenses were significantly reduced, and the use of ammunition, grenades and motorcycle hours have been significantly increased.

The air force is the big unit where the "prohibition" was first promulgated, and implemented early in 2008. "Alcohol should be strictly prohibited in an army with advanced technology and systems. Only in this way, can they operate valuable precision instruments, and carry out the most dangerous and complex combat missions," said Ren Yufei, the political commissar of one air force communications regiment. "It seems a small thing to prohibit alcohol in the army, but it means the Chinese army is transforming to higher standards across the forces."[32]

After the alcohol prohibition in the army and air force, the focus fell on their fleets of military vehicles. On May 1, 2013, the military license plates of the PLA were replaced by updated versions, and it was forbidden to use

---

tary of Chairman Xi Jinping, the Central Military Commission Leader," and "Advancing the Army's Political Work under the New Conditions," *Xinhua News Agency; Liberation Army Daily*, November 3, 2014.

32.   "The Completion of 'CMC Prohibition' for One Month," *The People's Daily*, January 27, 2013.

high-end luxury vehicles and private vehicles. Over the years, the privileged vehicles with military plates had a negative effect on the image of the army. Generals favored imported luxury sports-utility vehicles, and did not obey traffic rules; the emergency lanes on the loop of Beijing were even nicknamed "Bayi Road" by some military sources. Some non-military personnel even got military plates through their personal or professional networks and were proud to have the privilege. The friction between aggressive military vehicles and citizens was palpable.

This time, the issue of new military plates was reduced by more than 25,000. This was just the beginning of strict management on military vehicles. It is said that the plates of many generals on active duty and retired generals have been withdrawn for their vehicles, which were outside regulations and had to be parked in a garage. The use of military vehicles has also been tightened, with thorough checks on procedure, reason for travel, distance, and fuel consumption, and the private use of government vehicles is under strict control. In Beijing, special cameras have been established in the shopping centers, park attractions, and other places that have no obvious relation to military duties to investigate vehicles with military plates. By the end of 2013, the private and business vehicles registered to the PLA had been reduced by more than 29,000.

Legal Standards for Military Violation of Duty were jointly issued by the Supreme People's Procuratorate and the General Political Department and known colloquially as "40 Military Rules," which made detailed standards on crimes such as defection, negligently leaking military secrets, and maltreating subordinates. The rule of law has been involved since the beginning of military discipline reform.

At the annual sessions of the NPC and CPPCC in March, 2013, the changes in the PLA delegation were obvious: The entourages of army representatives were reduced, vehicle use was reduced, purely social engagements were reduced, and courting of visitors was reduced. The rectification of the Party advanced by Xi Jinping has received a fast and strong response in the army.

Where Will Senior Military Officers Go?

Another regulation, which came into force in April, 2015, states that officers and government cadres above regiment level are required to serve as soldiers in their companies; units at the division (brigade) level should arrange at least one time visit and inspect their companies each quarter, once every six months for division units, once a year for headquarters, and for higher units of military level for no less than fifteen days each time. It is required that they be equipped with the private ranks to serve as soldiers, live among the squad to help lead troops, and "dissection" of research is also necessary. This move was personally devised and promoted by Xi Jinping. He said, "Do what a real soldier does, experience the real life in the company, and develop a better style of work." According to the regulations, the staff who go down to the company to serve as soldiers should take their personal supplies and pay for their meals under the corresponding criteria of their troops. They are not allowed to receive banquets, travel stipends, and gifts. People immediately recalled the similar measures Mao Zedong had advocated in 1958. At that time, Mao Zedong said the military cadres at various levels should go to the company to serve as soldiers for one month each year.

In the Mao Zedong era, most of the PLA generals started out as soldiers, and the commanders were very close to the ordinary soldiers. In times of peace, however, many officers become complacent, easily gained promotion, and didn't have an understanding of their frontline officers and men, allowing a gap to emerge. It is the magic weapon of the PLA to unite officers and soldiers, when the generals of the Red Army were caught by the enemy in rags, and the color of their straw sandals had faded, they were as austere as soldiers, and there was only one bowl's worth of rice in their pockets. Now, however, the leading bodies at all levels have a shallow relationship with the grassroots infantry officers and soldiers.

The new session of the Central Military Commission arranges cadres to go down to the company not only to restore the fine traditions of the army, but take it as an act to realize the goal of strengthening the army and essential fighting units in a way that the Party can emphasize close ties with the masses.[33] In 2013, more than 820 cadres above army commander, and more than 56,000 cadres above regiment level, went down to the company level and served as soldiers. In 2014, over 86,000 cadres above the regiment level were equipped with a private rank. Senior officers remarked: "We can truly know how to love soldiers and lead them by eating with them often, sleeping on the beds they use, smelling their sweat, and listening to their complaints."[34]

Check Property, and No Offenders Can Flee

Another aspect of today's crackdown on corruption in the military involves "checking people" and "checking real estate," while vehicles that are against regulations are simultaneously under investigation.

---

33.   "Xi Jinping Rectify Military Discipline with Power," *Decision*, Issue 8, 2013.

34.   "Documentary of Promoting National Defense and Army Building under the Leadership of the CPC Central Committee Led by General Secretary Xi Jinping," *People's Daily*, December 28, 2013.

"Checking people" refers to checking numbers of secretaries or service personnel allocated to some leading cadres, numbers in excess of the prescribed standard; the task was finished quickly and the secretaries that military cadres actually used had been retained at the end of 2013.

But to clear up illegal housing is a difficult task lasting many years. In the 1970s, Deng Xiaoping criticized the attitudes of some senior officers, who believed "the bigger the house, the better it must be." The central government issued provisions on the lifelong treatment of senior cadres in 1979; each senior cadre was required to have only one "dormitory" allotted, and no one could take up two places at the same time. From the early 1990s until now, the controversial housing allocation battle has lasted for more than 20 years, but the effect has not been entirely good. On the one hand, a senior officer may have housing in different locations for long-distance transfer; on the other hand, housing prices in developed cities in China are very high, and after some officers left the army, they could not afford to move. In fact, many were reluctant to move out of army family housing. Of course, some cadres have multiple military residences after leaving the army; at the same time, the housing of some retired cadres is outside of regulations, or not returned to the government after death in accordance with provisions, but instead occupied by a family member or even sold or rented.

The military invests billions into the construction of affordable military housing and dormitories. However, in some cases, the military family areas are occupied by strangers, and the new cadres in active service have to stay in a long waiting list for housing allocations. This problem is very common in the entire army and seriously injures morale, particularly among young officers. Xi Jinping's housing clear-up mainly targeted retired cadres and demobilized officers, but it had the impact of a typhoon, especially in real estate.

In June 2013, a census of basic construction projects and real estate resources was implemented by the Minister of the General Logistics Department, Zhao Keshi, and was aimed at getting the true data. The military leadership listened to reports on clearing up illegal housing, and they emphasized they would proceed with powerful measures. The state media reported more than 27,000 cases of illegal housing had been cleared up in the entire army by the end of 2013. But this is obviously far from enough and represents only the tip of the iceberg.

The report, publicity and verification system of military personnel housing was issued in June 2014, and the penalties have been significantly increased. For instance, anyone involved in covering-up, falsification, and refusal to return illegal housing would be given Party disciplinary and military disciplinary punishments; the in-service cadres with illegal housing will not be promoted; and it is clarified that "compulsory measures could be taken when necessary" in the course of clearing up illegal housing. The new measures were allegedly approved by Xi Jinping.

Compared with the past, the scope measures addressing the housing issue was expanded, first being directed at the senior military officers in active service. Cadres above army commander had housing in multiple places because of official relocations. For example, a senior officer was transferred to another place without promotion, but the original forces would not take back the property, just to spare his feelings. In fact, illegal housing is possible to find and trace. Personal information on affordable houses and apartments have been available on the Internet, relevant data are stored in military security cards, and all the changes are very clear.

The officers in charge of the housing purge will go to the district housing agency with the ID numbers of officers and their families to sort it out and check the property registrations. High-level investigations also repeatedly emphasized that they would clamp down on cover-ups, falsification, and other problems. In mid-May, 2014, the PLA newspaper provided an example from the Baoding military sub-area in Hebei Province in an article entitled "Do Not [Be] Afraid of Pain for the Sake of Real Change."

Courtyard No. 100 is located in the center of Baoding city. It is the new courtyard of the Baoding military sub-area, and cadres in active service and retired veteran cadres, including some local cadres, are each allocated one house. Both Commander Jiang Yongliang and Director of the Political Department, Li Dazhong got a house of 165 square meters, and each of them bought a small house at their own cost. The military officers and men greatly objected to the disorderly and unfair housing distribution. In this military disciplinary rectification, the Party committee of the sub-area took the lead to redistribute unreasonable housing. Jiang Yongliang and Li Dazhong could only live in apartments, according to the rules, because they worked in different grounds. They took the initiative to return the big house distributed by the military sub-area and the small house they bought by themselves, and both had spent nearly RMB 100,000 on renovation. They moved to the guest-houses after the houses were returned. Indeed, they said they felt uncomfortable, but leaders must take the lead to correct illegal acts.[35]

Officers in active service acted quickly in consideration of the future, but it is hard to deal with the retired cadres and demobilized officers. According to public opinion, many demobilized cadres posted to complain that the link

---

35.   "Do Not [Be] Afraid of Pain for the Sake of Real Change," *Liberation Army Daily*, May 15, 2014.

with the security system was not smooth, and they found themselves in deep trouble due to the clearing-up of housing corruption.

However, new initiatives are being enforced without the slightest hesitation. It was regulated that a military house could be cleared up only after a subsidized house was provided, but new rules show that the military apartments must be returned as long as an officer already possesses housing in the area. In July 2014, the four general headquarters, military commissions, and a disciplinary inspection commission, jointly issued a circular which required further clearing-up of the illegal housing and vehicles of retired cadres: "The clearing-up must be completed without any slips." It confirmed the existence of strong resistance. This circular provided that a family in the same city could only have one apartment no greater than the rank standards; if the total area of more than two houses exceeded the rank standards, it should be returned or adjusted. In particular, a widow and children with housing must return army property.

For those who refuse to return houses, the military will charge rent according to the highest price in the market, and directly deduct the rent from the military salary by the financial department; at the same time all kinds of service pensions and welfare will also be suspended. If the widow and children refuse to return the house, the military will report to the unit of the person concerned, and administrative or legal measures should be taken when it is necessary.

A colonel defending the southeast coastal line said that most illegal occupiers of military housing were the children or relatives of retired or demobilized cadres. On the second-hand house market or related websites, you can often see advertising for a "military house for sale or rent."[36] In 2014, the Nanjing military region has issued special documents declaring that unreasonable or illegal housing occupied by the Party authorities above army commanders must be 100-percent returned before the end of that June.

It is extremely hard to clean up unreasonable housing in the subordinated Zhejing military region—it is the most economically developed area in China, urban property prices are high, and the employment of relocated cadres is difficult. In a base of the South China Sea fleet located in the resort of Sanya, Hainan, there is even forcibly occupied housing, high-rent housing units, and so-called "migratory bird houses for summer living." Measures such as exposure, and shut-downs of water and electricity were taken by the logistics department of this base against 48 households who refused to move after repeated requests and instruction; the demobilized cadres who did not

---

36.   "Great Housecleaning in Chinese Army," *Southern Weekend*, August 14, 2014.

want to return would be reported to their units and the higher commission for disciplinary inspection so as to get local support; there is even live video footage showing that the offenders' articles were packed for storage, and they were forced to return property in accordance with the law.[37] Ink was sprinkled over the door of the staff or trash was thrown in front of the door when the confrontation was fierce. Some "anti-movers" even lay obstinately in the staff's doorstep with a bedroll.[38]

The media also reported support from retired veteran cadres, such as the widow of an air force founding vice admiral and the widow of a former deputy commander who chose to move out of the government courtyard where they have lived for decades.

Initiatives to clean up illegal housing are not as thrilling as anti-corruption measures, but they have long-term significance in the rectification of military discipline, with wide-ranging impacts. A succession of policies and systems have sent a clear signal to the army: Anti-corruption measures at the highest levels are not merely "gusts of wind" or "publicity campaigns." China should not only purge exploitative people, but also purify its soil, send a warning to the entire army that corruption will not be tolerated under any circumstances.

In fact, the housing problem is one of the typical issues when reform in the army is not harmonious with societal developments. It is seen as the source of dispute that military housing property rights are not clear. Allegedly, the PLA is gradually implementing affordable housing, housing reform, and other preferential policies, enabling residents to obtain property if certain conditions can be met.

Money Is Not Necessarily Equivalent to Combat Effectiveness

Since 2000, the Pentagon has published a "China Military Report" every year regardless of the protests of the Chinese government, and "military expenditure" has always been one of the big issues. The military spending of the United States ranks highest in the world, its sum is equal to the total of more than ten countries after it, but it is still very keen to speculate on the military capacity of the PLA. On a visit to Germany in March, 2014, Xi Jinping said that China's defense budget conformed to the normal needs of national defense for a world power. China would never follow in the footsteps of superpowers seeking hegemony, but also, it cannot repeat the historic tragedy of being enslaved by colonial powers after the opium war.

---

37.   "Return 231 Illegal Houses with an 'Iron Hand,'" *People's Daily*, November 17, 2014.
38.   "Great Housecleaning in Chinese Army," *Southern Weekend*, August 14, 2014.

China must have enough force for self-defense.

China's military spending was less than RMB 810 billion in 2014. The figure is likely to get close to RMB 890 billion in 2015, a sum that has almost quadrupled compared with that of 2005, just ten years ago. But after 2010, the share of China's military spending in GDP always floated closely around 1.3 percent, the proportion was not only far lower than the 4 percent of the United States and Russia, but also lower than the 2 percent of most western countries, only slightly higher than Japan's 1 percent.

Per capita military spending levels were much lower. According to the data of 2014, it was about USD 57,000 per capita in China. The per capita spending of Japanese self-defense force was USD 210,000, and the United States reached as much as USD 430,000. Even this defensive troop reversed the trend of share decline in GDP after 1998, but a lot of money is still used to compensate debt in the "endurance period," and improve the basic living conditions of 2.3 million people. The military spending is divided into three parts: Living expenses, training expenses and equipment costs. However, when the army reform is increasingly urgent, the effective use of military spending becomes a key issue.

At the annual sessions of the NPC and CPPCC in March, 2013, when Xi Jinping communicated with the PLA delegation, he said the military spending should be well managed and effectively used so that it could be of the greatest benefit in national defense investment. This was regarded as an important reminder by military sources—it's not only based on the need of anti-corruption measures and strict discipline, but the need to improve management beyond a simple emphasis on frugality, just like the Chinese have often said, "use the best material at the key point."

Professor Jin Yinan of the National Defense University mentioned that there was a popular sentence in the army: "Money is a basket, anything can be put in it." If people questioned the battlefield effectiveness of the PLA, claiming it was not high, we could say that the army had no money, and the equipment allocations were affected; if people questioned the quality of the PLA, we could say the troops have no money, and that the military cannot acquire and retain key talents.

Deng Xaoping had a wish: "When the gross national product (GNP) reaches USD 1 trillion, we are able to invest USD 10 billion in the construction of national defense to improve the army's combat effectiveness." Now, our military spending is more than ten times the amount that Deng Xiaoping desired. We can never take a lack of funding as an excuse. Adequate funding is the driving force for the development of the army, and it is also a pressure point. If we cannot build combat effectiveness corresponding to the investment, how are we going to report to the central government and the common people?[39]

The whole army started a financial inventory in February, 2015, and plans to carry out a comprehensive inventory on revenue and expenditure management in 2013 and 2014, focusing on the rectification of long-standing financial violations, such as misrepresentation or false claims of funds, falsified invoices, spending transfers, private coffers, and other abuses. This has made a lot of people feel restless—some investigations are likely to reach a high-tension threshold if we check back as few as two years.

This inventory was the first "big move" by the audit office of the PLA after it was upgraded to the membership of the Central Military Commission. Since the 18th National Congress of the Communist Party of China, at least thirteen military spending supervision regulations have been issued by the army, the official reception, meeting training, account fund, approvals for reimbursement, and so on, are systematized, and the intensify of financial auditing has been strengthened. For example, in early December, 2014, the General Logistics Department set standards for the administrative expenses of units lower than army commander. The content is very specific: Desktop computers must cost less than RMB 4000, notebook computers less than RMB 6000, fax machines less than RMB 2000, and projectors less than RMB 2000, among other regulations. At the same time, as the budget system reform is implemented inside the army, the economic responsibility audits of the heads of divisions and regiments are strengthened.

In fact, as the governmental budget system reform has encountered heavy resistance in recent years, it will be more difficult to implement the reform in the army, which always pays attention to confidentiality and has a style all its own. The leaders of the four headquarters of the PLA made public commitments to manage well their spouses, children, and office staff ,who would not interfere with engineering, construction, materials procurement, and other matters. The People's Liberation Army newspaper reported in January, 2015, that more than 4,000 military officers above the regiment level were audited in the last two years, 61 people were deemed incompetent in accordance with the law due to their poor performance in economic responsibility, and 21 people were removed from office.

The military should start with savings in order to manage its funds. At the end of February, 2013, Xi Jinping signed and issued the *Rules on Practicing Strict Economy and Strengthening Fund Management*, which focused on specifying "what money can be taken, what money cannot be taken." It emphasized the priority of military combat preparedness, information

---

39.   "The Duties of Chinese Soldiers," *Global People*, February 2014.

security, construction of new and advanced-technology weapons and equipment, on-the-ground combat training, and more. Control on military infrastructure investment, centralized purchasing, conference receptions, memorial ceremonies, as well as overseas travel at public expense, self-purchasing of vehicles has been severely strengthened.

The Army will also implement military performance management, examining the actual effectiveness of military spending, rather than the profit of enterprises. To make a scientific determination on consumption standards, the General Logistics Department extended the scope of data collection to the units above the regiment level in the entire army. Military personnel say military spending should be invested to improve combat effectiveness, and that non-combat expenditures should be cut. The core mission of the army is "to fight, and to win." China can focus on this mission by, for example, reducing administrative expenses, investing funds in the direction of primary battlefield readiness, the main branches of the service, especially the high-technology sections of the service, such as the navy, air force, and second artillery.

Xi Jinping has an iron fist, but he is patient. He has repeatedly stressed that "where there is a will, there is a way."

However, although the relevant financial management doctrines have been frequently reissued, the achievements on refraining from luxury and reducing expenditures, efficiency improvement, and cultural adjustments have been made, the People's Liberation Army newspaper has continued to report that some large-scale harmful financial problems have still not been solved. "Flexible" implementation standards and unlawful acts such as "running a red light" have happened from time to time, and to act and spend money in accordance with the law has not always been the highest priority.[40]

IV. REFORM IS AN UNAVOIDABLE TEST

In the early summer of 2015, a lot of PLA officers were busy in weight control—the Central Military Commission led by Chairman Xi Jinping not only requires soldiers to be loyal, clean, and compassionate, but also requires them to have a strong body. All officers under the age of 60 should accord with the regulation weight without exception, otherwise they will encounter obstacles in promotion. This is just a minute aspect of the vast reform plans of the Chinese army.

The 88-year-old PLA has been invested heavily in reform. Especially in

40. "Make Efforts to Form a New Normal to Manage Finance and Act in Accordance with the Law," *People's Liberation Army Newspaper*, February 11, 2015.

times of war, when the army was still very weak, the reform had a direct relationship with life and death, so the power was stronger and the pace was quickened. In 1927, when the PLA was founded, a unit with more than 5,000 soldiers was left with less than 1,000 due to the failure of the Autumn Harvest Uprising: "like beans clutched in the hand, they vanish when you lose hold." In the "Sanwan adaptation," led by Mao Zedong, the Chinese Communist Party organization was embedded in companies, a military democracy system was built, and the precious seeds were retained and grew up gradually. The army of the Communist Party of China attaches great importance to reform not only because of its historical opportunities, but also because it pays special attention to the painful lessons of continuously being struck since modern times, and has attributed it to missing the precious opportunity to restructure its military affairs. This was discussed repeatedly in the last two years. For example, the Commissar of the National Defense University, General Liu Yazhou, believes that the old Chinese army had frequent reforms in modern history, but it could not avoid a destiny of decline and fall: "The biggest challenge the Chinese military is facing is not lack of ability to pursue the swelling tide of changes in the external world, but that the speed of decay is faster than the results of innovation. The modern western forces determined outcomes on the battlefield, but the old Chinese army was dead before they went to the battlefield."[41]

In the face of the modern military reform initiated by the western nations, the Chinese people of that time were saddled with mental burdens. "The modern military system first developed by westerners represented the unprecedented development of war violence which had a considerable gap with the military cultural concept held by Chinese people. Chinese people could not easily adjust their own military cultural mentality in a short time."[42] The processing time of a mental burden can be quite long, similar to the wavering attitude of the Chinese people toward modernization. After the People's Liberation Army escaped from the pressures of global war, they lagged behind in instituting reform for decades under a closed political ideology.

Professor Jin Yinan of the National Defense University believes that the change in the PLA was based on equipment before the reform and opening up. Three major shifts of development ideas and army-building dynamics occurred after 1978. The first was the disarmament of millions of armies led by Deng Xiaoping in 1985; the People's Liberation Army changed the combat

41.   Liu Yazhou: "Get out of the China-Japan War, Welcome Reform, Create Brilliance," *Liberation Army Daily*, May 15, 2015.

42.   *The Military Reform in Modern China*, People's Liberation Army Press, 2008, pp. 157–158.

strategy of depending on advantages in numbers of troops to carry out large-scale ground combat, and embarked upon the road to training better soldiers. The second period was from the Gulf War in 1991, until the Chinese embassy in Yugoslavia was bombed in 1999. The military restructuring plan was adjusted toward "winning the local war with a focus on intelligence." The third shift was the army reforms dominated by Xi Jinping after the 18th National Congress of the CPC.

This reform draws lessons from the experiences of foreign military transformations. The goal is to get rid of the disadvantages of outdated technology and systems, and build a modern military power dynamic in conformity with the national and military conditions. Liu Yazhou wrote in his essay that the military revolution with Chinese characteristics has experienced the initial period, a period of vigorously developing weaponry and equipment, and would next enter a crucial period.

Xi Jinping has repeatedly declared that the target of the reform was the long-term accumulation of deep-seated problems—the leadership management system was not scientific enough, the joint operational command system was not sound, the power structure was not reasonable, and policy reform was relatively slow: "You cannot fight and win the war without reform."

Deng Xiaoping reduced the ranks of the PLA from more than 6 million to more than 3 million and believed that we should simplify the army for revolution, and that improvement was entirely unworkable. Xi Jinping will also initiate a revolution. He reiterated the magic weapon of Deng Xiaoping: "emancipation of thoughts," explaining that, "Our bodies have entered the twenty-first century, but our thoughts cannot be left in the twentieth century."[43] He thinks there is a rare opportunity now, the opportunity is fleeting, we can ride it if we can catch it, or we may bypass a whole era if we don't catch on. Consequently, the reform of national defense and the army was written into the decisions of the Central Committee of the Communist Party of China for the first time in the history of the CPC.

The National Security Council, the leading group of the Central Military Commission for deepening the reform of national defense and the army, is a driving force behind the blueprint for security reform. The reform is regarded as the most profound, with the greatest potential benefit. The Chinese army had been committed to developing from mechanization and semi-mechanization to a tandem development of mechanization and intelligence over the past ten years, and will finally shift to an military system

---

43.   *Excerpts of Important Statements by Xi Jinping on Army Strengthening Targets under New Conditions*, PLA Publishing House, 2014, p. 110.

under the condition of information-based warfare. This reform was a radical reshaping, all efforts have been made to address the "pain points" of the Chinese army.

Jin Yinan believes the essence of this reform can be stated as: "all shall listen to the command of the party, consider winning battles as the goal, and enhanced fighting capacity as the fundamental standard," rather than pay attention to the balancing of interests and relationships between departments. This is bound to affect the actual interests of some people and some groups in the army, but we must make a determination to proceed with this thinking.[44]

The first key direction of reform is to adjust the military establishment. The current system "has a heavy head and long tail," huge institutions cannot be efficiently integrated, grassroots units are weak, the new combat strength ratio is not high, and the staffing numbers of non-combat agencies are high. Especially on the last point, the army is more easily exposed in the public eye and has been heavily criticized.

Each military zone, branch of services, and armed police all have their own professional art ensembles; at the same time, a lot of units of the army command or units lower than the army command have art ensembles. Some entertainers in military uniform not only consumed the national defense budget but also earned generous benefits for themselves; many female stars have been involved in corruption cases, which have led to public outrage. There was a time when some military literary groups were keen to recruit entertainers in order to improve public relations. The "recruits" were given high ranks short on true military service, and many soldiers rankings were uneven because of it.

Of course, the professionals are more focused on the fundamentals of the systemic adjustments—how to quickly change the outcome of a land-based battle, succeed in close combat, and national territory defensive military strength in the conditions of a massive ground war, accomplish the military fighting preparation standards issued in the 9th national defense white paper in late May, 2015.

It stands high in popular favor to set up a joint operational command system. The United States, Russia, and other countries are weakening the longitudinal command relations of all branches of military service, and strengthening the transverse command relations, but the Chinese army still has the problem of strong longitudinal relations and weak transverse relations. At the same time, there must be reform of the army structure based on the security requirements and operational tasks in multiple directions,

---

44.　　"The Duties of Chinese Soldiers," *Global People*, February 2014.

and strengthening the development of a new fighting force.

The second key direction of the reform is an adjustment in military policy. The essential goal is to enact the optimal allocation of human, financial, and material resources, especially to focus on strong measures directed at the military human resource policy and procedures. For example, the military professionalization called for a long time may be further promoted. A solution must also be found to the problem of the supporting policies of settlement procedures for civil servants, officers, and veterans. The systemic reform of military medical treatment, insurance, and housing will also be carried out, important areas of military security will be expanded, all of which are related to the vital interests of the military, and maintain a close relationship with the country's economic and social reforms.

The third key direction is the deep development of military and civilian integration. For example, the United States devotes much attention to the utilization of advanced technologies invented by Lockheed Martin and Boeing under market competition. They are used to update military equipment, save resources, and many advanced weapons are the product of excellent military and civilian integration. China will also try to introduce advanced private enterprises into R&D, production, and the ongoing maintenance of military hardware, and encourage the army to absorb the innovative technologies developed by private enterprises.

There are always radical voices when it comes to the reform and development of the PLA. For example, Liu Mingfu, a scholar of the National Defense University, believes that the Chinese army developed from a "revolutionary army" in wartime to a "national defense army" after 1949. In the face of the "final strategic period" between China and the United States today, China should become the most powerful army, in order to guarantee "the great rejuvenation of the Chinese nation and the lasting peace of the world."[45]

These voices mainly come from the new changes of international relations between world powers, and the expansion of national interests, and also reveal an anxiety that military strength is not consistent with economic strength. The most typical criticism is: Money is sufficient to build housing, but insufficient to build an aircraft carrier.

Liu Mingfu quoted a saying of Russian experts: "American leaders are observing China through a gun-sight." He argued that the next ten years would be a "final strategic period" and a "strategic collision period" between China and the United States. During this time, the biggest strategic risk

---

45.   "The 'Army-Strengthening Dream' accompanies the China Dream," *Decision and Information*, Issue 8, 2013.

China will face is not a political or economic risk, but a military risk; it will be extremely difficult for China to take the lead in the military game between China and the United States. There is a consensus achieved by Chinese military and western research institutions: The overall military weaponry and hardware of China fall at least 20 years behind in comparison with those of the United States.

Liu Mingfu said that China's rise in the last 30 years was primarily manifested as an economic success rather than a military triumph. China's "military crisis" means China's military power is not enough to guarantee it can effectively deal with a hypothetical military blockade, military siege, military containment, and even the "containment of war" from the United States. Thus, China must strengthen its army. He described several animals as examples: China neither wants to be a "tiger" as powerful and hegemonic as the United States, nor become a "fat sheep," in pursuit of wealth instead of power, or an "elephant," strong but not hegemonic—we do not invade and seek hegemony, but neither do we accept any provocations. We are able to maintain the safety of our own and our surroundings with sufficient deterrents.

Such an analysis has been partially verified in the 9th national defense white paper. This white paper, entitled *The Military Strategy of China,* is known for its unprecedented transparency, because the transparency of strategic intent is the greatest kind of transparency. The strategic principle of "active defense," determined after the founding of the new China, has been updated for several generations; analysts claim that the "active defense" mentioned today means "defense" in essence, but the main principle is embodied in the word *active.*

The United States and Japan were singled out in the white paper, the former for reinforcing the "military presence and military alliance system" in the Asia Pacific; "the external resistance and challenge" that China faces is growing. The strategic tasks that the Chinese army should accomplish are highlighted as "maintaining a new field of security and interests" and "maintaining the security of overseas interests." The concept of an "overseas interests zone" was put forward for the first time.

The navy emphasized strategic transformation for the first time—from offshore defenses to coastal defenses combined with a high seas guard; to embark toward the deep blue sea will soon become the norm of the Chinese navy, the right to maintain a maritime presence will exist to defend against the provocation of any "individual maritime neighbor" toward China's territorial sovereignty and maritime rights and interests, as well as the close reconnaissance of "individual countries" into the sea and air of China with high frequency.

On August 29, 2014, the Political Bureau of the CPC carried out a collective learning session focused on the new trends in global military development and promoting the military innovation of the Chinese army. Xi Jinping stated that international affairs were at a new turning point, a variety of strategic powers were restructuring for the conditions of the twenty-first century. "This worldwide new military revolution will directly affect the country's military strength and comprehensive national strength, and be related to the greater strategic initiatives."

In his view, deepening the reform of national defense and the military is "a great test that we must undertake…we should realize the opportunity to change boldly and with unwavering determination."

The People's Liberation Army Is Getting Closer to the Real Battlefield

After the end of World War II, control of Japanese sea was the key to the Pacific war. Staff officers of China's military operational sections gathered secretly to hold a "naval reflection meeting" and discussed the reasons for the defeat. The meeting was held once a month, and there were a total of 131 meetings through the eleven years from 1980 to 1991. Liu Yazhou presented this example as a warning to the Chinese people that we must have awareness of unexpected developments and cannot forget the war.[46]

Xi Jinping has said many times than an obvious disadvantage in the reconstruction of the People's Liberation Army was the fact that there had been no war for many years, and the PLA lacked operational experience and practical trials. Peace is, in a sense, debilitating to the military. If there is no war for many years and no strong fighting spirit, can a nation dare to fight? Once there is a true provocation, can China quickly mobilize for war, assemble all kinds of resources and powers, and align them into actual combat power? Can China fight? Are there suitable strategies and tactics in the face of a brand new form of war, and logistically airtight war planning with intelligence support?

In a drill held in July, 2014, the PLA Deputy Chief of Staff, Vice Admiral Wang Ning, said the distractions of cadres at all levels were too prevalent in peacetime, seeking undeserved reputations, and personal promotions, fearing punishment for any accident—all of these distractions caused many disadvantages in the field of military training. He demanded of the media: "You should reduce reports about going through fire drills, carrying logs, and crawling in ditches. They are just a show! They have no good influence

---

46.   Liu Yazhou: Get out of the China-Japan War, Welcome Reform, Create Brilliance, *Liberation Army Daily*, May 15, 2015.

on real combat training."[47]

The fundamental purpose of this national defense and army reform is to remove obstacles that restrict the upgrading of the PLA. The course of action taken by Xi Jinping to confront peacetime apathy is to forge the combat capacity of the army so that they can understand real combat and face the future battlefield. He sees clearly that the difference between the PLA and the forces of the world powers not only lies in equipment, but also in the military thoughts, ideas, and training levels. "If military training is a mere formality, we will pay the price of blood when a real fight comes!"

As opposed to the methods of the United States, the Chinese army, with peaceful development, must maintain and improve combat effectiveness through training alone. The emphasis on "actual combat" started in 2013, becoming the sole keyword of PLA training and reform, with the establishment of a new regime, contract combat training in the 1980s, the scientific and technical training in the late 1990s, and transformation from military training under conditions of mechanization to military training under the conditions of information-based warfare launched in 2006.

Very unusually, the Chinese media reported that marine corps soldier Xie Runzhen lost his life in the execution of an exercise code-named "Seal 2013." In fact, the number of casualties during training is on the rise, which proves that the intensity of training is increasing. In the past, military experts always mentioned the casualty proportion of the US Army was 3 to 4 percent when it came to the actual combat training. It is said that some senior leaders proposed undoing the restrictions aiming toward "passively safeguarding security by losing combat capacity" at the meeting for PLA senior officers, and, consequently, tolerate a certain amount of casualties in training.

The more important metric is how and what the army loses in the major exercises. It has been a long tradition in the PLA that the army can only win, but not lose. But it has been misunderstood to some extent, due to a variety of factors, under peacetime conditions. To break the convention "red will win, blue must lose" is considered to be the first step to really push forward the combat training in the PLA.

From May to the end of June, 2014, seven brigades from the seven military zones of the PLA traveled to the Zhu Rihe training base in the Beijing military region to participate in the important "Stride 2014 • Zhu Rihe" series of combat training exercises. In this, the largest military exercise of the year, the first professional blue army appeared; the red army lost six

---

47.   "Reform Expectations Behind the Annual Exercise," *Oriental Outlook*, Issue 30, 2014.

and won one. According to evaluations, this was the worst performance of the PLA since the Korean War.

The media has relentlessly reported on certain longstanding habits the army has formed, such as malfunctions frequently occurring with the equipment of an armored brigade, as its soldiers apparently lacked training; a few tanks withdrawing from the battlefield before the battle started; the commander of a mechanized infantry brigade not knowing how to lead the new fighting force; and some forces being misused to hold long meetings, which were convoluted and ultimately unnecessary. The People's Liberation Army newspaper, the *Liberation Army Daily,* pointed out that the standards of winning a war have changed: You could win before, but it's hard to say just how you can truly win now. In fact, assessment results of this exercise will not be posted, performances will not be rated nor included in annual assessments, in order to reassure the commanders that the key is not to win or lose, but to learn from the results of the actual combat.

Two months before the start of the exercise, the PLA launched the first guidance on combat-based military training in its history upon the approval of Xi Jinping, and also formed a joint training leading group and military training supervision group for the entire army. As the largest military action since the 18th National Congress of CPC, the Stride 2014 • Zhu Rihe series of exercises, and inter-regional base trainings in the entire army from 2014 to 2017, were all personally approved by Xi Jinping. Within four years, the operational capability of all brigades and divisions will be thoroughly assessed through highly realistic combat maneuvers. It will eventually be a part of the strategic considerations of the highest levels of state whether the PLA can fight, can win, and against whom—but only after thorough assessments.

Xi Jinping was allegedly very concerned about this exercise between the blue army and the red army. He called for tougher exercises with strict requirements and an improvement of the quality of the command.[48]

The combat training for the navy and air force have also been significantly augmented. From late October to early November, 2013, the Chinese navy organized the three fleets to carry out a military exercise code-named "Motor 5," for the first time in the western Pacific Ocean. This was described as "the first high-seas training of the People's Liberation Army Navy in the true sense." The previous "Motor" series of drills were conducted in coastal waters, and the focus on mechanical training was obvious. "Motor 5" emphasized the application of high-seas maneuvering and communications

---

48. "The Combat Training of the People's Liberation Army in the Xi Jinping Era," *Phoenix Military.* http://news.ifeng.com/mil/special/xjpsdjfjdszhxl/

methods. The red and blue sides continuously implemented "back-to-back" high-seas attack-defense combat, broke the earlier training modes to self-organize in accordance with the divisional system, and simulated "the fog of war"—neither side knew the other's position, navigation elements, and operational orders. The navy said similar offshore training exercises would be strengthened. In early winter of 2014, three large fleets jointly carried out the "Motor 6" exercise in the western Pacific Ocean. This true-to-life combat drill broke records—with the largest number of naval forces, the most complete training elements, the most difficult attack-defend scenarios, and the most realistic battlefield environments ever staged.

Oceans have an important position in the strategic planning of Xi Jinping. In August 2013, Xi Jinping went on board China's first aircraft carrier *Liao Ning*, which showed an initial signal of determination to proceed with ocean-going naval construction. The speed of the new ships was remarkable, and Xi Jinping gave special emphasis to the importance of combat training. The navy has also increased its training strength across all scenarios and conditions.

On May 21, 2015, Chinese airplanes flew across the Miyako Strait to the western Pacific for training, returning the next day. The air force spokesman said the training had achieved its stated goal, and such training out of the first island chain would be implemented in accordance with future necessities. The assessment of free air combat, marked by the awarding of a "golden helmet" in the air force has been well known since 2012. This attempt to get close to actual combat has been transformed from the technical and tactical level to systematic battle training and systematic navigational training, and become the norm for military training of the air force.

In August, 2014, the East China Sea fleet and an air force unit organized a free air fight exercise, the first in the history of the navy and air force. The *Liberation Army Daily* claimed that this drill aimed to lay the foundation for joint training of different services under standardized conditions. Multi-service joint training exercises based on system operation levels will now occur more frequently. In the fall of 2014, military drills were held in the Bohai Sea, the Yellow Sea, East China Sea, and the Northern Gulf at the same time, and there were ten army trans-regional base ammunition drills in the interior area of Gansu Province and other places for three months or so. Warm-up military exercises covered the anniversary of the victory against Japan on August 15, the anniversary of the September 18 Mukden Incident, and other major historical events. This year, the army and armed police forces held more than 200 combat-based exercises above division and brigade, and also attended 31 bilateral and multilateral training activities;

such military strength has rarely been seen in the past.

In July, 2014, the four headquarters of the PLA jointly developed and issued *Regulations on Reward and Recognition in the Army*, linking honor and recognition to actual combat performance. In Xi Jinping's words: "A person who can't fight and just wants to seek an official post and treatment in the army will not be promoted, only criticized." Almost at the same time, the PLA General Political Department issued documents to emphasize the cultivation of fighting capacity. A military expert asserted that true fighting spirit is the most important factor in combat effectiveness.

According to reports from foreign media, China has set up a Central Military Commission joint operation command center at the highest strategic level. In addition, joint operation command centers established by the PLA in warzones have taken shape, including the East China Sea joint operation command center.

Guo Wujun, director of the battle and command teaching and research office of the National Defense University, said that the commander authorities at all levels should first bear the brunt as military command centers in the face of the new military revolution in the world. Xi Jinping required the building of a new command authority when he met representatives of the army Chiefs of Staff. "Many people say it is the war of tomorrow, but what we are actually preparing for is yesterday's war." The scholar thought command authorities at all levels must advocate and aggressively promote innovative military theories.[49]

Some scholars thought innovation in military theory must be strengthened in this round of military reform. It has been a controversial topic for a long time: how best to absorb foreign experiences for reference. The point of view held by Professor Jin Yinan, of the National Defense University, is to build a "modern military power system with Chinese characteristics." The army needs to draw lessons from the latest methods of fighting, but it depends on their abilities alone to win the war. "We don't just accept rules, but also make rules."

In fact, after the Gulf War in 1991, the US had a huge impact on the PLA's tactics. The operational regulations and military reports of the US Army were largely translated, and the American war planning and tactical standards gradually became the reference point for the PLA. However, more and more military experts mentioned the unique Chinese military thoughts pioneered by Mao Zedong in recent years; many people thought the national

---

49.   "The Construction of the Army Calls for New Commanding Authority—One of the Series of Construction of the New Commander Authority," *China National Defense*, October 27, 2014.

conditions, equipment, and missions are unique, and we should not lose ourselves by blindly following others.

Professor Jin Yinan gave an example; there was a very eye-catching sentence in the chapter "Strategy and Tactics of the Chinese People's Liberation Army" from the *Chinese Military Report* written by the United States from 2007 to 2008: "You fight your way; I fight my way." This was Mao Zedong's military philosophy, but the Americans believe "it toppled the standards of success and failure in the world." The battle standard since ancient times is to "annihilate the enemy's effective strength and occupy cities." But Mao Zedong's standard was: As long as the guerrillas are not destroyed, it is victory. It is a failure if the regular army of the other side, which cannot win; as long as I live, the enemy fails. The short formula: "The enemy advances, we retreat. The enemy camps, we harass. The enemy tires, we attack. The enemy retreats, we pursue" is the standard set by China which has subverted the military system of the whole world.[50]

The People's Liberation Army in Xi Jinping's era is increasingly showing its ability to leave home and go abroad, maintain peace, and assume international responsibility in all overseas missions. For example, within two months of Malaysian Airlines flight MH370 being reported missing, China sent nine naval vessels and five air force planes in a bid to help trace the plane. The total search ranges reached 50,000 miles—equivalent to traveling around the earth more than twice.

As of December, 2014, 2,600 people had been sent to the 24 UN peacekeeping missions by the PLA in the Democratic Republic of the Congo, Liberia, and Sudan, and nineteen naval fleets were sent to Somali waters to escort nearly 6,000 ships as a guard against pirates. Support was given to the Philippines typhoon disaster area, warships and air transport were sent to supply water for desalination plants after a fire in the Maldives capital Male, and thousands of aid workers, backed by an army hospital, were sent to support West Africa in the fight against the deadly Ebola virus.

The Chinese people favor the art of dialectics. In the dialectical relationship between war and peace, the one who can start fighting can also stop fighting, the weaker you are, the easier it is to be beaten, you may fight when you are ready for it—these are lessons we draw from the painful history of more than 100 years, and also the real connotation of "fight the victorious war" advocated by the Supreme Commander Xi Jinping.

---

50.   "The Duties of Chinese Soldiers," *Global People*, February 2014.

Soldiering Will Become a Respectable Profession

On January 21, 2015, Xi Jinping visited the base of the second artillery in Kunming and when he saw a photograph of an ordinary soldier in the military museum, he said, "I know this soldier." The veteran recognized by Chairman Xi Jinping was 46-year-old Master Sergeant Wang Zhongxin, who had a 29-year career of military service. He was called the "gold trumpeter" and "coach" in the army, had operated three kinds of missiles, mastered the operating skills of nineteen positions of measurement control, and conducted live-fire operations more than 1,200 times without a mistaken password nor a wrong action.

On March 11, 2013, Xi Jinping met a cross-section of the NPC delegates from the grassroots army units, including Wang Zhongxin, at the annual session of the NPC and CPPCC. Chairman Xi Jinping asked him details about his age and service time, and told him: "The army reconstruction needs more officers with technical backgrounds like you."[51] The non-commissioned officer system has 500 years of history in foreign countries, and has a unique status in the armies of all nations. While staff reduction is an increasing trend in the army, the proportion of sergeants is becoming larger and larger. The scale of the non-commissioned officer systems symbolizes the professional level of the army, and also reflects the level of advancement of military weaponry and equipment. There are more 800,000 officers in the PLA with experience of nearly 30 years, the proportion of non-commissioned officers in the high-technology units of the PLA exceeds 60 percent. In 2014, the reform of the non-commissioned officer system had a key development—the master sergeant.

In early 2014, the pilot creation scheme of instituting a rank of master sergeant was carried out in a mechanized infantry brigade of the Beijing military area and an infantry brigade of the Shenyang military area. Some 36 non-commissioned officers were appointed as master sergeants after several rounds of assessment, tests, and training at the end of the year, and became the first batch of PLA master sergeants to start formal service. In March 2015, the first master sergeants appeared in the Guangzhou military area. They organized a monthly extended field tour of a special brigade in the 42nd Army instead of the officers. The level-3 officer Liu Hui, who served in the special brigade for six years, said there was no senior non-commissioned officer establishment in war camps in accordance with the previous provisions, but now troops would have more opportunities to become senior non-commissioned officers after serving as sergeants. The longest service length

51.   "The Veteran Recognized by Chairman Xi at First Sight," *Liberation Army Daily*, February 4, 2015.

a master sergeant can reach is 29 years—they have an RMB 400 monthly allowance, more than other ordinary non-commissioned officers, with an average wage of RMB 7,000 and above, and have independent offices and accommodations.

A Chinese defense ministry spokesman said in March, 2015, that the pilot study of the non-commissioned officer system will be further expanded according to military deployments. Master sergeants are called "sergeant majors" in many countries. They primarily assist officers with basic training and daily management at the grassroots level, reduce the work of basic military officers so that they can focus on military strategy and command, implement the upgrading of officer abilities, and generally serve to optimize the structure of the military force. At the same time, the role can also can promote officers' self-identity, improve the use of modern advanced equipment, strengthen military skills, inherit combat experience, and encourage grassroots officers to establish careers. Some people expect that the establishment of the non-commissioned officer system will lead to a great transformation in the study of Chinese military doctrine, achieve the transition from military technical study to the comprehensive transformative study of military affairs.[52]

The establishment of the non-commissioned officer system is seen as an important symbol of a new professionalism in the Chinese army. Chinese military personnel have experienced the transformation from revolutionary, to liberator, to builder, to professional soldier in the past 88 years. In fact, since China's reform and opening up, the value of the army was seldom mentioned during the "endurance period." Many military institutions have condensed in size, the rapid development of the market economy has made the low pay of Chinese soldiers pale by comparison to private careers, and the charisma inherent in the military image has dropped greatly.

After 2,000 years, the conditions of the army have been gradually improved, but the appeal of a military pay-grade still pales compared with the new opportunities of economic development in the whole society. On many military bulletins, discussion is focused on several questions: soldiers' wages, demobilized army cadres' futures, and the appointments of army cadres. "Soldiers will no longer be inspired by patriotism, they are more interested in working conditions, and even exhibit decreased trust for the state and military system."[53]

52.   "Observation of PLA Grassroots Reform from the Master Sergeant System," *Phoenix Military*. http://news.ifeng.com/mil/special/sgzzd/

53.   "The Military Cultural Identity of the Modern Contemporary Military in the Management of Modernization, Philosophy, and Sociology." Assembly of The Eighth Special Academic Conference in Jiangsu Province: November 1, 2014.

According to a survey of new recruits in the fall of 2013, 18 percent of them claimed "to live for themselves," 25 percent believed in the principle of "equal exchange," and thought they should get a corresponding reward for pay. When they were asked "are you ready to die for the country and its people," 25 percent of the recruits said "they would hesitate because of family." A subject even directly stated: "Everyone is thinking about making money in this society, it is difficult to understand why the army always educates us to be loyal to the Party with sacrifice and dedication, but only give us a little allowance."[54]

There is a consensus that the culture of pure devotion and sacrifice is difficult for the soldiers, and dedication cannot constrain the moral high grounds of others. In fact, the army faces many conflicts. For example, according to military law, the treatment of a soldier in active military service should be coordinated with the development of the national economy and societal progress. As a matter of fact, economic benefits gained by the soldiers have large differences. Apart from the allowance given by the state each year, subsidies will be given by the local government, including a family subsidy and some other forms of economic aid. The urban compulsory serviceman earns RMB 27,000 more than those with rural residences. After they return home upon the expiration of service, the subsidies they gain may also have very large differences on the basis of the financial resources and manpower demands of the local government; for example, a retired soldier may get more than RMB 100,000, or various rewards of RMB 200,000 in a business- and industry-developed region like Dongguan, Guangdong Province. But in a western region like Gansu Province, the economy is relatively backward, and retired soldiers may only have subsidies of little more than RMB 30,000.

One of the key points of the great reform promoted by Xi Jinping is the adjustment of the policy system in the army. Based on the sizable adjustments to the military service system, the adjustment of military policy and logistics is one of the major pivots of military reform in the detailed planning of the new reforms determined at the Third Plenary Session of the 18th Central Committee of the Communist Party of China. This also includes the strengthening and perfecting of the military human resource system, in accordance with the demands of military mission requirements, and innovations in policy at the national level, forming a scientifically sound and standardized military cadre system, civil servant system, military service system, non-commissioned officer system, and veteran emplacement system.

On December 27, 2013, Xi Jinping stated at an important meeting that

---

54. Ibid.

the military human resource policy system is the highlight of military policy reform, as it is closely related with the interests of officers and enlisted men. Due to various reasons, the cadre evaluation, selection, appointment and training system is not sound enough, a lot of problems still exist such as recruitment difficulties, emplacement of retired soldiers, and the treatment of injured, sick, and disabled personnel, among others. He asked to intensify policy reform, revitalize the military human resource departments, and attract more excellent talents. The core of the military human resource reform is officer professionalization, namely the technical and specialist training of officers, which is closely related to the army's combat effectiveness and cohesion. Starting in 2014, the discussion on officer professionalization, and introduction of the relevant methods adopted by foreign armies, have been frequently reported by the media.

In January 2015, according to the People's Liberation Army newspaper's microblog, Chairman Xi Jinping spoke at a meeting of the army, saying that the future income of officers will depend primarily on wages, otherwise they will be investigated if any "gray-market income," or illegal income is discovered.

The wages of the PLA are among the lowest in the world. Officer, civilian cadre, and non-commissioned officers have different salary standards; the salary of officers and civilian cadres includes a basic salary, military appointment salary, military rand salary, military service salary and allowance. The media estimated that the monthly salary of a platoon commander is RMB 3,000–4,000, a grade officer is RMB 5,000–6,000, and there exist some special allowances and subsidies for certain services in the army. In China, this level is similar and slightly higher than that of civil servants. However, there is a great gap in comparison with the US Army. For example, a senior US colonel with 30 years' service has a monthly salary of nearly USD 10,000, whereas an army officer with equivalent qualifications in the PLA receives about RMB 8,000–9,000.

Of course, unity between officers and enlisted men is a great tradition of the PLA. The income gap between officers and soldiers is very small; the salary of a senior general is 20 times higher than a private at most, but in South Korea, the highest-level four-star general will receive an income 95 times that of a private. While Xi Jinping has, on the one hand, emphasized that officers should depend on their salaries, on the other hand, he raised the salaries and benefits for soldiers at the end of 2014. As he has always thought that all things have their own place and every man his own post, he hoped to integrate a complete set of institutional arrangements, including new salaries, into the orbit of the law. On March 18, 2015, a new rule was issued to make detailed regulations on relevant military benefits; for example, some family members go to the army and temporarily have no housing. The new rules explicitly provide rent subsidies according to a certain proportion of the average rent charged in the locality; and allow to arrange transportation for the families who temporarily come to visit or go to the hospital. There is a relief system for the injured, sick, and disabled personnel and officers, and for soldiers who have special difficulties, and the headquarters will also set up special relief funds for special-circumstance cadres. At the same time, specifications have been made to improve the quality of life of officers and men, instituting major holidays, organized worship activities, and the distribution of souvenirs to retired soldiers.

It is said that the new rules were approved by Xi Jinping. In addition as to the implementation of reasonable benefits and clear, detailed, standards, questions that are not always easy to grasp were addressed—for example, after the implementation of strict management on vehicles, there was fierce debate on whether army vehicles should be arranged to meet and see off visiting relatives. Officer professionalization has become a reform consensus, the ultimate goal being to attract talented recruits to serve in the army. Growth of benefits and rational promotion resources can greatly arouse the enthusiasm and strengthen the responsibility of the army, and have an important effect in the improvement of military efficiency.

The military media and research institutes have frequently highlighted the relevant experience of the foreign armies. For instance, the People's Liberation Army newspaper reported that the Chinese army has paid a lot of attention to Russia in recent years, while the proportion of the contract army has expanded, they are not evenly allocated: the high-cost contract soldiers are focused in the key forces: Soldier positions of navy surface ships, submarines, and airborne posts are all supplemented by contract soldiers.[55]

National Defense Reference revealed a pay raise for officers in Britain, France, Germany, and Korea. It also mentioned that in addition to the treatment of army personnel in active service, the pensions of officers in these countries is even higher than the income of in-service officials of the same level in other places; military service veterans also enjoy a preferential loans policy in the purchase of housing, retired officers are awarded with medals and honorary certificates, and special ceremonies are held for retired senior officers, which greatly inspires the sense of pride and honor of veterans.[56]

In fact, formulating policy arrangements for veterans and improving

55.   The Quantitative Change and Qualitative Change of Russian Reforms, the People's Liberation Army newspaper, on March 7, 2014.

56.   "The Main Methods of Strengthening the Appeal of the Professional Military in Some European and Asian Countries," *National Defense Reference*, April 27, 2015.

their treatment is not only an important guarantee of continuous fighting capacity, but plays an important role in embodying the status of soldiers, motivating them to dedicate themselves, and strengthening army teamwork and cohesion. The unsatisfactory resettlement and treatment of retired veterans in China is a major source of controversy over the years. Xi Jinping has had an experience of career change from the army to a locality. In May, 2014, on the Sixth National Military Transformation Commendation Congress and Military Transformation Resettlement Work Conference of 2014, he said to the delegates: "I was also a military-into-civilian cadre."

In the discussion of officer professionalization, general restructuring, and efficiency-building measures, nurturing a sense of honor was also a hot issue. Professor Jin Yinan, of the National Defense University, told the media about his experience of how a hero shaped America: "General Douglas MacArthur was a controversial person within the US Army for a long time, his domineering and overweening acts used to be unpopular in America. But it's different now. I have visited the Pentagon four times, and the image of MacArthur is taller and taller, and has currently become a perfect hero. His pipe, soft brim hat, pistol, and pen can be seen everywhere in the Pentagon. There is a MacArthur's office in the American army command and the staff college. When I made a visit, they stuck my name under the sign of 'MacArthur office,' and it became Jin Yinan's office for one day, and I was told that 'this is the highest honor I obtained here.'"[57]

But nowadays the erosion in Chinese popular culture is deconstructing and pushing back against its heroes. For example, the bravery of soldiers Lei Feng and Qiu Shaoyun, who sacrificed their lives for their country in the Korean War in the 1960s, is being vandalized by historical nihilism. Professor Jin Yinan asked earnestly: "If a nation betrayed its own glory and dreams, what can it be expect, but to become nothing more than loose sand?"[58]

In January 2015, when Xi Jinping visited the 14th Army in Kunming, Yunnan Province, he recalled a poem written by the martyr Wang Jianchuan to his mother on the battlefield, and praised his courage "to dedicate himself to the country." The martyr was just nineteen years old when he sacrificed himself in the border war, only three months after he joined the army. What kind of hero should be shaped to encourage the soldiers who grow up in the Internet era for today's Chinese army?

57.   "The Duties of Chinese Soldiers," *Global People*, February 2014.
58.   Ibid.

The Army and the People Should Be Integrated

Facing the world's new military revolution, Xi Jinping is leading military reform in China. If we are determined to make real progress in the aspects of establishment systems, combat-effectiveness guidance, and officer professionalization, pursuing a "civil-military integration" seems not so onerous, and full of new ideas. On March 12, 2015, Xi Jinping's remarks focused on civil-military integration at the Third Session of the 12th National People's Congress, the Plenary Meeting of PLA delegation. He had talked about this problem on many occasions before, but this was the first time he clearly put forth the concept of raising "civil-military integration to the priority level of the national development strategy."

Economic growth and security have always been strategic problems faced by large countries. Someone once described the national dilemma in these terms: "resources are available, but cannot be shared; quality is available, but without ability." The China Dream, and by extension the Army Dream obviously cannot be stuck in such a stalemate.

In Xi Jinping's opinion, the development of military and civilian integration is a significant result of China's long-term exploration of coordinating development between economic growth and national defense restructuring. Professor Jiang Luming, of the National Defense University, believes the purpose of the pursuit of civil-military integration is to truly achieve the future development. "Civil-military integration is essentially a battle for comprehensive national strength and military dominance in the next 20 to 30 years, clashes of ideas and competition of philosophies should not stand in the way."[59]

He wrote an article in the *People's Daily*, stating that military technology was ahead of the civilian technology. But since the mid-1970s, society entered a new technological revolution characterized by digital information and intelligence and, so far, the commercial revolution is ahead of the military revolution, the societal level of adoption of new technologies is generally higher than the military's. At present, the proportion of military special technology in developed countries is less than 15 percent, and the proportion of military and civilian general technology is more than 80 percent.

The purpose of a national defense innovation initiative put forth by America is to discover important advanced technologies ahead of competitors through disruptive innovation. Nationalized innovation support institutions are founded in Russia to be responsible for disruptive

---

59.　"Why the Civil-Military Integration to National Strategy has Arisen," *People's Daily*, May 31, 2015.

innovation. Japan also established special funds to support the development of new technology. In fact, it has been very popular in developed countries to commit to civil-military integration of weaponry and military equipment development. America is the most typical example. It is said that the national defense department paid more than 60 percent of spending to contractors every year, including military supplies, weapons R&D, manufacturing, logistics services, and private contractors. And the proportion of military business is increasing in the outsourcing sector, such as training soldiers, camp security, even interrogations and intelligence-gathering missions are performed by contractors.

The army does not have to pursue such totality, as market-oriented military outsourcing will let them become "the most selective buyers." In the Chinese army, vegetable farming, raising pigs and ducks, and a self-sufficient mode of food supply are still quite common aspects in some military forces.

In this case, "civil-military integration" has a magnificent connotation, but it conflicts with reality. Professor Jiang Luming thought the development of civil-military integration would be a long-term plan to lead the country to develop from being simply large, to being strong. It has been a historical problem of how to plan security and development as a whole. During the 5,200 years from 3,200 BC to the 1990s, there were a total of 14,513 large wars in the world, about three each year. "A rising power must maintain strong economic development and strong military development, otherwise the nation will decline if the relationship between 'guns and butter' cannot be balanced well."[60]

He stated that France, Germany, Japan, and the Soviet Union, which attempted to challenge the world's leading powers, had experienced painful lessons. Today China is also facing a similar test: Economic development is entering the "new normal," fiscal revenue growth enters an adjustment period, and the conditions of national defense resources are tight. At the same time, the pressure of national security is increasing.[61]

Civil-Military Integration

Civil-military integration is considered as an option to plan the national security and development as a whole. It cannot only promote economic development through a national defense buildup, especially the development of national high-tech industries, but also provide support to the national defense via the economy.

---

60.   "Why the Civil-Military Integration to National Strategy has Arisen," *People's Daily*, May 31, 2015.

61.   Ibid.

The military scholar even shared the illustrative example that "carriages have wheels of the-same size; all writing is with the same characters" of the first unified country Qin more than 2,200 years ago to depict the urgent reality that the long-divided army and people must be deeply integrated. According to Xi Jinping's analysis, the connotations of civil-military integration in his mind are obviously more abundant, namely the so-called "big picture" perspective.

The military and civilian integration with a focus on new science and technology, as well as information-based warfare and economics, is obviously one of the essential ingredients. In today's China, the relationship between national defense and the economy is no longer simply "waxing and waning;" they can realize an increase of battle effectiveness and productivity growth at the same pace through adjustment of resource allocation and the promotion of independent innovation. For example, China's manned space flight project is an exemplar of military and civilian integration. It is expected that the Bei Dou system will bring the economic and social benefits of at least RMB 4.5 trillion in the next five years after its peak of industrialization is reached.

Xi Jinping stressed to incorporate the military innovation system into the national innovation system for mutually compatible and synchronous development, so as to provide strong support and continuous encouragement to military innovation.

Many people also put forth that the key areas and techniques of great significance to national security and strategic development of the country, such as sea, air and space, information, and earth and atmospheric physics, must be organized and implemented in a market economy according to market rules, no matter if they are accomplished through military-civilian cooperation or undertaken unilaterally. Then we can be certain to apply the most advanced technology in the service of national defense based on the market rule "survival of the fittest." However, the innovation and fusion of high and new technology is not the whole story: The fusion of people and the fusion of hearts is indispensable. The civil-military integration promoted by Xi Jinping particularly emphasizes the unification of the military and the government, as well as the unity of the army and the people—the army should actively support local development, the local party committee and government should "understand that the support of national defense and army building is a matter within their duty."

The so-called "matter within their duty" has practical pertinence. A typical example is that local economic development has caused serious dangers to military installations. It was widely reported by the media that a large stretch of European-style villas were built close to an important navy port in the northern coastal city Dalian. The number of ships in the port and their access times could be seen clearly from the third-floor terrace without use of any satellite reconnaissance. The base had to invest more than RMB 10 billion to build a wall up to 800 meters long and 22 meters high to keep the naval port out of sight of the villas. But hundreds of meters away from the port, its status can still be seen clearly from some tall buildings.

According to military sources, it's not uncommon that such a serious problem can affect the safety of military installations. When the economy of coastal regions is relatively developed, and military ports and naval bases conflict with the development of local tourism, agriculture, and shipping, disputes can arise. Problems like jammed sea channels, and occupation of berth and anchorage grounds exist to different degrees around all kinds of military ports. The poor planning and coordination of some local governments has seriously damaged national security.[62]

The deep meaning of civil-military integration is visible when recalling Xi Jinping's ruling experience in economically developed provinces of the southeast coast for so many years, and his measures to support national defense.

On September 3, 2015, to mark China's War of Resistance against Japanese Aggression and the 70th anniversary of the end of World War II, Xi Jinping will hold his first big parade after taking office. The previous big military parades in China were often arranged on the National Day in October and there is usually one military parade for each generation of leaders. This time it is of extraordinary significance that the Victory Day on September 3 was chosen as the day of the big parade to show our national pride and national spirit.

On September 3 of 2014, Xi Jinping delivered a speech at the commemoration of Victory Day: "The Chinese people have a mind broader than the sea and the air, but we cannot stand a grain of sand in our eyes."

On the Victory Day of 2015, the most advanced weapons and equipment, and the most elite troops will appear in Tiananmen Square. When China is striding toward its historically destined time and place as a superpower, the significance of the display will be not simply to flex its muscles, but to instill pride in its people.

Since Xi Jinping took over as Chairman of the Central Military Commission, he has reviewed troops during inspection, such as the naval forces in Sanya and Changsha National University of Defense Technology in Hunan Province. This time, as he enters the parade car in Tiananmen Square, the PLA Ground Force, the PLA Navy, and the PLA Air Force will be

---

62.   "Military Facilities Protection is an Obsession," *Oriental Outlook*, Issue 2, 2015.

in formation, and aircraft will roar past overhead, injecting more powerful energy into his arduous and progressive military reforms, as well as his reforms for the whole of China.

CHAPTER
8

Xi Jinping's New International Thinking

Before Xi Jinping took over supreme power in China, China had emerged as the world's second-largest economy, but China's diplomacy has been criticized for a long time. In other countries, it is widely suspected that China's diplomacy might allow the country to become a new hegemony, forming a threat to neighboring countries. In China, the mainstream public opinion is that China's foreign policy is too weak, and functions at a disadvantage in negotiations over disputed territories. The Chinese tend to believe the government is too submissive in the face of the United States' bullying.

Xi Jinping faced up to these challenges by starting with a whirlwind of "Xi-style Diplomacy." To allay the concerns of other countries, he was able to lessen the threat by making special trips to the Republic of Korea and Mongolia to pay his respects. Even in India he visited the hometown of Narendra Modi, prime minister of India, and talked with him. So far he has shown more flexibility than his predecessor. But he is more hardline than his predecessors in what should be the tough stances of a leader. He has categorically refuted Japanese politicians' denials of history, and expanded a public opinion battle through international diplomacy. Regarding the South China Sea dispute, he was not afraid of fueling more conflict by facing up to the struggle with the Philippines and Vietnam, and then approved the land reclamation. Even for China's old little brother, the Democratic People's Republic of Korea (DPRK), Xi Jinping denied an arbitrary visit upon entering office in order to clamp down on them publicly when the DPRK was too blindly proud in persisting in its old ways. He is a new geopolitical master. Perhaps we will see his influence on current Asia and the world in the next 50 years.

I. ATTACKING A VITAL POINT

To both Xi Jinping and Park Geun-hye, the current president of South Korea, Chinese philosophy and the board game Go are topics they both enjoy. They are more like a pair of close siblings. They remember each other's birthdays and never forget to send timely blessings. Xi Jinping was born in June 1953 while Park Geun-hye was born in February, 1952, a difference of less than two years. They also have similar family backgrounds, in that Xi Jinping's father, a veteran Chinese politician, used to serve as the vice premier of the State Council and Park Geun-hye's father, Park Chung-hee, used to serve as the president of South Korea.

Although born into powerful families, there were vicissitudes. During the unrest of the Cultural Revolution of China, Xi Jinping was put into a detention center as a "child of the gang," and later was sent to the countryside, where he experienced a harsh life for many years. After the 1979 assassination of Park Chung-hee, Park Geun-hye underwent a deep depression that she described in her biography, writing sadly: "If I need to live such a life again, I would rather choose death."

An "Old Friend" of the Chinese People

Similar experiences and backgrounds made Xi Jinping and Park Geun-hye feel like old friends at their first meeting as if they had known each other long before they moved towards the political pinnacles of their respective nations. Xi Jinping, who was the secretary of the Zhejiang Party Committee, visited South Korea in 2005, and met Park Geun-hye, who was the representative of the Grand National Party, which was not in power at the time. On February 2, 2014, Park Geun-hye's 62nd birthday, Xi Jinping personally wrote to his big sister to wish her good health and good luck.

So, when Park Geun-hye paid a state visit to China in 2013, Xi said to her, "You are an old friend of the Chinese people's and of mine." In China's political lexicon, the word "old friend" is the highest title given to a foreigner, and had only been used previously across the whole Korean Peninsula for the former President of North Korea, Kim Il Sung, and the former Supreme Leader of North Korea, Kim Jong Il. Naturally, the term "old friend" conveys Xi Jinping's personal favor to Park Geun-hye, but also conveys more profound considerations in respect to international politics. Before guiding Chinese politics, he studied international politics and had a clear insight of world politics.

The world's strategic patterns are going through a turning point from a unipolar development mode to a multipolar one. Only the United States constitutes a strategic threat to China, and to get rid of the threat, China must befriend the United States as much as possible. In doing so, Xi Jinping proposed to build a "new relation between great powers." At the same time, China must stabilize the periphery, including South Korea, with which China has had deep ties throughout history.

One and a half years after Xi Jinping became China's top leader, he decided to visit South Korea, and only South Korea, on July 3 and 4, 2014. It was a meaningful trip. During most of the past 2,000 years, South Korea acted as a dependent state of China, which was called the Central Empire.

Even in the twentieth century, the successor of the Central Empire, China, has followed this practice in its diplomacy activities. Before China and Japan established diplomatic relations, Japanese Prime Minister Kakuei Tanaka first visited China in 1972. After China and South Korea established diplomatic relations, South Korean President Roh Tae-woo also visited Beijing first in 1992. Even regarding Sino–US relations, despite the fact that the United States was much stronger than China, Nixon was the first head of state to visit China when he flew to Beijing in 1972 and held talks with Mao Zedong and Zhou Enlai.

Since the reform and opening up in 1978, China's leaders have visited foreign countries more frequently. However, from Jiang Zemin to Hu Jintao, including Deng Xiaoping, they all visited more than one country every time they made a trip abroad. But Xi Jinping broke the convention in 2014 when he traveled from Beijing to Seoul, and then flew back home from Seoul. For two days, he and Park Geun-hye held several rounds of talks.

A Chinese saying recommends: "When drinking with a bosom friend, a thousand cups will still be too little." When the conversation gets disagreeable, to say one word more is a waste of breath. The situation of Xi Jinping and Park Geun-hye is undoubtedly the former. Even at the negotiating table, in the absence of wine, they still had a lot of issues to discuss and almost all of their talks were extended, including the wide-range meeting of major officials which was extended to 170 minutes from the originally set 90 minutes; and the separate meeting between the two leaders was scheduled for 45 minutes, but 100 minutes had passed when the two finally left the conference room. Park Geun-hye said to Xi Jinping: "time seemed to be too little for tonight's long talk."[1]

Park Geun-hye made a detailed and thoughtful arrangement for the China's top leader. At the state banquet, the Korean chefs offered Xi Jinping's favorite lamb. Xi Jinping's ancestral home is Shaanxi Province, which is located in northwest China, and he lived also in the countryside of Shaanxi, where there is a local tradition of lamb meals, which remind him of his childhood.

Xi Jinping was quite surprised that Park Geun-hye also specially invited the top Go player of South Korea, Lee Chang-ho, who was born in 1975 and praised as the "Stone Buddha" in China, which means that he stays still without any movement when he is playing Go. This stillness is considered indicative of the highest level of Go. Xi Jinping recognized the lean Korean immediately, and praised him saying: "hardly any of China's outstanding players have defeated you." Go, or *Wei Qi*, which originated in China, is considered to be the most complex strategy game. It has only two colors, black and white, each player holds one color; the board is composed of a simple cross grid on which both players fight for territories, and whoever occupies the larger territory will be the winner. Lee Chang-ho entered the elite realm of the world's super-class Go masters in 1990. Almost all of the top Go players in South Korea, Japan, and China could not beat him.

The reason why Park Geun-hye invited Lee Chang-ho was that she knew that Xi Jinping likes Go. The game is similar to the art of war, with infinite variations, and poses a hard test of players' computing skills, especially regarding layout and strategy.

Xi Jinping and the Chinese Go master Nie Weiping were good friends in his youth. In the 1980s, the Japanese Go players were considered the world's best. But the young Nie Weiping defeated almost all Japanese players, and became China's "national hero." He is also called the "Grandmaster" by the Chinese people.

General Geng Biao was interested in playing Go, so he asked his staff members to learn to play it and considered that this could exercise their ability to see the bigger picture. He requested his secretary, Xi Jinping, to learn Go as soon as possible so they could play Go chess together. Xi Jinping specifically asked for Nie Weiping's help, hoping to learn a way toward quick improvement. Nie Weiping said that he did not teach Xi Jinping, because "I was afraid the level of Xi may be too poor and bring shame on me." But the contact between them must have promoted Xi Jinping's skills and deepened

---

1.   Hong Kong: *Wen Hui Bao*, July 9, 2014.

his study of the game. At South Korea's state banquet, Xi Jinping said to Park Geun-hye and Lee Chang-ho with emotion, "Go contains life philosophy and the world's strategy."[2]

China Provides Special Diplomatic Treatment to South Korea

The visit to South Korea is one of Xi Jinping's manifestations of the mentality that comes with appreciating games of Go. In East Asia, where China is located—the United States, Japan, and South Korea are allies; China and the Soviet Union used to be allies, but the relationship was broken in the time of Mao Zedong, and intense military conflicts took place in the border area. This pattern of change, in fact, culminated in the round of "ping-pong diplomacy" and eased Sino–US relations.

But after the "Tiananmen incident" of 1989, China and the US's "honeymoon" was over. After the collapse of the Soviet Union, China became the largest country ruled by a communist party, and the United States saw China as its largest rival. Although the relationship between Japan and China was good, when Junichiro Koizumi, who held a conservative political outlook, took up the post of Japanese prime minister, the Chinese have always believed that Koizumi denied the history of aggression, and that he implements military expansion, hence Sino–Japanese relations have continued to deteriorate.

In the game with the United States, China seemed quite isolated. China pursued a "non-alignment policy" in that it almost made too few allies. But Xi Jinping needs new friends.

In the 2,000 years of China's imperial history as the center of East Asia, the Korean peninsula has always been China's closest ally. During the Japanese annexation of Korea, the DPRK's leaders were exiled to China, and then they launched the struggle against the Japanese invaders in Chinese territory. For the past tragic history and hatred against Japan's denial of history and of the comfort women, China and South Korea share many common grounds.

Xi Jinping's diplomatic strategy is to "dig to a tiger's heart though its mouth." By taking a wise strategy, he would hold the target from the other side of the camp in his own hands. South Korea is the target. Although the United States and South Korea are allies, there are still 30,000 US troops stationed in South Korea. Furthermore, the United States has been partial to Japan in terms of historical issues. South Korea feels very martial from top to bottom.

The ultimate goal of Koreans is one of strong self-esteem and the complete reunification of the Korean peninsula. China is the DPRK's biggest backer.

---

2.   Ibid.

Just as the annexation of East Germany to West Germany required the consent of the Soviet Union, if South Korea wants to occupy the DPRK, the China factor must also be considered. Especially when the DPRK supports the development of nuclear weapons, it constitutes a more serious threat to South Korea, so Park Geun-hye needs support from China.

China's and South Korea's closeness also has economic aspects. By 2014, China was already South Korea's largest trading partner. According to the data of the Ministry of Education of China, China's total foreign students of 37.7 million in 2014 included 6.3 million from South Korea, which ranks first in all countries. The Wangjing area located in the northeast of Beijing near Capital International Airport, has a large number of Korean shops and settled Koreans, so this area is also known as "Korea Town" to Beijing residents.

Seeking out trends, paying attention to strategy, and focusing on planning and management are Xi Jinping's insights into the surrounding diplomacy. Specifically, it is the "talk of equality and feelings; more meetings and visits; take more popular and heartwarming actions."[3] He decided to make a special visit to South Korea, and bring his wife to visit South Korea only, so that Koreans feel his special respect for them. He explained that this would enable neighboring countries to be friendlier, more intimate, more recognizing, and more supportive of China with enhanced affinity, appeal, and influence.

This special courtesy to South Korea is a major feature of Xi Jinping's diplomacy. In June, 2013, Park Geun-hye visited Beijing. In addition to providing his "big sister" with a formal state dinner, Xi Jinping also specifically visited Beijing's Diaoyutai State Guesthouse, Park Geun-hye's residence, to have lunch with her. This special diplomatic privilege was unprecedented compared to when previous South Korean presidential visits to China.

This special visit was the best card Xi Jinping's diplomacy played in the first round. Japan's newspaper *Yomiuri Shimbun* noticed that this card had three effects: it dealt with the historical issues with Japan; it exerted pressure on the DPRK by virtue of its involving South Korea; and it even drove a wedge among the alliance of the United States, Japan, and South Korea.[4]

Yomiuri Shimbun also noted that many South Korean media used many "praising words" to describe Xi Jinping's visit, such as "Xi Jinping, as one of the faction that knows South Korea", and "the visit to South Korea is like a visit to relatives." Wang Yi, Chinese foreign minister, called such short,

---

3.   Xi Jinping's Speech on the Work Meeting of Neighboring Diplomacy, December 24, 2013:.

4.   Japan: *Yomiuri Shimbun*, July 4, 2014.

adaptable, and fast overseas visit as the diplomacy of "Attacking a Vital Point."[5] In Chinese martial arts, martial arts experts always know the best Kung Fu master because when he points at a significant part of the opponent's body, the opponent often feels tingling and cannot move. The vital point is sometimes called the "Achilles heel;" once pointed at, the opponent can immediately be killed.

Using "attack points" to describe Xi Jinping's style of diplomacy also shows his capability to plan, manage, and control the diplomatic game. He is not afraid to break the routine, brave to reveal his true personality, and better at closer personal relationships. For example, when Park Geun-hye asked when Xi Jinping and his wife met, they were delighted to tell her: "28 years ago, introduced by a mutual friend of ours."[6]

Xi Jinping Pays Full Respect to Mongolia

In July 2014, Xi Jinping visited South Korea. A month later, he visited Mongolia. Mongolia and China have a very special relationship. Under the iron heel of Genghis Khan and his descendants, China became a part of the Mongol Empire; in 1260, the great-grandson of Genghis Khan, Kublai Khan became the Khan of Mongolia after some power struggles, and he, who was fond of Chinese culture, became the founder of the Yuan Empire in Chinese history in 1271.

The Mongols' rule in China did not last long. In 1368, Ming emperor Zhu Yuanzhang, who had been a monk, captured the capital of the Yuan Dynasty (today known as Beijing), and the Yuan Dynasty was over. The Mongols retreated to the northern grasslands and the Ming Empire sometimes talked, and sometimes fought, but lasted almost 300 years.

Prior to the establishment of the Qing Dynasty after the capture of China, Manchu had incorporated Mongolia into its own territory. Throughout the Qing Dynasty, the royal family and Mongolian leaders made alliances by marriage, making Manchu and Mongolia the Chinese aristocracy. But after the Qing Dynasty collapsed in 1911, the Mongolian nobles refused allegiance to the Republic of China, and gained independence with the support of Tsarist Russia.

Leaving the embrace of China, Mongolia had been a vassal to the Russians in the subsequent 100 years. It is clear that the Mongolians and the Chinese people share a complex history. In China, there is still a large population of Mongolians, so they often refer to Mongolia proper as "Outer Mongolia."

---

5.   Xinhua News Agency, February 9, 2014.
6.   Hong Kong: *Wen Hui Bao*, July 9, 2014.

To balance China and Russia, in particular the influence of China, Mongolia, after getting rid of Soviet control, positively introduced their "third neighbors," which were the United States and Japan. Mongolian President Tsakhiagiin Elbegdorj used to study at Harvard University. In 2012, the then US Secretary of State Hillary Clinton visited Mongolia and delivered a speech, praising Mongolia as a "model of democracy" in Asia, in stark contrast to some countries.[7] Listeners would know it was Mrs. Clinton's allusion to China

The Japanese have always made a good impression on Mongolia, and the Japanese Kamikaze attack team's name is related to the Mongols. Over 800 years ago, Kublai Khan, who had taken control of China and Korea, decided to attack Japan, but a sudden typhoon destroyed the powerful Mongol fleet, and thereby Japan was preserved and the term Kamikaze, meaning "divine wind," was born.

After shaking off the Soviet Union's control, Japan quickly became a close friend of Mongolia and is the latter's largest foreign aid supplier. "Sumo" wrestling is very popular in Japan, and two of its highest-level Henggang players came from Mongolia. In March, 2013, Japanese Prime Minister Shinzo Abe visited Mongolia; he called on the two countries that shared common values of freedom and democracy to strengthen cooperation. Naturally, China would consider that Japan was drawing Mongolia to its side against China.

To prosper, China's backyard should be secure. Xi Jinping decided to use his diplomatic skills to resolve the gap between China and Mongolia, and bring Mongolia in as a part of China's development track. After all, China is Mongolia's largest trading partner. Mongolia is rich in iron ore, coal, and copper, but it has no big market, which is in southern China.

Xi Jinping still adopted the diplomatic strategy of "Attacking the Vital Point." To do so, he is willing to pay full respect to Mongolia.

Looking back, the last time a leader from China visited Mongolia was Wen Jianpao, the then Premier of the State Council in June 2010. The last Chinese President's visit as head of state was in 2003, when President Hu Jintao visited Mongolia as one country out of many destinations.

Although the territory of Mongolia covers an area of 1.56 million square kilometers, its population is only 3 million while in China with 1.3 billion people, a randomly chose average city's population is far more than all of Mongolia. Therefore, Xi Jinping's humble and special visit also moved the leaders of Mongolia. Mongolian Prime Minister Altankhuyag and his wife as

---

7.   Perlez, Jane. "From Mongolia, Clinton Takes a Jab at China," *The New York Times,* July 9, 2012.

well as the Foreign Minister Batbold and other officials welcomed Xi Jinping at the airport.

What surprised the outside world was that on the day of March 22, 2014, it was the 120th birthday of Deng Xiaoping, China's "Chief Designer of Reform and Opening Up," and China would hold a commemoration of the highest standard. Xi Jinping, as China's supreme leader, should attend. But in order to visit Mongolia on March 22, the forum to commemorate Deng Xiaoping was held in advance on March 21.

Xi Jinping likens his visit to visiting relatives. In Mongolia, he said that, "more open lines of communication and visits will bring us closer and closer, with deeper and deeper friendships." He also invited Mongolian friends to visit China and look around. This type of dialogue as if casually chatting, has been Xi Jinping's style. Naturally, his smile, coupled with China's huge financial resources captivated Mongolia's heart. During the visit, China and Mongolia signed a number of energy-related and financial cooperation agreements, including one in which China promised it would invite 100 young people from Mongolia to visit China, provide Mongolia with 1,000 training sites, increase the availability of 1,000 Chinese government scholarships, and invite 250 Mongolian media representatives to visit China in the next five years.

Although the visit to Mongolia lasted only two days, we can still see that Xi Jinping pays close attention to neighboring diplomacy. In his own words, "only if we willingly open the door can we feel at ease and run our own affairs." As an aspiring leader, Xi Jinping believes China must be a promoter of peace in the world.[8]

To compete in the world, we must manage affairs with our neighbors because China does not want more territory, but instead more friends.

The "Genghis Khan of our Time?"

During Xi Jinping's visit to Mongolia, one picture caused extensive heated discussions among the world's Chinese people, when the President of Mongolia, Elbegdorj, accompanied Xi Jinping to the Mongolian Nadam Fair. Xi Jinping took over the bow handed to him by a Mongolian valiant fighter, and crooked the bow as if shooting condors.

Over 800 years ago, relying on this simple but practical crossbow, strong Mongols with amazing arm strength swept across Eurasia and established an unprecedented empire well-known to history. In Chinese culture, the "crooked bow shooting condors" and Genghis Khan are linked as expressions

---

8.　　Xi Jinping. *Neighborhood Watch—to Create a New Era of Sino-Mongolian Relations in the Mongolian State Great Hural,* August 22, 2014.

of the aspirations of the world's ambitions. To Xi Jinping's supporters, his embodiment of the "crooked bow shooting condors" displays his ambition to regain the Chinese empire. A Hong Kong newspaper claimed that his action, in fact, meant he wanted to be "the Genghis Khan of our time."[9] Xi Jinping is certainly not Genghis Khan, but he does want Mongolia to be a part of China's development track. He is clearly aware that in China's 2,000 years of history, the most deadly threat has been always from the north; hence Mongolia must not become China's enemy.

He delivered a speech in the State of Great Hural in Mongolia where he said that China was willing to provide opportunities and space for common development for neighboring countries including Mongolia. He also welcomed others to take the train of China's development, either on board the express train or stowing away. His statement, apparently without naming, is a response to Obama's accusation that China is hitchhiking on the back of the United States.

Under his smile offensive, Mongolia is carefully connecting with China. The most outstanding performance is regarding track width. In Asia, the width of tracks is a very sensitive political issue. In Russia, Mongolia and other former Soviet countries, the track width is 1520 millimeters, which is the broad gauge. And 1520 is also known as the "Russian gauge," which originated in England, but flourished in Tsarist Russia, and has been maintained until now. Ironically, an important reason the broad gauge is still flourishing is war. In the vast territory of Russia, the railway is the most important mode of transport, but unlike other countries it has a broad gauge. An enemy army would be helpless to invade Russia by railway using its own trains.

In today's Asia, Russia, Central Asian countries under the control of the Soviet Union in the past, and Mongolia, still use broad gauge. China uses the standard gauge. Thus, the international intermodal trains from Beijing to Ulan Bator and to Moscow have to have the bogie and wheel set reassembled each time before entering Mongolia so as to continue to travel on the broad gauge.

In March, 2014, Xi Jinping reached an agreement with Mongolia to strengthen the railways and other infrastructure. This helps Mongolia, a landlocked nation, to transport cargo quickly. Clearly, China cannot change to the broad gauge, and if Mongolia continues to use the broad gauge, it will be such a waste of time and money. There is only one reasonable result— Mongolia needs to change its gauge and adopt Chinese standards.

Gauge is a technical issue and also a major political issue. In Mongolia,

---

9.   *Apply Daily*, August 24, 2014.

in fact, ten years ago, many people called for the introduction of the standard gauge, but they were immediately accused by opponents as being "pro-China," and it is difficult to promote such politically sensitive issues. Xi Jinping's visit promoted a shift in the policy of Mongolia. On October 24, 2014, the State of Great Hural in Mongolia finally ended several years of intense debate, and the final vote agreed to use the same standard of gauge in the two sections of railway adjacent to China. Votes in favor of this resolution accounted for 84 percent of the total membership. The railway starting from the Chinese border has been extended to Mongolia's largest coal mine Tavan Tolgoi, where it is estimated that there are 6.4 billion tons of high quality coal. Their main purchasing target is China; therefore, the construction of railways with the same rules as Chinese railways will allow direct loading and transport to China's coal plants. It is estimated that, due to the need to replace the wheels and rails, it would save a significant amount of funds per ton of coal.

This change is considered to be Mongolia's first step toward moving closer to China. In the long run, with the continued weakening of Russia, China is bound to become the most important decision-maker in Asia. In addition to Mongolia, other countries like Kazakhstan, Kyrgyzstan, and Tajikistan will also remove their original broad gauge and replace it with international standard track like China. There might even be a possibility that Russia abandons the broad gauge and adopts the same standards with China, especially when China has the competitive advantage of high-speed rails. This is what Xi Jinping would like to see; he is a politician with a long-range perspective that is not limited to one school of thoughts; in order to help other countries close to China, he specializes in lowering himself to appease others' anxieties.

In the Mongolian Parliament, in order to appease the Mongols' fear of China, he said, "the Chinese people often say 'a good neighbor is worth more than gold.'" China has the most powerful neighbors in the world, and they treat this as a valuable asset. China's modern history is a history of humiliation full of tragedies and disasters, a great history of the struggle against foreign aggression and for national independence, and "the Chinese people after suffering hardships cherish peace and will never impose what they have suffered onto other peoples."[10]

In the joint declaration issued by Mongolia and China, both countries stress that they will neither participate in alliances and groups that may cause damage to the other party, nor allow any third country that would

---

10. Xi Jinping. *Neighborhood Watch—to Create a New Era of Sino-Mongolian Relations in the Mongolian State Great Hural,* August 22, 2014.

prejudice the interests of another country in the proximity of their national territory. Xi Jinping is quite adept at lobbying. In his youth, he loved to read, even in the countryside during labor training, he would read all kinds of books in his time off work. He is quite familiar with historical anecdotes and proverbs. He has his words at hand for his speeches which he delivers with a smile, which makes it easy to be impressed by his sincerity.

The late Prime Minister Lee Kuan Yew, Singapore's founder, commented that Xi Jinping is actually introverted, not that he does not communicate with you, but that he does not reveal his likes and dislikes easily. "Whether or not you said something to make him angry, his face is always filled with a pleasant smile. Compared with Hu Jintao (Xi Jinping's predecessor), he has more of an iron will."[11] Lee Kuan Yew is known to be good at reading people. He thereby classified Xi Jinping at the level of Nelson Mandela, and praises them both for having strong emotional self-control and not allowing personal misfortune and misery to affect their judgment.

This feature of Xi Jinping is also reflected in his various speeches. On March 27, 2014, he attended the 50th anniversary of Sino–French diplomatic ties in Paris. In his speech, he quoted the words of Napoleon, "China is a sleeping lion, when the lion wakes up, the world will all tremble." But Xi Jinping said "the lion has been awakened, but it has a head of peace, and is an amiable and civilized lion." He is recognized as China's most powerful leader in the last 20 years, but privately, he is an honest friend.

Even to some troublesome western countries, Xi Jinping seems to respond freely. For example, Xi Jinping chose Moscow as his first visit as the supreme leader and met Russian President Vladimir Putin, a contemporary tsar that makes the West very unhappy. He held Putin's hand and said: "our characters are alike." Indeed, to Cheng Guoping, China's vice minister of foreign affairs, Xi Jinping and Putin's personalities share many similarities— they have the demeanor of leaders and strategists, global visions, the courage to venture outside norms, but are not reckless; they take deep consideration over everything, reflecting their wealth of political experience, but are also very approachable.[12]

World leaders do not usually pay attention to small details, but Xi Jinping is an exception. He keeps his friends' big days in mind. October 7, 2013, marked the birthday of Putin, and Xi Jinping and Putin were attending the APEC summit in Bali, Indonesia. That night, Xi Jinping ordered a specially prepared cake and drank vodka with Putin. Putin said at the time the state

11.   Lee Kuan Yew, Belfer Center for International Studies. *The Grand Master's Insights on China, the United States, and the World.* Cambridge, MA: The MIT Press.

12.   Hong Kong: *Wen Hui Bao*, March 21, 2013.

of the two were "like college students."[13]

To promote mutual trust and cooperation between countries with this private friendship and interaction is both Xi Jinping's real personality and an important aspect of his diplomatic style. As a foreign leader that interacts heavily with Xi Jinping, Park Geun-hye has certainly experienced it. During his visit to South Korea in July 2014, Xi Jinping and his wife carefully selected gifts for her, including a glass ornament decorated with hibiscus embroidery, which aligned with the "hibiscus" in the name of President Park Geun-hye. It is said that the president's parents, Park Chung-hee and his wife, were looking through a Chinese dictionary to pick Park Geun-hye's name—in Chinese "Geun" means the Korean national flower "Mugunghwa" and also means "nation", while "Hye" is a symbol of "grace."

In Xi Jinping's gift bag there was a portrait of the famous hero of the Three Kingdoms. Zhao is the legendary Chinese hero from the time of the Three Kingdoms, with a heroic spirit, wisdom, and bravery—he once rescued Prince A Dou from an army of millions. Park Geun-hye said in her autobiography that the hero was her favorite historical figure, and whenever Zhao Zilong enters the narrative, her heart would beat faster. She suspected that the hero was her first love.[14]

After the end of the Mao era, Chinese leaders' visits began to follow international practice in which leaders take along their families. However, no other first lady displays diplomacy quite like Peng Liyuan. She is one of the most famous Chinese military singers, and her elegant manners, decent words, and loving role as a mother, make her sometimes become the focus over Xi Jinping. If you want to evaluate China's soft-power diplomacy, Peng Liyuan is the fully deserved first lady. At her first public appearance in March, 2013, she escorted Xi Jinping in the international arena, stunning people immediately with her stylish clothes. It also caused share prices of China's domestic textile stocks to soar.

Xi Jinping employs the help of Peng Liyuan to bridge the gap between them and the people of all countries. Among the gifts for Park Geun-hye, there was a DVD of Peng Liyuan's songs. Worried Park Geun-hye made a special arrangement, singing Peng Liyuan's famous song "On the Hopeful Field," at the state banquet, and Xi Jinping and his wife were delighted.

---

13.   Hong Kong: *Wen Hui Bao*, May 20, 2014.
14.   Hong Kong: *Wen Hui Bao*, July 16, 2014.

II. MAJESTY WITHOUT ANGER

When Xi Jinping and Park Geun-hye were drinking and laughing in Seoul, less than 300 kilometers away in Pyongyang, a young leader's heart was filled with tension, anxiety, and possibly a little anger. He was Kim Jong-un, the third supreme leader of the DPRK, the two former leaders being his grandfather and his father.

Out of all the neighbors of the People's Republic of China, the DPRK is one of the closest in history. In the Korean War from 1951–1953, the DPRK and Chinese troops fought fiercely against South Korea and the United States forces; ultimately, realized the military demarcation of ceasefire. Although Chinese troops withdrew from the DPRK soon after, they still maintained a military alliance. Article II of the *China-DPRK Friendship Cooperation and Mutual Assistance Treaty* provides that: "Both parties will take all measures to prevent any attack on either party from any countries, and if either party is subjected to attack by other countries and states war, the other party will take any necessary means at its disposal to provide military assistance to the party at war."

Saying No to the DPRK

In the past, China's top leader would certainly choose to promptly visit the DPRK after taking office. What made Mr. Kim disappointed was that after Xi Jinping became China's top leader at the end of 2012, his first choice was to visit Russia; in 2014, he even crossed the border of the DPRK and went to South Korean's capital Seoul. South Korea and the DPRK have been in a stalemate since they signed a truce rather than a peace agreement between the two countries. Theoretically, they are still at war.

In China's diplomatic world, the DPRK has been a sensitive topic. Since Kim Il Sung and Kim Jong Il thought traveling by train was more secure than by plane, when they visited Beijing, the Beijing Railway Bureau had to dispatch a large number of civilian trains. China always used the highest standard of hospitality, including insisting that all the members of the Standing Committee of the CPC Political Bureau attended the banquet to emphasize the value of the Korean camaraderie.

But in the era of Xi Jinping, it all changed. He did not play by the rules. On April 7, 2013, just after taking over as the Chinese president, Xi Jinping went to China's southernmost province of Hainan, a tropical island, to participate in the Boao Forum for Asia. This is similar to a Chinese-built new version of the Davos World Economic Forum, realized with the intent of expanding China's voice and influence in international affairs.

In the keynote speech, Xi Jinping emphasized: "No one should be allowed to throw a region and even the whole world into chaos for selfish gains."[15] One must admit that Chinese is a very obscure language; the same words can often have multiple interpretations.

Who was Xi Jinping truly referring to? He did not disclose. It might be the United States, because it is the country most qualified to throw the world into chaos, and there were disagreements between China and the United States on many issues, then and now. It also might be Japan, as China and Japan have been in a stalemate over the Diaoyu Islands dispute and their understandings of history. But more likely, Xi Jinping was warning the DPRK. Because the day before, Wang Yi, the Chinese foreign minister also gave a similar and vaguely phrased warning at the Boao Forum. He had stressed, "trouble is not allowed on China's doorstep."

Almost at the same time as Xi Jinping took the office of the general secretary of the CPC Central Committee, the DPRK also underwent a power shift. In December 2012, 29-year-old Kim Jong-un succeeded his father who had died of illness and became leader of the DPRK. It is interesting that in the four countries in East Asia, the rulers are all the children of former politicians. In China, Xi Jinping is the son of the Party senior Xi Zhongxun; in Japan, Prime Minister Shinzo Abe's grandfather Kishi served as Japan's Prime Minister; in South Korea, Park Geun-hye became Korea's first female president, and her father was the assassinated former President of South Korea, Park Chung-hee; in Korea, Kim Jong-un was the third generation leader of the Kim family.

All of these leaders learned different political cultures from their ancestors. In China, when Xi Jinping conducted drastic reforms and proposed the China Dream to bring about China's rejuvenation, while in South Korea, the policy became more conservative than risk-taking. In April, 2012, the DPRK's test-fired long-range missile failed, and eight months later, another DPRK missile launch was a success. The DPRK insisted that they were launching a carrier vehicle, but it was widely believed in the international community that DPRK was actually carrying out a trial of a long-range missile, which was in violation of relevant bans of the Security Council.

On February 12, 2013, the DPRK ignored China's opposition and conducted a third nuclear test. The DPRK's propaganda machine was also loaded with comments reeking of gunpowder and aggression. For example, on April 9, 2013, the Korean Asia-Pacific Peace Committee issued a statement that, because of the US and South Korea's hostile and war-provoking moves, the Korean peninsula was sliding into a "thermonuclear war." Once the

---

15.   Xinhua News Agency, April 7, 2013.

war was ignited, it would be developed into a full-scale war, and the DPRK would launch "a merciless retaliation." In the event of war, according to the Alliance Treaty, China would be forced to support the DPRK. Moreover, a large number of DPRK refugees would be bound to flock to China, bringing a threat to the stability of northeast China, which would also disrupt the efforts underway to rejuvenate China.

In particular, the nuclear tests infuriated the Chinese people. In some cities in China, there were even protests against Korea's nuclear tests. The Ministry of Environmental Protection uncommonly held a press conference on the day after the DPRK's nuclear test, announcing that China had set up dozens of data monitoring stations to monitor the DPRK's nuclear test site near the northeast border of China and its surrounding areas, and China had initiated the emergency response plan of environmental radiation in response to the DPRK's nuclear test.

The Chinese people's worries are realistic. China's well-known nuclear expert Wei Shijie said: "The first principle for the selection of a nuclear test site is to keep it away from the crowds, prevent pollutants from harming people, and a choice of underground sites for nuclear tests also needs to avoid contamination of groundwater sources. This is also why nuclear test sites in the world are selected in deserts or isolated islands. Strictly speaking, North Korea covers a narrow territory and does meet the above conditions. The current choice of site is probably the most appropriate place for DPRK, but for China, it is very inappropriate."[16]

In his view, the DPRK's nuclear test "was the same as twice before: that they are tunnel-entrance nuclear tests, rather than shaft nuclear tests with better sealing," and therefore, the leakage of radioactive material would be inevitable.

In the opinion of some who are concerned that once a DPRK nuclear test incurs an accident in the densely populated areas in northeast Asia, like the accident of the Soviet Union's Chernobyl nuclear power plant, a large area of land will no longer be fit for human residence and the fertile northeast China will be turned into a barren area. The greater danger perhaps is not just nuclear leakage. Some South Korean experts worry that the DPRK's nuclear test has a scope of up to 300 kilometers, while it is only 110 kilometers away from Changbai Mountain, which is a dormant volcano that has had ten eruptions in the past 1,000 years, most recently in 1903. If the DPRK's nuclear test reached the same level as a 6.0 earthquake, it could lead to the eruption of Changbai Mountain.

According to associated studies, in the case of an eruption of Changbai

---

16.   *Oriental Morning Post*, February 22, 2013.

Mountain, the intensity index could be up to 7.4, a disastrous level, while in April, 2010, a volcanic eruption in Iceland that caused great disaster had an intensity index of only 4.0. According to simulation results based on the Federal Office of Disaster Management of the USA, the Korea Institute of National Disaster speculated that if the outbreak of the Changbai Mountain occurs in winter, the ash would cover Ulleung Island, South Korea, within eight hours, arrive in Japan within twelve hours, and cause the paralysis of airplane routes in northeast Asia.

Analyzing these potential consequences, Professor Zhang Lianmei, International Institute for Strategic Studies, Central Party School, believes that the DPRK's nuclear tests are a serious threat to China's national security, and may suffer a serious nuclear leakage, sooner or later, which would be disastrous. His article was published in *Leaders* magazine. In the past, it was unthinkable to publish articles criticizing the DPRK in China, but with the increasingly aggressive policy of the DPRK, there have been more and more criticisms. Xi Jinping may not agree with these publications but apparently has tolerated such criticisms.

After the DPRK's third nuclear test, Yang Jiechi, the then Foreign Minister, summoned the DPRK ambassador to China immediately, and made solemn overtures to express China's strong dissatisfaction and resolute opposition to DPRK's behavior. Such public attitude of criticism towards DPRK is very rare in China's diplomacy with the DPRK.

On the same day, the UN Security Council immediately held a meeting to strongly condemn the DPRK's behavior. In the past, on Security Council resolutions concerning the DPRK, China, as the DPRK's ally, has mostly objected to sanctions by other countries, or has tried to be a "peacemaker" to alleviate the expressions of the resolution; but this time, China clearly voted in favor of condemning the DPRK.

China Is Stunned by the DPRK's Transition

Chinese people are surprised that DPRK did not stop this risky policy and further bloody reprisals. On December 8, 2013, the late DPRK leader Kim Jong-il's brother-in-law, Jang Song-Thaek, North Korea's number two, was found guilty of conspiracy against Kim Jong-un. He was taken away by the soldiers from the scene of the General Assembly and was subsequently sentenced to death and executed immediately. In the verdict, the Special Court of DPRK accused 67-year-old Jang Song-Thaek of planning a coup. When Kim Jong-un was elected as the supreme leader, he was "reluctant to stand up and clap his hands and could barely cope with the arrogant and contemptuous attitude." The verdict was covered with DPRK-style acerbic vocabulary, for example, criticizing Jang as an "eternal usurper," and "human scum inferior to a dog." There is also a statement in the verdict saying that Jang Song-Thaek hoped to emerge as a reformer after the coup and gain foreign recognition. This must have drawn close attention from China.

China is the only country that may recognize the DPRK's regime change. China has been encouraging the DPRK to follow China's reform and opening up instead of maintaining a closed state. Jang Song-Thaek had the most contact with Chinese leaders. A year before he was sentenced to death, he made a special trip to visit China, and then held talks with China's top leader Hu Jintao. His mission was to promote both China and the DPRK's joint development zones to make progress, while the zone is to emulate China's special economic zone with the first economic take-off. The role of "China, an old friend" is clear, and the risk of the nuclear tests will be borne by China. Moreover, the DPRK's radical and risk-taking policy directly stimulated the strengthening of the military in Japan and South Korea, which in turn poses a threat to China.

Smiling is one side of Xi Jinping; the other side is a firm character behind a gentle appearance and a majesty without anger. He does not accept the DPRK's threatening actions and fired back at the young Kim Jong-un. In June 2008, his first visit after he was elected as the first Vice President was to Pyongyang. But by the end of 2012 when he became China's top leader, he began to grow cold toward the DPRK. He refused to visit DPRK, and also did not welcome Kim Jong-un's visit.

In a joint statement during his visit to Korea in July 2014, China and South Korea stressed that "they objected to the development of nuclear weapons in the peninsula." Though they did not mention the name of the DPRK, the target was self-evident.

Some Chinese officials have also publicly expressed their dissatisfaction with the DPRK. Wang Hongguang, deputy commander of the Nanjing Military Region, the former lieutenant general, wrote an article in the *Global Times*, "Chinese people do not have to fight the DPRK's war," "China is not the Messiah, if the DPRK collapses, China cannot save it." Although he does not represent the official position, this kind of speech can be published to show Xi Jinping and China's decision-makers' internal dissatisfactions with the DPRK.

On May 7, 2013, the Bank of China suddenly issued a press release announcing it had closed the account of the DPRK Foreign Trade Bank and stopped accepting transfer business related to the account. Although in the past the United States had always persuaded China to increase the intensity of sanctions against DPRK, China always gave a low-key response based on a variety of considerations, but seeing the DPRK ignore China's suggestions and gamble blindly, it was clear that China could not wait and see any longer.

In Xi Jinping's dictionary, there are no second chances. Whoever offends the dignity of China will receive a *no* from him!

On November 10, 2014, in Beijing's Great Hall filled with Soviet-style architecture, Xi Jinping held talks with Japanese Prime Minister Shinzo Abe. This was Abe's first meeting with China's leaders in the 2 years since he took the office of Japan's prime minister again in 2012. Prior to this, China and Japan had experienced tense relations due to historical issues and the issue of the Diaoyu Islands.

Xinhua News Agency used an ambiguous phrase, "meet-up after appointment," in a report. It can be understood as both sides agreeing to meet later after an appointment, or it can be understood as a requirement that is to be held upon the request of Japan; apparently the meanings were largely different, while the latter seems to highlight Abe's urgent mood.

It did not appear to be a pleasant meeting, as shown on CCTV. Xi Jinping, who usually smiles, was extremely serious, and did not even smile during their handshake. Japanese media reported that Abe met with Xi Jinping, immediately greeted in Chinese, and that they were happy about the meeting, but they did not report on Xi Jinping's response.

The formal conversation was more of a warning. Xi Jinping said to Abe that, in the past two years, whether the Sino–Japanese relations undergoing serious difficulties was right or wrong both countries had to deal with and improve Sino–Japanese relations by issuing a four-point consensus, and China hopes that Japan effectively acts in accordance with the spirit of consensus and handles the relevant issues properly. Xi Jinping did not mention Abe's visit to the Yasukuni Shrine. However, he noted that the historical issues were related to more than 1.3 billion Chinese people's feelings, related to overall regional peace, stability and development. Only when Japan abides by the Sino–Japanese bilateral political documents and the "Murayama Statement" as promised by previous governments, can Japan develop friendly relations with their Asian neighbor for development in the future.

The Yasukuni shrine honors several of Japan's military leaders that were convicted as war criminals after World War II, including Hideki Tojo, who was sentenced to death by Tokyo Trial Court. Abe has repeatedly visited the Yasukuni Shrine, although he argued the purpose was to cherish their memories and pray for peace. This caused great indignation in China and South Korea as this is seen as a spiritual place for celebrating war criminals. It is difficult for Chinese and Koreans to understand that, in the West,

German politicians publicly apologized for the crimes of the Nazis, and it is absolutely impossible to pay homage to Hitler; but in the East, a visit to Yasukuni Shrine by Japanese leaders is claimed to be for peace.

In China, to describe a person who hates evil with a passion, one would say, "his eyes cannot tolerate a grain of sand." Indeed, Xi Jinping is such a person, as he launched a massive action against corruption in China. He also holds quite a tough attitude against those who act to violate China's national dignity and sovereignty.

When inspecting the army, as the supreme military commander, Xi Jinping will always say that the army should be able to win the war. He stressed that the army must restructure and upgrade, and be prepared in accordance with the standards of wartime to ensure that the Chinese military will always assemble upon calling, be able to fight, and be able to win.

On October 14, 2014, the *People's Daily* published a lengthy review, which was an overview of Xi Jinping's military thinking. The commentary stated: "Historical experience shows that any country will not be really strong without a strong military power backing." It continued: "Now, we are in the center of the world arena we have never been closer to bring about the unprecedented great rejuvenation of the Chinese nation, and to have unprecedented ability and confidence to realize the goal. Without solid national defense, without a strong army, there will be no security for the great rejuvenation of the Chinese nation."

There must be a strong army to back China as a great country. Xi Jinping understands the challenges China is faced with; for a rising power, the conservative powers set up multiple obstacles, the United States' warships cruise offshore of China, which makes Chinese people think of the Opium Wars and other instances when western powers invaded China in the past. With Japan, the Japanese always holds an ambiguous attitude or even denial to the history of aggression against China, even though it continues to expand the military. "One day there will be a war between China and Japan;" there is no lack of such radical rhetoric on the Chinese Internet.

Other than for historical questions, which make the Chinese people angry, Japan's practice on the Diaoyu Islands issue also greatly hurt China's self-esteem. The Diaoyu Islands are near China's Taiwan, with an area of about 4 square kilometers. In 1972, the United States handed "administrative jurisdiction" of the Diaoyu Islands together with Ryukyu to Japan. However, the Chinese people believe that the Diaoyu Islands have always been part of China's territory, and the US–Japan move was through "backroom deals." In 2012, the Japanese government's move to nationalize the Diaoyu Islands infuriated China.

On November 23, 2013, the Ministry of Defense in China suddenly issued an announcement claiming that China has delineated the East China Sea Air Defense Identification Zone, announcing the airspace over the Diaoyu Islands as an area of territorial dispute with Japan. The announcement requires that flying aircraft in the area must provide identification and obey China's instructions; if not recognized or if there is a refusal to comply with instruction, "China's armed forces will take defensive emergency measures." On the same day, China dispatched two large-scale military reconnaissance plans to execute the first patrol at the identification zone.

For China's move, the Ministry of Defense Ministry of China's spokesperson, Yang Yujun, said that this was in accordance with internationally-accepted practice and the purpose was to safeguard China's national sovereignty and territorial airspace security, and further maintain order in the air; he said that this is not directed against specific countries or regions, and does not affect the flying freedom in the airspace concerned.

Although the Chinese military stressed that the air defense identification zone "is not directed against any particular country," but it is widely believed that the move is directed against Japan, precisely because, once Japan's fighters enter the defense identification zone, China will grant about ten minutes of warning. Chinese military experts Li Feng said that, in doing so, it is meant to further treat the Diaoyu Islands as China's territory, "and it also shows that the authorities have been prepared for military struggle, and are not afraid of conflicts with Japan."[17]

Such a bold move is unthinkable in the previous two terms of China's government. Hong Kong media reports even said that China's military has had the intention of establishing an air defense identification zone in the East China Sea for a long time, but the report was placed on hold after it was submitted to the Central Military Commission. When Xi Jinping holds the highest military power, however, he gives the green light.[18]

Actually, the core of the identification zone is the Diaoyu Islands waters. As the Japanese even refused to acknowledge the existence of the dispute over the Diaoyu Islands, China's move is to retreat in order to advance and force Japan to acknowledge the dispute over the Diaoyu Islands. This is also in line with Xi Jinping's tough style.

This naturally caused a strong reaction in Japan. On the same day, Junichi Ihara, the Director of Asian and Oceanian Affairs Bureau of the Japanese Foreign Ministry, called on Han Zhiqiang, the Chinese Ambassador to Japan, to express "solemn protest." Two days later, Japanese Prime Minister

---

17.   Hong Kong: *Sing Pao Daily News*, November 24, 2014.
18.   *Yazhou Zhoukan*, November 2013.

Shinzo Abe expressed publicly that China marks Japan's inherent territory of the Senkaku Islands (namely the China Diaoyu Islands) as if it is China's airspace. This is completely unacceptable to Japan; we will request China to withdraw. Japan is determined to defend the inherent territories, territorial waters and territorial airspace. China immediately responded, claiming that China's practice was consistent with the *Charter of the United Nations*, and furthermore Japan was "making irresponsible remarks for no reason whatsoever," and China firmly opposed.

When Japan summoned the Chinese ambassador to express a strong protest, China also summoned the Japanese ambassador to express their dissatisfaction of Japan's "unreasonable provocations."

Many people are more worried that China's identification zone over the Diaoyu Islands will inevitably lead to intensified confrontation between aircrafts of both countries, and increase the likelihood of an accidental weapons discharge.

January 31, 2014 marked the Spring Festival, the most important festival in China. Two Su-30 fighters belonging to the Eastern Sea fleet scrambled with live ammunition, and forced two Japanese fighters away from entering the East China Sea air defense identification zone. Chinese media called them foreign military aircraft in their report. As the details were gradually exposed, originally it was two F-15J fighters belonging to Japan's Air Self-Defense Forces and stationed in Okinawa who entered the East China Sea air defense identification zone designated by China, and China's Su-30 fighters began to drive them apart. In the interception process, Chinese and Japanese fighters competed in many tactical air operations including rising, diving, left turns and right turns over the East China Sea, and finally as the Japanese fighters still could not get rid of the Chinese fighters, they had to fly away.[19]

This exercise, with active payloads and ammunition, could have been highly likely to spark a conflict accidentally with even a slight mistake. So a few days later, US former Secretary of State Kissinger warned in Germany at the Munich World Security Forum that due to the increasing tension between China and Japan the ghost of war was hovering in Asia. He judged that, since the current situation was very similar to that between Asia and Europe in the nineteenth century, the possibility of explosive military conflict could not be ruled out.

Asian diplomacy observer Hu White at the University of Australia previously thought that if the United States and Japan went to battle with China due to the Diaoyu Islands issues of further escalation, it could lead

---

19.   Hong Kong: *Economic Daily*, February 6, 2014.

to confrontation between China and the United States and Japanese forces and "the situation will fall into a vicious cycle until the outbreak of a war no one can stop." The cause of a war could be trivial; perhaps the captain of a Chinese or Japanese ship suddenly loses his senses in a maritime standoff, makes a reckless decision to open fire. If one side shoots first, the other side will return fire, and neither will concede.[20]

But for the Chinese people, toughness towards the Japanese, including dispatching warships in the waters of the Diaoyu Islands, is in line with China's national dignity and national interests. In various maps and historical records, the Diaoyu Islands are Chinese territory belonging to Taiwan Island; in the open seas of the Diaoyu Islands, Ryukyu Islands were China's vassal state in the past. But with the decline of the Manchu Dynasty, these territories became gradually occupied by Japan.

After the defeat of Japan in 1945, Taiwan was returned to China, naturally including the Diaoyu Islands. Although the United States on the surface did not intervene in the Diaoyu Islands dispute, it actually transferred the Diaoyu Islands to Japan, and generated the current dispute over them. Taiwanese leader Ma Ying-Jeou was a "Diaoyu Islands protection" activist in the 1970s. To get back the Diaoyu Islands from the hands of Japan, the power of Taiwan is clearly not enough, they must rely on the People's Republic of China.

Letting the Chinese become generally disappointed in order to avoid an intensification of conflict, China, from the era of Deng Xiaoping, has begun to take the attitude of suspending disputes. When Japan nationalized the Diaoyu Islands and denied they had an agreement on suspending disputes with China, the Chinese began to become angry, and some cities organized anti-Japanese marches. Some radical people even compared the Chinese government to the late Qing government, which was always tough on domestic problems but weak towards international ones. Acting when China needs to act is the tough stance of Xi Jinping on the Diaoyu Islands issue, which has changed the diplomatic style of China fundamentally.

On the issue of national dignity and sovereignty, he stands firm. On January 28, 2013, Xi Jinping stressed in his first public foreign policy speech after becoming China's top leader: "China will never use 'core' interests of territory and security to make trade-offs."

He said, "We want to adhere to the path of peaceful development, but we must not give up our legitimate rights and interests, and must not sacrifice the core interests of the country. All foreign countries must not expect that we will make transactions with our core interests, and will not expect us to swallow the bitter fruit of damaging China's sovereignty, security, and

---

20.   *South China Morning Post*, January 7, 2013.

development interests."

On the surface, Xi Jinping's speech did not cross the basic principle of Chinese policy. But his clear description showed China's tougher stance on the international arena, and this is also a warning to Japan and other countries that in territorial issues China will not make concessions! Compared with words spoken to South Korea and Mongolia, this demonstrated Xi Jinping's firmness and flexibility.

Denying a History of Aggression

As for a high profile fight back against Abe's words and deeds denying the history of aggression, Xi Jinping has launched a public opinion war toward Japan with a more positive attitude. September 3, 2014 was the 69th anniversary of the Chinese Anti-Japanese war victory. Xi Jinping led all Standing Committee members of the Political Bureau to the Memorial Museum of the Chinese People's Anti-Japanese War near Marco Polo Bridge, and presented wreaths to the martyrs of the war. On July 7, 1937, Japan used the excuse of the missing soldiers and attacked the Chinese army near Lugou Bridge, and this day was considered the beginning of the full Sino–Japanese war. In fact, before this, Japan had occupied many places including northeast and northern China.

On the day of the memorial meeting, Xi Jinping delivered a strongly worded speech. He said that correct treatment and deep reflection on the aggression history of Japan's military, was an important political foundation for the establishment and development of Sino–Japanese relations. Entering the modern age, the war of aggression waged by Japanese militarists brought about tragic disaster to the Chinese people and the people of the majority of East Asian countries, and these were facts which were undeniable and could not be denied.

Xi Jinping swears that China will, with the greatest determination and hard work, together with people all over the world, resolutely defend the victory of the Chinese people's Anti-Japanese War and World Anti-Fascist War, resolutely safeguard the postwar international order, never allow the denial and distortion of the history of aggression, never allow a resurgence of the military, and never allow a replay of this historical tragedy.

As for the practice of the Japanese government continuing to deny the history of aggression, Xi Jinping stresses that fact is fact, and axiom is axiom. Black is black, even spoken 10,000 times, "black" could not become white; white is white, even spoken 10,000 times, "white" could not become black. All the practice of calling white "black" and vice-versa only amounts to self-deception.

Compared with his two predecessors, Xi Jinping is better at diplomacy. On overseas visits, he uses all the occasions he can to expose the evil of Japan denying their history of aggression. When Park Geun-hye visited China in June 2013, she suggested to Xi Jinping that An Jung-geun was a historical figure with common worship in China and South Korea, and hoped that China could establish an An Jung-geun monument in Harbin. On October 26, 1909, An Jung-geun entered the Harbin railway station, in northeast China and used a pistol to kill the first Japanese Resident-General of Korea Secretary Ito Hirobumi. An Jung-geun was arrested by Russian military police on the spot, transferred to Japan, prisoned in Lushun prison, and sentenced to death by hanging, and died at the age of only 32 years old. His heroic act enshrined him as an "anti-Japanese national hero" in South Korea and the DPRK.

After Xi Jinping listened, he immediately instructed relevant departments to cooperate and implement the memorial. Half a year later, on January 19, 2014, the Chinese people in Harbin railway station opened an An Jung-geun Memorial, with an area of more than 100 square meters, including an An Jung-geun story showroom, and markers revealing the location at which An Jung-geun killed Ito Hirobumi. This made the Japanese government angry, but the South Korean people were greatly moved.

On March 28, 2014, Xi Jinping delivered a speech in Germany for the Körber Foundation, and pointedly said, "history is the best teacher, it faithfully records the footprint of every country, and provides inspiration to the future development of every country. In more than 100 years from the Opium War in 1840 to the founding of the new China in 1949, war has been frequent in Chinese society, and internal war and foreign invasion have occurred in cycles, bringing painful suffering to the Chinese people.

He said, "the war of aggression launched by Japanese militarists caused great tragedies with casualties of about 35 million. This tragic history left an imprint engraved on the Chinese."

Xi Jinping chose Germany to deliver his speech attacking Japan, and this was clearly a clever strategy; Germany is known by neighboring countries for its thorough introspection into history. Germany and France have also become the backbone of the EU. Looking at East Asia, due to the words and deeds of Japanese politicians from time to time denying the aggression history, the relationship between Japan and China and Korea often creates difficult situations.

The choice of the Körber Foundation was also made because the person responsible for the fund was former German President Richard von Weizsäcker, whose father was sentenced in the postwar era for his role in Nazi Germany. While Weizsacker served as president, he held a clear opposition attitude to Nazism. The speech delivered by Xi Jinping at the Körber Foundation, in addition to China's peaceful development concept, is intended to put pressure on public opinion towards Japan.

But the United States, because of their allied relationship with Japan, and attempts at balancing China's influence, maintained tolerance and an indulgent attitude to Abe's right-wing views, and this further encouraged Japanese hardliners towards China. According to media reports, in 2014, Abe sent a message of condolence to a memorial ceremony for more than 1,000 Japanese soldiers convicted as guilty in World War II. Contents of the message called the war criminals "the foundation of the country," and "offered the most sincere memorial to those victims sacrificing their lives for today's peace and prosperity and depending on a new national spirit to become the cornerstone of the motherland."[21]

This behavior of Japan also stimulates China and South Korea to refuse to have a summit meeting with Japan. Xi Jinping sets two bottom lines for this, firstly, Japan must admit the dispute with China on the Diaoyu Islands issue; secondly, Abe must promise not to visit Yasukuni Shrine, otherwise he will not hold talk with Abe.[22]

The APEC summit held in November, 2014, in Beijing was a grand international conference hosted by Xi Jinping. A summit without the prime minister of Japan would certainly not be complete; Abe ultimately did not attend the summit and also made Japan appear isolated in the international community. China and Japan began to carry out measures to appease each other and seek a path of reconciliation.

After intensive negotiations, on November 7, 2014, China and Japan reached a consensus on four principles. In order to find the wording acceptable to each other, the negotiators of the two parties racked their brains, and the debate continued until the final signing of the agreement.

This is an agreement filled with delicate diplomatic art. On the core issue of the Diaoyu Islands issue, the third consensus stated that both sides recognized different views existing on tensions around the Diaoyu Islands in the East China Sea in recent years, and agreed through consultation and dialogue to prevent deterioration of the situation, establish crisis management mechanism, and avoid the occurrence of unexpected events. On the surface, Japan made concessions, admitted the situation in the related waters of the Diaoyu Islands, and agreed that China had a different view. Of course, Japan could also have admitted the tension, but not declared there

---

21.   *Japanese Asahi News*, August 27, 2014.
22.   *Kyodo News*, August 27, 2014.

was a sovereignty dispute or any controversy.

The same subtle language was also expressed in the issues of history. The Chinese side said that in the spirit of "facing up to history and facing the future" both sides should overcome political obstacles in the relationship between the two countries to reach consensus. Since there was no direct mention of the issue of the Yasukuni Shrine, this gives the two sides room for maneuver. In the Chinese version of events, however, this clearly includes the Yasukuni Shrine.

So on November 10, 2014, Xi Jinping finally shook hands with Abe. For this meeting with no smiling faces, Abe later told Japan's Fuji TV that he felt Xi Jinping shouldered responsibility for 1.3 billion people. Each country had its own difficulties but were hoping to gradually improve the relationship in the future, and building mutual trust was also the expectation of people in many regions.

Having tempered justice with mercy and been tough and flexible, Xi Jinping firmly controls the trends of Sino–Japanese relations, and holds a moral advantage in the international opinion fight. As for Japan denying their history of aggression against China, Xi Jinping prefers to arouse the common memory of the nation and forces Japan to respect the past history.

December 14, 2014, was the 77th anniversary of the Nanjing Massacre. To punish the tenacious resistance of the Chinese armed forces at the time and deter stubborn resistance, the Japanese army carried out a massacre in Nanjing, the capital of China. According to Chinese statistics, about 300,000 Chinese people died under the knives of Japan, many women were raped and then killed as well. But for this period of history, the Japanese government have always guarded this secret, or maintained a disagreement on the number of deaths and did not admit the massacre.

Countermeasures enacted by Xi Jinping include more high-profile commemorations of the dead. December 14, 2014 was defined by official China as the first national Memorial Day. On that day, Xi Jinping and the chairman of the National People's Congress Standing Committee Zhang Dejiang flew to Nanjing and attended this Memorial Day. Commemorative activities were held at the Nanjing Massacre Memorial Hall, and he supported 85-year-old survivor Xia Shuqin with his hand as they jointly unveiled a national memorial statue.

Xi Jinping solemnly delivered a speech in the field. The Nanjing Massacre was one of the world's three major tragedies, with irrefutable evidence that the memory could not be tampered with, "history will not change just because of the changing times nor will it disappear if denied."

International leaders have also expressed dissatisfaction with Japan's denial of history through various means. On March 9, 2015, German Chancellor Angela Merkel in Tokyo delivered a speech saying that war was Germany's painful memory, and Germany would never forget the history. This was the 70th anniversary of the ending of World War II; for both Germany and Japan, it was a meaningful year.

In answer to how Japan deals with the opposition of China and South Korea over these historical questions, Merkel said that Germany is saddled with the history of the Nazis carrying out a massacre of the Jewish people, and that it is because Germany has faced up to the history of the past that it was accepted by the international community. "This is because while Germany is facing the past, the United Nations has been guarding the 'overcoming of the past' for Germany." She noted that facing up to history is particularly important in the international community and for international relations.

As for how Japan should improve relations with its neighbors, Merkel said with euphemism, she could not help the Japanese. But she said: "as the German Chancellor, it is hard to give you advice on how Japan should deal with its neighbors. But in my opinion, history and experience tell us that we must find peaceful means to reach a settlement."

Some countries also expressed dissatisfaction with Japan through action. In April, 2014, Denmark's Queen Margrethe II visited China, she particularly went to the Memorial Hall of the Victims in the Nanjing Massacre, and became the first foreign state head to visit this Museum while in office.

III. MAKING THE RULES IN THE SOUTH CHINA SEA

To defend Chinese interests, Xi Jinping has no hesitations. If in the Diaoyu Islands issue, it is mostly competition between China and Japan, a more difficult problem may lie in the South China Sea, where China is facing challenges from many neighbors. In this vast sea, there are hundreds of islands, many of which are small reefs sometimes only exposed when the tide is low. The Chinese people discovered them first and have recorded the earliest use of them and they should belong to China. In December 1946, the Chinese government appointed senior officials to go to the Spratly Islands to hold a reception ceremony on one of the biggest islands where troops were stationed. The island was named Taiping Island because of the Taiping ships visiting there.

Because these reefs are far from the Chinese mainland, Chinese naval power is weak and the mainland and Taiwan are in a constant state of hostility over the sovereignty of these islands. In the 1970s, a large number of islands and surrounding reefs were occupied by the Philippines, Vietnam, Malaysia, and other countries. With attention from China to its maritime rights and interests, disputes in the South China Sea gradually became acute.

A Strong Response to the Huangyan Island Standoff

On April 8, 2012, the Philippines Navy found eight Chinese fishing vessels in the waters of the Huangyan islands. The Philippines Navy boarded Chinese fishing boats with guns, inspected the Chinese fishermen, and accused them of illegal fishing. In the past, China has often only protested meekly because, since Huangyan Island belonged to China, the behavior of the Philippines seriously violates China's sovereignty and the interests of the Chinese fishermen. After the protest, the Philippines continued to enforce the law, and Chinese fishermen were searched, fined and even detained by the Philippines regularly.

This time, the Philippines underestimated China's will. Two days later, two maritime surveillance ships from the China State Oceanic Administration rushed to the waters of Huangyan Island to protect Chinese fishing boats and fishermen on the site. Under the pressure of the Chinese ships, the Philippines had to release the arrested Chinese fishermen, but Philippine and maritime surveillance ships of China were in confrontation near Huangyan Island, and neither side compromised with the other. Confrontation between the two sides began to be upgraded. The Philippines sent more warships and aircraft into the sea, and the Chinese deployed cruise ships to counter them. China continued to exert pressure on the Philippines. On May 10, 2012, China on the grounds of security, warned the Chinese people not to travel to the Philippines, and reminded Chinese citizens in the Philippines to pay attention to safety, and avoid any demonstrations. By May 16, all Chinese tourists in the Philippines had left. Bananas grown in the Philippines were rejected by China with the excuse of agricultural damage.

Then there were rumors that the Guangzhou Military Region and the South China Sea fleet responsible for the South China Sea area had entered a second level of war preparedness, and all personnel leave was canceled. Naval aviation began to transition, and the naval fleet was brought into combat duty. Naval, Second Artillery Corps, and the 15th Airborne Corps of Nanjing military region adjacent to Guangzhou military region also upgraded to level three war preparedness at the same time. However, on May 11, the China Ministry of National Defense denied the Guangzhou military region and the South China Sea Fleet had entered into war preparedness mode. Taking into account the standoff in Huangyan Island, China was likely to take a sudden move to expel the Philippine ships by force and destroy them.

On May 14, 2012, the Chinese Navy amphibious fleet undertook military exercises near the northern Philippines in the Luzon region of the Western Pacific. China's defense ministry had said earlier that the Liberation Army Naval Fleet going to train in Western Pacific waters was a routine arrangement within the annual plan, and was not targeted at any particular country or target. China has the legal rights of navigation freedom in the relevant waters, and abides by the relevant international laws.

On May 14, China announced a moratorium from the second day lasting for two months, including the South China Sea and Huangyan Island. Under strong pressure from China, after confrontations lasting a few months, the Philippines had to withdraw. Although the Philippines foreign minister condemned China's stance on Huangyan Island and claimed the Philippines would never give up the sovereignty of Huangyan Island, and the Philippines indirectly admitted China's control over Huangyan Island.

The struggle to victory over Huangyan Island has demonstrated adjustments China has made in the South China Sea issue. In the past, China has been very worried that friction in the South China Sea would deteriorate and damage China's strategic opportunity. This round game helped China dispel most concerns, and also chastened China's grasp of the friction scale. After the Party's 18th National Congress, Xi Jinping paid more attention to this strategy. On April 7, 2013, when he visited Hainan Province, he went to Tanmen town in Qionghai and visited local fishermen. Among the Chinese fishermen in the Huangyan Island confrontation at that time, there were many from Tanmen town. Xi Jinping asked the fishermen whether it was safe to go to the South China Sea, and said the country will further care for them. This was publicly considered as encouragement and support for the Chinese fishermen.[23] Xi Jinping is no longer afraid of confrontation, he dares to fight to win peace, and without curbing the Philippines, the military could not defend China's interests in the South China Sea.

Demonstrating the Strength of Chinese Engineering

Compared to the Huangyan Island dispute between just China and the Philippines, the Spratly Islands are controversial and vied for between many countries. In the Nansha Islands, Vietnam claims the most with 29, the Philippines has eight, Malaysia has five, Brunei has two, and China only has nine, including the largest island, Taiping Island in Nansha, controlled by Taiwan.

The South China Sea islands controlled by China are mainly small reefs, there is no fresh water, and they can be submerged by the tide. Chinese soldiers guarding the island are very tough, they live in high houses on stilts,

23.   Hong Kong: *Sing Tao Daily*, April 10, 2013.

and they must wade for a long distance through shoulder-high water to transport fresh water, vegetables, meat and other substances from supply ships which are unable to dock close to the islands. Many people have arthritis because of this. This is not what Xi Jinping wants to see.

A western satellite monitor found that, from the end of 2013, China began to operate large-scale reclamation in reefs of the South China Sea. Taking Yongshu Reef as an example, the area before was about 0.08 square kilometers, and by the end of 2014, the area had expanded to 1.3 square kilometers, which was more than Taiping Island and became the largest island of Nansha. The satellite also found that a 5,000-ton dock and helicopter platform had been built on the island, with radar, a radio monitoring system and oil reserves set up, which could be enough to supply a small- to medium-sized naval ship.

In addition, there is a 3,000-meter long runway on the island, which is enough to land various types of Chinese fighter and transport aircraft, a deterrent to the United States and neighboring countries.

Yongshu Island is located in the center of the Spratly Islands, and its location is very advantageous. It is only 700 kilometers from Yongshu Reef to Hu Zhiming, Vietnam, less than 1,500 kilometers across the Philippines, and 1,400 kilometers to the Malacca Strait.

China, in fact, is planning to turn the island into a Chinese version of the Diego Garcia military base, and greatly expand China's deterrence abilities to countries around the South China Sea, the Philippines' foreign secretary Del Rosario said, this move by China is "in fact" controlling the South China Sea.

Moreover, land reclamation in China is not only in the Yongshu Reef, but it also includes reefs controlled by China such as Nanxun Reef, Chigua Reef, Huayang Reef and Dongmen Reef.

In the Deng Xiaoping and Jiang Zemin eras, China in the South China Sea issue adhered to "shelving disputes and joint development" principles, and took a more resigned attitude, but results were always passive, reefs being thought as having sovereignty were occupied, American warships prowled unhindered around the outskirts of China, and the voices of the surrounding small countries were louder and stronger than China.

In Chinese civil society this is considered an insult to China. Xi Jinping clearly saw this and decided to take offense. In addition to allowing no concession to the Philippines over the Huangyan Islands, the reclamation issue has made fast progress.

China is rapidly changing its weak position on the South China Sea issue, which depends on the engineering strength of China's economic power, but is more dependent on the will and determination of the highest leaders. After all, it takes massive human, material, and financial resources, and it may also affect a change in geopolitics in which leaders must repeatedly weigh up before making any decisions.

Taiwan's National Security Bureau Director Li Xiangzhou confirmed at the legislature's Foreign Affairs and National Defense Committee meeting in October, 2014, that this generous action was approved by Xi Jinping, and the goal was to "make these small islands into fortresses" and "make the island a statement of purpose."[24] And Chinese Admiral Wu Shengli took a battleship to travel to the South China Sea and to instruct reclamation work in September 2014, which showed there was overall strategic planning to be done in the South China Sea.

Tough, but not reckless; forceful, and at the same time measured. This is becoming an important principle for the South China Sea strategy of Xi Jinping. The expansion of the Chinese military in the South China Sea naturally makes the United States uneasy. But as for the warnings by the US, China refutes them and thinks this is an attempt by America to contain China.

If outsiders think the Chinese government is just bluffing, they underestimate the strength, courage and intention of Xi Jinping. He likes to take the initiative, and even uses force without fear when required.

Issues of Sovereignty

On May 3, 2014, the Maritime Safety Administration of the People's Republic of China announced that the 981 oil-drilling platform of China's National Offshore Oil Corporation would carry out a three-month drilling operation in the Paracel Islands in the Nanhai Sea. The 981 platform is regarded as the "Scales of the State" by the whole of China. But Vietnam immediately reacted angrily. Li Haiping, the spokesman of the Vietnamese Foreign Ministry, lodged a strong protest that the operation area of the Chinese platform was in Vietnam's exclusive economic zone only 120 nautical miles from the coastline. But China refuted this immediately: "the Paracel Islands belong to Chinese territory, and before the reunification of Vietnam, the communist party of the north Vietnamese government has always recognized China's sovereignty over the Paracel Islands.

Argument breeds action. Vietnam sent dozens of warships and maritime police boats to the area to confront the Chinese patrols. The two sides of the maritime police boats shouted to each other, and fired water cannons. The nationalist sentiment intensified rapidly in Vietnam, and anti-

---

24.   Taiwan: *United Daily*, October 16, 2014.

China demonstrations occurred in Ho Chi Minh and many other cities. Demonstration later turned into riots, and some rioters shouted slogans against China. Some even set fire to dozens of factories, including Taiwanese- and Korean-owned factories. Several Chinese people were killed.

According to past practices, if the other party protested strongly, China would gradually soften its stance. But Vietnam's attitude seemed to enrage China more. China immediately launched a massive evacuation operation, sending aircraft to pick up Chinese citizens in Vietnam. Chang Wanquan, the Chinese defense minister, examined the defense at the Vietnamese frontier. As for the 981 oil-drilling platform that triggered the problem, Fang Fenghui, chief of general staff of the People's Liberation Army, declared clearly during a visit to the United States, "The construction of the oil-drilling platform must be completed without any external interferences and destruction."[25]

War seemed all too likely. The Register of Fishing Vessels of Vietnam even said that China had deployed plenty of warships around the area of the 981 platform, removing their gun covers and being ready to fire.

Fortunately, the Chinese and Vietnamese senior officials did not get carried away with anger. Two months later, when China announced that the related drilling operations had been finished and the 981 drilling platform was towed off the Paracel Islands, the storm subsided.

Tough toward Vietnam and the Philippines, and angry toward Japan, these stances reveal the personality of Xi Jinping, that is, "dare to draw the sword." The word "sword" in this case refers to a quite well-known Chinese drama, recounting the legend of an anti-war general. He dared to assault, and was surpassingly resourceful and full of courage and moral stature.

Many times in his speeches, we can see his preference for the frontal assault tactics of the "sword". On June 30 2014, when it comes to the issue of anti-corruption, Xi Jinping said, "we must are to sword to all the unhealthy tendencies;" a month earlier, when it came to the Xinjiang issue of East Turkistan terrorists frequent activities, Xi Jinping said, "On the issue of promoting cadres, a standard is that the person dares to speak up and draws the sword at a critical moment."

There is a saying in China, "two meet and the bravest wins." In the era of Jiang Zemin and Hu Jintao, China's diplomatic style was partial to low-key conservativism, which lead to the Chinese diplomatic policy suffering criticism from both sides. One is the foreigners accusing China of being too hard on the problems of the Diaoyu Islands, the other is the domestic criticism considering that China is too weak—often by protest more than action.

---

25.   Taiwan: *China Times*, May 17, 2914.

Xi Jinping is burly enough, but he revealed his sophisticated methods: "Swords are drawn when needed, but smiles have an equal power." Drawing the sword serves as a deterrent, which complies with Sun-Tzu's wisdom: "Soldier are battling, but serving justice; kind people are experts at serving kindness." On issues of territory and sovereignty, China's position is firm and clear: If it is not ours, it is not a point of contention; if it is ours, the lands must be maintained.

A smile is an aspect of soft power, showing China's kind demeanor. During Xi Jinping's visit to France in 2014, he said that, "China is a peaceful, amiable, civilized lion." In Beijing at the APEC meeting in 2014 and at the 70th anniversary of the Bandung Conference in Indonesia in 2015, he showed friendliness toward the Japanese Prime Minister Shinzo Abe.

IV. CHINESE DIPLOMATS LEARN GAME THEORY

On October 24 and 25, 2013, Xi Jinping hosted the symposium of China's peripheral diplomatic jobs. He pointed out that, thinking about the peripheral issues and conducting peripheral diplomacy should have a three-dimensional, diverse, wide-ranging perspective, and put forth the concise idea to develop peripheral diplomacy, that is "friendliness, sincerity, reciprocity, and inclusiveness," which reflected Xi Jinping's strategy of managing the peripheral area, with the aim to dispel the concerns of the "China threat" in surrounding countries, and to seek the establishment of a security mechanism beyond the Cold War era.

With these four words, the interpretation of Qu Xing, the director of the China Institute of International Studies, has stated that manifestations of this include: "blood shared, treating people with sincerity, benefiting the surroundings, and showing tolerance." Xi Jinping's "three-dimensional approach" refers to globalization, recognizing that we need to go beyond the traditional concepts of the surrounding nations, and consider the countries by land and sea and every available vantage. "Multiplicity" involves politics, economics, military, culture, humanity, and other aspects that need to be coordinated to make comprehensive judgments. "Wide-ranging perspective" means not only looking at the current situation, but also looking at situations from a historical perspective to compare, and to extrapolate the future from now on.

Xi Jinping's guidance, in fact, will shift more focus to the periphery. In the past, the top priority of China's diplomacy has been the United States, and looking forward to establishing a special relationship with the United States, but under the background of America's "Return to Asia" to deal with the rise of China, China must pay more attention its surrounding areas. It is said that in the age of the empires, China had a sense of superiority and gifts for surrounding countries, but under the leadership of Xi Jinping China sometimes shows more respect and tolerance.

His first visit to a foreign country after he became the Chinese supreme leader was to neighboring Russia; he then went to the Republic of Tanzania, South Africa, and the Congo, and attended the fifth meeting between the leaders of the BRIC countries in South Africa. He has also visited neighboring South Korea and Mongolia three times, as well as participating in the Winter Olympics opening ceremony in Sochi on February 7, 2014. According to Foreign Minister Wang Yi, the first visit to Russia, focusing on the surrounding environment and the relations between big powers, attending the BRIC summit meeting, focusing on the world's fast-rising emerging powers, visiting three African countries, and focusing on developing countries, have all provided a solid foundation for China's diplomacy. In fact, it shows Xi Jinping's concerns about smart power, in view of the current unfavorable international environment surrounding China, it tempers justice with mercy, and resolves the strategic pressure from the United States and Japan. To Russia, giving crucial support in an attempt to make the North's largest neighbor become friends instead of a new enemy in Chinese history; to the other neighboring small countries, giving economic concessions in exchange for their support on China's core interests.

In Southeast Asia, China has a good friendship with Thailand, Cambodia, and Laos. Cambodia's Prime Minister Hong Sen was once an enemy of the Khmer Rouge that China supported, but when achieving national reconciliation in Cambodia, Hong Sen exchanged his position rapidly, and made efforts to develop relations with China. His attitude was recognized by China and China has given great assistance to Cambodia.

On the issue of the South China Sea, Vietnam and the Philippines stand to one side. In the last two ASEAN meetings in May, 2014, and April, 2015, the two countries that have territorial disputes with China made efforts to persuade their ASEAN partners to take a unified stance against China. In the boycott of other countries that had good friendships with China, the expected strong statements against China were not published. In fact the final declaration did not even mention China.

Behind the incentives and penalties lies Xi Jinping's diplomatic skill. While other countries tried to advance the "China threat" theory, he responded with his own notion of the "community of fate." When visiting Indonesia in 2015, he put forth the "China–ASEAN community of fate." At the Boao Forum for Asia in the same year, he proposed the "Asian community of fate;"

in previous visits to Africa and West Asia, he also proposed the "China–Africa community of destiny" and the "China–West Asia community of fate."

Undoubtedly, Xi Jinping uses vital interests to defuse distrust, and occupies the high moral ground of diplomacy, and he is very good at hunkering down. Although Indian Prime Minister Modi's tough nationalist stance made China unhappy, his visit to southern Tibet under China's sovereignty made Chinese people angry. Considering India's importance on the world stage in the future, as well as Modi's influence in India, Xi Jinping gave him enough respect.

On September 17, 2014, Xi Jinping and his wife Peng Liyuan first appeared in Modi's hometown in Gujarat where they enjoyed the sunset on the Sabarmati River with Modi. The two leaders even enjoyed a swinging bench together, which surprised the Chinese people, because in the past, leaders always showed a serious attitude.

Obviously, before Modi's visit to China, Xi Jinping's visit to India was a display of kindness to the Indian strongman. The Japanese Prime Minister Shinzo Abe, the US President Barack Obama, and Russian President Putin have all visited New Delhi, which highlights the importance of the world's second most populous country on the world stage.

But China found India haughty. Although Xi Jinping invited India to attend the APEC informal meeting in October, 2014, held in Beijing, Modi declined. In the Indian political arena there was criticism of China's voice from time to time. On January 26, 2015 India's Republic Day celebrations, President Obama was the most important guest and Modi personally greeted him at the airport. Inviting Barack Obama instead of Xi Jinping to visit India on this highly symbolic day may reflect the emphasis of India's diplomatic preference towards China or the United States.

With great patience, Xi Jinping made efforts to develop relations with India. In February, 2015, when Indian Foreign Minister Sushma Swaraj visited China, Xi Jinping altered the former practice of rarely meeting with a foreign minister, and met him in Beijing. As helmsman of the world's largest developing country, Xi Jinping tried to control the way the meeting went, but was dissatisfied with his stale, slow, sloppy diplomatic style.

On May 4, 2014, China's Youth Day, Xi Jinping went to Peking University, China's first university, to talk with Hou Yifan, who studied there. He said to the skilled chess player, who once won the international chess championship, "Chess is like life, it is a constant game," and he invited Hou Yifan to give classes to officials in the Ministry of Foreign Affairs, so that they could learn diplomatic principles and methods from the game of chess.

Xi Jinping's tough stances, unwillingness to back down, his devotion to the dignity of China, and his emphasis on diplomatic game theory—perhaps Xi Jinping's new international thinking brings fear to those Chinese diplomats still steeped in the passivity of bygone eras.

CHAPTER
9

*Building a New Model of
China–United States Relations*

It was a bitterly cold night; the north wind came from the Mongolian Plateau to the south, sweeping past Beijing city. On such a winter's day, without haze, the people of Beijing all stayed in their heated rooms. However, the two leaders of the world's most powerful countries were still walking in the cold wind in Zhongnanhai on the west side of the Forbidden City.

This was the most eye-opening part of Xi Jinping's diplomatic strategy during his two years in office; the person he was accompanying was the president of the United States of America, Barack Obama, and the day was November 11, 2014. A few hours before, the Asia-Pacific Economic Cooperation (APEC) meeting had just ended at Yanqi River on the northern outskirts of Beijing; Xi Jinping and Obama went back to Beijing by car, and Obama started his visit to China.

That day was also an online shopping holiday in China. Many Chinese people defied exhaustion to stay up all night to place their orders by Internet or phone to purchase their favorite items starting at midnight. The daily sales of China's largest Internet company, Alibaba, reached RMB 57.1 billion, more than the sum of "Black Friday" and "Cyber Monday" when the highest daily sales on the Internet are recorded in the US.

The winter was cold in Beijing, and Xi Jinping and Obama were both dressed in long black coats; one was burly and the other, lanky. After chatting, eating, and walking for five hours, Obama said to Xi Jinping, "Tonight, I received the most comprehensive and thorough insights into the history of the Communist Party of China, its ruling philosophy, and your ideology."

I. XI JINPING IMPARTS A LESSON

At 6:30 p.m. on November 11, 2014, Xi Jinping who is considered to speak the most standard Mandarin among the leaders of the new China, became a tour guide: He said he would like to introduce his "White House"—Zhongnanhai Yingtai—to the US President. Zhongnanhai used to be the West Garden of the Emperor of the Ming Dynasty; the Emperor ordinarily lived in the Forbidden City, and went to Zhongnanhai for amusement. After the establishment of the People's Republic of China, the Forbidden City became a museum, and Zhongnanhai became the living and office space of China's highest leaders. The south yard is the central location of the Communist Party, and the north yard is the site of the State Council.

In America, the White House is often open to visitors, but Zhongnanhai is a mysterious place to Chinese people; it is surrounded by high red walls, and the "red wall" is also considered to be another name for the highest leading authorities. Xi Jinping invited the US president into the core political realm of China, naturally hoping to show his sincerity to Obama.[1]

In international politics, the choice of conversational mode, meeting place, and subjects of the talks often have special meanings. Thus, it was even more extraordinary that Xi Jinping invited Obama to the mysterious Zhongnanhai and walked along the frozen lake on that cold night in Beijing.

A Walk at Night in Zhongnanhai

Xi Jinping told Obama that Emperor Qianlong of the Qing Dynasty once wrote a sentence here, a sentence meaning "to take a day of leisure." So, here was the perfect place to relax.

"I arranged to meet you here mainly because I thought of the meeting with you last June at the Annenberg Estate, and I wanted to create a similar atmosphere for this meeting," Xi Jinping said.[2]

That meeting had been Xi Jinping's first visit to the US as China's top leader, and the venue was arranged at the Annenberg Estate in California on the West Coast, a place where the then US President Ronald Reagan had once dined with British Prime Minister Margaret Thatcher. In the hot

1.   *People's Daily*, November 14, 2014.
2.   Ibid.

California sun, Xi Jinping and Obama met many times with each other, and Obama even gave the two redwood benches they had sat on to Xi Jinping as a national present.

Obama naturally understood the intention of Xi Jinping; the night walk in Zhongnanhai was just like the meeting at the Annenberg Estate, but instead of strolling in sunshine, this time both men walked in the howling wind without wearing ties. The two leaders walked and talked like old friends, which would naturally narrow the distance between them and create a better understanding of each other's real thoughts Unlike the last meeting, Xi Jinping had invited President Obama for a state visit to China this time and offered him the highest etiquette. In his last visit to the United States, Xi Jinping did not enjoy the ceremony of a national visit. Although Xi Jinping and his wife went to California together, the US First Lady Michelle Obama was absent because she wanted to accompany her two daughters to an unrelated event. As compensation, Michelle Obama and her two daughters made a special trip to China after that, and saw the giant pandas in Chengdu in western China.

On the whole, the two leaders had pleasant and carefree talks with each other at the Annenberg Estate and at Zhongnanhai. Obama was pleased to tell Xi Jinping that the effective cooperation between the two largest economies in the world, the United States and China, would benefit the whole world. He looked forward to open and fruitful communication with Xi Jinping, just like at the Annenberg Estate.

The informality, relaxation, chatting, and lack of formal dress were just some aspects of this special walk together; but on the other hand, Xi Jinping had a more profound political agenda.

Lights illuminating the palace architecture of Yingtai gave it a special aesthetic feeling. Xi Jinping told his American guest that Yingtai was built in the Ming dynasty of China, where the Qing Dynasty Emperor studied his documents, spent summers, and entertained guests. The great Emperor Kangxi of the Qing dynasty studied national strategies on how to pacify internal disorder and recover Taiwan in this place. In the reign of Emperor Guangxu, China was in decline, and the Emperor Guangxu intended to carry out the One Hundred Days' Reform to revitalize the country, but the reform failed finally, and the Emperor remained under house arrest in Yingtai by the Empress Dowager Cixi holding court behind a screen.

Obama immediately understood what Xi Jinping meant when he talked about history; he gave an immediate response that there were similarities between the histories of China and the United States. It was the same rule that reform always met with resistance, so we need to maintain our courage.

President Obama was engaged in a number of reforms in an effort to build a stronger US economy, which encountered a boycott on Capitol Hill, when the Democrats lost control of Congress in the midterm elections of 2014. Obama's response was apparently within Xi Jinping's expectations; he continued to say that it was very important to have an understanding of Chinese history since modern times because it would help the Chinese people to understand today's ideals and the road ahead.

Chinese top leaders often meet foreign heads of state for state visits in the great hall, but Xi Jinping especially arranged this one night to accompany Obama to walk in Zhongnanhai, which not only expressed his intention of developing a personal friendship, but also gave an historic education to Obama with the help of his familiar knowledge of Yingtai.

Harmony in Diversity

According to the original plan, the two world leaders would go for a walk at 6:30 pm in Yingtai of Zhongnanhai, before holding a brief meeting at Hanyuan Temple of Yingtai, followed by a small-scale banquet at Xiangyi Temple, and finally have tea at Yingxun Temple; it was originally planned that they would complete all activities of the day by 9:15 p.m.

But in fact, according to the records of the *People's Daily*, every event was repeatedly delayed as the two leaders had a great deal to talk about. For example, the meeting scheduled for 30 minutes lasted 90 minutes. Xi Jinping thought Obama might be hungry, and asked him to have dinner first. But Obama's response was that he still had a few more questions.

Informal leaders often make talks more free. The banquet scheduled for 90 minutes lasted nearly two hours. The tea gathering scheduled for 30 minutes lasted for nearly an hour. When Xi Jinping finally said goodbye to Obama as he got into his Presidential limousine, it was 11:00 p.m. The two world leaders had been together for five hours that night.

At the Annenberg Estate in California, Xi Jinping and Obama talked more about the bilateral relationship and their own claims, but this time the two leaders spent a lot of time talking about their own governing ideas. Xi Jinping said afterwards that they did not consider things as they stood, but carried out frank and in-depth exchanges on some fundamental questions, because they could comprehensively promote their mutual understanding, deepen mutual trust and respect, and avoid strategic miscalculations in only this way.

With this type of open and casual communication, the possibility of strategic miscalculation does still exist between China and the United States, although President Obama always said the emergence of a strong China was welcomed by the US, and the US had no intention of containing China. But in recent history there have been tensions between China and the US, particularly over the "Yinhe" incident in 1993, when the Chinese cargo ship Yinhe was halted in international waters by the US Navy, as well as the bombing of the Chinese embassy in Belgrade, Yugoslavia, in 1999 by a US aircraft, and territorial disputes in the South China Sea. To many Chinese people, the containment intention of the US is clear at a glance.

Although China's leaders have repeatedly clarified that China has no intention of challenging America's leadership, the boost of military power and economic development in China has made the point of view that China is the biggest threat popular in Washington, especially on Capitol Hill.

This is the reason that Xi Jinping chose Yingtai to give Obama a history lesson. In his words: "The different national conditions, history and culture, development path, different stages of development, all call for mutual understanding, mutual respect, mutual assimilation, and harmony in diversity."[3] "Harmony in diversity" was a famous saying of the Chinese sage Confucius. The original is "The gentleman aims at harmony, and not at uniformity. The vulgar man aims at uniformity, and not at harmony." It means that gentlemen maintain a harmonious and friendly relationship with others in interpersonal communications, but don't have to agree with each other in view of a specific problem; the mean men are accustomed to cater to others' psychologies and echo their speech, but do not have a harmonious and friendly attitude deep in their heart.

This is the wisdom of the ancient Chinese, and also the essence of Xi Jinping's diplomatic methods. He explained to Obama this "harmony in diversity" is the embodiment of the new power relationship between China and the United States. Both sides should strive for mutual understanding and mutual respect to achieve win-win cooperation without difference, conflict and confrontation.

"A Significant Achievement"

Five hours of intimate contact left a deep impression on President Obama. On December 3, 2014, when he was asked about his opinion of Xi Jinping in a business round-table meeting in Washington, Obama said the meeting with Chairman Xi Jinping, in terms of geopolitics, was very constructive, "obviously we both have reached a significant achievement."

Obama felt a deeper and more intuitive understanding of Xi Jinping and China's politics through the elaborate meeting organized by Xi Jinping, and voiced admiration for Xi Jinping's ability and power. He said to the audience

---

3.   *People's Daily*, November 14, 2014.

that Xi Jinping was probably a Chinese leader who has strengthened China's power in the shortest time and most intensive areas since Deng Xiaoping. "He took only one and a half to two years to gain such influence in China, and left everyone with a deep and lasting impression."[4]

China's development speed and potential have shocked Obama. He came to Beijing this time both for a state visit to China and to attend the APEC summit, held beside a beautiful lake in Huairou on the outskirts of Beijing where the haze and traffic problems of the city can be avoided. It is worth mentioning that Huairou means to 'bring calm and good governance' in Chinese, and China chose this venue as a meeting place to show its intentions were far removed from hegemony.

Obama saw a series of beautiful architecture works that had been built in Beijing for this meeting. He said to the American audience that the APEC summit venue was a luxurious conference center which took only one year to build and most other conference centers paled in comparison.

He said, "I want to say if they want to build something, it can really be built. It will erode our competitive advantage as time goes by. It's embarrassing to see the Chinese achievements by driving along the road."[5] Obama's remarks not only praised the fast development and high efficiency of decisions in China, but were also spoken out of admiration for Xi Jinping's control of power. The Democratic Party had just lost the midterm election, and although Obama has two years remaining in office, the fact is that he has become a lame duck in Washington politics. However, Xi Jinping's influence is increasing, and it is no wonder that Obama was "embarrassed" in comparison. Americans may also question whether simple pressure and containment is the best policy in the face of such a dynamic state and such a strong leader.

II. THE UNITED STATES: STILL NUMBER ONE

Although Xi Jinping and Obama were both very satisfied with the meeting in Beijing, it is worth noting that a phrase Xi Jinping began to talk about regarding the China-US relationship was "a new model of a major power relationship." President Obama just expressed his agreement, but never seemed to repeat it.

But what is the "new model of a major power relationship" described by Xi Jinping? Turning the clock back to June 7, 2013, at California's Annenberg Estate, at the press conference after the meeting with President Obama, Xi

4.   Washington, DC: *Reuters*, December 3, 2014.
5.   *Washington Daily,* December 3, 2014.

Jinping said he and Barack Obama agreed that China and the United States should be able to embark on a new path different from the conflict and confrontation among great powers in history, facing the rapid development of economic globalization, and the objective need of all countries to stay together.

In other words, the "new model of a major power relationship" in the eyes of Xi Jinping includes: no conflicts, no confrontations, mutual respect, cooperation, and benefits for both nations.

In a news release by the Xinhua News Agency, Xi Jinping explained in detail to Barack Obama about his analysis of these few key words: no conflict, no confrontation—China and the United States should objectively and rationally regard each other's strategic intentions, continue to work as partners instead of rivals; properly handle contradiction and differences through the ways of dialogue and cooperation rather than conflict and confrontation.

Mutual respect means China and the US should respect their choices of social systems and roads to development, and furthermore respect each other's core interests and major concerns, seek common ground while retaining their differences, tolerate and appreciate each other, and make progress together. Mutually beneficial cooperation is to abandon the zero-sum thinking between China and the United States, give consideration to the profit of the other side in pursuit of their own interests, promote common development in seeking their own development, and deepen interests' integration patterns.[6]

Both Barack Obama and Xi Jinping are worried that China and the United States may fall into the contradiction of the emerging power and the conservative power struggle. According to historical experience and lessons, the rising power often wants to get the international status to match its strength, but the conservative power always makes every effort to maintain their own interests. It might cause the outbreak of a war if the structural contradiction between the two cannot be effectively resolved. For example, before the outbreak of World War I, Germany rose rapidly and challenged Britain's hegemony; Britain desperately put pressure on Germany which resulted in the outbreak of the war.

The United States and China are nuclear powers; it will be undoubtedly devastating if war breaks out. A confrontation will also lead to the possible destruction of the world, and many small and medium-sized countries will be trapped in difficult situations. To resolve this confrontation, the leaders of China and the United States should have a long-term vision to make

6.   Xinhua News Agency, June 8, 2013.

responsible decisions for their own states and the world.

In the China-US strategic and economic dialogue of 2012, the American Secretary of State Hillary Clinton said the two countries must make "unprecedented" efforts to avoid a catastrophic war, and both sides needed to "write a new answer to the age-old problem, that is, what happens when a traditional power meets a rising great power?"

As an aspiring leader, Xi Jinping wants China to play a more active role in the world, and protect national dignity and sovereignty more effectively; at the same time he also clearly knows that the outside world, especially the United States, has doubt about China's rise. In 2013, he ignored the diplomatically cold reception of the United States and decided to have a talk with Obama in California without receiving an invitation for a state visit. He just wanted to set the direction of the China-US relationship and avoid any serious miscalculations.

China and the United States have conflicts and differences regarding Iran and North Korea's nuclear problems, as well as the network security issues. There have been recent tensions arising between the Chinese and US military over reconnaissance issues and a major fear is that a mutual trust deficit might cause a serious crisis because of a minor incident. Xi Jinping does not want any distrust to threaten the China-US relationship, nor destroy the development process in China in turn. Just as the close relationship he and Russian President Vladimir Putin have established, he hopes to also establish a similar relationship with Obama. Xi Jinping has told Obama he's very confident in the new model of power relations, based on five aspects of reasoning.

First, both sides have the political will for the construction of a new power relationship.

Second, the accumulation of more than 40 years of cooperation has laid a very good foundation for cooperation between the two countries in the future.

Third, the two sides have established a strategic and economic dialogue, high-level cultural exchange consultations, and more than 90 methods of communication, providing the dynamic for the construction of a new power relationship.

Fourth, the two sides have established more than 220 pairs of sister provinces/states and friendly cities. Nearly 190,000 Chinese students are studying in the United States, and more than 20,000 students from the United States are studying in China. Construction of a new power relationship between China and the United States has a profound basis in public opinion.

Fifth, the two countries will have a wide range of opportunities to cooperate in the future.[7]

Xi Jinping naturally understands the importance of showing the public the positive side as a politician, but the China-US relationship still simmers under the surface; many politicians take a tough stance against China in Washington DC, even believing that containing China will be in line with American interests. Therefore, they don't agree with the "new model of a major power relationship" put forth by Xi Jinping. Xi Jinping also acknowledges that the construction of new China-US power relations is unprecedented in history. Therefore, China and the United States need to continuously promote the formulation and importance of this "new model of a power relationship" in the process of strengthening dialogue, increasing mutual trust, expanding cooperation, and controlling the potential consequences of any differences in opinion.

In Xi Jinping's opinion, China and America are great nations, the people of the two countries are great people, and as long as the two sides have determination and confidence, maintain patience and wisdom, and bear both large and small interests in mind, the interests of both nations can be resolved in a manner beneficial to all concerned.

Maintaining a Distance

The United States deliberately maintained a distance from the zeal of China toward this "new mode of power relations." In July, 2014, US Secretary of State John Kerry went to Beijing to attend a China-US strategic and economic dialogue, and told the media: "I heard Chairman Xi Jinping mention many times 'the new model of a power relationship.' I think it cannot be defined only by words, but should be defined by action." The senior official in charge of Asia-Pacific Economic Cooperation Affairs in the State Department, Wang Xiaoming, said clearly: "It is a term proposed by China, not by the United States, so I'm not sure whether we can completely agree with its specific explanation."[8] The vague attitude maintained by Mr. Kerry is actually consistent with President Obama's deliberate avoidance of the phrase "new model of a power relationship." In the eyes of some American people, the promotion of "the new power relationship" is a political trap set by China so that the United States will acknowledge China's superpower status, and achieve the upper hand in the China-US relationship. This also means that the United States should respect China's "core interests," but the US believes that China's "core interests" such as Taiwan, Tibet, and the South China Sea are also related to the interests of the United States.

---

7.   *The Governance of Xi Jinping*, Chinese Foreign Language Press, 2014, p. 280.

8.   Bloomberg News, September 18, 2014.

As the world's leading superpower, the United States certainly does not want to see a strong contender. This means that the US admits that China is equal with it in assenting to "the new model of a power relationship," but a new form, a "G2" system, will lead to a downgrade of other US allies, which will inevitably create anxiety and discontent.

It is a fact of life that China is the most powerful competitor of America. The system of the Communist Party of China is not accepted by the United States, but it does not accord with American interests to have direct conflict with China, thus keeping a vague strategy will be in line with US interests.

After all, China is not the Soviet Union; military spending only accounts for a small fraction of GDP in China, and China is always trying to integrate into the international community. When Xi Jinping is making efforts to promote the "new model of power relationships," the United States has no need to discourage him, otherwise it may push China to a more unpredictable side if it is angered.

Harvard University Professor Joseph Nye remembered in the 1990s when the Clinton administration first considered how to deal with the rise of China, some politicians advocated a containment policy before China became powerful, but President Clinton refused. The reasoning contains two aspects: First, it was impossible to form an anti-China alliance, because most of the regions and countries wanted to keep a good relationship with both the United States and China; second, and more importantly, this policy would needlessly cause a hostile relationship with China in the future.[9]

The two reasons still exist today, and are even more strengthened with the rise of China. Former East Asia Affairs Chief Joseph Nye in the Pentagon said that if the United States treated China as an enemy, China would actually become a rival. It becomes a theme of America's policy toward China to contact within containment, and to reinforce the containment policy through its contacts.

Therefore, China and the US maintain different interpretations of the new power relationship; Xi Jinping could talk about his "new power relationship" concept during his meeting with Obama, and Obama seemed to be in favor of the idea, but did not repeat this phrase. Instead, he welcomed China's rise, and thought that a peaceful, stable, and prosperous China would be good for the United States and the world.

9.　　　Nye, Joseph. "The Future of the U.S.–China Relationship," *Hong Kong China–U.S. Focus*, March 10, 2015.

China Does Not Challenge the United States

Xi Jinping clearly knows the real face of the United States. But he also needs the cooperation of the United States, as the premise for an emerging power to rise is to dissolve the hostility of the conservative power structure. It cannot be denied that the United States takes advantage of its power, size, and number of allies.

Xi Jinping must consider the feelings of his home; he acted neither humble nor servile in the relationship with America but was full of sincerity and confidence. His officials try to take a more direct way to resolve the suspicions of China.

Wang Yang, China's vice premier, head of China's Foreign Trade and Finance, replaced the position of anti-corruption "Tsar" Wang Qishan. On December 17, 2014, in a speech made in the China-US commercial relationship forum in Chicago, Wang Yang told the American elites that when China adopted its reform and opening up policy, the United States had dominated the world economic system and rules. China's opening to the outside world means that China would like to join this system, basically acknowledge these rules and play a constructive role in the international economic system. He said that although China's economy was the second largest in the world, it only accounted for 55 percent of that of the United States, and the per capita GDP was only one eighth of the US figures. More importantly, the United States was still dominating the key technologies to lead the world in economic development, and shape the rules of world economic order. We should have a clear understanding of this.

"China neither has the motivation, nor the ability to challenge the leadership of America," Wang Yang told the US business elites: "We just hope the United States can better understand the position of China, understand China's national conditions, respect Chinese people's choice in cooperation with the United States, so that the difference of the political system will not become a barrier to cut off economic cooperation."

Wang Yang's words caused quite a stir in some Chinese circles, where some people interpreted his message as "China doesn't want to—and also can't—challenge the United States." Although some people thought what Wang Yang said was pragmatic, many were frustrated by the position he took and he was derided on the Internet, with shaming pictures comparing him to a pug raised by the United States.

Wang Yang once ruled Guangdong province, the strongest economic strength in China; he is not a career diplomat and is known for his frankness in speaking. Although his words appeared off-the-cuff and abrupt, in China's political ecology, it would obviously be impossible to make such a statement related to the China-US relationship without the consent of the highest levels. Wang Yang intended to pass information to the United States: in this world, the United States is still number one, and China has no intention of challenging it. At the same time, he also tactfully expressed criticism of some people's mindsets in the United States: The US cannot have doubts about China just because it is a communist country, China's current national condition and road are choices of the Chinese people; China and the United States can indeed coexist peacefully.

In that speech, Wang Yang also said frankly that when China has fully integrated into the global economy with the expansion of its economy, "the United States still needs to have a strategic vision on how to deal with China." History has shown that both confrontation and cooperation have a high price, but cooperation costs are low and the benefit is high.

China does not want to challenge the sincerity of the United States, which is also reflected in other leader's words and deeds. On April 15, 2015, the British *Financial Times* published an exclusive interview with China's State Council Premier Li Keqiang by Editor-in-Chief Lionel Barber. Barber remembered that Li Keqiang did not display arrogance even in the victory of the Asian Investment Bank against the United States. He has repeatedly insisted that China has no intention of building a new international order: "China is willing to work with other countries to maintain the international financial system," he said. "[The Asian Investment Bank] should be a supplement to the international financial system."

It was widely assumed that the establishment of the Asian Investment Bank in China was actually planned to replace the Bretton Woods System, but Li Keqiang's answer was an emphatic *no*. "The desire to break the existing order does not exist," he underlined. Li Keqiang insisted that "we cooperated with the World Bank and other agencies and learned a lot of advanced ideas; we joined the World Trade Organization so that Chinese enterprises knew how to better compete in accordance with the international rules. China is the beneficiary of the current international system for both peace and development."

Wang Qishan, the disciplined "Tsar" of the Communist Party of China, frankly told American guests that they could not avoid the fact that China was a country led by the Communist Party. On May 7, 2015, when he met the Democratic and Republican representatives of the United States at Zhongnanhai, he said the essential characteristics of Chinese socialism was the leadership of the Communist Party of China, "You have to know the Communist Party of China to deal with China."[10]

---

10.   Xinhua News Agency, May 7, 2015.

Xi Jinping and other leaders have a sober understanding of a strong America. National interests must be defended, and some problems can be argued through, but it is unwise to challenge the United States.

III. XI IS NOT ANTI-AMERICAN

On February 11, 2009, a financial tsunami swept through Wall Street and engulfed the globe. During a trip to Mexico to meet local overseas Chinese, Xi Jinping, still as the successor, introduced the countermeasures of the Chinese economy. He said we would see the dawn of China's economy if it can get through, "the greatest contribution to human society that the Chinese government can make is solving the problem of feeding 1.3 billion people."[11] But one passage of his speech sparked the attention of the international community, especially the west. Xi Jinping said: "There are some foreigners who have eaten their fill and have nothing better to do; just pointing their fingers at our affairs. China neither spread revolution, nor does it spread hunger and poverty."[12]

Smiling with Confidence

The impression Xi Jinping previously gave to the outside tended to be gentle. In Chinese political culture, the status of successor is special and sensitive; one should neither appear weak, nor surpass the superior, but always keeps a humble attitude.

But Xi Jinping voiced those strong words that other Chinese leaders have never dared to say, which reflected his diplomatic ideas: He was quite disgusted with the frequent criticism and pressure from the west. China respects other countries, but other countries must also respect China.

His manner of speaking is also related to his personality; he is strict with others, but even stricter with himself. Both abroad and at home, for example, when he has met the leaders of the United States, he always shows his affinity and good nature to greet people. But on matters of principle, he has a strong personality and appears impartial.

To deliver such a speech in Mexico, one must also take diplomacy into account. Mexico is near the United States, and at that time the criticism of China was mainly focused in the US-led western world, especially on issues such as human rights and Tibet. Just a few days before, at the UN Human Rights Council held in Geneva, several countries criticized China on the issue of human rights, including Mexico, which naturally made Chinese

11.   Hong Kong: *Ming Pao*, February 13, 2009.

12.   Ibid.

leaders angry.

Xi Jinping may also think of the 2008 Beijing Olympic Games. He served as vice president at that time and was the highest official of the Communist Party of China responsible for the Olympic Games. But when the Chinese cheerfully passed the Olympic flame on and it traveled overseas, it was boycotted by some nations and vandalized in France and the UK, which greatly hurt the dignity of the Chinese people.

To smile with confidence is a trait perfectly embodied by Xi Jinping. He is more confident toward the West, rather than having a hatred of the United States.

He is more familiar with the United States than any other supreme leader of China. In 1985, when Xi Jinping worked as a party secretary in a small area called Zhingding County in southern Beijing, he went to Iowa in America's Midwest with an agricultural delegation to inspect local farming and animal husbandry in the town of Muscatine—his first visit to the United States. The Executive Director of Iowa's sister province/state committee, Sarah Lande, asked the Dvorchak family of Muscatine to be a host family for Xi Jinping; at that time their sons were away from home at college, and Xi Jinping slept in their room for two nights. As a gift of thanks, he presented his hosts with a bottle of fine spirits on his departure.

The Chinese visit was big news in the small town of the Midwestern American agricultural state. The *Muscatine Journal* described the "Chinese visitors" as superstars in the town. Recalling the feeling at that time, Xi Jinping said: "We came here with a curious heart."

Who would have thought that the young Chinese officer back in 1985 would become China's top leader 30 years later?

On February 15, 2012, during his trip to the United States as China's Vice President, Xi Jinping paid a special return visit to Muscatine town and met his old friends again. He told them: "Those days left a deep impression on me because you are the American friends I first met, and I had a preliminary understanding of the United States after short investigation and through my stay in Muscatine."[13] In revisiting Muscatine, Xi Jinping was trying to tell Americans that he was a friend of the United States; the country he first visited 30 years beforehand. Apart from former US President George W. Bush, who went to Beijing at a young age with his father George H.W. Bush, the then top US diplomat in China, is there any other American president who visited China in his youth?

Xi Jinping has a strong family background, but he depends more on his ability and emotional intelligence (EQ). Once, during an inspection of local

---

13.   Xinhua News Agency, February 16, 2012.

officials, he asked them: "Which one is more important, IQ or EQ?" The local officials responded: "Both are important." Xi Jinping said: "EQ is very important to do practical work."[14] Xi Jinping shows a high level of emotional intelligence in contact with people of the United States. Although he only stayed for two days in Muscatine, the Dvorchaks made a positive long-lasting impression.

When he paid his surprise visit to their home 30 years later, Xi Jinping said to them: "I remember you are from New York. At that time, you prepared a rich breakfast for us, and you presented us with popcorn as a gift when we left."

Mr. Dvorchak asked, "Do you remember what gift you gave to us?"

Xi Jinping said, "A bottle of wine, soaked with white chrysanthemum"

"It is the most fierce alcohol I have ever drunk in my life," Mr. Dvorchak declared.[15]

Xi Jinping did not visit the United States frequently after that, but he has always cherished friendship with Americans. The Governor of Iowa Terry Branstad recalled that he met Xi Jinping twice—during his first visit to the US in 1985, when the young Chinese man visited Iowa state offices; and again in Beijing as a governor in 2011, when Xi Jinping met him in the great hall of the people as the successor, and recalled his original visit to America which he had treasured for 26 years.

The Charm of Chinese Leaders

Xi Jinping's short stay in America is enough for the average American to gain an insight into his personality. Mrs. Dvorchak said: "He was a polite and friendly man with a sense of precision." Moreover, during his visit to Muscatine, he "did not play golf like the other important people while visiting similar places."[16]

In China, golf is a noble and exclusive sport because the construction of a golf course takes a lot of land and water resources. Business leaders like to invite officials to play golf and obtain business interests in private. Xi Jinping prefers swimming and soccer rather than golf, which is loved by some notorious officials. In 2012, in an interview with *The Washington Post* before his visit to the United States, he said that exercise could keep a person in shape and healthy, and help people work more efficiently. He told the interviewer that he liked soccer better, but he said he also enjoyed the NBA, because it made people excited and had global appeal.

14.   Xinhua Viewpoint (blog), May 14, 2013.

15.   Xinhua News Agency, February 16, 2012.

16.   *Evening Post*, February 12, 2012.

During his five-day visit to the United States, Xi Jinping made a special trip to Los Angeles and watched a basketball match between the Los Angeles Lakers and Phoenix Suns. During halftime, Los Angeles Mayor Antonio Villaraigosa presented a Lakers jersey to Xi Jinping with Xi Jinping's name printed on the back. Former Lakers player Earvin "Magic" Johnson and English soccer star David Beckham, who was playing for the Los Angeles Galaxy team at the time, also met Xi Jinping.

Xi Jinping has a passion for football and other sports. After leaving Los Angeles, he traveled to Ireland, and at Dublin's Croke Park, the principal stadium for the Gaelic games in Ireland, he was invited to try his hand at hurling and Gaelic football, even though he was dressed in an overcoat and suit and wore leather shoes. The resulting photographs of him in action were seen across the world and helped project an image very different from other Chinese leaders. When his New Year's greeting was broadcast, people saw one of these photographs in the bookshelf beside his desk.

"What he has successfully shown to the world is not only his personal style and tolerance, but also China's image and charm," a foreign media spokesman appraised his diplomatic presence.[17]

In the basketball game Xi Jinping attended in Los Angeles, superstar Kobe Bryant scored 36 points in total, getting 18 points in the third quarter when Xi Jinping started to watch intently. Kobe happily gave his sneakers with his signature to Xi Jinping afterwards.[18]

According to informed sources, the China delegation proposed the visit to watch the NBA game at Los Angeles' Staples Center, as NBA games are not only an important event in the United States, but also very popular with Chinese people. China's first sports star, Yao Ming, has become a symbol of the friendly relationship between China and the US. Establishing a good image in the United States helps Xi Jinping to improve his leadership image in China. It also draws experience from Deng Xiaoping. In 1979, Deng Xiaoping visited the United States and put a cowboy hat on in an arena to show the open and self-confident image of a Chinese leader; on all of his visits, left a deep impression on the Americans.

For Americans, Xi Jinping's personal experience and personality is interesting, but more important is his influence on China and the world. On December 8, 2014, when China's Internet "Tsar" Lu Hui visited the Facebook headquarters in California, he noticed the book *The Governance of China* by Xi Jinping on the desk of CEO Mark Zuckerberg, who explained:

17.   Xi Jinping. "The people are the source of our strength." Xinhua News Agency, December 25, 2012.
18.   Associated Press, February 18, 2012.

"I also bought this book for my colleagues and I want them to have an understanding of socialism with Chinese characteristics."

The Governance of China is Xi Jinping's first best-selling book in the world, and was published in English, French, Russian, Spanish, Portuguese, German, and Japanese as well as other foreign languages in September, 2014. Former German Chancellor Helmut Schmidt wrote in a review that the book was intended to tell readers what kind of philosophy the Chinese leaders followed, and what kind of strategy the development direction of China was based on. Thus, the world could better understand the development of China, especially China's internal affairs and foreign policy.

"Western countries often cannot help playing the role of teachers in front of China and Chinese leaders, which is often originated from pride and is easy to hit a wall. Hopefully, western countries may put down the pretense and play the role of fair competition," Schmidt said.

In April, 2015, the Associated Press announced that the global circulation of *The Governance of China* had exceeded 4 million copies, and overseas circulation accounted for 400,000 copies, which set the highest record of overseas distribution for a book written by a Chinese leader apart from Mao Zedong.

Political Changes in China

When Xi Jinping made his US visit in 2012, he met President Obama in the Oval Office of the White House. Obama also expressed goodwill to the future Chinese top leader. He told Xi Jinping the United States welcomed China's peaceful development, and thought that a strong, prosperous and stable China was good for the prosperity and stability in the Asia-Pacific region. Moreover, US-China cooperation in international and regional issues was critical in the current situation.

That day, February 14, was Valentine's Day and the United States treated Xi Jinping as a high-profile guest. President Obama received Xi Jinping with a ceremony fit for a head of state; the Vice Secretary of State William J. Burns had previously met him at Andrews Air Force Base outside Washington. The US Secretary of Defense Leon Panetta held a grand welcome ceremony for Xi Jinping on the day he visited the Pentagon, including firing a salute of nineteen guns, and reviewing the three-service military honor guards.

The United States attached great importance to Xi Jinping's visit in terms of specification and content; however up until then, it was uncertain whether the visit would go ahead at all because of political events occurring in China.

On February 6, one week before Xi Jinping's visit, Wang Lijun, the Vice Mayor of Chongqing in southwest China, went to the US Consulate

General in Chengdu to seek refuge late at night. The incident sparked a serious political earthquake in China since the start of the twenty-first century. Wang Lijun was a trusted follower of Bo Xilai, and an ambitious Chongqing Party secretary in Chinese politics. Bo Xilai's father was also a founding member of the Communist Party of China and the former Vice Premier Bo Yibo. Wang Lijun worked as the chief of the Public Security Bureau and created a huge anti-mafia movement in Chongqing, along with the campaign to embrace Maoism initiated by Bo Xilai, making Bo Xilai an influential man at that time. Although these moves caused great controversy in China, some liberal scholars believed that it reminded them of the terrible Cultural Revolution.

On November 15, 2011, influential British businessman Neil Heywood, 41, was found dead in his hotel bedroom in Chongqing and it was later alleged that Bo Xilai's wife Gu Kailai had killed him and plotted with Wang Lijun to cover up the murder as a suspected heart attack or alcohol poisoning. She was later given a suspended death sentence after pleading guilty to Mr. Heywood's murder. Wang Lijun had allegedly had an affair with Gu Kailai, and when he reported Gu Kailai to Bo Xilai, it is said Bo Xilai slapped him, and then reassigned him to work as Vice Mayor of Chongqing nominally, but removed him from the post of Public Security Bureau Chief which had more actual power.

Wang Lijun took action immediately when he felt threatened. On February 6, 2012, he dressed as a woman and fled to the US consulate in Chengdu to seek asylum. Wang Lijun was a deputy ministry official in China, and if he was accepted for refuge, the US-China relationship was bound to be severely impacted, with a serious question mark hanging over Xi Jinping's visit. After weighing the pros and cons and coordinating with China, Wang Lijun left the consulate voluntarily and was detained by the relevant Chinese authorities, and Xi Jinping's visit to the United States went ahead as planned.

However, the incident continued to rumble on in the process of Xi Jinping's succession. After a month, Bo Xilai, who had been expected to become the top leader of China, was removed from his post. After Xi Jinping took office as the supreme leader, Bo Xilai was judged publicly and eventually sentenced to life imprisonment for bribery, corruption and abuse of power. Wang Lijun was charged with bending the law, abuse of power, defection, and bribery, and was sentenced to fifteen years in prison.

But some observers believed that the biggest crime Bo Xilai committed was to attempt a coup; he had close relationship with Zhou Yongkang, a member of the Standing Committee of the Political Bureau, and Ling Jihua, director of the General Office of the Central Committee. In the anti-corruption campaign launched by Xi Jinping, Zhou Yongkang and Ling Jihua received trials. Zhou Yongkang was one of nine members of the Politburo Standing Committee and had been in charge of politics and law. Under a new system of decentralization, each member of the Standing Committee had the highest power in their own field. Zhou was also the official with the highest level in the Communist Party of China to be charged with corruption. And with the fall of Zhou Yongkang, Xi Jinping gathered political power.

On November 11, 2013, at the British Royal Institute of International Affairs, former American Secretary of State Hillary Clinton spoke of the events which had occurred after Wang Lijun entered the US consulate in Chengdu. Chinese armed police surrounded the consulate, and his request for political asylum did not conform to the usual requirements for such cases. Wang Lijun was accused of corruption, had a brutal record, and was known as the "political fixer" of Bo Xilai. He was finally asked to leave; "they might have split up, so he tried to find a safe place."[19]

The situation quickly turned into a problem. Considering Xi Jinping was about to visit the United States, his status as a successor was important for the future China-US relationship. Hillary Clinton said that on this issue, "our disposal was very prudent, we did not want to embarrass any one, and we tried to deal with this matter in a professional way, and I think we did it." Xi Jinping did not have direct representation for the move of the United States in public. However, since he has taken office, China and the United States have carried out full cooperation on anti-corruption issues, and also enjoyed a tacit understanding on related issues.

IV. CHINA REFUSES FORCE

Xi Jinping has made many good friends in American politics. Former US Treasury Secretary Henry "Hank" Paulson is one of them. The tycoon used to lead the top investment bank Goldman Sachs on Wall Street, had visited China dozens of times before he was recruited into the Treasury Department by President George W. Bush in 2006, and is considered to be a China expert in the United States.

In September, 2006, Paulson visited China in his new position as the US Finance Minister, and his first stop was Hangzhou of Zhejiang province where his old friend, Zhejiang provincial party secretary Xi Jinping, was waiting for him. Their meeting place was the location of the China-US talks in 1972: the West Lake state guest-house.

Paulson says he appreciates some of Xi Jinping's peculiarities, especially

19.　　Hong Kong: *Wen Hui Po*, October 18, 2013.

his identification of free market values. In his opinion, Xi Jinping is a powerful and ambitious leader and is facing huge challenges. He has put his reputation and energy into creating significant transformations in the Chinese economy—from export-oriented and government investment-driven development model into a consumer-driven development model.

In Paulson's view, Xi Jinping neither takes America as a template, nor expects western values. "Xi Jinping thinks the future and stability of the country rely on a strong Communist Party of China."[20] Although Paulson thought this situation might not last, he gave a high mark to the government led by Xi Jinping, because the Chinese government can always understand the public opinion and today what they focus on is what people care about most: To combat corruption, restore the farmers' property rights, strengthen environmental governance, and make efforts to narrow the income gap.

Paulson's observation is correct—as a highly capable leader, Xi Jinping wants China to become a great country and must concentrate on solving a series of problems left in the country. He is looking forward to a peaceful and stable environment, and he hopes America can respect the choices of China, but he absolutely can't accept a situation if the United States forces China to do anything.

China's Focus on Sovereignty

Reviewing the foreign policies Xi Jinping has adopted since taking office, the dominant idea is clearly visible, and the professors of the National University of Singapore's Lee Kuan Yew School of Public Policy have summarized them into six points:[21]

> First, on the premise of resolutely defending China's core interests, establishing peace and development as a pillar of Chinese diplomatic policy. Xi Jinping made it clear that China is a strong advocate and vigorous defender for peace.
>
> Second, take the development of the China-US relationship as the reference point of Xi Jinping–style diplomacy, and keep the necessary strategic equilibrium in the process of shifting towards a multipolar world by vigorously developing the new type of power relationship.
>
> Third, actively establish a 'global partnership network', and ensure China's peaceful development is synchronized with the world.
>
> Fourth, tightly hold onto economic integration development

20.   Hong Kong: *Economic Daily*, May 4, 2015.
21.   *People's Daily*, April 22, 2015.

and seek improvement in the great tide of economic integration, put forward a series of foreign policies based on promotion of common development, seek security with development, maintain stability in development and promote peace with development.

Fifth, pay attention to morality and justice, follow principles, seek fairness and mutual benefits. It is important to firmly grasp the high moral ground in the international affairs, takes no concessions on the question of principle, and do not harm others.

Sixth, emphasize the fundamental position to solve the problem in a peaceful way. At the same time, actively develop national strength in varying aspects, provide a solid guarantee for safeguarding our own interests, and strengthen the ability to defend the peace.

This was the reason why Xi Jinping specially invited President Obama to Zhongnanhai to explain Chinese history and culture on his state visit to China in November 2014. For example, regarding the "new normal" for China's economy, he explained to the president that the essential idea was to focus on the transformation of the economic development pattern, structural adjustment, and sustainability, rather than the pursuit of high-speed growth according to the scientific development concept. He said, according to his calculation, to achieve the goal of doubling the per capita income by 2020, 7 percent of growth each year is enough.

For China's sovereignty, he told Obama, Chinese civilization attached great importance to "unification" right from the start. Chinese people pay attention to the cultivation of morality, family, ruling the country and uniting the world, in which uniting the country is the first step.

History has proved many times that as long as China can maintain a unified situation, the country will be strong, peaceful and stable, and the people will live a happy life. Once the country is in turmoil, it will be split, and its people will suffer the most severe disasters.

Xi Jinping told Obama that China pays more attention to sovereignty, because China had repeatedly suffered from foreign invasions in its history. The Chinese people are sensitive about external threats to their national sovereignty and security as a result of long-term historic suffering.

This was a conversation full of sincerity and wisdom. Xi Jinping emphatically introduced the history of Yingtai to Obama, particularly mentioning how the great Emperor Kangxi of the Qing dynasty studied national strategies on how to pacify internal disorder and recover Taiwan in this place. The issue of Taiwan has been a key problem in China-US relations, creating many crises in the relationship between the two countries. Xi Jinping meant to remind Obama that China cannot accept Taiwan's independence, and they should use their best judgment on China's intentions and will regarding the Taiwan question.

Divergent Views Must Be Addressed

President Obama may have comprehended some of his political arguments, but he might not have been able to identify with Xi Jinping in all aspects. On the issue of democracy, Xi Jinping reiterated to Obama that democracy in China was not only embodied in the direct election of "one man, one vote," but the pursuit of public opinion was sought even more than in western countries. A political party in the West represents one class or interest, but in China it must represent all the people. To this end, China has a wide range of democratic consultation processes, and go up or step down for a few times.

In the West, mainstream public opinion does not believe China is a democratic country, but a state where high-level politics are conducted more like backroom politics. But some scholars see the genius of the system from the promotion of Xi Jinping. Leaders like Xi Jinping are used to working at all levels of management, such as county, city, and province, and when he stands up to govern the whole country, he has more experience and more skills to govern the nation.

Although the Chinese media did not disclose Obama's views on democracy as explained by Xi Jinping, this face-to-face in-depth communication obviously contributes to the understanding of each other's views.

In some cases, it is certainly more complex than the leaders' cheerful talks. In the economic field, the United States has accused China of undervaluing the RMB from time to time, and also of carrying out a double negative survey for Chinese products—measures considered as the implementation of trade protectionism by China. The important part of the "return to Asia" strategy is to build the "Trans-Pacific Partnership Agreement" (TPP). The TPP negotiation countries include Japan, Australia, and even Vietnam, but not China; no matter how earnestly America says it is, it is hard to avoid the suspicion that it is in a bid to isolate China.

The United States was cold on the issue of the Asian Investment Bank at the very beginning, and even put pressure on its allies such as South Korea, Australia, and Canada to prevent these countries from joining the Investment Bank, a move which was deemed not particularly friendly to China. In April, 2015, when President Obama met the Japanese Prime Minister Shinzo Abe, he tried to reassure China that the US did not reject other countries from joining the Asian Investment Bank, but standards and transparency should be considered in the related operations.

In the military field, American warships and aircraft have conducted a series operations just outside China's seas and borders, and their "snooping" has regularly incurred China's disfavor, creating inevitable friction. In December 2013, China's first aircraft carrier *Liaoning* arrived in the South China Sea for testing, and the US military immediately conducted a comprehensive monitoring operation. On December 5, the *USS Cowpens* missile destroyer sailed close to the *Liaoning* and was intercepted by a Chinese escort ship. The Washington Freedom Beacon website quoted a US military official who said that China sent a tank landing craft to intercept it, and as the distance between the two ships closed to less than 500 meters, the *Cowpens* was forced to change course in an emergency maneuver.

The US felt the incident was a deliberate and dangerous action; it said that the *Cowpens* was sailing on the open seas, and had warned the approaching ship that its distance was too close, and it should stop, but its pleas were ignored. However, China thought the US was carrying out military provocation because the *USS Cowpens* had entered the defense zone of the *Liaoning*, and US ships were sailing in China's coastal waters. China argued: How would America react if Chinese warships sailed in the open waters off Los Angeles or the Gulf of Mexico?

Less than a year later tension mounted again when, on August 18, 2014, a US navy P-8 Poseidon anti-submarine patrol aircraft flew in international airspace near China's Hainan Island and was intercepted by a China J-11 B fighter jet. The distance between them was at one point only six meters; the Chinese fighter did a barrel roll over the US patrol aircraft and the missiles on its belly showed up. US defense officials thought the encounter was intentionally "threatening," and they lodged a protest against China.

After Xi Jinping took office, large-scale sea reclamation began in the South China Sea. China's powerful engineering and economic strength quickly brought the Fiery Cross Reef under the control of China, which become the biggest island controlled by China in the Nansha Islands (also known as the Spratly Islands).

The US Pacific Fleet commander, Admiral Harry Harris, compared it to a "Sand Great Wall," referring to the fact that China was reclaiming land from the sea, building a port, barracks, and even a runway on a remote rock through large-scale sand-excavating.[22]

On April 8, 2015, President Obama voiced US concerns to China, which threatened the surrounding South China Sea with "great size and strong

---

22.   Charles Clover, "How to Measure China's Military Power?" *Financial Times Chinese*, April 13, 2015.

muscle," and warned China not to "squeeze its neighbors." The US State Department also issued a warning that it would threaten regional stability if China continued reclaiming land from the South China Sea.

Chinese leaders see the South China Sea as a part of China; other countries have already carried out reef construction on a large scale, and missile bases had even been established in Vietnam and the US, but the US has never paid much attention to them, so why did it start arguing when China wanted to strengthen its construction? Was this not interference and bias? China's reply was that it was not acceptable. On April 10, Chinese Foreign Ministry spokeswoman Hua Chunying retorted: "I'm afraid it is obvious to everyone who has the largest 'size and muscle' in the world. Some countries kept silent when other countries built largely on the illegally occupied reef of the South China Sea for a long time, but made irresponsible remarks on the normal activity of China on its own territory. It is undoubtedly a double standard."

On March 8, 2015, Chinese Foreign Minister Wang Yi also joked that the land infill in the South China Sea reef is a construction in China's own back garden that is not affecting anyone: "We will neither construct illegal buildings in others' territories like some countries, nor accept being nagged by any other country when we build in our own back garden."

However, China maintains a prudent attitude on its relationship with the US on the whole, and always gives a good response as soon as possible with very few sharp criticisms in public. On the issue of sea reclamation in the South China Sea, on April 29, 2015, when Chinese navy commander Wu Shengli met the US chief of naval operations, Admiral Jonathan Greenert, he said China welcomed the United States and other countries to share these facilities in China for international humanitarian relief. Admiral Greenert might not be particularly adept in diplomacy, so he expressed affirmation and recognition. The US State Department spokesman Jeff Rathke urgently made a clarification afterwards, saying, "To artificially build facilities in disputed areas will not contribute to regional peace and stability, as some Chinese officials claim." Mr. Rathke complained that no invitation had been received from China to make use of these facilities.

American Provocation Is Unacceptable

The highest-ranking officials of China and the United States are certainly very clear; some contradictions between a rising power and existing power are irreconcilable, so the United States will still be trying to seek "rebalancing," including sending more naval ships to cruise in the coastal waters off China and applying pressure to China; but China will increase military strength and better defend its homeland. When the United States is determined to promote the TPP, Xi Jinping will try to resolve it by forming an Asia-Pacific free trade area and proposing The Belt and Road Initiatives.

The tensions between the United States and China are due to mutual distrust on both sides, as well as different cultural backgrounds. US diplomat Henry Kissinger felt that the two countries have different cultural inheritances—the American people are pragmatic, while Chinese people have a consciousness of suffering; the Americans hope to find a solution immediately after an event has occurred, and the Chinese feel that doing so may lead to new problems. He stressed that the fundamental challenge both China and the US are facing is to fully recognize the importance of cooperation, the need to manage daily problems every day, and keep them in control efficiently.[23]

Complaints against the United States are the inevitable impact of the existing order meeting the rise of China; if the US continues to maintain hegemony, frictions between both sides in the economic, political, and diplomatic fields will rise in the future.

China does not challenge the United States, but China will never accept provocations. Xi Jinping expects to maintain a good relationship with the United States and tries to achieve this through diplomatic abilities, but it needs the cooperation of the US. Moreover, the premise to solve a lot of problems in the world is to achieve cooperation between China and the United States. Both countries have reached unprecedented climate agreements after President Obama's visit to China in 2014. The United States plans to reduce emission by 26 to 28 percent on the basis of worldwide measures in 2005, and will ultimately try to reach a goal of 28 percent; China plans to reduce its carbon dioxide emissions and has set a deadline of around 2030, which it will try to beat. It also plans to increase non-fossil energy to about 20 percent of the total energy consumption by 2030.

China made a first commitment to limit emissions of carbon dioxide before a specific date. This agreement is popular in the international community; it shows that two of the world's largest greenhouse gas emitters are taking serious and earnest actions to halt the catastrophic events of global warming.

On the issue of North Korea, the American government has been trying to persuade China to increase pressure on it for years. Obviously, the magnitude of the pressure given on North Korea has been unprecedented since Xi Jinping took office; it can be seen that Xi Jinping delayed a visit to North Korea and North Korea's leader Kim Jong-un could not visit Beijing for a long period of time. Denuclearization of the Korean peninsula is in line

---

23. Hong Kong: *Da Kung Pao*, March 22, 2015.

with the common interests of China and the United States.

After five hours of conversation with Xi Jinping in Zhongnanhai in 2014, Obama said he was greatly surprised to see the ambitions of Chinese leaders, as well as his experience in governing. He said, "I can further understand why the Chinese people cherish national unity and stability. The United States supports China's reform and opening up, and does not mean to contain China, because it would not conform to the interests of the United States to do so. The United States is willing to work with China through open communication and dialogue, enhance mutual understanding, learn experience from each other, effectively control and avoid misunderstanding and miscalculation."

Xi Jinping said, "Now the strategic goal of a China-US 'new power relationship' is clear, we can neither let it stay in the conceptual phase, nor be satisfied with premature execution. We need to continue to move forward and proceed from a strategic and long-term perspective, constantly promote the construction of the China-US 'new power relationship' step by step."

The words of the two most influential politicians in the world might have elements of diplomatic language; but it will be a human catastrophe if the two countries cannot handle disagreements and ignite fighting and war. To avoid the tragedy of war, China and the United States must explore a new road—that is, to build a "new power relationship." After all, the United States and China will be the strongest, and the second strongest, countries in the world for a long time to come. China is bound to rise, but should not take the initiative to challenge the United States; the United States should not be afraid of China strategically, but should respect China on strategy.

This was an important night in the history of China and the United States. No president of the United States has ever enjoyed such courtesy in Zhongnanhai, and had such an intimate private conversation with the top leader of China. It was already 11:00 p.m. at night, and Beijing was shrouded in a boundless darkness. President Obama finally got into his official black sedan and Xi Jinping stood in the cold wind for a long time to watch Obama's entourage leave Zhongnanhai.

In the night sky, a bright moon was shining on Zhongnanhai and Beijing.

AFTERWORD
The Peaceful Chinese Century Arrives

Will the twenty-first century belong to China? This was the title of the June 17, 2011 Munk Debate held in Toronto's Roy Thomson Hall, the largest concert hall in Canada.

The participants of this debate, a debate quite relevant to the whole world, were a distinguished lineup: "old China hand" Henry Kissinger, the well-known CNN host Fareed Zakaria, the renowned historian Niall Ferguson, and prominent Chinese Scholar David Daokui Li. While those arguing against the premise of the "Chinese century" ultimately gained the upper hand, both the proponents and opponents came up with convincing arguments, confronting the reality that China faces both opportunities and risks in the course of its rise.

If the question of the "Chinese Century" was ahead of its time just a few years ago, the blueprint of China's return to the world stage has been made clearer since Xi Jinping's avowal of the "China Dream" as the goal of the great revitalization of China. China is in pursuit neither of twenty-first century hegemony, nor for the "China Dream" to manifest itself as a "nightmare" for other countries. China aims for peaceful development and to maintain the balance and cooperation of all the great powers, including the United States.

In today's world, nothing can obscure the rise of China. Even President Obama referred to China as a "big man." To deliberately cloak the advancement of China would only arouse the suspicions of other countries, suspicions that China would hide ulterior motives.

Now, the world's primary concern is: How will the "big man" show his strength? How will China flex its muscles? How will china use its powers? These issues have become the major concerns of US strategists.

In his book *The Hundred-Year Marathon: China's Secret Strategy to Replace America as the Global Superpower*, American scholar Michael Pillsbury claims that China maintains a century-long plan, secretly executed for 80 years, to replace the US as the world's preeminent superpower. What is not examined is whether the rise of China is an explicit plan, or just the expression of ambitions cherished by all nations and people, and not only China, that they will become stronger someday. China indeed has a one-hundred-year national recovery plan, manifested as the China Dream, but China's rise does not aim to overtake the United States among the world's superpowers, but to become a leader of global civilization and the defender of world peace and development.

There are two great maxims on the Tiananmen rostrum in Beijing; one reads "Long Live the People's Republic of China," and the other, "Long Live the Great Unity of the People of the World." The former is equivalent to the China dream, the latter is equivalent to a "World Dream" of the Chinese people. The aims and pursuits of the Chinese people are expressly written on Tiananmen rostrum, the political heart of China. Could any plan be clearer? The one-hundred-year marathon of the Chinese ascension is not a conspiracy, but a plan open to everyone.

The question can be asked: China's ambitions to develop and elevate itself on the world stage are understandable, but won't China then overtake the United State as the world's leading power? To answer this question, we must examine the China Dream against the background of Chinese history and literature.

Scholars from all over the world can acknowledge that China once led the world. In Niall Ferguson's words, China was one of the world's leading powers for about eighteen of the past 20 centuries. In the Han, Tang, Song, Yuan, and Ming Dynasties, the comparison of China's economic strength with the global economic power was more than the United States' share of the wealth today; as for military power, we must recall the strong military deployment of the First Emperor of Qin, Emperor Wu of Han, Emperor Taizong of Tang, and Genghis Khan.

In other words, China has been number one of the world for more than 1500 years, but it is less well known that China has never achieved the status of a "superpower," as the United States has, with its capacity to conquer, promote American values, and pursue power across the globe. China ruled the western regions in China's Han Dynasty: the Han Dynasty was primarily responsible for the order and peace of the western regions, and made the 36 countries of the western regions live and work in peace and contentment. The foreign policy of the Han Dynasty was to play the role of a "night watchman," and provide security so that the western countries could trade and prosper.

The former chair professor of the University of Hawaii and Duke University, and historian Xu Zhuoyun, in his book *Comparison of World Order in the Han and Tang Dynasties*, describes the governance of the Han and Tang Dynasties as open societies, with great emphasis on inclusiveness. It is easy to see on a map of China how the Korean Peninsula could have been incorporated into the jurisdiction of the Han Empire early in the dynasty, and the territory of Vietnam and Mongolia belonged to the sphere of the Han empire since ancient times, but China did not absorb these territories; instead it implemented a looser policy that allowed local autonomy in accordance with local customs and folk traditions.

Historians and scholars of international affairs acknowledge that an "East Asian Tributary System" existed for more than two thousand years in East Asia. The system was created during the Zhou Dynasty, and made good use of through the Han Dynasty, until the late Qing Dynasty. The Ming Dynasty established classical diplomatic relations with Japan, Korea, Ryukyu, Annan, Myanmar, Laos, Siam, Luzon, and other peripheral countries, as well as southern Asia and the eastern kingdoms of Africa, ushering forth the era most associated with the Tributary System. The Qing Dynasty was the last to end the tributary relationship, but maintained peace and quiet goodwill with Korea, Ryukyu, Burma, Annan, Laos, Siam, and other eastern Asian countries.

In an era predating globalization, China had successfully maintained the order, peace, and tranquility of the East Asian countries, fulfilling its duties as the steward of the international order for thousands of years.

It was said that the sun never set on the British Empire. But Britain's colonial expansion had its subject peoples boiling with resentment, and the empire eventually fell apart—even Great Britain's own territories Scotland, England, and Northern Ireland could not be united. Such an empire is not a competent steward of the international order. The United States became a global leading power after World War II, though at first it was in competition with the Soviet Union. During the Cold War, the world would reach the "Final Crisis," the brink of nuclear war, many times. Following the collapse of the Soviet Union, the United States launched or took part in wars in Iraq, Afghanistan, Kosovo, Libya, and other countries. The world of today is even more volatile than that of the Cold War. The US could hardly maintain the world order for 20 years; it is obviously not a competent leader.

John Mearsheimer is a professor of political science at the University of Chicago, and a representative of the neorealism theory of international relations. Mearsheimer has publicly acknowledged: The international system of today's world is a brutal arena; each country has no choice but to compete for power in order to live. Even countries content with a peaceful existence may become involved in the ruthless power struggle. According to Mearsheimer, nothing can refute the fact that today's international political relations, led by America, follows the law of the jungle; the strongest takes all, the weak must submit to the rule of the strong, and anyone refusing to surrender must suffer relentless bullying and suppression.

Since 1840, China has suffered the bullying of the world's powers, almost no country could know more than China about the pain of being pressured and denigrated. Now that China has risen and can claim the opportunity to lead the world once again, will it also mimic the world's earlier powers and do more harm to the vulnerable countries? The Chinese people hate and oppose totalitarianism. China has a maxim: "Never do to others what you would not like them to do to you." The Chinese people do not favor dominating other ethnic groups. Hegemony is akin to oppression in China. Those powers that bully the weaker countries are referred to as "hegemonic" powers. Since the eighteenth century, all superpowers have pursued hegemony, such that *super*power has become synonymous with *hegemonic* power.

China can announce to the world that it seeks to become the world's largest economy and most prosperous nation, but it is unwilling to become a superpower in the mold of Britain or the United States—this is why China has long claimed not to be in pursuit of total dominance.

Mao Zedong put it plainly in the 1970s: "China does not seek hegemony, and China will not become a superpower. China will not bully and threaten others even if it becomes rich in the future."

Mao Zedong believed that even if China dominates the world one day, the people of the world could bring it down.

When Deng Xiaoping met with foreign guests, he offered a more sincere explanation of the fact that China will never seek hegemony: As a socialist country, China belongs to the third world forever, and will never pursue predominance. Now people can understand the concept because China is still a quite poor and simple third-world country. The quandary is whether China, as a nation, will seek hegemony when it are developed in the future. As long as China is a socialist country, it cannot enact hegemonic ambitions and still belong to the third world. If China seeks hegemony in the world, it will be expelled from the third world, and will certainly no longer qualify as a socialist country. This is the foreign policy formulated by Chairman Mao Zedong and Premier Zhou Enlai, to be used for educating the nation's children.

China does not aspire to predominance, not only for emotional and ethical reasons, but also because history demonstrates that the hegemonic country cannot survive long.

Authority and hegemony were the subjects of heated debate for thousands of years of Chinese history. There were the famous "Five Hegemonies in Spring and Autumn Period" and the "Seven Powers in the Warring State Period" of Chinese history. During the life of Confucius, many states aspired to true hegemony. But no one could avoid the end foretold by the words "prosperity is a vigorous rise, decline is a sudden fall." The Chinese people recognize this as a law of the historical cycle. Totalitarian countries will never exist for long; they soon perish, inevitably. In Chinese history, the most exemplary state was the Qin. During the reign of the First Emperor of Qin, the Qin Empire defeated the warring state powers, and attained the dominant position. But the Qin Dynasty was one of the shortest lived in Chinese history, existing for only fifteen years after unifying the whole country. The politician Jia Yi of the Han Dynasty saw the root cause of the failure as "an aggressive posture changed to a defensive one, but policies of justice and humanity were not implemented."

History has taught the Chinese people that hegemony cannot last, persecution breeds resentment, and seeking hegemony will lead to destruction. It can be seen as a special wisdom of the Chinese people: to spurn hegemony, never aspire to be the domineering superpower. The best of men are like water: like water, they benefit all things and do not compete with them. Water does not compete with anyone; no one in the world can compete against it. Wisdom heralds the survival of water, reminds us to be open-minded like the sea. All rivers eventually run into the sea. A stream is unafraid of stopping, undaunted by repeated setbacks, so it will return to the sea. China's rise should embrace and nourish the natural advancement of all nations, gently as water. China's rise will be expressed in tenderness.

The Chinese people do not admire America's legacy of dominance, a legacy that pursues absolute power, and does not allow the existence of competitors. American hegemony is not a suitable model for China to follow. China will not compete directly with the United States for world dominance. An old proverb argues that, when encountering an angry lion, the best way to avoid conflict is to stand down. This is the Chinese way.

Acknowledgments

To understand the direction of a nation, one must understand its leaders. The late-twentieth-century renaissance of Chinese civilization has dramatically altered the political and economic structure of the world. Xi Jinping is instituting drastic changes through his highly personal style of leadership, in the footsteps of Mao Zedong and Deng Xiaoping.

Xi Jinping's greatest political goal is to realize the revitalization of the nation of China, through his strategic focus on the Four Comprehensive Initiatives. His lofty ambitions, political accomplishments, and promising style of diplomacy has, in the short time since he has taken office, ranked him among the leaders of the international community, who place the same high hopes in him as the Chinese people.

In recognition of the American people's and the international community's strong desire to understand the trajectory of China under Xi Jinping, we organized a group of experts and scholars engaged in China studies to write *The Xi Jinping Era*. The book systematically introduces the lived experiences, charisma, the advocacy for reform, and the strategic thinking of Chairman Xi Jinping, as well his appraisal of international affairs. Through this book, you can understand Xi Jinping; you can understand China's future.

The book was issued under the general editorship of the tenured professor of New York University, political science expert Dr. James C. Hsiung, co-authored by senior reporters Liu Hong and Chen Ying from the Xinhua News Agency of China, senior reporter Zhou Xingwang from the *Worker's Daily*, and Associate Professor Tan Huoshen from Tsinghua University. George, and Paul Harrington have generously contributed their labors toward the project, and more than a hundred experts and scholars from China and the US have provided valuable input. We would like to express our heartfelt thanks to all.

INDEX

adaptability, 156
administrative interference, 249
Afanasyev, Viktor, 275
aggression, denying history of, 398–402
aging of population, 131
AIDS orphans, 106–108
AIDS Orphan Salvation Association, 106
Airborne Warning and Control System (AWACS), 320
aircraft carriers, 361, 435
All-China Federation of Trade Unions (ACFTU), 257
allies, 379
ambitions, economic, 143
A Memorial of 20 Years for the Collapse of USSR and its Party, 132
American Academy of Engineering, 275
American Political Science Society, 232
An Assessment Study on the Health Hazards and Economic Losses of PM (2012), 278
ancestors, 17
And Quiet Flows the Don, 57
anti-American sentiment, lack of, 425–431
anti-corruption measures, 27, 32, 160. *See also* corruption
    cooperation with United States, 431
    internal reform (CPC), 167–171
    Korea, 161
    major reforms, 223–225
    military, 324, 325
    in Ningde, 88

policies, 168
    State-owned Enterprises (SOEs), 223–225
APEC Summit (2013), 147
Apple, 263
arbitrariness of power holders, 207–212
Army Day (2013), 333
Asian Investment Bank, 291–292, 424
    benefits of, 299–301
    membership of, 295–297, 300
    United Kingdom in, 297–299
Asia-Pacific Economic Cooperation (APEC), 296, 413
Association of Southeast Asian Nations (ASEAN), 295, 409
The Atlantic, 149
atomic bombs, 122
attack on Pearl Harbor (December 7, 1941), 125
automobiles
    China Association of Automobile Manufacturers, 268
    with GPS, 181
aviation, effect of pollution on, 279

Bacon, Francis, 243
Baekgang, Korea, 123
banks, 291–292. See also Asian Investment Bank
Bayi Road, 343
Beijing
    Capital International Airport, cancellations, 279
    Normal University, 68
    Railway Bureau, 388
    Water Resources Bulletin (2010), 282
    Xi Jinping escape to, 52
Belt and Road Initiatives, 291–316, 437
    Asian Investment Bank, 291–292
    benefits of Asian Investment Bank, 299–301
    influence of, 308–316
    membership of Asian Investment Bank, 295–297
    Silk Road Economic Belt, 302–308
    United Kingdom in Asian Investment Bank, 297–299
    Xi Jinping's initiative, 292–295
Berman, Harold, 246
best inventions, 269–272
Blanchard, Ben, 174
Blue Book of Rule of Law: Annual Report of China's Rule of Law, 162
Boao Forum, 308
bombs, 122
Book of Changes, 1
Boulding, Kenneth, 269
Bo Xilai, 430
Brazil, 21, 281

Bretton Woods System, 294
bribery, 163, 166. *See also* corruption
bubble economies, 253. *See also* economies
budgets, 230, 231, 351
bureaucrats, 89
Bush, George H. W., 426
Bush, George W., 426, 431
By Popular Demand: Revitalizing Representative Democracy Through Deliberative Elections, 229

California Institute of Technology, 271
Cameron, David, 297–299. *See also* United Kingdom (UK)
Canada, 281
Canrong, Jim, 142
Cao Zhiwei, 210
cars. *See* automobiles
Carson, Rachel, 288
Catalogue of Investment Project Subject to Government Verification, 208
Central Commission for Discipline Inspection (CCDI), 164, 174, 179
Central Economic Working Conference (2013), 137
Central Government, 10
Central Military Commission (CMC), 7, 32, 64, 319, 335, 342, 352
Central Organization Department, 187
Central Political Bureau, internal reform (CPC), 176–179
Central Work Leading Group, 195
Chairman Mao Memorial Garden, 326
Chairman of the Standing Committee of the NPC, 128
Chan, Margaret, 106
Chaoyang Studio, 115
Cheng Guoping, 386
Cheng Long, 209
Chen Yun, 16, 259
Chen Zhiwu, 266
Chiang Kai-shek, 4, 171
children
    AIDS orphans, 106–108
    policies for, 108–109
    Xi Mingze (daughter of Xi Jinping), 103
China. *See also* government; leadership
    the century of, 439–443
    democratization of, 233–236
    goals of, 125–129
    history of, 120–123
    new model of power relationships, 418–425
    political changes in, 429–431
    relationship with United States, 413–438
China and the World, 145
China Anticorruption Research Center, 157

China Association for Science and Technology, 281
China Association of Automobile Manufacturers, 268
China Central Television (CCTV), 79, 80, 148
China Dream, 119–154
    centenary goals, 142–147
    definition of, 119–129
    goals of, 125–129
    history of China, 120–123
    mental preparedness of people, 148–154
    reform, 130–138, 138–141
    strategy of, 129–141
    wars between China and Japan, 123–125
The China Ecological Urban Construction Development Report (2014), 280
China Economic Forum, 93
China Europe International Business School (CEIBS), 238
China Institute for Reform and Development, 258
China-Japan War, 323
China National Petroleum Corporation (CNPC), 218
China-Pakistan economic corridor, 311
China-Vietnam border war, 317
Chinese Academy of Engineering, 312, 313
Chinese Academy of Social Sciences (CASS), 157, 260
Chinese Century, 144, 441–446
Chinese Communist Party Disciplinary Regulations, 185
Chinese engineering, strength of, 404–406
Chinese Income Doubling Program, 135
Chinese Military magazine, 336
Chinese Military Report (2007/2008), 363
Chinese People's Political Consultative Conference (CPPCC), 126, 206, 208
Chronicle of Events in Zhengding County 1949–1983, 72, 80
Churchill, Winston, 251
civil-military integration, 370–374
Claremont McKenna College, 167
classification of State-owned Enterprises (SOEs), 217–218
Clinton, Hillary, 382, 420, 431
Clinton, William (Bill), 422
coal, 280, 285
Cold War, 444
college, years at, 60
college entrance exams, 54
combat training, 359
commander-in-chief of China, 70
commander in chief of the Chinese army, 318
Communist Party of China (CPC), 6, 37
    17th National Congress of (2007), 95
    18th National Congress of, 111, 134, 201
    democratization of China, 234
    internal reform (CPC). *See* internal reform (CPC)

    membership into the Standing Committee, 187–191

    party discipline, strictness of, 185–186

    qualified party members, 186–187

Communist Party of the Soviet Union (CPSU), 14, 156

Communist Youth League, 200

community of fate, 310

Comparison of World Order in the Han and Tang Dynasties, 441

Comprehensively Deepening Reform Leading Group, 195

confidence, 425

conflict with United States, 419

Confucian leadership traditions, 109

consultation, democratic, 226, 227

corruption, 28, 29

    fight against, 157–161

    illegal properties, removal of, 89

    Internet's role in, 164

    in the military, 342, 345–349

    tigers (corrupt officials), hunting, 157–171

    zero tolerance for, 161–165

county-level party chief, power of, 82

critical minorities, 246–249

cult of personality, 11

Cultural Revolution, 12, 49, 60

    college enrollment during, 61

Culture Interview, 98, 104

Davos World Economic Forum, 308

"death from overwork," 264

debt, 293

Decision on Amending the Employment Contract Law of the People's Republic of China (2012), 239, 240

Decisions on Pushing Forward Training and Educating Young Cadres, 189

defense identification zones, 395

deliberative democracy, 225–236. See also democracy

democratization of China, 233–236

democracy, 184

    United States' view of, 434

Democratic People's Republic of Korea (DPRK), 376, 388

Deng Jiaxian, 123

Deng Ken, 129

Deng Xiaoping, 4, 9, 13–22

    comparisons to, 110

    as designer of reform, 20–22

    role of ancestors in reform, 17–20

    Southern Talks, 174

    Soviet Union reform, 14–17

    "Up to the Mountains and Down to the Countryside," 50

Deng Xiaoping and the Transformation of China, 20

Department of Home News for Overseas Services, 39
Department of Student Affairs, 183
Deputy Party Chief of Zhengding county, 71
Deputy Secretary of Zhengding county, 69
development of economy, 258
Development Research Center of Resources and Environmental Policy Institute, 259
Diamond, Larry, 233
Diaoyu Islands, 394, 395–397, 400
Dickson, Bruce J., 156, 191
diplomacy, 375
    development of, 408–411
    to South Korea, 379–381
distribution channels, 129
dollar traps, 293
Dong Baohua, 239
Dong Biwu, 184
Dream of the Red Chamber, 79, 80

earthquakes, 106
East China Sea fleet, 361
Eastern China Non-ferrous Metals Investment Holdings Co., 220
ecological concerns, 276–289
    environmental sacrifices for growth, 285–289
    smog, 278–281
    water, 281–285
economic disorder, 204
economic innovations, 213
economic overheating, 204
"Economic Situation and Lessons Learned," 16
economic strategies, planning, 213–214
economies, 63. *See also* markets
    development of, 258
    environmental sacrifices for growth, 285–289
    growth of, 109, 131, 254
    innovation. *See* innovation
    modernization of, 252–264
    semi-suburban, 76
    Silk Road Economic Belt, 301, 302–308
    surpassing United States, 142–147
    ties to South Korea, 380
    zones, 84
educational revolution, 61
18th Central Commission for Discipline Inspection (CCDI), 169
Eight Rules, 173–176
elders, respect of, 75
elections, 234. *See also* democratization of China
Elstub, Stephen, 232
emotional intelligence (EQ), 427

Emperor Guangxu (Qing Dynasty), 41
Emperor Wu, 302
Employment Contract Law, 238
endogenous evolution processes, 236
endurance (military), 366
energy, 33
environmental pollution. *See* pollution
environmental sacrifices for growth, 285–289
ethics, internal reform of (CPC), 198–200
"Exchange Market for Technology," 267, 268
exercises, military, 360. *See also* military
expansion plans, 308–316
exports, 261–264
extremist left-wing inclination, opposition to, 46

Fair Labor Association (FLA), 263
fairness, 241–246
Fallows, James, 149
family background of Xi Jinping, 40–48
"farmers and soldiers," 61
farming skills, 53
Feng Lun, 207
Fifth modernization, the, 136, 137
First Emperor of Qin, 3
First Lady Peng Dehuai, 96–109. *See also* Peng Dehuai
First Opium War (1840), 121
First Sino-Japanese War (1892), 123
Fishkin, James, 227, 228, 229
food, conservation of, 182
force, refusal of use of, 431–438
foreign trade, 257
fossil fuels, 280
Four-Pronged Comprehensive Strategy, 129–141
Foxconn, 263, 264
Fox Hunting 2015, 170. *See also* tigers (corrupt officials)
fraud, 340
Free Trade Agreement of the Asia Pacific (FTAAP), 142
Friedman, Thomas, 127
Fujian Province, 33
    time in, 85
    Xi Jinping as Governor of, 91–92
Fukuyama, Francis, 197
Fuxing Road Studio, 115

G2, 150
Gang of Four, 64
Gan Li, 257
Gao Gang, 42

Gao Jun, 107
gasoline, 218
Gastil, John, 229
General Affairs Management Office of Yantai University, 183
Geng Biao, 63
Geng Yan, 64
Geng Ying, 67
The Genius of China, 270
Germany, 402
    Xi Jinping's visit to (2014), 349
Ghost Fear peak of Xiangshan, 52
giant pandas, 415
Global Competitiveness Report, 265
globalization, 20, 121, 408
global positioning system (GPS), 181
Global Times, 146, 392
Go (game), 65, 375, 378
gold mines, 286
Gorbachev, Mikhail, 14
governance
    elections and, 234
    laws and, 237–241
    modernization of, 237
The Governance of China, 429
government, 26
    limited-government theory, belief in, 92–94
    and market interactions, 203–207
    role of, 203–207
Governor of Fujian, Xi Jinping as, 91–92
Gramsci, Antonio, 109
Grand National Party, 376
Great Cultural Revolution, 4
Great Depression (United States), 150
Great Escape, 45
Great Leap Forward, 13, 127
The Great Wall, 88
greeting cards, 179, 180
    gross domestic product (GDP), 92, 135, 144, 255, 257
    contribution to innovation, 273
    growth of, 260
gross national income (GNI), 130
gross national product (GNP), 12, 350
Group of Twenty (G20), 294
growth
    of economy, 109, 131, 254
    environmental sacrifices for, 285–289
    gross domestic product (GDP), 255, 260
    of middle class, 135

Guangdong, 45
Guangdong Guanghong Holdings Co., Ltd., 210
Guangzhou city, 228
Guangzhou Military Region, 403
Gu JunShan, 337, 338
Gu Kailai, 430
Gulf War (1991), 332, 353, 363
Guo Jun, 264
Guo Wujun, 362
Gutian meeting (1929), 327

H-6K long-range strategic bomber, 332
Haihe River Basin, 284
Hainan Island, 435
Hainan Province, 141
Han Dynasty, 302
Hangzhou Wahaha Group Co., Ltd., 209
Harbin railway station, 399
harmony in diversity, 416–417
Hawkey, Joe, 297
haze. *See* smog
health, danger of pollution to, 277
Hebei Daily, 75
Hebei Province, 173
hegemonic power, 444
Heywood, Neil (death of), 430
history of China, 120–123
HIV/AIDS, 106–108
home truths, 113
homicide, 242
honesty, 198–200
Hong Kong, 32, 339
    Great Escape, 45
    Independent Commission against Corruption, 161
Hong Kong Commercial Daily, 39
housing allocations (military), 345–349
housing prices, 254
How China's Industry Will Develop, 145
How the Steel was Tempered, 57
Hua Guofeng, 70
Huaihai Campaign, 259
Hu Angang, 26, 31
Huang Weiding, 132
Huang Xiangqing, 210
Huangyan Island, 403, 404
Huang Yanpei, 225
Hubei Province, 283
The Huffington Post, 322

Hu Jintao, 22, 31, 71, 320
Huntington, Samuel Phillips, 133
Husák, Gustáv, 10
Huugjilt Case (2014), 242
Hu Yaobang, Xi Zhongxun in, 44–46
hydrogen bombs, 122
hyperinflation, 256, 259

illegal properties, removal of, 89
Implementation Plan, 237
incomes, average, 130, 131, 133
    Chinese Income Doubling Program, 135
Independent Commission Against Corruption (ICAC), 161, 171
India, 5, 21, 205, 410
Industrial and Commercial Bank of China (ICBC), 252
industrialization, 288
industrial output, 145
inflation, 256, 259
Inner Mongolia court, 242
innovation, 251–289
    best inventions, 269–272
    ecological concerns, 276–289
    military, 373
    modernization of economy, 252–264
    soft spot of, 265–276
inspections, military, 330
Institute of Economics and Management, 257
interference, administrative, 249
internal reform (CPC), 155–200
    anticorruption measures, 167–171
    Central Political Bureau, 176–179
    Eight Rules, 173–176
    engine of innovation, 191–194
    ethics, 198–200
    fight against corruption, 157–161
    leadership of CPC, 184–200
    membership into the Standing Committee, 187–191
    node by node, 179–182
    party discipline, strictness of, 185–186
    qualified party members, 186–187
    rules, 171–183
    ruling ability and level of CPC, 194–198
    tigers (corrupt officials), hunting, 157–171
    travel, 182–183
    zero tolerance for corruption, 161–165
International Monetary Fund (IMF), 143, 292–295, 305
international relations, 375–411
Internet, role in corruption, 164

inventions, best, 269–272
investment banks, 291–292
Iraq War, 148, 149
irrigation, 284

Jane's Defense Weekly, 332
Jang Song-Thaek, 392
Japan, 5, 380, 398–402
    defense identification zones, 395
    as export leader, 261
    Kamikaze attacks, 382
wars between China and, 122, 123–125
Japan as Number 1: Lessons for America, 20
Japanese Pirates Invasion in 1592, 124
Jia Dashan, 78, 79, 81
Jiang Luming, 371, 372
Jiang Qing, 11
Jiang Yukai, 139
Jiang Zemin, 22, 31, 71
Jiang Zhaohua, 227
Jiao Yulu, 83, 186
Jia Qinglin, 86
Jinan Airport, cancellations due to smog, 279
Jinggangshan Cadre College, 193
Jin Yinan, 322, 333, 350, 353, 370
joint operational command systems, 355
jurisdiction of laws, 245
justice, 241–246

Kamikaze attacks, 382
Kang beds, 54
Kapshin Coup in Korea, 124
Kazakhstan, 302, 303
Kerry, John, 421
Khan, Genghis, 383–388
Khan, Kublai, 382
Khrushchev, Nikita, 8–10
Kimball, Dan A., 251
Kim Il Sung, 377
Kim Jong II, 377
Kim Jong-un, 388–390
Kissinger, Henry, 29, 147, 437, 439
Körber Foundation, 399, 400
Komeito Party, 114
Kong Xiangxiu, 65, 66
Korea, 123. *See also* North Korea; South Korea
    anticorruption measures, 161
    Kapshin Coup in, 124

Kuhn, Robert Lawrence, 319
Kuomintang (KMT), 5, 122, 171
Kwok, Tony, 161

labor, skills learned by Xi Jinping, 53
Labor Law, 238
labor productivity, 267
Labor Union, 200
Lagarde, Christine, 305. *See also* IMF
lakes, 283. *See also* water, ecological concerns
land reclamation, 405
laws, 185
	Blue Book of Rule of Law: Annual Report of China's Rule of Law, 162
	jurisdiction of, 245
	market safeguards, 212
	rule of, 237–249
	trust of, 246, 247
leadership
	changes in, 94–95
	internal reform (CPC), 184–200
	style of Roosevelts, 150–154
	of Xi Jinping, 109–118
Leaders magazine, 391
leading group mechanism, 195
Lee Chang-ho, 378
Lee Kuan Yew, 117, 170, 308, 386
Legal Standards for Military Violation of Duty, 343
Legend of Mulan, 99
legislation
	market safeguards, 212
	taxation, 241
Legislation Law, 239, 240, 241
Le Monde, 198
Leninism, 17
Liangjiahe, Xi Jinping in, 53–56
Liao Ruilin, 181
Liberation Army Daily, 323
Li Chuncheng, 162
Lieberthal, Kenneth G., 157
Li Hongzhang, 124
Li Kai, 275, 276
Li Keqiang, 38, 141, 144, 195, 205, 206, 208, 214, 315, 424
limited-government theory, belief in, 92–94
Lin Biao, 11
Ling Jihua, 28, 157
liquor, consumption of, 341
Liu Ruishao, 135
Liu Shaoqi, 12, 338

Liu Yandong, 202
Liu Yazhou, 326, 353
Liu Yongtao, 151
Liu Yunshan, 155
Liu Zhidan, 42
Li Yang, 260
Li Zicheng, 59
Li Zuojun, 259
local protectionism, 246
Loessland, 49
Long March Flow Chart, 207, 211
The Long March: The Untold Story, 2
Longxing Temple (Zhengding), 79
Luan Songwei, 180
Lu Feng, 262
Lu Xun, 138
Luzyanin, Sergey, 304
Lv Hou, 116

Ma Chaoqun, 157
Mackinder, Michael, 315
major reforms, 201–249
    anticorruption measures, 223–225
    arbitrariness of power holders, 207–212
    deliberative democracy, 225–236
    economic innovations, 213
    economic strategies, planning, 213–214
    government and market interactions, 203–207
    market safeguards, 212
    monopolies, maintaining competition, 212
    rule of law, 237–249
    state-owned enterprise reform, 214–225
    use of power, 203–214
Ma Jun, 231
Mama Peng, 106–108. *See also* Peng Dehuai
management of State-owned Enterprises (SOEs), 216
Mandela, Nelson, 117, 308, 386
manufacturers, 266
Mao: A Biography, 17
Mao Zedong, 2, 4–13
    comparisons to, 110
    on economies, 259
    Gutian meeting (1929), 328
    on historical cycles, 225
    legacy of, 10–13
    lessons of, 30
    military standards of, 363
    New-Democratic Revolution, lessons from, 172

political power of, 5–10
predictions of, 127
on reform, 138–139
Sanwan adaptation, 352
"Six Rules," 173
surpassing United States, 145
Thought propaganda team, 61
Yuanjiagou Village, Qingjian County (1936), 34
March of the Volunteers, 3
Marcuse, Herbert, 115
Marine Silk Road, 304
Maritime Safety Administration, 406
Maritime Silk Road, 304
markets
government interactions, 203–207
regulations, 204
role of, 203–207
safeguards, 212
Marshall, George C., 313
Marshall Plan, 301, 313
Marxism, 17, 18, 136
Marxist economy, 63
Massachusetts Institute of Technology (MIT), 265
mass line, 199
master sergeants, 365
Mawei Economic Development Zone, 91
McKinsey Global Institute, 164
medical reform, 195
Meiji Restoration, 146
membership
into the Standing Committee, 187–191
of Asian Investment Bank, 295–297, 300
Memorandum to Build the Asian Investment Bank, 295
Merkel, Angela, 402
middle class, growth of, 135
military, 317–375. *See also* People's Liberation Army (PLA)
anticorruption measures, 324, 325
battlefield operations, 358–364
cadre and officer service in, 344–345
combat training, 359
corruption in, 345–349
defense identification zones, 395
expenditures of, 349–352
history of, 323
innovation, 373
integration of, 370–374
investment in, 337–352
loyalty to Xi Jinping, 326–337

non-commissioned officer systems, 36
    peace without dignity, 321–323
    professionalization of, 356, 364–370
    reform, 352–374
    salaries, 368
    senior officers, 341–344
    support for, 330–332
Military Procuratorate, 329
military service system, 367
The Military Strategy of China, 357
Ming Dynasty, 59, 414, 443
Ministry of Environmental Protection, 277
Ministry of Human Resources and Social Security (MHRSS), 255
minorities, critical, 246–249
Minxin Pei, 167
mixed ownership, 218–221
modernization, 14
    of economy, 252–264
money supply (M2), 256. *See also* economies
Mongolia (Xi Jinping's visit to, 2014), 381–383
monopolies, maintaining competition, 212
moon cakes, 179, 180
moral stature, 198–200
multi-party systems, 235. *See also* elections
Municipal Party Chief of Shanghai, 94
Municipal Party Secretary of Fuzhou (1990), 90
murders, 242
Muscatine Journal, 426
My Love from the Star, 67

Nanjing Massacre, 401
National Bureau of Statistics of China (NBSC), 254
National Chiao Tung University, 271
National Conference of the China Federation of Literary and Art Circles (1988), 102
National Defense magazine, 331
National Defense Reference, 369
National Defense University, 336, 350, 353, 371
The National Interest, 48
National Organization Working Meeting (2009), 186
National Party Congress (NPC), 206, 208
National People's Congress (NPC), 26, 126, 230
National People's Congress Standing Committee, 197
National Reform and Development Commission, 209
National Security Committee, 32
National Security Council, 354
Natsuo Yamaguchi, 114
natural gas, 280
Nature Publishing Index, 265

navy, 357, 361, 404, 435. *See also* military
Nazarbayev University, 303
NBA (National Basketball Association) games, 428
Needham Question, 269
Nehru, Jawaharlal, 205
networks, corruption, 159
New-Democratic Revolution, lessons from, 172
New Star, 81
New Year's Day traditions, 117
The New York Times, 71
Nian Nu Jiao, 186
Nie Weiping, 65, 378
"nine dragons managing the water," 26, 27
9/11 attack, 148
Ningde
anticorruption measures in, 88
Xi Jinping's transfer to (1988), 86–88
non-commissioned officer systems, 36
North Korea, 8, 305, 388–390, 438
nuclear capabilities of, 390
Northwestern University, 57
Notification on Deepening and Advancing Open Local Budgeting (2014), 169
nuclear force, 6
nuclear weapons, 122, 123
North Korea, 390
Nye, Joseph, 422

Obama, Barack, 119, 120–121, 298, 410, 413, 433. *See also* United States
visit to China, 414–418 (2014)
Obama, Michelle, 109, 415
October Revolution, 172
The Old Regime and the Revolution, 132
Old Zhong, 173
Olympic Games (2008), 315, 426
One Hundred Days' Reform, 415
opening policies, 44
Opinions about Strengthening the Socialist Deliberative Democracy Building, 232
Opium Wars (1840), 154, 399
opposition to extremist left-wing inclination, 46
orphans (AIDs), 106–108
Osborne, George, 297
outgoing warning (Zhu Rongji), 255. *See also* Zhu Rongji
"The Outline of Zhenguan's Reign," 8

Pakistan, 311, 312
Panetta, Leon, 429
Park Geun-hye, 309, 375–381
Party Chief of Zhengding, 74–76

party discipline, strictness of, 185–186
Party School of the Central Committee of the CPC, 42, 50
patrol systems, 340
Paulson, Henry, 319, 431
Pearl Harbor (December 7, 1941), attack on, 125
Peking University, 262
Peng Dehuai, 33, 96–109
    AIDs orphans, 106–108
    birth of Xi Mingze (daughter), 103
    courtship, 101
    education of, 97, 100
    as fascination of Chinese people, 97
    fashion of, 97, 98
    life of, 97–101
    marriage, 101
    operatic talents of, 97, 98, 99
    performances, 104–105
    policies for children, 108–109
    as President of PLA Arts Academy, 106
    service in army, 104
Peng Liyuan, 49
    diplomacy, 387
    marriage to, 85
pension scandal, Shanghai (2006), 94
People's Daily, 55, 75, 76–77, 416
People's Liberation Army (PLA), 68, 98, 317–375
    battlefield operations, 358–364
    discipline inspection commission, 338
    Peng Dehaui's service in, 104
People's Political Consultative Conference, 26
personality, cult of, 11
Philippines, 407
pictures of Xi Jinping, 67
Pilgrimage, 78
Pilot Program for Optimized Approval Process of Construction Engineering Projects, 210
poetry of Xi Jinping, 84
policies
    anticorruption measures, 168
    for children, 108–109
    technological advances, 267
Political Bureau Standing Committee members, 187–191
political mentors of Xi Jinping, 60–69
Political Order in Changing Societies, 133
political reform, 137
political strategies, 48
Political Tittle-Tattle, 70
politics
    changes in China, 429–431

and the military, 328–330
pollution, 251, 276. *See also* ecological concerns
 smog, 278–281
 water, 281–285
population, aging of, 131
power
 arbitrariness of power holders, 207–212
 balance of, 150
 hegemonic, 442
 interpretation of, 112
 military, 357. See also military
 use of, 203–214
pragmatism, 198–200
Premier of China State Council, 253–256
presidency (of Xi Jinping), first days of, 68
Presidential combo, 38
price distortion problems, 204
professionalization of military, 356
Proof of Domestic Dynamics, 182
protectionism, local, 246
Provincial Party Chief (2002), 92
public heath, danger of pollution to, 277
publicity, 80
public relations, 116
Public Security Bureau of Shenzhen Municipality, 211
Pudong Cadre College, 193
Putin, Vladimir, 318, 386. *See also* Russia

Qiao Yu, 99
Qing Dahe, 281
Qing Dynasty, 381
Qing Government, 124
Qi Xin, 42, 47
qualified party members, 186–187
"Questions presented by Geng Biao," 67
Quotations of Chairman Mao Zedong, 50

Reagan, Ronald, 15, 414
reception in Xiapu, 90
Red Army, 13, 41
reform, 81
 budgets, 351
 China Dream, 130–138, 138–141
 danger and hardship of, 354
 founders of, 44
 internal reform (CPC). *See* internal reform (CPC)
 major. *See* major reforms
 medical, 195

military, 352–374
National Reform and Development Commission, 209
political, 137
promotion of, 111
State-owned Enterprises (SOEs), 215–217
Reform, 201
Reform Plan for Payment Packages of Executives of Central SOEs, 222
Register of Fishing Vessels of Vietnam, 407
Regulation of Government Information Disclosure, 168
Regulation of the Commission of Politics and Law, 248
regulations, 176. *See also* rules
    Chinese Communist Party Disciplinary Regulations, 185
    markets, 204
Regulations on Reward and Recognition, 362
Renminbi (RMB), 283
research and development (R&D), 266
Resolutions on Historical Issues, 9
resources, strain on, 251
Revolution of 1911, 127
revolutions
    cultural. *See* Cultural Revolution
    innovation. *See* innovation
rice, watering, 284
rivers, 282. *See also* water; ecological concerns
The Road to Rejuvenation, 2
Roosevelt, Franklin D., 150–154
Roosevelt, Theodore, 150–153
rules
    Eight Rules, 173–176
    internal reform (CPC), 171–183
    laws. *See* laws
    for the military, 342
    rule of law, 237–249
Rules on Practicing Strict Economy and Strengthening Fund Management, 351
Russia, 21, 281. *See also* Soviet Union
    cooperation with, 303
    influence of, 314
    trains, 386
Russian Far East Institute, 304

salaries, military, 368
Salisbury, Harrison, 1
Sanwan adaptation, Mao Zedong, 352
SARS (Severe acute respiratory syndrome), 105
Schmidt, Helmut, 429
School of Public Policy and Management, 26
Science and Civilization in China, 269
Second Plenary Session of the Seventh CPC Central Committee (1949), 173

Secretary of the Central Commission for Discipline Inspection, 57

Secretary of the Jiangjiahe commune, 55

Seeking Truth, 112

Selected Statements on National Defense and Army Building, 336

Selected Works of Deng Xiaoping: Volume III, 21

Selected Works of Mao Zedong, 12

semi-suburban economies, 76

senior officers (military), 341–344

Sent-Down Youth Office, 58

Shaanxi-Gansu (Shaangan) Border Region Soviet Area, 41

Shaanxi province, 48, 49

Shaanxi Village, Xi Jinping in, 58–60

shale gas, 285

Shambaugh, David, 193, 202, 235, 236

Shandong Business News, 74

Shandong Yuncheng No. 1 High School, 100

Shanghai Cooperation Organization (SCO), 304

Shanghai International Group, 217

Shanghai International Port Group (SIPG), 220

Shang Yang, 138

Sheng Huaren, 238

Shen Peiping, 170

Shenzhen Special Economic Zone, 46

Shenzhen Special Zone Daily, 39

Sihinzo Abe, 393, 410

Shi Zhihong, 136

Sichuan Province, 163

Silent Spring, 288

Silk Road Economic Belt, 301–309. *See also* Belt and Road Initiatives

silver mines, 286

Sino-Japanese War, 41, 121–122, 398

"Six Rules," 173. *See also* rules

16th Central Committee of CPC, 214

small- to medium-sized enterprises (SMEs), 238

smog, 278–281

Snow, Edgar, 1, 7

soccer, 23

socialist deliberative democracy, 229

Song Dynasty, 79

Songmen Town, 226

songs, favorite, 66

South China Morning Post, 334

South China Sea, 422, 436

    dispute, 375

    fleet, 348. *See also* military

    rules in, 402–408

    tension in, 321

South Korea, 8, 309, 376–381

diplomacy to, 379–381
economic ties to, 380
South Talks (Deng Xiaoping), 174
South Tour Speeches (1992), 203
sovereignty, 400, 403, 406–408, 432–434
Soviet Union, 5
    collapse of Communist Party, 132, 155
    development of atomic bombs, 122, 123
    reform, 14–17
split-ticket voting, 235. *See also* elections
Spring Festival (2014), 396
Stanford University, 227
Standing Committee of the Political Bureau, 29, 59, 187–191
State of Great Hural (Mongolia), 384
State-owned Assets Supervision and Administration Commission (SASAC), 215
state-owned enterprise reform, 214–225
State-owned Enterprises (SOEs), 215
anticorruption measures, 223–225
classification, 217–218
reform, 215–217
statesmanship, maturity of, 84–92
Stiglitz, Joseph, 142, 143
stock market declines, 341
"Story of Fire," 56
strategy of China Dream, 129–141
student demonstrations, 41
Summers, Lawrence, 294, 301
Sun Liping, 24
Sun Tzu: Use of Energy, 33
Sun Yat-sen, 145
Supreme People's Court, 241
Su Rong, 28, 157, 170
sweatshops, 261–264

Taiwan, 394, 406, 422, 432
Ta Kung Pao, 32
Tang Dynasty, 123
Taoism, 288
taxation, legislation, 241
Taylor, Jon, 154
technological advances, policies, 267
Temple, Robert, 270
temptations, 83
Thailand, 130
Thatcher, Margaret, 415
theory of China collapse, 156
Third Plenary Session of the 18th CPC Central Committee, 24, 25
Three Gorges Group, 311

"Three Rules of Discipline and Eight Points for Attention," 172
Tiananmen Square, 374, 379
Tibet, 422
tigers (corrupt officials), hunting, 157–171
Time magazine, 269
Tocqueville, Alexis de, 132
"To the Old Version of Me" song, 125–126
Toynbee, Arnold J., 288
trade surpluses, 256
trains, 384, 385, 388
Trans-Pacific Partnership Agreement (TPP), 434
travel, internal reform (CPC), 182–183
Travels of Marco Polo, 304
Treaty of Shimonoseki, 124
truths, home, 113
Tsinghua University, 26, 60
tuberculosis (TB), 107–108
2013 China Environmental Bulletin, 283
Two Centenary Goals, 142–147

"Uncle Xi," 48–60. *See* Xi Jinping
United Kingdom (UK), 297–299
United Nations (UN), World Food Program (WFP), 182
The United Nations Charter, 396
United States
    anti-American sentiment, lack of, 425–431
    China as creditor, 293
    Chinese Military Report (2007/2008), 363
    exports, 262
    Great Depression, 150
    Liu Yandong's visit to, 202
    new model of power relationships, 418–425
    opposition of Asian Investment Bank, 297–299
    relationship with, 150, 306–308, 413–438
    surpassing economically not ultimate goal, 142–147
    unacceptability of provocation, 437
University of the West Scotland, 232
"Up to the Mountains and Down to the Countryside," 49–50
urbanization, 253
USA Today, 252

Vantone Group, 207
vested interests, reform overcoming, 138–141, 152
Vietnam, 407
Vogel, Ezra, 20
Von Kármán, Theodore, 271
voting, 235. *See also* elections
Wallace, Mike, 18

The Wall Street Journal, 33, 202
Wang Jianzhong, 221
Wang Lijun, 430
Wang Ning, 358
Wang Qishan, 29, 56, 57, 169
Wang Yang, 423, 424
Wang Yi, 313
Wang Youhui, 73, 74
Wang Yukai, 139
Wang Zhongxin, 364
Wan Li, 128
Wan Qingliang, 170
war, strategies of, 6
War of Jiawu, 323
Warren, Mark E., 233
wars between China and Japan, 123–125
Washington, George, 5
The Washington Post, 427
water, ecological concerns, 281–285
The Water Margin, 57
Weibo, 177
Wei Pengyuan, 157
Wei Zheng, 8
Wen Jiabao, 31, 270
Why Are The Chinese Industrious And Yet Not Rich?, 266
Womack, Brantly, 235
Women's Federation, 200
World Bank (WB), 32, 143, 257, 292–295
World Food Program (WFP), 182
World Health Organization (WHO), 106
World Intellectual Property Organization, 273
The World Post, 322
World Trade Organization (WTO), 63
World War I, 419
World War II, 125
Writers' Association of Yanchang County, Zhang Siming, 56
Wu Baoxin, 78
Wu Jinglian, 140
Wu Shengli, 361

Xiamen Special Economic Zone, 84
Xiangtan Hengdun Group Co., Ltd., 221
Xiao Gongqin, 110
Xiapu, reception in, 90
Xie Runzhen, 359
Xi Jinping, 2
    Belt and Road Initiatives, 292–295
    birth of Xi Mingze (daughter), 103

collective presidency, 26–30
courtship of Peng Dehaui, 101
Deputy Secretary of Zhengding county, 69
entering politics, 66
father (Xi Zhongxun) as hero, 40–48
gaining political experience, 81–84
as Governor of Fujian, 91–92
imprisonment of father, 42–44
influences of, 114
international relations, 375–411
interpretation of power, 112
leadership of, 109–118
in Liangjiahe, 53–56
life of, 37–40, 48–60
limited-government theory, belief in, 92–94
marriage, 101
meeting with Barack Obama, 120, 121
military loyalty to, 326–337
as Municipal Party Chief of Shanghai, 94
new era of, 22–35
Peng Dehuai (wife). *See* Peng Dehuai
poetry of, 84
political climb of, 69–84
political mentors, 60–69
as Provincial Party Chief (2002), 92
public relations, 116
reform, 138–141
second half of reform, 23–26
as Secretary of the Jiangjiahe commune, 55
self-restraint of, 46–48
in Shaanxi Village, 58–60
South Tour Speeches (1992), 203
statesmanship, maturity of, 84–92
"Story of Fire," 56
strategic economic focus, 256–261
targeting 2049, 30–35
transfer to Ningde (1988), 86–88
at Tsinghua University, 60
"Uncle Xi," 48–60
visit to Mongolia (2014), 381–383
in Yan'an, 188
youth of, 51–53
Xi Jinping: The Governance of China, 153
Xi Mingze (daughter), birth of, 103
Xing Yichuan, 141
Xinhe Town, 231
Xinhua News Agency, 38, 39, 77, 240, 393
Xinjiang Construction Regiment, 170

Xi Zhongxun
    father as hero to Xi Jinping, 40–48
    in Hu Yaobang, 44–46
    imprisonment of, 42–44
    self-restraint of, 46–48
Xu Caihou, 28, 157, 158, 329, 341
    capture of, 166
Xu Yaotong, 135
Xu Zhengzhong, 273

Yale University, 266
Yan'an, Xi Jinping in, 51, 188
Yan'an Cadre College, 193
Yan'an Correspondence, 56
Yang Yujun, 395
Yasukuni Shrine, 401
Yellow Book of World Economy, 142
Yingtai Bridge, 121
Yomiuri Shimbun, 380
Yongding River, 282
Youth Communist League, 183
Yuan Dewang, 100
Yuan Dynasty, 381
Yu Guangyuan, 76

Zakaria, Fareed, 439
Zeguo Town, 231
zero tolerance for corruption, 161–165
Zhang Lianmei, 391
Zhang Qian, 302
Zhang Wei, 201
Zhang Weiwei, 130
Zhang Wuchang, 238
Zhao Derun, 77, 111
Zhao Keshi, 346
Zhao Zilong, 387
Zhao Ziyang, 70
Zhejiang, 92
Zhengding
    crops in, 73
    history of, 79
    office in, 72
    Party Chief of, 74–76
Zheng Yongnian, 83, 191, 328
Zhongnanhai, 43
Zhongnanhai Yingtai, 414
Zhou Enlai, 63
Zhou Qiang, 241

Zhou Yongkang, 28, 157, 341
    arrest of, 165
Zhu Rongji, 31, 253–256
zones, economic, 84
zoning land, 45